The Survey
Research Handbook

McGraw-Hill/Irwin Series in Marketing

The Survey Research Handbook

Third Edition

Pamela L. Alreck
Perdue School of Business
Salisbury State University

Robert B. Settle
Perdue School of Business
Salisbury State University

McGraw-Hill
Irwin

Boston   Burr Ridge, IL   Dubuque, IA   Madison, WI   New York   San Francisco   St. Louis
Bangkok   Bogotá   Caracas   Kuala Lumpur   Lisbon   London   Madrid   Mexico City
Milan   Montreal   New Delhi   Santiago   Seoul   Singapore   Sydney   Taipei   Toronto

McGraw-Hill
Irwin

THE SURVEY RESEARCH HANDBOOK
Published by McGraw-Hill/Irwin, a business unit of The McGraw-Hill Companies, Inc., 1221 Avenue of the Americas, New York, NY, 10020. Copyright © 2004, 1995, 1985 by The McGraw-Hill Companies, Inc. All rights reserved. No part of this publication may be reproduced or distributed in any form or by any means, or stored in a database or retrieval system, without the prior written consent of The McGraw-Hill Companies, Inc., including, but not limited to, in any network or other electronic storage or transmission, or broadcast for distance learning. Some ancillaries, including electronic and print components, may not be available to customers outside the United States.

This book is printed on acid-free paper.

4 5 6 7 8 9 0 DOC/DOC 0 9

ISBN 0-07-294548-6

Vice president and editor-in-chief: *Robin J. Zwettler*
Editorial director: *John E. Biernat*
Executive editor: *Linda Schreiber*
Editorial coordinator: *Scott Becker*
Marketing coordinator: *David Kapoor*
Media producer: *Damian Moshak*
Project manager: *Charlie Fisher*
Senior production supervisor: *Michael R. McCormick*
Lead designer: *Matthew Baldwin*
Supplement producer: *Lynn M. Bluhm*
Senior digital content specialist: *Brian Nacik*
Cover design: *Joanne Schopler*
Typeface: *10/12 Palatino*
Compositor: *GAC Indianapolis*
Printer: *R. R. Donnelley*

Library of Congress Cataloging-in-Publication Data

Alreck, Pamela L.
    The survey research handbook / Pamela L. Alreck, Robert B. Settle. — 3rd ed.
       p. cm. — (McGraw-Hill/Irwin series in marketing)
    Includes index.
    ISBN 0-07-294548-6 (alk. paper)
    I. Settle, Robert B. II. Title. III. Series.
HN29.A46 2004
300'.72'3—dc22

                                      2003066453

www.mhhe.com

Preface

Survey research is one of those activities that cut across a dozen different boundaries. Those in business and public administration, the social and behavioral sciences, professional and family studies, journalism and communications, education and health services, politics, law and criminology, and many other diverse areas all find an increasing need for information based on survey research. Fortunately, the same basic tools, skills, and activities for doing surveys apply, regardless of the particular purpose or topics for any one survey research project.

As active survey research consultants for many years, we've designed and conducted projects in several areas for many different types of clients. Invariably, during the initial meeting with a potential new survey sponsor, those seeking the information will explain, with a good deal of sincerity and conviction, that their own particular organization, industry, or profession is unique—probably not much like any other we've encountered. This sometimes troubles potential survey sponsors because they wonder if they should seek out a survey research consultant or agency that has worked in their own area of activity and has substantial experience with the special nature of their information needs. Their concerns are genuine, but they're also unfounded. It's certainly true that the institutions and organizations that depend on survey information are often very different from one another in their goals, objectives, and operations. Yet by applying the same basic principles and techniques described in this handbook, we've surveyed many thousands of different types of respondents for dozens of very diverse clients with uniformly positive and valuable results. Perhaps you're wondering if you should seek a research book devoted exclusively to your own discipline, profession, or activity to guide you in a survey project. You need not be concerned because you'll find what you need here.

Fortunately, survey research *applications* cut across many institutional and disciplinary boundaries. Unfortunately, however, survey research also slices across many *technical* boundaries, as well. If you're going to do a complete survey project, from beginning to end, you'll find the diversity of skills rather demanding. You'll be working with people one minute and computers the next. At one time you may be concerned with how to phrase a question or word some instruction. A few days later you may be a little puzzled about some statistical method. You may have to deal with a printer who keeps telling you your work will be ready tomorrow or a computer that just doesn't seem to want to talk to you at all. Fear not!

One of our main purposes in writing this handbook has been to bring together all of the various techniques and principles, skills and activities that are required to conduct a really effective survey project. As university instructors, we've both been faced with one all too familiar situation far too many times. The typical situation is simply this: A student comes to the office or approaches one of us after class and declares with considerable gravity that he or she has decided to conduct a survey. Then comes the question: *"Where can I find a book that will tell me what to do?"* Often this same student has taken one or more university courses on research methods in his or her own area of study. Occasionally, they'll have a research textbook in their hand at the time. Yet we and they both know very well that neither the training they received nor the textbook they acquired would guide them through an entire survey research project from start to finish. We sincerely believe that with this handbook, we and they and you have the answer. This handbook isn't devoted to any one specific area, but it provides comprehensive coverage of the wide variety of things you'll need to know to conduct effective survey research.

We've been guided by two criteria when judging whether or not to include material in the handbook: Is this *sufficient* and is this *necessary?* We feel that both are important. When using a handbook, there's nothing quite so frustrating as finding it covers every conceivable situation *except your own.* Consequently, the breadth and scope of the handbook is, by necessity, very wide. It must be, in order to meet your own needs, whether you're a student who will conduct a single survey project to meet your academic requirements or a seasoned survey research professional seeking some new ideas or tools of the trade.

We've also avoided or eliminated a substantial amount of material often found in research textbooks. If we had never once used or seen the need for some technique, computation, or procedure in either academic or pragmatic survey research over many years of experience, we felt you probably wouldn't need it either, and it could safely be excluded. Perhaps there will be some who feel the handbook lacks dignity because the practical and technical aspects of survey research take precedence over the conceptual and the theoretical aspects. To us, that's the whole idea, and it's a small price to pay for a handbook that's understandable and useful.

Over 300 special exhibits are included to help you refer quickly and easily to the information you'll need to conduct a survey. They cover virtually every aspect of the survey process, from initiation to final report. Each of the five distinct types of exhibits has a special purpose and type of information:

- **Checklists** contain a series of questions followed by instructions on how to proceed, depending on the answers.
- **Guidelists** provide a series of instructions or directions, in sequence, to perform some task or follow a procedure.
- **Examples** contain typical elements or formats to use as models for creating various components of a survey.
- **Figures** portray verbal or graphic information, showing quantities or relationships according to their relative position.
- **Summaries** at the end of each chapter provide a sketch or outline of the most important things covered there.

As you examine the handbook, you should find there's little that's likely to get in the way of understanding. Some aspects of survey research, especially those involving computers, statistics, or the Internet, traditionally use a lot of buzz-words and obscure terminology. In our experience, that kind of vocabulary is intimidating and inhibiting, rather than helpful or enlightening. So we've deliberately avoided them wherever possible in favor of plain, ordinary words and phrases. If you find more here than what you need, at least it will be understandable. To the degree that we've been successful, you'll find everything you need for survey research and very little else.

Pamela L. Alreck

Robert B. Settle

Brief Contents

Contents

Checklists

Guidelists

Examples

Figures

Summaries

The Survey
Research Handbook

Planning and Designing the Survey

Part

1

1

Initiating a Survey

The Quest for Information

All economically and technically advanced societies run on the same fuel. That fuel is *information*. The organizations and institutions within which we live and work have an unquenchable thirst for data. They just can't operate without it. And much of the data they require concerns how *people* operate—how *we* operate: How we think and act, what we like and don't like, what we want and don't want, what beliefs and opinions we hold, what attitudes we maintain, what pictures or images have been etched in our mind's eye.

Some of this information about people is obvious and can be learned merely by casual observation. Some, but not much of it, and often not nearly enough. Organizations and institutions of every type—private and public, profit and nonprofit, government and commercial—need answers to important questions. Those answers must be *accurate, reliable*, and *valid*. Survey research is one way and often the most effective and dependable way to obtain that information.

Why Surveys Are Conducted

Surveys are often conducted simply because it's the only way to get the information needed. Even when the information is available through other means, survey research may be an easier, quicker, less expensive, or more accurate way to get the required information.

Individuals or organizations usually sponsor surveys for one of three basic reasons: (1) They want to influence or persuade some audience. (2) They want to create or modify a product or service they provide for a particular public. (3) They want to understand or predict human behavior or conditions because it's the focus of their academic or professional work.

Surveys of an Audience

Many who sponsor surveys would ultimately like to influence the beliefs or behavior of their audience—to persuade some group of people to think in a certain way or act in some particular fashion. Virtually everyone tries, at times, to influence and persuade others. There's nothing wrong with that because ordinarily the people they're trying to influence aren't being exploited or harmed in any way. Parents try to influence their children, spouses seek to persuade one another, employees attempt to influence their supervisors, and buyers try to convince sellers to reduce their prices. When ordinary people try to influence others, those doing the persuading can tell pretty easily from observation or conversation whether or not they've been successful. It's far more difficult for organizations or institutions that are trying to influence or persuade large audiences to gauge the effects.

Business firms promote their products or services. Political parties and organizations promote their candidates and issues. Government bureaus and agencies promote their positions. Social service institutions devoted to education, public health and medicine, religious belief, or social welfare promote their doctrines and services. All of these organizations communicate with their publics in a variety of ways. Yet promotion is one-way communication. The persuasive message goes out from the sender to the audience, but how does the audience respond? Are the messages effective? Is there resistance? Do those in the audience even understand? Is the information what they need to know? Do the messages "touch a nerve" or evoke a need?

When messages are directed to a large audience, survey research can be the other half of the conversation, so there's two-way communication between the message sender and the audience. Those who receive the messages ordinarily don't take the initiative to provide feedback. Even if they wanted to, there's often no convenient way for them to respond. Those who sponsor a survey of their audience are taking the responsibility for both halves of the conversation. They're providing a medium through which their audience can talk to them. They're not imposing on the respondents because nobody can be forced to respond if they don't wish to take the time or effort to do so. In fact, most people welcome the opportunity to respond, to record their opinions and reactions, and to have some effect on the sponsor.

Surveys of a Clientele

Most people's occupations involve doing or making something for others. So do the operations of most companies, organizations, and institutions. Individuals and organizations often seek survey information to discover the needs, wants, and desires of the people they serve. They often want to know the underlying human conditions that make their goods and services useful and valuable to others. The better the providers of goods and services know and understand their clients, the more they'll be able to serve them economically and effectively. Commercial and industrial firms, political parties and candidates, governmental agencies and units, hospitals and clinics, schools and colleges, churches and religious groups, and those in professional practices all provide products and services to their own publics. In almost every case, there are many alternatives concerning *what* they provide, *who* they provided it to, *when* and *where* it will be offered, *how* it will be produced, and the *cost* or charges for the goods or services. Survey research is often used to furnish information for making these decisions.

The producers of goods and services ordinarily have to take the responsibility for learning the needs and desires of their particular clientele. They usually have a fairly clear picture of what could be produced and delivered, but they're often uncertain about the needs and desires of the public. Similarly, the clients know what they need or want in a general way, but they don't usually know what goods or services could be produced or who might produce them. It's often desirable for the producers who sponsor surveys to learn about their clienteles. Such surveys typically benefit the clients or customers who respond to the surveys, as well as the producers who sponsor the research. The better the producers understand their clientele, the more effectively they will be able to serve them.

Surveys of Other Populations

The reasons for surveys identified above are *practical* ones. The results are directed toward decision making and executive actions. Sponsors may also be motivated by a desire for knowledge about people, in and of itself. People, themselves, are the subject matter—the focus of attention—for many academic and professional disciplines. Students, professors, researchers, and professionals within the social and behavioral sciences, the humanities and arts, business and public administration, and a wide variety of other professional studies focus partly or entirely on the behavior and conditions of the people in the society. This kind of survey information is sought not so much to assist in decision making as it is to enhance the body of theoretical and conceptual knowledge of the discipline. Rather than information to be applied to practical problems and actions, *theoretical* research seeks information to answer research questions and to test hypotheses about the propensities and predispositions of people. This type of survey information may apply directly to existing conditions or potential actions at the moment. Instead, it's used to enhance the literature and the state of current thought within the discipline or area of the sponsor.

The criteria for judging information needs differ between the two types of survey research. Nevertheless, the survey procedure itself is fairly standard, regardless of whether the purpose is practical or theoretical. Measurement tools are largely indifferent to what they're measuring. Those in many different occupations often use the same measurement tools. Carpenters, plumbers, and masons may all use a tape measure for lumber, pipe, or concrete, respectively. Similarly, surveys are measurement tools that can be used effectively by those in many occupations, and for a wide variety of purposes and topics. However, it's important to identify the general purpose of the survey project, not so much to indicate *how* the survey should be conducted as to show *what* information needs and survey topics should be considered.

Alternative Research Methods

There are two broad categories of research data: *primary data* and *secondary data*. Data are regarded as *primary* when they are collected for a specific purpose or inquiry. For instance, a company or government agency may initiate a research project to answer questions that have arisen because of a change in external circumstances. They may need data that apply directly and immediately to the new situation.

FIGURE 1–1
Primary versus Secondary Data Characteristics

Primary Data Collection	Secondary Data Acquisition
Relatively expensive	Less costly
Time consuming	Often can be obtained quickly
Demands expertise	Less expertise required
Requires respondent cooperation	Requires few participants
Specific to the information needs	Often for a general purpose
Directly applicable to the problem	Applicability may be only partial
Samples population of interest	Population may be too broad or narrow
Engages interest of users	Users detached from process
Reliability and validity can be assessed	Reliability and validity may be obscure

Data are regarded as *secondary* when they already exist and have been gathered for a different purpose than the problem at hand or were acquired to be shared by multiple clients. The U.S. Census data and other government databases, as well as institutional and industry data sources, are examples of secondary data. Secondary data are usually less expensive and quicker to obtain than primary data. Unfortunately they typically don't satisfy the information needs as well as primary data would. Primary and secondary data characteristics are compared in Figure 1–1.

Primary Data Collection Options

Surveys certainly aren't the only means of acquiring data about people's attitudes, opinions, preferences, experiences, and the like. While survey research is the most common method for obtaining such primary data, there are other methods that are sometimes used either independently or in conjunction with surveys. They include quantitative methods such as behavioral laboratory or field *experiments* and *systematic observation* methods, as well as verbal methods, sometimes called "qualitative" techniques such as *focus groups* or *depth interviews*.

Focus Group Discussions

Research techniques such as behavioral laboratory testing, systematic observation, or depth interviewing require special expertise and perhaps special facilities and equipment as well. By contrast, focus group discussions are less dependent on special training and expertise. They may be used independently, but they are often conducted preliminary to a survey. They can be extremely helpful in determining both *what* questions should be asked and *how* they should be expressed. Complete directions and guidelines for conducting focus group discussions are provided in Appendix A.

Field Experimentation

One of the most serious limitations of survey research is that it's difficult or impossible to measure *causality* with a survey. The research almost always involves *asking questions* and obtaining *self-reports* by respondents. Unfortunately, survey respondents are notoriously bad at assessing *causality*, either because they actually *don't know* why they or others behave in a certain way or because they *won't say* why.

Experimentation is ordinarily a much more capable method of measuring the *cause* of behavior. Surveys are usually good at measuring *what* happened or even predicting *what will* happen in the future, but experimentation, discussed in Appendix B, is often much better for discovering *why*. Fortunately, many of the same concepts and principles that apply to surveys are also applicable to field experimentation.

Expectations of Survey Results

Those who consider conducting a survey may wonder just what results they can and should expect. It may be difficult to assess the capabilities and limitations of survey research. Some prospective sponsors have overly ambitious expectations, while others think that surveys are much more limited than they really are. A survey's value depends on both the amount of resources devoted to it and the care and expertise that goes into the work. It's impossible to say exactly what should or shouldn't be expected of a particular set of survey results or to predict precisely what will or won't be accomplished in a given instance. Yet some broad guidelines may be helpful to compare surveys with other techniques for gathering information.

Survey Attributes

Survey research is an extremely popular form of inquiry. It would probably be difficult to find anyone who hasn't been asked to respond to some form of survey in the past, and many people are often approached by survey researchers. Surveys are so often used because they offer so many advantages to those seeking information.

Flexibility and Versatility

Surveys can be designed to measure things as simple as respondents' physical or demographic characteristics, or as complex as their attitudes, preferences, or lifestyle patterns. They may cover only one small aspect of the respondents' mentality or situation, or they may include dozens or even hundreds of questions about almost every aspect of the respondents' lives. Surveys can be designed to capture the respondents' personal history, their present life circumstances, their intentions and expectations for the future, or the entire scope of the time spectrum.

Survey data can be collected by personal interview, telephone interview, direct mail, or via the Internet. Respondents can be reached with only visual contact, only audible stimuli, or both. They can be reached in their homes, at work, while shopping, or even during their recreation. They can be presented with a response task that requires only a few seconds, or one that takes an hour or more. Survey research isn't confined to a single mode of inquiry.

The volume of data collected and the degree of complexity are a matter of choice. Simple surveys may require only a few tally sheets and limited spreadsheet computations, perhaps generating a single page report. Complex and exhaustive surveys may use highly sophisticated data analysis software to generate a large volume of precise information. The scope depends on information requirements and resource availability.

Specialization and Efficiency

When considering a survey, there are three questions that quickly arise: (1) How much will it cost? (2) How long will it take? (3) How much will be learned? They often can't be answered accurately at first. Much more specification is required because surveys vary widely and no two are exactly alike. This is an important advantage of survey projects. It means they can usually be customized to fit both the needs and the budget of those seeking information. A survey could cost only a few hundred dollars, or hundreds of thousands of dollars—take only a single day or extend over many months—generate only a single piece of data or cover a huge range of information. To answer the three big questions above, the project must be matched to the needs and resources of the sponsor.

Because survey research uses sampling, information about an extremely large population can be obtained from a relatively small sample of people. Rarely do surveys sample more than a thousand or so people, even when the results are to be generalized to many millions. The vast majority of surveys include only a few hundred respondents, and there are some projects where a sample of only a few dozen respondents is completely adequate. The use of well-designed and organized instrumentation also contributes to the efficiency of survey research. It isn't at all unusual for survey questionnaires to capture the answers to a hundred or so different questions or items in only a few minutes of each respondent's time. Without this careful and often artful instrument composition, that many individual questions asked in random order and in ad hoc fashion might take several hours to answer.

Survey Limitations

Despite the positive features of this type of research inquiry, survey research methods do have some intractable disadvantages and limitations. Aside from the most serious shortcoming, the limitations on assessment of causality cited earlier, survey research has other limitations that must be considered.

Threat and Sensitive Questions

There are some questions respondents won't answer because the information is so sensitive they're too embarrassed or threatened to give the information. For example, it's difficult to learn about issues associated with social taboos, such as sexual behavior, drinking habits, or drug abuse. Some such information may be obtainable with considerable expertise, effort, and ingenuity; however, it's usually impossible to get such information from survey research if the questions or issues seriously threaten respondents. For instance, questions about earnings and the amount of income listed on their tax returns are likely to elicit more heat than light from respondents. Other forms of inquiry, such as *behavior audits* or *systematic observations*, are often better means for measuring such things.

Cost, Expertise, and Error

Surveys should and almost always do generate information that's worth many times more than the cost of the project. Yet surveys take time, cost money, and require intelligent, well-directed effort. Survey research is extremely demanding in one respect: It requires complete planning and careful execution at virtually every step in the process. *One person* must take individual, overall responsibility for the survey project. That person certainly need not do all the work or make all the decisions. But that person, who is in charge of the project, does have to monitor and supervise the process continually and diligently. The survey process consists of a series of interactive steps or phases that have to be done in sequence. The researcher sometimes has to anticipate later phases and make decisions or commitments about them before completing the earlier steps. Unless the researcher has a clear picture of the entire process, there's always the chance some action or decision at an earlier phase will take the process down a dead-end street or have disastrous consequences at a later phase in the process.

As with any other kind of work, there will inevitably be mistakes, errors, and oversights along the way. These aren't reasons to forego a survey project until it can be done perfectly. It never will be. The objective of complete planning and careful execution is to avoid the *major* errors and oversights, to minimize the number of smaller ones, and identify ways to compensate or control the damage if the unexpected happens. So long as there's no serious jeopardy to the value of the survey information, minor mistakes can and must be tolerated. If minor errors show up during or after completion of the survey, they should be examined to see what effect they have on the survey information. It's never advisable to denigrate or discard survey results simply because some small mistakes were made during the process. Minor errors and inadequacies shouldn't be allowed to throw a dense shadow of doubt over the entire range of survey results. Rather, they should be treated for what they are: things that may require some modification in the interpretation and reliance on the survey findings.

Surveys Don't Dictate Decisions

Even if no errors or omissions are discovered and the survey project goes precisely as planned, the results won't be definitive. They won't dictate decisions or contain the ultimate answers. Instead, survey results should be treated as another body of evidence or set of indications. Survey results have to be evaluated in the light of experience, common sense, and other information. Human perception and judgment will always be required. The reason that survey results aren't definitive is simple but compelling: Respondents' answers are merely stand-ins for actual conditions or actions. It's typically important to know the answers to survey questions and understand the things they represent. Actions usually follow opinions. On the other hand, survey responses are never precisely indicative.

The Roles of the Participants

Surveys that are relatively limited in scope may be initiated, sponsored, designed, and conducted by the same individual, but that's not usually the case. Survey research often involves several people, and large surveys may require the services of a hundred or more people, sometimes employed by independent firms or agencies providing specialized services. Different aspects of the work each may have special roles and responsibilities to be performed by different people. During survey

For Sponsors Initiating a Survey   Guidelist 1–1

1. Furnish the researchers with sufficient background information about the setting and operations.

2. Provide a description of the issues, problems, or uncertainties that lead to consideration of a survey.

3. Indicate the type of information that would solve the problem or reduce the uncertainty.

4. Describe what decisions, choices, or actions will be based on the survey results.

5. Estimate the value of the information, based on potential risks or opportunity costs.

6. Specify the time requirements and level of funding and other resources allocated to the project.

planning and initiation, the major focus is on the roles of (1) those who sponsor the survey, pay for it, and seek the information it will generate, and (2) those who actually design and conduct the research.

The Sponsor's Role

Often those who sponsor a survey are unfamiliar with the survey process itself. They may be executives, managers, or professionals whose area of expertise lies elsewhere. They may be thoroughly familiar with the problems, decisions, actions, conditions, and perhaps the "conventional wisdom" of their own discipline, industry, or institution, but their understanding of the survey process may range from fairly accurate perceptions to only rather vague notions. Their role is to explain what information is needed and also why it's required. Some sponsors may expect the research team to operate in a vacuum of information about the purpose for the survey. They may feel it's satisfactory merely to provide a few basic questions to be addressed by the survey. They may fail to provide sufficient background. They may be reluctant to discuss frankly and openly the fundamental nature of the information needs or specific purposes to which the results will be devoted. Such a relationship between sponsor and researcher is almost never productive. The sponsor should indicate the ultimate purpose for the survey and provide the researchers with clear guidelines concerning the time requirements for the survey. They should also be prepared to indicate the general level of funding or resources that are allocated for the project. The role of the survey sponsor is outlined in Guidelist 1–1.

The Researcher's Role

Those who are to conduct the survey must be thoroughly familiar with the capabilities and limitations of the survey research process. In most cases, the researcher shouldn't try to *educate* the sponsor concerning the survey process. Instead, the researcher should inquire thoroughly about the information needs, the nature of the decisions and actions to be based on the research results, and the overall operation of the institution, organization, or unit sponsoring the survey. The researcher can then identify the alternatives for the sponsor and point out the survey procedures that might be used.

For Researchers During Survey Initiation Guidelist 1–2

1. Know the capabilities and limitations of survey research and indicate them to sponsors when appropriate.
2. Obtain background information about the operations, policies, and procedures of the sponsor.
3. Inquire about the nature of the uncertainty, problems, or issues to be the focus of the survey.
4. Ask what decisions, choices, or actions are to be based on the results of the proposed survey.
5. Make a preliminary assessment of the approximate value of the survey information for the sponsor.
6. Seek indications of the time requirements for the survey and the approximate funding and resources available.
7. Describe the type of cooperation and participation that will be required of the sponsor.
8. Explain what ethical responsibilities regarding the survey the researcher has to the sponsor and respondents.
9. Encourage the confidence and trust of the sponsor through candor and professional conduct.

The sponsors must have a sense of trust in those conducting the survey. They should feel free to provide the information the researcher seeks from them. The researcher may have to explain that those conducting the survey stand in a fiduciary relationship with the sponsor. The researcher is ethically bound to do nothing to harm or endanger the sponsors. This relationship is no different than that of physician and patient or attorney and client.

Unless it's otherwise stipulated in writing, the survey data, the information, the instruments, and even the knowledge that a survey is being conducted are all *proprietary* to the sponsor. In short, everything belongs to the sponsor. It would be highly unethical for those conducting a survey to discuss it with outsiders; reveal the sponsor; share the data, reports, or information; or to dispose of these *properties* in any way that might prove undesirable to the sponsor. If the researcher intends to publish the results or promulgate the information in any form, it's the researcher's obligation either to obtain approval in advance and include it as a provision of the contract or to obtain written permission later, but *before* releasing the information. These and other aspects of the researcher role are outlined in Guidelist 1–2.

Occasionally a potential sponsor will approach a researcher and propose a survey that's specifically designed to obtain certain results. In other words, the project is to *appear* to be an actual, unbiased survey, when in fact the process is *rigged* to yield specific findings. For example, the items may be worded in such a way that they will obtain certain results, the sample may be designed to obtain responses from those who are most likely to be favorable to the position of the sponsor, or the results may be analyzed to generate a positive picture. Usually such unethical motives and intentions become clear during specification of the information needs. They're totally improper and illegitimate and the prudent researcher will both refuse the proposed project and also avoid any working relationship with the sponsor in the future. These ethical considerations are outlined in Guidelist 1–3.

For Maintaining Professional Ethics   Guidelist 1–3

1. Maintain a fiduciary relationship, always seeking and protecting the best interests of the sponsor.
2. Treat all survey information, including the process and the results, as the sole property of the sponsor.
3. Obtain prior permission or approval before releasing, publishing, or using any survey information or data.
4. Refuse any project or relationship with a sponsor who seeks to bias the survey to get certain results.
5. Protect the privacy and anonymity of respondents if they're promised their identity won't be revealed.
6. Never permit the sponsor to identify individual respondents for reprisal for adverse survey results.
7. Don't identity respondents for solicitation unless they know in advance they may be solicited later.
8. Recognize the legitimacy of withholding sponsor identification to respondents and others when appropriate.
9. Return all data, reports, or other materials purchased by sponsors to them on completion of the project.

Often a sponsor will want a survey to be conducted by an independent researcher because the sponsor doesn't want to be identified to the respondents or to others. In other words, the *sponsor* wants to remain anonymous. If the respondents know who is sponsoring the survey, that may bias the results. If customers, competitors, vendors, or others know about the survey, that may have adverse effects on the sponsor. It's completely legitimate to conduct a survey without identifying the actual sponsor, either to respondents or to others. If potential respondents don't want to participate because the sponsor isn't identified, they can refuse. The researcher is under *no obligation* to reveal the sponsor to the respondents or to explain the nature or reasons for the survey if it's against the sponsor's wishes.

Respondent Rights

Both sponsors and researchers have some important ethical obligations toward respondents. Reputable researchers respect and maintain the privacy of respondents, as well as their anonymity if they're promised it. When the respondents are promised they won't be individually identified, that promise must be carefully kept. Sponsors must not request that individual respondents be identified unless the respondents have to be advised of it in advance, so they're free to decline participation if they prefer. If the respondents are to be assured of anonymity, only *aggregate* data or completely *unidentifiable* individual responses should be provided to the sponsor or made public.

There may be occasions when the sponsor would like to know the identity of the respondents after learning the results of the survey. For example, an employer who sponsored a survey of employees may want to identify individual respondents or units within the organization for the purpose of reprisal for negative attitudes or behavior. Similarly, a company may wish to identify potential customers, based on their survey responses, and solicit them to purchase goods. If the respondents have been assured of their anonymity, sponsors and researchers are bound by ethical principles to keep that promise. Even though the sponsor has initiated and funded the survey, they have no legitimate claim to the identity of respondents who have been promised anonymity.

The rights of all research respondents extend far beyond the time and place the research is conducted and the information reported. Computer and communications technology offer tremendous facility for the collection, transfer, and storage of data. In most cases, that's a very positive thing, but not always. The ease with which data can be stored, manipulated, and transferred carries with it a lurking danger that it will be conveyed to the wrong people or organizations or put to illegitimate purposes for which it was never sought or intended. The responsibility for careful maintenance and ultimate disposal of research data falls jointly on sponsors and researchers. The public in general and respondents in particular have a right to expect the data they provide will be safely protected and used as intended. Such information privacy rights are implied and irrevocable. All concerned are obliged to play by these roles.

Potential Survey Topics

Surveys can be designed to capture a wide variety of information on many diverse topics. Eight basic topic categories are described here: attitudes, images, decisions, needs, behavior, lifestyle, affiliations, and demographics. These categories aren't perfectly distinct from one another. Some may overlap and some issues or topics don't fit perfectly into one category. Yet the topics do differ in many ways and they're often measured by different types of survey questions or items.

Attitudes

Attitudes are often the subject of surveys. They predispose people to act in a certain way toward the object of the attitude. The attitude comes *before* behavior and affects the way the person will act. They're fairly enduring and usually last for weeks, months, or even years. But people may change their attitudes when they receive additional information or experience, or perceive the object of the attitude differently.

Attitudes are always focused on some object. It can be a physical or material thing, a person or group, or an idea or issue. They have three parts: (1) What the person *knows* or *believes* about the topic, (2) how the person feels about the topic or how it's *valued*, and (3) the likelihood that the individual will take *action* based on the attitude. When attitudes are measured, the survey questions should include all three attitude components. For example, it would be necessary to ask if respondents *know* about the object, how much they *liked or disliked* it, and how they *intend to behave* toward it. The basic recommendations for measuring attitudes are contained in Guidelist 1–4.

For Measuring Attitudes   Guidelist 1–4

1. Be sure to include all three components of the attitude: knowledge, feelings, and action tendencies, in that order.

2. Begin with awareness and knowledge. Ignore feelings and action tendencies if knowledge is insufficient.

3. Use unaided recall to measure awareness, if possible, to avoid false reports of recognition.

4. Measure depth of knowledge with an index of the number of correct statements about the topic.

5. Use ratings scales to measure feelings, so that both direction and distance from neutral are revealed.

6. Consider a comparative scale where relative, rather than absolute levels of feelings are appropriate.

7. Don't ignore the intensity of feelings or assume intensity is the same as distance from neutral.

8. Measure intensity by asking how strongly respondents feel or how sure they are of their position.

9. Measure past, present, and future behavior to assess the strength of the behavioral component.

10. Specify hypothetical conditions and ask intentions if respondents lacked opportunity to act in the past.

Knowledge Component

People base their feelings and actions on what they *know* about an object. So it's important to learn what they know or believe about the topic. Respondents should be asked about their knowledge of the topic first. If they've never heard of it, there's no reason to ask about their feelings or actions. People often give an opinion, even though they've no notion whatsoever of what the thing is. Nobody likes to admit they don't know, so they pretend. To measure the knowledge component, begin by measuring *awareness.* There are two ways to ask about awareness: *aided* and *unaided* recall. With aided recall, the respondents are asked, "Have you ever heard of _____?" The problem with this kind of question is that many will say they've heard of it, even though they haven't. To avoid this problem, ask for more detail concerning the characteristics of the object or else use the unaided recall method.

With the unaided method of measuring awareness, the respondent is asked to name all the objects in a given group or to identify the object based on a description of its characteristics. For example, people might be asked to name all the brands of a product they could recall. If they named the brand in question, they'd have awareness. Or respondents might be asked, "Do you know the name of the member of Congress from this district?" Naming the representative correctly would indicate awareness. Another way to get information about the knowledge component is to ask about the manner in which respondents learned of the object and the experience they've had with the topic.

Feeling Component

People are seldom completely neutral about anything they know about. The feeling component develops in one of two ways: through *reward* or *punishment,* or through *evaluation.* In the case of reward and punishment, they learn to like or dislike the object because their experience with it was positive or negative. For example, many have a negative attitude toward some food because they find it distasteful. The second way people develop feelings about objects is by evaluation. People automatically and often unconsciously compare what they know or believe about a topic with their own, personal values. If their knowledge fits their values, they develop positive feelings, and if it's contrary to their values, their feelings are negative toward the topic. For example, if someone knows that a particular brand is expensive and this person values economy highly, this would lead to the attitude becoming more negative.

To measure the feeling component of an attitude, two sets of things often need to be measured: *position* on the positive/negative spectrum and level of *intensity* of feelings. The two aren't the same. One person may feel that the object is very good but may be unsure of this, while another may feel slightly negative about the object but may hold that feeling with great intensity. It would be easy to change the first person's mind, but difficult to persuade the second one to take another view. Measuring the *position* of feelings requires measuring the *direction* and the *distance* of the feelings; to know if respondents *liked* or *disliked* the object and *how much* so.

It's easier to measure the direction and location of feelings than to measure intensity. Asking respondents to rate how certain they are of their good/bad or comparative rating provides a direct measure. Inquiring as to why they feel as they do or asking the likelihood of their changing their opinion are indirect measures.

Action Component

Even though two people have about the same knowledge about the topic of an attitude and share much the same feelings, they may behave differently toward the topic. For example, two shoppers who have the same knowledge and feelings about a certain brand may both find that the brand was out of stock at their favorite store. One may simply choose another brand, but the other may postpone purchase until the brand is available or seek that brand at another store. Why the difference in behavior? Because the action components of their attitudes toward the brand differ.

Measuring the action component usually requires asking how they've acted toward the object of the attitude in the past, what their current practices or habits toward the object are, and what they expect or intend to do in the future. Seeking indications of *why* they hold the attitude and how it relates to their motives, goals, plans, and aspirations also provides clues about the likelihood people will act on the attitudes they hold.

Images

People's images of things are exactly what the name implies: the mental *pictures* of the object they have in mind. But no picture is perfect. It may be blurred, as though the lens of the camera were not focused, or it may be sharp and resolute. It may be a close-up, showing every detail, or it may show only the most obvious features of the object. It may be accurate and precise, showing everything exactly as it is, or it may be badly distorted, as the image of someone looking at themselves in the curved mirrors of a fun house at the carnival. It may be complete, including the entire object, or it may show only a portion of it. And it may be a blowup or a reduction, showing the object as bigger or smaller than it really is. Each person tends to see things a little differently from others. Thus, no two images are apt to be exactly alike, although some may be very similar and others distinctly different. But an image is likely to take on a different form from the *real thing*, and when people lack some information, they tend to fill in the picture.

Image Dimensions

To get a verbal picture of people's images, they might be asked how they'd describe the object. They would be likely to name several characteristics and indicate their magnitude or the quality. These characteristics are actually the dimensions of their image of the thing—the features that define the image in the mind of each individual. There will be some variation from person to person, but many features will be included by nearly everyone, while some characteristics that might apply will be ignored by everyone. The tendency for most respondents to define images with about the same attributes allows researchers to measure and compare images. The first step is to ascertain what attributes or characteristic features (dimensions) are most common and important to *respondents.* That can be done as described earlier, by asking for a description of the object from several typical respondents. Alternatively, the researcher may elect to conduct one or more *focus groups.* The recording of the group can then be studied to learn how respondents think about the topic and what words or phrases they use to express those thoughts and images. The researcher mustn't be the *exclusive* source of ideas for identifying attributes because respondents may actually use a different set of dimensions. The image profile is accurate only if it includes those and only those attributes that are important to the respondents.

Image Profiles

The *configuration* of several attributes or characteristics defines a complete image profile. It's the constellation of ratings, rather than any single one, that's of interest. The individual attributes don't stand in any set pattern with one another, and the researcher determines the order in which the items are listed. They may be in random order or according to some other system. The most important ones should be in the middle of the list, rather than first or last. When some or all features have a good/bad connotation, about half should connote *positive* and half *negative.* The two types should be scattered among one another. This controls for the tendency for some people to be globally positive or negative. The most effective scales for measuring image profiles are described and exemplified in Chapter 5.

Image Comparisons

Image profiles often differ between respondents with different characteristics, such as men versus women or those in different occupations. The images for one or more objects can be compared among different groups or subsamples to reveal such differences in people's perceptions and evaluations. It's also often desirable

For Measuring Images   **Guidelist 1–5**

1. Use image profiles when several attributes or characteristic features of an object are to be measured.

2. Question some typical respondents about the objects to determine the attributes they use to define the image.

3. Don't depend on the sponsor to identify the relevant image dimensions.

4. Limit the number of items to only the attributes most meaningful to respondents.

5. Randomly order the items, being sure that about half can be seen as positive and half as negative.

6. Obtain ratings of more than one object in a class if comparisons of image profiles among objects are of value.

7. Have respondents rate an *ideal* object if there's uncertainty about positivity or negativity for some items.

8. Compare ideal image profiles for different respondent groups to reveal differences in preference patterns.

9. Plan to subtract ideal from actual ratings for each respondent to provide a *difference* profile.

10. Compare profiles of differences between ideal and actual object ratings to assess positive or negative valences.

to compare images of different topics or objects in the same general class, such as different companies in an industry or opposing political candidates. When the information needs call for comparison, each object must be rated separately by each respondent. This allows the researcher to compare the profiles with one another after the data have been compiled.

There may be several items that can't be readily identified as positive or negative. If so, this can be ascertained by asking the respondents to rate their *ideal* entity. The ratings for the actual object(s) can be subtracted from those for the ideal object for each respondent. The closer the actual ratings to the ideal, the more positive the ratings. Negativity can be judged by the absolute value of the difference between actual and ideal. These differences between actual and ideal for each of the actual objects can also be compared. This indicates which are more positive and which more negative. Measuring both the perceptions of objects and the valences makes the image measurement scales powerful devices. The guidelines for measuring images are summarized in Guidelist 1–5.

Decisions

When decisions are the topic of research, the focus isn't so much on the results of decisions in the past as on the *decision process* itself. Often people's choices require them to evaluate alternative courses of action. Their choices depend in part on their *information sources* and the *evaluative criteria* they use for judgment. Those seeking survey information are often keenly interested in these aspects of the decision process that people use to choose actions. Guidelist 1–6 outlines the main considerations for measuring decisions.

For Measuring Decision Making   Guidelist 1–6

1. Use when information requirements focus on the process of evaluation, not the results.
2. Determine how much the decision was based on preexisting information and how much was directly sought.
3 Classify information sources as direct experience, social influence, or media effects.
4. Measure the appropriate level of media effects: exposure, attention, content, or impact.

5. Measure abstract, global values only when information is required about decisions about many different objects or those of profound importance to respondents.
6. Expect to identify only a very limited number of evaluative criteria for any one individual.

Information Sources

Decisions are conscious choices based in part on information. In some cases the decision maker already has all of the information required for the decision. In others, the person will need more information, and that will require an *information search*. Survey research can measure both the information content on which a decision was based and also the nature of the information search process. Information can also be measured in terms of the source from which the decision maker obtained it. Generally, three different categories are useful: direct personal experience, social influence, and media sources.

Information obtained from nonpersonal sources is called *media* information. A survey inquiry might focus on several different levels of media effects. Respondents might be asked about mere *exposure* to some medium, such as whether or not they subscribe to a particular publication or listen to a certain radio station. They might also be asked how much *attention* they paid to a medium, such as whether or not they actually saw or read a particular advertisement. They can also be questioned about their comprehension or recollection of *content* of a message presented through the medium. Lastly, the most detailed inquiry would measure the *impact* the message had on choices or actions.

Although valuable data on information acquisition can be obtained through surveys, a note of caution is needed. The history of survey research indicates that most people are only vaguely aware of the information they actually apply to a decision and where they obtained it. Generally, direct experience is *overstated* and media influence is *understated*. In general, people are likely to recognize that media influence other people's decisions, but they often won't admit they, themselves, are influenced.

Evaluative Criteria

When someone evaluates something, the person is assigning a value to it. It's judged according to the attributes the decision maker feels are relevant. Any object of evaluation can be viewed as a *package* of different characteristics. Ordinarily, the object to be judged has many more attributes or characteristics than people actually consider. Thought processes are limited to consideration of only a handful of things at one time, usually about seven at most. There is seldom the necessity for judgment of more than a few attributes, and research has indicated that people typically use only a few features to judge and select among alternatives, even for very important decisions.

The identification of the evaluative criteria people use to select among alternatives is a major task of survey research. One of the most common ways to do this is simply to question respondents about why they made the choice they did. This requires composing a list of attributes of the chosen object and asking respondents to rate the importance of each. Another method of detecting evaluative criteria is to present respondents with a hypothetical choice situation and ask what information they'd seek about the alternatives. The attributes for which they seek information are those they'd use for evaluation. This method doesn't require previous choice experience.

Needs

Sponsors are often concerned with why people behave as they do. Most behavior is directed toward the satisfaction of one or more human needs. Thus, the answer to the question of *why* is often obtained by measuring the relationship between actions and needs, desires, preferences, motives, and goals. People generally act with intent. This doesn't imply that they know, consciously, what personal motives and needs lie beneath the surface of their actions. Consequently, it can be a difficult job to dig out the needs that underpin behavior and the motives that prompt action. The picture may be complicated further by the fact that (a) many different actions can serve the same motive or provide satisfaction for the same need and (b) several needs or motives may be served by one action or behavior pattern. To cope with these problems, the researcher must be willing to recognize the difficulties and to understand the nature of needs, desires, preferences, motives, and goals.

Needs can be viewed as categories of things that most or all people require for existence and contentment. They can be specified in terms of basic things that must be provided to sustain human life. Such things as food, shelter, clothing, and the like are basic human needs. Needs can also be classified according to the requirements for psychological and social conditions. For example, they might include love, prestige, or power. Finally, needs can be viewed in terms of specific categories relating directly to different types of activity. Such a list might include such things as play, nurturance, achievement, or recognition.

Desires are closely related to needs. When a person consciously focuses on some object, activity, or state of being that might provide satisfaction for a need, the person has a desire for that thing. The individual may not be aware of exactly what need is beneath the desire. *Preferences* are often treated as desires that have less drive or energy behind them. In other words, both imply a conscious focus on something, but desires are stronger while preferences imply less urgency regarding the object. *Motives* are also related to needs, but they're more closely associated with actions. Motives arise from unsatisfied needs, and they trigger behavior or energize the person to perform some action to get satisfaction. They might be seen as a *push* away from some negative condition or a *pull* toward some desirable

For Measuring Need-Related Concepts   Guidelist 1–7

1. Determine the needs, desires, preferences, motives, or goals that are relevant to the information requirements.

2. Specify the items or categories in terms that will be easily understood by all respondents.

3. Use a fixed sum, comparative, or forced ranking scale to avoid most or all items being rated as equally important.

4. Remember that multiple needs and related variables can be served by the same behavior, and different actions can serve the same need.

5. Use projective methods when measuring or assessing motives that are likely to be sensitive.

situation. *Goals* or objectives are also related to needs. A person's goals represent some *end state*, some destination or condition that the person seeks to reach through behavior. Goals are related to needs because the objective is often the satisfaction of one or more needs.

Several types of scales are commonly used to measure needs, desires, preferences, motives, and goals because they fit the nature of the concepts being measured. These question formats and scales are described in Chapter 5. Summary recommendations for measuring needs and related concepts are provided in Guidelist 1–7.

Behavior

The measurement of behavior involves four related concepts—what the respondents did or did not do, where the action takes place, the timing of the behavior, and the frequency or persistence of behavior. In other words, it often means assessing "what, where, when, and how often." When research is used to establish which actions were taken by respondents, the alternative courses of action can be listed in categories to be sure the responses are comparable. Simple multiple choice items can then be used, with either a single or a multiple response permitted.

The location of some particular form of behavior is often of interest. The places might be designated as geographic areas or by some other means, such as at home versus away. If only a few specific locations can be identified, a multiple-choice question can be used. Maps, graphs, or displays can also be shown to respondents to obtain their indication where the action takes place. It's best to provide the respondents with a specific set of possible locations, rather than depending on them to indicate a place in their own words. That's because each respondent tends to use different terms to describe a location, and probably no two respondents will use exactly the same phrase to describe any one place.

Respondents may be able to indicate a location by using a designation that has been assigned to the places, such as the ZIP codes or political jurisdictions. Maps are often available to show such geographic areas. The researcher may have to translate these numbers indicating geographic areas into different categories than those

For Measuring Behavior   **Guidelist 1–8**

1. Identify information needs in terms of "what, where, when, and how often."
2. Specify the actions and locations in categories to make responses comparable.
3. Determine if respondents might have engaged in only one or several categories of action, and use single or multiple-response items accordingly.
4. Remember that frequency of behavior is often best expressed in terms of time, such as times per day or week.
5. Keep in mind that *individual* intentions or predictions are ordinarily not as reliable as they are in aggregate.
6. Be sure to use such items as verbal frequency or fixed sum scales when proportions or behavioral policies are to be measured.

used by the source of the designations. This is an effective means of measuring location, provided that the individual designations apply to areas that are about equal to or smaller than those required by the survey information needs. Areas can be combined if necessary, but they can't be divided into smaller increments or blocks than those specified when the data are collected.

Respondents are often questioned about *when* they performed a certain action and whether or not they're presently engaged in such behavior. Future intentions to act can also be the subject of survey inquiry, but of course these predictions by respondents may not be completely accurate. Individual predictions of future actions are less reliable than the collective or aggregate predictions of the proportions who say they will act in a certain way. Some may change their mind and do something else, but others may elect to do so when they had no such intention. So aggregate predictions are often more reliable than any one expression of intent.

The *persistency* of behavior may be important to measure. Many actions are habitual, while others are performed routinely because a single decision has led to continuity until something changes the routine. Habitual or routine behavior of a respondent is often of great interest to sponsors. People might be questioned about their policies or practices concerning some action, such as their favorite place, their political party, or religious preference.

People also change patterns or deviate from their former or usual actions on some occasions. It's often important to determine just what proportion of the time they act in a certain way, *given the occasion to act*. In such cases, the researcher is often less interested in the *absolute* number of times the action is taken as in the frequency, *relative* to the number of occasions or opportunities to act; in other words, in the *proportion* of opportunities at which the action is taken. Chapter 5 identifies scales that work effectively to measure the proportion of behavior, based on the number of opportunities. The main issues regarding measurement of behavior are listed in Guidelist 1–8.

For Measuring Lifestyle Patterns   Guidelist 1–9

1. Seek out lifestyle libraries of items or compose items that are directly relevant to the information requirements.

2. Use multiple items to identify individual lifestyle patterns among respondents.

3. Choose questions about activities, interests, opinions, or possessions that are indicative of a particular lifestyle.

4. Keep in mind that lifestyle measurement requires many variables or items and may increase questionnaire size and response task time and difficulty.

5. Remember that lifestyle analyses focus on clusters and require substantial analysis to identify patterns.

Lifestyles

Surveys can be used to determine the lifestyles of respondents. Lifestyle consists of the *pattern* or *configuration* of things people do, believe, and own. Groupings of the population by lifestyle can be used to identify an audience, constituency, target market, or other collectivity of interest to the sponsor. Often, those with different lifestyles will react differently toward issues of key interest to sponsors. Different lifestyle patterns can be identified by four kinds of variables associated with respondents: (1) activities, (2) interests, (3) opinions, and (4) possessions. Researchers interested in the measurement of lifestyle can obtain lists of lifestyle items from the literature on the subject. Most such libraries of items have been used successfully in the past and often define meaningful lifestyle segments or groups. Another alternative is to compose a family of lifestyle items to define the lifestyle segments that are the most meaningful and relevant to the information needs. Such lists must contain enough items to ensure that patterns are fairly reliable. No single item will define lifestyle adequately.

In summary, a given lifestyle is a collective or conglomerate factor. The objective is to identify a pattern or profile. Consequently, respondents must be questioned about many items that relate to a given lifestyle or pattern of living. While this can be a potent method of identifying and distinguishing groups or segments, the measurement will often require many questions. In terms of questionnaire space and response time, this may be costly and in some cases, uneconomical. Guidelist 1–9 outlines the main points to be considered when measuring lifestyles.

Affiliations

Social contact and interaction are often the focus of survey research or bear heavily on other issues that are relevant to the survey. So the family setting, memberships, social contacts, reference groups, and communications of respondents are frequently measured or assessed within the survey research process. The main issues regarding the measurement of affiliations are listed in Guidelist 1–10. Those within the same nuclear or extended family often think, behave, and live similarly. Of all social groups, the family probably exerts more influence on individuals

For Measuring Affiliations **Guidelist 1–10**

1. Consider membership in both formal and informal groups as sources of influence for respondents.

2. Define groups clearly and concisely for respondents (e.g., such terms as "family" might include only parents and siblings, or more distant relatives as well).

3. Select the appropriate type of reference group for identification, either comparative, normative, or informative.

4. Consider both opinion leaders and key influentials when determining sources of influence on respondents.

5. Remember that identification of sources of influence is only approximate because people are often unwilling or unable to provide precise data.

than those of other groups or units to which the person belongs. The most simple measurement is specification of family status, including marital status and children in the home. This method is discussed in the next section, on demographics. Other family issues, including the roles played by various family members, group decision making, and authority relationships within the family, can also be measured by surveys. The types of questions and scales depend on what data are being sought. The researcher must select from among the available items and scaling techniques to obtain the most appropriate device.

Both formal and informal affiliations relationships are often the subject of surveys. Their measurement ordinarily consists of the specification of the groups in terms that can be easily understood by the respondents, who are then asked to indicate any groups to which they belong. The importance of the group to the individual and the importance of the person to the group are also assessable through survey questioning. Leadership or officer status are often topics of inquiry as well.

Social integration can be measured by indications of the frequency and duration of contact and interaction with others. The propensity to interact with others can be assessed directly or indirectly. Direct measurement requires listing the groups, and respondents are asked to indicate those with whom they interact. There are also *indirect* methods for measuring affiliations, described in Chapter 5, that might be used to reveal the importance of affiliation.

The *individual referents* or *reference groups* used by respondents may be of interest to the sponsor. These terms refer to an individual or group that serves one or more of three major functions: normative, comparative, or informative. A *normative* reference group is one that establishes or provides norms of conduct or behavior that the individual is expected to follow. Normative reference groups tell one *what* should and shouldn't be done.

By contrast, a *comparative* reference group provides a standard or benchmark to show *how* an individual is doing in some respect. People often comment about "keeping up with the Joneses," and the Joneses are obviously the comparative reference group. Surveys often identify just who the Joneses are and why they serve

For Measuring Demographic Status   **Guidelist 1–11**

1. Include all demographic items that may be systematically associated with other items of importance in the survey.

2. Specify categories clearly and concisely for respondents.

3. Choose categories and items that will be comparable with other, external, secondary data or information.

4. Use sample demographic items where possible and make only necessary modifications to avoid risk.

as a referent. Comparative reference groups are often used whenever people lack an absolute, concrete standard by which to judge their own standing.

An *informative* reference group conveys information about alternatives and conditions to respondents without suggesting a pattern of appropriate behavior or showing relative standing. For example, sports enthusiasts or auto experts may constitute informative reference groups for someone unfamiliar or less familiar with athletic or automotive equipment or services.

Reference groups can be identified by using several techniques. The most common and direct method of identifying reference groups is to ask the respondent to identify them. A less direct means is to question respondents about affiliations with those in similar conditions or with similar opinions, so reference groups are specified only by inference.

Surveys may be used to identify opinion leaders and those within their sphere of influence. An *opinion leader* is one who has special expertise, experience, or credibility in the eyes of others. The attitudes of the opinion leader are often amplified and extended to many others. Those known as "key influentials" occupy a special position or have special recognition that permits them to influence the attitudes of many others within a specific social setting. If key influentials can be identified prior to the survey, based on their position or office, the degree of influence or impact they exert can be measured. Respondents may rate the importance of the key influential, relative to other sources of information or influence. These data are useful, but they're never very precise because people are unwilling or unable to express influence patterns with much precision.

Demographics

Demographic factors often used in survey research include such variables as age, sex, marital status, family status, family life cycle stage, education, employment, occupation, income, and residential location and type, among others. Such data are often valuable to sponsors because (a) demographic groups often differ significantly on the issues of importance and (b) demographics can be used to identify segments, groups, audiences, or constituencies of people who are both identifiable and behave in similar ways. Guidelines for measuring demographic status are contained in Guidelist 1–11.

The key to accurate measurement of demographic status is the clear, concise statement of the categories or dimensions. This depends on clarity and meaningfulness to respondents and the degree of precision required by the information needs. Several examples of demographic items are shown in Chapter 6. They include some items that are broad and comprehensive, and others that are relatively precise and fine-grained. Select among these items and modify them as required. Previously tested items have less inherent risk than newly composed items, scales, and formats.

Conclusion

The list of topics discussed here isn't comprehensive or all-inclusive. Other topics might arise that could not easily be classified into the categories provided. This doesn't preclude their use. There are two purposes for including this outline of topics: (1) They help those seeking survey information to recognize the range and type of information that can be obtained from survey research, and (2) they assist the researcher to classify information needs and make tentative, preliminary plans for the survey process to follow.

Summary
Survey Sponsorship and Potential Topics

A. Evaluate survey potential. The same measurement methods are useful for many occupations and needs.

B. Maintain realistic expectations. Survey research is neither impossibly difficult nor precisely definitive.

C. Expect and evaluate errors. Minor mistakes may affect some results, but they seldom ever invalidate them all.

D. Recognize the potential topics. They indicate what can be measured and suggest ways to obtain information.

E. Allow for other topics. The list provided here isn't all-inclusive, and others might be used productively.

F. Consider suggestions carefully. The methods of measurement identified here are thoroughly tested.

2

Planning the Project

The Survey Process

A survey project is a process with a series of steps linked with one another. The decisions made during the early stages affect the choices open at later stages. The information needs specified at the first stage indicate what type of sample will be required, what type of measurement instruments will be needed, what data collection methods will be most appropriate, and more. This forward linkage among the steps is shown in Figure 2–1 by the solid lines running downward and to the right, on the left side of the diagram. If there were only these forward linkages, the researcher could take one step at a time, performing each set of tasks in turn. Only the effects on following steps would have to be considered at each step. But this would assume there are no limitations on the options available at the later steps. In reality, that's seldom so. There are usually limitations on data collection and data processing resources. These limitations restrict the alternatives open at the *earlier* stages. So there are *backward* linkages in the survey process. They're shown by the dashed lines running upward and to the left in Figure 2–1, on the right side of the diagram. Ignoring these limitations during the earlier steps in the process may lead the researcher to a dead end when some restraints are encountered later.

Figure 2–1 shows that the backward linkages in the survey process run from the data collection phase and the data processing phase back up to the sampling design and instrumentation steps. Major decisions concerning data collection always have to be made *before* designing and selecting a sample or composing and constructing the questionnaire and other materials. Some information needs can be satisfied more effectively with one method of data collection than with another. Yet data collection is typically the most expensive phase of the process. It would not make sense to design a sample without first selecting the data collection method and estimating the cost of collecting the data because different data collection methods will require very different sampling designs and questionnaires. The availability of data entry and processing facilities also influences the early stages of the process. The data processing method has to be planned so that sampling and instrumentation will be compatible with both the capabilities and the limitations of the data processing method chosen.

FIGURE 2–1
Linkage in
the Survey
Process

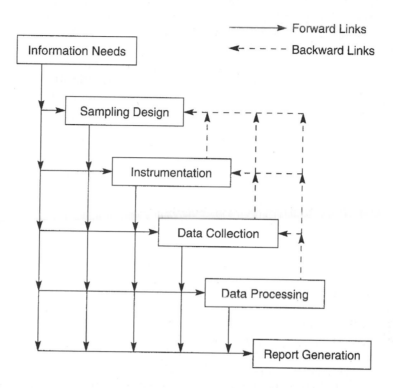

MAJOR STEPS IN THE SURVEY PROCESS

———————▶ Forward Links
◀ – – – – Backward Links

Information Needs

Sampling Design

Instrumentation

Data Collection

Data Processing

Report Generation

Specifying Information Needs

The sponsor's information needs are first determined in the dialogue between the researcher and the sponsor described in Chapter 1. Those needs for information must now be listed in more concrete and specific terms. For example, the researcher may have determined that the sponsoring organization may be seeking information about its workers' reactions to a new benefit program. But "worker reactions" is a relatively ambiguous term. It doesn't describe precisely what's to be measured. A survey could be designed to measure the workers'

- *Attitudes*—knowledge, feelings, and expectations regarding the program.
- *Images*—the mental picture they've developed of the program or employer.
- *Decisions*—regarding whether or not they'll avail themselves of the program.
- *Behavior*—such as how the program might change their work habits.
- *Affiliations*—to indicate the group consensus and communications patterns.
- *Demographics*—indicating what type of employee wants the new program.

To specify the information needs effectively, the researcher has to learn exactly what *kind* of information the sponsor wants in terms of the survey topics discussed in Chapter 1. The specification of information needs plays a key role in the survey process. As Figure 2–1 indicates, virtually every aspect of the survey project from beginning to end is geared to the nature of the sponsor's information needs. Everything has to be tailored to satisfying them. That's the whole purpose of the project. Accurate and effective specification is one of the most difficult of all the tasks associated with a survey. It often receives too little attention and effort. Errors or inadequacies in the specification of the information required from the survey will be amplified during the later stages of the survey process.

Survey Information Value

The value of survey information to the sponsor depends on three main factors: (1) the cost of making an error, (2) the degree of uncertainty surrounding the decisions or actions, and (3) the amount of uncertainty the survey may reduce. Each of these factors should be assessed carefully to gauge the expected value of survey information. Then the *expected value* can be compared to the funds and resources available for the project and to the *expected costs* of the survey.

The potential value of the information should be *at least* two or three times the entire cost of the survey project, and preferably much, much greater than that. That's because the estimates are only the *potential*, and not the actual value and costs. The value of information virtually never can be determined precisely. It may prove to be of greater or lesser value than estimated. The estimate of the information value will sometimes turn out to be too conservative, and sometimes it will turn out to be too liberal.

Similarly, it's almost impossible to obtain an exact estimate of the projects' actual costs. In almost every case, there will be "cost overruns." The actual costs nearly always prove to be greater than anticipated, even with an allowance or "safety factor" built into cost estimates. There are always some hidden costs associated with survey research as well. They're items that have costs which aren't measured, such as the time and efforts of sponsoring executives or managers.

The value of information from *academic* survey research can only be estimated by scholars familiar with the concepts being tested by a survey. Estimation of information value depends on expert judgments concerning the value of the potential contribution of the research to the scholarly literature. Information from those research projects that make strong contributions in critical areas of interest are more highly valued than that which has more finite implications or deals with more trivial issues.

The Cost of Errors

The value of information from *applied* survey research depends on its potential to avoid two broad types of decision errors. They might be labeled "go" errors and "no-go" errors. Go errors are more obvious while no-go errors are more obscure. A go error results when a decision maker takes a course of action that proves to be costly or unsatisfactory. A no-go error results when the decision maker either fails to take some action that would have positive results, or ignores an alternative that would be most positive, choosing instead some less positive course. (In some areas, the possibility of go errors is called *down-side* risk, while the chances of no-go errors are viewed as opportunity costs.)

For example, assume that a company is considering a new venture. The most basic question is *whether or not* to proceed with it. A go error, the most obvious kind, would result if the firm went ahead with the new venture and it *failed*. The potential cost of a go error includes everything the company might loose as a result of *going ahead* with the plan. Whatever funds they had expended and weren't recovered would show up as monetary losses. Other resources expended and not regained would be part of the nonmonetary costs of the failure. Most of these losses would be very obvious and fairly quantifiable.

The less obvious no-go error associated with this decision would result if the company decided *not* to go ahead with the venture when, in fact, it would have been successful. The potential cost of a no-go error includes any benefits—monetary and otherwise—that might have been gained if they had elected to proceed with the venture. Unfortunately, if the action is not taken, it's extremely difficult to recognize, comprehend, or appreciate what might have been gained. So most sponsors are far less cognizant of the costs of no-go errors than they are of the costs of go errors. The greater the potential gains or losses inherent in a decision or set of decisions, the greater the cost of uncertainty. Surveys that promise to reduce very costly uncertainty have commensurately more value.

The Amount of Uncertainty

The *amount* of uncertainty is a separate issue from the *cost* of uncertainty. In some cases, the sponsors are already fairly sure about what decision to make or what action to take. They may have a large amount of existing information about the issues in question, or they may be guided in part by information from other sources—observation, experimentation, deduction, previous experience, and the like. In other situations where there is a large amount of uncertainty surrounding the issues, those seeking survey information may be highly or even completely uncertain about what decision to reach or what action to take.

The evaluation of information value comes down to two basic questions: (1) How costly might either a go or no-go error be? (2) How much uncertainty surrounds the issues in question? When a great deal rests on the quality of the decision because there's much to be gained or lost, and when there's a high degree of uncertainty about the issues, additional information would have greater value. Often, only the sponsor will know the facts about go and no-go errors. Usually only those seeking the information can assess their own degree of uncertainty. The research designer may have to question them carefully to ascertain the potential value of the information.

Reduction of Uncertainty

Like any other source of information, survey research doesn't provide *perfect* information. Sometimes surveys can address nearly all the issues or problems that face the sponsor. There are also situations where only some—perhaps only a few of the existing questions—can be answered by survey information. For instance, if the sponsor wanted only to know, just before an election, the proportion of voters who intend to cast their vote for Candidate A versus Candidate B, a well-conducted survey would probably reduce nearly all of that sponsor's uncertainty. By contrast, sponsors who seek to learn the relative importance potential voters place on a complex set of political issues and candidate characteristics are likely to discover that a survey will reduce only a relatively small part of the total body of uncertainty they face.

Even when a survey can comprehensively embrace a specific set of questions, the degree of reduction in uncertainty may vary, depending on whether the survey information is *descriptive* or *predictive*. *Descriptive* survey data may sometimes be almost absolutely definitive, while *predictive* information is usually far more tentative. A survey of householders to determine what major appliances they own would be very likely to answer that question with a high degree of certainty. There would be little doubt remaining in anyone's mind about the existing situation. By comparison, a *predictive* survey to determine what major appliances they *intended* to purchase in a specific period in the future would lack the same degree of certainty. It would provide only tentative indications of what might actually transpire, since a wide variety of factors might alter intentions and sharply reduce the predictability contained in the survey results. Thus, a large amount of uncertainty would remain regarding what the sponsor might expect for the future.

Information Value and Priority

The three factors that determine the overall value of a survey to the sponsor and the justifiable level of expenditure on a survey are the *cost of errors*, the *amount of existing uncertainty*, and the *reduction in uncertainty* promised by a survey. These factors are summarized in Figure 2–2.

The specification of information needs should meet two objectives: to *include* all of the information that's genuinely required or highly valued, based on priority,

FIGURE 2–2
Factors
Determining
Information
Value

Factors Indicating High Value
1. The cost of selecting a "bad" alternative (go error) or failing to select the best alternative (no-go error) would be relatively high.
2. There's a very high degree of uncertainty about which alternative to choose, based on existing information.
3. Survey research information is very likely to reduce a large proportion of the existing uncertainty.
Factors Indicating Low Value
1. The cost of making either a go error (selecting a "bad" alternative) or a no-go error (rejecting a good alternative) would be relatively low.
2. There's relatively little uncertainty about the decision, based on existing information or information from other sources.
3. Survey research information will remove only a small portion of the uncertainty surrounding the decision or action.

For Classifying Information by Priority	Guidelist 2-1

1. There are two basic objectives to be met:
   a. Obtain *all* of the essential information.
   b. Obtain *only* what is directly applicable.

2. Information can be classified into three categories.
   a. *High priority* items that are *absolutely essential* to the project.
   b. *Medium priority* items that are *highly valuable* for decision making.
   c. *Low priority* items for *supportive data* to enhance understanding.

and to *exclude* any questions that are redundant or provide information that's of little or no value. The *priority of information needs is based on the value of information items*. Items of information can be classified into three levels of importance: (1) *absolutely essential*, constituting the main reason for the project, (2) *highly valuable* for making important decisions, and (3) *supportive data* to enhance the understanding of decision makers and clarify the picture portrayed by the survey results. Anything of lesser value should be culled from the list.

It's essential to prioritize the information needs because time and resources are always limited. Inevitably, it will be necessary to eliminate items or reduce the number of questions. Such deletions are more readily made when there's a clear indication of item priority. The least valuable items can be discarded and all of the most valuable questions will still be retained as the plans are modified and the project moves forward.

The priority of the survey questions has another function as well. When those who design and conduct the survey and compose the questionnaire or survey instrument have a clear indication of the importance of the various items, they'll be able to place greater time, effort, and emphasis on the most critical and valuable items of information. When the structure and sequence of items within the survey questionnaire require compromise, the least valuable items—those with the lowest priority—are more likely to be moved or adjusted. In that way, the most crucial questions will maintain the most prominent place within the instrument, where they're likely to receive the greatest thought and attention by respondents. The major considerations for assigning priority are shown in Guidelist 2–1.

Planning the Survey Elements

At this point, the researcher must plan the elements of the survey process and compose the project outline. The outline will guide, direct, and coordinate the tasks required to initiate and complete the survey. The sponsor should inspect and approve the outline before the project is continued. The project outline is more

FIGURE 2–3   **Elements of the Project Outline**

1. List information needs by priority.	6. Note the scope of the response task.
2. Indicate the value of the information.	7. Describe the data collection method.
3. Identity internal resource requirements.	8. Outline the data processing method.
4. Specify sample size and design.	9. Describe the type of reports required.
5. Provide a mockup of instrumentation.	10. Summarize final costs and the timetable.

essential than it may seem. It's even more important for less experienced researchers than for those with considerable experience. The elements of the project outline are listed in Figure 2–3.

The elements of the project outline aren't usually planned in the same sequence as they're listed. That's because the backward linkages in the survey process make it mandatory to consider some of the later phases before making decisions about those that come earlier in the process. Usually the researcher has to make several passes or iterations through the survey process, making only tentative decisions about *sampling design, instrumentation, data collection method,* and *data processing.* This circular process is shown in Figure 2–4. Data collection is typically the most expensive aspect of a survey. It often becomes the compelling factor, requiring direct modifications to the sampling design and instrumentation, as well as the data processing procedure.

Data Collection

Because data collection is usually the most expensive (and time-consuming) aspect of the survey project, it's the logical starting place for estimating project costs. The choice of a method for collecting the data depends on the information needs and

FIGURE 2–4
Circular
Nature of
Survey
Planning

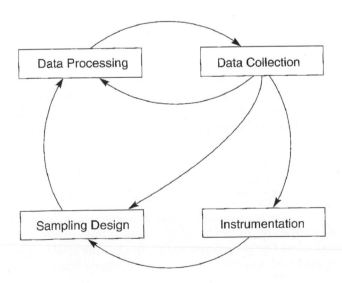

FIGURE 2–5 **Comparison of Data Collection Methods**

	Personal	Telephone	Online	Mail
Data collection costs	High	Medium	Low	Low
Data collection time required	Medium	Low	Medium	High
Sample size for a given budget	Small	Medium	Large	Large
Data quantity per respondent	High	Medium	Low	Low
Reaches high proportion of public	Yes	Yes	No	Yes
Reaches widely dispersed sample	No	Maybe	Yes	Yes
Reaches special locations	Yes	Maybe	No	No
Interaction with respondents	Yes	Yes	No	No
Degree of interviewer bias	High	Medium	None	None
Severity of nonresponse bias	Low	Low	High	High
Presentation of visual stimuli	Yes	No	Yes	Maybe
Field-worker training required	Yes	Yes	No	No

value, as well as the budget and resources available, access to the population to be sampled, and the timing requirements. Collecting the data requires contact with respondents, and that can be accomplished through interviewing—speaking with them in person or by telephone—or by self-administered questionnaires—online or by postal mail. Thus, personal interviewing, telephone interviewing, postal mail, and online surveys are the four principal methods of data collection used in survey research. The selection of the most appropriate method for collecting the data is a key decision for the researcher. Each of the four basic methods of data collection has its own special capabilities and limitations. There are some types of information that can only be obtained by one method, but often the researcher has a choice between two or three of them, while one or two others lack the capability required.

The basic differences among the four data collection methods are in the accessibility of the respondents and the intensity of contact between the researcher and the respondent. The closest contact and the greatest opportunity for two-way interaction between those collecting the data and those providing it are provided by personal interviewing, followed by telephone interviews. The most remote contact is obtained by postal mail, while online surveys are somewhat less remote than mail. The costs and resource requirements of the four methods also differ markedly. One may require much more time than the other. One particular method may be far more or far less expensive than the others. Each demands a different type of expertise from the research staff and field data collection team. The physical facilities that are needed differ for each method of data collection. Travel and media requirements vary from one method to the next. The degree of control over data collection also differs widely.

In summary, the data collection method that's selected is likely to result in a very different survey project from that which would ensue if another method were chosen. The contact and interaction requirements, the nature of the inquiry and information sought, and the timing and geographic circumstances of respondents are important considerations for making a choice. Figure 2–5 provides a sketch of the major factors.

Personal Interviewing

The size of the survey sample may vary from a few dozen to several thousand respondents. Personal interviewing usually requires a field force of interviewers. The field-workers may be recruited and trained by the researcher, or outside field data collection agencies may be hired to collect the data. If the interviewers work directly for the researcher, they must be trained in both the general procedures for selecting respondents and interviewing them and also the specific characteristics and requirements of the project. When field data collection agencies are used, they need only be instructed concerning the specific nature of the task. This data collection method requires the most interviewer training to avoid the most common sources of interviewer bias. It also requires a substantial amount of supervision in the field, and there's still a good possibility of bias because field-workers may fail to adhere to instructions. The project supervisor has less control than with other methods.

Personal interviewing provides the most complete contact with respondents because face-to-face interaction permits both audible and visual communication with respondents. They can examine, touch, handle, or try objects relevant to the questions. The interviewer can present visual materials such as rating cards, pictures, or displays. Physical objects can be presented to the respondents for them to see, feel, hear, taste, smell, handle, and even consume. Personal interviewing is often able to win respondent cooperation and hold it for a long time. Nonresponse bias is minimal, and this method is quicker than mail surveys for small, geographically concentrated samples.

This method is usually the most expensive per respondent because of the travel expenses and interviewer costs, especially if the respondents are dispersed over a wide geographic area or difficult to locate. But personal interviewing can reach respondents at home, at work, or at special locations, such as intercepts at polling places, the shopping mall, or some other place close to the location of an activity that might be the topic of the survey. So the advantages may outweigh the disadvantages of this means of data collection. The flexibility of this method sometimes makes it the only choice for projects that demand direct contact, a special location, or special selection of respondents who qualify for the survey.

Telephone Interviewing

With telephone surveys, the interviewers don't have to go into the field. The interviewing can either be done from one or more central locations or perhaps even from the interviewers' homes. Much depends on the location of the respondents and the long distance charges for the calls, as well as the degree of trust in the interviewers and the need to supervise them. While personal interviews may take weeks or months, telephone interviewing is usually completed much more quickly. But there are some important distinctions between the two methods. Telephone interviewing allows only audible contact, not visual. The interviewer can't see the respondent and must gauge the mood and demeanor of the respondent merely by the tone of voice, vocabulary, and other audible cues. Nor can the respondent see visual material such as rating scales or the color, size, shape, and texture of some object. They can't try some device or touch, taste, smell, or handle it.

There are also important psychological differences, as well as physical. Eye contact and the physical presence of another person affect a respondent's attitude, mood, and cooperation. It's more difficult for the interviewer to build strong rapport on the telephone. Physical presence usually helps to build trust and confidence. There are also some situations and topics for which telephone interviewing leads to *greater* cooperation than personal interviewing. Telephone respondents feel they have greater anonymity, so they may be more confident and at ease if they're asked to answer personal or sensitive questions. There are also some respondents, such as the elderly or handicapped, who may be physically fragile or psychologically vulnerable. They might be threatened by the physical presence of a stranger asking questions, but they may be willing and able to respond on the telephone.

Telephone interviews usually have to be completed more quickly than personal interviews. Considerable resistance or premature termination (hang ups) by the respondent can result from interviews of more than 15 or 20 minutes. Since the interviewer can't be seen, interviewer bias may be less with telephone interviewing. Physical appearance, dress, facial expressions, gestures, and other visual aspects aren't a consideration on the phone. The interviewers ordinarily require less training and instruction. If the telephone work is done from a central location, there's a greater opportunity to monitor interviewer performance and more control by the supervisor. This method is much more limited in its ability to reach respondents at special locations. Since they must be near a telephone, respondents to telephone surveys are usually at home or at work.

Mail Data Collection

Mail survey data collection differs from interviewing in many important respects. First and foremost, these surveys are "self-administered," so respondents fill out the questionnaires themselves. Since there is nobody present—in person or on the phone—the "cosmetic" aspects of the mailing piece are extremely important because its form and appearance will affect the rate of response and the quality of the data. Very high rates of nonresponse are typical of mail surveys. It may be necessary to provide an *inducement to respond,* either included in the mailing or promised and sent after receipt of a completed questionnaire. Such inducements can be effective, but unfortunately they also increase mail data collection costs dramatically.

The composition, production, printing, and mailing of the questionnaires can often be done by one researcher and a small staff or by external services. The researcher usually has much greater control with a mail survey than with interviewing. Contact with the respondents is less intense with mail surveys. In one respect this method is the reverse of the telephone interview survey. The telephone provides for audible, but no visual contact, while mail provides visual, but no audible contact. Interviews often vary greatly, and any differences may be reflected in the responses as error or bias. With the mail survey, the day, time, and location where respondents complete the questionnaires may differ from one respondent to the next, but the questionnaires are identical to one another. Each respondent is presented with *exactly* the same instructions and tasks, eliminating the chance of interviewer bias.

Interviewing is ordinarily more expensive than collecting data by mail, although direct mail often takes longer because respondents must have time to complete and return their questionnaires. For a given budget, mail surveys usually yield a much larger sample size than interviewing, providing the response rate is satisfactory. Perhaps the greatest advantage of the mail survey is its ability to reach widely dispersed respondents inexpensively. Mailing costs are identical whether the respondent is three blocks or three thousand miles from the mailing point. The geographic dispersion of respondents is often the compelling reason for selection of this data collection method. With postal mail, respondents can ordinarily be reached only at home or at work. The amount of data that can be collected from each respondent is usually more limited than it is when interviewing is used.

Mail surveys don't permit interaction with the respondents, except through the medium of the questionnaire, so the mailing piece must be constructed very carefully, the instructions must be clear to virtually all potential respondents, and the questions or sections contingent on an earlier question (known as "branching") must be kept to an absolute minimum. Normally, the questionnaire should be pretested to ensure its effectiveness and clarity, unless the researcher is thoroughly experienced and knows well what to anticipate from the particular group to be surveyed. The standardization of the communication to respondents eliminates bias due to variance among interviewers. On the other hand, the demand for covering all possible contingencies "up front" is a heavy responsibility with this form of data collection.

Online Data Collection

Online surveys, those that collect data by presenting the questionnaire on a web page, share many of the characteristics of mail surveys, but there are also very important differences. Like mail surveys, online surveys are self-administered, so there's no interaction between respondent and interviewer. Thus the contact with respondents isn't as intense as with telephone or personal interviewing, but neither is there the chance for bias and error that can be introduced by interviewing.

Compared to mail surveys, online data collection provides much *more intense* interaction with respondents. True, there is only the *possibility* of audio contact with respondents because most will probably only be looking at the questionnaire, not listening to the sound, even if it's available. On the other hand, the online visual contact can be far more stimulating than with mail surveys. Very simple online surveys may be quite similar to self-administered, paper-and-pencil questionnaires. But more elaborate and sophisticated online questionnaires may include very colorful, graphic material as well as text. There is even the ability to include animation or short video clips if necessary or desirable.

Survey Nonresponse Bias

The single most serious limitation to direct mail data collection is the relatively low response rate. Mail surveys with response rates over 30 percent are rare. Response rates are often only about 5 or 10 percent. That means that more than 9 out of 10 people who are surveyed *may not respond!* If so, the cost of each completed response will be about 10 times the cost of preparation, printing, and mailing for each questionnaire originally sent. The reliability of the data depends on the size of the sample *obtained*, and not the number of surveys sent, so the researcher must make an estimate of the response rate and mail enough questionnaires to yield the approximate number of responses required.

By far the most important consequence of a low mail response rate is the *nonresponse bias* that's likely to result. If respondents *randomly* complete or fail to complete and return the questionnaire, there will be *no* nonresponse bias, but that's seldom the case. Whether the survey recipients complete and return the questionnaire, set it aside and forget it, or just throw it away depends in part on their characteristics, attitudes, opinions, and interest in the topic. As a result, some types of people are likely to be overrepresented and others underrepresented in the sample received, creating biased results.

Some general principles can help the researcher gauge the degree of nonresponse bias, but they don't provide a definitive solution to the problem. Ordinarily, those who are highly involved with the topic are more likely to respond than those who aren't. That includes those who feel strongly *positive* about issues or topics and those who feel strongly *negative* as well. The more neutral the respondents or the less experience or involvement they have with the topics or issues, the more often they'll discard the questionnaire. Then, too, certain demographic groups are more likely to respond than are others. Those who are less pressured for time, such as the very young or the elderly, the unemployed, or those outside large urban areas, are more likely to respond.

Nonresponse is a *very* serious problem when there's a direct connection between the purposes of the survey and the information needs, on the one hand, and likelihood to respond, on the other. For example, if the survey is to measure the proportion of people who own a certain product, and owners are more likely to respond than nonowners are, the results will be *worse* than useless—*much* worse. The variable being measured—ownership—would directly affect the likelihood to respond. To avoid such bias, the researcher should judge the degree to which nonresponse will interact with the topics or issues of the survey. If the interaction is thought to be too strong, the data have to be collected in interviews. Even if this interaction is negligible, overrepresentation and underrepresentation of some population segments may preclude a mail survey.

Like mail surveys, online surveys are subject to very substantial levels of nonresponse and the bias and error associated with it. Only a fraction of those solicited to visit the website containing the survey questionnaire or who visit it voluntarily or by chance are likely to take the time and exert the effort to complete and submit the questionnaire. And as with mail surveys, these are likely to be those with the strongest positive or negative feelings and those with higher levels of involvement with the topics of the survey. Thus, there is likely to be substantial, and perhaps prohibitive, levels of self-selection and nonresponse biases.

Aside from the sources of bias that sometimes plague mail data collection, online surveys have another shortcoming: They are able to sample only those who have Internet access and use the web. This situation is of no consequence for those projects where the population to be sampled are *all* routinely online. It is a *major* stumbling block for survey projects where only a portion of the population of interest uses the Internet. Each year, a higher proportion of the general public connect to and use the Internet than that of the previous year. But even when a very large part of the population that's the focus of the survey is routinely online, there can be substantial bias. That's because there are likely to be substantial differences between those who are and those who aren't online. Thus, as with all online surveys, the results represent only those with Internet access and experience and can't be generalized to those who are not on the Net.

Selection Factors

The basic characteristics of the major data collection methods have been identified and compared. To select the most appropriate method, the researcher should decide whether or not interviews are required or preferred. Aside from the contact and interaction requirements and conditions, assessments of the degree of nonresponse and selection biases are extremely important. Even if a self-administered survey is feasible in terms of contact and interaction, it would be totally inadvisable to use either mail or online data collection if the results might be highly biased. The factors that influence most heavily the choice between interviewing and self-administration are outlined in Checklist 2–1.

If interviewing is required or preferable, the next step is to decide whether personal or telephone interviews would be most appropriate. The choice is based on comparison of the information needs and interviewing task with the attributes and characteristics of the two types of interviews. For some surveys, one method will be completely precluded and the other will be absolutely necessary. Usually the decision won't be dictated and the advantages and disadvantages of each must be weighed against one another. Checklist 2–2 lists the major considerations in outline form.

If a self-administered survey is feasible and required or preferable, the researcher must choose between a mail survey or an online survey. The latter isn't feasible unless a very high proportion of those to be surveyed routinely use the Internet. If all or very nearly all the prospective respondents are regularly online, an online survey is feasible. If the information needs specify topics or issues directly related to the Internet or its use, an online survey would probably be preferable to a mail survey. If presentation of colorful visual material or animation is required, only an online survey provides that facility. The main considerations for choosing between online and mail data collection are highlighted in Checklist 2–3.

While there are times when the information needs or availability of resources clearly dictate one particular data collection method, there's usually a choice to be made. Selection must come after specification of information needs, but there may be times when the data collection method chosen may necessitate changes in the information needs themselves. This might be either because some data can't be obtained, or because more is available than originally anticipated. Nonetheless, information needs should be the predominant consideration.

Sampling Design

The actual selection of a sample comes later in the survey process. Only the basic strategy and design must be chosen at this point and included in the project outline to guide the project. Sample size and design are discussed in detail in Chapter 3.

To Choose Between Interviews and Self-Administration

1. Does the task require interaction with the respondents? If there must be a two-way conversation, interviews will be required and a self-administered data collection method isn't feasible.

2. Is there the likelihood of interaction between the tendency to respond and the issues or topics being measured or assessed? If so, serious nonresponse bias precludes the use of a mail or online survey and interviewing is needed.

3. To what degree can the population be reached with a self-administered questionnaire? Lacking the ability to: (a) include a full representation of the population to be surveyed, and (b) exclude unqualified individuals, interviewing will be necessary.

4. Must the survey be conducted in a specific location, such as a store, workplace, or polling place, or at a specific time such as in the morning or on a particular day, or after a specific activity? If so, interviews are needed.

5. Can the respondents provide and record their own responses, or must it be done by an interviewer? The more complex and intricate the recording of the data, the less likely a self-administered survey will provide satisfactory data.

6. Is it more important to collect a large amount of data from each of a small number of respondents, or to obtain a more limited amount of data from each of a very large number of respondents? In general, the larger the sample required, the more appropriate a self-administered survey becomes.

7. Are the respondents widely dispersed over a broad geographic area or concentrated in groups in a confined area? The more widely dispersed, the less appropriate interviewing becomes in terms of the cost of travel or of long distance telephone calls.

8. Might nonresponse or selection bias associated with self-administered data collection jeopardize the survey results? If so, telephone or personal interviewing should be used.

9. Would respondents be more embarrassed or threatened by talking to someone than merely recording their own responses? The higher the degree of psychological threat, the more appropriate self-administered data collection becomes.

10. Are respondents likely to be highly sensitive to information privacy? The greater the respondents' need for confidence in complete anonymity, the more appropriate self-administered data collection becomes.

Response Task and Sample Size

Survey research strategy tends to lean in one of two directions: Obtain a large amount of data from a small sample, or obtain a small amount of data from a large sample. Usually the resources are limited while information needs are insatiable. The trade-off between the amount of data to be obtained from each respondent and the number of respondents in the sample is shown in Figure 2–6. The size of the response task and the size of the sample pivot on the fulcrum, a fixed level of funding. The more data to be collected from an individual, the greater the costs per respondent, and the larger the sample, the greater the expense. So, for a fixed level of funding, the larger the response task the smaller the sample must be, and vice versa.

The choice of which strategy to take depends on the information needs. When very precise estimates are needed, larger samples are required and that limits the

---

To Choose Between Telephone and Personal Interviewing

Checklist 2–2

1. Must the data be collected at some special location outside the home or workplace, such as a shopping center, polling place, meeting, or event? If so, personal interviews will be required.

2. Does the interview task require showing the respondent something? If so, telephone interviewing is precluded and personal interviews are required.

3. Must the respondent be seen to judge if they're qualified to respond? If there's a quota based on the physical appearance or observed behavior of respondents, personal interviews will be necessary.

4. Are interviewers likely to include or exclude certain types of people, based on their appearance or visible characteristics, contrary to quota specifications? If such selection bias is likely, telephone interviews are more appropriate.

5. Is there a likelihood of psychological threat or intimidation in a personal encounter with an interviewer? If so, the more remote telephone interviewing method is indicated.

6. Is contamination of responses by the respondents' companions during the interview session likely? If so, telephone interviewing is more appropriate because others are less likely to overhear the conversation or interrupt it.

7. Will the interview take an exceptionally long time? If so, personal interviews are preferred because greater rapport and cooperation can be achieved with personal presence.

8. Does the telephone directory or other telephone number list serve as an adequate sample frame? If not, telephone interviews are precluded.

9. Are the respondents spread throughout a wide geographic area? If so, time and travel costs for personal interviews are likely to be prohibitive and long distance telephone interviews are advisable.

10. Is there the necessity for very rapid data collection? If so, telephone interviews can normally be completed much more quickly than interviewing in person.

To Choose Between Online and Mail Data Collection

Checklist 2–3

1. Will nearly all those to be surveyed routinely be on the Internet? If not, a mail survey will be necessary.

2. Does the sponsor or research team have access to a website for presenting the questionnaire and collecting the data? If not, a mail survey will be necessary.

3. Does the researcher have the technical skill to create an online questionnaire or the resources to hire a specialized web survey agency? If not, it will be necessary to use postal mail.

4. Is the focus of the survey on topics or issues directly related to the Internet? If so, an online survey might be preferable to mail data collection.

5. Does the survey require the presentation of colorful illustrations, animated material, or video clips? If so, an online survey is required.

FIGURE 2–6
Response
Task versus
Sample Size

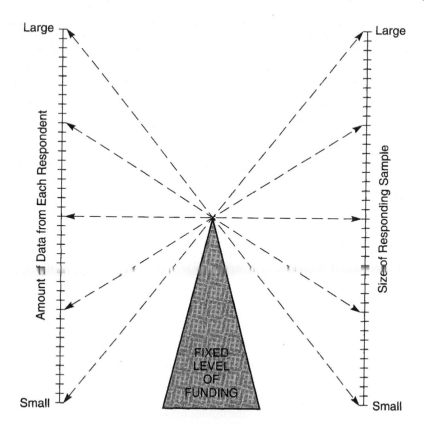

amount of data that can be collected from any one respondent. When the information needs depend heavily on the relationships among the survey questions so patterns can be detected, a large amount of data must be collected from each respondent. This limits the number of respondents that can be sampled at a given cost.

It's important to estimate the amount of data required from each respondent at this point in the survey planning process. This will determine the duration and difficulty of the response task and that will affect the estimate of cost per respondent. High cost per response will require a precise and perhaps elaborate design for a small sample. Low cost per response will permit sampling of a larger proportion of the population. The next step is to decide the approximate size of the *responding* sample; that is, the number of respondents who provide complete responses. The general considerations indicating the size of the sample and the size of the response task are listed in Figure 2–7. Once the approximate sample size and the cost per respondent have been estimated, data collection costs can be estimated and listed in the project outline. This is vital to the budgeting process, since data collection is often the single, most costly phase of the survey research project.

FIGURE 2–7
Factors
Determining
Sampling
Strategy

Indications for Large Sample and Small Response Task	Indications for Large Response Task and Small Sample
1. Very precise estimates of numeric values are required and there must be a high degree of confidence in them.	1. Estimates of numeric values for the population need only be approximate within a fairly broad range.
2. Individual survey items are of more interest than are patterns of response among many survey items.	2. Focus of information needs is more on patterns or configurations among responses to items than on individual items.
3. The range and volume of information required from each respondent is fairly limited.	3. The range and/or volume of information required from each respondent is relatively large.
4. The data are to be collected by mail, so a simple response task is likely to increase the response rate.	4. The data are to be collected by telephone or personal interview rather than by mail.

Population, Units, and Frame

The population includes all those of interest to the sponsor—the group from whom a sample will be selected. For example, a store might sponsor a survey of its *existing customers*, so only those who shopped at the store would be included in the population. Only *registered voters* might be included in the population if a political organization wanted to conduct an opinion poll. The actual *elements* of the population have to be defined to indicate exactly what constitutes a *sample unit* and what doesn't. For most surveys, the *sample units* will be individual people; however, sometimes *families, households, companies,* or *organizations* are surveyed, rather than just individuals. If so, the *sample units* would be defined in those terms and the *population* would consist of those sample units.

The *sample frame* is a list or set of directions that identify all the sample units in the population. For instance, a company may decide to conduct an employee survey. The *population* may be described as all existing nonunion, full-time employees. A list of them might be compiled from personnel records. That list could serve as the *sample frame* from which a sample of a fraction of respondents would be chosen. But suppose the store mentioned earlier wants to conduct a personal interview survey but doesn't have a customer list to use as a sample frame. In that case, a *set of directions* that identifies the population of customers could be composed. The *sample frame* may be all those who visited the store and made purchases during a specific, future time period. A *sample* of them may then be interviewed.

Sampling Design Alternatives

The researcher typically has several options regarding the basic sampling *design—random* or *convenience, stratified* or *unstratified, clustered* or *unclustered,* in any

FIGURE 2–8
Sampling
Design
Options

Random	Convenience
Every sample unit in the population has an equal chance of being selected. The sample represents the population well. The probability of sampling error can validly be computed statistically.	Some sample units have a greater chance of being selected than others. The sample's represenatation of the population is *inferior*. It's *invalid* to compute the probability of sampling error.

Stratified	Unstratified
The proportion of various types of sample units in the sample is controlled by selecting a series of *subsamples* of specified sizes.	The proportions of various types of sample units will be approximately the same in the sample as they are in the entire population.

Clustered	Unclustered
A series of physical or geographic areas are selected, then a specific number of sample units are selected proportionally from each "cluster."	Respondents are selected randomly (or by convenience) *regardless* of their physical or geographic location.

combination. These alternatives are outlined in Figure 2–8. They need only be discussed briefly here. They're discussed more fully in Chapter 3.

Random versus Convenience.   When sample units are selected randomly, each unit has an equal probability of being chosen. There's a very compelling reason to strive for a random sample: With random selection, the probability of a specific amount of sampling error can legitimately be computed statistically. For instance, the report can indicate to those seeking the information that there's a 95 percent probability that the value in the *population* is within a given range of the corresponding value for the *sample*.

There are times when it's exceedingly difficult or even impossible to choose a sample randomly. So those who conduct surveys may sometimes have to revert to a *convenience* sample—selecting those respondents from the population that are obtainable or convenient to reach. Confidence levels and the degree of sampling error can be computed, but these statistical values are technically invalid. They'll be inaccurate to the degree that the convenience sampling deviates from random selection, including sample units that overrepresented or underrepresented that type of respondent in the entire population.

Stratified versus Unstratified.   It's sometimes important to be sure that a sufficient number of certain kinds of respondents or sample units are included in the sample, even though they're a relatively small proportion of the population. An *unstratified* random sample would have to be extremely large to obtain enough respondents of a certain type. A *stratified* sample can be designed to reduce the required total sample size radically. The population is divided into specific *strata* containing certain types of respondents. Then a *subsample* of the required size is obtained for each strata. The stratification procedure is explained in more detail in Chapter 3.

Clustered versus Unclustered. A *clustered* sampling design is appropriate when respondents are widely dispersed in space or time. If the population is sparsely located over a wide geographic area, the entire area can be divided into sections or "clusters." The researcher can first select several such clusters (preferably at random) and then select a specific number of respondents from each cluster. If sampling is to be done over a long time, the periods during which respondents are to be interviewed can be clustered similarly. Cluster sampling may dramatically reduce data collection costs because of the savings in time and travel. The procedure for clustering a sample is discussed more fully in Chapter 3.

Sample Selection Methods

Regardless of the basic sampling design chosen, the researcher must decide just how the respondents will actually be selected. If a sample of 200 respondents is to be selected from a sample frame of 20,000 members of the population, exactly *how* should the 200 names be chosen? If 12 in-home interviews of urban residents are to be conducted within each of 30 neighborhood clusters, which clusters should be chosen and which homes within each cluster should be included? The most basic methods of random sample selection—n*th name sampling, random number generation, random number tables,* and *physical selection methods*—are discussed fully in Chapter 3. The choice depends on the nature of the individual survey project and no one method is universally preferable to the others.

When the data are to be collected by telephone or personal interviewing, there are many cases where some of those originally contacted *won't* be eligible for inclusion. For example, the sampling design may *exclude* those under 18 years of age, or it might *include* only those employed full-time outside the home. Similarly, a *stratified* sample may require half the respondents to be married and half unmarried. If so, each interviewer may be assigned a *quota* of a certain number of respondents of each type. The interviewers may have to ask those they contact one or more preliminary questions to qualify the respondent before continuing. The procedures for *quota assignment* and *qualification questioning* are explained in Chapter 8. The researcher should study these issues carefully during the planning phase if it appears that *prequalification* or *quotas* may be required.

Instrumentation

The information needs are expressed in terms appropriate to the sponsor. They're also listed in the order of their priority or importance to the user of the information. Survey instrumentation involves translating the information needs into a form that will elicit data from respondents. The survey instruments, themselves, include the survey questionnaire, as well as ancillary materials—cover letter and mailing materials, rating cards and display materials, or illustrative web page content that might be required. Part Two of the handbook, devoted to survey instrumentation, will provide a more thorough view of questionnaire development and instrument composition.

Survey Topics

Classifying the information needs into survey topics serves two purposes: It groups items that are similar to one another into the same topic categories, and it suggests the type of questions and scales needed to obtain the information. When the information needs have been classified into topic categories, the entire task of inquiry is expressed in terms more appropriate and meaningful to the researcher. This process also assembles the items into groups, so items that require about the same kind of task from the respondent are listed together. This is the first step in arriving at a sequence that will facilitate response and assure more reliable, accurate data.

To classify the information needs into topic categories, each item specified in the list of information needs must be identified as relating to one or more of the seven basic topic categories identified in Chapter 1. At times, the topic that's inherent in the question will be obvious. Careful thought and judgment are required when more than one topic is implied or where the identification of one particular topic is ambiguous. The translation of information needs into survey research topics should meet two important criteria: First, every item of information required should be classified into one or more of the topic categories and expressed in those terms. Redundancy should be limited and deliberate, so the exact same information should not be sought more than once unless that's intentional. Second, nothing should be neglected or it won't be collected. The list of information needs should be checked against the list of topics very carefully to be sure nothing has been ignored.

Instrument Specification

The principal measurement instrument is the survey questionnaire. A detailed description of the intended instrument should be composed to guide the rest of the project plan and the subsequent project tasks. Aside from the questionnaire itself, the description should also identify any ancillary elements of the survey instrument. The main items to be considered are listed in Checklist 2–4.

It may be necessary to compose a rough draft of the questionnaire so it can be checked and approved by the sponsor. A rough draft is also useful for completing the project planning. When the survey instruments have been described and perhaps drafted, the researcher should be able to estimate the size and scope of the response task. The approximate number of survey items or variables should be noted in the project outline, together with the total time it will require of a typical respondent and the ease or difficulty of the response task. It's also important at this point to estimate the costs for composition and production of the survey instruments. Thus, it may be necessary to obtain cost estimates or bids from internal or external sources, such as typesetters, printers, and the like. When these costs have been obtained, they should be listed in the project outline, together with the other information that's relevant to instrumentation.

To Describe the Survey Instruments   Checklist 2–4

1. How will the questionnaire be organized and why? What's the main principle of organization? Will the items be congregated by topic, type of question or scale, type of response required, or some other criterion?

2. How many parts or sections will be included and in what sequence? What comes first and why? What questions will be at the end of the questionnaire and why?

3. What type and level of language will be used—technical or lay, simple or sophisticated vocabulary?

4. What kind of grammar and composition will be used—formal or casual, scholarly or colloquial wording?

5. What types of questions and response scales will be included? Will respondents answer with words, letters, or numbers? Will they choose from the specified answers or respond spontaneously in their own words?

6. What are the most sensitive or threatening questions? What will be done to reduce resistance and why will it elicit respondent cooperation?

7. What ancillary instrumentation will be used—cover letter, pictures or displays, rating cards or other visual, audible, or animated material?

8. What's the expected size of the questionnaire? How many questions or items in total? How many parts or sections? How many pages? If printed, how much weight and physical bulk?

9. How will the questionnaire be produced?[1] If printed, what size, color, weight, and grade of paper stock? In what print format? How will it be reproduced and bound or attached?

10. What will be retained by the respondent and/or interviewers? What will be returned for data recording and processing?

[1] This item assumes a standard, "paper and pencil" questionnaire. If the questionnaire is to be presented on electronic media or in some other form, see Chapter 6 for detailed guidance.

Data Processing

Surveys generate *quantitative,* rather than only *qualitative* data. Responses are almost always recorded in the form of numbers, rather than words. The *objective* of data processing is to convert the *data* into *information.* The *product* of data processing is a set of tables and graphs that portray the results of the survey. They may be presented directly to those seeking the information or incorporated into written reports. Often both forms of reporting are used.

The primary objective of data processing and analysis is to *suppress superfluous detail* and to *make the most relevant and important facts and relationships apparent.* Too much detail is confusing. It hides, rather than reveals, the meaningful information. For instance, it would be difficult to learn much about the age of the group of 1,000 people by looking at a list of their birth dates or even their individual ages. But if these data were processed to compute the average age of the group, that *information* would be more *meaningful.* A table or graph showing the *distribution* of the age of the group might be even more informative.

Nearly all surveys include only a *sample* of the entire population of interest to the sponsors. When only a sample is surveyed, another objective of data processing is to perform *statistical analysis* so that *inferences* can be made about the entire *population*, based on the survey *sample*. For example, if the group of 1,000 people mentioned earlier constituted a sample of all those in the city, their average age could serve as an *estimate* of the average age of that population. But samples are never perfect, so this sample might include a slightly younger or older group, on average, than the population as a whole. In other words, there's likely to be some *sampling error*.

Statistical analysis allows the researcher to compute the *probability* that the values obtained from the sample are within a specific range of those for the entire population. In other words, statistical analysis reveals *both* the estimated values for the entire population *and* the range of possible error at a given level of probability, as a result of sampling.

Computer Facilities

The computer programs that can be used for survey data processing vary markedly. They range from simple, unsophisticated spreadsheet programs and database managers all the way up to highly capable and advanced statistical analysis packages and graphics programs. Spreadsheet programs, one of the staples on almost all desktop or laptop systems, can be used by anyone familiar with them to make simple transformations in the survey data where necessary. Spreadsheet programs can also be used to compute simple statistics such as averages and to portray distributions of data by category in tabular form. Spreadsheet programs may also reveal relationships between pairs of variables by cross-tabulating one variable with another or performing correlation or regression analysis. Nonetheless, spreadsheet programs are "general purpose" programs. They're designed to do a wide variety of analysis tasks, not just survey data processing or statistical analysis. Consequently, their ability is limited to only the basic forms of survey data analysis.

Statistical analysis software packages such as SPSS™ are composed of many integrated routines that allow the analyst to perform a wide array of analyses using the same basic format and set of instructions. Many corporate, government, and organizational survey sponsors may already have such software resident on their local area networks. These statistical packages are available for desktop or laptop computers, although their sophistication means they can also be rather expensive. The cost of purchase may be prohibitive unless it can be spread over several projects. For researchers undertaking only a single research project, it may be more economical to use online analysis routines that can, in effect, be "rented" based on the time and intensity they are used.

Report Generation

The nature and format of the reports to the sponsor must be specified and the costs of reporting must also be estimated in advance. A wide variety of report mechanisms and formats are used for survey projects, depending on sponsor preferences and information needs.

| For Composing Written Reports | Guidelist 2–2 |

1. Begin with a one- to three-page *executive summary* listing only the major highlights in telegraphic, bullet format beginning with the material that's most important to those seeking the information.

2. Include a *response summary,* a clean copy of the questionnaire containing brief indications of the percentage distributions of response to alternatives or the average values obtained from the sample.

3. Report the most important information first in the body of the document arid organize it in the *categories* or *sections* that are the most relevant to the reader seeking the information.

4. Provide attractive, clearly labeled, readily readable *tables and/or graphs* that summarize the survey results visually and portray relationships among the items or questions and patterns of response for various types of respondents.

5. Compose *narrative text* that explains the tables and/or graphs in clear, easily readable terms, avoiding technical jargon and highlighting the most important values or relationships.

6. Attach a *technical appendix* describing how the survey was conducted in detailed terms, as well as any relevant *computer print output* of statistical analyses where either or both are appropriate or requested.

Written Reports

The written report is both the most common report medium and the least expensive and time-consuming. The typical elements of a written survey report are described in Guidelist 2–2. The composition and production of written reports can be more expensive and time-consuming than might be anticipated. It's important to consider the size and the complexity of the reports of written documents when planning them and estimating costs.

Report Presentations

Sponsors often prefer the researcher or research team to make a visual and verbal presentation of the survey results and to respond to questions about the survey and its findings. If only one or a very few people are seeking the information, such report conferences may only require multiple copies of the report document. More formal report presentations, often made to larger groups, usually require composition and production of visual materials, including bullet charts, tables, graphs, and perhaps illustrations. The cost of producing such visual materials and the demands on the researcher or research team's time and efforts vary widely, depending on the sponsor's needs. Thus it's vitally important to identify the need for report presentations during the planning phase and determine the costs and timetable associated with this form of reporting.

Project Costs and Timing

The primary objective of the project plan is to guide and direct the entire process as the survey is conducted. The secondary objective—nearly as important as the first—is to determine in advance the cost of the project and the time schedule for the work.

FIGURE 2–9
Project Costs by Stage of the Process

1. Survey Initiation
   a. Information Need Determination
   b. Preparation of Project Proposal
2. Sampling Procedure
   a. Sampling Design
   b. Sample Selection
3. Instrument Composition
   a. Draft Document Preparation
   b. Questionnaire Production
   c. Ancillary Material Production
4. Interview Data Collection
   a. Training and Supervision
   b. Interviewer Compensation
   c. Travel or Telephone Charges
   d. Return and Verification
5. Data Processing
   a. Editing and Data Transfer
   b. Analysis Programming
   c. Statistical Analysis
6. Report Generation
   a. Narrative Text Composition
   b. Table and Graph Composition
   c. Production and Duplication
   d. Report Delivery or Presentation

Cost Estimation

Survey costs ordinarily fall into four basic categories: (1) direct labor, (2) direct materials and supplies, (3) external service fees, and (4) overhead expense allocation. The amount and proportion of each category of cost differs sharply from one phase of the project to the next. So cost estimation should be done by *stage*. One model of the stages of the interview survey process is shown in Figure 2–9. The data collection expense categories would differ somewhat for self-administered online or mail surveys.

Budget Preparation

The budgeting process consists of estimating the cost of each of the four categories, for each stage and substage from the beginning to the end of the survey project. For example, using the model presented in Figure 2–9, the researcher would begin by calculating the *direct labor costs* for *information need determination*. It might be necessary to break that substage down into even smaller increments, identifying such tasks as *sponsor conference time, facility inspection time, travel time, telephone conference time, office work time,* and so forth. These smaller increments can then be aggregated to determine the *direct labor cost* for item 1a. The costs for direct materials and supplies, external service fees, and overhead expense allocation for *information need determination* may be estimated in a similar way. The aggregate costs for all four categories is the estimated total for that substage. Finally, the sum of 1a and 1b constitutes the total *direct labor costs* for the first stage. Example 2–1 depicts a typical, small-survey budget outline based on the model shown in Figure 2–9 for an *interview* survey.

Budget Modification

As with other budgets, the original survey project budget is often modified after composition and inspection by the researcher and/or sponsor. While the plans for virtually every aspect of the project are subject to change at this stage of the

Survey Project Budget Example 2–1

Survey Initiation
Information Need Determination . . . . $_____
Preparation of Project Proposal . . . . _____
    Total Survey Initiation . . . . $_____

Sampling Procedure
Sampling Design . . . . _____
Sample Selection . . . . _____
    Total Sampling Procedure . . . . _____

Instrument Composition
Draft Document Preparation . . . . _____
Questionnaire Production . . . . _____
Ancillary Material Production . . . . _____
    Total Instrument Composition . . . . _____

Data Collection
Training and Supervision . . . . _____
Interviewer Compensation . . . . _____
Travel or Telephone Charges . . . . _____
Return and Verification . . . . _____
    Total Data Collection . . . . _____

Data Processing
Editing and Data Transfer . . . . _____
Analysis Programming . . . . _____
Statistical Analysis . . . . _____
    Total Data Processing . . . . _____

Report Generation
Narrative Text Composition . . . . _____
Table and Graph Composition . . . . _____
Production and Duplication . . . . _____
Report Delivery or Presentation . . . . _____
    Total Report Generation . . . . _____
TOTAL COST OF PROJECT . . . . $_____

process, the aspect that perhaps deserves the most careful consideration is the *sample size*. Figure 2–10 shows the relative cost levels for six cost categories on the vertical axis, plotted against various sample sizes shown on the horizontal axis. Over a range from 20 or 30 respondents to several hundred, the costs are fairly constant for every cost category *except data collection*. Data collection costs increase in a near-linear fashion with increases in sample size. Consequently, sample size is often adjusted, either to meet budget constraints or to take advantage of the economy of enlarging the sample.

When sample size is relatively large—perhaps several hundred respondents— decreasing sample size reduces total project cost sharply in percentage terms. That's because data collection costs represent a large part of the total project budget. Yet this sample size reduction isn't likely to increase sampling error or decrease certainty in the estimates very much at all. But a very different result occurs with relatively small samples—those of less than about 200 and especially samples

FIGURE 2–10
**Project Cost
Elasticity**

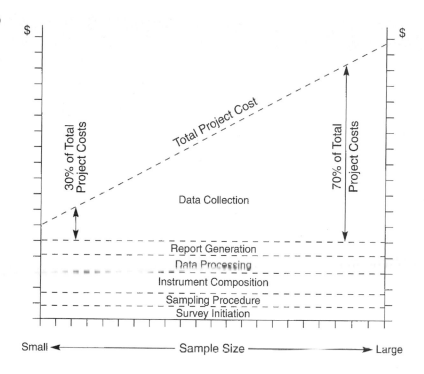

of under 100 respondents. Even a large percentage reduction in sample size at this level has very little effect on *total* project costs because data collection is a relatively small part of the total cost structure. Even more important, sampling error increases dramatically when small samples are reduced even further. By the same logic, *increasing* the size of small samples adds very little, in percentage terms, to the total cost of the project. As Figure 2–10 suggests, initiation, sampling, instrumentation, data processing, and reporting usually cost just about as much for a sample of only a few respondents as they do for much larger samples. Yet there's an important benefit of increasing the size of a small sample—sampling error drops sharply and confidence levels increase commensurately. Consequently, there's a strong tendency for survey researchers to prefer sample sizes in a range from one or two hundred to one or two thousand respondents, working most often with sizes toward the middle to lower part of that range.

Project Timing

The time schedule for a survey project is often as critical as the budget—sometimes even more so. Just as they tend to underestimate costs, researchers and sponsors alike are prone to underestimate the time requirements. Good work takes time! When tasks have to be rushed, errors and mistakes are much more likely. Simple mistakes that occur early in the process—whether they involve timing or not—tend to be amplified with each later phase of the work. Thus, they may jeopardize

Simple Project Schedule Chart   Example 2–2

Weeks from Start

Task	1	2	3	4	5	6	7	8	9	10	11	12
Determine Information Needs	▓											
Draft Project Proposal	▓											
Get Sponsor Approval		▓										
Design Sampling Procedure			▓									
Write Respondent Selection Instructions				▓								
Write Questionnaire Items and Scales				▓								
Compose Complete Questionnaire					▓							
Have Questionnaire Printed						▓						
Prepare and Copy Rating Scale Cards					▓							
Select Data Collection Agency					▓							
Ship Materials to Data Collection Agency						▓						
Train Field Supervisors and Interviewers							▓					
Data Collection Period							▓	▓				
Receive and Sight-Edit Questionnaires									▓			
Verify Response of Part of Sample									▓			
Key Data to File and Process Edit								▓				
Write Analysis Programs and Instructions								▓				
Run Statistical Analysis Routines										▓		
Inspect and Analyze Computer Output										▓		
Compose Report Tables and Graphs											▓	
Write Narrative Text of Report											▓	
Assemble and Duplicate Report												▓
Deliver Final Report to Sponsor												▓

the reliability and validity of the survey results. So careful timing is critical to both small and large survey projects.

Scheduling Tasks

Many survey tasks have to be undertaken *consecutively; others* can be done concurrently. Because of the complexity of the survey process, it's virtually mandatory to formulate a survey *project schedule*. Graphic schedule charts, such as the one shown in Example 2–2, are vastly more effective than tabular schedules. Such schedules

---

For Scheduling the Project   Guidelist 2–3

1. Break down each phase of the survey project into *independent* tasks if:
   a. the nature of the work is different or distinctive,
   b. they're to be done by different people,
   c. different equipment and materials are required, or
   d. the work is at different locations.
2. Estimate the *time duration* for each task, including:
   a. the actual work time on the task,
   b. time spent waiting for external materials or services, and
   c. an allowance for unexpected delays.

3. Identify the *dependency* of each task on completion of another when:
   a. the work product of one serves as input to another,
   b. the same person or people must do them both,
   c. the same facility or equipment is required for both, or
   d. approval of one task is needed before doing another.
4. On a *scheduling chart,* list the tasks in time sequence, graphing them:
   a. from the start, to determine the date of completion, or
   b. from the due date, back-timing to determine the date to begin.

---

range in sophistication from simple calendar notations for very small, uncomplicated projects to computer project management and scheduling routines that identify critical paths and track the work as it's performed. But regardless of their simplicity or complexity, all project schedules have the same two basic objectives: *planning* and *control.* The schedule ensures that each task will be done and done when it should be. It also serves as a benchmark or standard to compare performance with the plan and adjust the work or change the schedule when necessary. The directions for composing a simple project schedule chart are listed in Guidelist 2–3.

Monitoring and Controlling

Like any plan, the project time schedule shouldn't be something that's done one time and then set aside and ignored. It's not etched in stone. It's a working document to which the researcher refers more or less constantly. Very little gets done ahead of schedule, while everything and anything is prone to fall behind. If delays extend the duration of a task, the project manager has two options: Change the schedule, shifting the subsequent, dependent tasks to a later time; or *change the work* by arranging to do it or later tasks in a shorter time.

Finally, the survey project manager would be well-advised to share both the original time schedule with the sponsor and to update the sponsor periodically regarding the progress of the work. Sponsors rarely understand why a survey takes as much time as it does—they tend to want everything *yesterday!* If they "sign off" on the schedule, they're less likely to push researchers to hurry the work. Experienced researchers also work by another, iron-clad rule:

If there's a delay, notify the sponsor IMMEDIATELY!

Keep in touch. There's nothing more unnerving to those awaiting information than silence. Sponsors seem to detest a *surprise* even more than a delay. If the information seekers know there will be a delay, they may not like it but at least they can plan for it.

The Final Project Plan

The important factor for the researcher to note when completing the survey project plan is the necessity for an integrated project. Each element must fit together and be compatible with the others. When inconsistencies or incompatibilities are discovered, the elements must be changed. It's always advisable to express the elements of the project plan in written form. This plan will be the basis for later decisions and choices as the work is done and the project continues to completion. It may be necessary to edit and refine the project outline and append any questionnaire drafts or other relevant materials. The project outline should be submitted to the sponsors, with whatever annotation they might require. When approved, it serves as the basis for an agreement or contract for the survey project work to be performed by the researcher. For those projects where the researcher sponsors the survey, it's advisable to submit the project outline and obtain comments and suggestions from others who might provide insight by virtue of their training or experience.

Summary
Completing the Project Plan

A. Consider first things first. The survey objectives and information needs should be the basis for selecting instrumentation, data collection, and processing methods.

B. Value control very highly. The chance of catastrophic error increases dramatically with the number of people involved in survey data collection.

C. Communicate with others. Maintain a dialogue with the sponsor and obtain comments from those who can assist.

D. Evaluate options thoroughly. Questionnaire, data collection, and processing alternatives must all be identified and examined to make the best choice.

E. Choose alternatives carefully. If there's doubt about instrumentation, collection, or processing, turn to later chapters on these topics for direction.

F. Place trust in sampling. Don't use large samples when careful sampling design will obtain precise information from smaller numbers of people.

G. Budget very carefully. Most things cost more than anticipated and the budget should have a safety factor to allow for error.

H. Match costs and information value. Revise project tasks or increase the funds allocated so that there's an adequate margin of safety between costs and benefits.

Chapter

3

Designing the Sample

The Purpose of Sampling

Nearly every survey uses some form of sampling. The concept of sampling is easily understood. It simply means taking part of some population to represent the whole population. The alternative to sampling is enumeration—counting the entire population. The census of the U.S. population conducted each decade and political elections where all qualified citizens who register and vote are counted at the polls are both examples of enumeration. Sampling is much more common. Even though the Census Bureau uses enumeration for the decennial census, they generate a gigantic volume of data about citizens, companies, and organizations by surveying only a sample of the population under study. The news media, political parties, and candidates generate predictive data, using sampling, before the actual election. Sampling is a key factor for virtually any survey project.

The main reason for sampling is economy. To survey every individual in a population using enumeration is ordinarily much too expensive in terms of time, money, and personnel. There's really no need to survey every individual. Only a small fraction of the entire population usually represents the group as a whole with enough accuracy to base decisions on the results with confidence. While sampling is extremely practical and economical, it has to be done correctly or it will introduce error and bias in the results. The sample must be selected properly, or it won't represent the whole. It has to be large enough to meet the requirements for reliability—but not too large, or it will waste resources.

Specification of the Population

The actual specification of a sampling design begins with identification of the *population* to be surveyed. The three main tasks are shown in Guidelist 3–1. This may appear to be a simple task, but it seldom is. Suppose a survey is to be conducted to measure community attitudes toward a municipal, political issue. Then the population to be surveyed would include all those within the city. Are those who are temporarily living outside the city to be included or excluded? Should only registered voters be included in the population? Must respondents be 18 or 21 years of age or older? What about those who own property in the city but live elsewhere? Should businesses and organizations be included, or only individuals?

For Identifying Populations   Guidelist 3–1

1. Be sure the population consists of those people who actually possess the information sought by the survey.

2. Identify all the major factors that would qualify those knowledgeable respondents and make their responses meaningful to the sponsor.

3. List the criteria for inclusion and exclusion of respondents, together with the decision rules to be used.

It's important for the researcher to anticipate the decisions that are likely to arise during actual sample selection. Respondents must be qualified on the basis of two criteria: (1) they have to possess the information, and (2) they may need to have certain attributes or characteristics to make their responses meaningful.

Sample Unit Specification

A sample unit is the smallest entity that will provide one response. Ordinarily, survey sample units consist of individual people. Each person in the population might be a sample unit. This isn't always the case. For some surveys, the appropriate sample unit might be a household, consisting of all those living in one housing unit. For another, the sampling unit might be a family, consisting of parents, their children, and relatives. Some surveys may require sample units that are individual companies or government units. Others may use organizations or institutions as sample units.

Specification of a sample unit, outlined in Guidelist 3–2, must be neither too broad nor too narrow. If it's too broad, it won't be the smallest single unit. For example, it wouldn't be appropriate to use the family as a sampling unit for a survey of political attitudes because different family members may hold different opinions about the issues. If the specification of a sampling unit is too narrow, it would produce redundancy or be misleading. For instance, a survey to learn what policies various municipal police departments have instituted should specify what *one*

For Specifying Sample Units   Guidelist 3–2

1. The sampling unit should be specified so it's the smallest single entity from which the data can be obtained.

2. If the unit contains several individuals who might provide different data, the specification of the unit is too broad and should be narrowed.

3. If responses from individuals would be redundant or overrepresent some entities, the specification is too narrow and should be broadened.

4. If the survey data are to be compared with existing survey or secondary data, the same sample units must be used for the survey or the data won't be comparable.

For Selecting a Sample Frame	Guidelist 3–3

1. The sample frame is necessary to identify the entities or units to be surveyed.
2. The sample frame should be all-inclusive, so every unit in the population to be surveyed is included.
3. The frame for the sample should exclude any units that aren't part of the population being surveyed.
4. The entries listed in the sample frame must be specified in exactly the same way as the sampling units were specified.
5. When the sample is clustered, stratified, or both, the sample frame must indicate cluster boundaries and/or strata membership for the individual units.

person within each department should respond. In this case, the sample unit is the *department,* not the individual. If multiple officers or administrators from a department responded, the data would be redundant and the results misleading.

There's one other factor that must be considered when specifying sample units. There are times when the new survey data will be compared with existing survey data, such as data from an earlier survey or secondary data from some other source. If so, it's important to be sure the specification of the sample unit for the new survey is the same as for the data to which the survey results will be compared, to ensure comparability.

Sample Frame Selection

The sample frame is a list or set of directions identifying all the sample units in the population. Individual respondents will be selected from the sample frame when the survey data are collected. The sample frame might be a list of names and telephone numbers for a telephone survey, a map showing a specific residential area for in-home interviews, a list of names and addresses for a mail survey, or identification of certain kinds of visitors to a website for an online survey. There are other types of sample frames used for special surveys or data collection methods. Assume that interviews will be conducted at a location such as a store. The sample frame might consist of all those who enter the store during the sampling period, even though these shoppers can't be individually identified in advance.

It's seldom possible to obtain a perfect sample frame. The more complete and accurate the sample frame, the better the sample will represent the population as a whole. There are three criteria for selecting a sample frame for a survey: The frame should be all-inclusive, it should be exclusive to the population under study, and the units identified in the frame should be defined in exactly the same way as the sampling units. An *all-inclusive* sample frame is one that includes every member of the population to be surveyed. The frame should be *exclusive* in the sense that *only* those in the population are included. Lastly, it should list or identify the entities in the population the same way as the sampling units are specified. There are times when the sample frame should contain other details as well. The basic rules for selecting the sample frame are listed in Guidelist 3–3.

FIGURE 3–1
The
Reliability/
Validity
Diagram

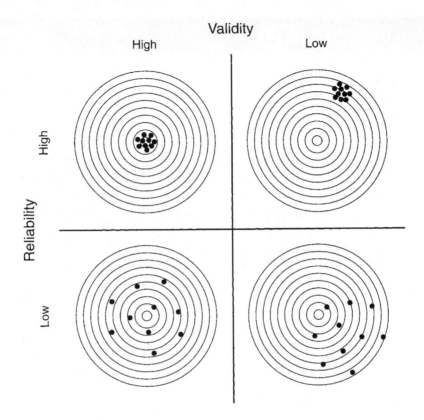

Reliability and Validity

The concepts of reliability and validity can be clarified by an analogy. Figure 3–1 shows four different patterns. Each of the four pictures shows a target—a *bull's eye* on a dartboard. The dots on the diagram are the marks of the darts thrown at each target. Each of the rows and columns on the diagram are labeled to show what they represent. The top row shows the results when reliability is high, and the bottom row shows low reliability. The column at the left contains the patterns for high validity (or at least *potentially* high validity), and the one at the right shows low validity.

Validity and Bias

Both targets in the left column of the diagram contain marks that are *centered* on the bull's eye. Although the marks on the lower target are spread over a wider area, they're in a random pattern, *centered* around the bull's eye. Nothing is *pushing* or *pulling* all the marks in one direction. By contrast, the patterns on both targets in the right column are off the mark. All tend toward one direction. The person throwing the darts at the target at the upper right had a steady hand, but consistently threw the darts high and a little to the right of the bull's eye. The player who threw the darts at the target on the bottom right was less steady and consistent and also persistently threw too low and to the right. Thus, the effect of *systematic bias,* often called just plain *bias,* is to push or pull the results in one or another *specific direction.* The two targets in the column on the right side of the diagram represent the results of survey data with low validity.

The pattern of marks on the lower left target of the diagram are identified as low in reliability but with *potentially* high validity, because the pattern is *centered* on the bull's eye. Technically, *no data can be more valid than it is reliable. Validity* requires hitting the bull's eye. In this case, *random error* caused the dots to miss the mark, resulting in low reliability. Thus, *the degree of reliability limits the degree of validity.*

A measurement of any kind is valid to the degree it measures *all* of that which it's supposed to measure and *only* that which it's supposed to measure. To be valid it must be free of extraneous factors that systematically *push* or *pull* the results in one particular direction. If something other than what's being measured affects the results by introducing a systematic *bias,* the results are less valid. Unfortunately, the effects of sampling, as well as many other factors, can bias the results of a survey. For example, the way a question is written may bias the answers. Interviewers may bias their respondents' answers if they aren't careful. Bias can also be introduced during recording, processing, and even reporting the survey results. Later chapters will identify and discuss other sources of bias and their effect on validity. Sample validity and sampling bias will be discussed in more detail later in this chapter.

Reliability and Error

In the top row of the diagram, the marks from the darts are all closely clustered. The person throwing the darts managed to place them all in very nearly the same place on the target. Thus, there's very little *random error* in these data. By contrast, the marks on the targets on the bottom row are spread over a wider area. This dart thrower wasn't doing exactly the same thing from one throw to the next, and the darts were randomly scattered on the targets. They're not very good *replicates* or representations of one another. They lack *repeatability.* These pictures illustrate the relationship between *reliability* and *(random)* error—the more error, the lower the reliability. High reliability implies a low level of error.

Reliability means freedom from *random* error. The most fundamental test of reliability is *repeatability*—the ability to get the same data values from several measurements made in the same way. For example, if a survey question obtained the same response, time after time, from one particular respondent who was asked that same question several times in one month, that would mean there was high reliability *over time.* If the answers varied in a random pattern, the reliability over time would be low. If a survey item yielded the same data from one respondent to the next when they did actually hold identical positions on the issue, that would indicate high reliability *over respondents,* and if there were random differences, reliability over respondents would be low. Similarly, if a survey yielded the same distributions of data from one sample of a given size to the next when they were drawn in the same way, there would be relatively low *sampling error* and high reliability *over samples. The greater the random error, the lower the reliability.*

Random error can result from a host of measurement factors. For instance, if a survey item used a term that was completely unfamiliar to many respondents, they would probably guess at the meaning. Even though they don't have any idea what it really means, respondents usually give answers. If those answers were merely random guesses, the reliability of the data for that item would be reduced. Similarly, interviewers may make *random* errors in recording results. Random error might also be introduced during processing or at other phases of the project. These kinds of error will be discussed in later chapters. *Sampling error* is the focus of attention here.

It's impractical to measure the entire population, so usually the researcher knows nothing about the whole population except what's learned from the sample itself. Thus, researchers and statisticians usually think of sampling error in terms of comparisons between similar samples. Data from a sample are relatively free from sampling error—are *reliable*—if other samples of the same size selected the same way from the same population provide the same or very similar results. If different samples provided very different results, there would be a lot of sampling error and the data from the original sample would be unreliable.

Sample Size Determination

The sample size depends on the budget and degree of confidence required. The sponsor and researcher can *buy* higher reliability, lower sampling error, and greater confidence for additional time, money, and effort. Ordinarily, though, there's some minimum sample size, below which the data are worthless. Similarly, there's a point of diminishing returns, above which additional confidence is negligible. The object of sample size determination is to find the optimum point between those two extremes for the survey project at hand.

Sample Size and Error

Smaller samples are more likely to be different from the population than larger ones. So smaller samples have more sampling error and lower reliability. Suppose only 5 people out of 10,000 were interviewed on some subject. There's a fairly good chance most or all of them would happen to hold views that aren't typical of the whole group. By comparison, it's very unlikely that a sample of 1,000 people would happen to include a high proportion of people who were very different from the other 9,000 in the population. Thus, the larger the sample, the lower the sampling error. Box A of Figure 3–2 shows that sample size and sampling error go in different directions—they're *inversely* related to one another. Box B of Figure 3–2 indicates that sample size and sample reliability go in the *same* direction—there's a *direct*, rather than inverse, relationship between sample size and reliability. The larger the sample, the *less* sampling error and the *greater* the reliability.

FIGURE 3–2
Sampling
Factor
Relationships

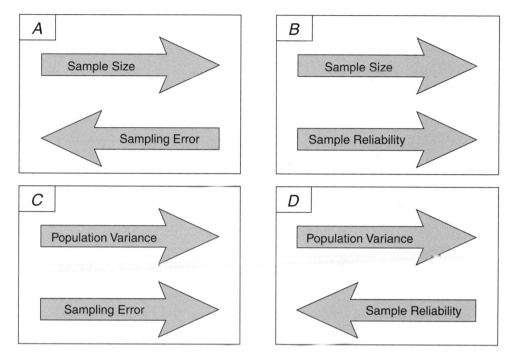

Confidence Level

Confidence level has a rather precise meaning for statisticians and survey researchers. It can be expressed as the *probability* that a value in the *population* is within a specific, numeric range from the corresponding value computed from a sample. For example, if the mean value of some variable computed from a *random* sample is 50, it wouldn't be logical or safe to assume that the mean for the entire population is exactly 50 as well. There's likely to be some *sampling* error. The pertinent question is *"How much error?"*

Standard Error

If the sample was, in fact, *randomly* selected, the probability of a *certain amount* of sampling error can be computed. The value that indicates the range of error or *confidence interval* is called the *standard error of the estimate*. As Figure 3–3 shows, the researcher can be 68 percent sure that the actual population value or *parameter* is within plus or minus 1 standard error of the corresponding sample statistic. Similarly, there's a 95 percent chance the parameter value is within plus or minus 2 standard errors and a 99 percent probability it's within plus or minus 3 standard errors.

Thus the value of standard error and the corresponding breadth of the confidence intervals are quantitative measures of sample reliability and sampling error. The more reliable the sample, the lower the value of the standard error will be and

FIGURE 3–3
Confidence
Intervals and
Probability
Levels

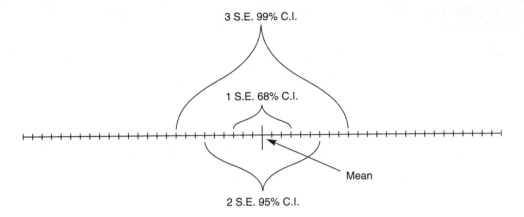

the more narrow the confidence intervals will be. Conversely, the greater the sampling error, the larger the value of standard error will be and the wider the confidence intervals will be. The determinants of confidence intervals will be discussed in more detail in the next section.

Key Variable Analysis

Surveys ordinarily include several items or variables, and occasionally they may have as many as a few hundred. Despite this multiplicity of variables, the specification of information needs and assignment of priority will ordinarily identify only a few *key* variables that are the most important—those that constitute the major reason for the survey. The researcher should have a sense of the level of confidence desired for these key variables.

The confidence requirements can be assessed by asking a series of *"What if . . ."* questions about various levels of confidence and error. For example, the sponsor might be asked, "What if the average value for this item is off by 1 or 2 percent?" Usually the answer will be that it would make no real difference—that it wouldn't matter. The next question might be, "What if it were off by 5 percent?" The researcher will soon discover both the consequences of basing decisions on estimates that are somewhat inaccurate for the population, and also the *critical points,* below which the error wouldn't be important, and above which it would have very negative consequences. These estimates of the desired confidence level serve as target values during sample size determination.

The Outside Limits

There are maximum and minimum *practical* sample sizes that apply to virtually all surveys. Ordinarily, a sample of less than about 30 respondents will provide too little certainty to be practical. Figure 3–4 depicts a plot of the upper and lower 95 percent confidence level for samples (from the same population) ranging from 20 to 300 respondents in increments of 20. The values are expressed as a percentage of the mean. So there's a 95 percent chance the actual population mean is within about 37 percent of the sample mean for a sample of only 20 respondents. Similarly,

FIGURE 3–4
Sample
Size and
Confidence
Intervals

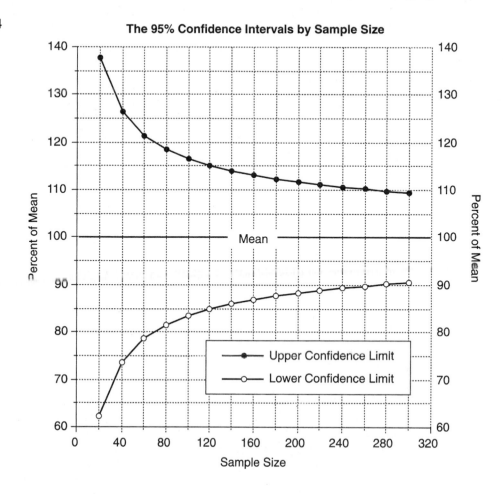

for a sample of 300, there's a 95 percent probability of a range of error less than 10 percent of the sample mean.

Minimum Limit

Usually experienced researchers regard a sample of about 100 respondents as the minimum sample size for large populations, though there are exceptions. Figure 3–4 indicates that confidence intervals narrow sharply when very small sample sizes are increased, up to about 100 respondents. So small increases in sample size at lower levels yield big reductions in sampling error and big increases in confidence. In short, it's well worth it to increase the size of very small samples.

Another reason survey samples seldom contain fewer than one or two hundred respondents is related to the cost structure for survey research, discussed in Chapter 2 and shown in Figure 2–10: Project Cost Elasticity, on page 51. The *fixed* costs will be incurred regardless of sample size. Thus, the additional or *marginal* cost of including at least 100 or so more respondents is often very small in comparison to the value of the fixed costs that will inevitably result.

Maximum Limit

The maximum *practical* size for a sample under ordinary conditions is about 1,000 respondents. Contrary to popular belief, the maximum practical size of a sample has *absolutely nothing* to do with the size of the population if it's many times greater than the sample. This fact may be difficult for a novice to accept, but it's statistically sound and indisputable. A simple analogy makes this fact intuitively understandable. Suppose you are warming a bowl of soup for yourself and you want to know if it's hot enough. You would probably *sample* it by stirring the soup, then trying a spoonful. The *sample size* would be *one spoonful.* Now assume that you are to warm a hundred gallons of soup for a large crowd, and you want to test it to see if it's hot enough to serve. You would probably stir it and take a sample of *one spoonful*, even though the so-called *population* of soup was hundreds of times larger than when only one serving was sampled. Thus, the size of the population has *nothing* to do with the size of the sample that's required.

It's seldom necessary to sample more than 10 percent of the population to obtain adequate confidence, providing the resulting sample is less than about 1,000 and larger than the minimums noted earlier. Thus, for a population of 1,000 units, the experienced researcher would probably consider a sample size of about 100 or so. For a population of 5,000 units, the minimum practical sample would be 100 or so, and the maximum would be approximately 500, or 10 percent. For populations of 10,000 or more, most experienced researchers would probably consider a sample size between about 200 and 1,000 respondents.

The futility of using extremely large samples is demonstrated by Figure 3–5. For this population, a sample of 2,000 provided a 95 percent confidence interval of only plus or minus 2 percent of the mean. A sample of 10,000—five times that size—reduced the confidence interval only slightly to just over plus or minus 1 percent. Above a sample size of about 4,000, confidence intervals decrease only very slightly and at a decreasing rate with each increment of 1,000 respondents. So, aside from some special circumstances discussed below, samples of more than a few hundred are seldom required. Those over one or two thousand are very rarely justified.

Variance in the Population

There's always a chance that a sample will include many individuals who are atypical, who are different from the most typical members of the population. The degree of sampling error is partly a function of the *variation,* from one individual to the next, within the population. The more similar the individuals in the population, the smaller the sampling error. The more they *vary* from one another, the greater the sampling error. Box C of Figure 3–2 indicates that population variance and sampling error are *directly* related to each other.

If there's more sampling error when the variance in the population is large than when it's small, then there's also *lower* sample reliability. Box D of Figure 3–2 indicates that population variance is *inversely* related to sample reliability—the *larger* the variance in the population, the *lower* the reliability of the data for a sample of a given size.

FIGURE 3–5 **Standard Error of Large Samples**

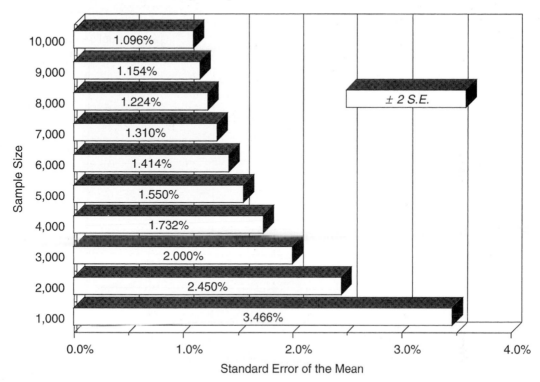

Variance and Reliability

A simple example shows how variation in the population affects sampling error. Suppose the sponsor wants to know the average age of all high-school students in a particular school district. If a sample of about 200 student records were randomly selected from the files, the average for the sample would probably be within only a few weeks or months of the average age that might be computed from all the records. That's because nearly all the students will be between 14 and 18 years of age—there isn't very much *variation* in the population on this variable. So the *sampling error* will be small.

Now suppose the sponsor wants to know the average age of *all* the students in the school district, from kindergarten to high school senior. The average from the same size sample of student records would probably differ from that of the entire student population by several months. There's more *variation* in age within that population. By extension, if the sponsor wanted an estimate of the average age of *all residents* in the district, from the most recent newborn to the very eldest, the range of *sampling error* would be denominated in years, rather than merely weeks or months. Again, the reason is more variation in age in the population of *residents*

FIGURE 3–6   **Population Variance and Reliability**

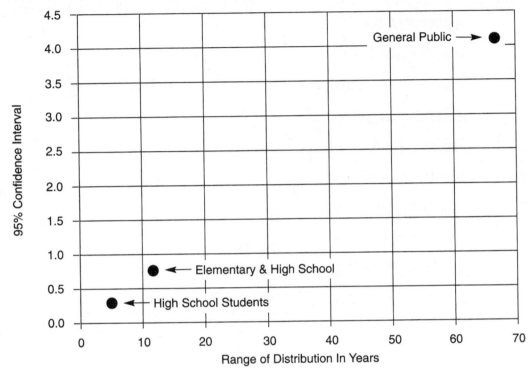

than in the population of *students,* just as there's more age variation in *students* than there is in *seniors.*

The *age ranges* for these three populations are plotted on the horizontal axis of Figure 3–6. The 95 percent *confidence intervals* are plotted on the vertical axis. When the variation is less than 5 years, for high school students, the 95 percent confidence interval is very small, indeed. It increases only slightly with an age range of just over 12 years for students from first grade to high school senior. The age range for the general public in this population was about 67 years. With that much variation, the 95 percent confidence interval jumped to almost 13 times that for high school students and over 5 times that for all students.

Assessing Variation

Since confidence level is partly a function of variation in the population, the researcher must make an estimate of the amount of variation that's likely to exist in the population for the *key* survey variables. These estimates might be based on the previous experience of the researcher or sponsor. Casual observation may also provide some indications. Data from previous surveys or from other secondary sources may be available. If there's no indication whatsoever of the population variance for

For Controlling Sampling Error   Guidelist 3–4

1. Sampling error results because those in the sample aren't perfectly representative of the population as a whole.
2. Any sample of less than the entire population will virtually always have some sampling error.
3. The larger the proportion of the population included in the sample, the smaller the sampling error.
4. Sampling error is *random* error, but it affects *both* the reliability and the validity of the data.

5. The greater the sampling error, the lower the reliability and validity of the sample data.
6. The greater the variation among individual members of the population, the greater the sampling error.
7. Therefore, the greater the population variance, the larger the sample size must be to attain a given level of reliability.

some key items, a simple pilot survey on only those items for a fairly small number of respondents from the population may be necessary to obtain an estimate.

The more the respondents are likely to differ on the key items of the survey, the larger the sample must be to reach a given level of confidence. If all responses are almost identical, fewer respondents need be surveyed. If responses vary widely among respondents, there will be a greater chance of selecting people who aren't typical and a larger sample will be needed. These relationships are outlined in Guidelist 3–4.

After identifying the key variables, assessing the tolerable error for each, and making an estimate of the amount of variance among those in the population for each, the next step is to combine this information. This process will require some judgment and perhaps just plain guesswork. The objective is to identify one or, at most, two or three items that will require the *largest* sample size to provide adequate confidence. If there's one item for which there are *both* a very high need for confidence *and* a high level of variance in the population, that's obviously the determining variable for selecting the sample size. Any sample large enough to meet the confidence requirements for that item will be sufficiently large for all the others. If the key items requiring the most confidence are likely to have the least variance in the population, and vice versa, the items must be considered as a group or the researcher must make a *judgment call* and pick one or two as a guide.

Subsample Sizes

Some survey samples may be divided into subsamples and analyzed separately. When that's the case, the size of each subsample must be determined separately as well. In the majority of cases, the entire sample will be used for analysis and interpretation, to estimate the values and distributions in the population. Ordinarily, though, most survey data is *implicitly* divided during analysis into what might be called subsamples. So it's necessary for the researcher to anticipate the types of analysis that will be used and the size and number of the implicit subsamples that might be created.

The two most common techniques used for data analysis that implicitly create subsamples are cross-tabulation and breakdowns of averages. For example, respondent age might be broken down to show the average for men and for women, or the sex of the respondents might be cross-tabulated with their response to a yes/no question. In the first case, two subsamples would be created: males and females. In the second, four implicit subsamples would result: men responding positively, men responding negatively, women responding positively, and women responding negatively.

The reliability and confidence that result from these types of analyses depend in part on the size of the implicit subsamples. The size of the subsamples depends, in turn, on both the nature of the variables or items used for cross-tabulation or breakdowns, and also on the distributions of response obtained from the survey. Items with only two alternatives or levels create fewer and larger subsamples than those with many response options or levels. Thus, the size of subsamples or cells within the analysis is of less concern when there are fewer categories for the item, providing that respondents are about equally divided among the levels or subsamples. This is certainly not the usual case. For example, on a simple, dichotomous, yes/no question, only 10 percent or less may fall in one category. That would create a very small subsample. This problem is confounded even further because cross-tabulation creates individual cells which may become even smaller. For example, suppose the item cited above was to be cross-tabulated with another, similar variable. Assume that it also has a distribution of 10/90 as well. If there were no relationship between the two items, only 10 percent of 10 percent, or 1 percent of respondents, would reside in the smallest cell of the cross-tabulation.

Certainly the researcher designing a sample and determining the appropriate size can't fully anticipate all the breakdowns and cross-tabulations that will be used for analysis. Nor can the researcher predict accurately the distributions of response that will result for items with response categories. On the other hand, the researcher must be aware of the implicit creation of subsamples. In addition, those designing a sample must anticipate the *potential* for subsamples inherent in the survey task. If the analysis is likely to generate many, small subsamples, the total sample size must be relatively large to ensure adequate numbers within them.

Judgment and Determination

There are statistical formulas for the computation of a specific sample size to yield a given level of confidence for a single variable. Unfortunately, they're of little value, even to experienced, practicing researchers, for several reasons. The computations require fairly accurate estimates of population variance, and that's seldom known in advance. In addition, most surveys include dozens or even hundreds of items or variables, and it would be virtually impossible to complete the calculations for each. If such computations were performed for each item and the largest required sample size were used for the survey, the sample would very likely be much larger than that required for all but a few survey items. Lastly, sponsors usually know and can verbally express the degree of confidence in the data and the estimates they desire, but rarely if ever will they be able to express these requirements numerically as confidence intervals.

Most surveys don't call for a precise sample size. So it takes study and judgment of the conditions listed in Figure 3–7 to make an intelligent choice. If most or all the factors indicating a large sample size are present, the researcher would choose a sample size very near the maximum practical limit for the population, as noted earlier. By contrast, if most or all the conditions indicating a small sample size applied to the survey, the sample size selected would appropriately be very near the minimum limit noted above for the particular population to be sampled. When there are factors that indicate a large sample but others indicating a small one, the actual sample size must be in the mid-range between the maximum and minimum values suggested. It may be advisable for the researcher to consider each of the factors listed, to determine the importance of each for the particular survey task at hand. Obviously, the most salient and important factors for the project would be the determining ones to be weighed most heavily in the decision.

FIGURE 3–7
Factors Determining Sample Size

Factors Indicating a Large Sample

1. The decisions to be based on the survey data have very serious or costly consequences.
2. The sponsors demand a very high level of confidence in the data and estimates.
3. There's likely to be a high level of variance among the units in the population to be sampled.
4. The sample is to be divided into relatively small subsamples during analysis and interpretation.
5. Project costs and timing vary only slightly with increases in the size of the sample.
6. Time and resources are readily available to cover the costs of data collection.

Factors Indicating a Small Sample

1. There are few if any major decisions or commitments to be based on the survey data.
2. The sponsors require only rough estimates concerning the parameters of the population.
3. The population to be sampled is very homogeneous, with little variance among units.
4. The analysis and interpretation will be based on the entire sample or only a few, large subsamples.
5. A large proportion of total project costs are for data collection or costs increase dramatically with sample size.
6. Budget constraints and/or time requirements limit the volume of data that can be collected.

Preliminary Sampling

To make the necessary decisions concurring the appropriate sample size for a survey, the researcher must somehow anticipate at least two types of results beforehand: variance in the population for the key variables to be measured, and distributions of response for items that will form implicit subsamples during analysis. There may be cases when it's virtually impossible to anticipate one or both of these two types of results. If so, the researcher has two options—a *pilot survey* or a *progressive sampling* design. Either might provide the data necessary to the decision.

The Pilot Survey

One option is to conduct an informal *pilot survey* to obtain responses to only the key variables in question. These results can be tabulated to show the degree of variance and confidence intervals that might be expected from the actual survey, as well as the percentage distributions of response to categorical items. The advantages of a pilot survey are simplicity, speed, and economy. Only a small number of respondents and a few questions are required.

The pilot survey need not even use the same data collection method as that for the main survey, and such pilot surveys can often be completed easily, quickly, and inexpensively. It may also provide useful information about other aspects of the survey process. For instance, the survey instruments might be tested, the alternative data collection methods might be compared, and so forth.

Progressive Sampling

Another alternative open to the researcher in doubt about the most appropriate sample size is known as *progressive sampling*. With this technique, the researcher proceeds with the project as though a sample size had been determined. Any quotas are expressed as percentages, rather than numbers of respondents. The necessary analysis routines are prepared in advance, and the survey is begun without precise determination of when it will be terminated. As the data are obtained, they're submitted to analysis, the confidence intervals around estimates computed, and the size of the implicit subsamples noted. By observing the decrement in the confidence intervals and/or the increases in subsample sizes as data are added to the file, the researcher will be able to predict more accurately the point at which the values will be adequate. If so, that number of respondents would be set as the point at which data collection would terminate. If prediction isn't feasible, the data collection would continue until the results were satisfactory, then terminated at that point.

Progressive sampling is especially effective and practical for online surveys where the data are collected directly into computer files. Similarly, when interview survey data are collected using data entry programs such as SPSS Data Entry Station,™ the data are accumulated in computer files as they're gathered. Such programs screen and edit the data on entry and it can be submitted to analysis at any point the researcher desires. In effect, this provides a "running tally" of the number of cases collected, the degree of variance in the data, confidence intervals, and implicit subsample sizes. Data collection can then be terminated when sufficient confidence levels and subsample sizes have been reached.

The disadvantage of progressive sampling, compared to a pilot survey, is that this method takes more time, effort, and resources for those projects that don't key the data directly to computer files as it's collected. Nor does progressive sampling permit testing of other survey decisions, such as the questions' wording or scaling techniques, while these can be tested in a pilot survey. The major advantage of progressive sampling is its precision and accuracy. As the cliché says, "What you see is what you get!"

Sampling Designs

The simple, random sample is the most straightforward form of probability sampling. There are also *systematic* designs that yield a sample where the probability of inclusion of respondents is equal or known to the researcher. Stratified and clustered samples are the most common of these systematic sampling designs. Their advantages and applications will also be discussed here.

Random Sampling Benefits

A pure *random* sample is the most desirable kind for almost every survey. *Random* in this context doesn't mean haphazard. Random samples are important to the reliability and validity of the data. When the respondents are picked at random, the probability of any one person being included in the sample is precisely equal to the probability of including any other. (In a technical sense, the probability of inclusion need not necessarily be equal, but the probability must be *known*. A random sample is merely a special case of a *probability sample*. The random sample is best because it's most representative of the entire population. It's least likely to result in bias. It has statistical properties that allow the researcher to make *inferences* about the population, based on the results obtained from the sample. Random samples permit the computation of *confidence intervals* indicating the probability the population average or other parameters are within a certain range around the sample statistics. With random sampling, the researcher can calculate and report the *statistical significance* of relationships between survey items, based on the probability that such relationships would result only from sampling error.

Without random selection, none of these statistical coefficients or values would be accurate or legitimate. This isn't to say they can't be computed. They can be. The analytical computations can be performed for *any* numeric data, regardless of how it was obtained. But the more the sample deviates from purely random selection, the less representative it's likely to be, and the less legitimate the results of statistical computation will be.

Stratified Sampling

There are times when it's useful to divide a population into two or more segments or *strata* and sample a different proportion of each. The selection of sample strata is often based on some demographic characteristic, but other variables are also used to divide the population into strata, depending on the reason for stratification. The conditions that encourage the use of a stratified sample can best be explained by examples.

Different Base Rates

Suppose a retail store wants to measure and compare the preferences of existing patrons as well as of nonpatrons with an interview survey. The researcher determines that a sample of 200 from each group would be sufficient. If only 10 percent of the people in the area are patrons, a simple, random sample would require 2,000 respondents to be interviewed in order to obtain the 200 patrons needed in that group. Yet, only 200 nonpatrons are required. In effect, there would be 1,600 "extra" or unneeded respondents. To avoid this unnecessary expense, the researcher could use a stratified sample, based on whether each potential respondent was a patron or not. By asking a simple, qualifying question to determine if they were or weren't a patron, the interviewers would have to contact about 2,000 people, but actually interview only 400.

Differential Confidence

Assume some company wants to measure employee preferences for several different fringe benefits that might be included in a labor contract. Some employees belong to a union whose contract will expire soon. Negotiation of a new contract is to begin shortly. Another group's union very recently signed an agreement. It will be many months before that contract could be changed. The sponsor needs to be very precise about the first group's opinions. They need only a general overview of the second group's attitudes.

If simple, random sampling with no stratification were used, the result might be less confidence than desired for the first group and more than necessary for the second. Resources would be wasted and the results wouldn't be optimum. In this situation, the population of employees can be divided into two mutually exclusive groups or strata, based on their union affiliation. A *large* proportion of the first stratum and a *smaller* proportion of the second would be surveyed. As a result, there would be an appropriate level of confidence for each group. Checklist 3–1 identifies the conditions for choosing a stratified sample.

Inter-strata Variance

Another situation exemplifies the use of stratification to markedly increase the reliability and confidence obtainable from survey data. Suppose a political survey will be conducted on a particular issue, and the researcher knows the population is sharply divided or *polarized* about the issue. The voters in one municipality tend to hold one position very strongly, and those in another are likely to take an opposing view with equal vigor. There are also indications of very little variation among the voters *within* each community.

With an unstratified, random sample, a very large sample of the whole population would be needed to provide the required degree of certainty about the combined views of those in both communities. That's because the degree of reliability is partly a function of the *variance* in the population. In this case, the variance would be large because of the polarization. If the population is divided into strata by community of residence, the variance within each will be small, so a smaller proportion of each can be sampled. The necessary reliability and confidence intervals for the

---

To Choose a Stratified Sample Design   Checklist 3–1

1. Is there a requirement for greater reliability and a larger sample for some strata than for others? If so, stratification would be practical.
2. Are there indications of little population variance *within* strata and large variation *between* strata? In such cases, stratification is recommended.
3. Is it possible to obtain a sample frame showing strata membership for individuals? If not,

   stratification isn't feasible without quota sampling.
4. Can respondents' strata memberships be determined in advance by observation or questioning with a quota system? If they can't, stratification isn't possible.

---

combined results would be obtained, yet the sum of the two subsamples would be much smaller than the number required for an unstratified sample.

Differential Strata Variance

In yet another example of stratified sampling, suppose the needs of the male clients of a social service organization are very similar while the needs of the female clients differ vary widely within that group. In other words, there is very little *variance* among the men, and a high degree of *variance* among the women. If a need assessment survey was conducted with a simple, random sample (no stratification), there would be an approximately equal number of men and women in the survey. The sampling error would be substantially lower and the reliability would be markedly higher for the men than for the women in the sample. The researcher could use a *stratified* design to obtain a much larger sample of women than men. This would result in approximately equal levels of reliability and confidence.

With stratified sampling, either the sample frame must indicate strata membership on the variables used to define the strata, or strata membership must be identified by observation or questioning. In the example of patrons and nonpatrons, strata membership was identified by asking qualification questions to fulfill a quota. The example of union and nonunion respondents didn't require qualification questions because the strata membership was identified in the sample frame. The steps for designing a stratified sample are outlined in Guidelist 3–5.

For Designing a Stratified Sample   Guidelist 3–5

1. Select the variable(s) or characteristic(s) on which to base or define the strata.
2. Obtain a sample frame that shows the stratum membership of each sample unit.
3. Estimate the variance *within* strata and the variation *between* strata.
4. Determine the confidence level needed for each stratum, based on information needs.
5. Specify the sample size for each stratum to obtain the desired confidence level for each.

To Choose a Cluster Sample Design   Checklist 3–2

1. Is the data to be collected by personal or telephone interviewing? If not, clustering isn't necessary.

2. Are the respondents spread over a wide physical or geographic area? If so, clustering may be appropriate.

3. Will travel time and costs be high, relative to the actual interviewing time? If so, cluster sampling will be economical.

4. Is the total sample size large enough to permit selecting many clusters? If not, clustering shouldn't be used.

Cluster Sampling

Sometimes the population to be surveyed is physically or geographically separated or widely dispersed. That doesn't matter to self-administered mail or online surveys because the geographic location doesn't affect the cost of obtaining a response. The concentration of the population is very important for personal interview surveys because the field-workers can spend more time and effort traveling from one respondent to the next than on the actual task of interviewing. Long-distance charges for telephone interviewing can also be substantial if respondents are geographically dispersed. Cluster sampling is a method for reducing cost and time requirements by surveying groups of respondents who are geographically close to one another.

Travel Economy

An example of a typical situation where cluster sampling can be used effectively may clarify the technique. Suppose a company would like to survey potential buyers of their product within a single area. The sample units are households, and a detailed street map of the entire area will provide the sample frame. Fifty-two consumers are to be interviewed. Individual households might be selected at random based on their location on the map. With a design such as the one shown in the upper box of Figure 3–8, even the two respondents who are nearest to one another may be several blocks or miles apart. Some outlying respondents may require many miles of travel.

To reduce travel time and cost markedly, the researcher may decide on a clustered random sample, such as that shown in the lower box of Figure 3–8. The design might specify that each of four clusters will contain 13 respondents, all from the same neighborhood. The location of each neighborhood would be chosen at random from the map, just as an individual respondent might be selected. The interviewers would then be instructed to begin with a particular household, then move five household units in a specific (randomly determined) direction, and obtain a second interview from the sixth household. They would continue until all 13 interviews in the cluster were obtained, then travel to the next cluster location. With the use of the cluster sampling design in Figure 3–8, the driving time and travel costs would be reduced to a small fraction of those for an unclustered random sample. Checklist 3–2 identifies the conditions for selecting a clustered sample.

FIGURE 3–8
Cluster
Sampling
Economy

Unclustered Random Sample

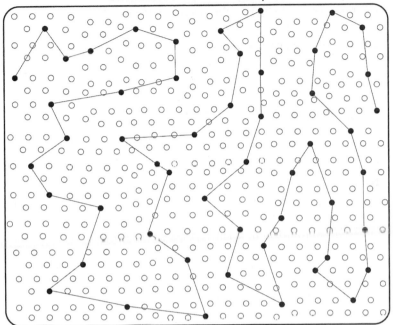

Clustered Random Sample

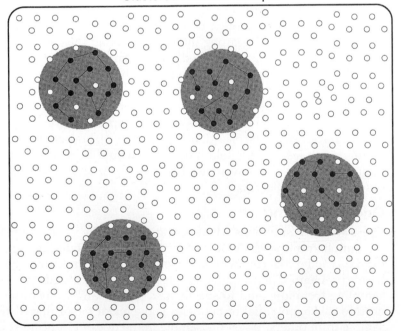

Telephone Economy

Cluster sampling can also be used effectively to reduce costs for telephone interviewing. Rather than placing many long distance calls with relatively high toll charges, clusters can be specified within particular, randomly selected communities, area codes, or exchanges. Interviewers within those communities can then place local calls that have only small toll charges or none at all. Guidelist 3–6 outlines the steps for cluster sample specification.

Other Economies

Cluster sampling isn't *limited* to geographical clustering, although that's most often the reason for using such a design. Clusters might also be selected on some other basis, such as groups of consecutive records from a paper file or very large computer file, rather than an *n*th name sampling design. This might be done to save time and costs associated with counting or *passing* every individual record to select a sample from a very large file contained in different places or on different media devices.

Another situation that isn't based on geographic areas or distance is the case of cluster sampling *over time*. For example, if visitors to a certain location were to be surveyed over an extended period, the total time might be divided into clusters, such as four-hour periods, and the cluster periods during which sampling were to occur could be selected randomly. This would reduce the amount of time required of interviewers and thus might reduce data collection costs substantially.

Clustering Provisions

It's important to note those within one cluster must *not* be too close to one another or very similar to one another because they share the same location or position in space or time. If there's strong interaction among those in the same cluster, or if those within a cluster are markedly more similar to one another than are those from different clusters, responses within a cluster would be redundant. Estimates of population variance would be erroneous and statistical inference would be illegitimate. The clusters should also be small enough so many areas are surveyed. If only 3 clusters of 100 respondents each were specified, the design would be faulty and the data likely to be biased. If 30 clusters of 10 households each were specified, there's much less chance that most or all would be atypical of the entire region than if 3 clusters of 100 were used. The steps for cluster sample specification are outlined in Guidelist 3–6.

Quota Sampling

There are often situations where a stratified sample would be most desirable, but the sample frame doesn't indicate the strata membership of the sampling units. If the data can be collected with interviews, a quota sample may be the best solution to this problem. When a quota sample is employed, it's advisable to use a random sampling technique and to specify a stratified sample, as described earlier. The need to *qualify* potential respondents is the major factor that distinguishes a *quota* sample from others. When the sample frame doesn't indicate strata membership, the interviewers don't know the stratum or group to which a potential respondent belongs. Thus, interviewers are assigned a *quota*—a given number of people from

For Specifying a Cluster Sample   **Guidelist 3–6**

1. Determine the degree to which those within one area are likely to be similar to one another or to interact.
2. Decide on the number of units to be *skipped* between individual units, based on similarity and interaction.
3. Consider the degree of variance that's likely to exist from one area to another.
4. Specify a minimum number of clusters that would still be large enough to sample the entire region adequately.

5. Divide the total sample size by the minimum number of clusters to obtain the number to be within each cluster.
6. Select the first or *key* unit in each cluster on a random basis.
7. Determine the procedure for moving from the key unit to others within the cluster, maintaining random selection.

each stratum. The interviewers are instructed to contact potential respondents and ask *qualifying* questions before beginning the inquiry itself. If the interviewers need a respondent for the stratum to which the person belongs, they continue with the interview. If they don't need a respondent for that particular stratum, they politely terminate the interview with an explanation, then continue to contact other potential respondents until they identify one belonging to one of the strata that still requires another respondent.

Interviewers may not always need to ask qualifying questions. They may be able to identify membership when they see or hear the respondent. For example, if the quota is based on sex, both telephone and personal interviewers need only see the people or hear their voices. With stratification variables such as age, employment status, occupation, and the like, interviewers have to ask the potential respondents about their status before they're accepted as qualified.

Quota sampling can also be based on observation or questioning about some incidence of behavior. For example, stratification might be based on whether a shopper makes a purchase or not, or buys brand X, brand Y, or brand Z. Quota specifications may be based on virtually anything that can be observed by the interviewer or ascertained quickly with a few questions. The quota sample design procedure is outlined in Guidelist 3–7.

Economy is the principal advantage of quota sampling designs. This technique can often be nearly as economical for stratified sampling where the sample frame indicates strata membership. On the other hand, if the sample isn't designed properly, quota sampling can become exceedingly expensive. This is because it may require very many contacts to identify those in the most obscure strata. For example, telephone interviewers may have to call many thousands of people before finding "a black, Protestant woman over 70 who drinks more than a liter of cola a day." Such a strange quota assignment may sound bizarre, but it can arise by combining quotas on race, religion, age, and consumption habits. Combined quota variables must be used with care.

For Designing a Quota Sample   Guidelist 3–7

1. Select the variable(s) or characteristic(s) on which to base or define the quotas, just as with stratification.

2. Use combinations of variables to define quotas carefully and be sure it's economical to locate such respondents.

3. Estimate the variance that's likely to exist among individuals within each quota category and the variation to be expected between quota categories.

4. Decide on the level of confidence required for each quota category based on the information requirements.

5. Specify the sample size for each quota category to provide the desired confidence level for each.

6. Provide instructions for interviewers to qualify respondents by strata membership and assign individual or group quotas to interviewers.

Special Designs

There are many very acceptable variations of the sampling designs discussed above. Such special sampling procedures are used to cope with problems or achieve special objectives. Researchers are encouraged to handle such unusual problems by combining some of the techniques or devising new ones that will be effective. There are no hard-and-fast rules, so long as the sample is random and sufficiently free from sampling error and bias. When selecting or creating special sample designs, the researcher should continually seek the answer to two questions: Will the design being considered violate random selection resulting in bias? Will it seriously distort the inferences and estimates of variance among the population? If either is likely to result, the design should be abandoned in favor of another or modified until these two prime requisites are met. The main considerations for choosing and creating special sampling designs are listed in Guidelist 3–8.

For Developing Special Sampling Designs   Guidelist 3–8

1. Inspect the conventional designs to determine if any might he modified or extended for the special case.

2. Attempt to combine designs, such as clustering and stratification, to meet special needs.

3. Remember that random sampling can be done over time, entities, or occurrences, as well as over sample units.

4. Be certain that any special sampling design doesn't violate random selection or distort variance estimates.

Sample Selection Procedure

Once the basic sampling design has been chosen and the sample size has been specified, the task of actually selecting respondents remains. In some cases, such as mail surveys and most telephone surveys, the actual selection of sampling units from the sample frame will be done entirely in the central office. In other situations, such as telephone or personal interview surveys that use *quotas,* the actual selection will be made at the point and time of contact with potential respondents. In those cases, the selection procedure should be specified and translated into a series of instructions for interviewers. The potential sources of bias and the guidelines for avoiding selection bias are identified later in this chapter. The actual instructions for telephone or field-workers to qualify respondents and fill their quotas during data collection are discussed in Chapter 8.

Random Selection Methods

Random sample selection sounds easy, but it's difficult in actual practice. Without careful adherence to a well-specified procedure, systematic bias is likely to creep in undetected. The procedure chosen has to be tailored to the demands of the individual survey situation. No one procedure is generally preferable to another. Guidelines for selecting random samples are shown in Guidelist 3–9.

Nth Name Sampling

When the sample frame consists of a list of sample units, the most common method of selecting a random sample from the list is to select every 11th name. *N* is calculated by dividing the sample size into the number on the list. If a sample of 200 were to be drawn from a list of 10,000, every 50th name would be picked. Technically, this is systematic, rather than *pure* random sampling, but it's completely legitimate, providing certain requirements are met.

For Selecting a Random Sample   Guidelist 3–9

1. For *n*th name sampling, divide the number in the population by the number to be sampled for the value of *n.*

2. Randomly pick the first unit for an *n*th name sample from the first one through *n* entries of the frame.

3. Random number generators often produce near-perfect random lists, usually without duplicates and ordered from lowest to highest.

4. When a seed number is required by a random number generator program, it should be picked at random.

5. In Appendix B, Table B–1 contains a random number table and Example B–1 contains instructions for selecting random numbers from the table.

6. When units from the sample frame can be identified on physical objects, mechanical devices can be used to create a random sampling list.

When *n*th name sampling is used, it's important to be sure there isn't any regular fluctuations or "periodicity" in the data corresponding to the value of *n* or a multiple of it. For example, if the value of *n* were 49 and the data were acquired one case per day, the sample would consist of data from the same day of every 7th week. There are several ways to resolve this problem. Perhaps the simplest is to *decrease* the value of *n* slightly, then *randomly* discard the *extra* sample units selected by the procedure.

With *n*th name sampling, the researcher shouldn't begin counting with the first name on the list. Those who happen to be the first on a list, such as the first name on the page of a telephone directory, are contacted much more often than others, because of their position on the list. In the example, the researcher should begin with one of the first 50 names. The actual starting point should be picked *randomly*. If the number drawn happened to be 37, the first unit for the sample would be the 37th name on the list, the second, the 87th, and so on.

Random Number Generators

There are many computational routines and computer programs that generate lists of random numbers. When a random number generator is used, it will usually be possible to discard duplicate numbers and sort them in sequence from lowest to highest. The units to be included in the sample would then be picked from the sample frame according to the random list.

If the sample frame consists of a computer file, many database management programs and other computer routines can be instructed to select a random sample of a certain size. If so, the sample list can be printed or displayed directly and the researcher is relieved of the task of making the actual selection.

Physical Selection Methods

There are several mechanical devices to select numbers randomly. One such device is commonly used to select *bingo* numbers, others are used to pick lottery winners, and some use small balls, cubes, tags, and the like. These physical random selection methods are quite acceptable, providing the selection is truly random so every unit has an equal probability of being chosen.

Sample Selection Bias

Selecting sample units from the sample frame on a random basis may appear to be simple and easy, but it's often difficult to select them on a *purely* random basis. No systematic patterns must evolve. Extraneous sampling factors that affect survey results produce systematic bias and reduce the validity of the data. Any factors that would change the probability of any one unit or type of unit being selected must be ruled out.

Sampling Bias Sources

The way the sampling units are selected may lead to overselecting or underselecting respondents of a certain type. If so, their responses wouldn't accurately represent those of the entire population. For example, suppose a survey were conducted

---

For Identifying Sources of Sampling Bias   Guidelist 3–10

1. *Accessibility bias.* Some respondents are more readily selected or included in the sample so they're overselected.

2. *Affinity bias.* Respondents who are most attractive to the interviewer are more often selected, so they're overrepresented.

3. *Cluster bias.* The respondents selected are too closely clustered, so they're more similar to one another than to the population as a whole.

4. *Nonresponse bias.* Respondents of a certain type more often refuse to participate, so they're underrepresented.

5. *Order bias.* The order of respondent selection overselects or underselects those of a certain type because they're in a certain place.

6. *Self-selection bias.* Respondents are allowed to *volunteer* and those of a certain type more often do so, so they're overrepresented.

7. *Termination bias.* Respondents of a certain type more often prematurely withdraw their participation in a continuing task, so they're underrepresented.

8. *Visibility bias.* Some types of respondents are more easily identified or recognized than others, so they're more often selected.

---

to measure how satisfied or content people are. If all the field workers were quite shy and would only interview people who looked like they were very friendly, the data would reflect two things: How satisfied people in general really are, and also the *positive* effects of picking people who look friendly and happy. Selecting only friendly people to interview would produce a bias in the direction of greater satisfaction. The greater the bias, the lower the validity of the data. Eight sources of sampling bias are identified in Guidelist 3–10. The sources listed here are the most common, but they don't constitute an exhaustive list. Every survey is subject to other, specific sources of bias as well. The sample selection process itself should be examined carefully to identify any additional sources of bias.

Controlling Bias

If the sample is to be selected *at random,* the probability that any one respondent will be selected must be exactly equal to the probability of selecting any other. For instance, if 10 percent of the population is to be sampled, then the probability of randomly selecting any one respondent is 1 in 10, or 10 percent. Any factor that alters that probability, either increasing or decreasing it for some respondents, will create *bias* in the selection process. It's important to protect against factors that bias random selection. The statistical inferences about the population depend on random selection and the equal probability of selecting each sample unit. There's a danger the presence of serious, unrecognized biases may lead to inaccurate estimates and errors when making interpretations and drawing conclusions.

Even when a *convenience,* rather than a random, sample is to be used, it's still necessary to avoid any unnecessary sources of bias. The more closely the convenience sample selection procedure approaches a random selection, the more valid the survey results will be.

Accessibility Bias. For many surveys, the actual selection of units takes place in the field, rather than at the survey headquarters. If so, some respondents may be more easily reached than others. Fieldwork tends to pick the most readily available respondents. When all units aren't equally accessible, controls and incentives are necessary to ensure there will be no overrepresentation or underrepresentation of some types of respondents.

Affinity Bias. When the selection of individual respondents is performed in the field by interviewers, there may be affinity bias. This is especially true if the selection plan fails to identify *precisely* which individuals are to be picked, so there's some choice on the part of the field-workers. Interviewers tend to select certain types of respondents because they have an affinity for them. For example, they'll ordinarily ignore those who are:

—apparently very busy or hurried,

—appear to be crabby, grouchy, or unpleasant,

—in groups or in the company of others,

—adults caring for small children,

—physically handicapped or impaired,

—wearing unusual or bizarre dress, or

—otherwise different in any way.

By contrast, they may tend to approach and include people who are:

—of the same social class as they are,

—of the same age and sex as they are,

—more leisurely in their movements,

—more friendly or cooperative, or

—more physically attractive.

When respondents are selected on the basis of their affinity to the interviewer, bias is introduced into the process. This affinity bias can be avoided by very precise specification of who is to be selected and contacted and by strict supervision and enforcement of the instructions to field-workers.

Cluster Bias. Some sampling designs include clusters of respondents, rather than individuals. Cluster sampling is legitimate and often very practical. Cluster bias occurs when the clusters are specified too closely. If respondents from 10 households next door to one another were interviewed, that may lead to bias because of two things: *membership* and *interaction.* People of the same type or status tend to live and work near one another. Those who live near one another are likely to interact, sharing their attitudes and opinions with one another. This tendency for consensus formation would bias the survey results because units within one cluster would provide redundant responses and there would be less variance among those in one cluster than among the population as a whole. Respondents in geographic or progressive clusters must not be too close to one another or be directly interconnected. The responses from each individual must be completely independent of those from all others. To obtain that independence, cluster designs should specify enough distance so there's no connection between individuals within a cluster.

Nonresponse Bias.   Nonresponse may be *independent* of the survey content, or it may *interact* with it. If people decide to respond to a survey or not to respond, *purely* on a random basis, then the nonresponse will be independent of the survey content and there won't be nonresponse bias. In such a case, the response rate need only be estimated and a sufficient number contacted, so the data collection yields an adequate number of respondents to satisfy the sample size requirements. The selection of respondents would remain a random selection.

Unfortunately, nonresponse is virtually never entirely independent of the survey issues. Interaction between survey issues and nonresponse can be direct or indirect. With direct interaction, the very things to be measured affect whether or not people will respond to a survey. Suppose a survey were conducted to measure purchase probability for a new consumer product. Those who have a need for the product are more likely to respond to the survey than are those who see no need for it. The latter group is likely to notice the topic, conclude they have no interest, and discard the questionnaire or refuse the interview. The survey results would portray the product as much more popular and with much greater potential for acceptance than actually exists in the population as a whole.

There may also be indirect interaction, mediated by the demographic or psychographic status of some respondent groups. For example, those in some demographic categories have more time than others. Elderly, retired respondents often feel less time pressure than younger people who are fully employed. They may respond in greater numbers than others. There may not be a direct interaction between the issues measured by the survey and the willingness to respond, but there's an indirect interaction. If those who are retired are *both* more likely to respond *and* more likely to answer in a particular way, this would be a serious source of nonresponse bias.

It's almost impossible to avoid nonresponse bias entirely, and so some such bias must usually be tolerated. It's the researcher's responsibility to assess the degree of direct and indirect interaction that may exist between the survey issues and topics, on the one hand, and the propensity to respond, on the other. At times, it may be virtually impossible to predict the direction of the effect: whether a particular attitude or opinion would tend to increase or decrease the response. When there are no clear indications of the direction of the bias, it may be advisable to conduct a pretest or pilot study that focuses directly on the issue of nonresponse. Another alternative is to use dual data collection methods.

Nonresponse is likely to be *very* high and the effects can be quite severe for self-administered online and mail surveys. So some survey projects use a self-administered survey to obtain a sufficient number of respondents within the budget or resource constraints, while also doing a limited number of interviews. By comparing the results from the two types of respondents, the online or mail response results can usually be adjusted or modified to compensate for the nonresponse bias that's detected and measured.

Order Bias. Most lists of the population that serve as sample frames contain sample units that are listed or appear in an orderly pattern. A telephone directory lists names in alphabetical order. A list of credit card holders may be in sequence from the earliest to the latest applicants. The selection routine has to take into account any such order in the sample frame. The sequential order of the units shouldn't be allowed to increase or decrease the probability that any particular unit or block of units are selected for the sample.

Self-selection Bias. Some sampling designs permit the self-selection of respondents. The most common type of self-selection occurs with online and mail survey, where respondents can easily refuse or ignore the invitation to respond. This *nonresponse* bias was discussed earlier. Aside from that kind of bias, self-selection can occur whenever respondents have a choice of attending or participating. To avoid self-selection bias, the researcher may need to deemphasize or reduce potential respondents' perceptions that they can freely volunteer or easily decline. While they can't be coerced or forced to participate, it's often possible to give the *appearance* that participation is mandatory—that those who decline will suffer some cost or be disqualified from receiving something of benefit or value to them.

Termination Bias. Some personal and telephone interviews take a lot of time to complete. The respondents who are the most cooperative, patient, or submissive will rarely terminate prematurely. By contrast, less cooperative, more impatient, or aggressive respondents may terminate the interview prematurely more frequently than others. If so, they will be underrepresented in the sample—a potential source of bias. The same precautions that are used to avoid *self-selection* also apply to this source of bias.

Visibility Bias. Often some types of units in the population are more visible than others. If the telephone directory serves as the sample frame, those who have unlisted or unpublished numbers and those without telephones wouldn't be included. The researcher has to be sure that such frames or lists are complete. Similarly, some potential respondents are more visible to field interviewers than others. For instance, some shoppers exiting a store may take a different route from most others. They might easily be neglected by those conducting *intercept* interviews. The researcher has to be sure the selection system doesn't pick the more visible units at a higher rate than those which are more obscure. Checklist 3–3 contains the key questions to ask to avoid all the main sources of bias.

Science and Art of Sampling

While there are scientific principles and statistical procedures associated with sampling, the task of designing a sample, choosing a sample size, and selecting respondents remains largely an art. Researchers designing survey samples should follow the guidelines and apply the recommendations, but ultimately they must be somewhat creative and willing to trust their own judgment.

To Avoid Sample Selection Bias   Checklist 3–3

1. Are some units in the population more visible than others? If so, be sure the more visible units are selected in the same proportion as the more obscure units.

2. Are the units in the sample frame presented in systematic order? If so, the sequence must not alter the probability of selection of some units over others.

3. Are some respondents more accessible than others? When they are, controls and incentives must be used to obtain equal proportions of those with high and low accessibility.

4. Are sample units clustered, either deliberately or accidentally? When clusters exist, there must be no more interaction or similarity within clusters than between them.

5. Will field-workers have more affinity for some respondents than others? If so, incentives and controls must be used to avoid overselecting those with greater affinity.

6. Is there an opportunity for respondents to select themselves or decline? If so, the opportunity should be reduced or concealed from potential respondents.

7. Will there be a high proportion of nonrespondents? If so, there should be as little interaction as possible between nonresponse and the issues being surveyed.

8. Are some types of respondents *both* more or less likely to respond *and* likely to respond in a certain way? If so, the nonresponse bias must be reduced or controlled.

Summary

Sampling Design and Size Determination

A. Strive for reliability and validity. Check each decision to determine if it will increase sampling error or introduce a systematic bias into the data.

B. Identify components quite precisely. The population, sample units, and sample frame must be described with clarity and precision.

C. Determine sample size carefully. Consider confidence required, population variance, analysis techniques, and the resources available for the project.

D. Depend upon random sampling. The greater the deviation from random selection, the less legitimate and accurate the statistical analysis and reports will be.

E. Evaluate design refinements. Use stratification, clustering, quota sampling, and special designs to increase reliability and decrease costs.

F. Use trial when necessary. A pilot survey or sequential sampling will indicate the appropriate sample size if it can't be determined in advance.

G. Identify sources of bias. Be aware of the major sources of bias, but constantly inspect the design to be sure additional sources of bias aren't introduced.

H. Be creative and confident. Sampling design and size determination is more of an art than a science!

Developing
Survey Instruments

Part

2

4

Composing Questions

The Core of the Survey

The questions asked of respondents are the ultimate core of the survey project. The entire effort is directed toward inquiry, and the questions are the elements that perform the actual interrogation. The reliability and validity of survey results depend on the way that every aspect of the survey is planned and executed, but the questions addressed to the respondents are the most essential component. Their performance ordinarily has a more profound effect on the survey results than has any other single element of the survey. Thus, it's vitally important that this fundamental task of composing the questions be done carefully and properly.

This and the following two chapters form a trio because they're all devoted to the broad topic of asking questions and obtaining answers. The more general principles and practices regarding question composition will be discussed first in this chapter because they apply to virtually all types of questions that might be asked in a survey questionnaire. Then, the most common mistakes and threats to reliability and validity are identified and recommendations for avoiding them are provided. Several more technical aspects of writing questions are also discussed, and a wide variety of examples are presented. The scaling techniques used with many survey questions are presented and discussed in Chapter 5. Chapter 6 contains guidelines for construction of the survey instrument, including question sequence, the questionnaire structure and format, and the introduction and instructions to respondents. While studying the material concerning question composition presented in this chapter, it may be useful to refer to the following two chapters to see how the questions relate to the scales and how they fit into the questionnaire as a whole.

Basic Attributes of Questions

Effective survey questions have three important attributes: focus, brevity, and clarity. The questions should focus directly on the issue or topic specified in the statement of information needs. They should be as short or brief as possible while still conveying the meaning. The questions should be expressed as simply and clearly as they can be.

The Focus of the Question   Example 4–1

Wrong: Which brand do you like the best?

Right: Which of these brands are you most likely to buy?

Wrong: When do you usually go to work?

Right: What time do you ordinarily leave home for work?

Wrong: Are you going to vote Democratic or Republican?

Right: Which candidate will you vote for on election day?

Focus

Every question on a questionnaire should focus directly on a single, specific issue or topic. This appears to be very obvious, but in practice it isn't as easily achieved as it might seem. Example 4–1 shows three sets of questions. The first of each set lacks focus, and the second is focused directly on the issue or topic in each case. In the first set, the researcher seeks to measure purchase preference. It would be a mistake to ask which respondents liked best, because they may *like* a very elegant and expensive brand, but be unwilling to buy it because of its price. In the second example, asking when the respondent usually goes to work also lacks the necessary focus. It doesn't indicate the point from which the respondent "goes" to work, nor does it ask for a time of day. Thus, some respondents might say, "Just as soon as I get to the shop" or "It depends on how much traffic I run into." The third example listed is supposed to determine voting preference for a particular office. The first question of the set is focused on party preference, rather than the individual choice of a candidate. The two need not be the same.

The best way to be sure that a question is focused directly on the issue at hand is to ask as precisely as possible exactly what the sponsor needs to know. Each of the correct examples shown is a direct expression of the information need; they focus directly on one issue.

Brevity

There are several reasons for keeping survey questions as brief as possible. The longer the questions, the more difficult the response task will be. Short questions are less subject to error on the part of both interviewers and respondents. When questions become too long and cumbersome, respondents are likely to forget the first part of the question by the time they read or hear the last part. Also, long questions are more likely to lack focus and clarity.

In Example 4–2, the brief form of each question is more likely to provide reliable data than is the longer form. If a person is asked the brief form of the first question, the respondent might reply, "I have a nine-year-old boy and a four-year-old girl." The interviewer would know the age of the boy and that of the girl. If the longer version of the first example were used and the respondent could remember everything that was asked, the response might be, "I have two children. A boy and a

The Brevity of the Question

Example 4–2

Wrong: Can you tell me how many children you have, whether they're girls or boys, and how old they are?

Right: What's the age and sex of each of your children?

Wrong: If you own one or more automobiles, please list the year and the make of each one, starting with the newest one:

Right: Please list the year and make of each car you own:

Wrong: When was the last time that you went to the doctor for a physical examination on your own or because you had to?

Right: How many months ago was your last physical examination?

---

girl. They're four and nine years old." The interviewer might either assume the boy was four and the girl nine, or else the field-worker would have to ask which child was which age. In the second set of questions, there's no need for the respondent to put the cars in sequence because that can be done by the analyst later. The item doesn't have to be conditioned on car ownership because those who have no car will leave it blank. For the last pair, the brief form is more straightforward and the longer form would receive answers in weeks, months, years, or by date.

Clarity

The meaning of the question must be completely clear to all respondents. Clarity demands that virtually everyone interprets the question in exactly the same way. In Example 4–3, the correct version of the question in each pair has only one interpretation while the incorrect version has two or more.

The Clarity of the Question

Example 4–3

Wrong: What do you have to say about the charities that your church contributes to?

Right: How much influence do you, yourself, have on which charities your church contributes to?

Wrong: About how much of the storage space in your home do you and your spouse use?

Right: What proportion of the storage space in your home is used for your things and what's used for your spouse's?

Wrong: Ordinarily, do you take aspirin when you feel some discomfort or when you feel actual pain?

Right: Do you usually take aspirin as soon as you feel some discomfort, or only when you feel actual pain?

To Construct Effective Questions | Checklist 4–1

1. Does the question focus directly on the issue or topic to be measured? If not, rewrite the item to deal with the issue as directly as possible.

2. Is the question stated as briefly as it can be? If the item is more than a few words, it may be too long and should be restated more briefly.

3. Is the question expressed as clearly and simply as it can be? If the meaning won't be clear to virtually every respondent, the item should be restructured.

In the first incorrect example shown, the phrase "What do you have to say" can be interpreted in different ways. The phrase might be perceived as asking, "What do you have to say (to me, right now) . . ." If that were the case, the respondent is likely to indicate how much he or she agreed with the selection of charities, rather than indicating his or her own degree of influence.

In the second example, the researcher intends to measure the proportion of storage space used by each head of household. The correct version of the question makes that clear, but the incorrect version doesn't. There's nothing in the wording to indicate that the proportion of each person's space should be indicated, and the respondents are likely to assume the question concerns the use of storage space by both spouses, combined. Thus, they're likely to respond with such a statement as, "We use all of the storage space we have!"

The third example is supposed to present a dichotomy. It assumes that the respondent does use aspirin, and that the individual *either* takes aspirin at the first sign of discomfort or *else* waits until there's the perception of actual pain. The dichotomy is lost in the unclear version of the question, and respondents might simply respond, "Yes, I do." The researcher wouldn't learn at which point the aspirin was consumed, and such data would be useless.

When constructing questions, the researcher must ask again and again: Does this question *focus* precisely on the issue? Is this as *brief* as the question can be stated? Is it completely *clear* what's being asked? If the researcher returns several times to questions that were written earlier to consider the issues outlined in Checklist 4–1, he or she will ordinarily detect some defects and find several questions that can be improved. It's also advisable to have one or more other people check each question for focus, brevity, and clarity. Checking one's own work is difficult because the writer knows what's intended, but others can only approach the questions strictly on their content and wording.

Expressing the Questions

Survey questions are, of course, expressed in words. To obtain meaningful answers, questions must be expressed with the appropriate words. In addition, the words must be combined and arranged in a way that's appropriate to the

The Use of Core Vocabulary | Example 4–4

Wrong: Are you cognizant of all the concepts to be elucidated?

Right: Do you know about all the ideas that will be explained?

Wrong: With what frequency have you experienced this of late?

Right: How many times have you had this happen recently?

Wrong: What emotions were evoked by perceiving the spectacle?

Right: What kinds of feelings did you have when you saw it all?

respondents. Thus, both vocabulary and grammar are important when forming survey questions.

Vocabulary

If the words used in a question aren't in the vocabulary of some respondents, they won't understand what's being asked. This will introduce error or bias in the data. Individuals have three levels of vocabulary. Respondents have a *core* vocabulary of words with which they're very familiar. These are words they use in common speech. They also have a wider vocabulary of words that they recognize when they hear or read them. They seldom, if ever, use such words in common speech, but they have a fairly good understanding of what they mean. Then, of course, there are many other words in the language that individuals don't recognize or understand. Such words have little or no meaning for them.

The researcher should use words that are in the *core* vocabulary of virtually *all* respondents. The reason can be explained very logically. *Comprehension of very pedestrian vocabulary is universal, while that of sophisticated vocabulary is peculiar to the elite.* The reader may well understand the last sentence, but most respondents from the general public wouldn't! Nor would anyone use such a sentence in common speech. The sentence should have been expressed this way: *Everybody understands common words, but only very well-educated people understand words that aren't used in everyday speech.* The conclusion is obvious: If common words from the core vocabulary of the least sophisticated respondents are used in the questions, everyone will understand. If bigger words or words that are seldom used in speech are used in the questions, many won't know what they mean or what's being asked. The researcher has everything to gain by using simple, core vocabulary and avoiding difficult wording, as shown in Example 4–4.

Sometimes people who write survey questions unconsciously want to appear well-educated or sophisticated, so they use fancy words and complex sentences. Also, many people were taught as students to use a special vocabulary or sentence structure for writing—one different from their speech. In either case, there's

The Use of Compound Sentences   Example 4–5

Wrong: What would you do when you had only a few things to buy and there were a lot of people in the checkout line?

Right: Suppose you have only a few things to buy. There are a lot of people in the checkout line. What would you do?

Wrong: How do you work it out when you want one thing and your spouse wants another and you both feel very strongly about it?

Right: How do you settle disagreements with your spouse when you both have strong feelings about it?

Wrong: If you didn't have a reservation ahead of time and you found out that the only seats that you could get were at the very top of the upper balcony, what would you do?

Right: What would you do if the only seats available at show time were at the top of the upper balcony?

a temptation to use a vocabulary that's beyond the core vocabulary of many respondents. The researcher should keep firmly in mind that the ultimate measure of sophistication in survey research is to generate data that are reliable and valid—data that are free from error and bias. That can best be done by using simple, core vocabulary.

Grammar

When writing survey questions, arranging the sentences in the right way is as important as using the right vocabulary. There are four basic kinds of sentence structure: simple, compound, complex, and compound-complex. Simple sentences have a subject and predicate, and sometimes an object or complement. Compound sentences are just two simple sentences linked together by a conjunction. Complex sentences are simple sentences with a dependent clause taking the place of a word, and compound-complex sentences are a combination of the two. The most effective questions are simple sentences. When a simple sentence can't be used, a complex sentence may be required. Compound sentences and compound-complex sentences should be broken down into simple and complex sentences. Three examples of effective and confusing questions are shown in Example 4–5. The correct phrasing in the first example broke the compound sentence into three simple ones. In the second pair, the correct expression of the question uses different wording to avoid the compound-complex sentence structure. The third correct example eliminated several superfluous words.

The choice of both vocabulary and grammar for expressing survey questions should be based on what the *least sophisticated* respondents will understand. The basic rules are contained in Guidelist 4–1.

Instrumentation Bias and Error

The way questions are expressed can all too often introduce systematic bias, random error, or both. Even questions expressed with focus, brevity, and clarity may jeopardize reliability and/or validity. Use of the proper vocabulary and grammar doesn't guarantee that they'll be free from bias or error. Consequently, several kinds of instrumentation bias and error and the means of avoiding them must be noted.

Unstated Criteria

If the criteria by which respondents must judge some issue or respond to some question aren't completely obvious, the criteria must be stated in the question. If an item might be judged by multiple standards and the criteria aren't explicitly stated, some respondents will use one set of criteria and others will use another.

In Example 4–6, there's no clear indication of the criterion in the incorrect question. Thus, some people may respond based on their own needs and others may consider what the stores need to do to win customers in general. The correct question clearly indicates the criterion to be the personal preference of the respondent only.

The Use of Unstated Criteria   **Example 4–6**

Wrong: How important is it for stores to carry a large variety of different brands of this product?

Right: How important is it to you that the store you shop at carries a large variety of different brands?

The Use of an Inapplicable Question   Example 4–7

Wrong: How long does it take you to find a
parking place after you arrive at the plant?

Right: If you drive to work, how long does it take
you to find a parking place after you arrive
at the plant?

Inapplicable Questions

The questions must be applicable to all respondents in the sense that they can reply, based on their own experience or condition. In Example 4–7, those who walk to work, ride a bike or motorcycle, or take a bus or cab would often indicate that parking was no problem to them. The researcher in this case wants to include only those people who drive to work. Thus, to include those who don't drive would provide biased results. The data obtained from the incorrect question would indicate a less severe problem or need than actually existed among those who drive.

Example Containment

When the question contains an example that consists of a response alternative or identifies a class or type of response alternatives, it's likely to interject bias. Many respondents may choose or include the example but fail to include others because the example brings that particular response or type of response to mind. In Example 4–8, the incorrect question would lead many to identify toasters, mixers, or blenders. They're likely to exclude such appliances as vacuum cleaners, power tools, and hair dryers. It's important to identify the entire class of alternatives and avoid examples that are among the possible choices for the respondents.

Over-demanding Recall

The researcher must not assume that respondents will recall their behavior or feelings over an extended period. Often the topics or issues of the survey are very important to those conducting the project, so the researcher assumes they're equally important and memorable to respondents. That's rarely the case.

   The first question in Example 4–9 assumes that respondents would remember the actual number of times they had gone out with their spouse before their

The Use of Examples in Questions   Example 4–8

Wrong: What small appliances, such as countertop
appliances, have you purchased in the past
month?

Right: Aside from major appliances, what other
smaller appliances have you bought in the
past month?

The Use of Overdemanding Recall   Example 4–9

Wrong: How many times did you go out on a date with your spouse before you were married?

Right: How many months were you dating your spouse before you were married?

marriage. Very few would recall that. Yet many wouldn't want to admit that they did not remember, so most respondents would probably estimate the number. Thus, there would be a large amount of error in the data. By contrast, most married respondents are likely to have good recollection of both the day when they met their spouse and the date of their marriage. These are fairly important anniversaries for most married couples. Thus, virtually all could report the number of months they were dating before their marriage.

Overgeneralizations

There are times when it may be appropriate and acceptable to ask respondents for generalizations. When a survey question seeks a generalization, it should represent a policy, strategy, or habitual pattern of the respondents, rather than specific behavior. Whenever specific incidents can be identified, the survey question should be specific. In Example 4–10, the incorrect item asks the respondents to generalize about their behavior. The question is much too general as well. It doesn't state whether the respondent is to use the immediate past as a frame of reference, go back well into the distant past, or indicate expectations for the future. By contrast, the proper wording of the item includes the past 10 incidents of the action. They would ordinarily be easily recalled by virtually all respondents, and the data are far more precise and accurate, so error is reduced and reliability is improved greatly.

Overspecificity

A survey question is overly specific when it asks for an actual or precise response that the respondent is unlikely to know or unable to express. In Example 4–11, virtually all respondents will be able to indicate their *policy* concerning the action in broad terms. Few respondents could report an exact number of times they had behaved in that way. In addition, the incorrect example would be of little value in

The Use of Overgeneralizations   Example 4–10

Wrong: When you buy "fast food," what percentage of the time do you order each of the following type of food?

Right: Of the last 10 times you bought "fast food," how many times did you eat each type of food?

The Use of Overspecificity   **Example 4–11**

Wrong: When you visited the museum, how many times did you read the plaques that explain what the exhibit contained?

Right: When you visited the museum, how often did you read the plaques that explain what the exhibit contained? Would you say always, often, sometimes, rarely, or never?

---

many cases, because there's no *base* number of opportunities. Two people might both report they read 30 such explanations. One may have visited only 30 exhibits and read the plaque on each, while the other may have visited 300 and only read 1 in 10. They would appear from the data to be identical, yet their policies toward this issue would be very different, indeed. If the information needs were concerned with the policies, the data would lack validity.

Overemphasis

If the wording of a question is overemphatic, it's likely to introduce bias by calling for a particular type of response. When it's necessary to describe some condition in the question, it's advisable to use words that lean toward understating, rather than overstating, the condition. Respondents are then free to reach their own conclusions about the degree of severity. If the condition is described in overemphatic terms, a judgment or conclusion is imposed on the respondents. Such words as *catastrophe* or *tragedy* suggest that a potent remedy is required, while words such as *predicament* or *mishap* don't. An example of such a case is presented in Example 4–12.

The correct and incorrect examples are identical except for the last word in each: *crisis* versus *problem.* The use of the word *crisis* implies a conclusion on the part of the researcher. In addition, it's always desirable to avoid or to end a *crisis* as quickly and completely as possible. On the other hand, a *problem* isn't something that necessarily requires immediate or dramatic action. Each question must be examined carefully to avoid wording that overemphasizes or overstates the condition. Words that are overly dramatic or constitute a conclusion must be avoided.

Ambiguity of Wording

Many words and phrases designate different things for different people. Often those who write questions are totally unaware that others may have a completely

---

The Use of Overemphasis   **Example 4–12**

Wrong: Would you favor increasing taxes to cope with the current fiscal crisis?

Right: Would you favor increasing taxes to cope with the current fiscal problem?

The Use of Ambiguous Words   Example 4–13

Wrong: About what time do you ordinarily eat dinner?

Right: About what time do you ordinarily dine in the evening?

different understanding of the term. In Example 4–13, the researcher is referring to the evening meal. Those from the eastern or western areas of the country eat breakfast, lunch, and *dinner*. In many areas of the Midwest, people eat breakfast, *dinner,* and supper. A researcher native to New York or Los Angeles might be shocked and surprised by the results if the incorrect example were used in a national survey. To avoid such ambiguity, virtually every questionable word or phrase must be checked carefully to be sure that it has a common meaning for everyone in the survey sample.

Double-barreled Questions

When two questions are contained within one item, the item is known as a double-barreled question. In Example 4–14, the incorrect item actually asks two questions: Do you take vitamins, and, if so, do you take them to avoid sickness? Those who take vitamins regularly but for some reason other than to avoid sickness would be in a quandary as to *how to* respond. To obtain the required data, the researcher should first ask if the respondents take the action. A second question might be expressed as in the correct example, or it might be *conditioned* on an affirmative response to the first item. Thus, it might be stated: "If so, why?"

Probably the most common form of the double-barreled question includes both the action and the reason or motive in the same item. This is certainly not the only form of double-barreled question, however. Simply asking about two things at one time also creates a double-barreled item. For example, "Do you often get headaches and stomachaches?" Those who get one but not the other would be puzzled by that item. Consider the question, "Do you and your family often go to the movies?" Singles who enjoy the movies could not answer accurately, nor could respondents who do one thing when their family does another. The key to detecting double-barreled questions is to determine if part of the item might be true and part false.

The Use of Double-Barreled Questions   Example 4–14

Wrong: Do you regularly take vitamins to avoid getting sick?

Right: Do you regularly take vitamins? Why or why not?

The Use of Leading Questions   Example 4–15

Wrong: Don't you see some danger in the new policy?

Right: Do you see any danger in the new policy?

Leading Questions

When questions lead the respondents to a particular answer, they create a very strong bias and often result in data that are completely invalid. The incorrect question in Example 4–15 would result in the identification of much greater danger than would the use of the correct form. Respondents are actually being led to identify dangers, while the information requirements seek only to measure the degree to which respondents, themselves, perceive danger.

In many situations, those conducting the survey are hired by a sponsor. Some sponsors may underwrite the survey to prove a point or obtain certain kinds of results that are in their own best interests. Such sponsors may try to insert leading questions or insist on such wording to produce data that are favorable to their position or in their own best interests. Survey data that purport to be "independent and objective" when such leading questions are used are actually fraudulent. This applies as well to other deliberate sources of bias, such as the use of "loaded" questions. Thus, the researcher who maintains an honest reputation through ethical behavior must not allow the deliberate "rigging" of survey results. When sponsors insist on such unethical practices, the researcher is best advised to resign from the project, no matter how attractive it might otherwise appear.

Loaded Questions

While leading questions direct the respondents' attention to a specific type of response or suggest an answer, loaded questions are less obvious. The loaded question includes some wording or phrase that constitutes a more subtle form of influence. Often loaded questions take the form where a "reason" for doing something is included in the item. Notice the phrase "to save human lives" in the incorrect question shown in Example 4–16. Saving lives is, of course, a very desirable goal. The question is phrased in such a way that those who would respond in the negative would appear not to value human life. The correct version of the question in this example is more objective. It deals directly with the issues and avoids

The Use of Loaded Questions   Example 4–16

Wrong: Do you advocate a lower speed limit to save human lives?

Right: Does traffic safety require a lower speed limit?

To Avoid Instrumentation Bias	**Checklist 4–2**

1. Does the question state the criterion for answering? If not, the criterion must be clearly indicated.

2. Is the question applicable to all respondents? If not, it must be reworded or some respondents exempted by using a detour around it for those to whom it doesn't apply.

3. Does the item contain an example that's also a possible answer? If so, change or discard the example.

4. Does the question require respondents to remember too much detail or recall distant events? If so, it must be modified or generalized to make recall easier.

5. Is the question as specific as it can reasonably be? If the item is too general, state it more specifically.

6. Is the item more specific than the way respondents think? If so, it should be expressed in more general terms.

7. Does the question overemphasize some condition? If so, it must be stated in less dramatic terms.

8. Are some of the words in the item ambiguous? If so, reword it using more commonly recognized phrasing.

9. Is the question as free from threat to respondents as possible? If not, change it to reduce the threat.

10. Does the question include only one issue? If it's a double-barreled item, it must be split or modified.

11. Will yea-sayers or nay-sayers always choose one answer? If so, revise the item to include both "yes" and "no."

12. Does the question lead respondents toward a particular answer? If so, the leading phrase must be removed.

13. Is the question *loaded* with a reason for responding in a particular way? If so, the reason must be deleted.

weighting one response with the feelings or emotions associated with "life-saving" policies.

The most common sources of bias and error resulting from the composition of questions are summarized in Checklist 4–2. Some introduce a systematic bias, "skewing" the answers in one particular direction. Others lead to random error because they result in answers that might "go in any direction." Some create both bias and error. The greater the amount of error or bias that's introduced, the lower the reliability and/or validity of the survey results will be. Probably no survey question is completely free of error and bias, but the goal is to approach that as closely as possible.

Sources of Response Bias

When the questionnaire instructions, questions, scales, or response options introduce bias, it's called *instrumentation bias*. The major forms of such bias were discussed in the preceding section. When bias is introduced because of the mentality or predispositions of respondents, it's called *response bias*. Those composing survey

FIGURE 4–1
Sources of
Response Bias

1. *Social desirability.* Response based on what's perceived as being socially acceptable or respectable.
2. *Acquiescence.* Response based on respondent's perception of what would be desirable to the sponsor.
3. *Yea- and nay-saying.* Response influenced by the global tendency toward positive or negative answers.
4. *Prestige.* Response intended to enhance the image of the respondent in the eyes of others.
5. *Threat.* Response influenced by anxiety or fear instilled by the nature of the question.
6. *Hostility.* Response arising from feelings of anger or resentment engendered by the response task.
7. *Auspices.* Response dictated by the image or opinion of the sponsor rather than the actual question.
8. *Mental set.* Cognitions or perceptions based on previous items influence response to later ones.
9. *Order.* The sequence in which a series is listed affects the responses to the items.
10. *Extremity.* Clarity of extremes and ambiguity of mid-range options encourage extreme responses.

questions must consider this type of bias as well because it can be reduced or controlled in part by the wording and sequence of questions. The many different sources of response bias can be classified in a variety of ways. Ten of the major types are listed and identified in Figure 4–1. Each of them will be discussed briefly below.

Social Desirability

When personal preferences, opinions, or behavior deviate from what's socially prescribed, respondents are very prone to report what's socially acceptable, rather than their true answers. This is a serious problem, and even the most experienced researchers find it a difficult problem to overcome. Some issues, such as sexual deviation, drug or alcohol abuse, or tax evasion, may require some other form of investigation because survey data would be useless.

The wording and the format of the question may increase or decrease the degree to which it will evoke a socially desirable response, rather than the true answer. For example, if the spouses of working women were asked, "Do you earn more than your wife?" nearly all would respond that they do, because of the social role prescription that the male be the main "breadwinner." The same question can be expressed in a way that's less likely to obtain a socially desirable response: "Are your wife's monthly earnings usually somewhat more, about the same, or somewhat less than your own?" The first version states the social norm and, in effect, asks if the respondent conforms. Most will indicate they do. The second version provides all three alternatives without stating the norm, and it "softens" the phrasing by using the words *somewhat* and *about.*

Acquiescence

People are usually cooperative. Their agreement to respond to a survey indicates their tendency to cooperate. If they feel that a certain response will be more welcome to the sponsor, researcher, or interviewer, then many will almost automatically provide it. There are two things the researcher can do to reduce such bias: (1) Assure respondents that candid, honest answers are much more helpful than purely favorable ones. They must understand that cooperation requires honesty, not flattery. (2) Provide no indications of which answer is *positive*. If questions are worded so the respondents can't detect what answer is positive in the eyes of the sponsor, researcher, or interviewer, their tendency to cooperate won't affect their responses.

Yea- and Nay-saying

Some people have a more or less global tendency to agree or answer positively and others to disagree or respond negatively. When an entire series of survey items or scales seek responses on a positive/negative dimension, yea-saying or nay-saying may become a source of bias. One method of controlling such bias is to avoid yes/no or positive/negative options. For example, rather than asking the question, "Would you prefer to go?" it might be expressed, "Would you prefer to: (a) go to that place, or (b) remain where you are?" In the second version, there are no positive or negative options. When many questions must be answered on a positive/negative basis, this form of bias can be partially controlled by "reflecting" roughly half of the items. For example, if attitudes toward some issue were to be measured by listing a series of statements and asking about agreement or disagreement, then half the statements might be negative toward the issue and half positive. Thus, yea-saying or nay-saying would, in effect, automatically compensate or "equal out."

Prestige

Virtually everyone likes to "look good" in their own eyes and in the eyes of others. When respondents inflate their income, shave a few years off their age, or amplify the importance of their job on a survey questionnaire, their desire for prestige becomes a source of bias. If every aspect of the survey shows respect and admiration for people of all walks of life, the likelihood of this type of bias will be reduced. This bias can be reduced further by avoiding questions that invite respondents to seek prestige. Asking "How would you rate yourself on self-reliance?" would invite a high rating and introduce serious bias. The same information could be obtained by seeking a rating along the continuum from "Depend entirely on myself" to "Depend mostly on others." Assigning the lower numbers to self-reliance and the higher to dependency would also help to compensate for the remaining bias from the pursuit of prestige.

Threat

Survey questions can constitute a psychological threat to respondents when they deal with issues and outcomes that have very negative consequences for them. Most people don't like to think about such things as their own death, disease, serious accidents, the loss or separation of a loved one, and the like. When the survey requires information concerning such issues, it's important to avoid the more graphic words and phrases, using euphemisms instead. It's less threatening to speak of having a "hearing impairment" than to talk about being "partially or totally deaf" Other means of reducing threat bias are either to "depersonalize" the issue either by referring to it in the abstract or by "projection," referring to the experience or condition of some other person. For example, rather than asking what the *respondents* would do if they lost their job, it may be necessary either to ask about how people might cope with unemployment (the abstract) or what they might suggest if a friend (another person) were temporarily unemployed.

Hostility

There are some situations where either the topics or issues included in the survey or the response task itself may engender strong hostility or resentment in some respondents. Once these strong feelings have been evoked, respondents won't focus exclusively on the thing that evoked their feelings or be able to dissipate their feelings very quickly. In such cases, the respondents who feel hostile may generalize these feelings to other questions that follow. They are, in effect, responding more to a previous item than to the ones that follow. One way to avoid this form of bias is to word questions in a manner that's less likely to create feelings of hostility. When it isn't possible to avoid evoking some hostility or where these negative emotions must be measured by the survey, there are two ways to keep them from contaminating the items that follow. One way is to allow the respondents to dissipate these feelings as fully as possible directly on the issues that created them. If respondents are allowed adequate opportunity to express these feelings before continuing, they're more likely to "get them out of their system," and then to relax and continue. Another helpful technique is to provide some means of separating one section very distinctly from the next. If respondents clearly understand that the next set of items deals with an issue or topic that's completely separate, they're less likely to carry their hostile feelings over to this new area.

Auspices

When respondents know in advance who is sponsoring the survey, their feelings toward the sponsor may bias their answers to the questions. For example, a survey of employees sponsored by the company may generate very different answers than if it were sponsored by the labor union. To avoid such auspices bias, many surveys are conducted by an independent agency or research team. There's often no necessity to tell respondents in advance who is sponsoring the survey. When information about the sponsoring organization must be obtained or when respondents might easily infer the identity of the sponsor from the questions, such questions should come as late in the questionnaire as possible. Such bias can also be avoided by "clouding" or "smoke-screening" the identity of the sponsor. For example, if the survey focused on the sponsoring company's brand of products, the same questions might also be asked concerning some other brands as well. That way, respondents wouldn't be sure which company was seeking the information and auspices bias would be controlled.

Mental Set

When respondents are asked to perform some mental task, they develop a set of perceptions and assumptions that serves as a frame of reference for responding. Usually, they'll maintain that same frame of reference or mental set until they realize it no longer applies. For example, the survey might include two questions: "How many times have you moved in the past five years?" and "How many times have you owned the home in which you lived?" Their frame of reference for the first question would cover only the past five years. When responding to the second question, many would use the same frame of reference, considering only the past five years when they answer, even though the question doesn't limit the history to that period. If the researcher intended the second question to include the entire residential history of the respondents, rather than only the past five years, the obsolete mental set of the respondents would create a bias. This bias can be avoided or controlled by making it perfectly clear to respondents when they're to shift their frame of reference or make a new set of assumptions to respond to the next item That can be done by beginning a new section with new instructions or by stating the new assumptions or frame of reference as a preface to the next question.

Order

The order or sequence in which survey questions or scaled items are listed will often affect the response, even though respondents are to respond to each in turn. There are three things that might induce order bias in these cases: *initiation, routine, and fatigue.* With the first item or so, initiation requires that respondents learn how to handle the response task. Samples or items of little importance should be listed first, so any bias from initiation won't affect the most important items.

When several similar items appear in sequence, the routine nature of responding may lead to a response strategy or policy. If that happens, each item won't be viewed or evaluated independently, as they should be. Bias from routine response can be reduced by varying the list to make individual items distinct and to require separate consideration of each. Rather than composing all items on a list to ascend in one direction, the list should be composed so some items ascend in one direction while others descend in that direction. For example, a list of statements might consist of a random mix, so some are positive about the issue and others are negative. Recognizing this, respondents would then have to read and evaluate each statement independently, rather than developing a "policy" of agreeing or disagreeing with all of them.

When respondents must rate or respond to a long list of items, the rote nature of the task may cause fatigue. In short, they get tired of the process. If that happens, they may respond carefully to the earlier items and carelessly to the later ones on the list, causing error, bias, or both. This form of bias can be controlled by keeping any one list or sequence short enough so even the least motivated respondents won't be affected by fatigue when responding to that section.

When responses are required for each item on a list, initiation, routine, and fatigue may cause order bias. Two kinds of order bias apply when respondents are given a list of alternatives and asked to pick one from the list: *primacy* effect and *recency* effect. People often remember the first items of any list, simply because they're first. This is called a primacy effect. They also recall the last items more readily than others because they have been presented more recently. Thus, this is called a recency effect. Usually, both apply for any long list, but not always with equal strength. In any case, the general principle indicates that people are more likely to recall the first and last things that are presented in sequence than they are those which come between. Consequently, there's a bias toward respondents picking the first or last alternatives from a group, simply because they're more easily remembered. There are two methods for reducing or controlling order bias from primacy and recency effects. One way is to be sure lists are fairly short. This is especially important for interview surveys, where respondents are read the list and must keep the whole set of alternatives in mind while they choose one. Ordinarily, only four or five options can be recalled at one time. When a longer list of alternatives must be evaluated relative to one another, it's usually advisable to provide a scale and have *each* item rated. Ratings can be compared during analysis, and the most preferred option can be identified by its highest rating.

Another method of controlling order bias resulting from primacy and recency effects is to vary the order or sequence of items from one respondent or subsample to the next. This is ordinarily not feasible for mail surveys, because more than one form of questionnaire would be required and that would be costly. It may be more feasible to instruct interviewers to read a list in random order (checking off each as it's read) for each respondent. This method should be used only when order bias is regarded as a serious threat to the validity of the data because it puts a burden on the interviewers and requires that they be instructed and monitored carefully.

Extremity

This form of bias is similar in some respects to primacy and recency effects. When scales are used, respondents sometimes tend to "dichotomize" the scale by picking only the extremes. Thus, if a scale contained numbers from 1 to 10 with the extremes labeled "Extremely good" and "Extremely bad," some people may answer only with a 1 or a 10. In effect, they're refusing to make a more fine-grained discrimination. It's easier to think in terms of black and white than it is to distinguish between shades of gray. (Ironically, the result is the exact opposite of "fence-riding," or picking a neutral, middle value, so the respondent actually avoids making a choice entirely.)

The careful choice and composition of scales will help to reduce or control extremity bias. Such bias may result because the scales have too many numbers or points. The number of scale points should be about the same as the number of categories in the respondents' mind. For example, when looking at a product, buyers may think in such terms as: terrible, unacceptable, poor, fair, good, and excellent. A scale of five, six, or even seven points would be appropriate, but one with a hundred points isn't. It's also important to label the ends of the scale with the *ultimate extremes*. In the example above, if the extremes were labeled "poor" and "good" rather than "terrible" and "excellent," a bias would result because the mid-range would cover only products that were viewed as fair.

Controlling response bias requires checking and rechecking the survey questions and items again *and* yet again. Sometimes correcting for one source of bias

---

To Control Response Bias | Checklist 4–3

1. Is the question subject to any of the 10 sources of response bias listed in Figure 4–1? If so, consider each of the methods for control noted below.

2. Can the question be reworded to reduce or eliminate the bias? Compose a few alternative forms of the question and select the version that's least likely to be subject to bias.

3. Might the instructions be changed so the item isn't subject to the bias? Examine and substitute instructions for the question, section, or scale to reduce bias.

4. Does the source of bias arise from the choice or form of a scale? Consider alternative scales from the examples in the following chapter or modify the scale to reduce bias.

5. Does the structure of the section or questionnaire induce or encourage bias? Try reforming the section or moving it to another location in the questionnaire.

6. Do the presence or nature of preceding or following questions or items make the question subject to bias? Tentatively rearrange the items in the section or move the question to another section to control the bias.

7. Do the modifications in the question or questionnaire to reduce one form of bias make it more subject to another? Check the revised item against the sources of response bias to be sure the changes have not created another problem.

---

inadvertently causes the introduction of another. Checklist 4–3 outlines the process for controlling response bias.

Question Format

There are two basic formats for survey questions: unstructured and structured. Unstructured questions are sometimes called "open-end" questions because only the question is expressed and no alternative answers are listed for the respondent. Structured survey items do two things: They ask a question and they list the alternative answers the respondent might choose. Experienced researchers prefer to use structured questions whenever they're feasible because they have many important advantages.

The Dimension of Answers

Unstructured questions often don't clearly indicate the dimension along which respondents are supposed to answer. In Example 4–17, an unstructured item is listed in the top section together with seven verbatim answers from different respondents. Notice that some respondents are selecting reasons for visiting *that* particular store, while others are indicating why they visited *today,* rather than another time. The unstructured version of the item doesn't indicate the range along which respondents should answer, while the structured version clearly indicates it.

In the structured form of the item used in the example, the list of alternatives clearly indicates to respondents that they're to base their answer on the attributes or characteristics of the store. In effect, they know more precisely what's being

Structured versus Unstructured Questions   Example 4–17

Unstructured Item

Q. Why did you visit this store?

A1.   "I happened to be in the neighborhood."
A2.   "I didn't have anything better to do."
A3.   "I like the merchandise they have here."
A4.   "I have an account at this store."
A5.   "I always shop on Wednesday."
A6.   "A friend recommended the store."
A7.   "It's fun to shop. I enjoy it."

Structured Item

Q. What's the one *major* reason you visited this store?

A1.   _____ The price of the goods.
A2.   _____ The selection of merchandise.
A3.   _X_ The location of the store.
A4.   _____ Friendly, helpful staff.
A5.   _____ Availability of credit.
A6.   _____ Some other reason. Specify what: _____
A7.   _____ No particular reason; don't know.

asked or what information is sought. Experience clearly indicates that respondents seldom answer the way they're expected to respond when they're free to provide any answer they wish. Even when it appears to the researcher that the dimension along which respondents are to answer is plainly evident, respondents are likely to be in a different frame of mind and thus to respond along some completely different dimension.

Comparability of Data

Unstructured items often produce data that aren't directly comparable from one respondent or group to the next. When structured items are used, the data are comparable among respondents. Thus, data processing and analysis can compare and contrast the answers of various individuals or subsamples.

The unstructured question in Example 4–17 may produce as many different verbatim responses as there are respondents in the sample. It would be necessary to "group" answers into categories when editing and postcoding the data, after the information was collected. This can be a laborious and time-consuming process. In addition, the editor or analyst must make many judgments about the meaning or intent of the respondents when grouping the responses into categories. On the other hand, when a structured item is used, this process of selecting categories is done in the field, at the time the information was collected. Furthermore, the judgments are made by the respondents, themselves, rather than by another person who must interpret their meaning or intentions.

Some survey projects instruct interviewers to read only the question but not the alternatives, and then select the category to check. This procedure isn't recommended unless special circumstances make it necessary. Nonetheless, this method is preferable to completely unstructured questioning because in such cases the selection of the category takes place while the interview is in progress. The field-worker can question the respondent further if there's uncertainty. If, on the other hand, the categories are to be selected during editing and postcoding, there's no way to obtain additional information if it's needed.

Recording Accuracy

It's difficult and time-consuming for either the interviewer or the respondent to record verbatim responses to questions. The answers listed in the top section of Example 4–17 are quite short, but in actual practice respondents might provide two or three sentences to explain why they visited the store. If the structured version of the same item listed in the bottom of the example were used, the respondent or field-worker would only have to check the appropriate category. Thus, there's much less likelihood of error in recording.

The Response Task

When a self-administered questionnaire is being used, or when the alternatives are listed for the respondent, the response task is much quicker and easier with structured items. Thus, there's likely to be greater cooperation, a higher response rate, less missing data, and fewer "random" responses when structured items are used.

Inappropriate Reasons

There are several reasons why unstructured survey questions are often used when structured items would be superior. It takes considerable time and effort in the beginning to compose structured questions effectively. It takes only a few minutes to write an unstructured question. There's a tendency for the researcher to hurry the composition task and worry about the editing and coding later, after the data have been collected. Thus, the work is both amplified and procrastinated.

Another reason for the frequent and inappropriate use of unstructured questions comes from sponsors and information seekers. Often those who sponsor a survey feel that the exclusive use of structured items will limit the "richness and variety" of people's answers. This is, of course, quite true. Because they aren't trained or experienced in survey research methods, they fail to recognize the enormity of the task of interpretation. Invariably, when presented with several hundreds or thousands of verbatim responses, they're overwhelmed by the volume and, by necessity, abandon the effort entirely. The researcher has the responsibility to explain the problems associated with verbatim answers and provide assurance that structured items will obtain the required data. The guidelines for using (or if possible, avoiding) unstructured questions are provided in Guidelist 4–2.

If it's necessary to hear people's answers to important questions *in their own words*, the best course of action is to conduct one or more *focus group discussions* prior to conducting the survey. That way, sponsors and information seekers can better perceive the richness and texture of the participants' extemporaneous

For Using Unstructured Questions   Guidelist 4–2

1. Structure the question whenever it's possible to do so, even though it requires time and effort.

2. Resist requests by sponsors for verbatim responses, explaining the difficulty of interpretation.

3. Be sure the dimension or range of alternatives is crystal clear to respondents when an item is unstructured.

4. Be sure the interviewers or respondents can record verbatim responses to unstructured items accurately.

5. Estimate the degree to which using an unstructured question will increase the response task.

6. After all is said and done, go back and see if it may not be possible to use a structured item, anyhow.

answers and comments because the number and volume of responses are much smaller. The advantages of this approach and the recommended procedures are discussed in Appendix A. If the focus groups are conducted *prior* to the survey, the results may be helpful in building the questionnaire and doing the other survey tasks. If the focus group discussions take place *after* the survey has been completed, participants can be questioned about those areas of the survey findings that appear somewhat ambiguous or would benefit from extension and clarification.

Composing Categorical Items

When a structured question is used, the researcher has to choose the categories or response alternatives to be used by respondents. Questions of this kind are called "categorical" items because all responses must fall into a particular category. (Alternative forms of structured items using numeric scales are presented in Chapter 5.) It takes considerable time and effort to compose a categorical question and select the proper categories. On the other hand, if the task is done carefully and thoroughly, it will save a great deal of time and effort later and increase the reliability and validity of the data. Categorical items ask a question, followed by a series of alternative answers. When composing the question itself, the researcher applies all the principles and guidelines discussed earlier. Thus, the same things are required of the question itself, whether it's structured or unstructured.

An All-inclusive List

The categories used with a structured item form a classification system. There are three rules or principles to observe when choosing the categories for such an item: (1) the list must be all-inclusive, (2) the categories must be mutually exclusive, and (3) there should be more variance in the meaning *between* categories than within them.

The first rule is that the list must include every possible response. Every answer a respondent might possibly give must fit into a category, and there must be no conceivable answer that doesn't fit into a category.

Structured Category Questions   **Example 4–18**

Incorrect Classification

Q. How did you *first* learn about the new clinic?

A1. _____ From a friend or co-worker.
A2. _____ From a relative or family member.
A3. _____ From a newspaper or magazine.
A4. _____ From the radio or television.
A5. _____ From a news story.
A6. _____ By seeing a sign, billboard, or poster.
A7. _____ By some other announcement or advertisement.

Correct Classification

Q. How did you *first* learn about the new clinic?

A1. _____ From a relative or family member.
A2. _____ From an associate or acquaintance.
A3. _____ From a newspaper or magazine *advertisement*.
A4. _____ From a radio or television *advertisement*.
A5. _____ *Read* a news story in some publication about it.
A6. _____ *Heard* a *news* story about it on radio or TV.
A7. _____ Some other way. *Specify how:* _____

In Example 4–18, the incorrect classification scheme shown in the top section doesn't meet the requirement of an all-inclusive set of categories. Suppose some respondents had actually seen the new clinic building. There's no category for recording that means of learning about the clinic. By contrast, the correct version shown in the lower section of the example includes an "other" category, so those responses that don't fit into any of the first six categories can be recorded and identified in the seventh. It's very advisable to include an open "other" category in such lists. Even though the questions are pretested in a pilot survey, there are likely to be a few exceptional or unusual responses that won't fit into any category listed.

When an "other" category is used, the nature of the "other" may or may not be specified, depending on the information requirements. There are times when those seeking information may be interested *only* in a few certain categories, but answers might range widely beyond them. When that's the case, the answers that don't fit into the categories of interest may all be lumped into an "other" category without specification of just what the other things are. For some situations, the nature of the "other" responses may be useful or required by those seeking the information. When they are, they should be specified so they can be identified, categorized, and postcoded when the completed questionnaires or online data files are being edited.

A Mutually Exclusive List

There must be a *unique* association between any given answer and one category or alternative. No response should fit into two or more categories. In Example 4–18, the incorrect version of the item has overlapping categories. Those respondents who first learned of the clinic through a news story could be recorded in that category and/or as having gained awareness from newspapers or magazines or from radio or television. The correct version of the item in the lower portion of the example not only makes a distinction between broadcast and print media, but also between paid advertising and publicity through news articles. Thus, no answer would fit into more than one category, and the requirement for a mutually exclusive list has been met.

Meaningful Clusters

When answers are recorded in categories, the alternatives used should cluster responses similar to one another. Answers substantially different from one another should fall into separate categories. Lacking such a classification system, the data wouldn't be especially meaningful, or at least some value will be lost. In Example 4–18, the categories used in the improper example don't make a distinction between print media publicity and broadcast media publicity. "News stories" consist of one category, and both types would be clustered together, although they might be regarded as having significantly different meanings for the sponsors. Also, the incorrect version makes a distinction between "signs, billboards, and posters" and "some other announcement or advertisement." Such a distinction doesn't appear to be valuable or meaningful.

The incorrect list of alternatives in the example would result in too much variation in meaning in the category for news stories and too little meaningful variation in the last two categories. There are no set rules for forming categories with more variance in meaning between than within them. The task requires a thorough understanding of what distinctions will and won't be meaningful to the sponsors. The choice also depends on what would be meaningful to *respondents*. Thus, the task is something of an art, requiring judgment and perhaps a pilot test.

Size and Number of Categories

The researcher composing structured, categorical items must also decide the number of categories to be used and how broad or narrow each should be. The simple, dichotomous question with only two categories is the lower limit on the number of categories. The upper limit is ordinarily about six or eight categories. With more than that, the response and recording task increases greatly, and it's seldom necessary or advisable to exceed that limit. The choice of the number of categories between these two extremes depends on how "fine-grained" the sponsor would like the data to be. The general rule should be to have no more categories than are actually required. Too many categories make the response task more difficult and time-consuming.

There's one *very important* precaution when determining the size and number of categories for a structured item. If there's doubt about how precise or fine-grained the data must be, it's best to use the larger number of more narrow categories. The

For Composing Categorical Items	**Guidelist 4–3**

1. For composing the question itself, the same rules and principles apply to structured, categorical items as to unstructured questions.

2. The categories must be "all-inclusive," so there's an appropriate category for any conceivable response.

3. If all possible answers can't be anticipated or when some types are of no interest, exceptional responses should be clustered into an "other" category.

4. The categories must be mutually exclusive, so no answer would fit into more than one category.

5. There should be more variance in meaning between categories than within them, so answers are clustered into categories on a meaningful basis.

6. Ordinarily, there should be no more than six or eight categories for any one question.

7. Categories should be broad enough to capture a sufficient number of responses and to provide adequate frequencies during processing and statistical analysis.

8. The categories shouldn't be more "fine-grained" than required by the sponsors.

9. When in doubt, choose the more narrow categories because they can always be combined later but they can't be split after data collection.

reason is simple, but compelling: Categories can easily be *combined* during processing, if necessary. On the other hand, if they prove to be too broad, there's no *way* to disaggregate the broad categories into smaller ones after the data have been collected. Once clustered, the answers must remain so.

Categorical items are sometimes the backbone of the survey questionnaire. Sometimes they're only a small part, but some categorical questions are almost always included. The recommendations for composing effective categorical items are summarized in Guidelist 4–3.

Verbal and Numeric Items

Structured, categorical survey items are only one type of survey question. It's *always* advisable to use an ordinary numeric item when it's feasible. Less experienced researchers sometimes tend to use structured, categorical questions in place of numeric items. They may feel that categorical items will facilitate the analysis, or they may hold the mistaken notion that respondents would prefer the categorical type. Neither is so, and when there's a choice, numeric items should be used, with very few exceptions.

In Example 4–19, discrete categories are used in the incorrect example. The categories are inappropriate because the data can readily be obtained in numeric form, as shown in the correct item. In addition, the categories are too broad and the data can't be disaggregated after data collection. Ordinarily, it's important to distinguish between those who had "some high school" or "some college" and those who completed the course of study and obtained a degree or diploma. That discrimination is forever lost with the categorical form of the intern.

Numeric versus Categorical Items   Example 4–19

Incorrect Categorical Item

Q. What level of education have you attained?

A1. _____ Elementary school only.
A2. _____ High school only.
A3. _____ College education.
A4. _____ College postgraduate.

Correct Numeric Item

Q. What's the last year of education you have completed? [For example, high school graduate equals 12 years.]

A. _____ years of formal education.

By contrast, the numeric data can easily be grouped into categories if required by those who seek the information. Those with 8 years of school or less could be grouped into the "elementary only" category, those with 9 to 11 years into "some high school," those with 12 years into "high school graduate," and so forth. In addition, the correct version of the item is less threatening and presents the respondents with a much simpler and easier task than does the categorical item.

Survey questionnaires usually include both structured, categorical items and numeric items and scales. This is especially so for self-administered questionnaires, whether sent by mail or presented on a web page. Several thoroughly tested and commonly used verbal and numeric items and scales are presented and discussed in Chapter 5. They're extremely efficient and effective when they're used appropriately.

Summary

The Composition of Survey Questions

A. Focus very precisely. Every item should zero in very directly on one specific issue or topic.

B. Keep each item brief. The longer the question, the greater the response task and the more error and bias.

C. Strive for clarity. Every respondent must know exactly what's being asked.

D. Use "core" vocabulary. Use the same words as the least sophisticated respondents would use in common speech.

E. Use simple sentences. Two or more simple sentences are far preferable to one compound sentence.

F. Avoid specific sources of bias or error. Be sure items are free from the factors that create bias and error.

G. Use structured questions. Unstructured items ordinarily provide large quantities of poor quality data.

H. Classify answers carefully. Observe the three rules for an effective classification system.

I. Choose appropriate categories. Be certain they're neither too broad nor narrow, too many nor too few.

J. Use scaling effectively. Refer to the following two chapters for guidance on numeric and verbal scales and to combine survey items into groups.

5

Creating Item Scales

Why Scales Are Used

Answers to survey questions are typically a choice of *position*, either within some category or along some continuous spectrum. A response scale is merely a representation of the categories or continuum along which respondents will arrange themselves. When scales are used, reports describe the *distribution* of respondents along the scale or in the categories. The positions of various individuals or groups can then be compared with one another. Scales can be coded with numbers. The numeric codes that represent answers to questions are more easily manipulated than words. The use of a numeric database saves time and money and helps to ensure accuracy, reliability, and validity. Scales can be arranged so they capture answers to many questions quickly and in very little space. They're both *efficient* and *practical*.

Specificity of Scales

Scales are used to obtain responses that will be comparable to one another. All responses should be expressed in the same terms. Sometimes the scale will be obvious to the respondent, and sometimes it will be necessary only to name the scale. There are also times when the scales will have to be clearly portrayed.

Implicit Scale Dimensions

For some questions, the scale already exists in the minds of the respondents. For example, when someone is asked their age, they'll respond with the number of years. There's a common understanding between the questioner and the respondent about the scale to be used. This is an *implicit* scale because it's *implied* by the question. Other examples include weight, height, eye color, distance between cities, and simple, dichotomous questions such as yes or no.

Explicit Scale Dimensions

At other times, there is no common understanding between the questioner and the respondent. If people were asked, "How long has it been since your last visit to a physician for treatment?" some might respond in days, some in months, and some in years. A few may even say, "Oh, it's been a long time" or "I go whenever I'm sick." Such answers are difficult to manipulate or compare to one another. It would be better to ask, "How *many months* has it been since . . ." rather than, "How long has it been since . . ." That way, the scale is *explicit.* All responses will be expressed in calendar months and they're comparable.

For common denominations, such as months, pounds, dollars, degrees of temperature, or the number of a certain thing, such as trips taken during a given time, virtually everyone will be familiar with it if it's named in the question. When this is the case, and the question can be asked by merely specifying the scale in the question, it should be done that way, so long as the respondents understand the scale specified.

Depicted Scale Dimensions

When scales can't be specified within the question, they must be *depicted* as response options, verbally, numerically, or graphically. For example, if the question were, "Where are you going when you leave here?" answers wouldn't be comparable. There's no scale that can easily be specified within the question, so the response options must be listed or depicted following the question: home, work, shopping, recreation, and so forth. When seeking qualitative evaluations, preferences, images, perceptions, or judgments, the scale dimensions may be depicted in the form of rankings, ratings, graphic figures, or some other set of response alternatives. In the examples that follow, several of the most popular scaling devices are shown.

The scale should be depicted only when necessary. Implicit scales should be used when respondents are sure to understand them and are as willing to respond to an implicit scale as to a depicted one. This is usually the case. When specification is required, common, simple dimensions should be used. Some researchers inappropriately specify age *groups* when it would be more simple and accurate to ask, "What's your age?" Three words in the question and one number for the answer—what could be simpler? No specification is necessary, and the scale is implied.

The question concerning level of education is another example. Here, the scale must be explicitly specified, but many researchers will list an elaborate set of categories, including: elementary only, some high school, high school graduate, some college, college graduate, some postgraduate school, or postgraduate degree. A simpler way to ask would be, "How many years of formal education have you completed?" In almost every case the researcher can safely assume that 8 years means elementary school, 12 means high school, and so on. Where an underlying dimension is commonly understood by both questioner and respondent, it should be used without elaboration.

Scale Data Types

The structured questions and scales described here provide four different kinds or "levels" of scale data: *nominal, ordinal,* (equal) *interval,* and *ratio* data. These scale data types are thoroughly explained and illustrated in Chapter 9. Nevertheless, a preliminary look at these data types might be helpful in understanding the characteristics of the various scale types described here.

To Select the Scale Category   **Checklist 5–1**

1. Will the respondents clearly understand the dimensions they're to use? If so, dimensions need only be *implied*.

2. Will the respondents be familiar with the scale dimensions if they're named, such as years,

times, or miles? If so, the dimensions need only be *explicit*.

3. Will the respondents be uncertain or unfamiliar with the scale? If so, the scale must be *depicted*.

Structured questions such as multiple-choice items provide data that merely identify categories. These data are called "nominal" because the numbers are merely names for the categories and don't stand for a quantity. This is the lowest level of scale data and the most limited with regard to the kinds of statistical techniques that can be used legitimately to analyze it.

The next higher level of data is called "ordinal" data because it indicates order or sequence. For example, if a child has 2 older siblings, that child's *ordinal position* in the family would be 3. The ordinal value indicates the order, but not magnitude. It doesn't indicate *how much* older the siblings are, so the "distance" between ordinal values is undetermined. Ordinal data can be analyzed with special statistical methods, generally known as "nonparametric" statistics.

The two highest levels of scale data are "equal interval" and "ratio" data. These are both data from scales where the interval between integer values are equal. Equal interval scales are often called merely *"interval"* scales for short. The only difference between interval and ratio scales is that with the latter, zero means *nothing*—the *null set*. With interval scales there may not be a zero value and if there is, it may not stand for *none*. For example, with the Fahrenheit scale of temperature, zero doesn't mean the absence of heat. With a ratio scale—distance, dollars, weight, etc.—zero means none so it's legitimate to form ratios such as 1/2 or 2:1. Interval and ratio scales have the fewest limitations on the kinds of statistics with which they can be analyzed.

Multiple-Choice Question

Multiple-choice questions are very common because they're simple and versatile. They can be used to obtain either a single response or several. Multiple-choice questions of both single response and multiple response are shown in Example 5–1.

Multiple-Response Items

In the multiple-response case, the respondents can indicate one *or more* alternatives, and they're instructed to check *any* within the question, itself. In this case, *each* alternative becomes a *variable* to be analyzed. Thus, this one item actually asks seven questions. They could be expressed individually, one at a time: 'Do you regularly read the paper for business news?" for each of the six, and "What other

The Multiple-Choice Item   Example 5–1

Multiple Response

Please check *any* type of newspaper you regularly read for business news.

——— Local, morning paper
——— Local, evening paper
——— Local, weekly paper
——— Regional, weekly paper
——— National, daily paper
——— National, weekly paper
——— Other (What kind?_____)

Single Response

What kind of newspaper do you *most often* read for business news?
(Check only one.)

(1) ——— Local, morning paper
(2) ——— Local, evening paper
(3) ——— Local, weekly paper
(4) ——— Regional, weekly paper
(5) ——— National, daily paper
(6) ——— National, weekly paper
(7) ——— Other (What kind?_____)

papers do you regularly read for business news?" That would take much more time and space, and so this multiple-response item is very economical.

Single-Response Items

When only one alternative is to be singled out from among several by the respondent, the item is a multiple-choice, but a *single-response* item. No "ties" are allowed, and the respondent is supposed to pick only one. Respondents don't always follow instructions if they're unclear. Consequently, single-response items can be used only when: (1) the choice criterion is clearly stated and (2) the criterion actually defines a single category. Notice that the words, "most often" and "one" are italicized in the item shown in the lower section of the example. This clearly states that only one option is to be designated. Note also that few if any respondents are likely to read two or more publications with exactly the same frequency, so ties are unlikely and there's a *unique* answer to the question. The selection of a single-response, rather than a multiple-response item, depends on the researcher's needs and the respondents' ability to identify one answer.

It's important to note again that the multiple-choice item is ideal for responses that fall into individual categories. On the other hand, multiple-choice items shouldn't be used for numeric data. When the answers can be expressed as numbers, a direct question should be used, and the number of units should be recorded. If it's desirable to *group* responses into categories within certain ranges,

For Using Multiple-Choice Items   Guidelist 5–1

1. The entire range of response should be classifiable into a few discrete categories. About 8 or 10 are usually the maximum.

2. The category names should define a set of discrete alternatives, so there's a clear distinction between them in the minds of interviewers and/or respondents.

3. The named categories should be mutually exclusive, so no possible answer could fit into more than one of the categories used.

4. There should be certainty that the labeled alternatives will capture over 90 percent of all answers that are likely to be given to the question.

5. An "other" category should be listed last to include any answers that don't fit into the named categories, unless there's no possibility of other answers.

that can easily be accomplished later, during data processing. The guidelines for writing effective multiple-choice items are presented in Guidelist 5–1.

Conventional Scale Types

The types of scales that are most commonly used in surveys are described below. While all of them have been used extensively in survey research, some are much more common than others. Nor are they equally effective for a particular kind of measurement. Some can be used to measure a broad range of topics and objects. Others are recommended *only for very specific* tasks. Nearly every information need or survey question can be scaled effectively with the use of one or more of the scales described in this chapter. Some special scales, less conventional than these, are presented in the following chapter. Thus, the researcher's scaling decisions are more a matter of *choice* among the conventional scales than of invention of scaling devices.

The Likert Scale

There are times when it's necessary to obtain people's *position* on certain issues or conclusions. This is a form of opinion or attitude measurement. An unstructured or *open-ended* question might be used for this purpose, but that type of question has many problems associated with analysis and interpretation. Answers are seldom comparable. The Likert scale, named for its creator, states the issue or opinion and obtains the respondents' degree of agreement or disagreement. This scale provides answers in the form of coded data that are comparable and can readily be manipulated.

When a Likert scale is used, the question is stated in the instructions, above the scale. The question becomes, "How much do you agree with this statement?" The actual items aren't questions, but statements that represent particular opinions. Respondents indicate their agreement or disagreement to each, so responses are on a single dimension or continuum. The instructions for such a scale, the scale itself, and 10 item statements are shown in Example 5–2.

The Likert Scale   Example 5–2

Please pick a number from the scale to show how much you agree or disagree with each statement and jot it in the space to the right of the item.

Scale

1 **Strongly agree**
2 **Agree**
3 **Neutral**
4 **Disagree**
5 **Strongly disagree**

A man should never cry in public . . . . ____
Higher education is more important for men than women . . . . ____
Women should receive equal pay for equal work . . . . ____
A man shouldn't resent a woman supervising his work . . . . ____
A woman's place is in the home . . . . ____
A man should help and protect a woman in public . . . . ____
Women should pay their share when dating . . . . ____
The husband should make the major family decisions . . . . ____
Women should never put career before family . . . . ____
Men should always take the lead in sexual matters . . . . ____

Because both the extremes—*Strongly agree* and *Strongly disagree*—as well as the intermediate scale points—*Agree, Neutral,* and *Disagree*—are labeled, the data are *ordinal* values, rather than *interval* data. If equal interval data are required, the Likert scale can be modified so only the extremes are labeled and the intermediate scale points are listed only as numbers with equal distance between them.

Likert scaling is very popular with researchers because of the power and simplicity of the format. The principal advantages of this type of scale include flexibility, economy, and ease of composition. The procedure is flexible because items can be only a few words long, or they can consist of several lines. Vocabulary can be technical and sophisticated or it can be very simple and primary, depending on what's appropriate to the population to be surveyed. The method is economical because one set of instructions and scale can serve many items, and once the respondent understands what's required, he or she can complete the items very quickly and easily. Likert scaled items can often be composed by the researcher quickly and easily, especially when the issues have been articulated in advance as statements.

A major advantage of this scale is the ability to obtain a summated value. In the example, the research is measuring attitudes toward sex role prescriptions. Some of the statements prescribe something for one sex but not the other, and some others state that no distinctions should be made between the sexes. Besides obtaining the results of each item, a total score can be obtained from this set of items. Some of the items would have to be reflected by reversing the numeric scores, so all items ascend toward either pro or con. Then, the total value would be an index of attitudes toward the major issue, as a whole. This ability to measure a more general construct

---

For Using Likert Scale Items   **Guidelist 5–2**

1. The Likert scale should be used for several items, rather than just one or two, to obtain the inherent economy.

2 The researcher should be able to identify or compose statements that are opinions *typical* of a global issue.

3. The items should be sufficiently diverse, so they represent an adequate range of the global issue.

4. There must he reasonable certainty that many respondents won't pick only a neutral value.

5. If a summated score is to be computed, about half the items should be inclined toward the pro side of the issue and half toward the con side, to avoid *yea-sayer* or *nay-sayer* bias.

---

is a major advantage of the Likert scale. Guidelines for using Likert scales are provided in Guidelist 5–2.

The Verbal Frequency Scale

The format of the verbal frequency scale is fairly similar to that of the Likert scale, with a couple of important exceptions: Rather than strength of agreement, the verbal frequency scale contains five words that indicate *how often* an action has been taken. Rather than statements about issues, the items of the verbal frequency scale indicate some action the respondents might have taken. Example 5–3 contains 10 items to measure the degree of political activism of respondents.

The Verbal Frequency Scale   **Example 5–3**

Please pick a number from the scale to show how often you do each of the things listed below and jot in the space to the right of the item.

Scale

1 Always
2 Often
3 Sometimes
4 Rarely
5 Never

Seek out information about candidates and issues . . . . ——
Actually vote during a strictly local election . . . . ——
Actually vote during a state and national election . . . . ——
Vote along strict party lines . . . . ——
Contribute money to a local political campaign . . . . ——
Contribute money to a state political campaign . . . . ——
Contribute money to a national political campaign . . . . ——
Volunteer to work on a local political campaign . . . . ——
Volunteer to work on a state political campaign . . . . ——
Volunteer to work on a national political campaign . . . . ——

There are times when it might be necessary to know the frequency of some action or behavior by respondents. Under some conditions, the question to measure this might simply ask, "How many times in the past have you . . . ?" Such a simple, straightforward question is recommended when the *absolute* number of times is appropriate and required. However, there are many occasions when the absolute number is of little use, or when the respondent would be unable to specify an absolute number. In the example provided, the absolute number of times wouldn't be of very much interest or value. Suppose there had been three or four elections in the districts of some of the respondents, and none in the districts of others. In that case, some groups would *appear* to be very inactive, based on the absolute level of participation. In fact, this inactivity wouldn't be the *choice* of the respondents. It merely reflects a *lack of opportunity* to participate. In this case, the researcher wants to know the proportion of activity, *given an opportunity* to perform it. The verbal frequency scale provides this more meaningful measure.

For some measurements, the respondents might not be able to say with any precision of recollection exactly how many times they have behaved in a certain way. For example, respondents could be asked, "What percentage of the time did you vote for a political candidate who was a member of your own political party in the past six elections in which you voted?" Besides the protracted length of this question, there are other difficulties. To answer accurately would require remarkable powers of recollection. Most respondents would be reluctant to try to recall each election and to complete the tedious computations to obtain an accurate percentage. With the use of the verbal frequency scale, this difficulty is avoided.

In the example and in many real situations, the focus isn't on the actual number or percentage of performances. Instead, it's on the respondents' *policies* concerning the frequency of certain actions. Thus, the item that seeks to measure how often the respondent votes along strict party lines provides an overall measure of loyalty to a political party. The general policy and underlying motivation are more important and valuable than the actual number or percentage of times the respondent has voted in that particular way in the past.

Guidelines for using verbal frequency scales are contained in Guidelist 5–3. The advantages of the verbal frequency scale include the ease of assessment and

---

For Using Verbal Frequency Scale Items   Guidelist 5–3

1. The verbal frequency scale should be used for several items, not just one or two, to obtain the economy.

2. The researcher should be able to compose items that assume the opportunity to perform the action.

3. The items should be used when only an approximation of percentages is required, with limited precision.

4. These scales are most appropriate when respondents are unable or unwilling to compute exact percentages.

5. If a summated score is to be computed, each item should have approximately equal *weight* in determining the overall index, or a weighted average should be computed in place of a *total* score.

response by those being surveyed. The number of opportunities to perform the action is automatically assumed within the question. It serves as the basis for picking the frequency category. There are two strong incentives for using the verbal frequency scale: (1) The ability to array activity levels across a five-category spectrum for data description, and (2) the ease of making comparisons among subsamples or among different actions for the same sample of respondents.

Verbal frequency scale data are *ordinal* values. Perhaps the major disadvantage of this type of scale is that it provides only a *crude* measure of proportion. For example, "sometimes" can mean anywhere from about 30 to 70 percent of the time. Also, different groups may assign different *breakpoints* between categories. In the example shown, the research could *reflect* all items, so the values ascended toward political activism, and then sum the values for all 10 items. This would provide an overall index of political involvement. In this case, the researcher would be *assuming* that seeking information about a candidate is as much a contribution to overall political action as contributing money or volunteering to work on a campaign. To the degree that this assumption is appropriate, such an overall index has considerable value in many research areas. Thus, the ability to obtain an overall measure of a construct is an advantage that the verbal frequency scale shares with the Likert scale, but individual weighting of items may sometimes be necessary.

The Ordinal Scale

There are times when it's important to measure when a particular thing occurs or takes place within a *fixed sequence* of events in a *predictable series*. It's not so much a matter of time of day, month, or year. Those aren't the relevant denominations. Rather, it's a matter of learning *at what point* in a series of events that the thing in question happens. The ordinal scale is designed for that kind of measurement.

With the ordinal scale item, the response alternatives define an ordered sequence. So, the choice listed first comes before the second in time, the second precedes the third, and so on. The item is ordinal because each time category listed comes *before* the next one. The principal advantage of the ordinal scale is the ability to obtain a measure *relative* to some other benchmark in a fixed series. The *order* is the major focus, not merely the chronology. As the name implies, the ordinal scale provides *ordinal* data.

Example 5–4 contains two items intended to measure when in the day the family first turns on the television set. They might have been phrased, "About what time do you or someone in your family first turn on the television set in your home on weekdays?" Then, the respondent would simply record a time of day. While the simple, direct question would obtain an absolute time of day, it wouldn't indicate the time *relative* to waking or eating. Thus, if this relationship between TV viewing and other daily activities were important, the typical time for each of the other activities would also have to be obtained.

Note that in the example, if two respondents both indicated they turn on the television a little while after awakening, they would appear as identical on this question. They would be seen as the same, even though one individual or family may arise at five o'clock in the morning and the other not until nine o'clock. Thus, the item obtains a *relative* measure, but some information is lost concerning the

---

The Ordinal Scale   **Example 5–4**

Ordinarily, when do you or someone in your family first turn on a television set in your home on a weekday?
(Please check only one.)

(1) ——— The first thing in the morning
(2) ——— A little while after awakening
(3) ——— Mid-morning
(4) ——— Just before lunch
(5) ——— Right after lunch
(6) ——— Mid-afternoon
(7) ——— Early evening before dinner
(8) ——— Right after dinner
(9) ——— Late evening
(0) ——— Usually don't turn it on.

Ordinarily, when do you or someone in your family first turn on a television set in your home on Saturdays?
(Please check only one.)

(1) ——— The first thing in the morning
(2) ——— A little while after awakening
(3) ——— Mid-morning
(4) ——— Just before lunch
(5) ——— Right after lunch
(6) ——— Mid-afternoon
(7) ——— Early evening before dinner
(8) ——— Right after dinner
(9) ——— Late evening
(0) ——— Usually don't turn it on.

---

distance or span between categories. The ordinal scale shouldn't be used when a numeric chronological value would be more meaningful and respondents can provide it. Thus, there's no reason to use the less economical and more complex ordinal scale when a direct question that can be answered based on the clock or calendar will serve as well. Guidelist 5–4 summarizes the requirements for using ordinal scales.

The Forced Ranking Scale

Forced rankings of items produce ordinal values, just as the ordinal scales do, only the items are *each* ranked relative to one another and they needn't represent a temporal sequence. In Example 5–5, the brand most preferred is ranked first. The forced ranking scale obtains not only the most preferred, but also the sequence of the remaining items.

With forced ranking scales, the *relativity* or relationship that's measured is among the items. This is one of the main advantages of this scaling technique. People are sometimes faced with choices among goods, services, ideas, individuals,

---

For Using Ordinal Scale Items   **Guidelist 5–4**

1. This scale is appropriate when the researcher wants to obtain a relative measure of when something occurs in a *fixed sequence* of events.

2. The researcher must be certain that the list of events will always occur in a fixed order for virtually all the respondents.

3. The ordinal scale should be used when a question about the time of an event based on the clock or calendar wouldn't be satisfactory.

4. This type of scale assumes that the clock or calendar time at which the items in the sequence occur is irrelevant.

5. The time interval between the list of fixed events on the ordinal scale need not be equal, nor are they required to be the same from one respondent to the next.

---

institutions, or actions. They're constantly making choices among a limited set of options. The forced ranking scale indicates what those choices are likely to be, from an *ever-shrinking* number of alternatives. While the parallel between the actual life choice situation and the measurement format is an advantage of forced ranking, this scale has several disadvantages. Forced ranking data is *ordinal* level data. The major limitation is the failure to measure the *absolute* standing and the *interval* between items.

Suppose two respondents to the sample item both rank Coca-Cola first and Pepsi-Cola second. This suggests they would choose Coca-Cola if they were given a choice among all four. It also suggests that if Coke were not available and the others were, they would both select Pepsi. This may or may not be the case, however. While the two appear identical, they may differ. The first of the two hypothetical respondents may regard Coke and Pepsi as almost equally preferable. The second may see Coca-Cola as far preferable to any of the others, including Pepsi. Thus, if Coke were not available, the first individual may substitute Pepsi without hesitation. The second person may refuse a cola beverage if Coke weren't available. In effect, then, the forced ranking reveals the *order* of preference, but the *distance* or *interval* between ranks for different respondents or between different pairs

---

The Forced Ranking Scale   **Example 5–5**

Please rank the colas listed below in their order of preference. Jot the number 1 next to the one you prefer most, number 2 by your second choice, and so forth.

      _____Pepsi-Cola
      _____Coca-Cola
      _____RC Cola
      _____Jolt Cola

For Using the Forced Ranking Scale   Guidelist 5–5

1. The number of things to be ranked should be less than 10, to avoid making the response task too difficult.

2. The major focus should be on the *relative* standing of the entities, not their absolute position.

3. The researcher must be willing to forgo measurement of the *distance* between ranks.

4. A single judgment criterion must be clearly stated, so all entities are arrayed on the same dimension.

5. As with other scales yielding ordinal data, analysis is confined to a limited set of statistical procedures that don't require equal intervals.

may differ markedly. That information is lost with ranking, or more precisely, it's ignored. If the researcher chose to obtain *ratings*, rather than rankings, the absolute value, interval between items, and relative standing are all easily computed and reported. So, the only time *forced* ranking is preferable to rating is when *no ties* can be tolerated.

The number of things that can be ranked is also a limitation with this type of scale. Respondents must first go through the entire list and identify their first choice. Then they have to go through the list again, eliminating their first choice, and selecting the alternative they would rank second, and so on. To rank 20 items, respondents would have to make 19 *passes* through an ever-decreasing list of alternatives, until only the last choice remained. Consequently, forced ranking scales are limited to only a few items. If too many are included, the response task becomes too tedious and time-consuming. This problem can also be avoided by using ratings, rather than rankings. Ratings don't require several *passes* through the list, and each item need be considered only once. Guidelines for using forced ranking scales are listed in Guidelist 5–5.

The Paired Comparison Scale

At times a researcher may want to measure simple, dichotomous choices between alternatives. The paired comparison scale is appropriate to such a need. The same basic assumptions apply to paired comparisons as to forced ranking scales. The focus must be almost exclusively on the evaluation of one entity *relative* to one other. In this sense, paired comparisons can be regarded as a special case of ranking, where only two items are ranked at a time. The same brands of cola beverages used to exemplify the forced ranking scale are also used in Example 5–6. In this case, each brand is compared with each other brand. Paired comparison scale data is only *ordinal* level data.

There's a major problem with paired comparisons when several pairs are ranked, known as *intransitivity* or *failure of transitivity*. Logically, if a respondent prefers A to B and prefers B to C, then obviously A must be preferable to C. It isn't unusual, when paired comparison scale data are analyzed, to find that many respondents fail to provide this transitivity.

The Paired Comparison Scale   Example 5–6

For each pair of soft drinks listed below, please put a check mark by the one you most prefer, if you had to choose between the two.

(1) _____ Pepsi-Cola
(2) _____ Coca-Cola

(1) _____ RC Cola
(2) _____ Pepsi-Cola

(1) _____ RC Cola
(2) _____ Jolt Cola

(1) _____ RC Cola
(2) _____ Coca-Cola

(1) _____ Coca-Cola
(2) _____ Jolt Cola

(1) _____ Jolt Cola
(2) _____ Pepsi-Cola

If "ties" or equal rankings can be tolerated, and especially if the determination of absolute distance or interval between pairs is useful, a numeric rating scale is strongly recommended. Virtually all the limitations and problems inherent in paired comparisons are avoided by using ratings, rather than rankings, of items taken two at a time.

Guidelist 5–6 contains recommendations for using paired comparisons. Despite their limitations, paired comparisons can be useful when only certain comparisons are sought and the relative distance between rankings is unimportant. While

For Using Paired Comparisons   Guidelist 5–6

1. The number of things to be compared should be less than 10, to avoid making the response task too difficult.

2. The method is most effective when actual choices in the real situation are always between two things.

3. The researcher must be willing to forgo measurement of the *distance* between items in each pair.

4. A single judgment criterion must be clearly stated, so all entities are arrayed on the same dimension.

5. The less sophisticated and careful the respondents, the greater the lack of transitivity will be, and the researcher must always expect some failure of transitivity.

they're not frequent, there are some situations in the real world where people are faced with *dichotomous* choices, such as candidates from each of two political parties. Paired comparison can be used appropriately in such cases because they closely parallel the actual situation. But when only *one* item must be compared with several others, and no direct comparisons among the others are required, a simple comparative scale, described next, can be employed using the one item as the standard by which all the other items are judged.

The Comparative Scale

In those situations where the researcher is most interested in the comparison(s) between one object and one or more others, the comparative scale is most appropriate. With this type of scale, one entity can be used as the standard or benchmark by which several others can be judged. In Example 5–7, the previous management group is the standard by which respondents are to judge the new management group.

There are two very important advantages of using a comparative scale. Note that with this method, no *absolute* standard is presented or required, and all evaluations are made on a *comparative* basis. Ratings are all *relative* to the standard or benchmark used. Thus, where a relative measurement is of greatest interest, or where no absolute standard exists, the comparative scale is applicable. Researchers are often most interested in comparisons of only their own sponsor's store, brand, institution, organization, candidate, or individual with that of others that are competitive. The comparative scale meets the requirements for such measurement.

Unlike such methods as ranking or paired comparisons, the comparative scale doesn't produce ordinal data, even though a relative measure is obtained. The scale consists of a *rating*, rather than a ranking of items. The results indicate the *interval* between the standard and the item being compared to it. Thus, this scale yields *equal interval* data for analysis. The *rank* or position of an item relative to other items rated on the same scale can also be determined by comparing the values of the ratings.

Another advantage of the comparative scale is its flexibility. The simple example shown here can be extended in two ways: The same two things can be

---

The Comparative Scale   **Example 5–7**

Compared to the previous management group, the new one is . . .
(Check one space.)

Very Superior		About the Same		Very Inferior
1	2	3	4	5

For Using Comparative Scales   Guidelist 5–7

1. The major research emphasis should be the comparison of a single standard entity with one or more others.

2. The actual rating scale should have an even number of alternatives, if *fence-riding* is likely.

3. The researcher must be sure the respondent is very clear about which is the standard and which is to be rated.

4. This method is advisable only if all or nearly all respondents are very familiar with the standard.

5. The method is particularly applicable when interval data are desired, but a relative measure is required. Both ranking and distance between entities are generated.

compared on several dimensions or criteria or, alternatively, several different things can be compared with the standard on a single dimension. For example, by listing several scales with different labels beneath them, such as "Much more progressive" and "Much less progressive," and so forth, an entire *profile* of the new management could be obtained, with the perceptions of the previous management team serving as the standard for judgment.

A second type of modification is to list the same scales but include several different entities. Each would be judged on the same criterion. In the example, the question would read, "How would you rate each management group, compared to the present one? Compared to the present one *this group is . . .*" Then, each management group would be listed with a scale beside or below it. Each group could be compared with the present, and only indirectly with one another.

It's important to note one caution when using comparative scales: The instructions and format must be presented *very clearly.* Every respondent has to understand which thing is the standard and which is being rated in comparison. If anyone gets the standard and the things being compared to it reversed, the data will be exactly opposite of what that respondent thinks.

Rankings are used (inappropriately) much too often, while the comparative scales aren't used as much as they should be. The comparative scales are more powerful in several respects: They present an easy, simple task to the respondent, ensuring cooperation and accuracy. They provide interval data, rather than only ordinal values, as rankings do. They permit several things that have been compared to the same standard to be compared with one another, and economy of space and time are inherent in them. Guidelines for using comparative scales are contained in Guidelist 5–7.

The Linear, Numeric Scale

When items are to be judged on a single dimension and arrayed on a scale with equal intervals, a simple, linear, numeric scale with the extremes labeled appropriately is the most straightforward method of scaling. The scale provides *equal interval* data and Example 5–8 contains a sample of the way this common scaling method is used.

The Linear, Numeric Scale   Example 5–8

How important to you is each of the public issues listed below?

If you feel the issue is extremely important, pick a number from the far right side of the scale and jot it in the space
   beside the item. If you feel it's extremely unimportant, pick a number from the far left, and if you feel the
   importance is between these extremes, pick a number from someplace in the middle of the scale to show your
   opinion.

Scale

| **Extremely Unimportant** | 1 | 2 | 3 | 4 | 5 | 6 | **Extremely Important** |

The protection of endangered species of animals . . . . _____
The improvement of the quality of the air . . . . _____
The discovery of additional petroleum reserves . . . . _____
The development of *renewable* sources of energy . . . . _____
The reduction or elimination of water pollution . . . . _____
The development of additional nuclear power . . . . _____
The protection of overall ecological balance . . . . _____
The industrial and technical growth of the nation . . . . _____
The provision of social services to those in need . . . . _____
The improvement of national defense and security . . . . _____

In the example, the question is listed first, and the indented instructions are
quite detailed, perhaps more so than would be necessary for most adult respondents. If those in the responding sample are fairly sophisticated, the instructions
might simply say: "Pick a number from the scale to show your opinion and jot it in
the space beside each item below."

In the example provided, the researcher seeks to measure the *importance* of 10
public issues. In effect, the respondents' values are being tapped and compared.
Notice that this scaling technique is very economical, since a single question, set of
instructions, and rating scale apply to many individual items. It's also important
to note that the linear, numeric scale provides *both* absolute measures of importance and relative measures, or rankings, if responses among the various items are
compared. (Of course, there's the possibility of identical ratings, yielding "tied"
ranks.) Yet, even though ranking is available, the rating scale is an equal interval
scale and provides data that are relatively unrestricted compared to ordinal data
from forced rankings or paired comparisons.

There has been some controversy among researchers about whether the intermediate points on the scale should be labeled with words, such as "Somewhat important" or "Slightly important." Labeling the intermediate levels of the scale isn't
recommended except in special circumstances. There are several reasons not to label intermediate points: First, consensus concerning the meaning of such words as
"very" or "slightly" is less likely than for the interpretation of only a series of numbers. Second, the graphic spacing and the common understanding of the equal

For Using Linear, Numeric Scales   Guidelist 5–8

1. This method is most applicable where evaluative responses are to be arrayed on a single dimension.

2. The scale is most economical where several items are all to be rated on the same dimension.

3. Scale extremes should be labeled "Extremely" to define the dimension, and the words used must be bipolar opposites.

4. In the vast majority of cases, the intermediate scale values shouldn't be labeled with words, and only numbers spaced at equal intervals should be used.

distance between numbers form a conceptual *mapping* of the underlying evaluation. Third, with only numbers, there's no possible mistake about there being only a single dimension or continuum. Most surveys don't require labeling of intermediate points, and there's little or no misunderstanding when only numbers are used.

Simplicity, clarity, and economy are all among the major advantages of the linear, numeric scale. The format is clean and straightforward. Respondents have little or no difficulty understanding the task they're to perform. The same question, instructions, and scale can be used for many items. Rankings can be computed with the use of this scale, but it provides equal interval data for statistical analysis and an absolute level of measurement. Guidelines for using linear numeric scales are listed in Guidelist 5–8.

The linear, numeric scale has few limitations, compared to other scaling methods. Of course, it isn't applicable to all situations. For example, it's less effective than the verbal frequency scale for measuring approximate frequency, and not applicable when direct comparison with a particular standard is required. This scale is a powerful device, and it has become very conventional and popular among survey researchers.

The Semantic Differential Scale

Researchers would often like to learn the *image* of an entity in the minds of the public. The most commonly used device for measuring such images is shown in Example 5–9. Using this scaling device, the image of a brand, store, political candidate, company, organization, institution, or program can be measured, assessed, and compared with that of similar objects.

To use the semantic differential scale, the researcher must first select a series of adjectives that might be used to describe the object to be rated. This can be a difficult task. It's very important to select the adjectives specifying attributes important to the respondents. The attributes used in the survey should be the major ones actually used by respondents to judge and evaluate the object. The actual attributes and adjectives most relevant in the minds of respondents are seldom obvious to the researcher. If there's any uncertainty, a preliminary inquiry can be used to identify

The Semantic Differential Scale   Example 5–9

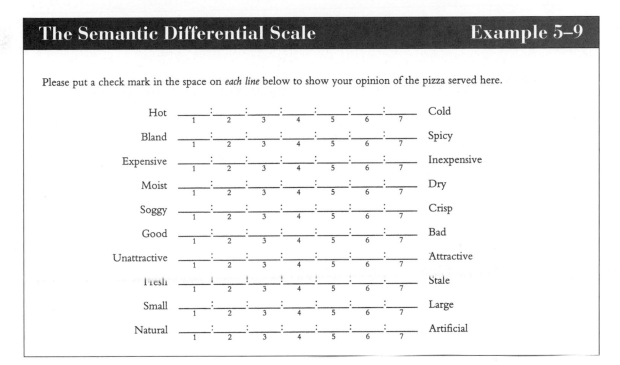

Please put a check mark in the space on *each line* below to show your opinion of the pizza served here.

Hot	Cold
Bland	Spicy
Expensive	Inexpensive
Moist	Dry
Soggy	Crisp
Good	Bad
Unattractive	Attractive
Fresh	Stale
Small	Large
Natural	Artificial

the most appropriate terms. If important attributes are neglected, an incomplete picture is developed. If unimportant attributes are included, some aspects of the profile that result will be irrelevant.

Once the attributes and the adjectives associated with them have been selected, the polar opposites of each adjective must be determined. This, too, can be something of a problem, and some substitutions to the list may be necessary. For example, is the opposite of "good" the word "poor," the word "bad," or the word "evil"? Once the attributes have been identified and descriptive adjectives and their polar opposites have been chosen, the semantic differential scale can be composed. About half the items should list the more positive adjective first and the others should list the more negative first. Items are ordinarily listed in random order on the actual scale. This scale provides *interval* level data.

The major advantage of the semantic differential scale is its ability to portray images clearly and effectively. Since several pairs of bipolar adjectives are used, the results, when processed and sorted, provide a profile of the image of the object that's been rated. When a series of semantic differential scales is used to measure the image of several objects, entire image profiles can be compared with one another. Still another advantage of the semantic differential scale is the ability to measure *ideal* images or attribute levels. In Example 5–9, the researcher wants to measure the image of pizza served at a particular restaurant. If another semantic differential scale were used to measure the image of a competing establishment, the two could be compared. Yet, some additional information might be very helpful.

For Using the Semantic Differential Scale   Guidelist 5–9

1. This method is most effective for measuring image profiles, people, things, organizations, or concepts.

2. Adjectives must define a single dimension, and each pair must be bipolar opposites labeling the extremes.

3. Precisely *what* the respondent is to rate must be clearly stated in the introductory instructions.

4. No more than about 20 items should be used, and about half should begin with the most positive word.

5. If the same scale is used for several topics and/or for rating an *ideal* entity, image profiles can be compared among real entities and between real and ideal ones.

For most items used in the example, the *positive* and *negative* adjectives can be identified easily. Obviously it's better to be "good" than "bad" and "fresh" than "stale." Suppose, however, the sponsor's pizza is more moist or more spicy than a competitor's. Is that good or bad? Where several scales can't be identified as positive or negative, respondents can be asked to rate their *ideal*, whatever the object. In this case, they would be asked to rate their *ideal* pizza on exactly the same set of items as that used for rating images of the real object. To determine differential preference patterns, it's often very useful to compare only ideal images among respondent groups. Images of real and ideal objects can also be compared, and the closer a real image corresponds to the ideal image, the more positive the profile.

Guidelines for using semantic differential scales are presented in Guidelist 5–9. The requirement for bipolar adjectives presents a serious limitation to the use of the semantic differential. The adjectives must be on the ultimate extremes of the spectrum and they must define a single dimension. It's sometimes difficult to identify antonyms. For example, is the opposite of spicy "bland" or "mild" in the minds of potential respondents?

The Adjective Checklist

It's sometimes necessary to ascertain just how an object is viewed by respondents and what descriptive adjectives or phrases apply to it. This can, of course, be measured with the semantic differential scale, but such an application may not be appropriate. The semantic differential technique is limited in the number of items that can be used and requires the specification of bipolar opposites. The adjective checklist is a very straightforward method of obtaining information about how an object is described and viewed.

In Example 5–10, the instructions ask respondents to check any of the adjectives that describe their jobs. There are 24 adjectives listed, but because of the economy of space and time and the ease with which respondents can complete the task, many more could have been included. Simplicity, directness, and economy are the major virtues of the adjective checklist. The adjectives listed can be many and varied. Short, descriptive phrases can even be used. This is especially valuable for

The Adjective Checklist   Example 5–10

Please put a check mark in the space in front of any word or phrase that describes your job.

_____ Easy	_____ Safe
_____ Technical	_____ Exhausting
_____ Boring	_____ Difficult
_____ Interesting	_____ Rewarding
_____ Low-paying	_____ Secure
_____ Strenuous	_____ Slow-paced
_____ Routine	_____ Enjoyable
_____ Dead-end	_____ Rigid
_____ Changing	_____ Pleasant
_____ Important	_____ Satisfying
_____ Demanding	_____ Degrading
_____ Temporary	_____ Risky

exploratory research work. The greatest disadvantage of the adjective checklist is the dichotomous, nominal level data it yields. There's no indication of *how much* each item describes the object. Recommendations for using adjective checklists are provided in Guidelist 5–10.

The Semantic Distance Scale

The major advantages of the adjective checklist, discussed above, are simplicity and economy, but the *profiles* it provides are only nominal data. The values only name categories indicating whether the item was checked. It doesn't show how *well* or how *poorly* the adjective described the object. By comparison, the semantic differential scale does measure this *distance* between the descriptive adjective and the thing rated. Yet, the semantic differential requires bipolar adjectives and is limited in the number of items that can be used because the response task is more difficult than with the adjective checklist. Example 5–11 shows a scale that combines the best of both.

For Using the Adjective Checklist   Guidelist 5–10

1. This method is appropriate for measuring images.
2. The instructions and response task are quick and simple, and many adjectives can be included.
3. Precisely *what* the respondent is to rate or judge must be stated very clearly in the instructions.
4. The scale yields a profile, but only in the form of discrete, nominal, dichotomous data.
5. If several topics and/or an ideal entity are rated using more than one adjective checklist, profiles among real entities and between real and ideal can be compared.

The Semantic Distance Scale   Example 5–11

Please pick a number from the scale to show how well each word or phrase below describes your job and jot it in the space in front of each item.

Scale

Not at all   1   2   3   4   5   6   7   Perfectly

_____ Easy	_____ Safe
_____ Technical	_____ Exhausting
_____ Boring	_____ Difficult
_____ Interesting	_____ Rewarding
_____ Low-paying	_____ Secure
_____ Strenuous	_____ Slow-paced
_____ Routine	_____ Enjoyable
_____ Dead-end	_____ Rigid
_____ Changing	_____ Pleasant
_____ Important	_____ Satisfying
_____ Demanding	_____ Degrading
_____ Temporary	_____ Risky

The semantic distance scale is very similar in appearance to the adjective checklist. The major distinction is that the semantic distance scale includes a linear, numeric scale below the instructions and above the descriptive adjectives or phrases. Rather than merely checking or not checking an item to indicate whether or not it applies to the object, the semantic distance scale requires that the respondent provide a *rating* of *how much* each item describes the object. In that way, the data generated by the scale is the *interval distance* from the item to the object. The *interval* data are similar to that obtained by the semantic differential scale.

The semantic distance scale can be used to portray an image, just as the semantic differential scale and the adjective checklist can. The major advantage of the semantic distance scale over the semantic differential is that the adjectives or descriptive phrases used need not have *polar opposites*. The researcher could specify "dry" without being concerned if the opposite is "wet" or "moist." The advantage of the semantic distance scale, compared to the adjective checklist, is the quality of the data provided by the former. Semantic distance scale data are interval data, rather than dichotomous data indicating only yes-or-no categories. Consequently, it can be manipulated and statistically processed with all the facility associated with any other equal interval scale data. The only drawback of the semantic distance scale is that it's a little more difficult to explain than the semantic differential scale or adjective checklist.

Guidelist 5–11 summarizes the main points to be observed when using semantic distance scales. All the same capabilities inherent in the semantic differential and the adjective checklist are included with the semantic distance scale. Profiles can be compared among real objects, an ideal entity can be rated, and ideal profiles of

---

For Using the Semantic Distance Scale   **Guidelist 5–11**

1. This method is appropriate for measuring images.
2. Many words or phrases can be included.
3. Precisely what the respondent is to judge and rate must be stated very clearly in the instructions.

4. The scale yields a profile indicating *how much* each phrase describes the topic, with continuous data.
5. If several topics or an *ideal* entity are rated with multiple semantic distance scales, profiles among real entities and between real and ideal can be compared.

---

preference can be compared among different respondent subsamples or respondent groups. Of course, real entity profiles can be compared with ideal profiles, by subject, if computer analysis is used, and the degree of correspondence will indicate the *overall favorability* of the ratings of actual objects.

The Fixed Sum Scale

There are times when it's important to learn what *proportion* of some resource or activity has been devoted to each of several possible choices or alternatives. The fixed sum scale is an excellent device for this purpose. It provides *ratio* level data. It would be possible simply to ask, "What percentage of the time do you do each of the following?" However, respondents are likely to have difficulty with such a question. The data from many respondents won't total to 100 percent. Example 5–12 shows a more effective format. The scale is most effective when it's used to measure actual behavior or action in the *recent* past. Ordinarily, about 10 different

---

The Fixed Sum Scale   **Example 5–12**

Of the last *10 times* that you ate lunch or dinner at a casual or fast food restaurant, how many times did you have each of the things listed below?

(Please be sure to make the total equal 10.)

_____ Hamburgers
_____ Hot dogs or sausage
_____ Chicken
_____ Pizza
_____ Chinese food
_____ Fish or seafood
_____ Deli sandwiches
_____ Hot sandwiches
_____ Mexican food
_____ Other (What?_____)

Total = 10

For Using the Fixed Sum Scale   Guidelist 5–12

1. The scale is used to measure proportions, rather than absolute values.
2. The occurrences must be apportioned into not more than about 10 categories.
3. The instructions must state very clearly the value to which the responses must total.

4. The scale provides continuous data so proportions can easily be compared among alternatives.
5. The data can be converted to percentages by dividing each value by the actual total, so every case will total a hundred percent and be comparable.

categories are the maximum, but as few as 2 or 3 can be used. The number to which the data must total has to be *very* clearly stated.

Recommendations for using the fixed sum scale are listed in Guidelist 5–12. The major advantage of the fixed sum scale is its clarity and simplicity. The instructions are easily understood and the respondent task is ordinarily easy to complete. It's important to list an *inclusive* set of items for this type of scale. If there are several options missing, respondents would have to list several "other" alternatives. There would be no way to break down the total number of "others" among the individual things represented.

Scale Combinations

Many of the scales described thus far have been shown in *listed* form. By listing items together in the same format, they can share a common scale. This saves valuable questionnaire space, but that's not the most important reason for using scale lists. Listing scales together reduces the response task and facilitates recording, and that's the greatest benefit of the *list* format. Once the respondents have read the instructions and learned how to respond to the first item or so, they can do the rest on the list very quickly, easily, and accurately. They don't have to stop and study the item. They can just answer it and move on to the next. They mentally carry the same frame of reference and judgment criteria from one item to the next, so the data are closely comparable.

The Multiple-Rating List

The multiple-rating list shown in Example 5–13 is a commonly used variation of the linear, numeric scale described earlier, but there is an important distinction. With the linear, numeric scale list shown in Example 5–8, the respondent has to pick a number from the scale shown above the item and then *write the number* beside the item. The multiple-rating list has the labels of the scale extremes at the top. The scale, itself, is *listed beside each item*. This has two advantages: (1) all the respondent has to do is circle a number, and that's easier than writing it; and (2) the

The Multiple-Rating List   Example 5–13

Several savings or investment vehicles are listed below. Please indicate how safe or risky you feel each one is by circling a number beside it. If you feel it's very safe, circle a number toward the left. If you feel it's very risky, circle one toward the right, and if you think it's someplace in between, circle a number from the middle range that indicates your opinion.

	Extremely Safe					Extremely Risky	
Bank savings account	1	2	3	4	5	6	7
Savings and loan savings account	1	2	3	4	5	6	7
Money market account	1	2	3	4	5	6	7
Certificates of deposit	1	2	3	4	5	6	7
Treasury bills	1	2	3	4	5	6	7
Corporate common stocks	1	2	3	4	5	6	7
Corporate preferred stocks	1	2	3	4	5	6	7
Corporate bonds	1	2	3	4	5	6	7
Municipal bonds	1	2	3	4	5	6	7
U.S. government bonds	1	2	3	4	5	6	7
Foreign government bonds	1	2	3	4	5	6	7
Credit union shares	1	2	3	4	5	6	7
Commodity futures	1	2	3	4	5	6	7
Corporate stock futures	1	2	3	4	5	6	7
Precious metals	1	2	3	4	5	6	7
Precious gems	1	2	3	4	5	6	7

responses form a *visual pattern,* so the juxtaposition of the responses on a horizontal spectrum is a closer mapping to the way people actually think about the evaluations they're making. For instance, "safe" is to the *left* and "risky" is to the *right* in Example 5–13. The actual numbers have very little to do with the evaluations. Guidelist 5–13 contains the directions for composing multiple-rating lists.

For Using a Multiple-Rating List   Guidelist 5–13

1. The scale, itself, is similar to the linear, numeric rating scale and it's used in much the same kind of measurements.

2. The listing format is most applicable where evaluative responses are to be arrayed on a single dimension.

3. The list is most economical where many, very brief items are all to be rated on the same dimension.

4. Scale extremes are at the top and they must define a single, bipolar dimension on which all items can be rated or *placed.*

5. The intermediate scale values shouldn't be labeled with words, and only numbers, spaced at equal intervals, should be listed beside each item.

The Multiple-Rating Matrix   Example 5–14

The table below lists four types of PRO brand baseball equipment along the top, and several characteristics of sports equipment along the left side. Please take *one product at a time!* Working down the column, pick a number from the scale indicating your evaluation of each characteristic and jot it in the space in the column below the product label and to the right of the characteristic. Please fill in *every space*, giving your rating for each product on each characteristic.

Scale

Very Poor	1	2	3	4	5	6	Excellent

	Bats	Balls	Gloves	Shoes
Price	____	____	____	____
Design	____	____	____	____
Selection	____	____	____	____
Durability	____	____	____	____
Appearance	____	____	____	____
Availability	____	____	____	____
Service	____	____	____	____
Packaging	____	____	____	____
Construction	____	____	____	____

The Multiple-Rating Matrix

The multiple-rating matrix shown in Example 5–14 is a very *condensed* format for using a combination of linear, numeric scale items. The scale, itself, is the same as the linear, numeric scale discussed earlier. The distinction between it and the matrix lies in the way the items are listed in a *matrix* of rows with *multiple columns.*

The multiple-rating matrix has two important advantages: First, it saves questionnaire space. The multiple-rating list in Example 5–13 obtains only data points. The multiple rating matrix in Example 5–14 takes less questionnaire space, yet it captures 36 data points. In addition, the objects and their characteristics that are rated are all very close to one another. So the respondents can easily *compare* their evaluations from one rating object to another. Each item is more likely to be rated using the same criteria and frame of reference as those of the others. Ratings obtained in this format are very comparable.

The principal handicap of the multiple-rating matrix, and a rather formidable one, is its *complexity.* The instructions are complex and the task is a bit difficult. There's a good chance some respondents will be confused and make mistakes—both obvious ones and errors that aren't so obvious. Some may refuse the section and skip it because it looks too hard to do. Others may fill in only one space in each column or each row. Such data are useless. Even more serious is the likelihood that some respondents will work *down the columns* while others will work *across the rows*! If that happens, there's no way to tell who did it one way and who another way, and the data would be less reliable than it should be. The main considerations for using a multiple-rating matrix are summarized in Guidelist 5–14.

For Using a Multiple-Rating Matrix   Guidelist 5–14

1. The scale, itself, is identical to the linear, numeric rating scale and it's for exactly the same kind of measurements.

2. This format is applicable only if evaluative responses are to be arrayed on a single dimension.

3. The matrix is effective only where a few items are to be rated on the *same* set of several *criteria* or *attributes*.

4. The rating matrix is most useful when closely comparable objects are to be rated with exactly the same judgment criteria and frame of reference.

5. This complex, difficult format should be used *only* when respondents are expected to be both bright and cooperative.

The Diagram Scale

Diagram scales can be used for many special situations. They're especially useful for measuring *configurations* of several things, where the *spatial relationships* convey part of the meaning. Example 5–15 shows one type of diagram scale to capture a *complete picture* of the family. Asking the respondent to circle his or her own age after listing it in the diagram has an additional advantage. Respondents are *less likely to lie* about their age because they ordinarily list the correct age with the others in the family and they're reluctant to change it afterward.

This is just one example of a diagram scale, and there are an almost infinite number of possibilities, depending on the measurement needs. Other types of

The Diagram Scale   Example 5–15

Please list the ages of all those in your family living at home in the spaces below. Jot the ages of the men and boys in the top circles—the ages of the women and girls in the bottom circles. Use as many as you need, listing them in order from oldest to youngest in each row.

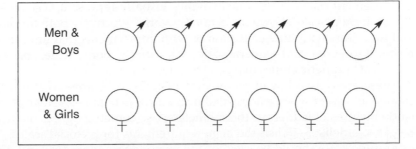

Now draw a big circle around the space with your own age in it.

diagram scales or items include line drawings depicting geographic areas, buildings, housing complexes, malls, or shopping centers. They can be used to measure traffic patterns or the location patterns or preferences of respondents. Diagrams might contain such things as maps, illustrations, and charts. Researchers should be encouraged to create such devices for special information needs or measurements. They would also be well advised to test their creations thoroughly in pilot studies with respondents similar to those who will ultimately provide the data.

Nonverbal Scales

The survey items and scales discussed and shown in examples earlier have all contained verbal and numeric content. There are some situations where *nonverbal* scales—pictures or graphs—must be used to obtain the data. For example, with a survey of young children, the respondents' ability to read or to understand numeric scales may be very limited. In other, special situations, the survey might include respondents who are illiterate or who aren't literate in the language of the survey. It may not be feasible to measure the evaluations or reactions of children or others who don't read well with the scales described earlier. These situations require *nonverbal* scaling.

The Picture Scale

Section A of Example 5–16 shows happy and sad faces that are very familiar to very young children. Even though they may have very little experience with letters, numbers, and other symbols, they have learned to recognize facial expressions very early in life. The interviewer would first ask the child to point to the face that's very happy, then to the one that's very sad, to be sure the child understands the pictures. Then the children would be asked to point to the face that shows how they feel when they do each of the things listed in the items, such as going to school or watching TV cartoons.

The Graphic Scale

For older children or adults in special situations, the Bottle Scale, shown in Section B of Example 5–16, may be more acceptable. It provides somewhat more useful measurement data because the extremes visually represent *none* and *all* or *total.* The Stair-Step Scale, shown in Section C, works effectively both for older children and for adults with little education or with impairments that limit their ability to respond to verbal and numeric scales. As with the bottle scale, space or distance represents numeric values that can be coded and recorded.

   These are only a few of many such pictorial or graphic scales that might be created and used when a nonverbal instrument is required. Other possibilities include pictures of ladders or thermometers, or geometric figures of various size or height. Guidelist 5–15 lists the main requirements for pictorial scales. Any picture or graphic scale should be easy for the respondents to understand. They should be based on some phenomenon with which the respondents would be *very* familiar. Picture and graphic scales are typically used for personal interview surveys,

Picture and Graphic Scales   **Example 5–16**

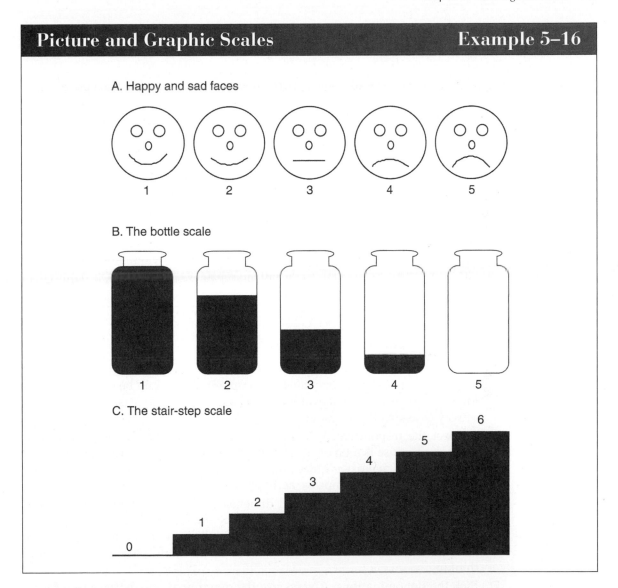

A. Happy and sad faces

B. The bottle scale

C. The stair-step scale

although they are sometimes used in self-administered questionnaires for mail or online surveys.

Scale Selection Criteria

There's seldom a single, clear-cut choice of a scale for any given question or information requirement when composing a questionnaire. Thus, it's impossible to list a set of rules that dictate exactly what scale should be used in each situation, even if every circumstance could be anticipated. Yet clearly, some scales are easily

For Creating Pictorial Scales	Guidelist 5–15

1. They must be very easy for respondents to understand.
2. They should show something respondents have often seen.
3. They should represent the thing that's being measured.
4. They should be easy to draw or create.

identified as potential tools for some common information needs and questions, and there are often other scales that are clearly inappropriate.

The criteria and considerations listed in the summary are merely guidelines. There are no ironclad rules that would limit the creativity and effectiveness of the researcher. While the conventional scales are nearly always adaptable, others should be invented for special needs and circumstances when they're required.

Summary
How to Create Effective Scales

A. Keep it simple. Given a choice between a very short, concise scale and a more elaborate, sophisticated one, the less complex scale should be used. Even after identifying a scale to be used for an item, ask, "Is there an easier, simpler scale or way of asking this question?"

B. Respect the respondent. While respondents are ordinarily cooperative and helpful, response is a favor. They have little involvement with the task. Select scales that will make it as quick and easy as possible for them. That will reduce nonresponse bias and improve accuracy.

C. Dimension the response. In what dimensions do respondents and sponsors think about the issue? They'll not always be the same, so some commonality must be discovered. The dimensions along which the respondents are to answer must not be obscure or difficult, and they should parallel respondents' thinking.

D. Pick the denominations. Always use the denominations that are best for respondents. The data can later be converted to the denominations sought by information users. Feet and inches can be changed to metric or time converted to a 24-hour clock during processing.

E. Choose the range. Categories or scale increments should be about the same breadth as those ordinarily used by respondents. Normally, respondents classify things into a range from about 2 to about 7 or 8 categories, and seldom more than 10. Respondents often can't be as precise as researchers would like.

F. Group only when required. Never put things into categories when they can easily be expressed in numeric terms. People think in years, not decades or centuries. Data can always be grouped during processing, but if obtained in broad categories, it can't be desegregated later, no matter how desirable that might be.

G. Handle neutrality carefully. If respondents *genuinely* have no preference, they'll resent the forced choice inherent in a scale with an even number of alternatives. If feelings aren't especially strong, an odd number of scale points may result in *fence-riding* or piling on the midpoint, even when some preference exists.

H. State instructions clearly. Even the least capable respondents must be able to understand. Use language that's typical of the respondents. Explain exactly what the respondent should do and the task sequence they should follow. List the criteria they should judge by and use an example or practice item if there's any doubt.

I. Always be flexible. Scaling examples provided here are only that. They can and should be modified to fit the task and the respondents. The instructions, format, vocabulary, and number of scale points can all be changed to suit the needs of the survey. Scales should fit the task, not conform to the original authors' specifications.

J. Pilot test the scales. When there's any doubt about the ability of respondents to use the scales, a brief, informal pilot test is quick, inexpensive insurance. Don't wait until the entire questionnaire is written. Individual parcels can be checked with a few typical respondents.

6

Building Questionnaires

Function of the Questionnaire

The composition of individual survey questions and the scaling techniques used with them were discussed in the two previous chapters. It's time to bring these elements together into a complete, finished survey instrument. Whether the survey is self-administered, such as online or mail surveys are, or a telephone or personal interview survey, the data collection instruments will be called *questionnaires* here, as they ordinarily are by research practitioners. Most of the same principles and practices apply to construction of both self-administered questionnaires and interview survey questionnaires. In those instances where interviewing versus self-administered data collection methods affect the questionnaire construction, the differences will be noted.

The questionnaire has several functions or objectives. It's the *package* that presents the questions and later contains the record of response for one respondent. The first section of the questionnaire introduces the survey to the respondents. The internal sections contain the items and scales to measure the survey topics, in a logical and necessary sequence. The final section ordinarily has questions to measure the respondents' characteristics, so the individual cases can be grouped and compared. The questionnaire also includes several other elements that facilitate data handling. These include the spaces or places to record the data and often the codes that identify particular responses. The questionnaire may also show the position on the record in the computer file into which each data point will be keyed.

This chapter also identifies and discusses other instrumentation devices to accompany the questionnaire. They include such things as the mailing piece for mail surveys, website links for online surveys, or rating scale cards for interviewing.

Survey Introduction

Research surveys usually depend very heavily on the *voluntary* cooperation of respondents. Research experience consistently shows that nearly all who refuse to cooperate do so within the first few *seconds* after initial contact, whether that contact is in person, on the telephone, by e-mail, via a weblink, or by postal mail. The principle is simply this: If the prospective respondent agrees to participate immediately when the survey is introduced, only a small percentage will withdraw their cooperation later. Once they *begin,* they nearly always continue. They're very likely to complete the response task, except under very unusual circumstances. Consequently, the introduction has to be composed and delivered effectively. If the survey is introduced properly, the response rate will be increased and the reliability and validity of the survey will be enhanced. If it's done poorly, refusal and nonresponse will increase data collection time and expense. Error and bias will result and the reliability and validity of the data will be diminished.

A Sample Questionnaire

Example 6–1 contains an example of a seven-page self-administered questionnaire to demonstrate many of the principles and techniques discussed in this chapter. It is designed to illustrate how the various survey questions, scales, elements, and sections are organized and combined into a single, integrated, smooth-flowing questionnaire. It's substantially longer and more comprehensive than one would ordinarily expect such a questionnaire to be so that all the different kinds of survey questions and scale types could be included. Consequently, it presents respondents with a more daunting response task than would be ideal, even if a substantial inducement for survey participation were offered.

This questionnaire might be used to survey guests departing from a luxury hotel. While it's meant to be illustrative, rather than practical and usable, it closely parallels an actual survey instrument of this type. Obviously, the questionnaire would look different if it were to be used by interviewers or self-administered online at a website. Nonetheless, most of the same principles and techniques apply to all types of interview and self-administered questionnaires, with only minor changes that will be identified during the discussion that follows. The various elements of this sample questionnaire will be referenced throughout the discussion of questionnaire construction in this chapter.

Questionnaire Organization

The cover letter, introductory note, or interviewer greeting is the introduction to the questionnaire and response task. It's useful to view the questionnaire, itself, in three main parts: the introduction, the body of the questionnaire, and the conclusion. Each plays a different role. The composition of cover letters for mail surveys and introductory notes for online surveys are discussed in Chapter 7. In Chapter 8 the initial greetings used by telephone and personal interviewers are considered in detail.

The first part of the questionnaire initiates the task for the respondent. It sets the stage and suggests what kinds of questions will follow. It indicates the type of information sought and provides an indication of the response task. Usually, this first part contains the most general questions that will be asked of respondents. It's important to include only questions that apply to all respondents and are fairly quick and easy to answer in the introductory part of the questionnaire. It's especially important to avoid any questions or issues that may be threatening to respondents. This isn't the place to ask *delicate* questions or seek *sensitive* information.

Sample Questionnaire   Example 6–1

A

Please put an ✗ in the space before *any* and *all* words you feel describe your stay at this hotel.

◇ Active	◇ Aggravating	◇ Amusing	A-C
◇ Boring	◇ Busy	◇ Costly	D-F
◇ Delightful	◇ Disappointing	◇ Disgusting	G-I
◇ Disturbing	◇ Entertaining	◇ Exciting	J-L
◇ Fantastic	◇ Frustrating	◇ Healthy	M-O
◇ Informative	◇ Invigorating	◇ Lazy	P-R
◇ Memorable	◇ Painful	◇ Pleasant	S-U
◇ Productive	◇ Recreational	◇ Regrettable	V-X
◇ Relaxing	◇ Restful	◇ Sensational	Y-AA
◇ Stimulating	◇ Tantalizing	◇ Terrible	AB-AD

B

Please check *any* of our services you used during this visit.
(Please check (✔) *all* boxes below that apply.)

❏ Inside Self-Parking	❏ MiniBar in the Room	AE-AF
❏ Valet Parking	❏ Laundry or Cleaners	AG-AH
❏ Wake-up Call	❏ Business Center	AI-AJ
❏ Bellman or Doorman	❏ Health Club or Pool	AK-AL
❏ Lobby Coffee or Breakfast	❏ Room Service	AM-AN

C

Please pick a number from the scale to show how important *each* of these factors is *to you* when you're CHOOSING A HOTEL and jot it in the space to the right of *each item*.

Scale								
Extremely Unimportant	1	2	3	4	5	6	7	Extremely Important

Convenience of the location of the hotel within the area you're visiting.·····	_____	AO
Safety and security of the hotel and neighborhood in which it's located.····	_____	AP
Knowledge or experience with other hotels in the same chain. ·················	_____	AQ
Recommendations or suggestions of travel agents or representatives. ·····	_____	AR

The sample questionnaire in Example 6–1 begins with an Adjective Checklist—perhaps the quickest, easiest type of item there is. The respondents get the feeling they've done a lot very quickly and easily. Once started, they're likely to continue.

The body of the questionnaire is the middle part. It's ordinarily much larger than the introduction or conclusion. It contains questions or items that deal with the substance and detail of the survey topics. The specific organization of the body

Sample Questionnaire (continued)   **Example 6–1**

D   If *THIS* is your *favorite* hotel, please skip to **E** below.

Please check *one* space on *each line* to show how *this hotel* compares to *YOUR FAVORITE HOTEL.*
Compared to my favorite hotel, THIS ONE IS . . .

	Much Less		The Same		Much More	

	1	2	3	4	5	6	7	
Expensive								AS
Convenient	1	2	3	4	5	6	7	AT
Comfortable	1	2	3	4	5	6	7	AU
Neat, Clean	1	2	3	4	5	6	7	AV
Spacious, Roomy	1	2	3	4	5	6	7	AW
Attractive	1	2	3	4	5	6	7	AX

E   Please pick a number from the scale to show how much you *agree* or *disagree*
with each statement and jot in the space to the right of the item.

SCALE
1 = **Strongly Agree**
2 = **Agree**
3 = **Neutral**
4 = **Disagree**
5 = **Strongly Disagree**

I'm very concerned about safety and security when I stay at a hotel. ········· _____	AY
The size of a hotel room is more important to me than how it's furnished. ·· _____	AZ
I like hotels that have elegant, unusual lobbies and open areas. ·············· _____	BA
If it cost the same, I'd much prefer a suite to just one hotel room. ············· _____	BB
When I travel, I like to stay in a different kind of hotel at each place. ········· _____	BC
Even if some hotels in a chain are very nice, others might be terrible. ······· _____	BD
I like newer hotels much more than older ones, even if they're well-kept. ·· _____	BE
When picking a hotel, the most important thing to me is its location. ·········· _____	BF
I don't like to decide to stay at a hotel until I visit it first. ·························· _____	BG
I like to see what the rooms are like before I agree to stay at a hotel. ········ _____	BH

Sample Questionnaire (continued)   Example 6–1

F

How important to you is
each of these hotel facilities
or services?
*Please circle one number
on each line.*

	Don't Know	Extremely Unimportant				Extremely Important	
Gym or health club ················	0	1	2	3	4	5	BI
Laundry or cleaning service ·······	0	1	2	3	4	5	BJ
Mini-bar in the room ··············	0	1	2	3	4	5	BK
Business center facilities ···········	0	1	2	3	4	5	BL
Inside parking ····················	0	1	2	3	4	5	BM
Valet parking ····················	0	1	2	3	4	5	BN
Doormen and bellmen ··············	0	1	2	3	4	5	BO
24-hour restaurant or cafe ·········	0	1	2	3	4	5	BP

G

Please pick a number from the scale to show how often you do *each* of these
things *when you stay at a hotel* and jot it in the space to the right of *each* item.

SCALE
1 = Always
2 = Often
3 = Sometimes
4 = Rarely
5 = Never

Have a rental car delivered and/or picked up at the hotel? ··························	_____	BQ
Take early morning coffee when freely served in the lobby? ·······················	_____	BR
Obtain information from the concierge or tour desk? ·································	_____	BS
Visit the hotel bar or lounge? ···	_____	BT
Order pizza from outside the hotel to be delivered? ·······························	_____	BU
Swim or sunbathe at the hotel pool (when available)? ······························	_____	BV
Eat one or more meals at the hotel restaurant? ·····································	_____	BW
Use the physical fitness or exercise facilities (if available)? ·······················	_____	BX
Have drinks or "set-ups" from the hotel bar served in the room? ·················	_____	BY

Sample Questionnaire (continued)   Example 6–1

H

When you plan and go on a trip, *at what point* do you *usually* decide what hotel you'd like to stay at?   (Please check [✔] only *one* space.)

Before I know I'm going. (I have a favorite I always prefer.) ·························· ___ 1

As soon as I know the destination. (Before I make travel arrangements.) ·· ___ 2

After making travel arrangements or reservations. ······························· ___ 3

Sometime before I leave on the trip. ······································· ___ 4

While I'm traveling. (Along the way.) ······························· ___ 5

When I arrive in the city where I'm staying. ······························· ___ 6

Just before it's time to go to a hotel and check in. ······················· ___ 7

Only after visiting one or more hotels to see which I like. ·················· ___ 8

BZ

I

How well does each of these words or phrases describe your impressions of *our hotel staff?*

	Don't Know	Not At All		*Please circle one number on each line.*			Perfectly So	
Unfriendly ··········	0	1	2	3	4	5	6	7	CA
Prompt ··············	0	1	2	3	4	5	6	7	CB
Capable ·············	0	1	2	3	4	5	6	7	CC
Discourteous ······	0	1	2	3	4	5	6	7	CD
Caring ···············	0	1	2	3	4	5	6	7	CE
Too busy ············	0	1	2	3	4	5	6	7	CF
Helpful ··············	0	1	2	3	4	5	6	7	CG
Greedy ··············	0	1	2	3	4	5	6	7	CH

J

Which *one* courtesy bath product do you find *MOST* useful and enjoyable?
(Please put an ✗ in only *one* circle below.)

1 ◯ Shampoo
2 ◯ Cream Rinse
3 ◯ Bath Oil
4 ◯ Moisturizer
5 ◯ Sun Lotion

Which *one* courtesy bath product do you find *LEAST* useful and enjoyable?
(Please put an ✗ in only *one* circle below.)

1 ◯ Shampoo
2 ◯ Cream Rinse
3 ◯ Bath Oil
4 ◯ Moisturizer
5 ◯ Sun Lotion

CI-CJ

Sample Questionnaire (continued)   Example 6–1

K Please indicate below what type of hotel RECREATION and ENTERTAINMENT you like best.
(Put an **✗** in space before the *one* you *most* prefer for *each* of the *six pairs* listed below.)

RECREATION	ENTERTAINMENT	
❑ Tennis or Golf ❑ Swimming Pool or Gym/Health Club	❑ Vocal or Instrumental Music ❑ Comedy, Magic or Pantomime	CK-CL
❑ Golf ❑ Tennis	❑ Continuous by Various Soloists ❑ Periodically by Performing Groups	CM-CN
❑ Swimming Pool ❑ Gym or Health Club	❑ In the Bar, Lounge, or Restaurant ❑ In the Atrium Lobby	CO-CP

L Please *rank* each kind of music below in your order of preference.

(Please put a 1 in the space before the kind you like best, 2 in the space before your second favorite, and so forth.)

____ Classical
____ Country
____ Easy Listening
____ Jazz
____ Rock

Please *rank* each type of performer below in your order of preference.

(Please put a 1 in the space before the type you like best, 2 in the space before your second favorite, and so forth.)

____ Ventriloquists	CQ-CR
____ Mimes	CS-CT
____ Magicians	CU-CV
____ Jugglers	CW-CX
____ Comedians	CY-CZ

M Please check [✔] *one* space on *each line* to show your overall, general opinion of this hotel as a whole.

	1	2	3	4	5	6	7		
Expensive								Inexpensive	DA
Ugly								Beautiful	DB
Old								New	DC
Immaculate								Filthy	DD
Elegant								Commonplace	DE
Prestigious								Debasing	DF

Sample Questionnaire (continued)   **Example 6–1**

N Please rate *each* area of the hotel listed below on *each* factor—*cleanliness, attractiveness, comfort, and convenience*—by picking a number from the scale and jotting it in *each square*. (Fill in every square, recording a zero if you don't know.)

Don't Know	SCALE						
	Very Poor					Excellent	
0	1	2	3	4	5	6	

	Cleanliness	Attractiveness	Comfort	Convenience	
Main Lobby	☐	☐	☐	☐	DG-DJ
Guest Rooms	☐	☐	☐	☐	DK-DN
Halls and Foyers	☐	☐	☐	☐	DO-DR
Pirate's Lounge	☐	☐	☐	☐	DS-DV
Ship's Galley Restaurant	☐	☐	☐	☐	DW-DZ

O Of the *last ten times* you stayed at a hotel, *how many times* did you stay at. . . .

This particular hotel?	_____	times	EA
Another hotel in *this* chain?	_____	times	EB
A hotel that's part of *some other national chain*?	_____	times	EC
An individual, *independent* hotel?	_____	times	ED
Some other kind of hotel? (What kind? _____)	_____	times	EE

(Please make the TOTAL = 10)   **Total =** **10** times

P Please list the ages of all those who shared your room or suite during this stay with us in the spaces below, including *yourself*. Jot the ages of all the men and boys in the top circles and the ages of all the women and girls in the bottom circles.

Men & Boys ♂ ♂ ♂ ♂ ♂   EF-EJ

Women & Girls ♀ ♀ ♀ ♀ ♀   EK-EO

Sample Questionnaire (continued)   Example 6–1

Q Please put an ✗ in the box to indicate which head of household you are, then check or fill in the items below for *each* head of household in your home.

I am the . . .

☐ **MALE Head of Household**	☐ **FEMALE Head of Household**

Age .... _____ years	Age .... _____ years	EP
		EQ-ER
Formal education ·· _____ years	Formal education ·· _____ years	ES-ET
(For example, High school graduate=12 years)	*(For example, High school graduate=12 years)*	

EMPLOYMENT STATUS: *EMPLOYMENT STATUS:*

MALE	FEMALE	
1 ☐ company employed	1 ☐ company employed	
2 ☐ government employed	2 ☐ government employed	
3 ☐ self-employed	3 ☐ self-employed	
4 ☐ seeking employment	4 ☐ seeking employment	EU-EV
5 ☐ military	5 ☐ homemaker	
6 ☐ retired	6 ☐ retired	
7 ☐ student	7 ☐ student	

OCCUPATIONAL STATUS: *OCCUPATIONAL STATUS:*

MALE	FEMALE	
1 ☐ professional [med, law, etc.]	1 ☐ professional [med, law, etc.]	
2 ☐ managerial, executive	2 ☐ managerial, executive	
3 ☐ administrative, clerical	3 ☐ administrative, clerical	
4 ☐ engineering, technical	4 ☐ engineering, technical	EW-EX
5 ☐ marketing, sales	5 ☐ marketing, sales	
6 ☐ skilled craft or trade	6 ☐ skilled craft or trade	
7 ☐ semiskilled occupation	7 ☐ semiskilled occupation	

ANNUAL INCOME: *ANNUAL INCOME:*

Approximately $ ___ ,000.00	Approximately $ ___ ,000.00	EY-EZ

THANK YOU FOR COMPLETING THIS GUEST QUESTIONNAIRE. PLEASE TAKE IT TO THE REGISTRATION DESK WHERE YOUR V.I.P. BONUS GIFT IS WAITING FOR YOU TO CLAIM IT.

FIGURE 6–1
Sample
Questionnaire
Item Types

Section	Question or Scale Type
A	Adjective Checklist
B	Multiple-Choice, Multiple-Response
C	Linear, Numeric Scale
D	Comparative Scale
E	Likert Scale
F	Multiple-Rating List
G	Verbal Frequency Scale
H	Ordinal Scale
I	Semantic Distance Scale
J	Multiple-Choice, Single-Response
K	Paired Comparisons
L	Forced Rankings
M	Semantic Differential Scale
N	Multiple-Rating Matrix
O	Fixed Sum Scale
P	Diagram Scale
Q	Demographic Items

of the questionnaire is discussed below. Generally the items should be in a sequence that's logical and meaningful to respondents. There should be a smooth transition from one issue or topic to the next, with no sudden breaks or dramatic changes in the respondents' frame of reference.

Figure 6–1 lists the sections, by identifying letter, in the introduction and body of the sample questionnaire, preceding the demographic section. Each section contains just one type of survey question, item, or scale. This organization will be discussed more completely later in this chapter.

The final or concluding part of the questionnaire is reserved for two kinds of questions: those that deal with the most sensitive or delicate issues or topics, and those that measure the attributes or characteristics of the respondents. The *demographic* or *biographic* questions are almost always at the very end of the questionnaire. The reasons for putting these questions last are compelling. First, the respondent has become familiar with the inquiry and rapport should be maximum at this point. They have more trust and are less likely to be skeptical or uncooperative than at an earlier point. Second, some respondents may terminate at this point or refuse to answer some of the items. Nevertheless, they have provided the bulk of the data and their responses to the earlier items in the body of the questionnaire may still be usable.

The sample questionnaire in Example 6–1 concludes with the demographic questions—a very conventional method of closing. The most sensitive of the demographic questions, those on income, are reserved for last. Basic guidelines for organizing questionnaires are listed in Guidelist 6–1.

For Organizing the Questionnaire — Guidelist 6–1

1. Picture the questionnaire in three main parts: introduction, body, and conclusion.

2. Begin with the most general questions and avoid those that might be threatening or difficult to answer.

3. Remember the introductory part sets the stage and influences the respondents' expectations about what's to come.

4. Be sure the body of the questionnaire flows smoothly from one issue to the next.

5. Organize items in the body in a sequence that's logical and meaningful to respondents.

6. Save the most sensitive issues and threatening questions for the concluding portion, when rapport is greatest.

7. List demographic or biographic questions last, so if some respondents decline most data are still usable.

Creating Questionnaire Sections

For most surveys, and especially those of considerable length, the questions can be grouped into smaller sections than the three main parts just described. Some surveys may include only a dozen or so questions, but typically a survey will have 50, 100, or more individual items. Grouping them into sections simplifies the task of asking and answering the questions. It not only makes the task *appear* simpler and easier for respondents, it actually makes it so. The more effectively the items are grouped into sections, the more efficient the questionnaire will be.

Grouping Items by Topic

The most common way to group items is by topic. For example, a marketing research survey may contain questions about three different topics: purchase *behavior*, the *image* of one or more retail stores, and the *lifestyles* of the respondents. One section of the questionnaire might be devoted to each of these topics. Each section might contain all the items devoted to that particular survey topic. This would be an effective way to organize the items, providing that it appears logical or makes sense to the respondents. For example, it would make sense to ask all about the products they bought from various stores in one section; then, in another, to ask about their perceptions or images of several different stores. A section with several items to define their lifestyle based on their activities, interests, and opinions might follow this. This would be a much more meaningful organization than if all the various topics and kinds of questions were intermixed with one another.

A survey of employees may provide another example of grouping questions or items by topic. For such a survey, it would make sense to the respondents if all the questions about job satisfaction were asked in one place, all items about relationships with co-workers were contained in another, and all questions concerning occupational history were listed together in a third section. It wouldn't be appropriate to *jump around* from one to another of these areas of inquiry. After the first question or so about a particular area, the respondents' minds will have turned to that issue. They can easily respond to additional items about the same basic issue, but it would be difficult to shift abruptly to another, entirely separate issue, and then turn their attention again to the first.

Grouping Items by Scaling Technique

Often the same scaling technique can be applied to many questions or items. When that's the case, it's very practical and efficient to list them together in one section of the questionnaire. For instance, all the items composed as statements and using a Likert scale (Strongly agree, Agree, Neutral, Disagree, or Strongly disagree) can be listed in one place and the scale shown only once at the top of the section. Another section might contain all the items that use a verbal frequency scale (Always, Often, Sometimes, Rarely, or Never). Such grouping by scale type saves time and space and makes the response task easier. The respondents need only to read the instructions and get familiar with the scale one time. They can then continue through the list of all the items that use that type of scale.

Grouping Items Both Ways

Items can often be grouped by both topic and scale type. A set of items devoted to the same topic may also use the same scaling method. That's the ideal situation because there are both a logical sequence and a high degree of time and space economy. Several scaling techniques described in the previous chapter can be used to group items by both scale type and topic. The researcher may also devise special scaling methods to apply to many items dealing with a single topic. Then they can be grouped into one section, reducing the time and effort required to answer the questions.

The survey questionnaire for hotel guests shown in Example 6–1 is organized by topic and scale type, simultaneously. The broad topics or issues addressed by each section of the questionnaire are identified in Figure 6–2. Each section covers a fairly distinct set of topics or issues and each uses just one type of item or scale.

A questionnaire should be seen as the outline of a *conversation* between the researcher and the respondents. The respondents don't expect the conversation to switch abruptly from one topic or format to another. Each section should be integrated and consistent. There should be a *bridge* leading from one section to the next, to ensure the proper flow of the dialogue. Guidelist 6–2 contains recommendations for grouping questionnaire items into sections. The principal factors to consider when inspecting the organization of the entire questionnaire are listed in Checklist 6–1.

Directing Response Flow

For many surveys, every respondent will be asked every question in the questionnaire. But in some surveys, only certain questions apply to some respondents while other items do not. For instance, a survey might have some questions addressed only to men or only to women, even though both sexes are included in the

FIGURE 6–2
Sample
Questionnaire
Topics by
Section

Section	Issue or Topic of Items
A	General impression and image profile of the guests' visit to the hotel.
B	Experience and use of various hotel services during this visit.
C	Importance of four common evaluative criteria for choosing a hotel.
D	Comparison of guests' perceptions of this and their favorite hotel.
E	Measurement of common guest beliefs, values, and opinions.
F	Profile of the importance of eight ancillary hotel guest facilities.
G	Assessment of guests' general policies and practices while traveling.
H	Timing of hotel choice during the travel planning process.
I	Measurement of the guests' image profile of hotel staff personnel.
J	Identification of most and least preferred courtesy bath product.
K	Comparisons of hotel recreation and entertainment options.
L	Rank ordering of music and entertainment alternatives.
M	Measurement of the guests' image profile of the hotel as a whole.
N	Guest evaluations of five internal hotel areas on four criteria.
O	Profile of guests' experience and use of various hotel types.
P	Picture of the individual, family, or group occupying the room or suite.
Q	Demographic profiles of male and female heads of household.

sample. Similarly, the questionnaire may contain items or sections that apply only to people who respond a certain way to previous questions. In such cases, the *flow* of the questions has to be governed or directed carefully. Branching the flow of the interrogation according to specific criteria typically does that.

Conditional Branching

Often there are survey items that apply to some respondents but not to others, depending on their answers to a previous question. When that's the case, the questionnaire writer can use *conditional branching* or a "go to" statement so those for whom the items don't apply will skip them. This is called *"conditional* branching"

For Grouping Items into Sections   Guidelist 6–2

1. Group items into sections to save interviewer time or to save space on a self-administered questionnaire.

2. Always group items in a way that's meaningful to the respondents or facilitates answering questions.

3. Items that deal with the same survey topic or issue can often be clustered into meaningful sections.

4. Items that use the same scaling technique may be grouped together into a coherent section.

5. Special scale formats may be devised to apply to many items dealing with the same basic issue or topic within one questionnaire section.

6. It's very efficient and practical to group items so that many of them share the same scale and instructions.

To Organize and Group Items	**Checklist 6–1**

1. Does the initial section set the stage for respondents? If not, only general, nonthreatening items that apply to everyone should be retained in the first section.

2. Is each section in the body of the questionnaire organized around one topic, set of issues, or scaling technique? If not, items must be regrouped into meaningful sections.

3. Does the *conversation* flow smoothly from one section to the next? Rearrange the sections or insert a *bridge* between sections when necessary.

4. Have threatening or *sensitive* questions been retained for the latter sections of the questionnaire? If so, they'll more often be answered because rapport is greater.

5. Are the demographic or biographic items contained in the concluding section? Placing them there increases response and obtains the most data in case of refusal.

6. Does the entire dialogue flow smoothly in a manner meaningful to respondents? If not, any abrupt shifts or discontinuities should be identified and removed.

because the branch in the flow of questions is made *on condition* that a certain answer is given to the preceding question.

With most online surveys and those where the questions are presented to the interviewer or the respondent by a computer or PDA (*Personal Digital Assistant*, an electronic handheld information device), the conditional branching is programmed into the device in advance. When the respondent answers a question on which other items are contingent, the program *automatically* goes to the appropriate section or set of items to be answered next. With this kind of data collection, branching is almost entirely unlimited.

Four slightly different methods of conditional branching within a "paper and pencil" questionnaire are shown in Example 6–2. The instructions might be expressed a little differently, depending on whether the questionnaire was used for a self-administered mail survey or by a personal or telephone interviewer. In any case, the basic concept is the same. The examples assume the researcher intends to ask one or more questions about the Sunday newspaper. It wouldn't make sense to ask such questions of those who didn't subscribe. So the questionnaire must *first* ask whether the respondent subscribes. If so, the question(s) would be asked. If not, they wouldn't, and the process would move on to other issues and questions.

The first example is an implied branch because there are no specific branching instructions. The second question begins with the phrase, "If so . . ." implying that *if not*, the question need *not* be answered. This is the simplest form of conditional branching around a question that may not always apply. It's often used in self-administered questionnaires because it's simple, quick, and easy for the respondent to understand. Even if some respondents who need not answer the question do so anyhow, little time and effort is lost. The data for such cases can be ignored when it's transferred and processed.

The Use of Conditional Branching   Example 6–2

Implied Branch or Subquestion

Do you subscribe to the Sunday newspaper?   _____ yes _____ no
  If so, do you read it regularly?   _____ yes _____ no

Explicit Branch with a Single "Go To"

Do you subscribe to the Sunday newspaper?   _____ yes _____ no
  [If not, go to Question 30]

Explicit Branch with "Skip"

Do you subscribe to the Sunday newspaper?   _____ yes _____ no
  [If not, skip Question 20]

Explicit Branch with Multiple "Go To's"

What Sunday newspaper do you *most* often read, if any?   _____ yes _____ no

> _____ *Times* . . . .(Go to Question 30)
> _____ *Tribune* . . . .(Go to Question 35)
> _____ *Dispatch* . . . .(Go to Question 40)
> _____ *Chronicle* . . . .(Go to Question 45)
> _____ none . . . .(Go to Question 50)

The second example is very typical of an *explicit* branch. It contains instructions directing the interviewer or the respondent to go to a particular question, and any items between the instruction and that point would be ignored or skipped. Alternative forms of the instruction might specify a different page of the questionnaire, or some other mark or indication can be used in place of question numbers. For example, interviewers might be instructed: "If *NO*, go to the *X*, below," or some similar designation.

The third section of the example shows a similar branch with an *explicit* instruction, but rather than directing the interviewer or respondent to a particular place, it says what must be skipped. This form is recommended when only one or two items are to be skipped, but it gets too complex when several items are skipped. Obviously, the question(s) to be skipped must immediately follow the instruction. The interviewer or respondent won't remember to skip the items if they come later in the questionnaire.

The last example consists of an explicit, multiple branch. In this case, a different set of questions is asked, depending on which paper is most often read. (Note that the item seeks only one newspaper. If it asked about subscription, more than one might be identified and the branching would become extremely complex and intricate.) This type of branching instruction is acceptable for interview surveys, but it's ordinarily too complex for mail surveys that are self-administered by respondents. Notice, also, that this format will require a second branch after the set of five questions about any one newspaper. Presumably, an *unconditional* branch instruction

The Use of an Unconditional Branch   Example 6–3

Do you regularly read the:

	30. Magazine section?	_____ yes _____ no
	31. Sports pages?	_____ yes _____ no
	32. Editorials?	_____ yes _____ no
	33. Religious news?	_____ yes _____ no
	34. Home directory?	_____ yes _____ no

(Go to Question 50)

would be used to direct the questioning process to item 50, where a new set of questions or issues would be addressed.

As with the single "go to" branch statement example, the designation of where to go need not be listed as a question number. The instruction might refer to "Part A, B, C, etc.," to "Section I, II, III, etc.," to a page number, or to any other meaningful designation. The questionnaire writer may use color coding or shading of pages or sections, or any other device that would help make the place to which the process should move distinct and clearly identifiable, as it is in Section D of Example 6–1.

Unconditional Branching

An *unconditional* branch directs the questioning process to another place for *all* respondents who reach that particular location on the questionnaire. In the example of a branch with multiple "go to" instructions used in Example 6–2, some respondents might indicate they most often read the Sunday *Times*. The interviewer would then move to Question 30, shown in Example 6–3, and ask the next five questions. Since Questions 35 through 49 apply to other newspapers, the process would then branch *around* them and go to the next section, beginning with Question 50. A similar branch instruction would follow Questions 39 and 44. (Obviously, if the branch were to Question 50, none would be required after Question 49.) As in the case of conditional branch instructions, *unconditional* branches need not always use a question number. Any other clearly identifiable means of designating the location to which the questioning process should move would be acceptable.

Branching Limitations

The main considerations for using branching instructions are identified in Checklist 6–2. Branching instructions within the questionnaire can be very useful and helpful, and at times, some form of branching is inevitable. On the other hand, the use of branching is *strictly limited*. Each branch adds greatly to the complexity of the interviewing or response task. Too many branches may introduce bias and error, reducing the reliability and validity of the results. In self-administered mail surveys, the least sophisticated respondents often become confused or bewildered by the instructions and fail to follow them correctly. The respondents are voluntarily doing the task for the researcher. If it becomes too complex or difficult, many will give up and discard the questionnaire, rather than completing and returning it.

To Use Branching Instructions   Checklist 6–2

1. Is the questionnaire to be administered by a local or online computer? If so, the branches can be programmed and no instructions to interviewers or respondents are needed.

2. Are the data to be collected with a self-administered mail questionnaire? If so, branching must be strictly limited.

3. Does only one question immediately following another need to be skipped by some respondents? In that case, use an implied branch, such as "If so . . . "

4. Must some respondents skip an entire set of questions? If so, a conditional branch with *go to* should be used.

5. Do several different answers to an item require going to several different sections that must be completed? If so, a multiple, conditional branch and an unconditional branch after each such section except the last one will be needed.

6. Is the location to which each branch is to be made clearly designated and easily identified? If not, shading, color coding, or some other designation should be included.

7. Is it absolutely certain that the least sophisticated or least motivated interviewers or respondents can and will branch correctly? If not, modifications are necessary.

8. Are there more than a few branches required within the questionnaire? If so, multiple forms of the questionnaire (instead of branching) should be considered.

9. Are there several branches that are based on the same basic *condition* or response? If so, the conditioning question should be used as a *qualifier* in the greeting and multiple forms of the questionnaire used.

While branching can be used a little more liberally for personal or telephone interview surveys, it's still very limited. The people who *construct* questionnaires often, if not always, overestimate both the *ability* and the *willingness* of the interviewers to follow their instructions. It's also difficult for questionnaire or interview schedule writers to appreciate the conditions under which the field-workers or interviewers must ask the questions and record the responses. It's extremely difficult to hold the respondents' attention and maintain their interest while simultaneously recording answers, reading branching instructions, and finding the correct location of the next question. An occasional branch over one or a very few items is usually okay. When many branches are required and the task is very complex, it would be better to *prequalify* respondents and use *alternative forms* of the questionnaire for different groups of respondents.

Unlimited Branching

There's a notable exception to the restrictions and limitations on branching noted earlier. Some commercial data collection agencies have telephone interviewing facilities where the questions are presented one at a time on a computer display. Similarly, personal interviewers may be equipped with laptop or notebook computers or PDAs that are programmed to present the questions, item by item. In some special data collection facilities, respondents may be invited to sit down at a computer that will present the questions and allow them to respond on a regular or special keyboard or a touch-sensitive display screen. These programs may present a question and allow the user to enter the response before listing the next question.

With this kind of dynamic questionnaire, there are very few limits to the amount and complexity of branching, because the computer, rather than the interviewer or respondent, does it all. The program "looks at" each answer as it's recorded, or looks back at the record of earlier responses, then chooses the next item based on earlier answers. Neither the interviewer nor the respondent has to be concerned about the branching. Indeed, they wouldn't even be aware of it.

Computer-generated survey interrogation allows the questionnaire writer to devise a highly complex, dynamic flow of questions. In addition, data input is edited "on the spot," so if the user tries to enter an improper value or response, they will be prompted to enter a correct one and perhaps coached on what answers are acceptable. These computer applications are used mainly for online web surveys and by those who conduct frequent interview surveys. Many who conduct surveys only very infrequently will probably continue to depend on traditional paper-and-pencil methods. Nevertheless, programs such as SPSS Data Entry Builder and Data Entry Station are priced from a few hundred to several hundred dollars, bringing them within reach of many who only occasionally conduct surveys.

Instructions to Respondents

Whether the questionnaire is self-administered or administered by an interviewer, *instructions* will be required or helpful in many places. Instructions aren't really part of the actual questions or items. Rather, they tell the interviewer or respondent how to present or respond to the questions. Most often the instructions apply to a *set* of items or questions. For example, several items may use the same response scale, and the instructions indicate how to use that scale.

The indented paragraphs above the items listed in examples of scales, shown in Chapter 5, are typical instructions. They apply to all the items listed below them. Most scaling techniques require some instruction, at least for the first time they appear in a questionnaire. Instructions for using scales are the most common instructions found in questionnaires. Yet this is only one type of questionnaire instruction. Several other types may also be required or helpful.

Instructions for Using Scales

With a self-administered paper-and-pencil questionnaire, the more complex the scaling technique and the less sophisticated the responding population, the more elaborate the instructions must be. For example, the very common Likert scale with five categories ranging from "Strongly agree" to "Strongly disagree" ordinarily requires very simple instruction. Typically, it's sufficient merely to say, "Please pick a number to show how much you agree or disagree and jot it in the space beside each statement below."

The semantic differential scale, shown in Example 5–9 in the previous chapter on page 133, requires very brief instruction because of its visual or graphic nature. On the other hand, the semantic distance scale, shown in Example 5–11 on page 136, needs a little more elaboration because it's less graphic and depends on a linear, numeric rating scale from which numbers are selected and recorded. The fixed sum

Correct and Incorrect Scale Instructions   Example 6–4

Wrong: Please rate the importance of the following.

Scale

Unimportant 1 2 3 4 5 Important

_____ Dishwasher
_____ Kitchen range
_____ Refrigerator
_____ Washing machine
_____ Clothes dryer

Right: Please rate how important it's for you to own *EACH* of these household appliances. If it isn't at all important to own it, pick a low number from the scale and jot it in the space in front of the item. If it's very important, pick a high number, and if it's somewhat important, pick a number from the middle range and jot it in the space.

Scale

Unimportant 1 2 3 4 5 Important

_____ Dishwasher
_____ Kitchen range
_____ Refrigerator
_____ Washing machine
_____ Clothes dryer

---

scale shown in Example 5–12 on page 137 of the previous chapter is even more complex because the answers should total to a given, constant sum. Thus, that example provides the basic instruction at the top, an additional, parenthetical note just above the items, and yet another *cue* at the bottom indicating the total to which the numbers should sum.

The degree to which instructions should be simple and brief or elaborate and complete depends as much on the sophistication of the respondents as on the complexity of the scales. In Chapter 5, Example 5–13 on page 139 contains very thorough and complete instructions. It assumes that the respondents are relatively naive or unsophisticated. If this same scaling technique and set of items were to be used for a survey of certified public accountants, rather than the general public, the instructions might simply say: "Please circle a number for each investment vehicle to show your perception of financial risk." The rule is to compose instructions that meet the requirements of the *least* sophisticated respondents.

Elements of Instructions

Instructions on how respondents completing a self-administered paper-and-pencil questionnaire should use scales usually contain several elements: (a) what items or statements to rate; (b) what criterion or standard to use; (c) how to use the scale, and (d) exactly how and where to report or record the responses. In Example 6–4, the correct version contains all elements while the incorrect version contains none.

For Composing Scale Instructions   Guidelist 6–3

1. Clearly indicate which items are to be rated and if only one is to be picked or an answer recorded for all items.

2. Say what criterion or standard should be used to judge the items or answer the questions.

3. Describe how the scale is to be used and include an example if the task is complex or difficult.

4. State how the responses are to be reported or recorded, such as a check mark, number, circle, etc.

5. Use brief instructions for simple, easy tasks and more elaborate instructions for more difficult response tasks.

6. Make the instructions clear and complete enough to be sufficient for the least sophisticated respondents.

7. The less sophisticated the responding sample, the more complete and thorough the instructions must be.

8. Write instructions so the most sophisticated respondents need only read the first part and can skip the remainder.

The incorrect example doesn't indicate that respondents should rate each and every item. Many respondents would rate only some of them and ignore others or would rate all of them collectively, as a set. More importantly, this version of the instructions doesn't indicate the basis, standard, or *criterion* to be used when rating the items. The correct version indicates that importance of *ownership* should be rated. Many, if not most, respondents would agree that it's vitally important to have a refrigerator or a kitchen range available, and, in the incorrect version, these appliances would almost always be rated as highly important. On the other hand, many who rent homes where such appliances are provided wouldn't regard it as important to own those appliances.

The incorrect version doesn't indicate how the scale is to be used. Take note that there are five points on the scale and five items to be rated. Many respondents would probably *rank* the items, when the researcher's intention was actually to obtain ratings, so that two or more may be rated the same.

Lastly, the incorrect version doesn't indicate how or where the answers are to be recorded. Thus, some respondents are likely to check a space, others to circle scale numbers, and still others to write in the words "unimportant" and "important." To the inexperienced researcher, such responses might sound like absurdities that are highly unlikely. They aren't. Extensive experience demonstrates all too well that a surprisingly large proportion of respondents will provide very bizarre responses if the instructions aren't crystal clear. Guidelines for writing clear instructions are contained in Guidelist 6–3.

It's ordinarily better to err in the direction of providing instructions that are too thorough rather than too brief. If the instructions are well written, the more sophisticated respondents who quickly understand will need only read the beginning, while others have complete direction when needed.

Special Respondent Instructions   Example 6–5

A. Please read each item one time, then indicate your opinion. Remember, it's your first impression that counts.

B. Please answer the following questions about your favorite brand, even though you may sometimes buy others.

C. Please pick a number from the scale to show how often your spouse does each of the following things.

D. Please rate how satisfied or dissatisfied you are with each appliance that you now own. Leave the space beside the item blank if you don't now own one.

E. Let's assume that you have decided to buy a new car in the next few weeks. What brand would you be most likely to consider first?

F. If one of your children suddenly needed emergency medical treatment during the daytime, where would you be most likely to take the child?

Special Instructions

There are times when the respondents must be given special instructions on how to respond to one or more survey items. The need for such special instructions depends on the particular situation. Some examples of them are shown in Example 6–5. In Section A, respondents are instructed to read each item only once and not to study or compare the items. The instructions in Section B of the example list an *unconditional inclusion*. The favorite brand is to be rated, *regardless* of whether or not other brands are sometimes purchased. In Section C, the respondent is instructed to respond for his or her spouse, rather than for him- or herself.

The instructions in Section D list a *conditional exclusion*. Since the respondents don't rate appliances they don't own, these are *implied*, miniature branches around such items. The last two sections list *assumptions* that the respondent is to make when answering the questions. In Section E, the assumption is explicitly listed in the first sentence. The example in Section F implies an assumption with the use of the conditional clause, "If one of your children . . ."

These are but a few special instructions that might be needed for some survey items. Special instructions such as these are needed whenever the respondents are to make an assumption, answer for another person, base their responses on a special criterion, or otherwise act or respond in some *extraordinary* way. The same rules of grammar, vocabulary, and style for composition of survey items, themselves, also apply to the composition of special instructions. They must be crystal clear, and the key words or phrases should be underlined or highlighted to make them clearly recognizable.

Interviewer Instructions

For telephone or personal interview surveys, instructions for the interviewers, listed within the survey instrument, are often needed. They're designed for the interviewers only. They aren't read or shown to the respondents. Several such instructions are shown in Example 6–6.

Instructions for Interviewers Only   **Example 6–6**

 A. [If yes:] What store did you purchase it from?
 B. [If respondent is male, *skip* to page 5.]
 C. [If respondent is married, return to ★ above and ask each question about his or her spouse.]
 D. [Hand respondent the *pink* rating card.]
 E. [Check appropriate category below but DON'T read alternatives to respondent.]
 F. Are there any other reasons? [*Probe* for all others.]
 G. [Record ethnicity of respondent below. DON'T ASK!]

            _____ White   _____ Black
            _____ Oriental   _____ Hispanic
            _____ Other (Specify what: _____)

Sections A, B, and C are samples of branching instructions for interviewers. Branching was discussed in detail earlier in this chapter, but it's important to note here the exceptions that apply for an interview survey. First, the instructions should be enclosed in brackets or parentheses, written in uppercase letters, or otherwise distinguished from the items, themselves. The questionnaire writer should use one convention throughout the instrument to indicate to the interviewers that these phrases are *not* to be read to respondents. Any easily recognizable markings will do, so long as the *same* ones are used throughout and all interviewers know what they mean.

It's also important to note that branching must be limited and very clearly indicated. Some researchers are inclined to assume that the field-workers are more sophisticated and better motivated than they actually are. The branching can be *somewhat* more elaborate or slightly more complex for interviewers than if the questionnaire is self-administered, but not much. Interviewers receive training and instruction before going into the field. They can examine the questionnaire thoroughly before using it. Nevertheless, it's best to assume they're no more sophisticated than respondents.

Section D of the example is merely an instruction to give the respondent a visual display of a rating scale. Such supplementary materials will be discussed more fully later in this chapter. In Section E, the field-worker is instructed about recording the responses and reminded not to list the alternatives for the respondent. Similar instructions can be used to indicate that the alternatives should be read to respondents, when that's required. Notice that the word DON'T is both entirely uppercase and underlined, to be sure the interviewer sees this is a prohibition.

Section F of Example 6–6 shows a question followed by a general instruction for the interviewer to probe for more reasons. The use of probing is discussed more fully in Chapter 8. Interviewers are instructed on the methods for probing when they're trained or before going into the field. The questionnaire needs only to tell them when to do so, but they don't need to be told exactly how to do it each time a probe is required.

In the final example, Section G, the interviewers are conducting a personal survey so they can visually identify the respondents' ethnicity. They're instructed to

For Composing Special Instructions   Guidelist 6–4

1. Keep the instructions as clear and simple as possible.
2. Use uppercase letters, boldface type, italics, or underlining to highlight important words or phrases.
3. Set instructions slightly apart from actual items.
4. Use some convention, such as brackets or parentheses, for instructions to interviewers only.

record it without asking the respondent, to avoid any potential threat. Note the use of uppercase letters and underlining, so interviewers won't fail to see that part of the instruction.

These are only a few special instructions for interviewers. Many other types might be used, as they're needed. The same rules about clarity and simplicity apply to these instructions as to all others. Guidelines for writing special instructions are provided in Guidelist 6–4.

Interview Rating Cards

Surveys often require respondents to rate items using a scale. With self-administered questionnaires, the scales can be printed directly on the survey instrument. If personal interviewing is used, the various scales must be printed on cards that can be handed to the respondents, so they can see the scale and select their choice for each item as it's read. Three such samples are shown in Example 6–7.

In each case, the questionnaire would contain an instruction to the interviewer to hand the respondent the rating card. The cards should be color coded by printing each on a different color card stock, or they can be labeled with a name, letter, or number to distinguish the various types. When such identification is used, the labels should be printed on *both* sides of each card, to facilitate their recognition and use. It's usually not advisable to include more than one such scale on the same card. Ordinarily, the contents of the cards are printed in large typeface, so they're clearly readable to all respondents, including the elderly or those with poor vision.

In the first two examples, Sections A and B, two frequently used scales are shown. They're basically the same as those used for a self-administered questionnaire, shown in Example 5–8, page 131, and Example 5–3, page 122 in Chapter 5. The same type of instruction is given respondents, and they're used in the same way as described earlier. The last example in Section C shows a rating card for obtaining an indication of annual family income. This is a *sensitive* item. Many respondents are likely to refuse; those with high incomes tend to understate and those with low incomes tend to overstate income if asked the dollar amount. Thus, using random letters obtains more reliable data. Respondents are asked simply to report what letter indicates their annual family income. The basic guidelines for composing rating cards are listed in Guidelist 6–5.

Respondent Rating Cards   Example 6–7

A.
Linear, Numeric Scale Card

Scale **UNIMPORTANT   1 2 3 4 5   IMPORTANT**

B.
Verbal Frequency Scale Card

1 = Always **2 = Often** **3 = Sometimes** **4 = Rarely** **5 = Never**

C.
Annual Family Income Indicator

R = Under $20,000 **G = $20,000 to $39,999** **L = $40,000 to $59,999** **W = $60,000 to $79,999** **F = $80,000 to $99,999** **Q = $100,000 and Over**

For Creating Respondent Rating Cards   Guidelist 6–5

1. Put only one rating scale on each card to make identification easier and facilitate handling.

2. Color code the cards or label them with a name, letter, or number on both sides so they're easily recognized.

3. Have the cards computer-printed in a large typeface or use a copy machine that will enlarge the image.

4. Compose instructions using the same rules as for scales on self-administered questionnaires.

Concluding the Questionnaire

The conclusion of the questionnaire is reserved for two kinds of questions: (1) Items that are *delicate* or *sensitive*—*those* that are potentially *threatening* or *intimidating,* and (2) questions about the respondents' *demographic status.* Often the latter are *inherently* threatening to some respondents—especially those that fear they'll be identified or those who are reluctant to reveal facts about themselves.

To Identify Threatening Questions   Checklist 6–3

1. Does the question ask about financial matters? This society judges people by what they earn and own and most people fear the IRS above all else.

2. Does the question challenge mental or technical skill or ability? People often fear looking stupid or inept in their own eyes or to others.

3. Will the question reveal self-perceived shortcomings? People are highly sensitive to their inability to accomplish personally or socially desirable goals.

4. Is the question about *social status* indicators? Those with low-level educations, jobs, neighborhoods, and the like may be defensive about such questions.

5. Does the question focus on sexuality, sexual identity or behavior? Sexuality is a very private topic and many are embarrassed by even the mention of sex.

6. Does the question refer to consumption of alcohol or illegal drugs? Many will deny or understate such consumption or be insulted by the suggestion of use.

7. Are personal habits the topic of the question? Most people don't like to admit their inability to form or to break personal habits.

8. Does the question address emotional or psychological disturbance? Such illnesses are far more threatening to people than physical ailments.

9. Is the topic of the question associated with the *aging process?* Indicators of aging arouse fear and anxiety among many people of all ages.

10. Does the question deal with death or dying? Morbidity is often a forbidden topic and many refuse even to think about their own or their loved ones' death.

Minimizing Threat or Intimidation

Checklist 6–3 lists ten categories of questions that many respondents find threatening. Financial information heads the list because income and wealth are important status indicators and because almost everyone fears the IRS and other tax agencies. Some of the other sources of threat may not be as easy for the questionnaire writer to identify. For instance, any instruction, question, or scale that's unclear to respondents may suggest they're ignorant or incompetent. Questions that deal with failure to attain certain goals (e.g., losing weight, learning to play a musical instrument, or even keeping the house clean) may be threatening.

Some respondents—especially, but not exclusively those at lower levels of the social hierarchy—may be defensive about common social status indicators. That might include anything from the car (or truck) they drive to the fact that their spouse was a high school dropout. People also get highly resistive and defensive about questions concerning sex, alcohol, or illicit drugs. Inability to form socially desirable personal habits—healthy diet, exercise, cleanliness, orderliness, promptness, and the like—is a sensitive issue for many. Similarly, the inability to *break* socially undesirable personal habits—smoking, nail-biting, knuckle-cracking, fidgeting, and other such habits or mannerisms—evokes strong, defensive feelings and reactions among some people.

This culture and society also encourage people to hide, avoid, or retreat from other issues as well. Survey questions about mental or emotional illness often elicit

FIGURE 6–3
Commonly
Used
Demographic
Variables

A   Sex of respondent.
B   Sex of family members.
C   Age of respondent.
D   Age of each head of household.
E   Age of family members.
F   Age of youngest child in the home.
G   Education of respondent.
H   Education of each head of household.
I   Employment of respondent.
J   Employment of each head of household.
K   Occupation of respondent.
L   Occupation of each head of household.
M   Annual income of respondent.
N   Annual income of each head of household.
O   Annual family income.
P   Racial or ethnic identity of respondent.
Q   Race or ethnicity of each head of household.
R   Religious preference of respondent.
S   Religion of each head of household.
T   Type of family dwelling.
U   ZIP code or location of residence.
V   Time of residence at present location.
W   Self-designated social class membership.

resistance from respondents. Factors related to aging—such as the use of bifocals, hearing aids, or dentures—may yield a negative reaction or a response that's less than truthful. Lastly, death and dying are forbidden topics to many.

If the survey questionnaire includes questions dealing with any of these potentially sensitive or threatening issues, they should be worded very carefully to avoid bias, as suggested in Chapter 4. During construction and organization of the survey instrument, such sensitive items or sections should be identified, earmarked, and inserted near the end of the questionnaire. That way, rapport is at its highest, and respondents are less likely to lie or resist. Even if they do refuse to continue, the data they provided earlier may still be usable.

The Demographic Section

Almost every survey contains items indicating the status of the respondents. These are called *demographic* items. They're used in three ways: First, the profiles portray the nature of the sample. Second, the demographic profile of the sample can be compared to that for the population as a whole, when these parameters are known. Third, the items can be used to divide the sample into subsamples by age, sex, and so on. The data for the other survey items can then be compared among the demographic groups to determine the effect of demographic status on other responses.

Figure 6–3 contains a fairly comprehensive list of demographic items. Not all of them will be required for any given survey, and some other items, such as travel history or residential history, might also be included with demographics. For some surveys, demographic data for only the respondent would be necessary. For others, it may be valuable to obtain demographic data for both heads of household. (In years past, surveys sought data for *the* head of household, assuming the person was a male. That might create resentment today. Obtaining data for *both* heads of household is also more valid for many households.)

The age of the youngest child is often included because it can be used with marital status and occupation to determine the stage in the family life cycle. There are several different classifications of family life cycle, but one of the most common schemes is described in Figure 6–4. Often, the stage in the family life cycle is more likely to influence response than merely the age of the respondent. For example, a 35-year-old single male may respond in a manner more similar to a 20-year-old single male than to a 35-year-old who is married and has children in the home.

Demographic items are ordinarily clustered together in a single section and included at the end of the questionnaire. That way, respondents are less likely to refuse or terminate the process, since they've been cooperating for some time. Notice that income, ordinarily the most sensitive and threatening demographic item, has been listed last. Similarly, if racial or ethnic identity or religious preference is to be included, that should be listed just prior to annual income. Even if a small proportion should decide to refuse further cooperation, the data obtained earlier in the questionnaire may still be usable and valuable.

A typical demographic page is shown in the last page of Example 6–1. In the example, age, education, and income are to be obtained in continuous, numeric form. They can be grouped into appropriate categories during data processing if that's required. Employment and occupation are listed in categories. Different categories and more or fewer of them might be used, depending on the nature of the survey and the information requirements. The categories listed have proved to be both meaningful and easily understood in many surveys of the adult public.

The format in the example is typical of one for a self-administered questionnaire. Respondents can complete it quickly and easily. If there's only one head of household, the other column is simply ignored. This or a similar format would, of course, work effectively for an interview survey, with appropriate interviewer instructions included.

FIGURE 6–4 **Family Life Cycle Stages**

Stage	Description
1. Young Single	Under 45, not married or living with a spouse, no children in the home.
2. Young Couple	Under 45 years of age, married, no children in the home.
3. Full Nest I	Single or married parent, youngest child under six years old in the home.
4. Full Nest II	Single or married parent with youngest child in the home from 6 to 15.
5. Full Nest III	Single or married parent, the youngest child in the home between 16 to 23.
6. Empty Nest I	Over 44, married, no children in the home, one or both in the work force.
7. Empty Nest II	Over 44, married, no children in the home, retired, neither in the work force.
8. Single Elder I	Over 44, not married, no children in the home, still in the work force.
9. Single Elder II	Over 44, not married, no children in the home, retired, not in the work force.

For Precoding Survey Items	**Guidelist 6–6**

1. Use numbers for response codes, rather than letters, because they're more easily entered and processed.

2. Response codes aren't required for dichotomous items or items that are checked only if they apply.

3. Numeric items and scales containing numbers to be checked or circled require no response precoding.

4. Print response codes in very small typeface and place them inconspicuously so respondents will ignore them.

Precoding the Questionnaire

Printed, so called "paper-and-pencil" questionnaires should virtually always be *precoded*, whether they're used for a self-administered mail survey or an interview survey. Precoding means adding response codes for each alternative response to each structured question. Numbers are far preferable to letters because they can be keyed and handled more easily during data transfer and processing. Guidelines for precoding response alternatives are provided in Guidelist 6–6. Notice that in Example 6–1, Section Q, the employment and occupation categories are numbered from one to seven with small numerals to the left of each box. These are the code numbers that will later be keyed to a data file. Listing such codes on the questionnaire *before* the questionnaire is printed avoids the extremely laborious, time-consuming task of *postcoding* each item on each completed questionnaire after the data are collected. One of the major reasons for using structured questions is to make precoding possible.

Notice that in the example, *age, education,* and *income* aren't precoded because they don't need to be. No precoding is required for numeric items recorded by respondents because the values can be keyed directly to file. Nor are precodes required when respondents jot down a number to represent a scale category, such as in Example 6–1, Sections E and G. Similarly, some scales, such as those in Example 6–1, Sections F and I, have no precodes because the codes are a part of the scales, themselves. When respondents check a *position* on a scale, such as in Example 6–1, Sections D and M, the individual positions *do require* precoding so there's no confusion about what value to key for each response.

Aside from cases where the respondents, themselves, jot down or circle a numeric value, it's ordinarily desirable to precode virtually every response alternative on the questionnaire, except dichotomous response categories. For such choices as yes/no, checked/not checked, male/female, and so forth, precoding isn't really required. Instead, the code values are specified in the instructions for those entering the data. For instance, in Example 6–1, Sections A and B, those entering the data might be told to enter the number 1 for any item that's checked and a zero for those that aren't.

Online questionnaires, coded in HTML, the main program language of the web, require neither precoding nor record format listings, described below. Example 6–8 contains a sample section of an online questionnaire with a few of the same

Online Questionnaire Section   Example 6–8

Please check *any* and *all* words that describe your stay at this hotel.

☐ Active   ☐ Memorable   ☐ Relaxing
☐ Boring   ☐ Aggravating   ☐ Disappointing

How well does each of these words or phrases describe your impressions of our hotel staff?

	Not At All						Perfectly So	Don't Know
Unfriendly	O	O	O	O	O	O	O	O
Courteous	O	O	O	O	O	O	O	O
Lazy	O	O	O	O	O	O	O	O
Helpful	O	O	O	O	O	O	O	O

Which one courtesy bath product do you find most useful and enjoyable?

O Shampoo
O Cream Rinse
O Bath Oil
O Moisturizer
O Sun Lotion

Of the last ten times you stayed at a hotel, how many times did you stay at. . .
(Please make the total = 10)

This particular hotel?   [____]
Another hotel in *this chain?*   [____]
Some other hotel?   [____]

items used in Example 6–1. When a respondent is completing this kind of self-administered (or computer-administered) questionnaire, the data are automatically recorded in the proper places in the data file when the respondent "submits" the form.

In Section J of Example 6–1, if a respondent indicated that she found "Bath Oil" to be most useful and enjoyable, the person entering the data would enter the code value of 3 in column CI of the spreadsheet or data entry program. If a respondent clicked the radio button on the same item, "Bath Oil," on the online questionnaire in Example 6–8, that data would be stored in the proper place in the data file according to the way the web page and ancillary documents were programmed. Neither code values nor record format listings need appear on the questionnaire. In addition, there is no instruction on the online questionnaire in Example 6–8 reminding respondents to pick *only one* response. That's because the online version can be programmed so it won't allow multiple responses to single-response items. If someone tries to click on two buttons, the first one will go "off" when the second one goes on or is highlighted.

Listing Record Formats

Another kind of information should be listed on a questionnaire before it's printed. These are the letters that show the column position where the data for each item will be keyed to a computer spreadsheet or data entry program. No record format listing is required if a special data entry program to receive the data displays the questionnaire in the same format as that of the printed document. In that case, the data are keyed to the same physical location on screen as where it appears on the printed questionnaire. With online surveys, the data are automatically stored in the specified format when entered. But for "paper-and-pencil" surveys, the record format should be listed on the questionnaire before printing.

Precoding the responses can be done as the questions or scales are written; however, the letters indicating the record format in the far right-hand margin of the questionnaire should *never* be listed until the *entire* questionnaire has been assembled. When the questionnaire is laid out, it's important to allow space in the right margin for format indicators, but the actual letters should *not* be listed until the questionnaire is completely finalized. That's because any changes, such as adding or deleting an item or even changing an item, may require changes in *all* the record format positions that follow the modification.

Listing the record format on the questionnaire is simple and easy, but it must be done *precisely*. If there are any errors, it will be *very* difficult to cope with them after the questionnaire is printed. If errors are discovered after the data collection has been completed, a new record format may have to be listed *on each completed questionnaire,* from the point the error occurred to the end of the questionnaire. That's a very tedious and time-consuming process.

Spreadsheet Record Formats

Some limited data analysis can be done using spreadsheets alone, but larger surveys or those requiring more thorough analysis typically use statistical analysis programs such as SPSS. Nonetheless, spreadsheets are often used for data entry because analysis programs almost always allow spreadsheet data to be imported into them for analysis.

The spreadsheet with data from 10 respondents might look similar to the example shown in Figure 6–5. Each row of the spreadsheet is numbered and each column is designated by letters of the alphabet. If the data from the survey will be entered into a spreadsheet, the column letters where each variable will be entered in the spreadsheet should be listed beside each question or item on the questionnaire.

Spreadsheet Format   Figure 6–5

◇	A	B	C	D	E	F	G	H	I	
1	Rate1	Rate2	Miles	Own	Spent	Sex	Age	Edu.	Case	
2	3	3	8	1	77.50	1	28	12	201	
3	5	1	22	1		1	35	12	202	
4	4	2	40	1	0.45	1	61	13	203	
5	4	2	119	1	97.50	2	44	16	204	
6	5	1	27	1	22.50	1	41	12	205	
7	3	3	48	1	11.87	2	50	14	206	
8	2	4		2	9.16	2		12	207	
9	4	2	31	1	81.40	1	64	11	208	
10	3	3	4	1	35.55	2	27	16	209	
11	3	3	60	1	6.25	1	21	15	210	

Questionnaire or Case Numbers

Each questionnaire should be assigned a unique number, either before or after data collection. This *case number* will be keyed to the data file. Then, if an error is discovered or a problem encountered after the data have been transferred, the case number identifies the completed questionnaire from which the data were keyed. The researcher can return to the completed questionnaire and make any corrections needed. The case number is usually listed at the end of the questionnaire and entered at the end of the row for that case in the data file, as shown in Figure 6–5.

Note that it's a much less serious error to list too many, than too few, spreadsheet columns on the questionnaire. If too many are assigned, one or more columns can be skipped during data entry. They just remain blank and won't be used. If too few are assigned, there's no way to *reduce* the number of columns needed, and serious problems are likely to result.

Experience indicates that it's all too easy to make mistakes when listing the record format in the margin of the questionnaire. One common mistake is to fail to recognize *multiple responses* to an item and allow positions for *each alternative.* To clarify this point, refer to Example 6–1 and compare Section B with Section J. Both of these sections contain *multiple-choice* questions. Thus, they look very similar at first glance. Yet the amount of data they provide is *very different* because Section B contains two *multiple-response* items while Section J has two single-response questions. Notice that in Section B the alternatives aren't precoded. That's because respondents can check any or all alternatives. *Each alternative becomes a survey item or variable.* The number 1 would be keyed for that item if it were checked, and a zero if it were not. Notice also that *each* alternative has been assigned a position on the record. The danger is that it's extremely easy to glance at the item, assume it's a single-response item, and assign only *one* position to it. If the mistake weren't discovered until it was too late to correct it, all of that remaining record would be "off" by 8 columns. In other words, there would be no columns for 8 of the 10 items.

For Listing the Record Format   Guidelist 6–7

1. Don't begin listing the format until the entire questionnaire draft is complete.
2. Determine the first column in which actual data will be keyed and begin listing with the letter designating that column.
3. Remember that each alternative of a *multiple-response* item constitutes one variable and each requires a separate column.
4. Allow a column for any "other" or open-ended items to be postcoded.
5. Always perform the acid test, filling in maximum values, checking all options, and keying the data to a test file.

   In Section J of Example 6–1, each of the two items allows for only one response; one alternative must be selected. So, only one position is required for each. If the person precoding the record format made a mistake and assigned a column to *each alternative*, 8 columns would be "wasted" and data transfer would be a little less convenient, but no serious harm would be done. Again, the basic rule, "better too many than too few," holds true. Guidelines for listing the record format are provided in Guidelist 6–7.

The Acid Test

Testing the codes and record formats is absolutely mandatory for inexperienced researchers and highly recommended for even the most experienced. It takes only a few minutes to do so, and the testing usually returns many, many times its cost in time by catching errors before the data are collected. To test the codes and record formats, the questionnaire writer should make a copy of the final questionnaire draft. Then, the researcher should complete the questionnaire, listing the *maximum* value for each item. *Every* alternative on each multiple response item should also be checked. When that has been done, the data from the test questionnaire should *actually be entered* to a data file. Very often one or more errors will be discovered.

Pretesting the Questionnaire

When the entire paper-and-pencil questionnaire has been completed and all the items have been organized, the sections arranged, the instructions inserted, the responses precoded and record format listed—when it's all done and everything is complete, **don't send it to be printed!** Not yet. Instead, duplicate 20 or 30 copies and administer it to as many typical respondents. If it's an online survey, have a few people complete the questionnaire before publishing it online. See how it goes when they fill it out or when they're interviewed. See if they understand the questions, the scales, and the instructions. Observe how accurately they follow the branching, if there is any. See how long it takes them and how easy or difficult they find it. Ask them about their reactions and suggestions when they've finished. Then, actually try entering the data into a computer file. Maybe everything will work beautifully and the instrument is nearly perfect. Maybe. But very often, very often indeed, even well-trained and highly experienced researchers find some changes that will improve the performance of the questionnaire. And sometimes the pretesting of the questionnaire will reveal very serious errors, oversights, or problems that would have spelled disaster if they hadn't been detected and corrected before going into the field or the mail.

Summary

The Construction of the Questionnaire

A. Emphasize the introduction. Most refusals will come immediately and once respondents begin, they seldom terminate prematurely.

B. Check sequence carefully. Simple, interesting, informative items should come first, and sensitive or threatening items as late as possible.

C. Group items into sections. Combine items that use the same scales or put the same topics into sections to facilitate response and simplify the task.

D. Limit and control branching. Make branch instructions simple, clear, and concise and avoid complex branching or multiple branches as much as possible.

E. Use ample instructions. An instruction should be included if there's any doubt, and it must be simple enough for the least sophisticated respondents.

F. Don't overestimate interviewers or respondents. Sophistication and motivation are always less than the researcher is likely to expect.

G. Make good use of rating cards. For personal interview surveys, good rating cards will simplify the response task and increase reliable, valid responses.

H. Be sure to precode responses and list record formats. Precoding must be done very precisely and accurately and submitted to the "acid test."

I. Always pretest the entire questionnaire on a pilot sample of 20 or 30 respondents, observing closely as they respond to the instrument.

Part 3

Collecting and Processing Data

7

Self-Administered Surveys

Self-Administered Questionnaires

Self-administered surveys are distinct from interview surveys in several ways. Many aspects of data collection for the self-administered survey don't apply to interview surveys. Even those tasks or attributes common to both types of surveys typically require more or less emphasis for one type of data collection than for the other. Because of these distinctions, self-administered surveys are discussed in detail in this chapter. Surveys that collect data through telephone or personal interviews are considered in the next chapter. Those who are considering whether to conduct a self-administered or an interview survey may want to examine both chapters to compare the unique capabilities and limitations of each type of data collection. Those who intend to conduct a single study and have decided on either self-administered or interview data collection will find complete guidance in the chapter dedicated to that type of data collection.

Online Data Collection

The term "online data collection" used here refers to data collected by e-mail, e-mail attachment, newsgroup inquiry or invitation, or by a questionnaire published in the World Wide Web. Some of the terms and acronyms used in connection with the Internet and online data collection may be unfamiliar to many. A complete glossary of survey research terms is provided beginning on page 437.

Plain Text E-mail Surveys

The simplest and least sophisticated way to collect survey data via the Internet is by sending a questionnaire in a "plain text" e-mail message. The recipients are asked to type their answers on the document and return the completed instrument by clicking on "reply" or choosing it from the program's menu. The principal advantages of this method of data collection are its simplicity and universality.

Neither the production of the questionnaire nor the response and return require much technical ability. In fact, the typing of postal mail questionnaires or even interview survey questionnaires require more word processor skill than what's required or appropriate for a plain text e-mail survey. That's because any niceties often used for other questionnaires, such as bold or italicized type or even the use of tabs, will be lost when the document is copied or saved as plain text.

The other main advantage of plain text e-mail questionnaires is the fact that they can be read by *any* e-mail program, no matter what platform, operating system, or application program the recipient is using and no matter how dated the version of the software is. If the recipient can receive e-mail—any e-mail at all—they can open and read a plain text e-mail questionnaire. Virtually every e-mail program also allows the user to "reply" to the sender with just a click or menu choice, so returns can be directed to the correct address with very little effort on the respondents' part.

The simplicity and universality of plain text e-mail questionnaires are important attributes for small, informal surveys of a limited number of potential respondents; however, this method has some serious shortcomings that make it unfeasible for larger inquiries and mailings. The columns of print in plain text document are likely to be badly contorted unless the recipient happens to be using the same font as the one in which the document was composed. Even when the questionnaire is composed in a fixed width font, such as Courier, there are likely to be recipients whose e-mail programs won't recognize or distinguish fixed width from variable width type. The results might appear as in the two sections of Figure 7–1.

Aside from the bias and error these formatting problems are likely to create in the response data, the plain text limitations also severely restrict or prohibit listing the record format on the questionnaire. Consequently, editing, postcoding, and data transfer are likely to be arduous tasks if more than a limited number of cases are to be processed.

E-mail Questionnaire Attachments

Self-administered questionnaires can be delivered (and returned) by attaching them to e-mail messages. With this method, the questionnaire is composed on a word processor and attached to an e-mail message that seeks the recipients' cooperation and asks them to open the attachment, complete the questionnaire by inserting their answers, and attach the completed questionnaire to the reply. This method is sometimes used if some of the questionnaires are to be sent by postal mail and some sent by e-mail. That way, both subsamples receive exactly the same questionnaire.

Attaching survey questionnaires to e-mail messages should be used only in *very* special circumstances. The researcher must be very sure that virtually every recipient will have a computer system and word processor program that will open the attachment and present it in the way it was composed. When this method is used, the questionnaire is usually composed in Microsoft Word and saved as a Word document or in Rich Text Format (RTF) because that is the most common application program and format. Even when the survey is to be directed to a special population that is certain to have the software, the expertise, and the motivation to complete this rather complex series of steps, the researcher would be well advised to consider a Web survey rather than an e-mail attachment.

FIGURE 7–1
Plain Text
Formatting
Problems

Fixed Width Font Item

```
Please put an x in one space on each line to indicate if you would
welcome a free trip to:

Atlanta, Georgia. . . . . __Yes    __Maybe    __No    __Don't Know
Baltimore, Maryland . . . __Yes    __Maybe    __No    __Don't Know
Chicago, Illinois . . . . __Yes    __Maybe    __No    __Don't Know
Dallas, Texas . . . . . . __Yes    __Maybe    __No    __Don't Know
Edmonton, Alberta . . . . __Yes    __Maybe    __No    __Don't Know
```

Variable Width Font Item

Please put an x in one space on each line to indicate if you would welcome a free trip to:

Atlanta, Georgia . . . . . __Yes   __Maybe   __No   _ Don't Know
Baltimore, Maryland . . . . __Yes   __Maybe   __No   __Don't Know
Chicago, Illinois . . . . . __Yes   __Maybe   __No   __Don't Know
Dallas, Texas . . . . . __Yes   __Maybe   __No   __Don't Know
Edmonton, Alberta . . . . . __Yes   __Maybe   __No   __Don't Know

Web Surveys

Collecting data with a questionnaire on the Web is vastly superior to e-mail questionnaires or attachments. Nearly everyone who can be reached by e-mail also has access to the Web and uses a Web browser. Even those who often get their e-mail on a cell phone or Personal Digital Assistant (PDA) will almost always have access to the Web on a desktop or laptop computer with a larger display than hand-held devices. Thus, the reach of the two contact methods is about the same, but Web surveys have gained in popularity very rapidly. The main reasons for their growth are outlined in Figure 7–2.

FIGURE 7–2
Why Web
Surveys Gain
Popularity

1. Internet access and acceptance have grown rapidly.
2. More stable, wide-band connections are readily available.
3. A wide spectrum of demographic groups use the Internet.
4. Telephone survey refusal rates have grown sharply.
5. Mail survey nonresponse is usually *very* high.
6. Web surveys can reduce data collection costs greatly.
7. Web surveys can be conducted more quickly than others.
8. Web survey technology reduces data handling problems.
9. Web survey services are readily available and affordable.
10. International reach is both feasible and economical.

FIGURE 7–3
Who or What to Survey on the Web

1. Consumers who shop the Web
2. Those to be reached at work
3. Companies, organizations, and institutions
4. Computer- and Internet-related occupations
5. Professional users of Internet services
6. Educational and scientific occupations

Although Web surveys enjoy ever-increasing popularity, this doesn't imply that they are universally appropriate for surveys of every population or purpose. While a large proportion of the general public are connected to the Internet, there are still a substantial number who are not. So, Web surveys are particularly effective for the populations and purposes listed in Figure 7–3, but less so for others and not at all appropriate for some groups. Thus, the researcher's responsibility is to examine the feasibility of a Web survey relative to the other methods of data collection and choose that which promises to yield the most reliable, valid information that will satisfy the information needs.

Web survey instruments range from simple, linear questionnaires with little or no embellishment to highly sophisticated creations that include color, animation, sound, or video clips. On the Web the possibilities are almost unlimited. The choice of how much to include depends on a variety of factors, including the information needs, nature of the topics, population to be surveyed, budget limitations, and time requirements. Most of all, the decisions about every aspect of a Web survey should be governed by the researchers "judgment about how each choice will affect (1) the response rate, (2) the reliability of the data, and (3) the validity of the results. After all is said and done, these are the only things that *really* matter to sponsors and information seekers. An absolutely spectacular questionnaire website that yields unreliable or invalid results is worse than no information at all. The sponsor would be better off basing decisions and policies on executive judgment, conventional wisdom, or just plain intuition than on false findings.

Static Web Questionnaires

The most basic Web survey questionnaire is a simple, linear instrument written in HTML, the universal language of the World Wide Web. Although it's referred to here as "static," that doesn't imply that it's totally inert; however, the flow of interrogation (inclusion and order of items) is identical for every respondent. The questionnaire may be on a single page or may extend to several pages. The questionnaire consists of one or more "forms" containing the instructions, questions, and scales as well as response elements such as checkboxes, pop-up menus, list selection fields, radio buttons, text fields, and submit buttons. Some of these elements are shown in Example 6–8 on page 174.

Static Web questionnaires such as these can be composed by website creation and management programs such as Microsoft FrontPage® or Adobe PageMill®. These programs require some degree of computer skill and technical ability, but the user doesn't have to know much of anything about the actual HTML program language itself. If the researcher or survey sponsor's staff are already familiar with website creation and management, composition of a simple linear questionnaire would certainly be feasible.

Interactive Web Questionnaires

More elaborate Web surveys and those designed to collect data over substantial periods of time from large numbers of respondents benefit from use of more technically sophisticated Web questionnaires, referred to here merely as "interactive" questionnaires. Their programming and operation is more complex than the simple, linear, "flat form" questionnaire described above. There are interactive features that can be included in these questionnaires when the information needs and budget warrant them.

Multiple Question Formats

Complex questionnaires accommodate multiple question formats. If a multiple-choice question is designated as *single response* (check only one), it will allow respondents to select only one alternative choice. If a respondent clicks on another, the first is automatically unselected. If, on the other hand, the item is designated as *multiple response* (check all that apply), respondents can check as many alternatives as they wish and each will remain highlighted.

Dynamic Probing

These questionnaires may also include a single line text box or multiple line text area where respondents can answer open-ended questions or make comments in their own words. The more advanced questionnaire programs also provide dynamic probing. A "probe" is a question that follows another, often asking *why* the person responded as they did or seeking some other "follow-on" response. In the past, probing was used mainly with interview surveys, where the interviewer could listen to an answer and base the probing question on what the respondent said. With complex Web questionnaires, the program does much the same thing. Rather than a *general* probe, such as "Why do you feel that way?" the probe is specific, based on key words from the previous answer.

   An example may clarify the operation of a dynamic probe. Suppose the sponsor wants to measure the degree to which people identify the crime rate as a major problem in the community without suggesting crime in the question. An open-ended question might ask, "What do you regard as the most important problem facing this community today?" Respondents would answer in their own words in a text area. If they did *not* include the words "crime" or "criminals" or other terms suggesting crime, such as "lawbreakers," the dynamic probe might ask, "Aside from that, how much do you regard the crime rate as a problem?" If, on the other hand, they identified crime as the major problem, the dynamic probe might be programmed to ask, "How can the crime rate be reduced most quickly?" Thus, dynamic probes in a Web questionnaire function in much the same way as an interviewer, "listening," or looking at an answer to a question, then posing another, probing question based on the words that were used.

Skipping and Branching

In an interactive Web questionnaire, skipping and branching control the flow of interrogation in the same way as implied and explicit branching do in printed questionnaires, with one very important difference: Branching is *very limited* with a printed instrument, but there's virtually *no limit* to the number of skips and branches in an interactive questionnaire. Skipping and branching are very similar to one another. Skipping is akin to an implied branch. One or more questions or items are skipped, based on the answer to the preceding question. For example, the question might be, "Do you own a car?" If the answer was affirmative, the next question might be, "What is the make, model, and year of your car?" If the respondent didn't own a car, that question would be skipped by the program.

Branching also conditions the flow of questions on the answer to one or more previous questions, but it's similar to the explicit branch or "If so, go to . . ." item described in Chapter 6. Thus, if the respondent was a homeowner, he or she might be asked a series of questions in one section but if the person was a renter, another series of questions might be presented. The flow of questions follows one "branch" or another. The branches might reconnect at some point for additional questions common to all, or they may lead to separate conclusions to the questionnaire.

Response Piping

Taking the answer to a question and including it in the expression of a subsequent question is called "response piping." For example, a multiple-choice, single response question might ask, "What type of vehicle to you drive <u>most</u> <u>often</u>?" Options might include *"Sedan, Minivan, SUV, Truck, Motorcycle,"* etc. In a later question, the respondent might be asked the question, "What grade of gasoline do you most often use in your (<u>data</u>)?" where the data field would be filled with the type of vehicle they indicated earlier (i.e., Sedan, Minivan, SUV, etc.). Response piping makes the questionnaire more "conversational," but it also has a more practical function. In the example above, it would be awkward to ask, "What grade of gasoline do you most often use in the type of vehicle you most often drive?" On the other hand, if the questionnaire merely asked, "What grade of gasoline do you most often use?" without specifying a vehicle, those who had multiple vehicles would probably consider the gas they used in *all* of them when they answered, distorting the results. Response piping is designed to solve such problems as that.

Rotation and Randomization

Rotation or randomization means listing survey response alternatives, questions, or sections in a different sequence with each respondent. When a list is *rotated*, the order stays the same but the list begins with a different item each time it's presented. When a list is *randomized*, the order in which it's presented is randomly selected for each respondent. For example, suppose four cities, Atlanta—Baltimore—Chicago—Dallas are the response alternatives for a multiple-choice question. If the list is *rotated, it would* appear in that sequence for the first respondent. For the second, it would be shown as Baltimore—Chicago—Dallas—Atlanta; for the third, Chicago—Dallas—Atlanta—Baltimore; for the fourth, Dallas—Atlanta—Baltimore—Chicago, and then on to the next set of rotations. When the list is *randomized*, the probability of any sequence appearing is the same as the probability of any other.

In the list of response bias sources, Figure 4–1 on page 102 identified *order bias* and noted it occurs when "the sequence in which a series is listed affects the response to the item." The discussion goes on to say there are three things that might induce order bias: *initiation, routine,* and *fatigue.* Initiation means respondents are learning how to understand and handle the first item or so in any list. People normally react to the *first* of anything differently than they do to subsequent exposures or experiences. Routine implies that in a series of similar items, the respondent may (consciously or unconsciously) adopt a response strategy toward the entire series, rather than considering each item individually. Lastly, with a long list of questions, items, or questionnaire sections, respondents may become tired or bored with the task. They may treat the later ones with less care and consideration than the earlier ones.

When the sequence in which they appear is arbitrary, *randomization* of response alternatives, items, or sections is advisable. Randomization is preferable to simple rotation unless there is some specific reason for keeping individual items adjacent to one another. Randomization *won't eliminate* order effects. Respondents will still react differently toward these elements, depending on their sequence, but rotation will control the bias by *randomly distributing* the effects of the order over the list of options, items, or sections. The order effects will still create some random error, but the systematic bias created when the same response alternative, item, or section always appears first, in the middle, or last will be reduced or eliminated.

Data Validation

The researcher can specify parameters for text and numeric entry fields in an interactive questionnaire. If respondents attempt to enter values outside those parameters, the program will identify the incorrect entry and remind them of what's acceptable. For example, suppose a question asked respondents to enter a dollar value *to the nearest thousands* of dollars, when the maximum expected whole value is less than $100 thousand. Without data validation, if someone entered a value of 35000, the whole value in the file would be $35 *million* dollars when almost certainly the respondent intended to indicate $35 *thousand.* When data validation is in place, that respondent would be reminded they are to enter a value *to the nearest thousand dollars.* If response piping is also programmed, the respondent might even be asked if he or she *meant* to indicate $35 *thousand,* rather than $35 *million.*

Data validation parameters can be specified to check a wide range of data characteristics, from simple things as entering words or letters in a numeric field to much more complex combinations of data characteristics. For instance, Example 5–12 on page 137 contains the *fixed sum scale* question, *"Of the last 10 times that you ate lunch or dinner at a casual or fast food restaurant, how many times did you have each of the things listed below?"* It also includes the reminder, *"(Please be sure to make the total equal 10.)"* But of course, some respondents will enter values that sum to less than or more than 10. Without an interactive questionnaire and data validation, the typical way to resolve this problem is to program the analysis routine to convert all the entries to fractional values of the total. Unfortunately, that results in noninteger values for some respondents. For example, if the respondent in the example above entered values that totaled to 11, rather than 10, and indicated eating one kind of food 4 times, it would appear they had that kind of food 4/11 or 3.5 times, yet it's impossible to actually have fractional values in this case.

With data validation, the data entered by each respondent would be instantly summed. If the values were incorrect, the respondent would be reminded to make the total equal to the specified total and asked to reenter the values. Similar data validation might include dates or times, such as specifying a duration longer than would be possible, or other "impossible" responses, such as answers that result in a negative value for distance. Answers can also be screened to be sure they're compatible with earlier answers on the questionnaire. For example, a *homeowner* may not have a mortgage, but it's unlikely (though possible) that a *nonhomeowner* (such as a divorcee) would be paying off a home loan. With data validation, if such questionable compatibility between answers is detected, the respondent can be asked to recheck the answer or provide clarification. The possibilities for validation criteria are almost unlimited. The result is usually very clean, unconflicted data.

Qualification and Quota Control

Interactive questionnaires allow screening respondents for qualification. The program checks to see if a respondent is the type of person being sought and if the quota cell for that person is open. If respondents don't qualify or their cells are full, they are thanked for their participation and allowed to depart or return to the website from which they came.

Interactive questionnaires usually allow the researcher to set a quota total for a study and quota limits for individual quota cells. The quota variables might be either *independent* or *interdependent,* as described in Chapter 8 and shown in Example 8–2 on page 234. With interview data collection, quota variable combinations and the number of individual cells that result are more limited than with Web surveys using interactive questionnaires. The more complex the quota specification, the higher the *rejection rate* (the percentage who don't qualify). Thus, complex, interdependent quotas may prolong the data collection period and slow the rate of data acquisition, but there are no interviewers to become confused and the complexity won't increase costs as dramatically as low incidence rates for interview data collection.

"Real Time" Processing

Web surveys with interactive questionnaires often allow the researcher to receive "real time" reports of the results. If so, the researcher can monitor such things as the characteristics of the data distributions, the degree of variance in the data, and the confidence intervals (margin of error) that prevail at any given point for the number of cases in the database. The percentages of quota completion and the number of respondents or cases (*n*-size) for individual cells can be monitored, as well. That way, both the size of the total sample and the quota can be modified if necessary or appropriate, to include fewer or more than were originally specified.

Duplicate Control

A postal mail survey ordinarily delivers just one questionnaire to a potential respondent, so there is little chance of duplicate responses—that any one person will respond more than once. Similarly, there's very little chance that interviewers will call upon or encounter a respondent more than once. But this is not the case for Web surveys. Depending on the method of response solicitation, a potential

FIGURE 7–4
Methods of
Web Survey
Duplicate
Control

1. **Cookies:** A cookie is data sent to a computer by a Web server that records the users' actions on that particular site. If a respondent visits the Web survey site a second or subsequent time after being sent the cookie on the first visit, the server would recognize the duplicate response and politely refuse participation. This will only work if the respondent is using the same computer as the first time and the browser is set to accept cookies.
2. **Singular IPs**: The Common Gateway Interface (CGI), a set of rules for programs on a Web server, can be set up to accept only one entry from a particular IP address, the code number that identifies a particular computer on the Internet. This provides protection against repeated response to a questionnaire during the same session; however, if respondents log off their connection and come back again later, they would probably have a different IP address than initially.
3. **Unique URLs**: If invitations to participate are sent by e-mail, a unique URL system can be used. Each respondent would get a unique address for participation. For instance, the URL might be: http://www.domain.com/cgi-bin/websurvey.pl?54321. Then a different, unique, nonsequential number following the question mark would be assigned to each participant. That number must be used to access the questionnaire. If an invitee deleted the number or tried to use a different one, access would be politely denied. It would be almost impossible to guess a different, valid number.
4. **Unique passwords:** A username/password combination system can be used to allow each invitee to participate only once. Alternatively, multiple entries might be accepted, but the username and password can be captured in the data, so duplicates can be identified and deleted later.
5. **Later cleanup:** Perhaps the easiest way to handle duplicates is to allow them initially and clean them out later. Multiple entries can usually be identified and duplicates deleted by analyzing several criteria such as IP address, browser type, personal data entered, and patterns of response.

respondent might be invited to participate many times. There are several methods for controlling duplicate response. One or a combination of methods listed in Figure 7–4 might be used.

Complexity and Cosmetics

One of the reasons Web surveys are so popular among researchers of all types is because of the higher response rate, relative to mail surveys. And one of the main reasons for that response rate is the appearance and ease of response to a dynamic questionnaire. Somehow, clicking through a colorful, attractive Web questionnaire is vastly more interesting than checking off boxes on a black-and-white, printed form. Web survey research firms usually offer both off-the-shelf and custom designs that can be geared to the nature of the inquiry and population to be sampled. One company, Centrac DC (www.centracdc.com) offers colorful themes with colorful names—*Classic, Blue Note, Green Machine, Neon Dream*—and even the four seasonal themes. Questionnaires can be designed to include animation to capture attention and create interest, as well as video clips for demonstrations of survey topics.

The visual, and even the audio possibilities are limited only by the questionnaire designer's imagination and creativity—*and the respondent's connection bandwidth!*

FIGURE 7–5 Interactive versus Flat Form Questionnaires

Single-page "Flat" Form Questionnaires	
Advantages	**Disadvantages**
Server performance is less critical. Each time the "Continue" or "Submit" button is clicked, a server request is made. With a flat form questionnaire, if there are 20 questions on a single page and 2,000 respondents, there will be 2,000 server requests in total. By contrast, if *each question* is on a single page, there will be 40,000 server requests. The greater the number of server requests, the more potential problems respondents may have with the questionnaire. So, the fewer server requests, the better.	Connection time-out may occur. Some respondents may be using computers connected to Internet service providers (ISPs) through telephone MODEMS. Many ISPs set their host MODEMS to time out after a certain idle period. If it takes too long for the respondent to fill out one page before clicking on the "Submit" button, the connection could be lost because it timed out. That would result not only in a lost participant, but also probably an irate one.
Respondents know the length of a flat form questionnaire. An interactive survey with one question per page may seem like an endless task to respondents. Without some indication the end is near, many respondents may drop out with only a few questions remaining.	Interaction is very limited. While some features, such as single response radio buttons, are available in flat form questionnaires, skip patterns, questionnaire branching, and response piping are not possible.

Web questionnaire designers often sit at high-speed computers with high-speed connections to the Internet. It's easy to forget that a substantial proportion of the general public are still connected to the Internet by 56K telephone MODEMS. Cable, DSL, and satellite connections are increasingly popular, but if a large part of the population to be sampled has a slow Internet connection, website complexity can cause delays that encourage dropping out before completion of the survey. Researchers can check slow MODEM performance of a questionnaire before it's opened to the public. They need only go to a machine with such a MODEM on a weekday mid-afternoon and see just how long it takes to complete the questionnaire. If it's too long, some simplification is in order.

Multi-Page Considerations

Sponsors and researchers new to Web surveys and the technical sophistication they offer may be captivated by all the "bells and whistles" interactive questionnaire programs can provide. A word of caution is in order here. The picture of interactive questionnaires isn't *entirely* positive. Interactive questionnaires require multiple pages, but not because the content won't fit on a single page, as with printed documents. Rather, it's because the respondent must click on a "CONTINUE" button to send the entry to the host server and the server must respond with a new page to interact with the respondent. There are both advantages and disadvantages to using multi-page, rather than single-page Web questionnaires. The pros and cons are outlined in Figure 7–5. The researcher should consider the benefits

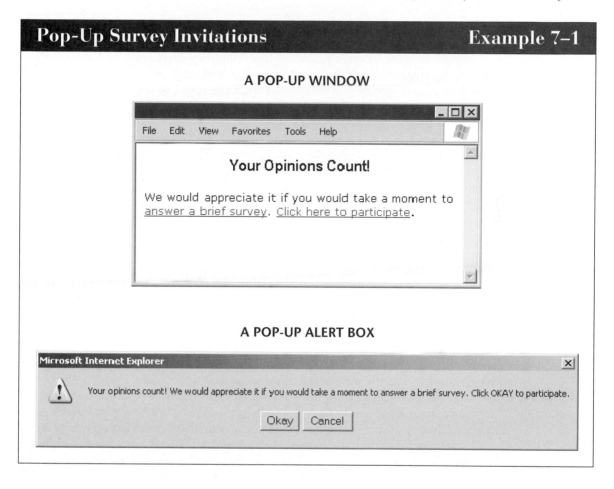

Pop-Up Survey Invitations   **Example 7–1**

A POP-UP WINDOW

Your Opinions Count!

We would appreciate it if you would take a moment to answer a brief survey. Click here to participate.

A POP-UP ALERT BOX

Microsoft Internet Explorer

Your opinions count! We would appreciate it if you would take a moment to answer a brief survey. Click OKAY to participate.

Okay   Cancel

and shortcomings of multi-page interactive surveys versus single-page flat form questionnaires very carefully before making a choice.

Web Survey Samples

Web survey samples can be classified according to: (1) method of contact and recruitment, (2) means of inducement, (3) degree of screening, and (4) duration of participation. The methods of original contact and recruitment vary greatly, ranging from mere chance encounters on the Web to very focused e-mail solicitations among newsgroups, discussion lists, or membership rosters.

Method of Contact

On the casual side of this spectrum, the researcher may use random website intercepts, posting or having posted pop-up windows or pop-up alerts such as those shown in Example 7–1 on the sponsors' or other websites. They may be presented to everyone who visits the site or page. Alternatively, if high traffic is likely to lead to too many respondents, the pop-ups can be programmed to appear to every *n*th visitor to invite only a certain proportion of visitors.

More focused recruitment programs may target specific groups with e-mail messages or newsgroup postings that invite participation. Tile.Net® (www.tile.net) is a comprehensive Internet reference that identifies discussion and information lists on the Internet, Usenet newsgroups, ftp sites, computer products vendors, and Internet and Web design companies. This site could be regarded as a *source for sources,* where vendors and brokers of e-mail lists for nearly every kind of population can be found.

Email Universe.com (www.EmailUniverse.com) is another resource, providing a directory of publicly accessible mailing lists. The site also features links to *"List-Lingo—The Newbie's Guide to Email List Terminology"* and *"List-Etiquette—The List Member's Guide to Email List Guidelines, Rules, and Behavior,"* both of which may be informative to both survey researchers and sponsors. Resources such as this allow the researcher to identify the specific target population for the survey and reach them quickly and effectively with an invitation to participate.

Means of Inducement

Because Web surveys are often quick, easy, and even fun to do, many invitees may be willing to respond without any inducement, whatsoever. At the other extreme are a few people who wouldn't respond to a survey if their life depended on it! The "best" respondents for most surveys, Web or otherwise, are those that are someplace between these extremes, but hopefully toward the *willing* side of the spectrum. There's an old adage that says, *"Free advice is worth as much as you pay for it!"* There may be times when the same thing could be said of survey data. It's certainly not *always* necessary to provide an inducement to respond. In fact, most Web surveys don't require one, but researchers should be wary of people who are *too* eager to participate. They're probably atypical of the population they are supposed to represent.

Guidelines for using inducements for postal mail surveys are provided in the following section of this chapter. Six criteria for selecting an inducement are described. They apply equally to Web surveys. Of the types of inducements that are listed, *drawings or sweepstakes* and *reports of results* are the most common inducements for Web surveys and often the most effective. They lend themselves especially well to Internet communication.

Degree of Screening

A Web survey sample may be *screened* or *unscreened,* meaning only certain respondents are allowed to participate or participation is open to anyone willing to respond. The latter tactic needs no explanation. If the sample is to be limited only to those with certain characteristics, it may be *prescreened* or *postscreened.* Prescreening can be either *invitational* or *participatory:* In other words, the recruiter can either contact *only those who meet the criteria* (invitational screening), or contact as many potentially qualified respondents as possible, but *accept participation* from only those who meet the criteria (participatory screening).

Prescreening participation is accomplished in much the same way for Web surveys as for postal mail surveys: Prospective respondents are asked one or more "qualification" questions. If they meet the qualifications, the survey continues with the substantial items. If not, they are politely thanked and released to go back to a previous page or to exit the site and go on to another.

Under some circumstances it's better to let anybody who's willing to participate. If so, postscreening can be used. It's called that because it takes place *after* the questionnaire has been completed. It merely involves checking on the key questions to determine qualification and deleting the cases that don't qualify. Postscreening is *never* used for other kinds of surveys because discarding mail or interview responses would be a costly waste. But when the questionnaire is quick and easy to complete, so it's not demanding on the host server, and when no inducement is provided (or there's no cost per respondent, as with sweepstakes or drawings), there's little lost in deleting unqualified responses. It's important to note that if drawings or sweepstakes are used as inducements, the "entry" or identity of *both* those who were accepted and those who were rejected must be retained and included.

Duration of Participation

Web survey respondents may participate on a one-time-only basis or they may be a member of a panel that responds to Web surveys regularly. There are dozens, if not hundreds, of Internet companies that recruit and maintain screened or unscreened panels of many types. Typically, prospective panel members are offered pay for each survey they complete, but they may also be offered other benefits, such as free products or services, entry into sweepstakes or drawings, or points toward premiums. Most such panels are composed of "consumers," but there are also industry panels, occupational panels, avocational panels, and panels based on religious affiliation, association membership, or special interests such as travel, ornithology, history, or music. A few minutes searching the Web will reveal the endless number and variety of panels available. The researchers' problem isn't so much to uncover the options as to cull the list and make an informed choice.

Web survey panels appear to be a quick, easy alternative for obtaining a survey sample, and, in fact, they are quick and easy to use. But they're usually not inexpensive and they may be unreliable. Perhaps the most serious shortcoming of such panels is the atypical nature of the members. They tend to attract people who literally have "more time than money." Yet often the population to which the results will be generalized is relatively "time-poor." They may also be substantially more affluent than the panel sample.

An even more serious source of bias is the *experience* the panel members often have in completing surveys. They very quickly become "professional critics" rather than naive respondents, as the people they will represent are. When response to surveys becomes a "job," rather than a favor or a courtesy, the opinions and reactions are likely to be seriously biased. Yet many panel members are likely to regard participation exactly that way—as a *job!* One Internet firm, PaidSurveys.com (www.paidsurveys.com) makes this self-explanatory recruitment statement on their home page:

> Paid Surveys are listed below! Over 15 survey and market research companies are listed that are absolutely free to join. The more survey companies you join, the more surveys you will receive. The more surveys you receive, the more rewards you will earn! So start sharing your opinion today and be rewarded for it! You will get to earn Cash and Gift Certificates, Free Samples and Prizes, and Entries into Sweeps For $$$.

This is not to imply that there's anything unethical about this approach to Web survey sampling. But it is important that researchers are aware of what they're getting when they purchase such a sample. In most situations, *some information is better than none.* But that's not true in the world of research, where the adage is (or should be) *No information is better than bad information.*

Software and Services

Researchers new to Web surveys need not "go it alone," so to speak, unless they wish to do so. Assistance is available in several forms that require various levels of expertise and involvement on the researchers' part. At the low end of external participation, there are several sources of very powerful, user-friendly, off-the-shelf software to create attractive Web survey questionnaires. At the high end, there are full-service Web research firms that do almost everything except specify the information needs and interpret the results, and they may offer substantial assistance even with those tasks.

If the researcher is seeking software only (or software mostly), companies such as SPSS, Inc.® (www.spss.com) provide questionnaire building and data entry programs that create both print and electronic questionnaires. The questionnaires can be used for Web surveys, but also for desktop computers used by interviewers. The questionnaire software is integrated with data entry and analysis with the SPSS suite of statistical analysis programs.

There are also more specialized firms, such as Infopoll, Inc.® (www.infopoll.com), geared to serve clients large and small, from Fortune 500 companies to individual students and educators. Their main product is a survey design, data collection, and analysis program that prospective clients can download free. The key features of the software, listed in Figure 7–6, allow researchers to create Web surveys without a great deal of technical skill. This company also offers Web survey hosting, consulting, and training services.

Most researchers with little Web survey experience will want, at the very least, to explore full service research service options, as well, before undertaking the project with only software assistance and technical advice. Full service research organizations such as iResearch (www.iresearch.com) and Centrac DC (www.centracDC.com) take almost the entire Web survey burden from the researcher. They and hundreds of others that can be identified with an Internet search also provide other survey research and focus group services to meet the needs of a wide array of clients. While using a full service research firm reduces the risk and the demands on the researcher for special technical skill or training, it also comes at a price. Consequently, the information value of one or more survey projects must be substantial to justify the cost of such services.

Postal Mail Surveys

Interview surveys are administered entirely by the field or telephone worker, but mail surveys are *self*-administered. Thus, the "cosmetic" aspects of mail surveys are much more important. The mailing piece is the only contact respondents will

FIGURE 7–6
Infopoll
Questionnaire
Designer
Features

Familiar interface for anyone to get started quickly:
    Both copy & paste and drag & drop are supported
    No knowledge of HTML or JavaScript required
    No knowledge of database design is required
Multi-lingual support for international surveys.
Built-in spelling check, multiple language dictionaries.
Built-in browser for WYSIWYG design.
Support most commonly used question types:
    Short text input (up to 200 characters)
    Long text input (unlimited free text)
    Numeric input with validation check
    Date field input with validation
    E-mail field input with validation check
    Single choice questions with skip logic
    Multiple choice questions
    Group input questions
    Group single choice/rating questions
    Group multiple choice questions
    Weighted (rated) single choice questions
    Weighted (rated) group single choice questions
    Unique matrix/spreadsheet questions
Users can specify "Other" for group and choice questions.
Built-in intelligent skip logic with no coding required.
Features include required field entry.
Data entry validation.
Large number of question banks and templates:
    Built-in templates of professionally developed question types
    Integrated question library to quickly build your questionnaires
    Quick-start with a template survey
Unlimited free-style questions and answers in one survey.
Eliminate duplicate submissions with the click of checkbox.
Unique built-in survey data simulator for better results.
Completely free to download and use with online support.

have with the researcher and the project. Consequently, it must perform effectively on its own. It has to be completely self-contained. It must "stand on its own" and do the entire job—winning cooperation, capturing the data, and returning it to the survey headquarters. Once the questionnaire and mailing piece are complete and the survey is mailed, there won't be an opportunity to make changes or corrections. At that point, the researcher is "locked into" the instrument and data collection process. Thus, the preparation and mailing of the survey must receive very careful attention, so that every detail will be handled properly and mistakes or inadequacies kept to an absolute minimum. This usually requires substantial testing and revision, and perhaps a "pilot" data collection project, to be sure the mailing will do the job reliably.

The relatively high percentage of *nonresponse* is by far the most important shortcoming of mail survey data collection. It's obviously important to do as much as possible to reduce nonresponse and encourage an adequate response rate. The appearance and quality of the mailing piece and its contents have a very important effect on mail survey response rates. Those conducting a mail survey should understand the alternatives from which they may choose.

It's always best to plan and create a mailing piece that's consistent in quality. If some components of the mailing are to be done very inexpensively, it's wasteful to do other parts lavishly. On the other hand, if most of the components are of very high quality, one or two parts that are obviously done cheaply will diminish or eliminate any advantages of the higher-quality parts. Usually the mailing piece is composed entirely of printed material. Before considering each individual component of the mailing piece, those aspects that apply to all of the components—paper, color, size, print, layout, attachment, and envelope—deserve attention.

The Paper Stock

Paper is the *vehicle* for mail inquiries, while the *printing* is the voice of the interrogator. The quality of the paper used in a mailing will affect the general impression the recipients have of the project. It isn't advisable to use very light paper stock to save postage costs. The paper should be opaque so the print on the back of a page or on the following page won't show through it. Paper with a *smooth* surface, such as regular typing paper, is acceptable for almost all surveys. *Slick* surface paper, such as that used for many magazines, isn't recommended for survey mailings. It tends to give the impression that the mailing piece is an advertisement, rather than a research questionnaire. If distinctive, textured paper stock is used, the cover letter and the mailing and return envelopes should also be of the same paper. It's most effective to use matching envelopes and paper stock for a survey mailing. Most mail surveys use paper and matching envelopes purchased "off the shelf" from a paper supply house, stationer, or printer.

Color

Inexperienced researchers are sometimes tempted to use bright or unusual colors in the hope of gaining more attention from the recipients. This isn't a good practice for survey research because bright colors will have a negative rather than a positive effect. They give the mailing the appearance of a direct mail advertisement. Many recipients discard such materials out of hand as soon as they pick up their mail. White paper is *always* perfectly acceptable. Off-white or *very light* gray or cream may be appropriate for high-quality mailings. Pink, blue, and yellow paper should be avoided.

Paper Size

The cover letter and questionnaire for a mail survey should ordinarily be on standard, 8-1/2-by-11-inch (letter-size) paper. Smaller sizes aren't usually advisable because they don't allow enough space. Smaller sizes may be appropriate for other kinds of printed, self-administered survey questionnaires, such as product inserts, customer questionnaires, and the like, but not for mail surveys. Some researchers may consider using 8-1/2-by-14-inch (legal size) paper to get more content on fewer pages. *Not* a good idea. Almost everyone except the legal profession is used to handling and filing letter-size paper. Legal-size paper too often presents problems. It would be better to include another page on the questionnaire if needed, rather than using larger paper.

Envelopes

The standard number 10 business letter envelope is recommended for nearly all surveys. It can contain several sheets of letter-size paper. The return envelope should be a *number nine* reply envelope, so that it will fit inside the mailing envelope without folding. Some mail economizes by using number 10 envelopes for both mailing and return. If so, the return envelope has to be folded twice and inserted sideways into the mailing envelope, creating an unattractive mailing piece.

Print Characteristics

The mail questionnaire should be composed with a word processor or desktop publishing program in a very conventional style. Such programs typically offer a variety of typefaces or "fonts" from which to choose. The more conventional the typeface chosen, the better. Avoid the more novel or unusual typefaces in favor of one that's totally unremarkable. The goal is to have the reader notice and pay attention to the *content* of the words, not the printing of the document.

Conventional fonts can be either *serif* or *sans serif*. The *serif* is the small stroke used to finish off the main lines of a letter. As a general rule, sans serif fonts such as Arial or Helvetica are appropriate for headlines and short phrases, but serif type such as Times New Roman or Palatino is easier to read when there's a substantial amount of text. Consequently, serif type is recommended for most mail questionnaires.

Type Size

Space is almost always at a premium on a self-administered questionnaire. Many questionnaire writers try to save space by using smaller print. Most people outside the fields of advertising and publishing don't realize that almost everyone over about 45 or 50 years of age needs reading glasses or bifocals. Almost everyone that age *needs* them, but they don't always *have* them or *use* them. Even when they do, small type can be very difficult and tedious to read. The alternative, of course, is to discard the questionnaire or at least set it aside, where it will probably be forgotten. This is a serious problem because this kind of nonresponse creates *systematic bias!* It systematically screens out those of a certain age group. The precoded numbers and record format letters may be in very small, 7-point type so they're not very noticeable to respondents, but the rest of the questionnaire should be in at least 10-point type and preferably 12-point for easy reading.

Color

Black ink is always acceptable for mail surveys. Two-color printings are only very rarely needed. When questionnaire sections have to be highlighted or set apart from others, shading or borders usually work effectively. If the cover letter for the survey will be individually hand-signed by the sender, the signer should use a *blue* pen rather than black. After expending the time and effort to individually hand-sign each, it's important to make that effort perfectly obvious.

Page Layout

The manner in which the print is organized on the paper is just as important as the type itself. The recipient will glance at the entire envelope or page and *immediately* gain a general impression of what's there, even before reading the first word. So the page layout actually "says" something to them before they begin to read the printing. The format of a mail questionnaire is important because it affects the likelihood the respondent will complete and return it. Formatting features such as boldface, italicized, and/or underlined type highlight words or phrases so that respondents are sure to recognize key words. Boxing items in cells helps to avoid confusion and errors by respondents. So do "leaders" on tabs that run from the end of an item or line to the space where the response should be recorded.

It's very important that every page of the questionnaire for a mail survey has an ample amount of "white space." The appearance should be clean and simple, rather than dense and cluttered. It's always advisable to use more pages than to fit the content too tightly. Plenty of white space makes the response task appear much easier and simpler for the respondent, so the response rate is increased.

Most questionnaires require more space than merely the front and back of a single, letter-size page. When multiple pages are required, they should be attached to one another so that they won't become separated or the questionnaire completed in the wrong sequence. Ordinarily, the cover letter need not be returned, so it doesn't need to be attached to the questionnaire, although it could be.

Multiple questionnaire pages can be printed on both sides and stapled together in the upper left corner. A more elegant alternative is to have the questionnaire printed on larger, 11-by-17–inch paper and folded down to letter-size pages. One such page can be folded once to produce two letter-size sheets on which four pages are printed. For larger questionnaires, a "booklet" format with several 11-by-17–inch sheets printed and folded together once down the middle forms a neat document. If there are only a few pages, the entire booklet can be folded twice and inserted into a number 10 envelope. If there are several pages, the questionnaire can be mailed in a larger envelope.

Vendors and Services

Everyone has had a great deal of experience preparing and mailing letters in the normal course of organizational or personal life. So, preparing and mailing a survey may not appear, at first glance, to be a difficult or time-consuming task. On the other hand, very few organizations or individuals have had the experience of preparing and mailing hundreds or perhaps thousands of identical mailing pieces to recipients with whom they have never before communicated. The sheer size of the task and volume of material can come as a surprise for those who haven't had such experience. Also, the fact that the mailing pieces are identical creates additional problems. The effect of any mistakes or inadequacies are automatically multiplied by the number of mailing pieces. Consequently, virtually every detail of the task deserves much greater attention and care than what's required for preparation of a single letter or a small group of mailing pieces.

For Using an In-House Namelist   Guidelist 7–1

1. Use the specification of the population and sample frame as a guide when selecting a source of names.

2. Use an existing in-house namelist if one is available and it meets the sample frame requirements.

3. If there's no existing list, see if a namelist can be assembled from accounting, personnel, or sales records.

4. Determine if it would be feasible for the survey sponsor to gather a namelist in the process of regular business.

5. Check existing directories and public records to see if a namelist can be composed from available records.

There are several service organizations that specialize in doing various tasks required for a survey mailing. They vary in their range and level of expertise, the quality of their work, the minimum volume they're prepared to handle, the range of goods or services offered, their price levels, and the time required for delivery or performance. It's the researcher's responsibility to assess the need for external services and check their availability and qualifications.

Namelist Sources

The "namelist" contains not only the names, but also the addresses of those to whom the survey will be mailed. For some mail survey projects, the researcher or sponsor may have a namelist already. In other cases, internal accounting or personnel records may contain the information necessary to compose a namelist. These "in-house" lists make it unnecessary to obtain a list from an outside source. For example, a retail store conducting a survey of store credit card customers could assemble the namelist accounting records. A political candidate who intends to survey those who recently volunteered their time or contributed to the campaign would have the list in-house. In these situations, the namelist may have to be transformed in some way, but there's no necessity to seek a list from an independent source. Guidelines for using an in-house namelist are provided in Guidelist 7–1.

There are many mail survey research projects that require mailing to the general public or some subsection of the general public, such as those in a certain geographic area or people with certain demographic characteristics. Other projects may require a mail survey of a special population, such as those engaged in a certain occupation, those in a certain position, or those with some particular condition or attribute. In these cases, the sponsors aren't likely to have the namelist in advance, and it must be obtained from those who specialize in assembling and providing such lists.

Namelists can be purchased or rented from firms who specialize in the management and sale of namelists. Some of these firms may have accumulated a namelist as the result of their principal business, such as a magazine that sells (or more correctly, rents) its list of subscribers. There are also many firms whose principal business is the creation, management, and brokerage of namelists. These firms have elaborate computer facilities, and they obtain namelists together with other coded information about those on the list. They may merge lists, match names, and overlay additional information, purge duplicates, make address corrections, and update the list to keep it current and timely. Some firms are strictly namelist brokers. They don't "own" the lists in which they deal. They merely serve as a source of lists for those who require them. They maintain records and relationships with a variety of firms who own and manage namelists. They're often able to locate and provide special lists, and they're paid for doing so on a commission basis.

The principal market for namelists consists of those who use direct mail advertising to market their goods or services directly to buyers. Nevertheless, the firms specializing in namelists provide a rich and varied source of names for mail surveys. Rarely is the population so specialized that a namelist isn't available from some commercial source. A broad Internet search for "mailing list brokers" or "namelist brokers" will yield thousands of "hits." A more narrow search is likely to yield the Web location and contact information for dozens of local or regional firms in the researcher's or sponsor's geographic area.

Namelists may cost less than $100 per 1,000 names, but most firms have a minimum order quantity of 5,000 or 10,000 names. This minimum covers the cost of initiating the job and picking the names from the master list, which may contain many millions of names in total. The namelist selected will probably contain many more names than the actual sample size. When it does, the supplier can usually use the nth name sampling procedure described in Chapter 3 to select the number needed plus a small surplus as a backup.

Usually, a commercial namelist takes a week or two to get, but sometimes it may take several weeks. So it's advisable to shop for a list, select one, and buy it well in advance. The supplier may require that the buyer provide a copy of what's to be mailed. Ordinarily, a preliminary draft of the mailing piece will suffice, so there should be no delay.

Namelists vary greatly in quality, measured in terms of recency, proportion of nondeliverable mailing pieces, correctness of names and addresses, and duplication of names on the list. Either the list supplier or the broker may be able to provide information about such list characteristics if they're questioned carefully about them. Perhaps the most important protection is to deal only with a highly reputable source.

The Post Office

Mail surveys are delivered by the postal service, and the post office personnel are valuable sources of information and assistance. They'll provide the necessary information about permit fees, postage costs, and mailing restrictions, but they also offer much more. Postal authorities are familiar with the details of metered postage, precancelled stamps, formats for printing permit information on mailing and return envelopes, size and shape requirements for mailing pieces, bulk mail regulations and preparation, presorting and addressing requirements, and mail box facilities for receiving returns. Those who anticipate conducting a mail survey should check with the local postal authorities well in advance. All the necessary information should be gathered and all the required approvals should be obtained *before* any component of the mailing piece is finalized and produced. By doing so, potential obstacles and expensive, time-consuming corrections can be avoided.

Printers and Suppliers

Printers often provide a variety of services besides the actual printing of the survey materials. Most have a variety of paper stock and envelopes available. Many offer layout and typesetting services as well. At times, the entire "package," including paper and envelopes, layout and typesetting, printing, and folding may cost less from a printer than when each task is performed separately. This is especially likely when the mailing is small, including less than 1,000 mailing pieces. In other situations, considerable savings may be realized by using separate vendors, especially for large mailings. It's important to check and compare both the cost and the time requirements and to assess the degree of expertise and quality of the work that might be obtained from various alternatives. There are two very real advantages to using a "full service" printing company: The research staff doesn't have to spend as much time and effort delivering, picking up, and dealing with several different vendors. The coordination is also likely to be better when a single firm does several tasks. These factors have to be balanced against any savings that might be obtained by using several different vendors for different tasks.

Mailing Houses

Direct mail advertisers and marketing companies are the principal customers of mailing houses. A mailing house is a service firm that specializes in assembling all the printed materials, then folding, inserting, sealing, affixing postage, presorting, and delivering the mailing to the post office. Many also provide additional services, such as namelist acquisition, graphics, typesetting, paper stock, envelopes, and printing. The chief service offering of mailing houses is, of course, the preparation of the mailing.

Mailing houses are typically geared for *very* large mailings—tens of thousands, hundreds of thousands, or even millions of pieces. So, using them may not be practical for small mailings of less than 1,000 pieces. On the other hand, it may be advisable to use a mailing house for larger survey mailings. Without special mailing preparation equipment, folding, inserting, sealing, metering, stamp affixing, and label affixing by hand may require hundreds of hours of individual labor.

Mailing Piece Components

The mailing piece for the typical survey consists of four or five different components: the mailing envelope, the cover letter, the questionnaire, the return envelope, and perhaps an inducement. Decisions about any one component can't be made independently of the others. The mailing piece has to be an integrated package, and the components must be consistent and compatible with one another. Thus, the researcher should always be aware of the effects of a decision about one component on the requirements for the others.

For Selecting Postage for Mailing   Guidelist 7–2

1. Regular, first class postage stamps on the mailing envelope will result in the highest response rate.

2. Precanceled stamps at the bulk mail rate are second most effective in obtaining response.

3. Metered postage on a mailing, even though first class, provides lower response rates than do postage stamps.

4. Using a bulk mail permit printed on mailing envelopes obtains the lowest response rate.

5. Bulk mailing is less expensive and allows for heavier mailing pieces than first class mailing.

The Mailing Envelope

The typical survey questionnaire would be mailed in a standard number 10 business envelope. Nothing should be printed on the back, and the front should contain only the name and address, the return address, and the stamp or metered postage.

The mailing envelope can be addressed either by typing or printing directly on the envelope, or by affixing labels. When personalized letters are used for the survey, "window" envelopes can also be used. They have a transparent window through which the name and address typed on the letter can be seen.

When an in-house namelist is used, the names and addresses may be typed directly onto envelopes from the namelist using the form letter and data merge features of a word processing program. They may also be typed onto preprinted, letter-size sheets and then transferred to pressure-sensitive label sheets on a copy machine that will accommodate the special forms. This is often useful when the same list will be used more than once. Commercially obtained mailing lists are usually available in several different label and electronic formats, depending on what's needed.

The type and amount of postage will affect the response rate. The response rate will be greatest when first class postage stamps are affixed. It's least with a bulk mail permit, and metered postage falls somewhere between the other two. Bulk mailing requires a bulk mail permit from the post office. The permit number and required indication are then printed directly on the mailing envelope. Bulk mail is slower than first class mail, but it costs much less per piece. For large mailings with many pieces going to the same ZIP code, bulk mail preparation provides additional savings. This requires sorting by ZIP code and bundling the mailing pieces for each ZIP code or state. That's fairly easy to accomplish if the namelist is sorted by ZIP code before the letters are addressed. The researcher should check with postal authorities *well in advance,* to allow time for printing and production. Guidelines for selecting the type of postage are listed in Guidelist 7–2.

The Cover Letter

The letter that introduces a mail survey or other self-administered questionnaire to respondents is usually called a "cover" letter. The function of the cover letter is to

FIGURE 7–7
Questions a
Cover Letter
Must Answer

1. What's this about?	7. How long will this take?
2. Who wants to know?	8. Will it cost me anything?
3. Why do they want this?	9. Will I be identified?
4. Why was I picked?	10. How will this be used?
5. How important is this?	11. What's in it for me?
6. Will this be difficult?	12. When should I do it?

explain the project and win the cooperation of the recipient. It should ordinarily contain several elements and accomplish multiple goals.

Figure 7–7 lists a dozen questions that will ordinarily be in the mind of the recipient of a mail survey. The items are listed in the same sequence they're likely to arise in the mind of the person who receives the letter. It's usually advisable to include the answers to each in the same order within the actual cover letter. Example 7–2 includes the answers to each of the 12, in 5 paragraphs and in this same sequence.

The cover letter should be geared to the nature of the responding sample. The same general rules concerning vocabulary, grammar, and style that apply to question composition also apply here. A good cover letter shouldn't be too stiff, formal, and demanding. Neither should it beg the recipient to respond. It shouldn't be "over the head" of the least sophisticated respondents, but it shouldn't appear to be patronizing or condescending to the most sophisticated respondents. Guidelines for composing an effective cover letter are listed in Guidelist 7–3.

A bulk printed cover letter is least expensive and most easily produced. It usually has a salutation such as "Dear Respondent:" It's printed on letterhead

---

The Mail Survey Cover Letter   **Example 7–2**

Dear Respondent:
A. The manufacturers have asked us to conduct a brief survey of a sample of hot tub owners. You were selected from those who have purchased a hot tub, and it's very important to learn your opinions because you represent many other owners who have similar experiences.
B. The questionnaire has been designed so that you can complete it very quickly and easily. It takes only a few minutes, and you need only check off your answers or jot down a number. A postpaid return envelope has been included for your convenience.
C. You can be absolutely sure that all of the information you provide is strictly confidential, and no individual hot tub owners will be identified. Your answers will be combined with those of many others and used only for statistical analysis.
D. As a token of the company's appreciation, we have included a gift to enhance your enjoyment of the hot tub. We genuinely appreciate your valuable assistance. Your honest impressions and opinions, whether favorable or unfavorable, are very necessary to be sure that the company serves the public as effectively as possible. We do appreciate your candid opinions.
E. Please complete and return the form right away. Again, thank you for your help.

For Composing a Cover Letter	Guidelist 7–3

1. Remember the respondent is likely to accept or reject the response task within the first few seconds.
2. Anticipate the 12 questions that recipients might ask and answer them in the cover letter.
3. Use a conventional business letter style format for the cover letter to meet respondent expectations.
4. Avoid an overly formal style and trite or hackneyed words and phrases in the cover letter.
5. Keep the vocabulary and sentence structure within the limits of comprehension of the least sophisticated reader.
6. Show respect for the readers, their time, and effort, and avoid being too demanding or presumptuous.
7. Don't beg the reader to respond or grossly overstate the importance of the information.
8. Keep the letter friendly and cordial and be confident that nearly all recipients are likable, cooperative people.

stock and each letter is identical, so respondents aren't individually addressed on the letter.

When the cover letter for each respondent is individually typed, including the individual's name and address and a salutation that greets the person by name, they're called "personalized" letters. Respondents are more likely to read a letter that's addressed directly to them and appears to be hand typed and signed. They're also more likely to do what the personalized letter asks of them, so response rates can be increased by including a personalized letter. The disadvantages of personalized cover letters are the cost of the letters and the time required to produce them. But with a good word processing program to merge the letter, names, and addresses and a reasonably fast printer, 1,000 or fewer letters can usually be printed in a day's time.

When potential respondents receive the mailing, the first thing they're likely to do is read the cover letter. The second thing (and sometimes the first) is likely to be a quick examination of the questionnaire itself. The more professional and important the questionnaire appears to be, the more likely the respondents will complete and return it. The easier and quicker they perceive the task to be, the more likely they'll begin answering the questions. Thus, the "cosmetic" aspects of the questionnaire and its appearance to recipients at first glance are vitally important to an adequate response rate. Checklist 7–1 identifies the main considerations for finalizing the questionnaire.

As noted earlier, the return envelope should be smaller than the mailing envelope so that it can be inserted into the mailing without folding. Nothing should be printed on the back of the envelope, and the front contains the same three elements as those on the mailing envelope. The return envelope should contain *both* an address and a return address, although they're usually the same. Guidelist 7–4 identifies the return postage options for the reply envelope.

To Finalize the Questionnaire   Checklist 7–1

1. Does the questionnaire appear, at first glance, to be quick and easy to complete?
2. Does the first page of the questionnaire contain only easy, nonthreatening questions?
3. Is there any uncertainty about the questionnaire's effectiveness that might be reduced by testing?
4. Will the questionnaire be the first thing recipients see after reading the cover letter?
5. Are the pages attached so they won't be lost or separated from one another?
6. Are all the pages clearly numbered and arranged so respondents can follow the sequence easily?
7. Does each page have a note at the bottom, directing respondents to the next page?
8. Is there a title at the beginning of the questionnaire and a note of thanks, urging a quick reply, at the end?
9. Do the sections within the questionnaire form simple steps or subtasks to be completed one at a time?
10. Does the questionnaire have ample white space, with an open, uncramped, uncluttered appearance?
11. Has all work done by others been checked thoroughly?

Inducements to Respond

Ordinarily, response rates for mail surveys are low. This has two negative effects: It increases costs because the number of mailing pieces must be several times the number of respondents required. It also increases the likelihood of nonresponse bias, reducing the survey's validity. Mail surveys may offer a gift or premium for the recipients: an *inducement* to respond to the survey. They needn't be of great value. They don't have to pay recipients for their time and effort. Rather, they're a token of appreciation. The inducement shows goodwill on the sponsor's part. Inducements tend to catch the recipients' attention and put them in a more positive frame of mind. For some, they can also create a sense of *obligation* to respond if the inducement is sent with the original mailing on the assumption that recipients will complete and return the questionnaire.

For Selecting Postage for the Reply   Guidelist 7–4

1. Use of postage stamps on return envelopes *encourages* rather than discourages response.
2. Metered postage on return envelopes is inadvisable because it's both too expensive and ineffective.
3. Business reply permits printed on the return envelopes are satisfactory for most mail surveys.

Inducements that are contingent on receipt of a completed questionnaire are less often appropriate. They require a second mailing or later delivery to all those who respond, and they may be seen by recipients as "pay" for completing the questionnaire. If so, it must be fairly valuable or it may actually *inhibit* response. Such inducements are also more likely to influence the *manner* in which people respond, introducing a serious source of bias. Thus, for most surveys the inducement should be sent with the original mailing, but, of course, there are exceptions.

Selecting Inducements

Six major criteria for selecting an inducement are listed below. Obviously, an effective inducement need not necessarily meet all the criteria exactly, but the closer it conforms to the criteria, the more effective it's likely to be.

Economy

When hundreds or even thousands of people are to be included in the mailing, the cost of an inducement becomes a very important factor. It's important to select an inexpensive item. The objective is to find something that the recipients will value highly, but that won't cost much for the sponsor to provide.

Nonreactivity

The inducement must not influence the nature of the responses to the survey questions. It shouldn't be directly associated with the topics, issues, or sponsor so that recipients "react" to the items in a certain way. To the degree that an inducement affects the *way* that people respond, it will create bias. For example, if the survey dealt with the way people evaluate a particular brand or product, it would be extremely inadvisable to use a sample of the same brand or product as an inducement.

Uniqueness

Inducements that aren't otherwise obtainable by the respondents tend to be more attractive. Such gifts may be relatively inexpensive, but they may be seen by recipients as quite valuable because they can't easily be purchased or acquired in some other way or from some other source.

Value

Even as a token of appreciation for cooperating, an inducement must be of sufficient value so that it doesn't demean the importance of the survey. Giving something obviously worth only a few cents for performing a task that requires considerable time and effort might serve to diminish rather than enhance goodwill and cooperation. Yet, the value doesn't have to be monetary. The monetary value is irrelevant if the inducement has personal, social, psychological, or emotional value to recipients.

Luxuriousness

Gifts which respondents would probably love to own but wouldn't be likely to purchase for themselves are the most potent and effective inducements. As with any gift, utilitarian items are less welcome or valued than are little luxuries or treats the recipients wouldn't otherwise obtain for themselves.

Individualization

While they may be expensive to obtain or produce, gifts and premiums that are individualized are more effective. If the inducement is "personalized" with the individual's name or otherwise directly related to the individual, such as referring to their profession, occupation, affiliation, or some other characteristic the recipient is known to have, it tends to have greater value.

Types of Inducements

Without attempting to include an exhaustive list, it might be helpful to discuss a few common forms of inducement. Studying the experience of others is a good way to avoid missed opportunities (or repeating their mistakes).

Cash Payments

The use of cash as an inducement fails to meet most of the criteria listed above. The disadvantages are several, but the most important is that it "disappears" into the individual's pocket without a trace. In other words, currency is homogeneous, and so the recipient is likely to forget about the gift very quickly. Also, there's danger cash may make it appear the respondent is being "paid" for participation, yet the amount isn't likely to compensate them very adequately for their time and effort. But despite these shortcomings, money can be used effectively with a clever approach, as Example 7–3 demonstrates.

Certificates or Passes

Many service organizations have very high fixed costs and very low variable costs for creating their services. For example, it costs little or nothing for a movie theater to serve additional patrons by giving away tickets. The only "cost" would be the lost revenue if recipients would have otherwise purchased them or if there were a "full house," so that tickets could have been sold for the seats occupied by the guests. Service providers (e.g., theaters, restaurants, airlines, public transportation, and so forth) who sponsor surveys can provide certificates or "passes" for free services as inducements to respond. These inducements cost the sponsor little or nothing, yet they're valuable to the recipients.

Drawings or Sweepstakes

Some mail surveys use the *chance* to win a drawing prize as an inducement to respond. Recipients must complete and return the questionnaire to be eligible for the drawing. There are some important advantages to this kind of inducement: Only *one* prize has to be delivered rather than hundreds or perhaps thousands of inducements for each and every recipient or respondent. When the budget is limited, the total amount available may constitute a substantial prize for the lucky winner, but only a pittance if divided among all the respondents.

Perhaps most important of all, this kind of inducement requires the respondents to identify themselves. They have to provide their name and address so they can be contacted if they win the drawing. So they have an incentive to relinquish their anonymity. But that's a two-edged sword. Knowing the identity of respondents may allow the researcher to redrop a mailing to only those who haven't responded, to avoid getting duplicate responses from the same people. It may also

Novel Inducements to Respond   Example 7–3

WORTHLESS MONEY THAT PAID OFF

A survey of U.S. residents sponsored by a Mexican bank included as an inducement a one-peso coin. One peso has so little value the coins aren't even used in circulation in Mexico. In U.S. monetary value, it was worth only an extremely small fraction of a cent. Yet recipients appreciated the gift and responded well to the survey because this little story of the peso and dollar sign was included. The gift had psychological rather than monetary value.

Your Souvenir Peso . . .

. . . while valued at just a few cents, it is rich in history. On the coin itself is the Mexican national seal, consisting of an eagle eating a rattlesnake while perched on a cactus. On the other side there is a likeness of Jose Maria Morelos y Pavon, a founding father of modern Mexico and hero of the struggle for independence from Spain a century ago.

The word peso comes from a Spanish term for the word piece. The name was given to Spanish coins used throughout her New World colonies during the 16th century. Pesos from Mexico—home of some of the world's greatest gold mines—were particularly valued. The Mexican peso was used as a medium of exchange throughout this hemisphere and in all lands bordering the Pacific Ocean.

The U.S. dollar sign is inherited from the peso. The original abbreviation for peso was PS. During handwritten correspondence to the famous American explorer George Rogers Clark, the finance minister of the Louisiana Territory listed payments in pesos, overlapping the P's and S's to look much like today's $ sign. Today, the peso and dollar share this same sign.

THE THREE-SCENT RESPONSE INDUCEMENT

A survey of spa and hot tub owners included, as inducement to respond, three "spa kisses"—small, pillow-shaped, plastic packets containing pink, yellow, and green scented oil to give the spa a pleasant aroma. The company that sold the product provided them free of charge, together with a promotional flyer. Although it required tremendous persuasion before postal authorities would accept the plastic liquid packs for shipment, recipients were delighted with the inducement and the response rate was superb.

LET ME BUY YOU A CUP OF COFFEE

One national mail survey arrived with a cover letter that began with the words, "Let us buy you a hot cup of coffee . . ." and below it a shiny, new half-dollar was attached to the paper. Below the coin, the letter continued, ". . . and perhaps while you're sipping it, you'll take just a few minutes to answer some brief questions." Many respondents did just that.

DISCOVERING A PAGE FROM THE PAST

A large, metropolitan daily paper was conducting a survey of small business owners in the city. The researchers found that the owners' birthdates were on the business license file from which the sample was selected. They also learned that the newspaper had electronic archives of every edition of the paper for the past 87 years. Each survey recipient opened the letter to find a small copy of the front page of the paper—*dated the day he or she was born!*

For Including an Inducement to Respond   Guidelist 7–5

1. Send the inducement with the original mailing rather than promising to send it later if the recipient responds.

2. Don't make the gift contingent on respondents completing and returning their questionnaires.

3. Be sure respondents will see the gift as a token of appreciation rather than meager pay for helping.

4. Avoid any form of inducement that might influence the way people answer questions, introducing a bias.

5. Evaluate potential inducements using the six criteria as flexible standards for judgment, not rigid rules.

6. Don't use money as an inducement unless it's perfectly clear that it will be effective.

be useful to combine the responses to the survey with other data about individuals that's already on file.

There are some serious disadvantages to using drawings or sweepstakes. Some people will absolutely refuse to reveal their identity, especially if the survey topics or issues are controversial or confidential in nature. So asking them to relinquish their anonymity may *decrease* rather than increase the response rate. There's also the chance that those who love to enter drawings and those who don't hold *systematically different* views on the issues or topics of the survey. If so, the inducement will cause *nonresponse bias*. Thus, the researcher should study the possible effects—both good and bad—before making a decision about inducement sweepstakes.

Reports of Results

For surveys of people in their occupational role, offering a report of some of the results of the survey may be a powerful inducement to respond. The respondents are often eager to learn how others in their position or profession will answer the questions—how their own experiences and opinions compare with those of their counterparts elsewhere.

This kind of inducement requires respondents to reveal their identity in order to get the report. If that appears to be a problem, the researcher can provide an entirely separate, preaddressed, postage-paid postcard on which respondents indicate they want the report of results and record their name and address. While many people might enter a drawing for a prize that way, *without completing and returning the questionnaire*, very few will seek the results without participating in the survey themselves. It should also be noted that while this protects respondent anonymity and the negative effects of revealing identity, it also costs more for the separate card and postage.

Guidelines for using an inducement to respond are listed in Guidelist 7–5. When an inducement to respond is to be used with a mail survey, the search for a suitable gift should begin several weeks before the mailing date. There are several specialized companies that deal exclusively with premiums, sales promotional items, and the like. They often carry a very large selection of inexpensive items and they can provide many hundreds or thousands of units. These goods are ordinarily not available in retail stores, but delivery may take a few weeks or more.

Mailing and Receipt

There are still a few tasks and decisions concerning the mailing that remain, even after all components have been prepared and the mailing piece is complete and ready. These factors deserve no less attention than the earlier preparation.

The timing of the mailing will make a significant difference in the response rate in some cases. Obviously, a lower response rate will result from mailing during a holiday period or some other time of year when respondents are likely to receive large quantities of mail or be very busy and pressed for time. Such periods may also induce bias and decrease the validity of the survey. When the survey is addressed to businesses or organizations, a higher response rate can be expected if recipients receive the questionnaire during the middle of the month than if it arrives at the very beginning or end of the month.

Ordinarily, over 95 percent of all returns that will eventually be received will arrive within a period of three or four weeks. Rather than waiting a long time to begin analysis, the researcher should monitor the number of returns received per day and decide on a cutoff date, beyond which returns will be ignored.

Some mailing pieces will be returned to the sender because they can't be delivered to the addressee. The number of nondeliverable pieces should be recorded. The percent of nondeliverable mail is an indicator of the quality of the mailing list. If the list is inferior, that source can be avoided in future surveys.

The raw response rate can be computed by dividing the number of returns by the number of pieces mailed, less the number of nondeliverables. This is the gross response rate, because some of those returned will prove to be incomplete or unusable. The net rate can be computed in the same way, after editing and data transfer, based on only the number of usable responses.

Remailing and Redropping

When the response rate is difficult or impossible to forecast, it may be necessary to follow the initial mailing with another, after computing the initial rate. This is called "remailing" because the same mailing piece is used, although it's sent to different individuals.

There may be some special situations where it would be useful to remind survey recipients to respond. This is called "redropping," and it can be done in two ways: One is to send a postcard or note, identifying the questionnaire sent earlier and urging those who haven't done so to complete and return it. The other is used when it seems likely that many respondents no longer have the questionnaire. If so, they're merely sent a duplicate mailing. This shouldn't be done, however, unless the researcher can identify *duplicate* responses from the *same individuals.*

As the returns are received, the research staff should open and discard the return envelopes, sorting the completed questionnaires and preparing them for data transfer and processing. When doing so, the questionnaires should be sight-edited,

Typical Self-Administered Questionnaires   Example 7–4

- **Application supplements.** Additional questions or sections on applications for credit, membership, or some other privilege, included to gain additional information about applicants.
- **Discount rebate coupons.** Questions about the purchase and buyer included on labels or package inserts offering manufacturer or store rebates to buyers. In effect, the rebate is not only an incentive to purchase, but an inducement to provide information about customers.
- **Order form supplements.** Supplementary questions included on order forms to gain information about buyers beyond that required for billing and delivery of the goods.
- **Patron questionnaires.** Often small questionnaires on card or paper stock asking hotel or restaurant patrons a few questions about their reactions to the service the establishment provided during their visit.
- **Periodical questionnaires.** Questionnaires printed in newspapers, magazines, or other periodicals seeking information from readers or subscribers. Results are often published in subsequent issues.
- **Premium request forms.** Questions included on forms for requesting premiums or to enter drawings or sweepstakes. The survey isn't the main purpose of the offer, but most entrants willingly supply additional information.
- **Statement insert forms.** Ordinarily brief questionnaires included with billing statements or invoices used to obtain additional information about customers or clients. They're often economical and effective because they cost almost nothing extra to send and almost everyone must respond with payment.
- **Warranty cards.** Brief questionnaires included with consumer appliances or equipment, asking the new owners to "register" their purchase. The implication (though false) is that the warranty won't be valid unless the information about the purchase and buyer is provided.

or examined to eliminate those that aren't usable. Additional editing and postcoding may be required, but the initial, cursory sight-edit permits computation of the net response rate and indicates the overall effectiveness of the measurement and quality of response. Additional guidelines for receiving, editing, and postcoding completed questionnaires and preparing the data for analysis are provided in Chapter 9.

Self-Administered Surveys

This discussion has focused on *mail* surveys because that's a very common method of survey data collection. Not all printed, self-administered surveys are delivered by mail. Several other types of self-administered questionnaires are identified in Example 7–4. These questionnaires are often smaller and more brief than mail surveys. Nevertheless, for very long questionnaires, self-administration may be preferable to interviewing because the respondents can complete the instrument when and where it's most convenient for them. Some questionnaires are also partially or entirely self-administered because the information is highly confidential. People may be more willing and open to respond honestly and candidly if they can sit down in complete privacy to record their answers and be absolutely assured of complete anonymity. Yet, if the survey was done by mail, most people would probably discard it. For such cases, the prospective respondents may be contacted and solicited by field-workers who gain the respondents' agreement to participate.

While the dimensions and ancillary materials for printed, self-administered questionnaires that aren't mailed to respondents differ from those for mail surveys, virtually all the same principles of composition and construction still apply. Whether the survey instrument is mailed individually to prospective respondents or delivered in some other way, the self-administered questionnaire is an excellent way to interrogate respondents and obtain information, provided the instrument is expertly and carefully crafted.

Summary

Self-Administered Surveys

A. Use Web surveys judiciously. Not everyone can be reached and not everything can be measured by a Web survey.

B. Give preference to the Web. Nearly everyone who has access to e-mail also has a browser and access to the Web.

C. Compare Web questionnaire types. Both static, flat-form and interactive, multi-page questionnaires have their advantages and shortcomings.

D. Balance appearance with performance. The website should be attractive, but it must also perform quickly and reliably.

E. Use external services when needed. A variety of survey software and services are readily identifiable and available on the Internet.

F. Coordinate mail questionnaires. Make the decisions about any one component in the light of their effects on the others and on the mailing piece as a whole.

G. Make production consistent. Select paper, print, page layout, and assembly that are consistent among the components of the mailing piece.

H. Use external services. Contact namelist sources, the post office, stationers, word processing shops, graphic artists, printers, and mailing houses.

I. Create an effective cover letter. Use the example and be sure that all 12 questions recipients might ask are clearly answered in the letter.

J. Select an effective inducement. Examine many alternatives and evaluate them using the six major criteria for selection.

K. Control timing and follow-up. Select an appropriate mailing date, allow sufficient time for response, and monitor returns as recommended.

8

Collecting Interview Data

Role of the Interviewer

When a self-administered survey will be conducted, the questionnaire is the media through which the researcher holds a "conversation" with respondents. With an interview survey, the questionnaire plays an important role, but it isn't the key element. Instead, the *interviewers* are the communication media between the researcher and the respondent.

Once a questionnaire that's to be self-administered has been finalized and produced, it's an inert and invariable medium. Each printed mail questionnaire is identical to all of the others, so exactly the same message reaches every respondent in exactly the same way. Similarly, each online questionnaire is programmed to respond in exactly the same way to a given input. By contrast, interviewers are neither inert nor invariable—quite the contrary! Thus, the messages that reach respondents through interviews *always* vary to some degree, both from one interviewer to another and from one interview to the next. This creates several major problems for those conducting interview surveys.

The reliability and validity of a study depend, in a large measure, on consistency. The more variation there is among interviewers and interviews, the greater the introduction of random error and systematic bias, and the lower the reliability and validity of the data. Consequently, the researcher must strive for consistency and control of the interview process in order to obtain reliable, valid results.

Mode of Interviewing

When conducting an interview survey, there's a choice between two basic modes of data collection: contract the interviewing to an external data collection agency, or manage an in-house data collection crew. Each has its advantages and disadvantages.

Agency Capabilities and Limitations

Perhaps the most important advantage of using a data collection agency is that these agencies are spread across the country. Every major metropolitan area has several data collection agencies. When an interview survey requires collecting data over a wide geographic area, it may be almost impossible to field a crew of in-house interviewers to conduct personal interviews. Even when the interviews are done by telephone, long distance charges may be prohibitive. When data collection agencies conduct telephone interviews from widely dispersed areas, several calling locations can be used, so each is closer to area respondents and long distance charges are reduced.

When external data collection agencies are used to collect the survey data, the task can often be accomplished more quickly than through an in-house crew of interviewers. This is because the data collection agencies are already "in place" and have trained interviewers on call. When it's essential to collect the data quickly, the data collection agency can often assign more interviewers to the project than would be available for an in-house crew, so the collection process can be done more rapidly.

Some data collection agencies conduct interviews using computer-generated questionnaires. They may use desktop computers at central calling locations for telephone interviews and laptop or notebook computers or personal data assistants (PDAs) for field interviewing. The cost of such technically sophisticated methods make them uneconomical for one-time survey sponsors, but data collection agencies can spread the cost of the training, software, and hardware over many surveys.

Computer-generated questionnaires have many advantages over traditional, paper-and-pencil interview questionnaires and very few disadvantages, aside from their cost and complexity. The principal advantage is in the reduction in the bias and error associated with interviewing. For example, the number and complexity of *branching*—modifying the flow of the questions based on responses to earlier questions—is of no consequence. The branching and flow are preprogrammed and controlled by the computer. Similarly, items in a series can be listed in a different (random) order for each interview, controlling any order bias that might otherwise exist with a fixed questionnaire. In short, the advantages are similar to those of on-line questionnaires compared to mail survey instruments. It may be worth a premium to select a data collection agency that has such capability.

There may be substantial economy in using data collection agencies. It would be costly to recruit, select, and train a large, in-house crew of interviewers to conduct a single project that may take only a few days to complete. In effect, only one project must bear the entire development cost for an in-house crew. By contrast, data collection agencies use their interviewers for many data collection projects. Thus, the recruitment, selection, and training costs for both field-workers and supervisors can be spread over many such projects. To the degree these savings are passed on to the client, there may be significant savings.

The two major disadvantages to using data collection agencies are lack of direct control and uncertain quality assurance. While many data collection agencies are well managed and maintain high standards of service quality, others may not. What's more, it's difficult to distinguish between the more capable and the less capable agencies before contracting the data collection project to them. In fact, it may be difficult to detect poor quality work, even *after* the data have been collected and analyzed.

It's difficult for the data collection agency's client to maintain control of the data collection process, especially from afar. There may be communications problems between data collection agency and research team. Even when instructions and directions are clearly specified by the researchers and thoroughly understood by the data collection agency personnel, there's no guarantee the agency or its interviewers will follow them closely. Thus, contracting with an agency to collect the survey data certainly doesn't offer an easy, automatic solution to the data collection problem. Using a data collection agency *changes* the nature of the decisions, tasks, and responsibilities of the researcher. It may alleviate problems, but it doesn't necessarily eliminate them.

Using In-House Interviewers

When a crew of interviewers are hired and trained by those conducting a research survey, the researcher has greater control over the data collection process. Because the interviewers are recruited, selected, trained, supervised, and compensated by the individual or organization conducting the survey, they're directly responsible to the researcher. Those conducting the research have a wider range of choice, authority, and control over most aspects of the data collection process. There's more direct focus and concentration of effort on the project at hand. Thus, quality control and assurance may be substantially greater.

There are some significant disadvantages to using in-house interviewers that accompany these advantages. With an in-house field crew, the researcher has a much bigger burden of responsibility. It requires more expertise and effort by the researcher to recruit, select, train, supervise, and compensate interviewers. There may also be diseconomies of scale for data collection projects that take only a short time. The entire cost of obtaining and training the interviewers must be borne by a single, short-term project. If the project offers employment for only a few days, it may also be difficult to recruit qualified people as interviewers.

For many interview surveys, there's no single, clear-cut choice as to which mode of data collection would be best. Rather, the researcher must weigh the pros and cons of the two modes. Before making a choice between an independent data collection agency and an in-house interviewer crew, the researcher has to be thoroughly familiar with the responsibilities and tasks associated with each mode. While the more seasoned researchers may have gained considerable insight from experience, those with less experience are well advised to study the process for both modes before making a final choice.

Data Collection Agencies

It may be useful at this point to describe data collection agencies and their operations before looking more closely at the process of data collection by an agency. Data collection agencies are often local firms, though there are also national and even international companies that provide data collection, often along with other research services. Many began as small businesses operated from the home, then

For Locating Data Collection Agencies   Guidelist 8–1

1. Visit the Market Research Association (MRA) website to examine the association's services, membership requirements, codes, and guidelines.

2. Use the MRA's online *Blue Book Research Services Directory* to identify and locate agencies with the services required.

3. Check the MRA chapter listing online to identify agencies or facilities in the area(s) where data are to be collected.

4. Conduct an online search for survey data collection services using search facilities such as Google, Yahoo!, etc.

5. Look for advertisements in trade publications, such as the A.M.A. *Marketing News.*

6. Refer to telephone book Yellow Pages and local business directories.

grew into larger firms. Even the larger, older companies are often entrepreneurships that remain under the direction of the person or family who began the business. Many such companies have gained their knowledge and expertise through experience and some may have little or no formal training in survey research. Their skills may be specialized in data collection rather than in the survey process as a whole.

Data collection agencies typically have a relatively small, permanent staff of supervisors and office workers who are full-time employees. Usually the agency has a large number of interviewers who are temporary, part-time workers who may be supplementing their family income by interviewing. These data collection agencies form a loose network that covers the metropolitan areas of the country. They can easily reach many nearby towns and rural areas as well. There are, however, some remote and sparsely populated areas that are difficult to reach through data collection agencies. Coverage is far from complete. In smaller cities, there may be only one or a very few data collection agencies, while the largest metropolitan areas may have over 100 such firms. Guidelist 8–1 suggests some ways to locate data collection agencies.

A large proportion of these agencies belong to an industry association called the Market Research Association (MRA) [www.mra-net.org]. The association name refers to *"Marketing" Research* only because the majority of their members' clients conduct marketing research or collect marketing data. It is important to note that neither the association nor most of its members confine their activity only to marketing surveys or marketing research. Thus, they are a very important source of data collection services for a wide variety of research sponsors and organizations, including governmental, political, military, law enforcement, medical, social service, arts and science organizations and units.

Membership in the MRA allows the members to work together, and it allows client firms to hire several agencies in order to cover a wide geographic area when conducting a regional or national survey. The MRA's annual *Blue Book Research Services Directory* [www.bluebook.org] is a comprehensive directory of members who provide interview data collection services. Its menu driven search engine will also locate focus group facilities, permanent mall (survey research) locations, and central telephone (interviewing) facilities, based on area and region to be included and the type of service or facility required.

Quality and Ethics

The quality of data collection service varies from one agency to the next, and even from one time to the next for any given agency. For example, if an agency is very busy at the time, it may use interviewers that are less well trained or experienced than those available during slack times. They may also take less time and effort to instruct them on the details of the project at hand. During busy periods they may be more lax about field supervision and verification than they would otherwise be.

Facilities and services offered by data collection agencies also vary greatly. Some are small, with very limited physical facilities. Others may have many locations, including fixed facilities in shopping centers for intercept and central location data collection. Facilities might also include test kitchens and dining areas for food preparation and taste testing, focus group facilities for observation during conferences with respondents, mobile field units, audio and video equipment for both recording and presentation to interviewees, and a host of other facilities. Some may *claim* to be able to provide a wide array of services to potential clients despite whatever limitations they have. Consequently, it's the researcher's job to check very carefully to be sure the claims are, in fact, reasonably accurate.

It's important that the survey researcher or research team and everyone providing data collection or other services understand the ethical principles that apply. The rights and responsibilities of everyone involved in the process are clearly articulated in the MRA's *Code of Data Collection Standards*, contained in Figure 8–1. These sound ethical principles should be followed not only by MRA members, but by all those involved in the survey research process, regardless of their affiliations or the data collection method used.

Agency Data Collection Process

When a data collection agency is used, the process can be divided into six broad phases:

1. Initial contact and cost estimation.
2. Agency selection, notification, and alert.
3. Delivery of materials and acknowledgment of receipt.
4. Training, instruction, and initiation.
5. Monitoring, control, and supervision.
6. Receipt, verification, and payment.

Each of the six phases will be discussed briefly below.

Initial Contact and Cost Estimation

The initial contact with a prospective agency might be by mail or personal visit to the facility, but most often it's done by telephone. The project and sample requirements, the nature and length of the questionnaire, the anticipated initiation date

FIGURE 8–1
MRA Code
of Data
Collection
Standards

RESPONSIBILITIES TO RESPONDENTS

Data Collection Companies . . .

1. will make factually correct statements to secure cooperation and will honor promises to respondents, whether verbal or written;

2. will not use information to identify respondents without the permission of the respondent, except to those who check the data or are involved in processing the data. If such permission is given, it must be recorded by the interviewer at the time the permission is secured;

3. will respect the respondent's right to withdraw or to refuse to cooperate at any stage of the study and not use any procedure or technique to coerce or imply that cooperation is obligatory;

4. will obtain and document respondent consent when it is known that the name and address or identity of the respondent may be passed to a third party for legal or other purposes, such as audio or video recordings;

5. will obtain permission and document consent of a parent, legal guardian, or responsible guardian before interviewing children 12 years old or younger;

6. will give respondents the opportunity to refuse to participate in the research when there is a possibility they may be identifiable even without the use of their name or address (e.g., because of the size of the population being sampled).

Interviewers . . .

1. will treat the respondent with respect and not influence him or her through direct or indirect attempts, including the framing of questions and/or a respondent's opinion or attitudes on any issue;

2. will obtain and document permission from a parent, legal guardian, or responsible guardian before interviewing children 12 years old or younger. Prior to obtaining permission, the interviewer should divulge the subject matter, length of the interview, and other special tasks that will be required.

RESPONSIBILITIES TO CLIENTS

Data Collection Companies . . .

1. will ensure that each study is conducted according to the client's exact specifications;

2. will observe confidentiality with all research techniques or methodologies and with information considered confidential or proprietary. Information will not be revealed that could be used to identify clients or respondents without proper authorization;

3. will ensure that companies, their employees and subcontractors involved in data collection take all reasonable precautions so that more than one survey is not conducted in one interview without explicit permission from the sponsoring company or companies;

4. will report research results accurately and honestly;

5. will not misrepresent themselves as having qualifications, experience, skills, or facilities that they do not possess;

6. will refrain from referring to membership in the Marketing Research Association as proof of competence, since the Association does not certify any person's or organization's competency or skill level.

FIGURE 8–1
MRA Code
of Data
Collection
Standards
(continued)

RESPONSIBILITIES TO DATA COLLECTORS

Clients . . .

1. will be responsible for providing products and services that are safe and fit for their intended use and disclose/label all product contents;
2. will provide verbal or written instructions;
3. will not ask our members who subcontract research to engage in any activity that is not acceptable as defined in this Code or that is prohibited under any applicable federal, state, local laws, regulations and/or ordinances.

RESPONSIBILITIES TO THE GENERAL PUBLIC AND BUSINESS COMMUNITY

Data Collection Companies . . .

1. will not intentionally abuse public confidence in marketing and opinion research;
2. will not represent a nonresearch activity to be marketing and opinion research, such as:
   - questions whose sole objective is to obtain personal information about respondents, whether for legal, political, private, or other purposes,
   - the compilation of lists, registers, or databanks of names and addresses for any nonresearch purposes (e.g., canvassing or fundraising),
   - industrial, commercial, or any other form of espionage,
   - the acquisition of information for use by credit-rating services or similar organizations,
   - sales or promotional approaches to the respondent,
   - the collection of debts;
3. will make interviewers aware of any special conditions that may be applicable to any minor (18 years old or younger).

and expected duration of data collection, and any other relevant details or requirements are described to the agency. They would inquire about any additional information they might need. It might take a day or two, or even longer for the agency to assess availability and compute a cost *estimate* or a fixed price for the job. Contracts or letters of agreement between data collection agencies and their clients are often flexible agreements, since there are many contingencies neither party may be able to anticipate. When the sponsor and the data collection agency have worked together on many projects over a long period of time, agreements tend to be very informal, as one might expect. On the other hand, if it's expected to be a one-time relationship the contractual agreement is usually more formal.

Agency Selection, Notification, and Alert

After obtaining the information on availability, timing, and costs from potential data collection agencies, the researcher can compare and contrast them, eliminating those that aren't acceptable. It's best to obtain references from the agencies, including the names and telephone numbers of current or former clients, rather than merely a client list. Before making the final selection, it's advisable to contact some

---

For Shipping Materials to Agencies   Guidelist 8–2

1. Indicate on the outside of each container:
   a. The project name.
   b. The number of the container.
   c. The number of containers in the lot.
   d. The nature of the contents.
   e. Special instructions for storage.
   f. When the container is to be opened.
   g. How the container is to be opened.

2. Notify agency in advance of:
   a. The project name use.
   b. The number of parcels shipped.
   c. How the materials were sent.
   d. Where they were sent.
   e. When they were shipped.
   f. When they'll be received.

3. Include in each parcel or container:
   a. A detailed packing list of contents.
   b. Complete inventory instructions.
   c. A check-off list for acknowledgment.

4. Instruct the data collection agency not to open packages when they arrive, but wait until instructed to open them.

5. Telephone the data collection agency if the proper acknowledgments aren't received within a day or so of when they're expected.

6. Retain copies of all materials sent, so replacements can be produced if required in an emergency.

---

of the agency's clients to get their recommendations and comments. The agency selected should be notified of the decision when it's final. The researcher should also alert the agency a week or so before sending the materials for a small project, and perhaps a month or more beforehand for a very large project. That allows the agency to obtain the required interviewers, schedule the project, and make any other preparations needed.

Delivery and Acknowledgment

At the time of the agency alert or shortly thereafter, the agency should be sent a *precise* list of what materials will be sent, how they're being shipped, and when they can expect to receive them. A name should be assigned to the project so both the client and the agency can refer to it by name. All materials should be clearly labeled with this name. The project name and description of contents should be listed on the outside of each parcel of materials shipped to the data collection agency, together with instructions on when and how the contents should be handled, stored, and opened. That's necessary because data collection agencies often have many containers of materials from various clients. Materials or supplies for a data collection project can be lost or misplaced, either during shipping or after receipt by the agency. If that happens, the project may be delayed or seriously hampered. Guidelist 8–2 lists the main tasks associated with shipping materials to agencies.

It's usually advisable to instruct the agency to inspect the *outside* of any packages for damage during shipment, and then to acknowledge their receipt intact. If the acknowledgment isn't received shortly after the expected date of receipt, the researcher should call the agency to be sure the materials have arrived in good order. The agency should be instructed *not* to open containers of materials until just prior to the beginning of data collection. If such containers are opened and inventoried in advance, there's a good chance that some of the contents will be misplaced,

For Training Interviewers   Guidelist 8–3

1. Train both supervisors and interviewers if possible.
2. Provide an overview of the project and its purposes.
3. Distribute a copy of all the materials for interviewing.
4. "Walk through" the instrument and other materials, describing each element and its use.
5. Do a "trial run" by conducting a mock interview of one of the supervisors or interviewers.
6. Answer any questions or solve any problems that arise.
7. Question supervisors and interviewers to be sure they understand each aspect of the interview task.
8. Distribute the necessary materials and supplies for the actual field or telephone work.

destroyed, or used for another project. An itemized packing list should be included in each container so that, when it's opened, the contents can be inventoried, checked off on a copy of the list, and the acknowledgment of contents returned to the client.

Training and Initiation

It's often advisable for a member of the research staff to visit the data collection agency and help instruct and train the agency staff when the data collection is to start. This may not be practical if several data collection agencies are used, if the agency is located far from the researchers' project headquarters, or if the data collection task is very simple and straightforward. In such cases, written instructions must be included. When no agency visits are planned, telephone conversations or conference calls among all agencies may be helpful.

When a member of the research staff visits an agency at the start of the project, all materials and supplies for the project should be inspected and inventoried to be sure everything needed is there and in good order. The researcher can then instruct and train either the agency supervisors or both supervisors and field-workers. The researcher should start with a general introduction to the project and its purposes. This is followed by a listing of any special, verbal instructions. The trainees should then be given a copy of the materials that will be used, including the questionnaire, written instructions, rating cards, and the like. (Equipment such as pens and clipboards are ordinarily provided by the interviewers or the agency rather than by the client.) When interviewers are being trained, it's helpful to "walk through" the complete questionnaire first, noting each question, instruction, branch, and recording detail. When the interviewing task is intricate, this can be followed by a "trial run," with the trainer conducting a mock interview of one of the interviewers or staff members. If any questions or problems arise, they're discussed and solved.

When interviewer training is done entirely by data collection agency supervisors, they should be instructed to proceed with the process *exactly* as it has been described here. Data collection agencies may try to abbreviate the training process, usually because they are pressed for time. Guidelines for training interviewers are contained in Guidelist 8–3.

Monitoring and Control

It's always advisable to monitor the process during the actual data collection. Waiting until the data collection project end date when the completed records and materials should have been returned may result in serious, unexpected problems or delays. The data collection agency should be given the name and telephone number of a research staff member and be encouraged to call for information or direction *whenever* a problem or question arises. Typically, researchers who often use data collection agencies find it necessary to take the initiative to telephone the agency daily or a few times a week to be sure the process is going smoothly and the agency is on schedule with the data collection. The researcher should maintain a log of the number and proportion of interviews completed at each point in time.

When personal interviews are to be conducted at a certain place, when only certain respondents are to be selected, or when quota requirements are based on qualifying questions, it's usually necessary to monitor the respondent selection process, along with the degree of completion. These special selection options and specifications are discussed in more detail later in this chapter. It should be noted, however, that data collection agencies are much less likely to cut corners or deviate from the selection instructions if they clearly understand they'll be monitored and *won't be paid* if they don't adhere to instructions.

When interviewees are selected from a specific list of respondents, provided by the researcher, it may also be advisable to "salt" the list with auditors. These may be members of the research staff or sponsoring organization, or others solicited to secretly play the role of regular respondents. Interviewers who telephone or visit such auditors think they're naive respondents. Thus, they're likely to conduct the interview and record the responses as they would others. Any cheating, skipping, false recording, or other anomaly will quickly be revealed.

Receipt, Verification, and Payment

When the completed survey instruments are received from the data collection agency, they should be sight-edited for completion and proper recording. Any questionnaires that aren't usable should be separated, and the reason for their removal should be noted. They shouldn't be discarded until later, because it may be necessary to refer to them when renegotiating final payment with the agency. The complete, usable questionnaires should then be numbered, counted, and prepared for final editing, postcoding, and data entry.

A sample of some proportion of the completed questionnaires should be used for verification of response. A questionnaire may appear complete, accurate, and quite satisfactory, but it may prove to be invalid on verification. The interviewer may have merely filled out the form him- or herself rather than actually conducting an interview. This is sometimes called "arm-chairing" in the industry, and the term is an apt metaphor. Other, less blatant forms of cheating or misconduct on the part of the interviewers or agency include skipping parts of the interview, cutting it short or terminating the interview early, or completing sections to which the interviewee refused to respond. The interview may also have been conducted at the wrong time or place, or with the wrong respondents, or those unqualified to respond may have been included. Incidents of blatant cheating are much more rare than are honest mistakes or errors from carelessness. Nevertheless, the effect of

For Hiring In-House Interviewers   Guidelist 8–4

1. Recruit from among those of the same sex, age group, and socioeconomic status as most respondents.

2. Recruit a much larger number of applicants than will actually be needed, to provide sufficient choice.

3. Request applicants to visit the office, complete an application, and be interviewed.

4. Check former employment and references very carefully.

5. Seek indications of personal responsibility, honesty, and integrity above all else.

6. Expect those who are relatively outgoing and gregarious to be most effective at the interviewing task.

7. Give preference to those with interviewing experience only if they're flexible and have been well trained.

either source of trouble is to introduce substantial bias and jeopardize the validity of results.

Verification requires the identification of respondents by first name and telephone number. A sample is then called and asked a few brief questions to reveal any of the forms of cheating described above. When such discrepancies are discovered, the individual questionnaire, all those from that interviewer, or all of them from the agency may be disqualified. Of course, the agency isn't paid for such inadequacy.

An itemized statement, in considerable detail, should always be required of the agency. When the invoice for payment is received, the amount may be greater than the original estimate. Each item can be examined closely for accuracy, each cost compared to the estimate, and each deviation noted. It's the agency's responsibility to justify the exceptions or cost overruns. Renegotiation of the final amount is fairly common. To save time and effort, such discussions should always be held, from the very beginning, with an officer of the agency who has the authority to make and approve billing adjustments.

Interviewer Management Functions

An in-house interviewing crew is the alternative to using a data collection agency. A relatively small data collection project may require only one interviewer. Ordinarily, several interviewers will be needed, unless the data collection process can be extended over a long time. The data collection and interviewing often make it necessary to hire temporary, part-time employees as interviewers. Even the organizations that continuously do interviewing usually use part-time rather than full-time interviewers. Thus, it's often necessary to *recruit* applicants for the interviewing, *select* those that meet the requirements, *train* them to do the job, *supervise* their work, and *compensate* them on the basis of their productivity or time, plus any expenses they incur in their work. Guidelines for hiring interviewers are listed in Guidelist 8–4.

Interviewer Recruitment

In most communities, there are two basic "pools" of temporary, part-time employment prospects: students and homemakers. Their composition obviously differs markedly by both age and sex, and these characteristics also affect the type and degree of interviewer bias that's likely to be introduced. The decision to recruit applicants from the student or homemaker populations, or both, should be governed in part by the "match" between the age and sex of interviewers and prospective respondents.

Ideally, a much larger number of applicants should be recruited than the project will actually require. This permits the selection of only the most qualified, and it provides a list of qualified applicants from which to hire any replacements or additional interviewers if needed. Usually only an advertisement or so in the "help wanted" section of the classified ads in the newspapers will produce enough applications. The advertisement can be brief, but it should indicate temporary, part-time employees are being sought. It should state the qualifications to be met and indicate when, where, and how the prospects should apply. It saves time to have prospects apply in person, to fill out an application, and to interview them immediately when they first apply.

Selection of Interviewers

The interviewers should be selected from the group of applicants based in part on the correspondence between their demographic characteristics and those of the intended respondents. In other words, it's usually advisable to use interviewers of the same sex, age range, and socioeconomic status as those of the majority of people they'll be interviewing.

Aside from correspondence with respondent characteristics, the principal consideration when selecting interviewers is their reliability. Their effectiveness depends on two factors: the degree to which they're *able* to follow instructions and adhere to directions and the degree to which they're *willing* to do so. In other words, both *skill* and *motivation* are prime factors, and both are absolutely necessary.

A great deal of attention should be paid to the way prospects fill out the application form. It's best if they do it immediately when they come in to apply. That's because an employment application is a *questionnaire,* and if they have difficulty completing it or if it's difficult to read or understand, they'll almost certainly have problems when they're in the field or on the phone with a respondent. Those who do a poor job with the application form shouldn't be considered further.

The task of interviewing respondents consists almost entirely of communication. Thus, capable interviewers are those who can both interrogate people effectively and also listen carefully to responses, perceive and interpret them correctly, and record them accurately. While it's usually desirable for interviewers to be gregarious, extroverted, or outgoing personalities who welcome and enjoy contact with others, they should not be too animated. If they're extremely verbose and talkative, they won't be able to pause, listen, and perceive the respondents' answers and comments accurately. In other words, they may not give the interviewee much opportunity to respond completely and thoroughly, nor grasp the more subtle verbal or nonverbal cues that constitute a part of the response.

Typically, interviewers are paid only minimum wage or slightly more than minimum, plus their direct expenses. The job is usually temporary and only part-time, so the pay doesn't represent a substantial proportion of their total income. Thus, strictly monetary considerations aren't at all sufficient to prevent them from cheating, cutting corners, or taking the route of least resistance, at the expense of the validity of the data. That depends mostly on the interviewers' own sense of honesty and integrity. Yet they may misbehave badly if they're paid so little they feel they're being exploited.

Interviewers almost always come to believe the risk of getting caught if they cheat is extremely small. In fact, it's difficult to detect cheating. So the temptation can be very strong. The honesty and personal ethics of the interviewers are the strongest and most potent inhibitions to cheating. That means only those applicants who show every indication of complete honesty and diligence should be hired. Checking with previous employers about their experience with the applicant, including the applicant's record of absenteeism, is certainly recommended. It's also advisable to get personal references and to ask about affiliations, community involvement, and other indicators of personal and social responsibility. It's far better to hire an interviewer who is completely honest and trustworthy, even though he or she may not be highly skilled or experienced, than to choose a highly skilled, experienced person of uncertain character.

Whether or not it's advisable to select experienced versus inexperienced interviewers is an open question. There are both pros and cons to using experienced interviewers. Obviously, if the researcher has used the interviewers for previous projects and they performed well, they should be hired again. On the other hand, experienced interviewers who worked for some other researcher or data collection agency in the past may not have been well trained, and they may have acquired many bad habits or practices that will be difficult to correct. Inexperienced interviewers require more training, but sometimes it's often easier to "begin from scratch" than to dispel inaccurate or inappropriate beliefs and habits. Experienced applicants must be evaluated just as thoroughly as the inexperienced, and perhaps even more so.

Interviewer Training

The interviewers who are working more or less continuously for a data collection agency receive some initial training when they begin and get additional training in the field through actual experience with many surveys. Thus, they ordinarily need only to be introduced to the project at hand and to become familiar with the particular questionnaire and materials being used. Interviewers who are hired by the researcher must be trained in both the general nature of interviewing and the particulars of the task for the project at hand.

There are two broad classes of information new recruits must have to be effective interviewers: the "how" and the "why." First, they must know *how* to (1) locate, (2) identify, (3) contact, (4) greet, (5) qualify, (6) interrogate, (7) record, and (8) terminate. Second, they must know *why* it's important to follow the instructions and procedures for interviewing. Most interviewer training programs are much more effective at conveying *how* to do it than *why* it must be done that way. Yet, it's essential to teach new interviewers both things, because there are usually many ways to do each of the eight interviewer tasks listed above. Often the way the interviewers are instructed to do each of the tasks is more difficult for them than other ways they, themselves, could find for doing the job. The reasons for doing each task in the prescribed manner won't be obvious to new interviewers. So, the reasons for the procedures have to be stated and the consequences of deviating from them should be made clear to the interviewers.

When the new interviewers have received their instruction and training on survey interviewing procedures in general, they can be given additional instruction in using the particular questionnaire for the survey they're to conduct. The same procedure should be used at this point as that described earlier for training interviewers from a data collection agency.

Supervising the Interviews

There are two aspects to interview supervision: monitoring the process and checking the results. The interview process can be monitored and supervised overtly or covertly. For example, supervisors should accompany personal interviewers during their first few trials and periodically throughout the process, to be sure they get off to a good start with the project and stay on track. It's also necessary to return to the field to be sure interviewers haven't become lax, picked up bad habits, or devised improper shortcuts.

When the interviewing is done by telephone, the first few calls should be done in the presence of a supervisor who might help or direct the placement of the calls and listen to the conversations on an extension beside the interviewer. Interviewing can also be monitored covertly, although that may not be necessary if the interviewers are both well trained and well motivated and there are no signs of cheating or other misconduct. If there's any possibility covert monitoring might be used during a project, it's absolutely necessary to inform the interviewers in advance this might be done.

Covert monitoring is helpful because interviewers are likely to behave differently when they know they're being monitored. This difference isn't necessarily intentional or deliberate. Covert monitoring of interviews can be accomplished by including accomplices unknown to the interviewers on the list or at the location where interviews take place. They can then report on how the interview was conducted. With telephone interviewing, a supervisor can listen to the interview without either the interviewers' or respondent's knowledge. If a recording is made of the call, respondents have to be told at the beginning of the call the conversation *may* be recorded for quality control.

While some deviations or discrepancies from required procedure or good practice can be detected only by observing the process of interviewing, others may be revealed in the results. Thus, effective supervision also requires checking the results as early and as often as possible. Daily checking is advisable in most cases if it's feasible to do it that often. Interviewers may be required to report to a supervisor at the end of the day and submit their finished work. The completed questionnaires are then counted and recorded in the day-log of finished work. That way, there's a "running record" of progress, and the researcher can tell if the interviewing is on schedule or if additional interviewers will be required. It's also desirable for the

For Supervising Interviewers   Guidelist 8–5

1. Monitor the process and also check the finished results.
2. Have a supervisor present during the first few interviews by each person to get them off to a good start.
3. Supervisors should return to the field or the phone room periodically to detect problems that might creep in.
4. Use covert monitoring only when necessary and always tell interviewers in advance it might be used.
5. Require completed work to be submitted in person to the supervisor daily when it's feasible to do so.
6. Finished work should be checked for completion, then counted and recorded in the day-log at the time it's submitted.
7. Check the day-log of finished work against the schedule to determine if more interviewers will he required.
8. Have supervisors sight-edit the questionnaires submitted while the interviewer is still present.
9. Provide coaching and make changes on work submitted while the case is fresh in the interviewer's mind.
10. Treat errors or problems in a matter-of-fact manner and never blame, deride, or insult the interviewers.
11. Compliment and praise the interviewers lavishly to enhance their confidence and motivation.

supervisor to sight-edit the questionnaires while the interviewer is present to be sure they're complete and the data appear to have been recorded correctly. This permits the supervisor to check with the interviewer about any unusual cases and to make any necessary corrections while the interview is still fresh in the interviewer's memory.

There's a very strong tendency for supervision to focus on any aspect of the interviewing that's wrongly or poorly done. This is a drastic mistake. Concentrating on the negative rather than the positive only discourages and demotivates those being supervised. Supervisors should express praise lavishly and compliment interviewers sincerely and often for what they do correctly. It's only necessary to identify errors and show how they can be corrected. Interviewing can be difficult, but confident, well-motivated interviewers always do superior work. Guidelist 8–5 provides recommendations for supervising interviewers.

Compensating the Interviewers

Interviewers are ordinarily paid either by interview or by hour. Each way has its pros and cons. Whichever method is chosen, interviewers must also be compensated for any direct expenses they incur. Paying interviewers a set amount for each interview they complete has several advantages. One of the main ones is the fact that those who are most productive receive the most pay. The interviewers who work very quickly, who are more effective in getting the cooperation of respondents, or who work longer hours will receive more for their efforts, and all the others are encouraged to do so. That benefits both the interviewers and the researcher. At the same time, this formula also discourages sloppy work, because the interviewers are

---

For Compensating Interviewers   **Guidelist 8–6**

1. Interviewers should be paid for their direct expenses, such as travel and other such costs.
2. Interviewers might be paid either by hour or per interview completed.
3. Payment per interview requires the task to be roughly equal per interview or among interviewers.
4. Payment per interview may encourage cheating, hurrying respondents, or avoiding people who should be included.
5. Payment per interview is more equitable if circumstances permit and it makes cost estimation more accurate.
6. An hourly wage requires more supervision because such workers may be prone to waste time.
7. Hourly wages are usually more equitable when different interviewers work at different times or places.

---

paid only for questionnaires that are complete and usable. This method of payment permits the researcher to compute the cost of the data collection quite precisely, based on the number of responses that are required. Also, the interviewers know exactly what they must accomplish to earn a certain amount and they can easily compute how much they have earned at any given point during data collection.

There are also some notable disadvantages to paying a set amount per interview to field or telephone workers. Doing so may encourage cheating. It may also cause the interviewers to hurry respondents or record responses too hastily. They may avoid qualified respondents who should be included, shying away from them because they appear to be too risky or too slow. When interviewers are to be paid per interview, the researcher must accurately assess the length and difficulty of the task in advance, in order to arrive at an amount that's equitable to both the interviewers and the sponsor. There may be some cases when the interviewing task differs from one interview or interviewer to another. For example, quota requirements may differ, or some respondents may have to complete several sections of the questionnaire that others don't. Paying interviewers a set amount per interview would be appropriate only when the interviewing task is roughly equivalent or when any differences would almost certainly average out.

The advantages of paying interviewers per hour are the same as the disadvantages of paying per interview. Paying an hourly rate is appropriate when interviewers might otherwise be tempted to avoid certain types of respondents that ought to be included or to cut corners to make it easier to get interviews. This method of compensation is also recommended when the task differs appreciably from one interview or interviewer to the next, such as when field-workers are stationed at different locations or telephone workers are assigned different calling times.

When interviewers receive an hourly wage it's more difficult for the researcher to arrive at an accurate cost estimate. Paying an hourly wage will also require more rigorous supervision because interviewers will be more prone to be idle on the job, to chat with one another, take long lunch and coffee breaks, and generally waste time. Recommendations for compensating interviewers are summarized in Guidelist 8–6.

For Controlling Interviewer Error	**Guidelist 8–7**

1. Monitor the interview process to detect instruction, interrogation, and response option error.
2. List both the scale card numbers and the words on the questionnaire to avoid scale interpretation error.

3. Use structured questions and avoid recording verbatim answers to control recording error.
4. Don't require interviewers to select response options based on verbatim answers to avoid interpretation error.

Interviewing Error

Random error reduces the reliability of the survey data, while systematic bias diminishes the validity of the results. These concepts were described and discussed in Chapter 3. Error and the bias that might arise as the result of interviewing and the methods of controlling them are major concerns. Guidelist 8–7 lists the principal methods for controlling interviewer error.

Instruction Error

If interviewers don't present the instructions in precisely the way they're listed on the questionnaire, the deviations will introduce error. Deviating from the written instructions is very common. After reading them a few dozen times, the interviewers may automatically memorize them. Interviewers are likely to repeat the instructions from memory without reading them directly. After doing so several times, without reference to the written instructions, they're likely to repeat them differently. After many such small changes in wording, the memorized instructions may be entirely different from the written form.

Interrogation Error

If questions are expressed differently from one respondent to the next, this will cause error. Even when asking for strictly factual information, people respond differently to different wording. For example, asking "What's your age?" will result in an older age, on the average, than asking, "How old are you?" Merely using the word "old" tends to cause some people to report a younger age. Interviewers don't realize how much even subtle differences in the wording affect respondents' answers.

Response Option Error

Interviewers may be instructed either to read or not to read the response options to the respondents. If interviewers read the alternative answers to respondents when they shouldn't do so, or fail to read them when they should, this will introduce error into the results.

Scale Interpretation Error

When scale cards are used, errors may result. Suppose a Likert scale card listed the option "Strongly agree" as number one, "Agree" as number two, and so on. Some respondents may reply with the numbers and others with the words. If both the numbers and the options aren't listed together on the questionnaire, errors are likely. In this example, some interviewers might record the number five for a response of "Strongly agree," rather than number one, as they should.

Recording Error

The more the interviewers are required to write, the greater the recording errors will be. The likelihood of error is higher when verbatim responses are recorded than when interviewers just jot down a number or letter. Interviewers tend to abbreviate verbal responses, often by necessity. The average respondent speaks at a rate of 120 to 150 words a minute. Thus, even a 10-second response may require the interviewer to write a 20- to 25-word, verbatim answer.

Interpretation Error

When interviewers are asked to interpret responses during the interview, errors are very likely. For example, interviewers may be instructed not to read the response options listed on the questionnaire to respondents. Instead, they may be asked to listen to the answers, then choose an option and circle it. Rarely will respondents use exactly the same words as those listed as response options. So the interviewers have to make judgments about the meaning of the response, and then record them. Such judgments are very prone to error when they're made in the field or while on the telephone.

Controlling Interviewer Error

The interview process must be monitored carefully, both at the beginning and periodically during the data collection process, to detect errors by interviewers. The supervisor should follow the conversation while reading a copy of the questionnaire. Any differences between the questionnaire and the interviewers' presentations of instructions, questions, or response options should be noted carefully. Simple observation of the interviewers at work in the field or at the telephone may also reveal whether they're reading the material precisely, or just speaking from memory. To reduce response option errors, a note in parentheses on the questionnaire should indicate if the options are or aren't supposed to be read to respondents, unless it's very obvious. If scale cards are used, the numbers and words should also be listed on the questionnaire just as they appear on the scale card, to reduce errors in scale interpretation.

Merely monitoring the interviewing won't detect recording error. The supervisor must monitor the conversation and also record some of the answers, and then compare the record with that recorded on the actual questionnaire by the interviewer. The objective is to *prevent* such errors in advance by composing questions and constructing a questionnaire to make recording quick, simple, and easy. It's usually not advisable to ask unstructured questions, where options aren't read to respondents, and then require the interviewers to interpret the answers and check an option. If such items are unavoidable, the interviewers should be trained and instructed very thoroughly on the criteria for choosing the response option. They should also be monitored carefully at the beginning and throughout the data collection to be sure they interpret answers consistently and correctly.

Interviewing Bias

The sources of interviewing *error,* discussed in the preceding section, affect survey results randomly. The effect of those sources of error is just as likely to "push" the results in one direction as another. Random error reduces the reliability of the data, and it also reduces the validity of the data indirectly, by reducing the reliability. There are also several sources of *systematic bias* associated with interviewing. Bias reduces the validity of the data directly, by consistently "pushing" the results in one specific direction. Because of this, bias is the more serious problem.

When the validity of the survey results is reduced by bias, it's very difficult to detect after the fact. There's a danger the researcher and sponsor will base decisions on the data, assuming it's quite valid when, in fact, it isn't. Consequently, it's essential to control interviewing bias as much as possible, before and during data collection. In other words, it's always advisable to exert more effort on the *prevention* of interviewing bias than on trying to detect it or correct it after the data have been collected.

Amplification of Response Bias

Twelve major sources of bias are identified in Chapter 4, Figure 4–1 on page 102. These sources apply both to self-administered questionnaires and to interviewing. However, the very presence of interviewers is likely to create or increase additional response bias. With a self-administered questionnaire, respondents feel greater anonymity. When they're interacting with an interviewer by telephone, and especially in person, any tendencies toward response bias are likely to be amplified rather than reduced. Thus, it's vital to guard against such response bias with even more effort when interviews are used to collect the data.

Creation of Response Bias

Aside from the effect of the mere presence of an interviewer, the telephone or field-workers' *performance* can create or increase response bias. For example, if the verbal or nonverbal actions of an interviewer are seen as intimidating by the respondents, this would create *threat* bias. If the interviewers were rude or overly pushy, *hostility* bias could be expected to affect the answers to questions, and so forth. To the degree interviewers are well trained, well motivated, and closely monitored, they're less likely to become a source of response bias in and of themselves. When training and monitoring interviewers, the trainer or supervisor should be especially aware of each source of response bias and must look for signs that the interviewers' actions are creating or amplifying one or more types of bias.

The Interview Questionnaire

Most of the principles for composing the survey questions and constructing the questionnaire apply equally, whether the questionnaire is self-administered or the data are collected by telephone or personal interviewing. Nonetheless, there are some elements of the questionnaire and the other survey materials that differ, depending on whether the questionnaire is self-administered or administered by an interviewer. The principles and elements that apply only to questionnaires

For Composing Interview Greetings — Guidelist 8–8

1. Keep the greeting as short and simple as possible, rather than including a lot of information about the survey.

2. Ask a question very quickly, to engage the respondents' attention and get them started right away.

3. Never ask the potential respondents if they have the time to answer questions or for permission to ask questions.

4. Ask questions to determine if respondents are qualified to respond if that can't be determined in advance.

5. Remember, anyone has the right to refuse, but the vast majority are friendly and cooperative and won't decline.

6. Be confident that once respondents begin the response task, they'll only rarely stop before completion.

administered by interviewers but not to those that are self-administered deserve special attention here.

The Interview Greeting

The most effective interview greeting is very short. Guidelines for composing interview greetings are listed in Guidelist 8–8. Four typical greetings are shown in Example 8–1. The two in the top section ask a question to determine if the individual is "qualified" to respond. A greeting with qualification questions would be used when only certain types of people are interviewed and they can't be identified in advance. The two greetings in the bottom section of the example don't ask

The Interview Survey Greeting — Example 8–1

With Qualification

1. Good morning [afternoon—evening]. My name is _____ [first name only] and we are conducting a brief survey of registered voters here in the county. Are you registered to vote? [If YES, continue. If NO, ask for others and continue or terminate if none available.]

2. Good morning [afternoon—evening]. My name is _____ [first name only] and I'm with Expert Research Company. I have a few quick survey questions for those who own certain kinds of automobiles. Is your car an American make or an import? [If at least one American, continue. If foreign or none, terminate.]

Without Qualification

3. Good morning [afternoon—evening]. My name is _____ [first name only] and I'm calling for Field Research, Inc. I'd like to ask you some quick survey questions about your favorite candidate for mayor. [Ask first question immediately.]

4. Good morning [afternoon—evening]. My name is _____ [first name only]. I have some survey questions to ask about your preferences and opinions concerning supermarkets. [Ask first question immediately.]

qualifying questions. They merely introduce the survey and move quickly and directly to the actual survey questions. Such greetings as these would be used when those who qualify to respond can be identified in advance.

Those with little or no survey research experience may be tempted to compose a greeting that's much longer and contains more information. Avoid that temptation. The general rule is to keep the greeting and introduction by interviewers as short as possible. The objective here is to get the respondent to begin answering questions immediately. As long as the person's mind is engaged in answering the survey questions, the respondents' thoughts won't turn to consideration of whether or not they should participate.

There's a cardinal rule about interview greetings: *Never, ever ask permission!* Beginning with such questions as, "Do you have a few minutes to answer some questions?" or "Will you take a little while to participate in this survey?" provides potential respondents with an open invitation to decline. The refusal rate will be much, much greater than it would be when using a more correct and effective greeting—one that doesn't ask for permission. Remember, the sooner respondents start answering, the better.

Qualification Criteria

The sample frame for an interview survey identifies the population from which the sample is selected. In some cases, the survey research staff may be able to select individual names and addresses or telephone numbers from the sample frame, according to the sampling design, prior to data collection. In such cases, the namelists provided to the interviewers would constitute the sample. It would, of course, be necessary to include a substantially larger number of names than the actual sample size needed because the interviewers may not be able to contact or obtain responses from all of those listed. When all individuals identified on such a sample list are qualified to respond, the interviewers need not "qualify" respondents with preliminary questions. In that case, a greeting such as those in the lower portion of Example 8–1 would be used.

For most interview surveys, it's impractical or impossible to select individual names and addresses or telephone numbers in advance. Consequently, interviewers are provided with a set of general directions concerning who and when to call on the telephone or when and where to go to conduct personal interviews. They're then instructed to interview only those who are qualified to respond and to ignore those who aren't qualified. To do so, they must be given a set of criteria by which to judge whether or not those they contact are qualified.

In some cases, qualification criteria for selecting respondents may be based on factors the interviewers can judge just by seeing or hearing potential respondents. For example, if only women were qualified, there wouldn't be a need to ask potential respondents any questions to ascertain their qualification. Simply seeing them or hearing their voice on the telephone would be sufficient to determine if they should be interviewed (although it may be necessary to ask their age to be sure they're adults). In many cases, however, it will be necessary for interviewers to greet potential respondents and ask them one or more preliminary, qualifying questions. In that case, a greeting such as those listed in the upper portion of

The Quota Specification Sheet   Example 8–2

Independent Quotas

	Variable	Groups	Number
1.	Marital	Married Not married	120 120
2.	Sex	Men Women	120 120
3.	Age	20–34 35–49 50–99	80 80 80

Interdependent Quotas

	Marital	Sex	Age	Number
1.	Married	Men	20–34	20
2.	Married	Men	35–49	20
3.	Married	Men	50–99	20
4.	Married	Women	20–34	20
5.	Married	Women	35–49	20
6.	Married	Women	50–99	20
7.	Not married	Men	20–34	20
8.	Not married	Men	35–49	20
9.	Not married	Men	50–99	20
10.	Not married	Women	20–34	20
11.	Not married	Women	35–49	20
12.	Not married	Women	50–99	20

Example 8–1 would be used. When the qualification of respondents must be judged by interviewers before they're actually interviewed, it's important to provide clear, concise criteria concerning who should and shouldn't be included. When qualification is based on such factors as sex, age, or employment status, there's very little ambiguity about who qualifies to respond. When the criteria are based on less concrete or quantifiable factors, such as occupation, mode of dress, or respondent experience or history, the interviewers must be given a clear set of rules for determining who are qualified and who aren't.

In order for the respondent qualification process to yield reliable, valid results, two requirements must be met: consistency and accuracy. The actual selection of respondents will be consistent if precisely the same individuals are included or excluded, from one time to the next and from one interviewer to the next. The selection process will be accurate if: (1) *all* those who are, in fact, qualified are included and (2) *only* those who are qualified are included. Thus, the consistency and accuracy of the selection process depends heavily on providing interviewers with clear-cut, unambiguous criteria.

Quota Specification

When a quota sampling design is used, quota specification is a special case of stating qualification criteria. Without a quota, each interviewer uses the same qualification criteria for every respondent interviewed. When a quota sample is required, the qualification criteria differ from one interviewer to the next or from one potential respondent to the next. Aside from this difference, the same principles concerning the specification of qualification criteria apply to quota specification. There are, however, some other factors that must be considered when a quota is used. An example of a typical quota may clarify the discussion.

Suppose an interview survey sampling design specified a quota based on the age, sex, and marital status of respondents, with a total sample size of 240. The quotas for all interviewers might be specified in two different ways, as shown in Example 8–2. Each variable might be considered independently of the others, as in the upper section of the example. If so, it will be somewhat easier for interviewers to fulfill the quota, but there's a "catch" to specifying the quota in this way. Because the three variables are considered independently of one another, it would be permissible for interviewers to fulfill this quota with all married men and all unmarried women, providing there were 80 from each age group. This is, of course, an extreme case, but if the quota variables are treated independently, interviewers aren't likely to provide closely proportional numbers of one category for each category of the other variables. Quota sampling is usually used to be sure the sample *proportionally* represents the various groups in the population. Thus, if the quota is based on more than one variable, the quota variables are ordinarily treated as *inter*dependent, and the quotas would be specified as they are in the lower section of Example 8–2.

The quota specifications shown in the example above are for the total sample or all interviewers. If more than one interviewer is required, it's also necessary to specify individual quotas for each interviewer. Suppose four interviewers were required to collect the data for the quotas listed in Example 8–2, and they're treated as interdependent quotas, as shown in the lower section of the example. There are two basic ways the quotas for individual interviewers might be specified:

The first method is to assign each one an equal portion of each quota. In the lower portion of Example 8–2, each of the four interviewers would be assigned a quota of five interviews for each from each group. This method can be somewhat inefficient because one interviewer may have fulfilled the quota for one stratum while another is striving to find respondents with those qualifications.

Another method of specifying individual interviewer quotas would be to assign the first three categories in Example 8–2 to the first interviewer, the next three to the second, and so forth. This technique is temptingly simple, but usually not acceptable. The reason for avoiding it is complex but compelling. No matter how well-trained and motivated the interviewers are, they're likely to introduce *some* systematic bias. In other words, some of the differences in the answers will be attributable to the individual interviewers, themselves. Chances are, when the data are analyzed, the groups resulting from the quotas will be compared with one another. Suppose all married men are interviewed by one interviewer, all married women by another, and the analysis showed significant differences in the answers between these two groups. Such differences might be attributed to either the sex of the respondents or to differences between the interviewers, or both. In other words, the analyst would not be able to tell if the sex of the respondent affected the answers or not. In technical terms, this is called a "confound" between individual interviewers and different groups. Thus, the other method of individual quota specification is superior.

Interview Questionnaire Format

The appearance and cosmetic aspects of a self-administered mail or online questionnaire are extremely important because they affect both response quality and response rate. Ordinarily, interview questionnaires are read and handled only by the interviewers, and so they need not be especially attractive to the eye. On the other hand, they have to be constructed in a format that makes them easy to use. If the interviewer must take time to study the questionnaire or hunt for the next item while conducting the interview, this may jeopardize the success of the interview. Thus, the interview questionnaire writer has to anticipate and appreciate the conditions under which the interviewing will be done. Any format or device that will assist the telephone or field-workers to conduct the interview quickly and smoothly, with a minimum of hesitation or delay, should be used when writing the questionnaire.

The Personal Interviewing Process

There are several aspects of personal interviewing that don't apply to telephone interviews, and vice versa. Those things of particular concern when personal interviewing is used to collect the data are discussed in this section, and those related to telephone interviewing are considered in the following section.

Timing

The time of day and day of the week when the interviews are conducted are likely to affect both the response and refusal rate and the nature of the answers to the questions. For example, it's advisable to conduct in-home interviews between the hours of nine o'clock in the morning and nine at night. It may also be advisable to avoid mealtimes when possible. When interviews are conducted during daytime hours on weekdays, homemakers and those who are retired are likely to be over-represented, while those employed outside the home will be represented in smaller proportions than in the population as a whole. Thus, it's often desirable to conduct a substantial proportion of the interviews during evenings and weekends. Field-workers must be instructed and monitored carefully to be sure they conduct

FIGURE 8–2
Common
Personal
Interview
Locations

1. **In-Home**
   The interviews are conducted at the residence of the respondents. They may be inside the home, at the door, or outside, on the property.
2. **Job Site**
   The interviews are conducted at the shop or office of the respondents. This location is ordinarily used only when the employer is the survey sponsor.
3. **Traffic Intercepts**
   One or more areas of pedestrian traffic are identified for field-workers. They then intercept all qualified respondents as they move through the area. Shopper intercepts are the most common. (It's ordinarily necessary to obtain permission to interview at proprietary locations, such as within a store or mall, or at a shopping center.)
4. **Mall Intercepts**
   These are similar to traffic intercepts, except the data collection agency may have an interviewing facility permanently located within the mall. Interviews may be conducted outside or inside the facility.
5. **Stationary Concentrations**
   Those attending or waiting at meetings, sports or entertainment events, and the like may be interviewed where they have congregated.

the interviews at the times specified. They ordinarily have a strong tendency to work when it's convenient for them rather than for the respondents or as directed by the supervisor.

The Interview Location

The locations at which the interviews are conducted must be carefully specified by the researcher, and the field-workers must be monitored to be sure they adhere to the location requirements. The interviewers aren't likely to realize that the location of the interview will affect the responses. In Figure 8–2, the most frequently used locations are identified and described. When the interviews require more than a few minutes and are conducted at the home of respondents, it's advisable for the field-workers to seek permission to enter the home and perhaps to sit at a table with the respondent. Most people will extend that courtesy, and doing so will facilitate accurate interrogation and recording.

Even when certain areas appear to be "public," in the sense that anyone is welcome to enter, they may, in fact, be proprietary to some company or organization. For example, most shopping malls, stadiums, and the like won't permit interviewing without prior written permission. If it has not been obtained in advance from someone authorized to approve it, the field-workers may be detected and ejected from the site. When such permission has been obtained, each interviewer should be given a copy of the written authorization, so no misunderstandings or delays result if they're accosted by authorities at the location.

Distractions and Interruptions

Field-workers should be instructed about how to handle the most common types of distractions or interruptions that are likely to occur during the interviews. For example, they should be told whether or not the interviewing may be done if one or more other people are present during the interview, so they could listen to the questions and answers (and/or contribute to the response). The directions given to field-workers should also indicate whether the interview should be continued if it's interrupted, and if so, how long an interval is acceptable. Ordinarily, interruptions of more than a few minutes require termination and rejection of the incomplete response. Whether respondents can or should refer to other people or to records or other materials in order to respond to the questions should be clearly indicated.

Rating Cards and Visual Aids

When personal interview surveys make use of rating cards or other visual or physical materials to be examined by respondents, the field-worker instructions clearly indicate how they're to be handled. For example, interviewers must know if they may hand the item to the respondent or merely show them the material, and they must also be told when such visual aids are to be withdrawn or removed. The appearance of such visual materials is very important, because they're viewed by respondents and their perceptions may affect the response. Thus, ordinarily the same such items are used again and again with each interview. It's vital to provide two or more "sets" of such material, because some are almost certain to be lost, destroyed, or defaced. It's also advisable to include a very prominent instruction at the end of the questionnaire to remind field-workers to reclaim any such visual materials from the respondent before leaving. They need the reminder because they're very likely to forget such things, fail to retrieve them, and then be unable to continue with the interviewing.

Recording Observations and Responses

When field-workers must record data they observe, they must be given firm criteria by which to classify or categorize the observational data. The same requirements for consistency and accuracy apply to these observations as to the qualification criteria noted earlier. When recording responses from the interviewees, it's advisable to compose the questionnaire in such a way that items need only be checked or circled or a number recorded, whenever possible. When unstructured or open-ended questions are included, field-workers should be instructed on what to record, such as whether they should record the complete, verbatim response word for word or only key words and phrases. Usually, field-workers must also record the time and location of the interview and provide an indication to identify themselves as the interviewer. The instructions for recording such data should be listed clearly and prominently at the end of the questionnaire.

The Telephone Interview Process

Telephone interviewing can be done either from a central location, such as the research headquarters, or from the interviewers' homes. It's always advisable to require interviewing from a central location when doing so doesn't add significantly to toll charges or data collection costs.

Calling Location

A central calling location greatly facilitates the supervision and monitoring of the data collection. When the telephone workers do call from their own homes or other locations, they must be selected and trained very carefully, and their work supervised as closely as possible. One of the main advantages of a central calling location is the fact that supervisors can watch and listen into calls to be sure the interviewers interview at the right times and in the prescribed manner.

The central calling facilities of data collection agencies usually provide the most efficient and effective setting for telephone interviewing. Interviewers are typically seated comfortably at desks or tables in partially enclosed cubicles lined with sound-absorbing material. They usually use headsets so both hands are free to handle the questionnaire and record the responses. With facilities such as these, one supervisor can easily monitor, assist, and supervise many interviewers simultaneously.

The best-equipped and most sophisticated data collection agencies may offer computer-equipped calling facilities. These systems may permit the researcher or supervisor to input the text of the questionnaire and the branching instructions, so individual questions are displayed to the interviewer in the prescribed sequence. The list of numbers to be called may also be entered in advance, so the numbers are dialed by the computer rather than manually. Usually the responses are keyed directly to a data file rather than recorded with paper and pencil. Such systems make the interviewers work much faster, easier, and more accurately. They also enhance the ability to monitor and control the entire telephone interviewing process for the project.

The Namelist or Directory

Telephone interviewing is often done directly from a telephone directory. Ordinarily, telephone workers are provided with directions concerning which names and numbers to select. Such instructions must be very clearly written and provided to each interviewer for reference when a question arises. It's never sufficient merely to require interviewers to call every nth number. Rather, they must be instructed concerning where to start in the volume, where to begin the count on the page and column, and so on. They must also be told how to handle listings that are clearly not qualified, such as business listings when only residential listings are to be included.

Timing

With telephone interviewing, just as with personal interviewing, the time of day and days of the week during which calls are placed will affect the type of respondents that are interviewed. It's especially important to supervise and monitor the timing of calls because telephone workers are much more likely to deviate from the prescribed timing than are field-workers conducting personal interviews. Respondents who are called after nine in the evening or before nine in the morning may agree to respond, but if the task is an unwelcome interruption or intrusion, this would certainly affect their answers to the questions.

FIGURE 8–3
Telephone
Collection
Results and
Options

Possible Call Results

1. Call answered by a qualified respondent.
2. Call answered by an unqualified person.
3. Number proves to be wrong location or subscriber.
4. Call isn't answered after 6 to 10 rings.
5. Busy signal is received for the number called.
6. Call answered by an answering service or device.
7. Call answered by a fax or computer modem.
8. Number has been changed and new number is listed.
9. Number not in service and no new number is listed.

Telephone Interviewer Options

1. Interview respondent and place next call.
2. Ask if a qualified respondent is present.
3. Terminate and place call to next number.
4. Terminate and call back in a few minutes.

The duration of the interview constitutes another important timing factor. Field-workers conducting personal interviews are ordinarily able to hold the attention and interest of respondents for substantially longer periods than are telephone interviewers. There's ordinarily little or no resistance or premature termination when telephone interviews are less than five minutes, and telephone workers experienced at building and maintaining rapport with the respondents may conduct interviews of 10 minutes or so in duration with few refusals or terminations. Telephone interviews of more than 15 minutes are likely to result in a very substantial number of refusals or premature terminations by the respondents.

Call Results and Options

The telephone workers must be provided with directions stating how to respond to the various outcomes that might result when a number from the list has been called. The eight possible outcomes and the four common options open to the interviewer are identified in Figure 8–3. Based on the sampling design and requirements, the researcher must compose instructions that indicate which of the four options should be pursued in case of each of the possible call results. Telephone workers should also be instructed to record the telephone number of the respondent, the date, time of the call, and their own identity. These instructions should be clearly listed at the end of the questionnaire.

Summary

Interview Data Collection Procedures

A. Understand the interviewer's role. The telephone or field-workers should be perceived as part of the measurement instrument, with the potential to create error and bias.

B. Consider the data collection agency. Study the agency data collection process and check on agency cost and availability and quality carefully.

C. Appreciate the interviewer management task. Study the interviewer management functions and weigh the advantages and disadvantages of an in-house crew.

D. Choose the mode of interviewing. Evaluate the capabilities and limitations of data collection agencies, compared to an in-house interviewing crew.

E. Reduce potential interviewing error. Consider instruction, interrogation, response, scaling, recording, and interpretation as possible sources of error.

F. Control interviewing and response bias. Check each element of the questionnaire and process for each of the major sources of bias.

G. Handle instrumentation carefully. Compose the greeting, qualification and quota criteria, interviewer instructions, and questionnaire format to avoid error and bias.

H. Identify the unique aspects of each process. Recognize the distinctions between personal and telephone interviewing, making required adjustments for the mode selected.

Chapter

9

Processing the Data

Receipt of Questionnaires

Data processing should be thoroughly planned at a much earlier stage in the survey process, but the work actually begins with the receipt of the first completed questionnaires from the field. The final preparation and testing of the computer programs to be used for data analysis can be done while the survey is still in the field and the data are being collected. With mail surveys and with interviewing done by a data collection agency or a separate interviewer team, the researcher will often have a few weeks during data collection when there's little else to do with the survey except prepare the processing system. This extra time gives the data analyst an opportunity to get a head start on the processing phase. By completing a few blank questionnaires with fictitious data, the research analyst can begin constructing files, preparing the analysis programs, and specifying the tasks that will be needed for data analysis.

Data Receipt

It's usually necessary to monitor the collection of the data very carefully. With interview surveys, reports may be obtained from the field on a *daily* basis, or at least two or three times per week, from *each* interviewer or agency working on the survey. That way, adjustments can be made and extra effort exerted when it's required to avoid delays or procrastination by the field-workers and supervisors. Mail survey returns should be collected daily or with each delivery. Any nondeliverable pieces should be checked to determine why they couldn't be delivered to the intended recipient. That way the researcher can assess the quality of the mailing list and its source. When there are many nondeliverable pieces marked with a notation such as "no such address," that indicates the list is inaccurate. If many of the questionnaires couldn't be delivered because many of the addressees have moved and there's no forwarding address, that usually shows the list is "dated." The namelist was probably from many months or years earlier and wasn't kept current. This information is useful to assess the namelist quality. It's also valuable to judge the potential quality and accuracy of the survey results and the degree to which the sample validly represents the population as a whole.

Mail questionnaire returns should be opened immediately, and the date the questionnaire was received should be recorded on the back, at the end of the questionnaire. Similarly, interview questionnaires coming in from the field should be checked to be sure the interviewer has recorded the date of the interview, and perhaps also to record when it was received in the office. It may be necessary later to compare results from the earlier data collection period with that from the later period. With mail data collection, this comparison indicates differences between those who were most motivated and willing to complete the task and those who delayed it for some time. When the data are collected by interviewers, the comparison can show what effect interviewer inexperience versus experience may have had on the answers obtained.

Online survey data and that collected with computer-generated questionnaires are typically edited "on the fly," so to speak, and recorded in a data file. Ordinarily the software can be programmed to record the date and time and the device or location that received the data. The early returns from such survey systems should be checked to insure that the data are being accumulated properly. Any adjustments required should be made immediately. After that, it's usually only necessary to check the volume of data collected from time to time for a web survey. When telephone or field interviewers use computer-generated questionnaires, the data should be transferred from their individual devices or workstations to a central file and examined to be sure it's being collected properly. Backup copies of all data files from desktop computers and especially from laptop or notebook computers and PDAs absolutely must be made regularly and often. The smaller and the more portable the device, the more susceptible it is to loss or damage.

During this period when the completed returns are received, it's always wise to keep a complete record of how many surveys were sent into the field, how many are still out at any given point, and how many have been completed and returned. This running record of data collection allows the researcher to anticipate the "cutoff" point, when collection can be terminated and additional responses ignored. It also shows whether the data collection process is on schedule and going according to plan. If there are serious delays, it may be necessary to take some action, such as assigning additional interviewers, extending the data collection schedule, or changing the procedure for contacting potential respondents and soliciting their participation. If such changes do become necessary, it's important to maintain a record of which responses were received through the original procedure and which were collected after the modification.

Handling Completed Questionnaires

The completed paper questionnaires are the documents from which computer files of survey data will be created. This period, during receipt of data, is usually the first time the researcher will actually experience the volume of data and documents created by the survey. With surveys of very limited scope there will be few surprises and little confusion. Larger survey projects are likely to produce more documentation than inexperienced researchers anticipate or for which they're prepared. The physical volume can be considerable. It's absolutely necessary to devise a system for handling the completed questionnaires and then stick by it throughout the receipt period.

The first step is to open mail returns or materials received from interviewers and record the date of receipt. After that, the extra materials that are returned, such as copies of the cover letter, envelopes, rating cards, interviewer instructions, and the like, can be discarded or filed for later use on another project. It may also be necessary to record the location of some mail survey respondents on the questionnaire by checking the postmark on the return envelope before it's separated from the completed questionnaire it contains.

Experienced researchers find it very useful to record consecutive numbers at the end of the questionnaires as they're received. Later this number can be recorded in the data file, together with the data, so the researcher can refer to a particular completed questionnaire at any time to make corrections in the data file, if necessary. These case identification numbers can be handwritten, applied with a consecutive number stamp, or printed on labels that can then be attached to the document. It's important always to note the *last* number used for each session, to avoid duplication.

When more than one person will be sight-editing documents and transferring data to computer files, a systematic record of who has which documents will be needed. That's especially necessary when those working on the completed questionnaires will be taking them away from the survey office or headquarters to some other place. These completed questionnaires are valuable and they aren't replaceable. Those working on them are much more likely to handle them with care and avoid misplacing or losing them if they have to "check them out" before taking them. They'll know they're being held accountable for the documents they have. Another advantage of such records is that they show which individuals performed the various tasks required. If problems or mistakes are discovered later, they can be attributed to those responsible. If necessary, the individuals who worked on the documents and files can be questioned for clarification, and all the documents or cases they processed can be checked for similar discrepancies or problems. The degree of control that's achieved by recording who has each completed questionnaire at any given time is well worth the little extra time and effort required to keep such records. Guidelines for initiating data processing are listed in Guidelist 9–1.

Sight-Editing Printed Documents

Once the completed questionnaires have been received, recorded, and sorted, the actual processing begins with a sight-edit of each document. Each one should be examined to see if it's acceptable for processing and to make any corrections or notations required. The initial sight-edit of early interview questionnaire returns also indicates whether the interviewers were instructed properly. Additional instruction or supervision can then be arranged if it's needed.

Judging Completeness

Some questionnaires returned from the field, especially from mail data collection, will be obviously incomplete. Some may contain a comment or note of explanation

For Initiating Data Processing   Guidelist 9–1

1. Plan and obtain data processing facilities, files, records, and programs while the survey is in the field.

2. When a large number of questionnaires are involved, prepare the physical setting so there's a separate place to shelve each group or set.

3. Monitor collection and receipt of data carefully, obtaining daily reports of completion and receipt.

4. Record nondeliverable mail surveys by reason for failure to gauge the quality of the namelist and representativeness of the sample.

5. Record the date of collection and/or receipt on the end of the completed questionnaires, so early and later returns can be compared during analysis.

6. Maintain a record of the number of surveys sent into the field, the number remaining, and the number returned.

7. Record a unique, consecutive identification number on each completed questionnaire returned from the field.

8. Keep a record of who has which completed questionnaires, by number, when others are to sight-edit and postcode documents and transfer data to files.

9. Be sure those who assist or perform the processing tasks know they'll be held accountable for both the loss of any documents and the quality of their work.

by the recipient or interviewer. If so, a brief record of them should be kept as an indication of the reasons for failure to complete the instrument. These incomplete documents can then be eliminated from the pile of forms to be processed. (Save several blank questionnaires, if none were retained earlier, to use as scratch working forms during coding and processing.)

Each document that appears at a glance to be completed must be checked thoroughly. The editor should examine each page and section of the questionnaire to be sure the interviewer or respondent followed instructions and recorded answers in the proper place. The researcher should establish fixed criteria concerning how much of the questionnaire must be completed to make the case acceptable. This is especially important when others will be assisting with the sight-editing. The editors probably won't be able to make judgments on their own, so they should be given guidelines concerning what to accept and what to eliminate. Have editors form three groups of documents: (1) the "yes" pile, those that are obviously acceptable; (2) the "no" pile, those that are obviously rejects; and (3) the "maybe" pile, those that are questionable. The editors should attach a note to every document in the "maybe" group, clearly indicating where in the questionnaire the problem is and why they think it's questionable. The researcher can then examine the questionable documents and make a more informed decision about them.

There will inevitably be individual items respondents fail to complete. Some missing data can almost always be tolerated. If the questionnaire is substantially complete, with only an occasional missing answer, it's usually usable. On the other hand, if entire sections are incomplete or the respondent has completed only the beginning and then terminated prematurely, the case should be rejected.

Multiple Questionnaire Forms

Occasionally, one survey will require different forms of the questionnaire for different respondent groups. For example, some interviews may be conducted in person, and others, to obtain only the most essential data, may be done by telephone. Two forms would then be needed. In such cases, the instruments of each type should be separated into two groups and treated individually in the initial phase of data processing. The more standard the task, the more efficient the editors and data transfer clerks will be. If multiple questionnaire forms are used, the researcher must also establish separate criteria for editing and accepting each form of the instrument.

Editing, Branching, and Exclusions

Some survey questionnaires may require a considerable amount of branching or contain many items with exclusionary conditions. For example, the respondent or interviewer may be instructed to skip an entire section or go to a later point in the questionnaire, based on response to a key item. There may be several items conditioned on the previous questions, such as a question beginning with "If so, . . ." If there are many such explicit or implied branches or exclusions in the instrument, the sight-editing becomes more laborious and demanding. The editors should mark out answers respondents have inserted for items they should have ignored. Inappropriate or superfluous responses shouldn't be keyed to the data file. They might not be detected and eliminated later. The most effective way to edit such questionnaires is to give each editor a "key" questionnaire. Items or sections that should sometimes be excluded should be boldly marked, as shown in Example 9–1. The "criterion" question or item—the one indicating whether the following item or section should be completed—should also be marked clearly on the key, together with an indication of the answers that include or exclude the following item or section. The editor should compare each page of the completed document with this key to be sure there are no inappropriate answers recorded. This is especially important for each editor to do for the first dozen or so questionnaires, until each one is thoroughly familiar with the sections or items that might be excluded and with the criteria for completing or excluding them.

When a respondent failed to complete an item or section of the questionnaire that *should* have been completed but wasn't because of a branching mistake, the editors should use the same criteria to judge acceptability or rejection of the case as they would for other items or sections. On the other hand, when a respondent has *completed* an item or section where they *shouldn't* have, it usually doesn't require rejecting the case. Often those answers can be safely ignored. The remainder of the data is usually acceptable. Guidelist 9–2 summarizes the procedure for sight-editing printed documents.

Postcoding the Data

If the questionnaire was written properly, most questions will be "structured." Almost all responses will fall into predetermined categories or the data will be scale values recorded by the interviewer or respondent. The questionnaire also should

Key Questionnaire Branching Notation   Example 9–1

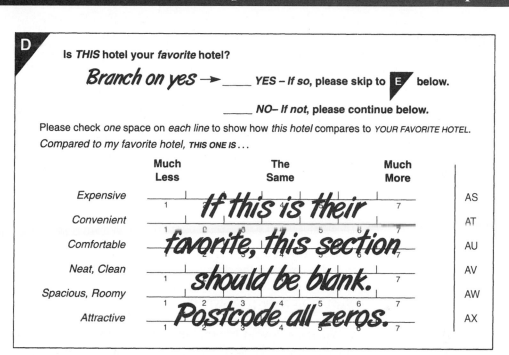

For Sight-Editing Documents   Guidelist 9–2

1. Early returns should be sight-edited promptly to detect data collection problems that might be remedied.
2. The objective of editing is to determine the data and cases to be accepted and those to be rejected.
3. Establish firm criteria for editors concerning the degree of completeness required to accept a case.
4. Instruct editors to set aside questionable documents to be examined by the researcher for an informed judgment.
5. Ordinarily some missing data from a few items can be tolerated and the remaining data will still be of value.

6. Usually cases where entire sections are incomplete or only the first part has been completed must be rejected.
7. When multiple forms of a questionnaire are used, they should be segregated and treated individually.
8. With many branches or exclusions in the questionnaire, editors should he given a key showing their location and the conditions when items shouldn't be answered.
9. When respondents or interviewers have mistakenly recorded answers to questions where they shouldn't have, the superfluous data should be marked out.
10. Inappropriate or superfluous data don't usually require that the case be rejected.

Key Questionnaire Postcoding Notation · · · · · · · · · · Example 9–2

O

Of the *last ten times* you stayed at a hotel,
how many times did you stay at. . . .

This particular hotel? ··································	_____ times	EA
Another hotel in *this* chain? ····················	_____ times	EB
A hotel that's part of *some other national chain?* ·········	_____ times	EC
An indiv~~*Postcode this*~~ ➝	_____ times	ED
Some other kind of hotel? (What kind? _____) ··	_____ times	EE
(Please make the TOTAL = 10)	***Total =*** **10** times	

---

have been precoded with numeric values for each answer printed on the questionnaire. The record format for the data file should be listed at the far right margin. Even if the questionnaire was written that way, substantial *postcoding* of responses will often be necessary. Postcoding consists of assigning code values to all responses that don't already have a precode. For example, an item may list several response categories followed by an "other" category and a note to specify what other response. Obviously, such responses couldn't be anticipated, so they have no individual precoded value associated with them. Consequently, the editors have to postcode such responses before the code values can be transferred to the data file for processing.

The postcoding can either be done simultaneously with the sight-editing or as a separate task. If there isn't much postcoding required and it can be done quickly, it's best to do both the sight-editing and the postcoding at the same time for each document. Doing so won't delay the sight-editing very much and the editors will handle each document only once. When the postcoding is more demanding and time-consuming, it should probably be done as a separate task *after* the sight-editing is finished. Those postcoding the questionnaires can devote all of their attention to this one complex task and it won't delay the sight-editing and recording of documents.

Those postcoding the questionnaires should have a blank, "key" questionnaire similar to that used for the sight-editing. It should highlight the items to be examined and postcoded, as shown in Example 9–2. If the same key is used to sight-edit and postcode the questionnaires, the two types of indications on the key must be *distinct* from one another, such as using different colors. Both must be easy to recognize.

The postcoding editors record two things: New codes for answers that have no precode values are inserted on the questionnaire so they can be keyed to the data file later. In addition and at the same time, the code value, *together with the answers themselves,* must be recorded on the code<u>list</u> for that item within the code<u>book</u> for that survey.

Postcoded Items   **Example 9–3**

O

Of the **last ten times** you stayed at a hotel,
how many times did you stay at. . . .

This particular hotel? ··	*1*	times	EA
Another hotel in *this* chain? ······································	*3*	times	EB
A hotel that's part of *some other national chain?* ············	*5*	times	EC
An individual, *independent* hotel? ······························	*0*	times	ED
Some other kind of hotel? (What kind? __Health spa resort__) ··	*1*	times	EE

(Please make the TOTAL = 10)   **Total =** **10**   times   EF   **3**

Hotel survey codebook, pg. 2
Section O – column 21   What other?

code	label
1	*Cruise ship*
2	*Conference center*
3	*Health spa resort*

Example 9–3 may clarify this process. In the example, respondents were asked how many times they had stayed in some other kind of hotel. They were also asked to write in *what kind* of other hotel. On this particular completed questionnaire, the postcoder noted that someone had recorded the number 1 for "Some other kind of hotel" and written in "Health spa resort," a response category not printed on the original questionnaire and therefore one for which there was no precoded value.

To postcode this item properly, the editor first referred to the codebook for the survey, turning to page two, which had the codelist for this section and item. Noting that two previous items were listed and assigned the code values of 1 and 2, the postcoder recorded the number 3 in the column for codes and wrote in the type of *other* hotel in the "label" column. Then the postcoder recorded a big, bold number 3 in the margin of the original questionnaire, just to the right of the record format column letters EF, where that value will later be keyed.

Later, when the data are transferred to computer file, the data entry clerk will key the value of 1 in column EE to show how many times that respondent had stayed in an "other" hotel. Then the code value of 3 will be entered in column EF to show *what* other kind of hotel. Meanwhile, the analyst preparing the analysis program will label the categories for a variable called "What other hotel" according to the codelist for that item: 1 = *cruise ship*, 2 = *conference center*, 3 = *health spa resort*, and so on.

As the example indicates, there must be a codelist for each item that may require postcoding. The codebook should be set up in advance to contain one or more *separate pages* for each such item, with the item number or questionnaire location clearly indicated at the top of the page. That's because the researcher can't tell how many new codes and answers will result from any one item. There has to be room to enter new ones until all completed questionnaires have been postcoded.

Postcoding is a fairly simple process when only one editor does the coding on any given day or at any one time. It's best to do it that way, either by assigning only one person to the task or by "staggering" the times and/or days when different editors will code the completed questionnaires. If that's not feasible, the editors must all work at the *same place* when they're coding at the same time. If two or more editors are postcoding at the same time and in *different* locations, they won't know what *new* codes the *others* have listed in *their* codebooks. A single code value will inevitably be assigned to two or more *different* answers.

The objective of the coding process is to provide a *unique* code for each acceptable answer. Inexperienced researchers may minimize the importance of this potential problem and ignore the recommendation in order to "save time." Experience clearly indicates it's very dangerous to permit editors to work independently from different codebooks in separate locations. Serious errors and data problems will almost certainly result. Ultimately, it will take a lot more time to put things right than it would to do the postcoding as recommended here.

If several people are to do the postcoding from different locations and share a codebook on a computer network, the system must be programmed so only one person can open the file at a time. When someone opens the codebook file, the system should prompt them to close the file after a brief period if they've left it open. Without that, others won't have access to the file. This may seem like a trivial problem, but it's not! Some people doing the postcoding may become impatient and fail to postcode items that require it, creating error and/or bias.

Criteria for Postcoding

The researcher should specify the criteria for identifying and categorizing answers and assigning codes to them. The editors need guidelines about how "fine-grained" the categories should be and how to group individual answers into categories. For instance, in Example 9–3, if someone indicated "Some other kind of hotel" and listed a *"convention* center," how should that be handled? Should it be assigned a postcode value of 2—the same as a *conference* center—or should it be listed separately and assigned its own code value?

Without specific guidelines and criteria for coding, editors who aren't familiar with the survey process are likely to err in one of two directions: Some will assign a new code to virtually every new alternative, based on the precise, verbatim word or phrase noted on the questionnaire. This will create far too many codes and categories. Probably there will be only one or two cases for each such code. Other editors may simplify their task by "lumping" all responses that are even vaguely similar to one another into the same, large category. That would discard distinctions and data that might be regarded as useful by the researcher. Thus, postcoding editors need specific guidelines. They should also be monitored closely during the initial phase of the work.

When deciding on the level of detail—on how "fine-grained" the new categories should be—it's much better to specify categories that might be too narrow rather than too broad. If too much detail is recorded, this will result in more code values than are really needed. That isn't serious because the data can easily be regrouped into larger categories during processing. By contrast, if the data are grouped into categories that are too broad, there's no way to separate out smaller categories, short of returning to the completed questionnaires, postcoding them again, and transferring the data to file a second time. Once distinctions have been lost by grouping into broad categories before data entry, they can't be regained without reference to the completed questionnaires. Thus, experienced researchers normally prefer that postcoding editors create a new category and code if they're in doubt about its fitting neatly into an existing category.

Maintaining the Codebook

If the data have been collected online or *directly* on a computer-generated questionnaire, either by respondents or by interviewers *during the interview,* the data will already be in computer files. If the questionnaire is such that *every item* is precoded or numeric and there are *no* fields into which verbatim answers are keyed, no postcoding is required and the data can go directly to computer processing and analysis. If, on the other hand, there are some unstructured items with fields into which respondents are permitted or requested to key in their answers, postcoding of these answers will almost certainly be necessary.

Online survey data as well as data that's entered directly during interviewing are usually accumulated with the use of database programs such as Microsoft Access or FileMaker Pro or data entry programs such as SPSS Data Entry Builder or Quinput 2. Survey data files created by such applications can be set up to accept postcoding and labeling within the same data file. While the same general principles regarding postcoding of paper questionnaires apply here as well, the precise procedure depends on the manner in which the database files have been structured and programmed.

When the codebook is a paper document, it's very important to be sure the entries in the codebook are very neatly and legibly made. This point seems trivial until it's time to use the information during the analysis phase. It's far better to avoid a potential catastrophe than to spend hours trying to remedy one. For large surveys, the editors often will be "clerical help" who aren't particularly interested in the survey results or familiar with the process. When there are several people postcoding, each will be making entries on the codelists. So there's likely to be many mistakes. The chance of errors increases markedly if the codelists aren't kept in a neat, orderly

For Postcoding the Questionnaires   Guidelist 9–3

1. Postcoding is almost always required because any answer that doesn't have a code value must be assigned one.

2. New codes should be listed on the questionnaire so they can easily be recognized when transferring data to file.

3. A separate codelist page for the codebook should be created for each questionnaire item that might require postcoding.

4. It's vital that editors record every new code category they create on the codelist so others don't use the same code value for a *different* answer.

5. If more than one editor does postcoding, they must all work from the same codebook, either at different times or simultaneously, at the same place.

6. Simple coding can be done together with sight-editing, but substantial postcoding jobs should be done afterward.

7. Coding editors should have a "key" questionnaire with the items to be postcoded clearly marked.

8. The researcher should provide the guidelines for when and how to create new codes and group answers.

9. It's better for editors to create too many small categories than too few overly broad ones.

10. The codebook must be maintained neatly and clearly and should be recopied if it becomes disorderly.

fashion. For example, editors may make "margin notes" when a sheet is full, rather than labeling and starting a new page. If they do, they or others probably won't notice the last entry. They may assign the *same* code to a *different* response. The necessity for neatness in the codebook is more than cosmetic—far more!

If the codelists become disordered or confusing, it's well worth the time and effort to rewrite them from the originals, creating a more orderly codebook. Note that the entries must not be changed in any way, and the same codes must apply to the same answers and categories. When categories are to be combined, that should be done only after the codes have been transferred to the data file, and not during the coding process.

The most common and detrimental error when coding completed questionnaires and making entries in the codebook is to fail to list a new code and category in the book. If that happens, the same code will be assigned to two different answers. That must be avoided at all cost. By contrast, if editors make the opposite error by failing to notice that a particular response has already been coded and entered on a codelist, they will create a *new* code for the *same* answer. That's not serious because the two can be recoded to a single value during processing. Little, if anything, will be lost. A sketch of the main considerations for postcoding questionnaires is provided in Guidelist 9–3.

Transferring the Data

When all of the completed questionnaires to be included in the data have been sorted, sight-edited, and postcoded, it's time to transfer the data to computer files. If the precoding and postcoding have been done properly, data transfer should consist only of reading the codes for each item and recording them in the file according to the record format printed on the questionnaires.

If the data are keyed to computer files by data entry clerks who are unfamiliar with questionnaire data entry, they must be instructed thoroughly on *precisely* how to enter the data. The research analyst should be present or readily available while the first few cases are being keyed to file, so the operators can ask questions and get additional direction if they need it. Inexperienced researchers often make the mistake of assuming too much expertise on the part of those entering the data. Even though they may specialize in data entry, they're not likely to understand the research process or be familiar with *survey* data entry. They may be very fast and accurate at data entry but know very little about the content of the data itself or its ultimate purpose.

Data Entry Documents

While a variety of different types of computer programs and files might be used to enter survey data, the formats almost all fall into two very broad categories: spreadsheet formats and database program formats. Regardless of the type of document, the objective is the same: The data entry operators must know *exactly* where they are in the record and file at *every* point. In other words, the same item on every questionnaire (or variable for analysis) must be keyed to the same field location in every case in the file. Analysis programs "recognize" a given item only by its location in the data file being read at input.

Spreadsheet Documents

The most common document for data entry is a spreadsheet table or worksheet. While there are many, Microsoft Excel is the most common. Figure 6–5 on page 176 shows a small portion of a spreadsheet containing a few cases of survey data. Each row in the spreadsheet should correspond to a single questionnaire or "case" for analysis. So the data are entered horizontally, and there will be as many rows as there are completed questionnaires. The rows of a blank spreadsheet are numbered by the program and the columns are designated with letters. To a spreadsheet for data entry, the record format printed on the questionnaire should indicate *letters* of the column in which each item is to be entered.

When the spreadsheet document has been initialized, data entry is accomplished merely by entering the code values for each item of the questionnaire while tabbing to the next column. The questionnaire or case number is usually entered in the last column of the spreadsheet, depending on the way the record format is specified on the questionnaires. There is no necessity to enter the questionnaires consecutively or in any particular order, since the data can easily be sorted at any time by those values or by the values keyed to any other column.

It's absolutely critical that the operator refer very often to the column designations to be sure the data are being entered into the correct column. That should be done at many points when entering data for each questionnaire. If the operator were to enter the wrong value for an item, only that one data point would be incorrect. That's an error, but usually not a very serious one. Another type of error results in misaligning the columns on a row or for a case. Thus, the operator may *double-enter* an item, causing all the data for that row to be offset one column to the right. Similarly, the operator may skip a variable on the questionnaire, failing to enter one value and causing all the remaining data on that row or for that case to be offset one column to the left. Either way, the mistake creates *multiple* errors, rather than just an error for a single data point.

To help those entering the data into a spreadsheet or similar format, some researchers include 3- or 4- or even 5-digit section or page numbers on the questionnaire and list a column number for them when listing the record format on the document. When those entering the data get to that point on the questionnaire, they would enter the page number, such as 1111, 2222, 3333, etc. in the appropriate column. That way, both they and anyone else inspecting the file can tell at a glance if the columns are aligned properly merely by looking down the page number columns to be sure they line up correctly. By using several of the same digits for the page numbers, they are obviously distinct from the adjacent data values.

Those entering the data should also be advised to save the file very frequently—perhaps after every case is entered. Data entry can be a tedious, if not laborious, process and any number of disruptions could cause unsaved data to be lost.

Database Documents

Database programs such as Microsoft Access or FileMaker Pro don't create files in a specific, preset format. Instead, these programs are designed to assist the user to structure files according to the characteristics of the data and the analysis or reporting applications to which the data will be submitted. Consequently, the procedure for entering the data depends on how the files were specified and initialized. In their simplest form, data entry may be similar to that for spreadsheets. With larger and more elaborate structures, the data entry tables may appear to be very similar to the actual questionnaire.

One of the principal advantages of database programs, compared to spreadsheets, is the fact that the former can be programmed to edit and screen the data as it's entered. In other words, the variable ranges can be specified so that if those entering the data mistakenly try to enter a value beyond that range of the scale, the program will signal an illegitimate entry. For instance, on a 10-key pad, mistakes such as entering a 7 for a 4 or an 8 for a 5 are common because the keys for the erroneous values are right above the correct ones. With data screening, if an operator incorrectly tried to enter an 8 for an item with a 5-point scale, the program wouldn't accept it.

Another advantage of database document data entry is that they can be programmed to move to the next field after a specific number of digits have been entered. With a spreadsheet, and with no special programming, moving from one column or variable to the next requires pressing the tab key. Since many survey questionnaire scale values are single digits, pressing the tab key each time nearly doubles the number of keystrokes needed. Database programs allow the user to specify the documents so entry of a single digit (or a specific number of digits) automatically moves the entry point to the next field.

Dedicated Data Entry Programs

Programs such as SPSS Data Entry Builder or Quinput 2 are designed especially for data entry, whether the data are from a survey or some other source.

Consequently, they are the most sophisticated and elegant forms of data entry. As with general purpose database programs (of which they are a special category), they permit data screening and manipulation. They make the job of those entering the data as clean and simple as possible, speeding the process and reducing fatigue and other sources of error. They are also designed to articulate very readily with statistical analysis programs that are from the same "family" or software suite.

Program Pros and Cons

Spreadsheet data entry has some advantages as well as shortcomings. Perhaps the main strong point of spreadsheets is the fact that they are ubiquitous. Spreadsheets are *very* common application programs, readily available on almost every computer system or network that's likely to be used for survey data processing. Since they are general purpose programs, performing a variety of tasks, a very large proportion of computer users are familiar with them. Spreadsheet data can easily be transported across systems and platforms and read or imported into analysis programs. So, there is much to be said for using a spreadsheet to enter survey data. This is especially so for relatively small-sample surveys with a limited number of cases, even though there may be a large number of items or variables.

While the advantages of spreadsheets are several, there are also some major disadvantages compared to database programs and data entry programs. Perhaps the most serious shortcoming of spreadsheets is that they don't screen data input without substantial programming. In addition, tabbing from one column or field to the next increases the data entry task appreciably.

Database programs and data entry programs are especially effective for surveys with large samples or for those who frequently conduct surveys. Their facility for screening and manipulating data is highly desirable for data entry projects of substantial size and scope. The main disadvantage is in the amount of expertise and the time and effort required "up front" to program them and format the database they create. Nor are they as readily available or inexpensive as spreadsheets. Thus, they can be regarded as most appropriate for those who are to conduct a very large survey, who do many surveys, or who can use a data entry application for data other than that from survey research.

Computer Data Editing

If the data have been keyed to a spreadsheet file, they must be edited thoroughly to be sure they're acceptable for analysis. This *is far more important* than it might seem. If the data aren't perfectly clean and in the proper condition for analysis, two serious problems can result:

First, the analysis routines may fail to run—that is, to accept the data—and even if they do, they may generate reports with obviously invalid values. Second, and far worse, the programs may run and generate erroneous results that appear to be okay.

Computer data editing should seek to identify and correct two kinds of errors: (1) Records that deviate from their prescribed format—where variables have been keyed to the wrong columns or fields, and (2) variables whose values exceed the acceptable range for the item.

Checking Variable Column Positions

One of the simplest and most effective devices for checking the column positions in a spreadsheet document was described earlier. By listing multi-digit section or page numbers and assigning columns for them, visual inspection of the spreadsheet will quickly reveal misalignments. Examining areas where adjacent columns should contain different numbers of digits will also reveal misalignment of columns. For example, sex—single digit data columns—may be adjacent to age, which are 2-digit entries. Thus, single digit "age" or a 2-digit indication of sex on a row would indicate it was misaligned.

When a spreadsheet contains hundreds of cases or rows, it may be tedious to scroll through the file from top to bottom again and again. It may be more efficient to highlight the entire data set and simply sort on the section or page numbers or other key variables, then check the top and bottom row values.

Checking Deviations from Variable Range

Each variable in the data file has an acceptable range of data. For example, if the item used a six-point scale, the range would be from one to six, and if missing data were tolerable for the item, zero (or perhaps blank) would also be acceptable. Similarly, if only adults were to be accepted as respondents, then no age keyed as a continuous numeric item should be below 18, 21, or whatever age was used to qualify young respondents. Every variable should be checked to be sure the data are within the permissible range.

If the data file is a spreadsheet and there are a limited number of variables, each variable range can be checked by sorting one column at a time and checking the top and bottom rows. As noted earlier, spreadsheets usually require that the columns to be associated with (moved with) the one being sorted must be selected or highlighted. Forget to highlight the entire data set and only the column being sorted or those highlighted will be moved, virtually destroying that version of the data. Such mistakes are another reason for saving multiple copies of the data and saving the work frequently so that damaged data sets can be discarded in favor of an earlier "generation" of the file.

If the extreme values for a variable are out of range, the data for any such case can be checked against the corresponding, completed questionnaire. The data entry operator may have merely entered the wrong value for one variable, but such errors may also result because *several* variables were entered into the *wrong columns*. Thus, it's important either to reenter the entire case or to check the values of the *other* variables for the case against the questionnaire.

While sorting spreadsheet columns may be an acceptable way to check the ranges of a limited number of variables, it would be far too time-consuming if there are a large number of survey items. Instead, the data should be submitted to a preliminary analysis merely to edit the data. Running frequency distributions for *all* the variables in the survey (including the section and/or page numbers) will generate a large output, but it's quick and easy and the results can be checked on screen, rather than printed.

SPSS was used to create the data editing table shown in Figure 9–1. The *Frequencies* task was run on three variables, all of which consisted of 5-point scales.

FIGURE 9–1
Data Editing
Table

Code	Var01	Var02	Var03
1	303	285	96
2	208	192	126
3	315	279	301
4	154	178	301
5	77	125	236
6	0	1	0
7	2	0	0
9	1	0	0
Total	1060	1060	1060

Of the 1,060 cases in the sample, Var01 had 2 cases with a value of 7 and 1 case with a value of 9. Var02 had 1 case out of range, with a value of 6, while none were out of range for Var03. If there were many more variables to be checked than just these 3, the SPSS statistical analysis program allows the user to list the table with the values across the top and the variables down the side. That makes it easier to list and inspect dozens or even hundreds of variables with a limited variable range.

The disadvantage to this process is the fact that when invalid values are found, there's no indication of the case numbers from which they were derived. The researcher may have to sort the cases in the spreadsheet of the analysis program database to locate the errant values. A quicker easier method when the data are in a spreadsheet would be to select (highlight) the column for that variable and search for the erroneous value, then shift to the case number on the right side of the row to identify the proper questionnaire. Complete guidelines for editing data by computer are outlined in Guidelist 9–4.

Data Processing

The data processing and statistical analysis are far less burdensome than in even the recent past. Analysis systems are increasingly user-friendly, freeing research analysts to turn their attention and effort to the content and meaning of the information. The discussion that follows assumes only a basic understanding of computers and doesn't assume a sophisticated understanding of statistics.

Statistical analysis software often makes it relatively easy to process data, even for those with little experience or training. That's a big benefit, but there's a danger in it, too. The analysis routines can't protect research analysts from *themselves!* The programs only recognize data, but don't know where the numbers came from or what they stand for. So if the analyst chooses the wrong statistical tool, the program will probably run but the results are likely to be entirely bogus. This is a real problem because it may be difficult for the analyst, and especially for those seeking the information, to recognize that the results are incorrect and misleading. Thus, it's the analyst's responsibility to learn exactly what kind of data each statistical tool requires and what conditions must be met to use the tool legitimately. The remainder of this chapter and all of Chapter 10 are devoted to providing that understanding.

For Computer Editing of Spreadsheet Data   Guidelist 9–4

1. Computer editing of spreadsheet data is required to be certain the data analysis won't produce erroneous results—especially errors which aren't apparent in the reports.

2. The editing should seek out two types of errors: deviations from record format, and deviations from the acceptable range of variables.

3. Record format deviations often result from one or more pieces of data being skipped over or keyed twice.

4. Editing should examine the columns containing section or page numbers or adjacent columns with data that has different numbers of digits (e.g., 3-digit next to 1-digit variables).

5. Format errors are more serious than field range errors because they may cause all the following variables on the record for the case to be incorrect.

6. Establish the "permissible range" of data for each item on the questionnaire, to establish acceptable variable range.

7. Each variable in each record of each case should then be checked to be sure it's within legitimate range.

8. The variable range of data in spreadsheets can be checked by sorting each column in turn (together with all the others) and checking the extreme values at the top and bottom of the table after each sort.

9. The variable range of data can be checked by running preliminary editing analyses producing frequency tables, then checking maximum and minimum values.

10. When errors are detected during process editing, refer to the completed questionnaire by case number to make the required corrections in the data file.

Purpose of Data Processing

Surveys generate a very large volume of "raw" data, but these are of little or no use to those who seek survey information. It would be extremely impractical for researchers to examine each such datum for each item on each completed questionnaire. Even if they did, it would be virtually impossible to glean any meaning from them as a whole. Thus, the difference between *data* and *information* is that data are meaningless on inspection, while those who examine information can understand it and obtain meaning from it. The primary purpose of data processing is to *summarize* the data into information. The objective of data processing and analysis is to *suppress* the detail and reveal the important and meaningful patterns and relationships contained in the data.

Scale and Data Types

The various statistical tools and procedures described in the following chapter require the data to meet certain conditions or be in a particular form. The type of scale and data dictate, in part, which statistical techniques are appropriate and which are inappropriate. Thus, before actually beginning the statistical analysis, the analyst must be able to identify the scale and data types for *each* questionnaire item. Then the analyst will be able to pick the appropriate statistical tools and avoid using the wrong methods.

FIGURE 9–2
Scale Data
Type Diagram

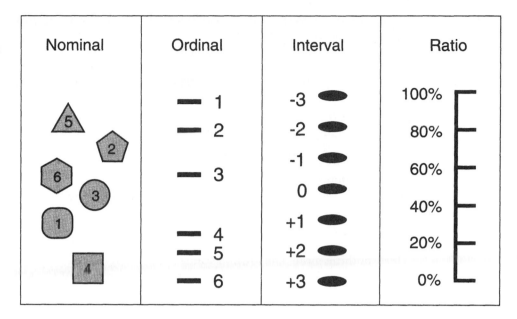

Four different types of scales are identified below and diagrammed in Figure 9–2: *nominal, ordinal, interval,* and *ratio.* Novice analysts are encouraged to study the description of the scale types, identify each item on the questionnaire as one of the four scale types, and note it on the *key* questionnaire beside each item or in each section of similar items. This key can then be used to identify the scale and data type for any given item when selecting statistical tools, without the necessity to reassess each item several times.

Nominal Scale Data

Computers handle numbers more readily than letters or words, so the different verbal meaning of answers to a survey questionnaire are typically assigned a numeric code value, even if it doesn't actually designate a quantitative of any kind. For example, respondents might check the word "male" or "female" to indicate their sex. Male may then be assigned the numeric code of 1 and female the value of 2 when the survey instrument is coded. In this case, the numbers don't designate a quantity. They're only *names* for the categories "male" and "female." Data values that don't stand for any quantity are called *nominal* data. The numbers are only the *names* of categories.

Other examples of nominal data might be the ZIP code of respondents or a person's telephone number or social security number. The assignment of the numbers is completely arbitrary, so long as every category is assigned a *unique* number. For convenience, the response category of questionnaire items are usually numbered in consecutive sequence, but they need not necessarily be so. No mathematical or arithmetic operations—addition, subtraction, multiplication, or division—can be legitimately applied to nominal data. For instance, it would make no more sense to calculate the average response to a multiple-choice question than it would to compute the average *ZIP code* for the sample.

Notice that in Figure 9–2 the *nominal* scale values are attached to different shaped objects and they don't appear in any orderly sequence—they aren't arrayed on a spectrum or dimension. The numbers only identify categories—in this case, shapes. Most analysis programs allow the analyst to attach verbal "labels" to each code to make the categories more easily identifiable on the reports. So, in the example, 3 might be labeled *circle*, 5 labeled *triangle*, and so forth.

Ordinal Scale Data

If respondents *ranked* several brands of a product, these rankings could constitute an *ordinal* scale. Similarly, if they were asked to indicate the order in which they did a series of tasks, that question would produce ordinal data. Ordinal values show the *sequence* or *order* in which things occur within the range of the scale. On a 5-point ordinal scale, a value of 4 indicates 3 things come before and 1 comes after—nothing more. The ordinal scale shown in Figure 9–2 shows 1 on top, 6 on the bottom, and the other values in order between them, but the spaces are *unequal*. Ordinal scales do *not* have equal intervals between the integers or scale points.

An ordinal scale is somewhat more powerful—it provides more information, in a sense—than a nominal scale. The numeric values have more meaning. With a nominal scale, the numbers are only names that make one category *distinct* from another, but they don't indicate any *relationship* whatsoever. Ordinal scale values do show relationship in terms of *sequence* or *order*, so the numbers have more meaning than nominal values. On the other hand, the values of ordinal data have less meaning than do those of the two other types of scale data described below.

Ordinal data can't legitimately be used in mathematical *equations.* They can only be manipulated in what are called *systems of inequalities*—systems whose terms consist of "greater than" and "less than." Statistical analysis of ordinal data requires what are termed *nonparametric* statistics, rather than more common and powerful statistical tools. Because of these limitations, survey researchers are well advised to avoid scales yielding ordinal values in favor of those providing *interval* or *ratio* data whenever that's feasible.

Interval Scale Data

A scale with numeric values equidistant from one another is an interval scale. To be precise, interval scales should actually be called *"equal interval"* scales because the interval between each integer on the scale is the same. Interval scales need not include the value of zero. If they do, as in the scale shown in Figure 9–2, the zero value doesn't really indicate the complete absence of whatever is measured—it doesn't represent *nothing*.

A typical example of an interval scale is the Fahrenheit scale of temperature. The interval between one integer value and the next is exactly the same, no matter where the value is on the scale. Yet the zero doesn't represent the *absence* of heat—it's not *absolute* zero (which is, in fact, about $-460°F$).

Because the zero may be absent from an interval scale (or, if it is present, it doesn't stand for the absence of the thing measured), the arithmetic operation of *division* isn't permissible for interval data. For example, if the low temperature last night was 40°F and the high temperature today is 80°F, this doesn't imply that last night was half as warm as today. Such a statement would have no meaning or validity. In short, the ratio of one value to another has no meaning for interval scale data. On the other hand, interval scale values can legitimately be added, subtracted, or multiplied. Interval scales used in survey questionnaires, such as a *linear, numeric scale*, permit the analyst to use all the most common statistical tools. Little is lost by the fact that zero isn't absolute.

The Ratio Scale

There's only one difference between an interval scale and a ratio scale: Zero is absolute on the ratio scale. For example, distance in miles or age in years are ratio scales. In this society, at the instant of birth the infant's age would be zero, and, if an object stays in the same place, it would have traveled zero distance. In both cases, the zero is absolute; it stands for no age or no distance. On the ratio scale shown in Figure 9–2, zero represents *none—no* part of the whole of 100 percent.

Because zero actually means nothing of what's being measured and the distance between any two points on a ratio scale is always equal to that between any other two, ratio scales impose the least amount of restrictions on the mathematics or statistics that can be used to manipulate these values. They're called ratio scales because ratios of one value to another have meaning. For example, if one person travels 20 miles and another travels 40, the first has traveled half as far (1:2 or 1/2) as the second, or the second has traveled twice as far as the first (2:1 or 2/1). Thus, arithmetic operations of division and multiplication are permissible with ratio scale data and the "quotient" or "product" that result from them, respectively, are both meaningful values.

Ratio scale data are least restrictive regarding the types of statistics that can be used. Yet, it's important to note that many things measured on a survey questionnaire don't lend themselves to the use of a ratio scale. Thus, interval scales are much more commonly used. There are ordinarily very few differences between interval and ratio scales, in terms of the ability to manipulate the data with statistical tools, so little if anything is lost by using an interval scale rather than a ratio scale. On the other hand, a substantial amount of information or meaning *is* lost or unmeasured by using an ordinal scale in place of an interval scale. A nominal scale even more strictly limits the use of statistical manipulation. These characteristics of scale data are summarized in Figure 9–3. Checklist 9–1 identifies the principal areas to examine to ascertain the type of data each scale yields.

Recoding the Data

There are some situations where the analyst may want to change the form of the data from that in which it was collected. Statistical analysis programs allow their users to regroup or *recode* the data to a more suitable form. Either the original variable can be altered or a *new* variable based on the same data can be created and modified. Often much of the recoding required is done as part of data preparation rather than waiting until the statistical analysis phase is underway.

FIGURE 9–3
Data Type
Descriptions

Nominal Scale

1. The numeric values are merely the names of categories.
2. The numbers are used only to make categories distinct.
3. The values don't indicate any magnitudes.
4. The values don't indicate any relationships.
5. No arithmetic operations can be used on the numbers.
6. Statistical manipulation is extremely limited.

Ordinal Scale

1. The numeric values show the order or sequence.
2. The values are not a measure of magnitude.
3. The interval between values doesn't indicate magnitude.
4. The values do show relationships by order or sequence.
5. The values can't be used in mathematical equations.
6. Statistical manipulation is somewhat limited.

Interval Scale

1. The numeric values show both order and magnitude.
2. The interval between integer values is equal.
3. A zero value doesn't indicate absolute zero.
4. The values show relationships by order and magnitude.
5. The values can't be used to form ratios.
6. Statistical manipulation isn't very limited.

Ratio Scale

1. The numeric values show both order and magnitude.
2. The interval between integer values is equal.
3. A zero value does indicate absence of the thing measured.
4. The values show relationships by order and magnitude.
5. The values can be used to form ratios.
6. Statistical manipulation isn't limited.

To Identify the Scale Data Type   Checklist 9–1

1. Are the values only names to designate independent categories? If so, and the categories don't represent some order of magnitude, the scale data are *nominal.*

2. Do the values indicate only sequence or order of magnitude? If so, and they don't indicate the actual magnitude or interval between values, the scale data are *ordinal.*

3. Do the values indicate actual magnitudes with equal intervals between the scale points? If so, and zero *doesn't* represent *absolute* zero or complete absence of the thing measured, the scale is *interval.*

4. Do the values indicate actual magnitudes with equal intervals between the scale points? If so, and a value of zero *does* represent *absolute* zero or complete absence of the thing measured, the scale is *ratio.*

Recoding for Fewer Values

Sometimes recoding is done to reduce the number or range of different values in the distribution of response to a survey item. For example, respondents may have been asked to record their age. That kind of question yields continuous ratio data. For a large sample of adults, there would be many different values, perhaps ranging from the late teens to the nineties or older. In this situation, the analyst can present the data in a more meaningful form by *recoding* the many different age values into only a few categories, such as by decades, labeled "teens," "twenties," and so on. Analysis programs ordinarily allow such recoding to be done quickly and easily with only a few statements or menu option selections.

Recoding to Meaningful Categories

In the sample questionnaire shown in Chapter 6, Example 6-1, Section Q (page 148), respondents were asked to record their formal *education* in years. Thus, there might be over 20 different values for this variable. For some information seekers, individual number of years may not be as meaningful as the *categories* associated with completion of certain levels. There's probably far less distinction between those who have 10 years of education and those who have 11 than there is between those with 11 and those with 12 years. The latter pair are distinguished by the fact that some have *graduated* from high school and some have not.

In this example, education was gathered as continuous ratio data simply because it's a better and easier way to *collect* the data. During data preparation, those with 8 years of education or less can be recoded into category *1—Elementary Only;* those with 9, 10, or 11 years into category *2—Some High School;* those with 12 years into category *3—High School Graduate;* and so on. The objective here isn't merely to *reduce* the number of values. Rather, it's to group the data into more *meaningful* categories.

There are three rules to follow when recoding a variable into new categories: (1) The categories must be all-inclusive, so every value must fall into a category. (2) The categories must be mutually exclusive so there's no overlapping. (3) There must be more variation in the thing being measured *between* categories than within them. In the *education* example, not having graduated "joins" some respondents—with 9, 10, or 11 years—and "separates" them from those who have—with 12 years of education.

Recoding and Category N-Sizes

The shorthand term used to designate the number of respondents or cases in a sample, subsample, or category of a variable is n-*size*. In other words, it just means the *number* of respondents or cases. Normally, the *broader* the categories and the fewer the categories into which the data for a variable are recoded, the *larger* their n-size will be.

During the recoding process, the analyst may run some preliminary data description routines, such as frequency or percentage tables, to determine how many respondents are in each category of certain variables. For example, assume a multiple-choice item has some alternatives that were each selected by only a very few respondents. If so, it would be appropriate to group those categories together into an "other" or "miscellaneous" category with a larger n-size.

To Recode Survey Data   **Checklist 9–2**

1. Would different categories be more meaningful for analysis and interpretation than those in which the data were gathered? If so, create new categories by recoding the variable.

2. Is there a need to portray continuous, numeric data with a large number of values in tables or charts? If so, recode the data into a limited number of categories.

3. Are the new categories *all-inclusive* so every original value can be recoded into a new category? If *not,* change the classifications or include a miscellaneous category.

4. Are the new categories *mutually exclusive,* so each original value can be recoded into only *one* new category? If not, change the recoding specification to eliminate the overlap.

5. Is there more variation in the underlying meaning of the variable *between* the new categories than within them? If not, select new categories that have greater distinction in meaning.

6. Do any of the new categories have very large proportions of the cases or respondents within them? If so, divide the large categories into meaningful ones with smaller numbers of cases.

7. Do any of the original or new categories have very small numbers of the cases or respondents within them? If so, combine them with adjacent or similar categories to form larger categories.

Statistical comparisons between variables, such as cross-tabulation (to be discussed in the next chapter), *require* a sufficient number of respondents within each category if they're to yield reliable results. Thus, the statistical tools themselves may demand that some variables be recoded to obtain a sufficient number of respondents in each category. There are other situations where statistical limitations make it necessary to recode continuous, numeric data into categories. That may not be discovered until analysis is under way. Such recoding will be discussed in Chapter 10. The main data recoding considerations are outlined in Checklist 9–2.

Report Labeling

Virtually all spreadsheet and statistical analysis programs allow the user to enter names or labels for the variables and categories to be analyzed. These names or labels are usually limited to a certain number of letters, so it may not be possible to list the entire item from the questionnaire. Instead, the analyst should create brief names or abbreviated labels to stand for each item or variable and each category of nominal data, including those created by recoding. The names and labels should be listed on the key questionnaire. Doing so will avoid mistakes or confusion at later stages of analysis.

Some inexperienced survey research analysts may be inclined to skip the rather tedious, time-consuming job of entering a long list of variable names and category labels into the spreadsheet or analysis program. The longer the list, the greater is the temptation to avoid the task. And the longer the list, the *more important* it is to do it! There's a very compelling reason: These names and labels ordinarily need to be entered only *once* at the data preparation stage. If it isn't done now, it might be necessary to do the naming and labeling *many, many times* on output and reports generated by analysis programs. Even more troubling is the possibility that without labels, the analyst or those reading the reports may mistakenly assume they're studying one variable, item, or question when they are, in fact, looking at another. Such mistakes could be extremely costly.

Summary

Survey Data Preparation

A. Get a head start. Prepare for processing while the questionnaires are still in the field.

B. Expect a large volume of paperwork. Surveys often generate more paper than many researchers anticipate.

C. Keep it neat and orderly. Have a place for everything and keep everything in its place.

D. Maintain adequate records. Record things promptly and make notes, rather than depending on recollection.

E. Sight-edit documents thoroughly. Establish criteria for acceptance or rejection of completed questionnaires and use them consistently.

F. Postcode questionnaires carefully. Every item that isn't precoded must be assigned a code value and be recorded in the codebook.

G. Monitor data transfer. Be sure the data are keyed to files promptly and accurately.

H. Edit the computer data files. Check to be sure the records conform to the format and the variable values are within range.

I. Identify scale and data types. Record the designations on a "key" questionnaire to use as a working guide.

J. Recode data with care. Select categories that are more meaningful and recode continuous items with many values into fewer but larger categories.

K. Enter names and labels. List variable names and category labels on the key questionnaire and enter them into the analysis routines.

Interpreting and Reporting Results

Part 4

10

Describing
Data Distributions

Statistical Data Description

Data analysis requires the use of a set of statistical tools that reduce the amount of detail in the data, summarizing it and making the most important facts and relationships apparent. The researcher need not know a great deal about the internal workings of the statistical tools in order to use them effectively. Nevertheless, the analyst must be able to select the correct statistical tool to generate the information required, based on the type of data. As with any tool, there are two types of things that dictate what statistical tool should be used or would work best: the nature of the data—the "material" to which the tool is applied—and the nature of the report—the "product" that's to be created. In other words, the researcher has to know what tool would work best for a particular type of data and a particular type of report. Ironically, those who learn a great deal about the tools themselves are often still in a quandary about which to use in a given situation. That's because they lack information about the types of data such statistical tools require and the type of information that can be obtained from each of the statistical procedures.

The types of scales and data were discussed in the previous chapter. There are two general categories of statistical tools used to analyze survey data: those used to describe individual survey items, and those used to measure associations or relationships between two variables. There are several statistical tools in each category. This chapter is devoted to those used for data description, while the following chapter discusses the tools used to measure the relationships between pairs of variables. It isn't as important for the research analyst to know how these statistical tools work as it is to know *how to use them correctly!* Since the choice of an appropriate statistical tool depends so heavily on the type of data to be analyzed, this discussion will focus more on the characteristics of the data distributions than on the workings of the statistics themselves.

It's almost never appropriate to use the same statistical tool for every survey item. Some scales are different from others, and they require different tools for their analysis. *Nominal, ordinal, interval,* and *ratio* scales were described in the previous chapter. The analyst has to be completely familiar with these scale types to select the proper statistical tools described in this and the following chapters.

The data from each, individual survey question or item is known as a "variable" because it can vary from one respondent to the next. Some statistical tools, called "univariate" statistics, are used to describe just *one* variable at a time. Others, known as "bivariate" statistics, may include *two* variables and show the relationship *between* them. Still others, called "multivariate" statistics, may include *several* variables and show the *pattern* of relationships among them. This chapter is devoted to the use of univariate statistics.

Category Data Description

Survey questionnaire items or variables form "distributions." The choices or values respondents provide for any item are *distributed* across some spectrum of *values* or response *categories.* Usually, the analyst's first analysis task is to run data descriptions for each variable.

Frequency and Percentage Tables

Frequency and percentage distributions of response, or just *frequency* tables for short, are the most common form of data description for a limited number of values or categories. All nominal scales yield *categorical* data, but numeric data distributions from ordinal, interval, and ratio scales can also be treated as categorical and be described in frequency tables if there are a limited number of different scale values. Frequency tables provide a very complete picture of the distribution of data for the variable. Their use is limited mainly by the number of scale points or categories that can be shown. When there are a dozen or fewer categories or scale points, frequency tables are ordinarily practical and meaningful to researchers.

Example 10–1 shows the frequency and percentage of respondents at five levels of education. The tables in this example are very typical of those generated by statistical analysis programs for analyzing survey data. Starting from the left, the first column of the frequency tables in Example 10–1 shows the labels for the various categories. When only numbers with a limited range are being reported, such as "trips to the bank in the past week" or "number of coffee breaks taken yesterday," no labels may be required and the column would be blank.

The second column of the frequency tables in Example 10–1 shows the code value, the code assigned to the answer and entered in the file. The third column, labeled "Freq.," is the *number* of respondents that indicated that particular response. The fourth column, labeled "Pct.," is the percentage of all respondents to the survey who chose each answer. These percentages are computed by dividing the frequency for each category by the total number of respondents to the survey and expressing the fraction as a percentage.

The next to the last column in Example 10–1 is labeled "Adj." for "adjusted" percentages. The *adjustment* is based on the missing values for the variable being reported. This *isn't* the same as those who failed to respond to the survey. There will ordinarily be some respondents who participate in the survey and provide

Frequency Table Print Output   Example 10–1

No Missing Values Specified

Category	Code	Freq.	Pct.	Adj.	Cum.
Some high school	1.	28	4.2	4.2	4.2
High school graduate	2.	191	28.5	28.5	32.7
Some college	3.	141	21.0	21.0	53.7
College graduate	4.	136	20.3	20.3	74.0
Postgraduate	5.	118	17.6	17.6	91.5
Refused	6.	57	8.5	8.5	100.0
Total		671	100.0	100.0	100.0

Zero Specified as a Missing Value

Category	Code	Freq.	Pct.	Adj	Cum.
Some high school	1.	28	4.2	4.6	4.6
High school graduate	2.	191	28.5	31.1	35.7
Some college	3.	141	21.0	23.0	58.6
College graduate	4.	136	20.3	22.1	80.8
Postgraduate	5.	118	17.6	19.2	100.0
Refused	0.	57	8.5	—	—
Total		671	100.0	100.0	100.0

completed questionnaires but fail to respond to some individual items. For example, they may refuse to list their education or income or they may simply skip the item by mistake. It's usually not practical to discard all questionnaires that aren't *perfectly* complete. That would probably eliminate many cases unnecessarily. So the adjusted percentages are computed in the same way as the previous ones, except they're based on only those who responded to *that particular item.*

Notice that in the upper portion of Example 10–1 the percentages and the adjusted percentages are identical. That's because those who refused to indicate their educational level were assigned a code value of six and weren't specified as "missing values." They're included in the adjusted percentage column. By contrast, in the lower section of Example 10–1, those who refused were assigned a code of zero and that value was listed in the analysis program as a missing value for that item. Thus, the 8.5 percent of respondents who failed or refused to answer the item are listed in the percentage column, but nothing is listed in the adjusted percentage column. The dashed line indicates the percentage isn't zero, but rather that the percentage for this alternative isn't applicable. In this table, the adjusted percentages differ from the unadjusted, and of course they're slightly larger because they're based on a smaller total.

The last column at the far right of the frequency table in Example 10–1 is labeled "Cum." to designate "cumulative percentages." The percentage for the first row of the table will always be the same as the adjusted percentage for that row. The cumulative percentage for the second row is the sum of the adjusted percentages for the first and second rows, and so forth. Each cumulative percentage is the total of the *adjusted* percentages for that row and those above it—those with a lower code value.

Cumulative percentages have little meaning or value for nominal data, where the categories aren't related to one another in any fashion. They're meaningful and they can be quite useful when ordinal, interval, or ratio data are shown in a frequency table. In the lower section of Example 10–1, the reader of the table can easily see that nearly 59 percent of those responding have less than a college education. When the rows are ordered from "lowest" to "highest," the value of the column for any row shows the percentage of respondents who are in that category or "less," and 100 minus the value shows what percentage were "greater." The cumulative percentages also indicate the approximate point or value on the scale at which those in the 50th or some other percentile resides. "Percentile" means those who rank at some place out of 100 typical cases.

Often several columns on frequency tables such as those shown in Example 10–1 are of little or no interest to the analyst or information seekers. The listing of the code values themselves is useful for checking and editing data to be sure it's correct, but once that's been done, they have no real meaning if the scale points have been labeled. So the codes aren't usually listed in final reports. The frequency distributions are more difficult to interpret than the *percentage* distributions, so they may or may not be included in the report table.

Percentage Distribution Tables

The percentage distributions are often more easily interpreted and of more interest than are the frequency distributions. This is because percentages can be compared from one item or survey to the next, even though they may be based on different total frequencies. More importantly, the sample percentages can be used directly as an estimate of the percentages of the total population that might indicate each alternative response. Thus, the percentage distribution is often the most important column on the frequency table for those interpreting the survey results.

Example 10–2 shows two percentage distribution table formats. Usually the *adjusted* percentage distribution is more meaningful than the unadjusted percentages. If only the adjusted percentages are shown, the *n*-size listed should be a number for *that variable or item*, rather than the number of respondents for the entire sample. The *cumulative* percentage distribution is useful only in special cases.

Graphic Data Description

Statistical analysis programs and spreadsheets can usually describe category data with graphs as well as frequency tables. Figure 10–1 contains two bar charts portraying the same data as that shown in Examples 10–1 and 10–2. Spreadsheets and analysis programs typically offer vertical plots, pie charts that show proportions, or other graphic displays of the categories in the distribution. These graphic formats are discussed in more detail in Chapter 12.

Percentage Distribution Tables   Example 10–2

Frequency and Percentage Reported

Educational Level	Number	Percent
Some high school	28	4.2
High school graduate	191	28.5
Some college	141	21.0
College graduate	136	20.3
Postgraduate	118	17.6
Refused	57	8.5
Total	671	100.0

Percentage Only Reported

Educational Level (*N* for Item = 614)	Percent
Some high school	4.6
High school graduate	31.1
Some college	23.0
College graduate	22.1
Postgraduate	19.2

Interpreting Category Data

When the variable being analyzed can only be considered as categorical, there's really no continuum or relationship between categories; the only statistic that's appropriate to describe the distribution is the mode—the category with the largest frequency and percentage of cases. When data from an ordinal scale are displayed in a frequency table, the *cumulative* percentages may be meaningfully interpreted. In Example 10–3, the cumulative percentage column indicates over 40 percent of respondents had at least a college education and over 95 percent graduated from high school. These proportions could have been calculated mentally if only the percentage column was shown, but the interpretation is quicker and easier with inclusion of the cumulative percentages.

Graphic plots of cumulative percentages are sometimes more readily interpreted than just the adjusted percentage values. Figure 10–2 shows two plots of

FIGURE 10–1
Frequency
and
Percentage
Bar Charts

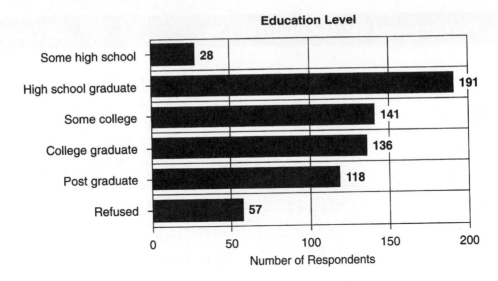

Education Level

Some high school — 28

High school graduate — 191

Some college — 141

College graduate — 136

Post graduate — 118

Refused — 57

0   50   100   150   200

Number of Respondents

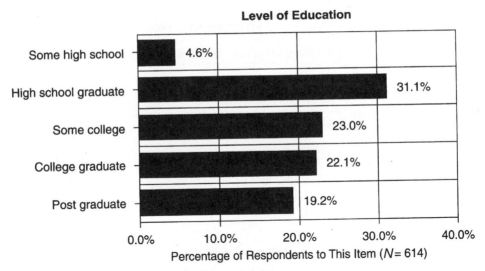

Level of Education

Some high school — 4.6%

High school graduate — 31.1%

Some college — 23.0%

College graduate — 22.1%

Post graduate — 19.2%

0.0%   10.0%   20.0%   30.0%   40.0%

Percentage of Respondents to This Item (*N* = 614)

data from a survey item that sought to learn what percentage of people were still awake and what percentage were asleep at various points throughout the first hour after "lights out." The bar chart in the upper section isn't very informative because it shows when during the hour various percentages fell asleep. By contrast, the plot of *cumulative* percentages in the lower section of Figure 10–2 provides precisely the information sought. The area in the upper left shows the proportion still awake and the area in the lower right depicts the proportion who have fallen asleep at each point.

When continuous ordinal, interval, or ratio data are obtained from scales with a limited number of scale points or values, this type of variable can be treated *both* as continuous and as categorical data. Each scale point can be treated as a separate

Interpreting Cumulative Percentages   Example 10–3

Level of Education	Frequency	Percentage	Cumulative Percentage
Postgraduate	118	19.2	19.2
College graduate	136	22.1	41.3
Some college	141	23.0	64.3
High school graduate	191	31.1	95.4
Some high school	28	4.6	100.0
Total	614	100.0	

category, even though they're on a continuum. Doing so isn't only permissible, it's advisable. Of course, the conventional descriptive statistics to be discussed below, such as averages, measures of the spread, and shape of the distribution, can also be computed for such items.

When continuous variables have too many values to be listed in a frequency table, it's often advisable to *temporarily* recode the variable into fewer, larger categories (or generate a "duplicate" and recode it into categories to preserve the continuous distribution). The range of the interval for each category should be identical, and there should be no more than a dozen categories, and preferably only six or eight. When a continuous variable has been recoded into categories in this fashion, it can be treated as *either* continuous or categorical, providing certain conditions are met. For example, if age in years resulted in 40 or 50 different values, the variable might be duplicated and recoded into five or six 10-year categories. The age can be shown in frequency tables and perhaps used for cross-tabulation later, when relationships between variables are analyzed. The original age variable that was retained in continuous form might also be described with the statistics appropriate for continuous distributions.

Another option is to recode the *original* variable into categories with equal intervals. Each category could be coded with the value of the *midpoint* of the interval. For example, if age was reclassified into 10-year categories—20s, 30s, 40s, and so on—then each category could be recoded with the values: 25, 35, 45, and so on. That way, the descriptive statistics for continuous distributions can be used together with the frequency tables. These statistics would be interpreted in the same way as they would when a strictly continuous variable was analyzed, except that all of the values and coefficients will be slightly different because all those in one group or category will be treated as identical during the computations.

It takes very little time and effort to recode continuous survey variables this way, and it's often worthwhile. The statistics for describing the data and measuring relationships between items are more complex and difficult to interpret for

FIGURE 10–2   **Plot of Cumulative Percentages**

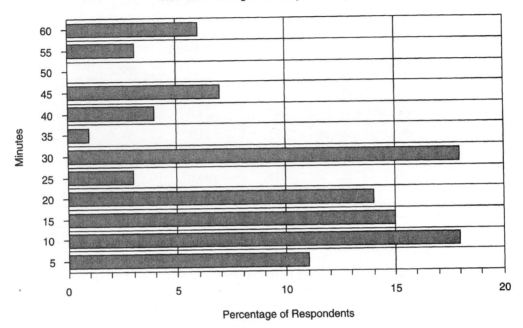

How soon after lights out do you usually fall asleep?

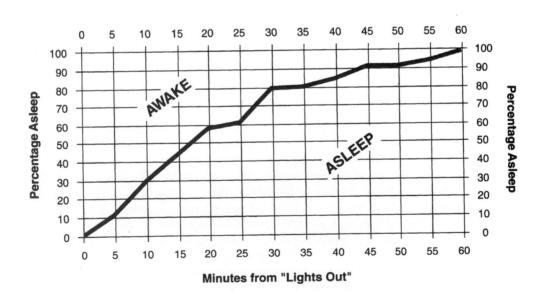

continuous variables than for categorical ones. For the vast majority of all survey data, percentage tables are used to describe the distributions, and cross-tabulations are used to measure the associations between items. These methods are usually more understandable to information seekers than the techniques for describing continuous numeric data and measuring the associations between such items. Some information is lost when recoding continuous data into categories, but the loss is usually negligible.

Continuous Data Distribution

Frequency tables cannot be used to describe continuous numeric distributions with a large number of values, but there are a variety of ways they can be described by statistics. Different types of scales require different types of statistics. There are three different characteristics of the distribution that researchers ordinarily measure and describe: (1) *average*—the most typical value; (2) *spread*—the amount of deviation from the average; and (3) *shape*—the form of the distribution. The technical term for a coefficient that indicates the most typical value is "a measure of central tendency." Measures of central tendency will be referred to here simply as "averages." The technical name for the amount of deviation from the average is *dispersion* or *variance*. The term *spread* will be used here to indicate the amount of deviation from the central point or average. The form of the distribution will be called its *shape* in the discussion that follows. The statistics to describe distributions of the four different types of data are shown in Figure 10–3.

In order to select the most appropriate statistical tool, the analyst has to identify which of the four types of scale data the variable represents. When more than one

FIGURE 10–3
Tool Selection for Descriptive Statistics

Scale Type	Average	Spread	Shape
Nominal	Mode		
Ordinal	Median	Interquartile Range	
	Mode	Range	
		Maximum & Minimum	
Interval	Mean	Standard Deviation	Skewness
	Median	Interquartile Range	Kurtosis
	Mode	Range	
		Maximum & Minimum	
Ratio	Mean	Standard Deviation	Skewness
	Median	Interquartile Range	Kurtosis
	Mode	Range	
		Maximum & Minimum	

coefficient could be used, the most common and most often appropriate is listed first, followed by the next most likely. In general, any tool that's appropriate for a "lower level" of scale data (one listed above in Figure 10–3) would be acceptable for the scales of a higher level (listed below it in Figure 10–3), although it may not be the most preferable. If no statistic is listed in the table, as in the case of spread or shape for nominal or ordinal data, this means no common statistical coefficient is appropriate to describe them, and the distributions may have to be described in tabular or graphic form.

Central Tendency and Averages

In most cases, the use of the term *average* refers to the *arithmetic* mean, but this is only one of three common averages that can be used. Each of the three averages has a different set of characteristics that make it more appropriate for some distributions and less for others. The average of a distribution is almost always reported because it represents the most typical response, or the researchers' "best guess" of how someone picked at random from the population sampled would respond. The choice of which average to use is based on the type of scale data that form the distribution and sometimes the "shape" of the distribution as well.

The Mean

The arithmetic mean, usually called simply the *mean*, is the most common average used to indicate the most typical response. While the median and mode can also be used to describe the central tendency for interval or ratio data, the mean is usually the most meaningful statistic. It's computed simply by dividing the sum of the values by the number of values or cases. While the mean is the most commonly used average, it has some restrictions and limitations that make other averages more appropriate in some situations. First, it isn't valid to use the mean for *nominal* data because the values are merely names. If unmarried respondents were assigned a code value of one and married respondents a value of two, it wouldn't make sense to compute the *mean* marital status, any more than it would to compute the mean telephone number of a group of people.

The mean shouldn't be used for *ordinal* data, such as that obtained from a set of rankings. That's because with ordinal data the code values indicate only that each sequential value is *greater than* those with a lower value and *less than* those with a higher value. Consequently, the intervals between code values on the ordinal scale aren't necessarily equal. A fractional value would have little meaning. Thus, the median or mode is a more appropriate average for ordinal data.

Even with distributions of interval or ratio data, there are some situations where the mean has limitations that may make another average a more appropriate and meaningful representation of the most typical case. The mean tends to be *overly sensitive* to influence by only one or a few *extreme* values in the distribution, known as *outliers,* because they lie outside the normal range. An example may clarify this. Example 10–4 shows two distributions of ratio data—contributions to a charitable fund drive. The maximum contribution on the frequency table at the left was $5. The distribution shown on the right is exactly the same, except that five people gave $50 instead of $5—there are five outliers.

Outlier Effects on Averages   Example 10–4

	No Outlier				One Outlier		
Amount	Number	Percent	Cum.	Amount	Number	Percent	Cum.
$1.00	25	6.3	6.3	$1.00	25	6.3	6.3
$2.00	150	37.5	43.8	$2.00	150	37.5	43.8
$3.00	125	31.3	75.0	$3.00	125	31.3	75.0
$4.00	75	18.8	93.8	$4.00	75	18.8	93.8
$5.00	25	6.3	100.0	$5.00	20	5.0	98.8
				$50.00	5	1.3	100.0
Total	400	100.0		Total	400	100.0	

Mean	Median	Mode	Mean	Median	Mode
$2.80	$3.00	$2.00	$3.38	$3.00	$2.00

Although these five cases constitute only about 1 percent of the sample, their presence changed the mean from $2.80 to $3.38. To be meaningful and useful, an *average* should be an indication of the most typical respondent. Yet, with outliers, the mean isn't very typical of either the vast majority of cases or of the outliers. Notice, however, that the median and mode are exactly the same for both distributions. Both are completely insensitive to changes in extreme values.

The Median

The median value for a distribution is another form of average or indication of the "most typical" case. The value of the median can be computed by the analysis routine, but it's easily understood. The median is merely the value of the "middle" case if the cases were arrayed from the lowest to the highest value. In both frequencies in Example 10–4, inspection of the *cumulative* frequencies shows the *50th percentile,* or the middle value, is $3.00 for both distributions. Since it's merely the middle value, the median isn't affected by changes in extreme values or the existence of outliers. To put it another way, the middle value or median will be the same, no matter how much greater or lesser the values on the extremes turn out to be. Consequently, the median is likely to be more typical of the *majority* of cases in the distribution and a better average to use than the mean with asymmetrical distributions where there are outliers. The *shape* of the distribution will be discussed more fully later in this chapter.

The Mode

The mode is simply the category or value with the greatest frequency of cases. It's the only acceptable indicator of the most typical case for distributions of nominal

FIGURE 10–4 **Distributions With and Without Outliers**

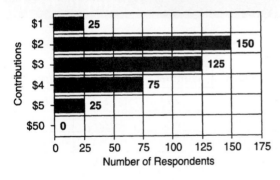
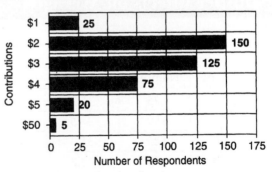

data. In Figure 10–4, based on Example 10–4, the mode is $2.00 for both distributions because that category has the highest frequency and percentage of cases in both. This category would be the "best guess" for predicting how much any one member of the population sampled would contribute. In other words, it's the *most likely* value an individual has contributed or would contribute.

Continuous numeric distributions of ordinal, interval, and ratio data also have one *primary* modal value. In the distributions shown in Figure 10–5 and Figure 10–6, the mode is the "peak" of the distribution—the high point, where the line tapers off toward a lower frequency in either direction. Often there will be just one such point—a primary mode only—but those cases where there are more than one will be discussed more fully later in this chapter.

Measures of Dispersion or Spread

Continuous numeric distributions of ordinal, interval, or ratio data have a value that's regarded as "most typical." They also tend to be spread out around that value in both directions. The amount of spread or *dispersion* around the average is often as meaningful to the analyst and information seekers as the value of the average itself. One way to gauge the spread of a distribution is to portray it graphically in a plot or chart. While graphic displays of distributions are often useful, they have some shortcomings that limit their value during analysis: They take considerable time and effort to create, they require a lot of space, and, most importantly, they can't be manipulated mathematically or statistically. Consequently, the analyst will often have to depend on numeric coefficients or values that describe the amount of dispersion or spread of the distributions of variables to be analyzed.

Maximum and Minimum

The minimum value indicates how far the spread extends toward the lower direction, and the maximum value shows the extent of spread toward the upper direction from the average. These values are often of interest simply because they define the *extremes* of the distribution. They describe the respondents or cases that represent the least and the most on whatever dimension is being measured.

FIGURE 10–5
Normal and
Skewed
Distributions

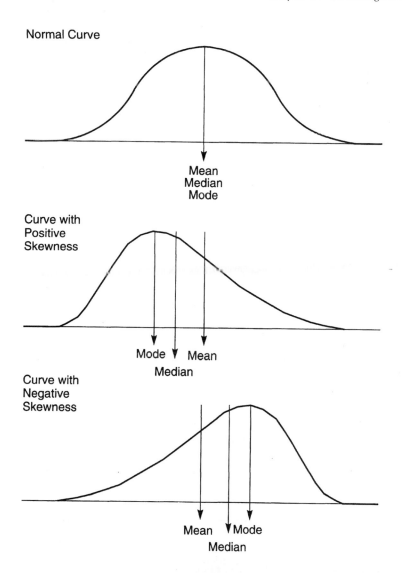

Range of the Distribution

The range is simply the maximum minus the minimum, showing the total spread between extremes. While the maximum, minimum, and range may certainly be of interest for many distributions, they're often lacking in one important respect: They're defined only in terms of the extreme values. Unfortunately, they say nothing about the spread of the cases within those boundaries.

Interquartile Range

A "quartile" is a fourth of the data if the cases are arrayed from low to high, just as a "centile" is a hundredth of the data if so arranged. The *interquartile range* is the

FIGURE 10–6
Normality and
Kurtosis of
Distributions

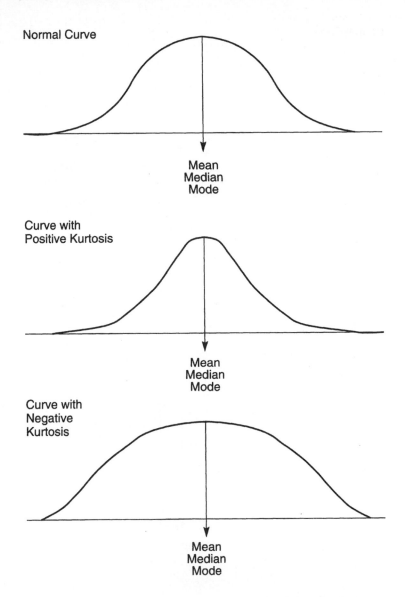

Normal Curve

Mean
Median
Mode

Curve with
Positive Kurtosis

Mean
Median
Mode

Curve with
Negative
Kurtosis

Mean
Median
Mode

distance from the first to the third quartiles. In other words, it's the range of the middle half of the data. The lower fourth and the upper fourth are ignored by the interquartile range. This is occasionally a useful measure of spread for nonnormal distributions where the standard deviation, described below, isn't appropriate. It's especially useful if there are extreme outliers on one or both sides. Their presence would make the maximum, minimum, and range misleading indications of spread.

Standard Deviation

Fortunately, there's a measure of spread or dispersion that permits the researcher to estimate and report the *proportion* of respondents or cases within certain ranges in the center part of the distribution, as well as toward the extremes, *providing that the distribution doesn't deviate very markedly from the normal, bell-shaped curve.* The *standard deviation* is a measure of the deviation or spread away from the mean. It's a single value that indicates the amount of spread in a distribution. It's routinely computed by statistical analysis programs and spreadsheets. (Mathematically, the standard deviation is the root mean squared [R.M.S.] deviations from the mean—the square root of the mean of the squared deviations.)

The standard deviation can be computed for any distribution, regardless of its shape, but when the distribution conforms closely to the standard normal distribution shown in the top section of Figure 10–5, a given proportion of the survey cases will always fall within certain ranges that are determined by the standard deviation (S.D.) of the distribution. Thus, the standard deviation is an excellent indicator of spread.

Shape of the Distribution

The shape of a distribution can be inspected by displaying it graphically. That's often useful, but the same limitations to graphic portrayal cited earlier still apply: It takes substantial time, effort, and space, and graphs can't be manipulated statistically. Thus, the analyst often depends on two coefficients that indicate the degree and direction for distributions of interval and ratio data with large numbers of values that deviate from a normal distribution. They're the coefficients of skewness and kurtosis.

Skewness of Distributions

The *skewness* of a distribution is a measure of the degree and direction of its *asymmetry.* If a distribution is symmetrical, such as the normal curve shown in Figure 10–5, one side of the distribution is precisely the "mirror-image" of the other and the coefficient of skewness will be zero. Often distributions of data for survey variables are somewhat asymmetrical; they "lean" toward one direction or the other.

In the middle section of Figure 10–5, the bulk of the distribution is skewed to the left, toward the lower values of the distribution. The extreme values tail out from the mode further to the right or higher side than toward the left or lower side. The coefficient of skewness for a distribution with such a configuration will have a *positive* value. In the reverse case, shown in the lower section of Figure 10–5, the coefficient of skewness will be negative. So the *sign* of the coefficient of skewness indicates which *direction* the distribution is skewed. The *absolute magnitude* of the coefficient of skewness indicates just how much the distribution deviates from symmetry—how much different one side is from the other.

It's often important to measure the degree of skewness in a continuous numeric distribution with many values when the data are analyzed to provide data description. That's because the standard deviation, as a description of spread, provides a close estimate of the proportion of cases within a given range around the mean *only* if the distribution is *symmetrical,* as with the normal curve. Thus, the sign and the value of skewness indicate the degree of *accuracy* with which the standard deviation can be used to estimate the amount of spread in the distribution. In addition, several statistical measures of the *association* between pairs of variables,

Data Distribution Statistics   Example 10–5

No Outliers	
Mean	2.183
Median	3.000
Mode	2.000
Standard Deviation	1.015
Skewness	0.383
Kurtosis	−0.488
Maximum	5.000
Minimum	1.000
Range	4.000

Some Outliers	
Mean	3.375
Median	3.000
Mode	2.000
Standard Deviation	5.344
Skewness	8.355
Kurtosis	70.707
Maximum	50.000
Minimum	1.000
Range	49.000

to be discussed in the next chapter, are inaccurate and illegitimate if one or both distributions deviate significantly from symmetry.

Kurtosis of Distributions

The *kurtosis* of a distribution is an indication of how peaked or flat it is, compared to the normal curve. The value of the coefficient of kurtosis for a normal curve is zero. In the middle section of Figure 10–6, the distribution has a higher, more narrow peak, with the tails extending out in each direction at a low level. The coefficient of kurtosis will be positive. By contrast, a negative value of kurtosis indicates a curve such as that shown in the lower section of Figure 10–6. It has a broad, low peak and "wings" that extend out at a rather high level before falling off. The distributions shown in Figure 10–6 are all symmetrical (with zero skewness), but either the coefficient of skewness or of kurtosis can be computed for any distribution, regardless of the value of the other.

Example 10–5 contains the data description coefficients for the two distributions of data shown in Example 10–4 and Figure 10–7. For both distributions, the median contribution is $3, the modal contribution is $2, and the minimum is $1. The mean increased over 50 percent from $2.18 to $3.38. All the other coefficients changed dramatically with the inclusion of the outliers. While the standard deviation and coefficient of skewness were extended substantially by the inclusion of outliers, the coefficient of *kurtosis* increased almost 150 times in absolute value.

At first glance, the bar charts for the two distributions shown in Figure 10–4 appear to be quite similar. That's because bar charts are designed mainly to display *nominal* data where the categories don't take on a magnitude or stand in any sequential relationship to one another. So the $5 contributions and the $50 contributions are merely treated as two different *categories* on a bar chart. There's no

FIGURE 10–7
Data Plots
With and
Without
Outliers

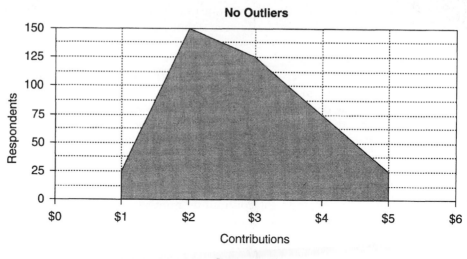

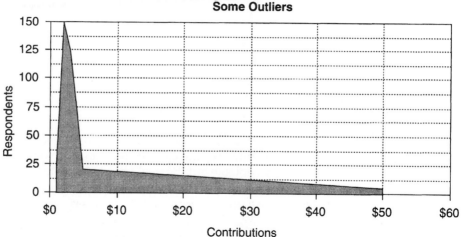

indication that one is 10 times the other. By contrast, examination of the descriptive coefficients in Example 10–5 clearly indicate that one distribution is markedly different from the other.

While bar charts don't display the *shape* of a data distribution, area plots such as those shown in Figure 10–7 do. They portray the shape of the distribution, taking into regard the *numeric value* of each data point rather than treating each as an independent category. Examination of these plots makes it easy to see why the coefficients of skewness, and especially kurtosis, are so different for these distributions.

When no outliers are present, as in the upper plot of Figure 10–7, the shape is a rough approximation of a normal distribution. The coefficient of skewness is near zero because the curve is fairly symmetrical. The coefficient of kurtosis is only very slightly negative, indicating there's a little less data in the tails of the distribution than there would be in a normal curve.

By contrast, the distribution containing outliers plotted in the lower section of Figure 10–7 is obviously very asymmetrical—skewed sharply to the left with a tail extending far out to the right. Thus, the value of the coefficient of skewness for that curve exceeds +8. Similarly, since there is much more data in the right tail of the distribution, because of the outliers, the coefficient of kurtosis exceeds +70, indicating radical departure from normal.

If the coefficient of kurtosis departs substantially from zero, that also excludes using the standard deviation as a meaningful measure of spread. The standard deviation will accurately indicate how much data is within given ranges of the mean only when the data distribution approximates a normal curve. The interpretation of skewness, kurtosis, and standard deviation is discussed more fully in the following chapter. It's only necessary to note here that these coefficients should usually be obtained for continuous numeric distributions with a large number of values during the data description phase of analysis.

Interpreting the Statistics

The most common averages and measures of the spread and shape of continuous distributions were identified and their relationships to one another were explained above. The interpretation of these characteristics and coefficients is discussed in the sections that follow.

Interpreting Averages of Distributions

The researcher has to decide whether the mean, median, and mode would be the best indicator of the most typical case. If the data were obtained from an ordinal scale, the mode is acceptable but the median is preferable. If the data were derived from an interval or ratio scale, the choice depends on the *shape* of the distribution. If the coefficient of skewness, described below, is very near zero, indicating the distribution is symmetrical, the mean, median, and mode will all be the same or nearly the same value. If the distribution is skewed to the left or the right, as in the upper section of Figure 10–8, the mean, median, and mode depart from one another in the directions shown. The lower section of Figure 10–8 depicts distributions with positive and negative kurtosis, which will be described fully below. But since they are *symmetrical*, the mean, median, and mode don't depart from one another. Thus, the choice of the most appropriate *average* is affected only by skewness or deviation from symmetry, but not by kurtosis.

Figure 10–8 indicates the mean is sensitive to extreme values on the high side, off to the right, for positive skewness and to the low, or left side, for negative skewness. The greater the amount of skewness in a distribution, the *less* appropriate the mean will be as a measure of the most typical case. In other words, the greater the skewness, the more likely the *median* will best represent the most typical case.

The median is the approximate value of the case that would be in the middle, if all cases were arrayed from low to high value on the variable. It isn't the center point on the horizontal axis of the plot shown in the upper section of Figure 10–8, because that's merely the midpoint of the scale. In the figure, the number of cases is represented by the *area* under the curve, rather than the horizontal distance on

FIGURE 10–8   Averages of Nonnormal Distributions

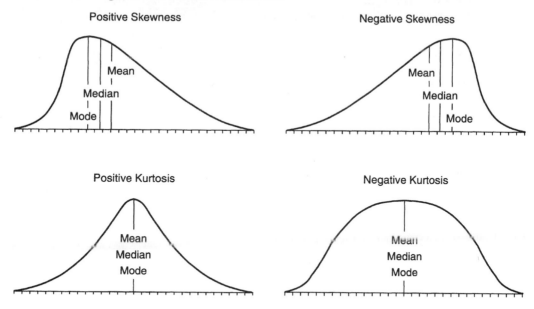

the scale. When the distribution is skewed, the *median* is the most appropriate average to indicate the most typical case. It's only influenced by the *number* of cases with higher values and with lower values, but it isn't sensitive to *how much* the values are higher or lower.

The mode was described earlier as the only proper measure of the most typical case for categorical data, where the modal category is merely the one with the largest percentage of responses. For continuous data, the mode is the "high point" in the distribution. In Figure 10–8, the mode would be the scale value where the distribution has reached its peak. It's often used as the best indicator of the most typical case when a distribution is *extremely* skewed to one side or the other. The mode is an especially appropriate average to use if the distribution both is very skewed to one side and also has a high peak, indicated by a positive value for the coefficient of kurtosis. This is because a large portion of the cases will be very close to the mode. Guidelines for selecting the most appropriate average are contained in Guidelist 10–1.

Interpreting Spread of Distributions

Figure 10–9 shows that when the distribution is normal, about 68 percent of the cases will be within 11 S.D. of the mean, 95 percent within ±2 S.D. On the extremes of a normal distribution, only 1 percent of the data lie beyond 3 S.D. above or below the mean, so 99 percent fall within ±3 S.D.

Suppose the survey data for a certain variable is normally distributed and there are 200 cases. If the mean value was computed to be 30 and the standard deviation was 5, this would mean that 68 cases would have values between 25 and 30 and another 68 cases would have a value between 30 and 35. In total, 132 cases, or 68

For Choosing the Best Average   Guidelist 10–1

1. If the data are from an ordinal scale, the median should be used.

2. If the skewness is zero or very nearly so, the distribution is symmetrical and the mean, median, and mode will all be the same or nearly identical.

3. If the skewness is positive, the mode or peak will be to the left of center, the median greater, and the mean the highest.

4. If the skewness is negative, the mode will be to the right, toward the high side, the median will be a lower value, and the mean, the lowest value.

5. If the distribution is nearly normal but there are a few very small or very large values, they are called "outliers" and the median is the best indicator of the most typical case.

6. If the distribution is skewed and the kurtosis is zero or negative, indicating a normal or flat curve, the median is the best average to show the most typical case.

7. If the distribution is skewed and the kurtosis has a high, positive value, the distribution has a high peak with many cases around the mode, and the mode is the best average to represent the most typical case or value.

percent, would be between 25 and 35. This is within 1 standard deviation above and below the mean. Similarly, 190 cases or 95 percent would be within 2 standard deviations of the mean, with values between 20 and 40. Only about one case would have a value of less than 15 and one a value of more than 45, because about 198 cases or 99 percent would be within 3 standard deviations of the mean. In this way, the research analyst can see the range and describe the spread of the distribution for the variable simply by knowing the mean and standard deviation, *providing the "shape" of the distribution is approximately* NORMAL.

The standard deviation provides a close estimate of the proportion of cases within a given range around the mean *only* if the distribution is symmetrical. The distributions shown in the middle and lower sections of Figure 10–9 are positively and negatively skewed, respectively. The mean and the approximate percentages of data within 1, 2, and 3 S.D. are listed. The *proportion* of cases is represented by the area under the curve for each section. So about 74 percent of cases fall within ± 1 S.D. rather than the 68 percent that would be in that range for a normal distribution. Nor are the 74 percent of cases evenly divided above and below the mean. Rather, 44 percent lie in one direction while only 30 percent are in the other.

The *absolute* value of the coefficient of skewness indicates the degree of accuracy with which the standard deviation can estimate the amount of spread in the distribution. When the coefficient of skewness is positive, there will be many more cases within 1 S.D. to the *left* of the mean than to the right of it. The opposite is true for negative skewness. Thus, the *sign* of the coefficient tells only in what *direction* the distribution is skewed.

Nor can the standard deviation be used to show the range within which a given percentage of cases will fall if the coefficient of kurtosis departs markedly from zero in either a positive or negative direction, as in the middle and lower sections of Figure 10–10. If the value of kurtosis is positive, indicating a more peaked distribution than normal, *more* than 68 percent of cases will fall within ± 1 S.D. of the mean. On

FIGURE 10–9   Zero, Positive, and Negative Skewness

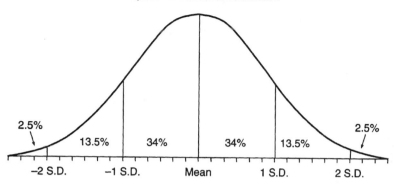

Spread in a Normal Distribution

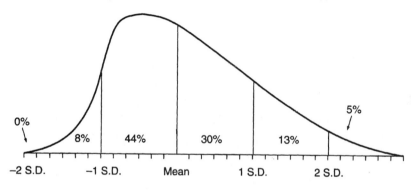

Spread in a Distribution with Positive Skewness

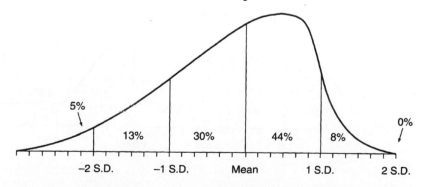

Spread in a Distribution with Negative Skewness

FIGURE 10–10 Zero, Positive, and Negative Kurtosis

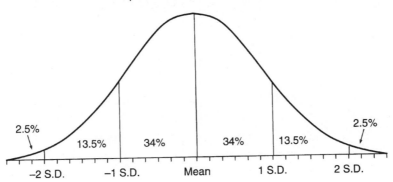

Spread in a Normal Distribution

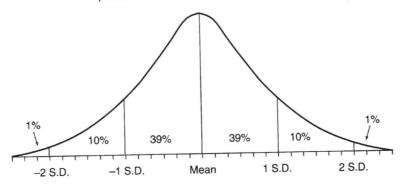

Spread in a Distribution with Positive Kurtosis

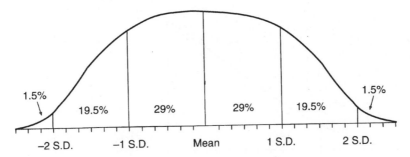

Spread in a Distribution with Negative Kurtosis

For Assessing Spread of Nonnormal Distributions

Guidelist 10–2

1. If either skewness or kurtosis depart significantly from zero, the distribution isn't normal and S.D. won't indicate the proportion of data in a given range.

2. If the scale has only a few values, obtain a frequency table and use the percentages and cumulative percentages to show proportions within ranges and above and below points on the scale.

3. If the variable has a large number of values, it or a duplicate may be recoded into fewer, larger categories of equal intervals displayed in a frequency table.

4. The distributions of continuous, numeric variables with many values can also be plotted to allow visual examination of the shape and spread of the distribution.

the other hand, if the distribution is flatter than normal, indicated by a *negative* kurtosis value, then fewer than 68 percent of cases will be within ± 1 S.D. of the mean.

In summary, the standard deviation can be computed despite how much the distribution departs from normal. But if skewness, kurtosis, or both deviate significantly from zero, the standard deviation does *not* indicate the *proportion* of data within a given range of standard deviations from the mean. If the distribution is skewed, there will be more or less cases above the mean than below it, depending on the direction of skewness. If the distribution has substantial kurtosis, *more* or *less* than two-thirds of the cases will be within 1 S.D. of the mean, depending on the sign of the coefficient. Thus, when using the standard deviation to gauge the proportion of cases within some range around the mean, it's important to check the skewness and kurtosis. Guidelist 10–2 summarizes the recommendations for assessing the spread of nonnormal distributions. Guidelines for the spread of normal distributions are listed in Guidelist 10–3.

For Using Standard Deviation with Normal Curve

Guidelist 10–3

1. About 34 percent of cases are between the mean and +1 S.D.

2. About 34 percent of cases are between the mean and −1 S.D.

3. About 68 percent of cases are within ±1 S.D. of the mean.

4. About 95 percent of cases are within ±2 S.D. of the mean.

5. About 99 percent of cases are within ±3 S.D. of the mean.

6. About 50 percent of cases will be above the mean.

7. About 50 percent of cases will be below the mean.

8. The percentage of cases above and below other points on the scale, defined by the standard deviation, can be determined by adding and subtracting these percentages.

Interpreting Shapes of Distributions

The coefficients of skewness and kurtosis do suggest the shape of a distribution of data, but it requires substantial experience to visualize a distribution based only on those values. It's advisable for less experienced analysts to inspect a plot of the distribution for any item in question if the software is capable of generating one. Such data plots are very helpful to both research analysts and information seekers to visualize and comprehend the shape of the entire distribution of data for a survey item.

Figure 10–11 contains the data plots and descriptive coefficients for six actual survey variables. The values are combined favorability ratings for phone or mail-order shopping via six modes: magazines, catalogs, newspapers, television, direct mail, and retail stores. The minimum possible score was 8 and the maximum was 40.

The descriptive statistics for each variable shown in Figure 10–11 are listed below the plot of each distribution. Careful comparisons between the coefficients and the plots will clarify many of the conditions discussed earlier. The averages indicate that *stores* were rated most highly, followed by *catalogs*. These two distributions are further to the right than those for the other four shopping modes. Each distribution is slightly skewed to the right, with a few cases of very low scores tailing off to the left. Thus, all the coefficients of skewness have slightly negative values. The distribution of ratings for *stores* is rather flat and the coefficient of kurtosis is slightly negative. All the others are more peaked than normal and the corresponding kurtosis values are slightly positive.

Floor and Ceiling Effects

Survey data distributions are sometimes asymmetrical or skewed to the left or right because of what are called "ceiling" or "floor" effects. Figure 10–12 displays two distributions of data from a seven-point rating scale. On the left, nearly 17 percent of respondents indicated the *minimum* scale value. It seems reasonable to assume their ratings would have been even lower if they were not limited by the *floor* of the scale. By contrast, more than one out of five respondents chose the *maximum* value for the variable described at the right of Figure 10–12. This suggests their reactions were bound by the upper limit or *ceiling* of the seven-point scale.

With strong floor effects, a large proportion of cases will be grouped at the lower boundary of the scale. The coefficient of skewness will have a *positive* sign because the distribution is skewed to the *left*. On the other hand, if there are strong *ceiling* effects, with a substantial proportion of respondents clustered at the *upper* limit of the scale, the distribution will be skewed to the *right* and the coefficient of skewness will be *negative*, as indicated in Figure 10–12.

Floor and ceiling effects on survey data distributions are highly disruptive. The departures from symmetry they create inhibit the use of the standard deviation as a meaningful measure of the spread of the data distribution. More importantly, such asymmetry prohibits the legitimate use of some measures of association, to be described in Chapter 11, such as analysis of variance or regression analysis. Thus, survey researchers strive to prevent floor or ceiling effects. Yet they aren't as easy to avoid as it might seem.

FIGURE 10–11   Six Distributions of Survey Data

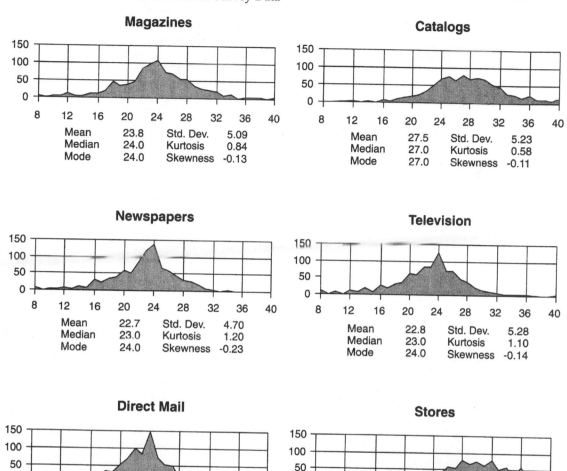

It may appear, at first glance, that floor and ceiling effects could be avoided by using a "wider" scale—a scale with more values. In fact, that's rarely the answer. For instance, in the example shown in Figure 10–12, if a 9-point or even a 100-point scale had been used, about the same proportion of respondents would probably have clustered at the lower and upper extremes, producing almost identical effects.

The answer to the avoidance of floor or ceiling effects lies not so much in the breadth of the scale as in the manner in which the question or item is expressed or the way in which the extremes of a scale are labeled. It's not always possible, but sometimes the researcher can *anticipate* the possibility of strong positive or

FIGURE 10–12   Scale Floor and Ceiling Effects

Floor Effect

Value	Frequency	Percent
1	121	16.6
2	203	27.8
3	184	25.2
4	120	16.5
5	60	8.2
6	35	4.8
7	6	.8
Total	729	100.0

Ceiling Effect

Value	Frequency	Percent
1	11	1.5
2	23	3.1
3	68	9.1
4	105	14.1
5	166	22.3
6	202	27.1
7	170	22.8
Total	745	100.0

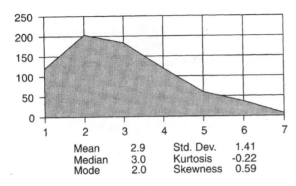

Mean	2.9	Std. Dev.	1.41
Median	3.0	Kurtosis	-0.22
Mode	2.0	Skewness	0.59

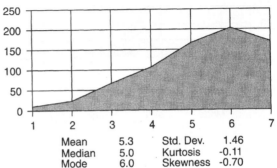

Mean	5.3	Std. Dev.	1.46
Median	5.0	Kurtosis	-0.11
Mode	6.0	Skewness	-0.70

negative reactions to an item. If that's the case, the wording of the question and/or the labeling of the scale's extremes can be expressed to capture the full range of potential response. For example, a scale labeled "Good—Bad" may produce floor or ceiling effects, while such effects would be mitigated somewhat by the labels, "Terrible—Superb."

There are other situations where floor and ceiling effects are virtually impossible to prevent because it's the nature of the underlying distribution in the population—for example, with such items as personal income, because nobody reports negative income. Almost everyone has a few thousand dollars per year of income, while most report many thousands. On the high side, a few respondents may report income in the hundreds of thousands of dollars or more, so there's virtually *no ceiling*. This causes the distribution to be skewed positively, toward the left or low side of the distribution. In effect, the "floor" of zero cuts off the distribution on the left, but it can extend far toward the right extreme.

The opposite tendency occurs when there are ceiling effects on the scale for the variable or item. For example, suppose respondents were asked to indicate how many days per month, on the average, they drive their automobile for any purpose at all. Some may report only a few days, but many are likely to report they use the car every day. Since there's a maximum of 31 days per month, nobody could report more than that ceiling value. The distribution would be negatively skewed toward the right or high side of the distribution. When asymmetry due to floor or ceiling effects can't be avoided, the analyst has little choice but to recode the variable into categories and use the statistical tools appropriate to ordinal, categorical data.

The Meaning of Bimodality

Most of the distributions shown in this chapter were "unimodal" (single mode) distributions. This isn't always the case. Sometimes a distribution of continuous numeric data will have two or more modes or peaks, such as that shown in the upper section of Figure 10–13. For such distributions, the coefficient of kurtosis will be quite negative, indicating a very flat curve, because that's the way the computational routine would "see" the distribution. In fact, the distribution dips sharply downward in the middle and then rises to a second mode on the right.

The distribution of categorical data shown in the lower left section of Figure 10–13 is also bimodal. The *primary* mode has a value of 6, while the *secondary* modal value is 3. Such bimodal distributions usually indicate there are two, fairly distinct "populations" or groups of respondents concealed in the responding sample. If so, each group might provide a fairly normal distribution of response for the item. Yet, when they're combined into one sample, the curves are, in effect, overlaid on one another. A bimodal distribution results.

This is precisely the case exemplified in Figure 10–13. In the upper section, the plots of the two, distinct distributions have been overlaid on the "combined" distribution for the variable. In the lower left section of Figure 10–13, the "combined" distribution is shown in a *stacked* bar chart. If the two distinct subsample distributions hadn't been identified and the data were displayed in an ordinary bar chart, it would appear just as it does but without the two segments for each bar. The two distinct distributions are plotted separately in a *split* bar chart in the lower right section of the figure to reveal that each is approximately normal in form. When the research analyst discovers a bimodal distribution, it's often a clue that some factor or characteristic serves to distinguish one group from the other within the responding sample. The important question is, *what* characteristic?

The content of the survey question or item may suggest what may separate the two groups, causing each to range around a different point on the scale. The analyst should note any bimodal distributions that are detected, examine the item or question generating the distribution, and perhaps analyze the relationship between the variable and others in the survey, such as the demographic items. Often, such demographic characteristics will prove to be strongly related to items with bimodality.

For example, a bimodal distribution of frequency of air travel may be strongly related to occupational groups, indicating higher frequencies for business travelers and lower frequency of travel by those in occupations that don't require it, even though there is some variation in the amount of travel *within* both groups. This may be of major importance to those seeking the information because the average amount of travel for the whole sample *wouldn't be typical of either group*, but

FIGURE 10–13   **Continuous, Bimodal Distributions**

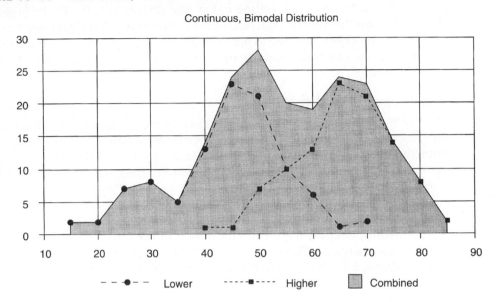

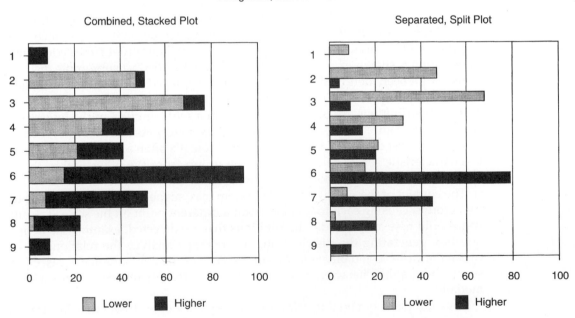

the average for each separate population might be very accurate and informative. Similarly, men and women often respond in systematically different ways, as do married and unmarried respondents, those with children in the family and those without, those who are and those who aren't employed outside the home, those with college degrees and those with less education, or those in blue-collar and those in white-collar jobs.

There may be no way to explain bimodality based on the survey results, but often an explanation can be found. If so, it might provide highly valuable information to the sponsor. The important point here is that recognition of bimodality should spark the analyst to examine the variable very closely to see if two underlying populations can be identified. One way to do that is to examine the potential associations between the item in question and other survey items. The statistical methods for measuring those associations are discussed in Chapter 11.

Statistical Inference

Ordinarily, researchers and sponsors aren't really interested only in the results obtained from a sample. Rather, they want to "estimate" the *parameters* of the population, based on the *statistics* obtained from a sample. This process of making inferences about the population from sample statistics is called *statistical inference*. It must be based on a random sample, or at least an approximation to random selection, to be fairly accurate. With a random sample, the respondents to be included in the sample are randomly selected, and each individual's probability of being picked is exactly equal to that for any other person. This discussion of statistical inference and reliability is based on the assumption the sampling was random or at least approximately so.

Suppose a researcher wants to learn the average age of those in a particular population, such as those living in a well-defined geographical area. A sample of some portion of the people within the area might be surveyed to learn the age of each, and the average age of the people in the sample could be computed. If the sample were selected at random from among all those in the population, the average age for the sample would be an unbiased estimate of the average age of all the people in the area. The average age of the population would be *inferred* from the sample. If, on the other hand, the sample were picked only from among those living in the part of the area closest to the survey headquarters, that wouldn't be a random sample and the sample statistics wouldn't be very representative of the entire population. It would be a biased estimate of the population, and inferences about the population as a whole would be questionable. Thus, statistical inference is based on random sampling. The more the sampling design deviates from random selection, the less legitimate any such inferences about the whole population would be.

Standard Error of the Estimate

The fact that no sample is likely to be perfectly representative of the entire population was noted earlier. In other words, no sample survey data are perfectly *reliable.* In the example above, the average age of the people in the sample is likely to be slightly different from the actual average age of everybody in the population. Those who seek survey data would often like to know just how "good" the estimate really is. In other words, they want to know about the *reliability* of the estimate. The term *reliability* is used here in exactly the same way as it was explained in Chapter 3. Reliability is determined by the ability of a procedure—in this case, sampling—to produce the same results with multiple replications.

To illustrate the reliability of estimates from samples, suppose a sample of 100 adult respondents were selected *at random* from a very large population and the ages of each were recorded. The mean age of the sample could then be computed. If this procedure were done hundreds or thousands of times, it would result in hundreds or thousands of sample means. Of course, they wouldn't all be identical. They would vary slightly from one another, since the sampling isn't perfectly reliable.

In effect, this procedure would result in a data distribution—a *distribution of sample means.* It would be a *sampling* of all possible samples of this type. So, statisticians refer to this hypothetical distribution as the *sampling distribution of sample means.* This distribution could be treated like any other data distribution. In other words, one could compute the *mean* of the *sampling distribution of sample means,* and this would be an unbiased estimate of the *population mean.* The *standard deviation, skewness,* and *kurtosis* could be computed, as well. One of the nice properties of this sampling distribution is that it tends to be normal or very nearly so, regardless of the shape of the population distribution from which the samples were randomly selected.

It was noted in Chapter 3 and earlier in this chapter that if the distribution is normal, about 68 percent of the data falls within ± 1 S.D., 95 percent within ± 2 S.D., and 99 percent within ± 3 S.D. of the mean. So, if the mean of this hypothetical distribution were 40 years and its S.D. were equal to 2 years, that means that 95 percent of random samples of 100 respondents would yield a sample mean between 36 and 44 years (i.e., ± 2 S.D.).

Now, suppose a research analyst selected one random sample of 100 adults from this same population and the mean age of the respondents was 45 years. *If* the analyst knew (without going through the entire process of selecting hundreds of samples) that the S.D. of the *sampling distribution of sample means* was equal to 2 years, that would be extremely helpful. Since 95 percent of the means of such samples as this will fall within ± 2 S.D. of the population mean, there's a 95 percent chance *this* sample mean is within 4 years of the population mean. Similarly, there's a 99 percent probability it's within 6 years of the mean for the entire population.

In fact, research analysts *can* learn the value of the standard deviation of the *sampling distribution of sample means* without going through the laborious process of multiple sampling. Virtually all statistical analysis routines and some spreadsheet and charting programs can compute and report the *standard error of the estimate of the mean,* usually called simply the *standard error* or abbreviated as S.E. The standard error is actually the standard deviation of this would-be *sampling distribution of sample means* computed from many different samples of exactly the same size from precisely the same population.

The standard error of the estimate is *directly* related to the *variance* in the population. In other words, the more the respondents tend to differ from one another or vary in their response to the item, the higher the standard error will be. The standard error is *inversely* related to sample size. The larger the sample, the more representative of the entire population it's likely to be. Thus, the mean from a large sample is less likely to be different from that for the whole population than the mean from a small sample.

Confidence Interval

The confidence interval is a range around the sample mean based on the standard error. Thus, the 68 percent confidence interval is the range from −1 S.E. below the mean to +1 S.E. above the mean. Similarly, the 95 percent confidence interval is the range within ±2 S.E., and the 99 percent confidence interval is the range within ±3 S.E. The range of the standard error is shown graphically in Figure 10–14. Since the mean is 10 and the S.E. is 1, there's a 99 percent chance the actual population mean is between 7 and 13 (±3 S.E.). Similarly, there's a 95 percent chance the population mean is between 8 and 12, and a 68 percent chance it's between 9 and 11.

Many statistical analysis programs routinely compute the 95 percent confidence interval by subtracting twice the value of S.E. from the mean for the lower value and by adding twice the value of S.E. to the mean for the higher value. When only the standard error is computed and reported, the analyst can easily compute the confidence interval in the same way. Guidelines for interpreting confidence intervals are provided in Guidelist 10–4.

To interpret the confidence interval to sponsors, the researcher need only indicate there's a 68 percent chance, a 95 percent chance, or a 99 percent chance the mean for the whole population is within a given range, depending on whether ±1, ±2, or ±3 S.E. is used for the calculation. All three confidence intervals might be reported for key variables. Reporting the confidence interval around a mean provides those seeking the survey information with a sense of the reliability of the estimate and the confidence they may have when making inferences about the whole population.

It's important to note here that the standard error of the estimate and the confidence intervals computed from it can be used for *both* normal distributions and those that depart from normality, no matter how much they depart. In other words, the distribution need not have a skewness and kurtosis value near zero for the *standard error* to be valid. There's no equivalent to S.E. for categorical data. That's why it may be desirable to retain the continuous form of a numeric variable, creating a new, identical one to be recoded into categories when it's desirable to treat it as categorical for some analysis.

FIGURE 10–14   Confidence Interval Diagram

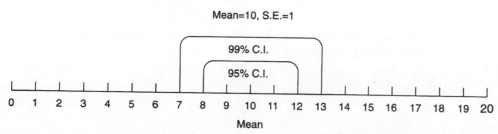

For Interpreting Confidence Intervals   Guidelist 10–4

1. Confidence intervals are based on the *standard error* of the estimate, often called S.E.

2. Confidence intervals apply only to continuous numerical variables.

3. A confidence interval is always based on a given level or probability, usually 95 percent or 99 percent.

4. A 68 percent confidence interval is the range from -1 S.E. below the mean to $+1$ S.E. above the mean.

5. A 95 percent confidence interval is the range from -2 S.E. below the mean to $+2$ S.E. above the mean.

6. A 99 percent confidence interval is the range from -3 S.E. below the mean to $+3$ S.E. above the mean.

7. Confidence intervals are used to indicate the probability the actual *population* mean is within a given range around the sample mean.

8. The standard error and the range of the confidence intervals are measures of reliability.

9. The more *variance* there is in the distribution, the lower the reliability, the larger the standard error, and the wider the confidence intervals will be.

10. The larger the *sample size,* the greater the reliability, the smaller the standard error, and the more narrow the confidence intervals will be.

Summary

Describing Data Distributions

A. Remember the objectives. Statistics are designed to suppress detail and reveal *important* findings.

B. Always identify the scale types. The nature of the scale determines, in part, the proper descriptive measures.

C. Treat variables both ways. Continuous items with only a few scale values can be treated as categorical.

D. Portray information when feasible. Showing the entire distribution is more effective than describing it.

E. Describe data with care. The shape of the distribution affects the choice and interpretation of descriptions.

F. Begin with data description. Organize and interpret the descriptions of individual variables before turning to measures of association.

G. Choose the best average. Consider both the type of scale and the shape of the distribution when selecting the best average.

H. Assess confidence carefully. Choose an appropriate level of probability for determining confidence intervals.

11

Measuring Item Interactions

Relationships Between Variables

The statistical tools and analyses discussed in Chapter 10 allow the researcher to describe or portray individual variables. Analysis of individual variables may satisfy many of the information requirements, but typically the analyst will also want to learn about the *relationships* between pairs of variables. There may be substantial meaning in the description of each of two survey items viewed *individually*, but there may be even more interest in how they're related to one another. In other situations, there may be very little value in the results of two variables viewed *independently*, but, when studied in conjunction with one another, there may prove to be substantial value to the information.

This latter situation is demonstrated in Example 11–1. The percentage distribution shown in the upper left section indicates half of the respondents were of each sex. The percentage distribution displayed in the upper right section of Example 11–1 shows that half of all respondents agreed with the issue and half did not. If only these percentage distributions were presented, the analyst and information seekers would remain ignorant of the relationship between these two variables—sex of respondent and agreement with the issue. They would probably *assume* that about half of all men and half of all women in the population were in agreement. Unfortunately, that would be a serious error.

In the lower section of Example 11–1, these same two variables are *cross-tabulated* with one another. The row and column totals at the right and on the bottom agree with the percentage distributions shown above. But the really *pertinent* information lies in the cells of the *body* of the table. It turns out that *three times* as many women as men are in agreement with the issue in question. Equipped with this information, the survey sponsor or information seekers may address the men and women in their audience very differently or otherwise adjust their actions toward their public, depending on their sex. If so, the principal value of the information doesn't

Interaction Between Variables   Example 11–1

Percentage Distributions of Response			
Sex of Respondent		**Agreement with Issue**	
Men	50%	Agree	50%
Women	50%	Disagree	50%
Total	100%	Total	100%

Cross-tabulation of Variables			
	Men	**Women**	**Both**
Agree	25%	75%	50%
Disagree	75%	25%	50%
Total	50%	50%	100%

lie in knowing about individual variables, but in knowing about their *relationship* to one another!

When the responses to a pair of survey items or variables are compared to one another, over the individual respondents, there are two possible results: Either the answers to the two items may vary or "move" together, indicating they're significantly related to one another, or they may be completely independent of one another, indicating there's no relationship between the two. The statistical tools to measure associations (relationships) between variables are designed to indicate precisely that: whether they are systematically related or completely independent.

Dependent and Independent Variables

When two variables are associated with one another, they may have one of two types of relationships: One can be regarded as partially *causing* or determining the value of the other, or they may be viewed simply as varying or changing together, *without* any causal implications. The statistics used to measure associations don't indicate whether or not one is causing another. That must be determined by the researcher, based on knowledge about the meaning of the items or variables, themselves. The statistics only measure the presence and degree of relationship between items. The existence and direction of causality must be inferred by the researcher, in advance, because the choice of an appropriate statistical tool often depends on whether or not a *causal* relationship is implied.

The selection of the proper statistical tool for the task at hand is just as important for measurement of association between variables as it is for portraying or describing individual items. When individual items are analyzed, the choice of the

FIGURE 11–1
Statistical
Measures of
Association

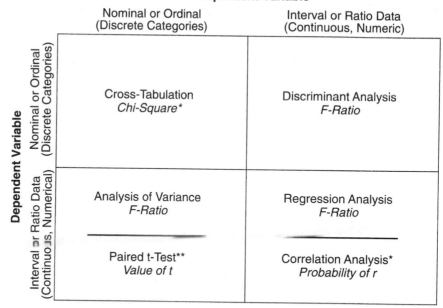

Independent Variable

	Nominal or Ordinal (Discrete Categories)	Interval or Ratio Data (Continuous, Numeric)
Nominal or Ordinal (Discrete Categories)	Cross-Tabulation *Chi-Square**	Discriminant Analysis *F-Ratio*
Interval or Ratio Data (Continuous, Numerical)	Analysis of Variance *F-Ratio* ——— Paired t-Test** *Value of t*	Regression Analysis *F-Ratio* ——— Correlation Analysis* *Probability of r*

Dependent Variable

* Either variable may be regarded as the dependent or independent variable.
** The *independent* variable defines the pairs. Both are *continuous, dependent.*

proper statistical tools depends on the type of variable described or portrayed. Similarly, the choice of an appropriate statistical tool to measure association does depend on the types of variables being analyzed, but it also depends on whether *causality* is implied. If it is, it also matters which item is being affected by the other. Thus, to choose the proper statistical tool to measure a relationship between two items, the researcher must determine two things: what type of variable each item is, and which item will be viewed as "dependent" and which as "independent" if causality is implied. The dependent variable is the one *being caused* or *affected*, and the independent variable is the one *causing* or *affecting* the other.

The analyst should first determine the variable types and direction of causality, and then refer to the simple matrix shown in Figure 11–1 to select the proper statistical measure of association. Nominal and ordinal data in categories and continuous numeric distributions of interval and ratio data were identified and described in the previous chapter. The analyst should be thoroughly familiar with these different types of data in order to select the proper statistical tool to measure association.

With some statistical measures of association, it doesn't make any difference whether one item is causing or affecting the other and, if so, which is affecting the other. Other statistical tools for measuring the association between variables do require the analyst to decide which one can be regarded as affecting the other. The variable that's causing the other to vary or affecting the other is called the *independent* variable. The variable that's being affected or that's presumed to vary because of the value of independent variables is called the *dependent* variable. The direction of causality is from *independent* variable to *dependent* variable.

Merely knowing the name of a variable or what it represents doesn't necessarily indicate whether it will be a dependent or an independent variable for a particular measure of association. The analyst has to know more than that about the meaning of the variables and the possible relationships or dynamics between them. The dependent and independent variables are *operationally* defined—they're identified by how they *operate,* not what they are. The analyst must study the nature of the two items and determine which, if either, is likely to cause or affect the other. At first glance, it might seem that such survey items as demographic characteristics will always be independent variables, while opinions or attitudes are nearly always dependent variables. While that's usually the case, it's certainly not always so in every conceivable situation.

Some survey items may be treated as independent variables for some measure of association or in relation to one set of other variables, and then be treated as dependent variables for another measure of relationships with another set of items. The analyst should identify a variable as dependent or independent for *each analysis* or "pairing," rather than merely identifying each survey item as dependent or independent for all measures.

Statistical Measures of Association

The most common statistical tools to measure the relationship between two survey variables are listed in Figure 11–1. To identify the proper statistical tool, the analyst should identify each variable by *type*—*categorical* or *continuous*—and by operation—*independent, dependent,* or with *no causality* implied. Where no causality is implied and the focus is merely on the degree of association between the two variables, it doesn't matter which is regarded as independent and which dependent. Note, however, that only cross-tabulation and correlation analysis don't require specification of causality. The others listed in Figure 11–1 do require identification of dependence and independence. Once the variable types have been identified and the direction of causality determined, the analyst can refer to the appropriate row and column of the matrix to find the proper statistical tool to measure association. It's important to note, however, that there are *other conditions* regarding the data distributions that have to be met before some of these tools can be used legitimately. They will be discussed below.

An example of the use of the matrix for selecting a statistical tool may prove helpful. Suppose one survey item to be analyzed is the marital status of the respondents and it's a categorical variable, *married* or *not married.* Another survey item might be a simple, *yes/no* answer to some question. If the sponsor wanted to know if the sex of the respondent affects the answer to the yes/no item, sex would be the independent variable. It's a nominal, categorical variable, so the appropriate tool will be in the first *column* of the matrix. The yes/no item is the dependent variable, defining the rows of the matrix, and it's also a nominal, categorical variable, indicating the *top row.* To measure this relationship, the analyst would use cross-tabulation of the two items, because it's listed in the first column, top row. (The technical name for cross-tabulation is *contingency table analysis,* but it's often simply called *"cross-tabs."*) The significance of the relationship would be indicated by the chi-square (pronounced kie-square) statistic. Thus, selection of the proper statistical tool is mostly a matter of finding the correct cell of the matrix by row and column.

In this example, if the analyst wanted to know if men travel further than women or vice versa, the independent variable would again be the sex of the respondent, a categorical variable, again indicating the first column. But in this case, the dependent variable, the one being caused or influenced, would be miles and that is a continuous, ratio data item. Because the dependent variable is continuous, it defines the bottom row. The cell containing the correct statistic would be column 1, row 2, containing Analysis of Variance (ANOVA) or Paired t-tests. In this case, ANOVA would be appropriate. The reason will be explained below.

Each of the statistical measures of association between variables listed in Figure 11–1 will be discussed in the remainder of this chapter. The focus here will first be on the selection criteria and data requirements for each statistical tool. Then the interpretation of the coefficients and values the statistic yields will be discussed and exemplified.

Statistical Significance

Virtually all of the measures of relationships between variables are designed not only to show the degree of association between the items, but also to report the *statistical significance* of the relationship. The word *significance* has a very special and consistent meaning when used in this context. It does *not* mean importance! If a relationship between two variables is statistically *significant,* this simply means it *signifies* or *signals* there's a good chance the two items are actually related to one another in the population, just as they are in the sample. By contrast, if the relationship is *not* significant, this means there's too high a chance this much of a relationship could result only from sampling error, even if it didn't exist in the population at large. Consequently, *significance* is required to make a *statistical inference* about the population, based on the sample. An example may clarify the meaning and interpretation of statistical significance.

Suppose the respondents to a survey are asked to record their age and sex in the demographic section. The sponsor may want to know if the men in the *population* tend to be older, the same age, or younger than the women surveyed. To answer that question, the analyst will need to assess the *relationship* between two variables: *age* and *sex* of respondents. Age is a continuous ratio variable and sex is a nominal, categorical item. The age of the men and women can be compared by computing the average age of each group. Suppose the average age of everyone was 40 and half of the respondents were of each sex. The men in the sample may have an average age of 41 and the women an average age of 39. This *suggests* the men in the *population* are about two years older than the women. That may or may *not* be true.

There's always a possibility the sample "happened," purely by chance, to include a group of men who were somewhat older than the actual average age for all men in the population. There's also some chance that the sample contained a disproportionate number of younger women from the population, also purely by chance. Because of this possibility, there's a chance the average age of men and of women in the population as a whole is exactly the same—40 years. Yet the sample seems to indicate the men were older. The research analyst needs a way to determine the *probability* the sample would produce such differences between men and women even if the average age of all men and women in the population were the same. If the sample has been selected *randomly,* there is a way to determine that probability. In this example, the analyst would use *analysis of variance* to assess the significance of the difference between the average age of men and women, but the interpretation of statistical significance is the same, regardless of the statistical measure that provides it.

The question regarding statistical significance is simply this: What's the chance of this much relationship between the variables resulting only from sampling error if there were no relationship whatsoever in the population? The *significance probability* is the answer to that question! Example 11–2 lists five ways to phrase the interpretation of statistical significance for each of the five measures of association to be discussed here. The same basic wording could be used interchangeably for any of the statistics. The only difference is the type of relationship being analyzed—differences in proportions for cross-tabs, differences in means for ANOVA and paired t-tests, or covariation for correlation and regression analysis.

The most important point is that the *smaller* the significance probability is, the *less likely* the association between the variables resulted *only* from sampling error. So the *smaller* it is, the *more* it *signifies* a similar relationship between the variables in the entire population from which the random sample was selected.

How sure does the sponsor or information seeker want to be? That depends on the *costs* of making either of two kinds of errors, described in Checklist 11–1. Statisticians call them *Type I* errors—rejecting the *null* (no relationship) hypothesis when it's actually true—and *Type II* errors—accepting the *null* hypothesis when it's actually false. This same dichotomy of potential error is common to other fields as well. Medical researchers refer to *false positives*—finding an indication of a condition when it does *not* really exist—and false *negatives*—*finding* no indication when a condition *does* actually exist. In most areas of predictive decision making, there are corresponding errors. There are *go errors* and *no-go errors*—*doing* something when it turns out one should *not* have done it and deciding against doing something that ultimately would have been beneficial, respectively. Anyone who has gone ahead with a picnic only to have it rain or canceled an outing for what turns out to be a beautiful day has an intuitive understanding of such errors. A major advantage of statistical analysis is computation of the *probability* of making the first kind of error—of assuming a relationship exists in the population when, in fact, it shows up in the sample only because of sampling error. Guidelines for assessing statistical significance are presented in Guidelist 11–1.

It's important to note here that significance is related to the importance of a relationship between variables, but the two aren't the same thing. In technical terms, significance is *necessary,* but not *sufficient* for importance. That simply means that if a relationship or difference isn't statistically significant, it can't be regarded as important. On the other hand, simply because it's significant doesn't imply that it will necessarily prove important. In the example used earlier, suppose the difference

Interpretations of Significance Probability   Example 11–2

Example A — Cross Tabulation

Chi-square = 11.5	d.f. = 4	Prob. = 0.050

There is a *five percent* chance this much of a relationship would result purely from sampling error if the two items were *not* related in the population.

Example B — Analysis of Variance

F = 8.2	d.f. = 1	Prob. = 0.002

Two times out of 1,000 this much difference in means between the two groups would result from sampling error if the means in the population were the same.

Example C — Paired T-Test

T = 1.9	d.f. = 932	Prob. = 0.049

This much difference between means for the two variables would result only from sampling error less than *one time out of twenty* if the means were identical in the population.

Example D — Correlation Analysis

r = 0.03	n = 933	Prob. = 0.333

About *one third* of the time, a sample of this size would show this much correlation between the variables due only to sampling error, if the items had zero correlation in the population.

Example E — Regression Analysis

Rsq. = −0.09	d.f. = 931	Prob. = 0.004

The independent variable would explain this much variance in the dependent variable due exclusively to sampling error *less than one half of one percent* of the time if the two items were completely unrelated in the population.

between the average ages of men and of women was rather large but it was *not* significant. The difference would then be attributed to sampling error, despite its size. It wouldn't make good sense to treat the two groups in the population as though they were different in that respect.

Now suppose the difference proved to be slight but it was statistically significant. That means one can be very sure the ages of the two groups in the population are indeed different from one another; yet that slight difference may not be of much *importance* to the sponsor. Statistical significance is a function of several

1. Would it be very costly to *mistakenly assume* the relationship actually exists in the population when, in fact, the two variables are unrelated in the population? If so, the results *shouldn't* be regarded as *significant* unless the probability is extremely low.

2. Is there much to lose by *mistakenly assuming* the relationship resulted only from sampling error and not because it exists in the population when, in fact, it does? If so, the results *should* be regarded as *significant* unless the probability is quite high.

3. Would it be extremely costly to make an error in *either way?* If so, the sampling reliability can be increased by subsequently sampling a larger proportion of the population on a random basis and combining the results to obtain a larger sample size.

things—the sample size, the amount of variance in the variable within the population, and the actual relationship between the variables in the population. These determine the value of the significance probability. The importance of a relationship depends on the meaning of the variables and relationships to the sponsor. It depends on the actions that are implied or the consequences that result.

Cross-Tabulation

Cross-tabulation is by far the most common measure of association between survey variables. It's used much more frequently than all of the other measures of association between variables, combined. Cross-tabulation is so common and popular in part because the method is effective, it can easily be understood and interpreted, and it can be tabulated very readily by both spreadsheets and analysis

1. Significance is determined by the probability that a sample would show such a relationship if it did *not* exist in the population as a whole.

2. If a relationship between variables is regarded as significant, it's taken by *inference* to *exist* in the population as a whole.

3. A relationship can't be viewed as important if it isn't significant, because there's too great a chance it resulted only from sampling error.

4. A relationship that's statistically significant may or may not be important, because importance depends on the strength and meaning of the relationship.

5. The researcher or sponsor must determine the critical value of probability below which the relationship will be viewed as significant and above which it will be attributed only to sampling error.

6. If the probability or significance value generated by an analysis routine is .05, this means there's only a 5 percent chance of such a relationship in the sample if it did not actually exist in the population.

programs. It's also very flexible and robust! In other words, it will readily accept any data that can be put into a limited number of categories. It does lack the power and sensitivity of other measures of association, but cross-tabulation makes up for it by placing very few demands on the type of data it can legitimately analyze. So cross-tabulation is to the statistician's tool chest what a monkey wrench is to the mechanic's toolbox.

Very often, survey items that are continuous are obtained from scales that have only a few scale points or values, so these variables can be treated as categorical and used in cross-tabulation. Even when continuous survey variables have a wide-ranging scale with many values, the data can often be recoded into meaningful categories to provide categorical data for cross-tabulation with other items. Lastly, cross-tabs are often the "method of last resort" for measuring associations between variables. The continuous, interval, or ratio data distributions of one or both variables to be studied may not meet the requirements of such methods as ANOVA or regression analysis. If not, they can be recoded into categories and then submitted to cross-tabs to determine the significance of the relationship between them.

Cross-tab tables indicate the relationship between two categorical variables. The procedure doesn't require one variable to be identified as dependent and the other independent, although that's often the case, as it was for the cross-tab table shown in Example 11–1. If it is, either variable can be listed to define the rows or the columns of the table. The analyst is free to set up the table the way it's most readily interpreted and understood.

There is only one basic requirements for using cross-tabs: The total *n*-size or *number of cases* must be large enough to provide a sufficient minimum *expected* cell frequency. The data can be nominal, ordinal, interval, or ratio, but there should be a *limited number of categories* for each variable. If there isn't, the *expected* cell frequency is likely to be below the minimum of 5 that's required. If an ordinal, interval, or ratio variable has a very large number of values, it can be recoded into a small number of categories by the analysis program. Thus, if the questionnaire asked the respondents to record their age or education in years or their income in dollars or thousands of dollars, there may be many different values for such variables. By recoding age into decades (20s, 30s, 40s, and so on), education into stages (some high school, high school graduate, some college, and so on), and income into broad categories of several thousands of dollars, these variables can be "reduced" into fewer than 10 or 12 categories for cross-tabulation with other variables.

It's important to note that with such recoding of continuous variables into categories, some information is lost. Namely, the information about the *differences* between values that are cast into the same category are obliterated. All the cases within a given category are seen and treated as identical to one another. Thus, it may not always be advisable to recode such data and use cross-tabs if another statistical measure of association could be used to assess relationships with other survey variables. When recoding into categories is required, it's *always* desirable to record into the smallest categories that will yield acceptable *n*-sizes for columns, rows, and cells. That way, the amount of information "lost" or ignored will be minimized.

When it is necessary or desirable to recode continuous data into categories, the analyst should take precautions not to *destroy* the original continuous variable in the process. If the recoding is temporary and does not permanently modify the data file, the analyst can return to the continuous values at a latter stage of processing if necessary. When recoding will permanently change the variable, the recommended procedure is to first create a new variable identical to the original continuous one. Then one can be recoded into categories, leaving the continuity of the other intact.

Row, Column, and Table Percentages

Many computer analysis routines permit the researcher to obtain row, column, and table percentages within the cell, as well as the frequencies, the expected cell frequencies, and the chi-square value for the cell. It's rarely if ever advisable to have all those values listed. Normally, only the frequencies and either the row or the column percentages are needed. Row percentages total to 100 percent across the rows; column percentages total to 100 percent down the columns. Table percentages are just the percentage of all the cases in the table that fall within a given cell.

Row or column percentages are usually required because it's very difficult to interpret the distributions in the cross-tab table based on the frequency or number of respondents in each cell. Ordinarily there will be different numbers of cases in each row and in each column. So the proportions and relationships are difficult to gauge. Table percentages are only rarely useful for some special situations where the researcher would like to infer the percentage in the population who answer each of two survey questions in a certain way. In the majority of cases, the researcher will use only either the row or the column percentages for the bulk of the analysis and interpretation.

Minimum Expected *Cell Frequencies*

The chi-square statistic computed from the cross-tabulation table will indicate the statistical significance of the relationship between the two variables. The meaning and interpretation of chi-square for cross-tabulations will be discussed more fully below. As noted earlier, the chi-square statistic won't be valid or accurate if one or more of the *expected* cell frequencies is less than five. In other words, there must be a sufficient number of cases in the rows and columns in order for the statistic to work correctly and accurately.

Most computer programs that compute chi-square for cross-tabulation produce a table and a statistic, regardless of whether or not the expected cell frequencies are adequate. They don't require a minimum cell frequency for their computations. If the lowest expected cell frequency is less than five, the statistic generated and the significance value based on it won't be valid. Thus, it's imperative the analyst checks the minimum cell frequency for each cross-tab table. Some analysis programs routinely report the smallest expected cell frequency for each table. If the program doesn't do so, the analyst can calculate it with a minimum amount of effort.

The cell of a cross-tab table with the lowest *expected* cell frequency is the one on the *row* with the smallest total and the *column* with the smallest total. Thus, it isn't necessary to calculate the expected values for all the cells. The three-step process is very simple: (1) Find the smallest *row* total, usually listed on the right margin of each row. (2) Divide it by the *table* total, often listed at the bottom right. (3) Multiply this value by the smallest *column* total, usually listed at the bottom of each column. The result is the smallest expected cell frequency.

If the smallest *expected* cell frequency is less than five, the analyst should recode a row or column variable, combining rows or columns until an adequate expected cell frequency is achieved. Notice that this requirement refers to *expected* cell frequency, *not* to the actual or observed cell frequency or number of cases actually in the cell. Untrained researchers commonly err by inspecting the table to see if the smallest actual cell frequency is five or greater. It doesn't matter if the actual cell frequency is *zero*, so long as the *expected* cell frequency is five or more.

As an example, assume the analyst has cross-tabulated education (6 levels) with most common mode of transportation to work (5 levels). There may be only a few respondents who have only an elementary school education. There may also be very few who ride a motorcycle to work. If so, the expected cell frequency for that column and row might be less than five. The analyst might elect either to combine "elementary only" education level with "some high school," or to combine "motorcycle" with "other" modes of transportation. There is no one correct way to combine rows or columns. It would depend on the distributions of data, the meaning of the variables, and the information needs of the information seekers.

Interpreting Cross-Tabulation

Cross-tabulation is used to assess the relationship between two categorical variables. It doesn't matter whether causality is assumed. If it is, it doesn't matter which variable is regarded as dependent or independent. Nor does it matter whether the data are nominal, ordinal, interval, or ratio variables. The only statistical requirement is that the minimum *expected* cell frequency for the table must be five or more. From a *practical* point of view, the only limitation on the use of cross-tabulation is that there should be a limited number of categories for each variable—preferably only 5 or 6, and certainly no more than 10 or 12. Very large tables are too bulky and complex to interpret effectively.

The Cross-Tab Table

The cross-tab table in Example 11–3 will be used to illustrate how cross-tabulation works. The top value in each cell is the *count or frequency*. The bottom number in the cells is the *total percentage*—the percentage of *all* cases that are in the cell. The row and column totals are self-explanatory. The row and column percentages printed below those values are the percentages of all data contained in each row and column. The middle values in each cell, the *expected* values, are the number of cases one would *expect* if the proportions in each cell were the same as the proportions for the row totals and column totals. In other words, the *expected* values are the frequencies that would yield the same *percentage* distributions for each row or each column as the *percentage* distribution for the row or column totals.

Cross-tabulation is a way to show how much the frequency or percentage distributions of one variable differ according to various levels of another variable. In the left section of Example 11–3, the *expected* and *actual* frequencies or counts are exactly the same in each cell. The column totals are 50:50 and so are the values in the cells of each row. There's *perfect* proportionality. In the right section of the example, proportion of

Significance of Cross-Tabulation Tables   Example 11–3

Proportionate, No Relationship				Disproportionate, Strong Relationship		
Count Exp. Val. Tot Pct.	Group 1	Group 2	Row Total		Group 1	Group 2	Row Total
Type A	60 60 30%	60 60 30%	120 60%	Type A	40 60 20%	80 60 40%	120 60%
Type B	40 40 20%	40 40 20%	80 40%	Type B	60 40 30%	20 40 10%	80 40%
Column Total	100 50%	100 50%	200 100%	Column Total	100 50%	100 50%	200 100%
Chi-Sq. = 0.0 d.f. = 1 Sig. = 1.00000				Chi-Sq. = 33.33 d.f. = 1 Sig. = 0.00000			

Group 1 respondents who are also Type A is *disproportionately* low. Instead of 60 cases in that cell, there are only 40. The counts in the other cells are also disproportionate to the row and column totals. So, the chances of an individual being Type A or Type B depends on whether the person is in Group 1 or Group 2. In other words, the two variables—*Group* and *Type*—appear to be related to one another.

Statistical Significance of Cross-Tabs

Visual examination of a cross-tab table (or a graphic picture such as a split bar chart) will reveal the amount of disproportionality to the analyst or information seeker. But the question of *statistical significance* still remains: *What's the chance of this much disproportionality among the rows or columns resulting only from sampling error if there were no disproportionality whatsoever in the population?* The chi-square statistic answers that question.

The chi-square statistic and the significance probability associated with it are based on the amount of difference between the *expected* values for each cell and the actual *count*. The *more* proportional the rows and columns are to the totals, the smaller the chi-square value will be. In the left section of Example 11–3, the differences between the *expected* and *actual* frequencies is zero and so is the chi-square value. In the table in the right section of the example, the differences are large and the chi-square value is also relatively large. The significance probability indicates there's virtually no chance this much disproportionality would result only from sampling error if the two variables—Group and Type—were unrelated in the population. The probability of the chi-square value is listed as zero, but there is

Cross-Tab Row and Column Percentages   Example 11–4

Time of Day Type by Age Group

Column Percentages	Under 35	35 to 49	Over 49	Total
Larks	44.5%	20.0%	21.2%	30.0%
Wrens	27.1%	30.6%	30.6%	29.2%
Owls	28.4%	49.4%	48.1%	42.4%
Total	38.7%	21.2%	40.0%	100.0%

Chi-square = 27.72   d.f. = 4   Prob. = 0.0000

Row Percentages	Under 35	35 to 49	Over 49	Total
Larks	57.5%	14.2%	28.3%	30.0%
Wrens	35.9%	22.2%	41.9%	29.2%
Owls	27.0%	25.8%	47.2%	42.4%
Total	38.7%	21.2%	40.0%	100.0%

Chi-square = 27.72   d.f. = 4   Prob. = 0.0000

always *some* probability the relationship is due merely to sampling error. The analysis routine printed only five significant digits beyond the decimal point, and the probability is so small it registers as zero—and for practical purposes, it can be treated as zero.

In Example 11–4, the column percentages are listed in the table in the upper section and the row percentages are used in the lower section. If the research analyst wanted to see how people in different age groups differ in their time of day preferences, the column percentages would be compared across rows in a table such as the one in the upper section. Thus, over twice the percentage of young people are "Larks" than those of other ages, and so forth.

If, on the other hand, the analyst wanted to see how people with each time of day pattern differ in age, the row percentages could be compared down the columns. For example, only about 28 percent of "Larks" were 50 or older, while nearly 42 percent of "Wrens" and about 47 percent of "Owls" were in the elder group. It would also be possible to reverse the bottom table so the time of day patterns defined the rows and the age groups defined the columns. Column percentages could then be listed and used to make the second type of assessment described above. Guidelist 11–2 summarizes the guidelines for interpreting cross-tabulation.

For Interpreting Significance of Cross-Tabs   Guidelist 11–2

1. Check the minimum expected cell frequency to be sure it's five or greater.

2. The significance probability of chi-square is the probability of this much disproportionality by row or column as the result of sampling error if they were proportional in the population.

3. If the significance probability of chi-square is *smaller* than the critical value chosen by the sponsor, the results are *statistically significant.*

4. If the relationship isn't significant, this can be interpreted to mean the variables are probably not related in the population.

5. If the relationship *is* significant, this implies that in the population as a whole, distributions across

the rows or columns are likely to be disproportionate.

6. If the relationship *is* significant, the two variables are assumed to be systematically related in the population.

7. Even if the relationship is statistically significant, one variable may or may not be *causing* the other.

8. If the relationship *isn't* significant, it can be attributed to sampling error and therefore it *can't* be important to information seekers.

9. Even if the relationship is statistically significant, that doesn't imply that it's *necessarily important* to the information seeker.

Analysis of Variance

When the independent variable is categorical and the dependent variable is continuous, the data can be described in a *breakdown* table or on a bar chart or graph. The appropriate technique to measure the statistical significance of the differences between two or more means is analysis of variance, often referred to by its acronym, ANOVA.

An example may illustrate the use of analysis of variance. The upper section of Figure 11–2 shows the plots of two groups of 170 men and 170 women from the same sample of 510 respondents. These distributions of ratio data are almost identical, but, on average, the men's scores are lower than the women's. The descriptive statistics for the two groups individually and for both combined are shown in the breakdown table in the middle section of Figure 11–2. The lower section contains a vertical bar chart portraying the difference in mean scores on the dependent variable in graphic form.

Breakdown tables and bar charts are very adequate ways to present data description, but they leave a very critical question unanswered: "What's the chance this much difference in mean scores between groups would result merely from *sampling error?*" In other words, how safe is it to make the *assumption* that men's and women's scores actually do differ this much or more in the population as a whole? How *significant* are the differences in mean values? That question can be answered by submitting the data to analysis of variance.

The assumption is that the reason one group has higher scores than the other is because they are of different sexes. So the sex of the respondent is *causing* a difference in scores. Thus, the continuous, numeric, interval scale *scores* constitute the *dependent variable*—the one being caused or affected. The *nominal categories* for

FIGURE 11–2
Association
Between Sex
and Scores

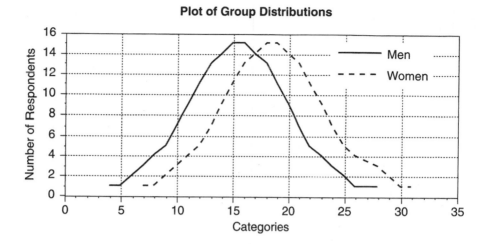

Plot of Group Distributions

Breakdown Table of Group Means

Group	Count	Mean	Standard Deviation
Men	170	16.5	4.6
Women	170	18.5	4.6
Total	340	17.5	4.7

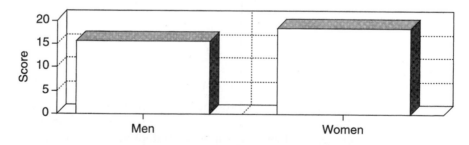

Bar Chart of Group Means

the sex of the respondents is the *independent* variable—the one that is affecting the other.

Obviously, the greater the difference between group means, the *less* likely it resulted merely from sampling error. The *smaller* the difference between group means, the greater probability there is that the sample just happened, by chance, to include one group with higher values and another with lower. These relationships are depicted in Figure 11–3. If these four sets of data were submitted to ANOVA, the differences in the lower section probably wouldn't prove to be significant. Those in the other sections probably or certainly would.

FIGURE 11–3
Differences
Between
Group Means

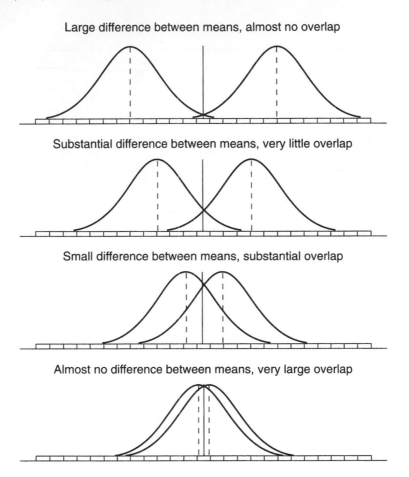

Large difference between means, almost no overlap

Substantial difference between means, very little overlap

Small difference between means, substantial overlap

Almost no difference between means, very large overlap

Requirements for Using ANOVA

Analysis of variance *requires* the data distributions to have certain characteristics: First, the *dependent* variable must be from interval or ratio scales. The second requirement is that each case must be independent of the others—each value of the dependent variable must be from a different person, responding independently of the others. When *two* interval or ratio values are obtained from the *same* respondents, a *paired t-test* can be used to assess the significance of the difference in means. When *more than two* interval or ratio values are obtained from the *same* respondents, testing the significance of the differences among the means requires a special, *repeated measures* design that's beyond the scope of this discussion of ANOVA.

Analysis of variance also requires that the distributions of data for each group have nearly the same variance or spread and that they don't depart significantly from a *normal* distribution. These conditions are depicted in Figure 11–4. Most statistical analysis programs allow the user to request the routine to analyze the distributions and report their *homogeneity of variance, skewness,* and *kurtosis.* The more

FIGURE 11–4
Distributions
Unacceptable
to ANOVA

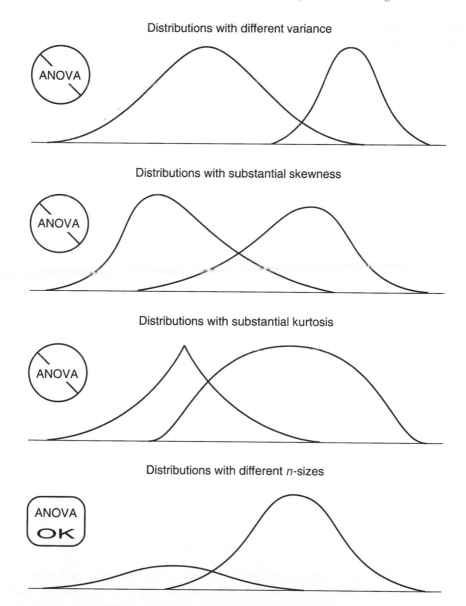

Distributions with different variance

Distributions with substantial skewness

Distributions with substantial kurtosis

Distributions with different *n*-sizes

the distributions deviate from these requirements, the more likely the significance level the routine reports will be erroneous.

ANOVA does *not* require the groups be of the same size. If some groups are very small, with only a few respondents in them, the independent variable should be recoded in the same way as that for cross-tabulation. The only other restriction on group size is that the ratio of the smallest to the largest group should not be extremely small. The results tend to be unreliable if the smallest group is less than about 4 or 5 percent of the largest.

For Using Analysis of Variance — **Guidelist 11–3**

1. The objective is to determine if the mean values of the dependent variable for each category of the independent variable are significantly different from one another

2. The independent variable must be categorical and the dependent variable must be continuous.

3. The dependent variable must be derived from either an interval or a ratio scale, but not an ordinal scale.

4. The values of the dependent variable must be obtained from different respondents, so they're completely independent of one another.

5. The variance in the dependent variable must be about the same within each category of the independent variable.

6. The distributions should be normally distributed or nearly so, with neither substantial skewness nor kurtosis.

7. The independent variable may have two or *more* categories for analysis of variance, but only two for a *t-test,* which is a special case of ANOVA.

8. The groups need not be of the same size, providing the smallest is of adequate size and is no less than about 4 or 5 percent of the largest group.

9. When two values of a continuous, dependent measure are obtained from the *same* respondents and their means are to be compared for significant differences, a *paired t-test* should be used in place of analysis of variance.

Occasionally, a survey will obtain ratings or other continuous interval or ratio data for two or more variables from the *same* respondents. The analyst may want to determine if the mean value for one is significantly greater or lesser than the other. If so, the values wouldn't be "independent" of one another, as noted in the fourth requirement for ANOVA listed in Guidelist 11–3. Analysis of variance shouldn't be used in such cases. Instead, the analyst should use a *paired t-test.* With this procedure, only one pair—two variables—can be compared with each analysis. The *independent* variable becomes, in effect, whether the value is that of the first variable or the value of the second.

Interpreting Analysis of Variance

Analysis of variance measures the degree and significance of a relationship between a categorical independent variable and a continuous numeric dependent variable. Figure 11–5 contains the description of job satisfaction score distributions by three employment types: government, corporate, and self-employed respondents. Based on inspection of either the plot of distributions, breakdown table, or bar chart, it would appear that job satisfaction is strongly related to the type of respondents' employment. But the question of *statistical significance* still remains: *What's the chance of this much difference among mean group scores resulting only from sampling error if there were no such differences whatsoever in the population?* ANOVA can answer that question.

The ANOVA table

The ANOVA table for the variables described in Figure 11–5 is shown in Example 11–5. This is a very conventional format for an ANOVA table. Statistical analysis routines almost always produce a table like this or something very similar, although

FIGURE 11–5   **Distributions for Three Respondent Groups**

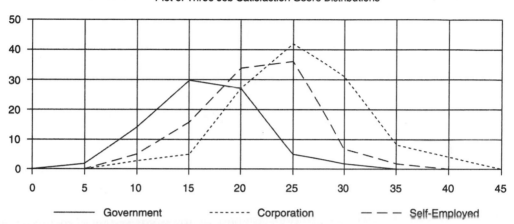

Plot of Three Job Satisfaction Score Distributions

——— Government   ------- Corporation   — — Self-Employed

Breakdown of Mean Job Satisfaction Scores by Employment Type

Employment	Count	Mean	Std. Dev.	Std. Error
Government	80	18.6	5.1	0.57
Corporation	120	27.4	5.7	0.52
Self-Employed	100	23.3	5.0	0.50
Total	300	23.7	6.4	0.37

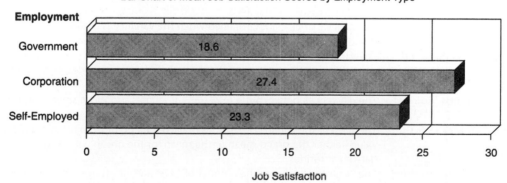

Bar Chart of Mean Job Satisfaction Scores by Employment Type

they may also, either optionally or by default, include additional coefficients such as *range* tests and tests of *homogeneity of variance*.

The terms and values contained in an ANOVA table are explained briefly in Guidelist 11–4. The steps for computing the ANOVA table values are very simple—they require only addition, subtraction, and multiplication. Nonetheless, there are

Analysis of Variance Table   Example 11–5

Analysis of Variance					
Source	Sum of Squares	D.F.	Mean Squares	F-Ratio	F Prob.
Between Groups	3713.42	2	1856.71	65.95	.0000
Within Groups	8361.57	297	28.15		
Total	12074.99	299			

usually so many computations it would be a tedious process to do manually. Nor is it necessary to do so. Analysis software for every budget is readily available, ranging from highly capable, high-end products (www.spss.com) to very inexpensive statistical software add-in for Microsoft Excel® spreadsheets (www.analyse-it .com) to completely free software (www.stat.umn.edu/macanova/).

For Understanding ANOVA Table Terms   Guidelist 11–4

Analysis of Variance
Comparison of all the variance around the grand mean with the amount of variance around the mean for each group.

Source (of Variance)
The "source" of the variance on each row, depending on what means were used to compute the variance.

Total [Source]
The total variance values obtained when the variance is computed around the grand mean without regard for the groups in which each case resides.

Within Groups [Source]
The variance values obtained by computing variance of each data point from around the mean of the group in which the data point resides, combined for all groups.

Between Groups [Source]
The differences between the *total sums of squares* and *mean squares* and the corresponding values from *within groups*.

Sums of Squares (S.S.)
The sums of the squared deviations of each data point from around a mean value—either the grand mean or the mean for the group within which the data point resides.

D.F. (Degrees of Freedom)
The "adjusted" value of the number of cases and/or groups in the analysis, as a divisor to convert total variance values to average variances.

Mean Squares (M.S.)
The sums of the squares for each source of variance divided by the degrees of freedom for that source to constitute an "average" variance for the source.

F-Ratio
The ratio of the *between groups mean squares* to the *within groups mean squares,* expressed as a decimal value.

F Probability
The probability of obtaining an F-ratio of a given value or greater, based on the F probability distribution for numerator and denominator degrees of freedom.

For Interpreting Analysis of Variance   Guidelist 11–5

1. The object is to compute the mean value of the dependent variable for each category of the independent variable and determine if the means for the groups in the analysis are significantly different.

2. If the probability is computed by the analysis routine, it's the probability that as much difference in means would be due merely to sampling error if, in fact, the groups had the same means in the population.

3. The larger the F-ratio value, the smaller the probability and the greater the likelihood of significance. The smaller the F-ratio, the less likely the relationship will be significant at a given probability.

4. If the probability isn't reported by the analysis routine, significance is judged by comparing the value of the F-ratio with the value in a statistical reference table for the F-distribution.

5. Such tables have rows and columns for various numerator and denominator d.f., and if the values listed there are smaller than the F-ratio value from the analysis of variance, this indicates significance.

Statistical Significance of ANOVA

The F probability of .0000 means there's virtually no chance this much difference in mean scores between groups would result purely from sampling error if the group means in the population were identical. Thus, in this case, the analyst would conclude that the two variables are significantly related—that employment type, the *independent* variable, has a significant effect on job satisfaction scores, the *dependent* variable. If the analysis routine reports only the F value and doesn't list the actual probability, the analyst must refer to a statistical table of critical values for the F-distribution. Such tables typically provide values only for specific probability levels, such as .05 or .01. If the F-ratio from the ANOVA is *larger* than the value listed in the table, the differences in means are significant. In other words, the *larger* the F-ratio, the *more* likely the differences in means between groups will be statistically significant. Guidelist 11–5 provides the guidelines for interpreting analysis of variance.

Interpreting Paired t-Tests

At times it may be necessary to check the significance of differences between two continuous variables that were *both* provided by the same respondents. If so, a *paired t-test* provides a better measure of statistical significance than ANOVA does. Figure 11–6 provides a comparison of results from the two statistical tools. The data represent the *initial* and *final* reaction scores of 220 respondents regarding a political issue, taken before and after they received a mailing about the issue. The results of the *paired t-test* are shown below the breakdown table in the upper section of Figure 11–6. The middle section contains an ANOVA table. Analysis of variance treats the *initial* and *final* scores as individual cases, as though they were obtained from different respondents, rather than two ratings by the same individuals. Of course,

FIGURE 11–6   t-Test versus ANOVA Results

T-Test Breakdown Table

Reaction	Count	Mean	Std. Dev.	Std. Error
Initial	220	23.80	4.87	0.33
Final	220	22.89	4.66	0.31
Total	440	23.34	4.78	0.23
Difference	220	0.09	5.19	0.35

t-Value=2.58   d.f.=219   2-tail Probability=.01

Analysis of Variance Table

Source	Sum of Squares	D.F.	Mean Squares	F-Ratio	F-Prob.
Between Groups	90.00	1	90.00	3.96	.05
Within Groups	9945.18	438	22.71		
Total	10035.18	439			

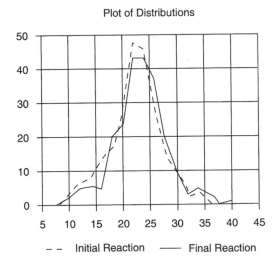

Plot of Distributions

– – Initial Reaction   —— Final Reaction

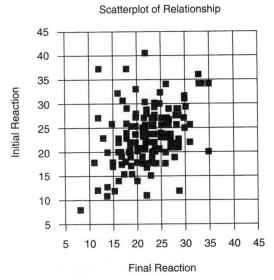

Scatterplot of Relationship

this is improper since ANOVA requires independent measures—each from a separate respondent. It's shown here only to demonstrate the difference in sensitivity.

The ANOVA results indicate the significance of the difference between mean values is .05—one chance in 20 that such results would be obtained purely because of sampling error if there were no difference in means in the entire population. By comparison, the t-test results proved to be a much more sensitive test. The significance of the t-value was .01, or one chance out of a hundred in obtaining such a difference due only to sampling error. Thus, the t-test provides greater assurance of significance than ANOVA for the same data distributions.

For Interpreting Paired t-Tests	Guidelist 11–6

1. The objective is to measure the statistical significance of the difference between two means when the variables are "paired" because the same respondents provided both.

2. The probability of as much difference (in either direction) purely by sampling error if there were no differences in the population is based on the t-value.

3. If the probability isn't listed, analysts can refer to a statistical reference table for the t-distribution, using the value of d.f., and the number of cases minus one.

4. If the absolute value of t, ignoring the plus or minus sign, is larger than that listed in the table, the difference is significant at the given level of probability.

The plot of the two distributions is displayed in the lower left section of Figure 11–6. The picture clearly shows there's only a slight difference between initial and final reactions. In the lower right section of Figure 11–6, the data are portrayed in a scatterplot with the initial reaction scores on the vertical axis and the final reactions on the horizontal. The two reactions appear to be correlated with one another. (The actual value of the correlation coefficient is 0.41.) The reason a *paired* t-test provides a better measure of significance than ANOVA for two measures when *both* are from the *same* respondents can be understood intuitively. ANOVA ignores the fact that some people tend to rate *both* measures relatively high while others rate *both* relatively low. By contrast, paired t-tests focus on the *difference* between each *pair* of scores. In effect, this controls for the variance in *both* measures from one respondent to the next. Guidelines for interpreting paired t-tests are listed in Guidelist 11–6.

Discriminant Analysis

When the independent variable is continuous and the dependent variable is categorical, Figure 11–1 indicates that d*iscriminant analysis* is the appropriate statistical tool to test the significance of the relationship between variables. The technical term for the procedure is *analysis of the linear, discriminant function, or discriminatory analysis.*

With ANOVA the *dependent* variable is a continuous, numeric distribution from an interval or ratio scale and the *independent* (causal) is a categorical variable. With discriminant analysis the *independent* variables are continuous, numeric distributions from an interval or ratio scales while the *dependent* variable is categorical. So in that sense, one is the opposite of the other. The object of discriminant analysis is to classify cases into categories based on the values of the independent, continuous variable.

If the analyst wants to measure the relationship between a continuous, numeric variable and a categorical variable when *no causality* is implied—when it isn't necessary to assume one is affecting the other—ANOVA should be used. Analysis of variance is preferable because it's far more common and understandable. In addition, statistical programs to do ANOVA are much more readily available, they're much easier to use, and it's easier to interpret the results.

Discriminant analysis is a complex statistical tool that's most applicable and useful only under rather stringent conditions. For example, if there are only two groups—two categories or levels of the dependent variable—and *multiple* interval or ratio scale variables, discriminant analysis can be valuable. Such multivariate analysis is beyond the scope of this discussion, but discriminant analysis and a host of other powerful, multivariate statistical tools can be studied in many texts devoted to statistical analysis.

Experienced researchers commonly prefer analysis of variance if there's no compelling reason to use discriminant analysis. The analyst who needs only to establish the significance of the relationship between a continuous numeric variable and a categorical variable would be well advised to use analysis of variance, even though technically the causality is "reversed," so to speak.

Regression and Correlation Analysis

When the objective is to test the degree and significance of the relationship between two continuous variables from interval or ratio scales, the appropriate technique is either correlation or regression analysis. Regression requires that one variable be identified as independent and the other dependent. Correlation analysis measures only the degree to which the two are related, or tend to move together, but there's no assumption that one is causing or affecting the other. If one or both variables are from *ordinal*, rather than interval or ratio, scales, a special form of correlation analysis, called *rank* correlation, can be used. Its interpretation is similar to that for the more common *product-moment* correlation method.

Correlation Analysis

A correlation between two continuous variables is just what the word implies, "co-relation," and it's based on covariance, or movement together. Correlation analysis generates a single value, the correlation coefficient, that shows how much the two variables move together. The correlation coefficient is usually symbolized by the letter r. It ranges from a value of zero, indicating there's no relationship between the variables, to a plus or a minus one, indicating a perfect linear relationship. Figure 11–7 depicts six scatterplots together with the correlation coefficient for each. An r value of 1.000 indicates a "lockstep" relationship between the two variables. In other words, if the value of one of the items increased by one unit from one case to the next, the value of the other item would always move by a given amount, although it need not be the same number of units as the other variable moved.

The plus or minus sign on the correlation coefficient indicates the *direction* of the correlation. If the correlation is positive, the two move in the same direction. If it's negative, they move in the opposite direction. In other words, the plus or minus indicates a *direct* or an *inverse* relationship between the two variables. The absolute value (ignoring the plus or minus signs) shows how much the two items are correlated or moving together. The closer to zero, the less the relationship, and the closer to one, the greater the relationship. Thus, both the sign and the value of the correlation coefficient provide information about the relationship between the variables.

FIGURE 11-7   **Scatterplots and Correlation Coefficients**

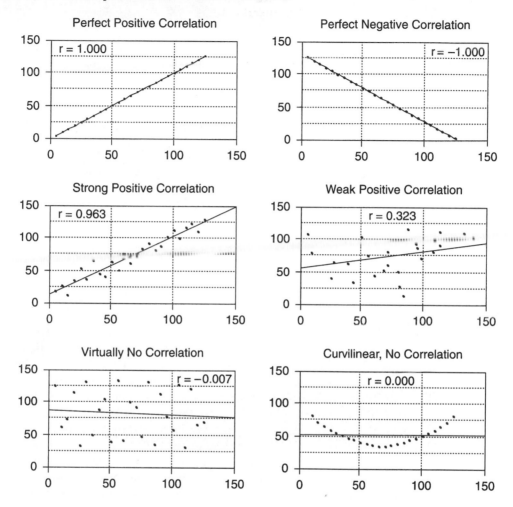

Interpreting the "degree" or strength of the relationship between two variables using the correlation coefficient can be a little misleading, because this coefficient doesn't show what proportion of a "perfect" relationship the two variables have. The proportion of *"shared variance"* is actually indicated by the *square* of the correlation coefficient, and that's called the coefficient of *determination*, symbolized by r^2 or abbreviated as RSQ.

To clarify this interpretation, suppose two survey items are submitted to correlation analysis and the coefficient of correlation is 0.50. This doesn't mean that they're "half" as closely related as they might be if they were perfectly associated with one another. If $r = 0.50$, then r^2, the coefficient of determination, is 0.25 and only 25 percent of the variance in the two items would be "shared" between them. In other words, one could think of them as "tracking together" from one respondent or case

1. The objective is to determine the degree to which two variables move or vary together from one case to the next, and to test the significance of the relationship.

2. Both variables must be continuous, but they need not be identified as dependent and independent.

3. Product-moment correlation requires that both variables are interval or ratio data, but rank correlation can be used when one or both are derived from ordinal scales.

4. The correlation coefficient ranges from zero—no relationship—to plus or minus one—a perfect relationship.

5. When the coefficient is positive, the variables move together in the same direction, and when it's negative, they move together in opposite directions.

6. The percentage of all possible shared variance or movement together is indicated by the *square* of the correlation coefficient, the *coefficient of determination*.

to the next only 25 percent of the time. Similarly, if the correlation coefficient was .70, they would share only 49 percent of the variance, not 70 percent.

The research analyst will also want to know whether or not r^2 indicates a statistically significant relationship between the variables. The significance level is the probability such a relationship would result purely by chance from sampling error if the two items were uncorrelated in the population. Virtually all statistical analysis routines will report that probability. If the significance level isn't reported, it can be checked by reference to standard statistical tables ordinarily appended to statistics texts. Such statistical probability tables can also be readily located with an online search. The analyst need only know the value of the correlation coefficient and number of cases or "degrees of freedom" reported by the routine.

The most common correlation method is called *Pearson product-moment correlation,* or just *product-moment (PM)* correlation. It requires the data be from either *interval* or *ratio* scales. When one or both variables to be correlated are *ordinal* data, *Spearman rank correlation,* or just *rank correlation,* must be used. Rank correlation isn't as powerful or sensitive as PM correlation because the data indicate only order but not the interval between scale points. Guidelist 11–7 summarizes the requirements for using correlation analysis.

Interpreting Correlation

Correlation measures the degree, direction, and significance of relationships between two continuous numeric variables *without* assuming causality—without identifying one as independent and the other as dependent. Figure 11–8 shows the tables and plots of two *pairs* of variables. In a sample of 300 men and 300 women, both sexes responded to a series of items that were totaled to produce a score indicating their degree of trust in the news media. Later in the questionnaire, they were asked to indicate the percentage of time they felt television news reports were totally accurate. Both variables were interval data, but neither was regarded as identified as causing the other.

FIGURE 11–8 **High and Low Correlation Plots**

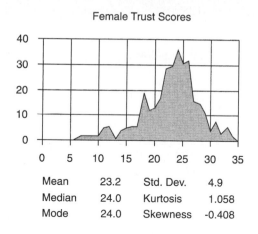

Female Trust Scores

Mean	23.2	Std. Dev.	4.9
Median	24.0	Kurtosis	1.058
Mode	24.0	Skewness	-0.408

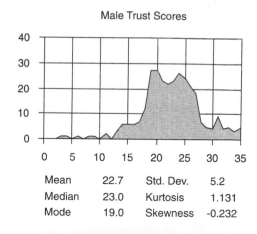

Male Trust Scores

Mean	22.7	Std. Dev.	5.2
Median	23.0	Kurtosis	1.131
Mode	19.0	Skewness	-0.232

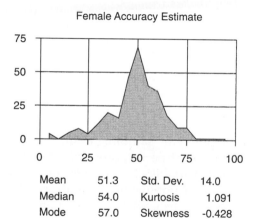

Female Accuracy Estimate

Mean	51.3	Std. Dev.	14.0
Median	54.0	Kurtosis	1.091
Mode	57.0	Skewness	-0.428

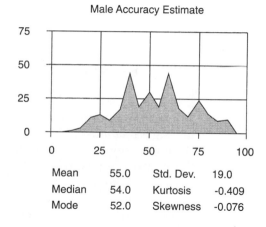

Male Accuracy Estimate

Mean	55.0	Std. Dev.	19.0
Median	54.0	Kurtosis	-0.409
Mode	52.0	Skewness	-0.076

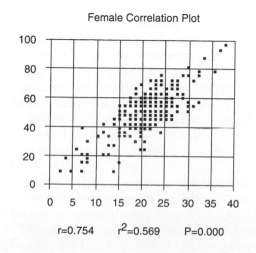

Female Correlation Plot

$r=0.754$ $r^2=0.569$ $P=0.000$

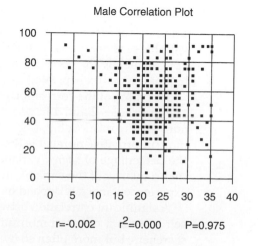

Male Correlation Plot

$r=-0.002$ $r^2=0.000$ $P=0.975$

Correlation Matrix Table   Example 11–6

	Var 1	Var 2	Var 3	Var 4	Var 5
Var. 1	1.000	.303	.011	.164	.094
	—	.001	.402	.001	.018
Var. 2		1.000	−.098	.479	.083
		—	.014	.001	.032
Var. 3			1.000	−.193	.425
			—	.001	.001
Var. 4				1.000	.010
				—	.408
Var. 5					1.000
					—

The scatterplots in the lower section of Figure 11–8 list the accuracy scores on the vertical (y) axis and the trust scores on the horizontal (x) axis. The coefficient of *correlation* (r) and the coefficient of *determination* (RSQ) are listed below each plot. The significance probability for women indicate there's virtually no chance of obtaining a relationship of this magnitude purely by sampling error if it didn't exist in the population. By contrast, there's a near-perfect probability of obtaining the minuscule relationship between these variables for the men in the sample strictly by sampling error if it didn't exist in the population. Thus, the two types of scores would be regarded as signifying a relationship in the population. The same pair of scores—accuracy and trust scores—were not significantly related for the male group.

Example 11–6 shows a *correlation matrix* for each pair of five variables. This is a common tabular format when all the two-way relationships among a group of variables are analyzed. In this example, the probability for assessing significance appears below the correlation coefficient in each cell. Often only the upper right half of the matrix is printed because both sides of the diagonal are identical.

The value of the correlation coefficient can easily be misinterpreted. In Example 11–6, variables 2 and 4 have a correlation coefficient of 0.479. This *appears* to be a fairly strong relationship, since it's *half* the maximum value of r. In *fact*, however, the more informative number is RSQ, the coefficient of determination, since it identifies the percentage of *shared* variance. In this case, RSQ equals only 0.229. Thus, less than a quarter of the variance in the two variables is "shared" between them. Most experienced analysts depend more on RSQ than r to interpret correlations.

A significant correlation between variables does *not* imply causality, in and of itself. This is a *very* common interpretive mistake, sometimes perpetrated by researchers, but more often so by the news media. In fact, if *A* and *B* are correlated,

For Interpreting Correlations   Guidelist 11–8

1. The object is to measure the direction, degree, and statistical significance of relationships between two continuous variables when no causality is implied.

2. Product-moment correlation analysis is used for interval and ratio scale data, and rank correlation analysis is used for ordinal data.

3. The correlation coefficient ranges from zero, indicating no relationship, to plus or minus one, indicating a perfect, linear (lockstep) relationship.

4. The sign of the correlation coefficient shows whether the variables are directly or inversely related (moving in the same or opposite directions).

5. The probability for assessing significance is the chance that such a relationship would result purely by sampling error if the variables weren't related in the population.

6. If the probability for assessing significance isn't listed, the researcher must refer to a statistical reference table for significance of correlation coefficients.

7. If the absolute value of the correlation coefficient, ignoring the sign, is larger than that listed in the reference table, the relationship is significant.

8. Correlation doesn't imply that one variable is causing the other, because A may cause B, B may cause A, A and B may interact, or C may cause A and B.

there are four potential causal relationships, aside from sheer chance: A may be causing B, B may be causing A, A and B may be *interacting* (dynamically causing one another in turn), or C may be causing both A and B. Guidelines for interpreting correlations are listed in Guidelist 11–8.

Regression Analysis

When there are two continuous interval or ratio variables, one of which can be identified as an independent variable and the other as the dependent variable, *regression analysis* is the appropriate technique to measure the relationship between them and assess its significance. When the analysis includes just one independent variable, the more precise term is *simple, linear regression*. This is the technique described here, but there are extensions of the method, called *multiple regression,* which include a single dependent variable and multiple independent variables.

There are usually two objectives of regression analysis: One is to measure the degree and direction of the influence of the independent on the dependent variable and, of course, to assess the statistical significance of the relationship. Another is to obtain a formula to *predict* the value of the dependent variable for a new case based on knowledge of the independent variable. A brief example may demonstrate these two objectives.

Suppose a clothing shop sponsors a survey to determine the age of their customers and the dollar value of their purchases during the recent past. Both age in years and purchases in dollars are continuous, ratio scale variables. Since the customer's age might affect the volume of purchases, but not vice versa, age is the independent variable and purchase value is the dependent variable. Figure 11–1 indicates that regression analysis is the appropriate statistical tool to assess the relationship between these two variables.

The first objective would be to determine if age had a *statistically significant* influence on purchase behavior. If it did, the analyst would want to know how much and in what direction. (If the analyst wanted only to measure the significance of a relationship, correlation analysis, rather than regression, would accomplish only that.) If a significant relationship exists, the analyst may also want to know how to predict the purchase level of customers of different ages and how accurate these predictions are likely to be. If purchases could be predicted with reasonable accuracy, the shop sponsoring the survey could adjust their merchandising and promotional policies to obtain the age group with greatest potential sales volume. It might also use the information to forecast sales based on the ages of those visiting the store or shopping center.

Regression analysis produces a coefficient that's practically the same as the coefficient of determination for correlation analysis. It's ordinarily called R^2 (R-square with an upper-case R) or abbreviated RSQ. With correlation analysis, the square of the coefficient indicates the proportion of variance in the two variables that's "shared" between them. With regression analysis, RSQ indicates the percentage of variance in the dependent variable that's "explained" by the values of the independent variable, as depicted in Figure 11–9. Thus, RSQ is an indication of how much influence the independent variable has on the dependent variable. Some statistical programs also compute and report the significance of RSQ, but if not, the analyst can refer to statistical tables to determine the significance level.

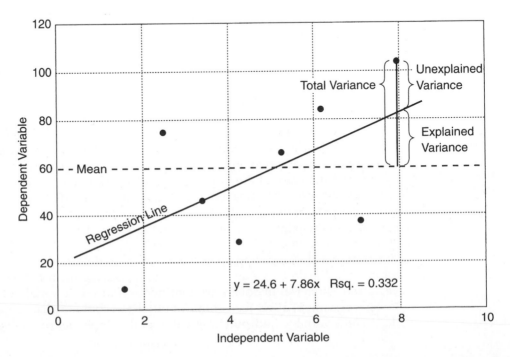

FIGURE 11–9
Variance Explained by the Regression Line

$y = 24.6 + 7.86x$ Rsq. = 0.332

While the correlation coefficient is either positive or negative, indicating the direction of the relationship, the RSQ value is always positive (because it's a squared value). The value of RSQ ranges from zero to one. A value of zero indicates the independent variable has no influence whatsoever on the dependent variable, as in the lower sections of Figure 11–7. A value of one indicates that the value of the dependent variable could be predicted exactly if the value of the independent variable is known, as in the upper sections of Figure 11–7. In other words, just as with correlation, the variables are in a perfect, linear, "lockstep" relationship with one another from one case or respondent to the next.

Regression analysis generates a "regression equation," as well as the RSQ value. The regression equation is the formula for computing a predicted value for the dependent variable, based on the value of the independent variable. There are only two values required in the equation for simple, linear regression: a constant and a regression coefficient. (This is merely the equation for a straight line: $y = a \pm bX$, where a is the constant y intercept and b is the slope of the line.) Using the equation shown in Figure 11–9 to predict the value of the dependent variable for a new case when only the value of the independent variable is known, the analyst would multiply that value by the value of the regression coefficient, 7.86, and add the constant, 24.6. Thus, if the value of X for a new case was 6, the computation would be $y = 24.6 + (7.86 \times 6) = 71.76$.

In Figure 11–10, the points are very close to the regression line, indicating that the RSQ value will be very high and that one could make very accurate predictions of unknown values for the dependent variable based on known values of the independent variable. An RSQ value of 0.96 means 96 percent of the variance around the mean is "explained" by the regression line. On the other hand, when the data points on a scatter plot "splay" widely from the regression line, the RSQ value and the ability to predict will be low.

Requirements for Regression

Regression analysis requires that both the independent and dependent variables are from interval or ratio scales. Each pair of values must come from an independent

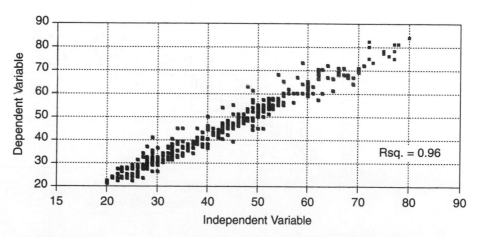

FIGURE 11–10
A Linear Regression Scatterplot

FIGURE 11–11
A Curvilinear
Scatterplot
Pattern

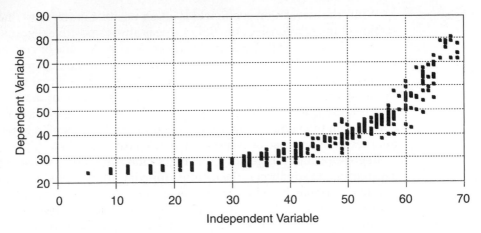

case or respondent. The relationship between the variables must be *linear*. That means if the cases were plotted, the points on the plot must be arrayed approximately in a straight line. Figure 11–11 shows a case where the corridor of data points are sharply curved rather than linear. If these data were used for regression, the RSQ value would be deflated and predictions for the dependent variable would be too high for low and high values of the independent variable and too low for medium levels.

Most statistical analysis programs include optional routines that indicate whether the scatterplot departs significantly from linearity. Such tests should routinely be run during analysis. It may also be advisable to plot the data points and visually examine the plot. Analysis routines will compute the statistics regardless of whether or not the plot is linear, but the results are very likely to be grossly misleading or completely erroneous if the requirements aren't met properly.

Another requirement of regression analysis is that the *vertical* spread or variance around the regression line (the spread of the dependent, Y variable) be approximately equal. If not, erroneous results will be generated. Figure 11–12 shows a

FIGURE 11–12
A Funnel-
Shaped
Scatterplot

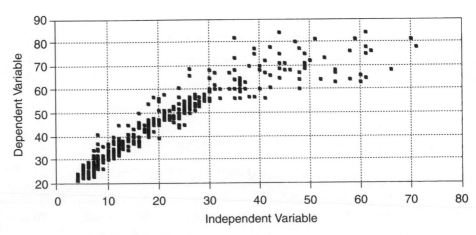

For Using Regression Analysis   Guidelist 11–9

1. One objective is to measure the degree and direction of influence the independent variable has on the dependent variable.

2. Another objective is to obtain an equation to predict an unknown value of the dependent variable, based on the known value of the independent variable.

3. One variable must be identified as independent and one dependent, and both must be derived from interval or ratio scales.

4. The strength of the influence of the independent on the dependent variable is indicated by r-square, ranging from zero (no influence) to one (perfect determination)

5. The regression equation consists of a constant and a regression coefficient, indicating the

direction and amount of influence, or slope of the regression line.

6. When the regression coefficient is positive, the relationship is direct and the slope is upward to the right. When it's negative, the relationship is inverse and the slope is downward to the right.

7. Regression analysis requires that the relationship be linear rather than curved or kinked.

8. Regression also requires the variance of the dependent variable around the regression line to be approximately equal from one end of the line to the other.

9. Both *linearity* and *homogeneity* of variance around the regression line can be checked by visual inspection of a scatterplot or by statistical tests during analysis.

---

pattern that's very common for survey data. Notice the data points are closely clustered around the regression line for the lower values of the variables, but they splay outward quite widely for the higher values. Again, the statistical analysis programs for regression usually allow the user to specify a test to determine if the variance of the dependent variable around the regression line is the same across the range of independent variable values or differs significantly from homogeneity. Guidelines for using regression analysis are provided in Guidelist 11–9.

Interpreting Regression Analysis

Linear regression analysis is used to measure the effect of one continuous variable on another. So, one must be specified as the independent variable and the other the dependent variable. Both must be from either interval or ratio scales. The other requirements for the legitimate use of regression analysis were discussed above.

The Regression Table

Example 11–7 contains a typical regression table report from a statistical analysis routine. The values and coefficients in the table are described in Guidelist 11–10. A scatterplot of the same data is shown in the upper section of Figure 11–13. These data provide an example of the interpretation of regression.

In this example, a group of resident *homeowners* in a planned development community were surveyed to measure their *expected* spending at one of the recreational facilities—the *independent* variable for analysis. During the following period, their *actual* spending was recorded—the *dependent* measure. The scatterplot, regression

Regression Analysis Table   Example 11–7

Descriptive Statistics					
Independent Variable					
Mean	22.450	Std. Dev.	4.700	S.E. Mean	0.271
N of Cases	300	Skewness	−0.371	Kurtosis	1.079
Dependent Variable					
Mean	22.663	Std. Dev.	4.660	S.E. Mean	0.269
N of Cases	300	Skewness	−0.425	Kurtosis	1.353
Regression Table					
Corr. (r)	.79538	N of cases	300	Missing	0
R-Squared	.63263	S.E. Est.	2.82923	Sig. R	.0000
Intercept (A)	4.958113	S.E. of A	.798464	Sig. A	.0000
Slope (B)	.788651	S.E. of B	.034814	Sig. B	.0000

Analysis of Variance					
	S.S.	**D.F.**	**M.S.**	**F**	**Sig.**
Regression	4107.65069	1	4107.65059	513.16657	.0000
Residual	2385.34608	298	8.00452		

equation, and RSQ value are shown in the upper section of Figure 11–13. The lower section shows the corresponding information for another group of 300 *renting* residents who were surveyed in the same way. The dependent and independent variables are significantly related to one another for both types of residents, but comparison indicates that expectations of *homeowners* are much better *predictors* of spending than those of *renters*.

Regression Analysis Predictions

The significance of r, the correlation coefficient, indicates the degree, direction, and significance of the relationship between two variables. Regression analysis and the resulting *regression equation* provide two additional kinds of information: It describes *how* the variables are related and it also provides a method for *predicting* the value of the *dependent* variable for new cases based on the value of the *independent* variable. Causality doesn't matter for *correlation* analysis. It *does* matter for *regression*.

For Interpreting Regression Tables	**Guidelist 11–10**

Corr. Coef. (r)	The product-moment coefficient of correlation between the two variables, described earlier in this chapter.
N of Cases	The sample size or number of cases in the analysis that's the basis for computation of the *degrees of freedom* for the analysis.
Missing Values	The number of cases for which one or both variables had missing or unacceptable values (e.g., zeros, blanks, outlying values, etc.).
R-Square	The coefficient of *determination* is the square of the correlation coefficient (r). It indicates the percentage of *explained variance* as described previously and shown in Figure 11–9, page 330.
S.E. Est.	Standard error of the estimate around the *regression line,* depicted in Figure 11–16. It determines *confidence intervals* around the regression prediction just as its counterpart is used for estimates of the mean.
Sig. R	The probability of obtaining r of this value or greater because of sampling error if the variables were unrelated in the population.
Intercept (A)	This constant is the predicted value of Y when X is zero. In effect, it's the height of the regression line on the Y axis.
S.E. of A	Standard error of the estimate of the Y intercept value.
Sig. A	The probability of obtaining A of this value or greater because of sampling error if it were the mean of Y in the population.
Slope (B)	The slope of the line, defined as the *rise over the run* in terms of Y and X values, respectively.
S.E. of B	Standard error of the estimate of the slope of the regression line.
Sig. B	The probability of obtaining a slope of this inclination or greater because of sampling error if the slope was zero (horizontal) in the population.
ANOVA (for regression)	Analysis of the proportion of *total variance* around the mean of Y *explained* by knowing the values of X. The regression ANOVA is analogous to *analysis of variance* around the means for groups, described earlier in this chapter. The terms of the ANOVA table are similar to those described in Guidelist 11–4. The F-value and significance level are computed and interpreted in the same way.

As the plots and regression equations in Figure 11–14 show, regressing *actual* spending on *expected* spending isn't the same thing as regressing *expected* on *actual*. The correlation coefficient is the same, but the regression equation and scatterplots are different.

In regression scatterplots, the causal independent variable is conventionally shown on the horizontal X axis, and the effected, dependent variable is plotted on the vertical Y axis. The regression equation refers to X and Y values, so the independent and dependent variables are often called the X and Y variables, respectively.

Another analytical factor that affects the values of the regression equation is the *range* of the independent (X) variable included in the analysis. Figure 11–15 contains four scatterplots, regression equations, and RSQ coefficients for the same variables—the expected and actual spending of homeowners. The plot in the upper left is merely a miniature of that in the upper section of Figure 11–13. It

FIGURE 11–13
The Strength
of Regression
Relationships

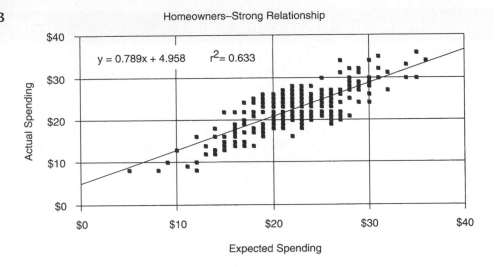

Homeowners–Strong Relationship

$y = 0.789x + 4.958$ $r^2 = 0.633$

Actual Spending (y-axis: $0, $10, $20, $30, $40)

Expected Spending (x-axis: $0, $10, $20, $30, $40)

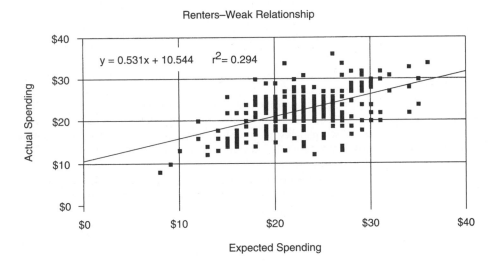

Renters–Weak Relationship

$y = 0.531x + 10.544$ $r^2 = 0.294$

Actual Spending (y-axis: $0, $10, $20, $30, $40)

Expected Spending (x-axis: $0, $10, $20, $30, $40)

includes the full range of nonzero expected spending. The remaining sections sequentially reduce the range of the X variable. As the range changes, so do the regression equation and RSQ value. Thus, when predictions are to be made based on regression analysis, it's important to be sure the analysis includes the proper range of the *predictive independent* variable.

An example of the use of the regression equation from the upper section of Figure 11–13 may clarify the application of this kind of analysis. The facility that sponsored the survey wanted to predict the demand for equipment and services in subsequent periods by *new* homeowners coming into new sections of the closed community as additional phases of development were completed. To do so, they surveyed new owners to learn the amount of *expected* spending. In one case, the

FIGURE 11–14
Direction of
Causality for
Regression

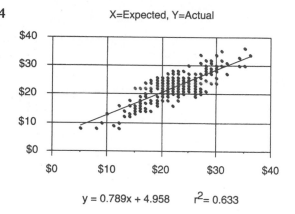

X=Expected, Y=Actual

y = 0.789x + 4.958 r^2 = 0.633

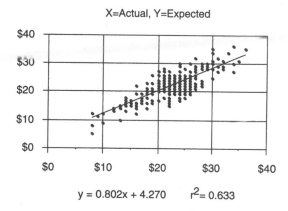

X=Actual, Y=Expected

y = 0.802x + 4.270 r^2 = 0.633

family *expected* to spend $33.00. This is the value of the X variable for prediction of Y, their actual spending. The regression equation is: Y = 0.789x + 4.958. Substituting the value of X, the prediction is Y = 0.789 (the slope) times 33.00 + 4.958 (the constant) = 30.995. So they can expect this new homeowner to spend about $31 per month at their facility. This example is shown graphically on the scatterplot in Figure 11–16.

The relationship between expected and actual spending isn't perfect—the RSQ value isn't 1. While a lot of the variance around the mean of Y has been "explained" by the regression line, there is obviously some error remaining. This raises the questions, "What are the chances the estimate is incorrect, and by how much?" Those questions can be answered by computing the *confidence intervals* around the estimate in much the same way as the confidence intervals around a mean value from a sample are calculated. In other words, the standard error of the estimate around the *regression line* is akin to the standard error of the mean. Ninety-five percent of the actual values will be within ± 2 S.E. of the regression estimate and 99 percent will be within ± 3 SE.

In the example the *predicted* value of spending was $31.00 and S.E. is $2.83. So, there's a 95 percent chance their actual spending will be between $31.00 ± $5.66,

FIGURE 11–15 **Variable Ranges and Predictive Ability**

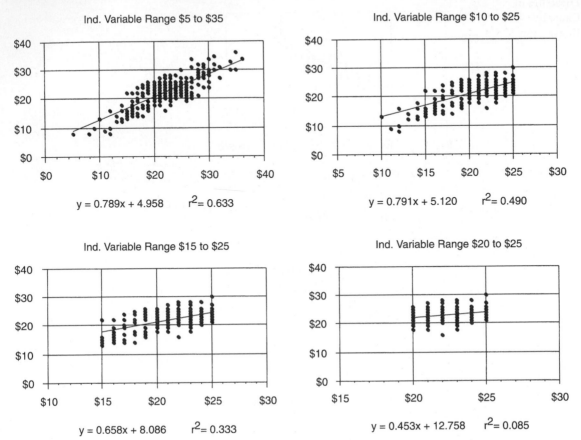

Ind. Variable Range $5 to $35

$y = 0.789x + 4.958$ $r^2 = 0.633$

Ind. Variable Range $10 to $25

$y = 0.791x + 5.120$ $r^2 = 0.490$

Ind. Variable Range $15 to $25

$y = 0.658x + 8.086$ $r^2 = 0.333$

Ind. Variable Range $20 to $25

$y = 0.453x + 12.758$ $r^2 = 0.085$

or between $25.34 and $36.66. Similarly, there's a 99 percent probability the actual spending will be between $22.51 and $39.49. These values could be verified visually by extending vertical and horizontal lines to the boundaries of the confidence interval corridors in much the same way as the estimate was plotted. Guidelines for interpreting regression analysis are contained in Guidelist 11–11.

Interpreting versus Reporting

The statistical tools described here are the most *fundamental*. They're designed for basic measurement of bivariate relationships. They're probably adequate for analysis and interpretation of the data from the vast majority of survey research projects. It's important to note, however, that there are a host of more complex, multivariate statistical tools readily available to those who know how to use them properly and effectively. If the survey project, information needs, and resources warrant more sophisticated analyses than those discussed here, the analyst may

FIGURE 11–16   **Standard Error of the Regression Estimate**

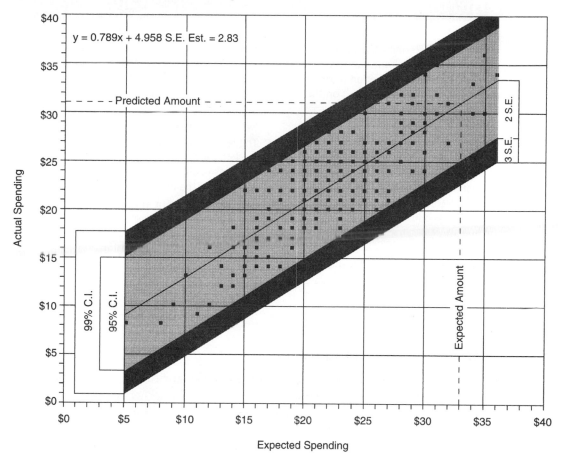

seek either guidance from advanced statistical texts or the advice and assistance of an expert.

This chapter has focused on helping the survey research analyst to understand the various terms, values, coefficients, and relationships revealed by statistical analysis. While it may be necessary for the analyst to comprehend such information, it typically isn't required of the *sponsors* or *information seekers* to whom the information will be reported. In fact, without a statistical background, most sponsors and information seekers won't find the "raw" reports from analysis routines much more meaningful or informative than they would the "raw" data. Thus, there's an important distinction between *interpreting* statistical results and *reporting* the information to those who seek it. While some components of the final report are very similar to what was shown and discussed in this and the previous chapter, most of the formats and language differ sharply. The formats, guidelines, and recommendations for *reporting* the statistical findings are provided in Chapter 12.

For Interpreting Regression Analysis   Guidelist 11–11

1. Regression is used to determine the degree, direction, and significance of one variable's effect on another *and to* obtain an equation to predict values of the dependent variable based on the values of the independent variable.

2. The r-square value ranges from zero to one and indicates the proportion of variance in the dependent variable that's *explained by the values* of the independent variable

3. *The assessment* of significance is determined by the value of r, the correlation coefficient, and significance is checked in the same way as for correlation analysis.

4. The regression equation consists of a coefficient to be multiplied by a known value for the independent variable, plus a constant to be added, to compute a predicted value of the dependent variable for a "new" case.

5. The constant, often designated with the letter A, is the intercept, the value of the dependent variable when the independent variable is zero.

6. The regression coefficient, often designated with the letter B, is the *slope* of the regression line, or the rise on the dependent variable scale for each unit of the independent variable.

7. A positive coefficient indicates a *direct* relationship and a regression line sloping upward toward the right, while a negative coefficient indicates an *inverse* relationship and a line sloping downward to the right.

Summary

Measuring Relationships Among Items

A. Determine the data type. Continuous and categorical data require different statistical measures of association.

B. Define dependent and independent variables. Examine the meaning of the items to determine direction of causality, if any.

C. Select the correct tool. Statistics that use continuous data provide more sensitive measures of associations between items.

D. Meet distribution requirements. Examine data distributions to be sure they meet the requirements of the intended analysis tools.

E. Depend on cross-tabulation. Use cross-tabs to measure associations between variables if the data conditions required by other measures of association aren't met.

F. Check causality carefully. Remember that an association between variables doesn't automatically imply that one is causing the other.

G. Use prediction cautiously. Be sure that equations for prediction from regression analysis are valid and stay within the range of the database.

H. Make inferences carefully. Choose an appropriate level of probability for assessing the statistical significance of associations between variables.

I. Consider practical importance. Make a clear distinction between statistical significance and the practical implications of relationships between variables.

12

Reporting the Information

Information Need Satisfaction

Report generation is the task of making the survey results respond directly and meaningfully to the information needs. When the questions, scales, and questionnaire were composed, the items were arranged to make it easy and understandable for respondents. During the reporting phase, they're usually rearranged to make the information understandable and easy to grasp by those seeking the information. The main information requirements and the most important items or facts should be listed first, followed by those of lesser importance, regardless of the order in which they appeared in the questionnaire.

The last two chapters discussed two kinds of statistics—data description and measures of association between items. The information is usually presented in that order in written reports and presentations. That means showing the results for all of the *individual items* or sections first. After that, the main *relationships* between items are presented. The most common way to report survey results to sponsors is with a written report containing tables and charts as well as explanatory text. Such reports may be copied and bound for distribution, but more often only a limited number of hard copies are printed. Increasingly such reports are posted on a network where those authorized to obtain the information are provided access.

In this chapter, the emphasis will be mainly on composition of an effective *written* report including text, tables and graphs. Such reports are the "work horses" for reporting survey information. They're typically written on a word processor but tables and graphs may also be produced and imported from spreadsheets, database programs, analysis programs, and charting and graphics programs.

Text and tables are the backbone of most written research reports, but charts and graphs have an important role to play in conveying survey information. Words and numbers have to be manipulated mentally by those reading or listening to the report. For instance, if the report says 40 percent of respondents answered in one way and 60 percent in another, the reader has to mentally *visualize* a 4 to 6 ratio. Such proportions would be clearly and instantaneously visible in a simple graphic such as a pie chart. Graphics of this kind don't rely on words or numbers. Instead, they use *space* and *position* to portray magnitudes and relationships.

This chapter begins with a discussion of the main features and organization of written reports and oral presentations. After that, guidelines and examples of *data description* reports for each type of question and scale discussed in Chapters 4, 5, and 6 are provided. The remainder of the chapter contains recommendations and examples for reporting each *measure of association* between variables discussed in Chapters 10 and 11. While text and tables get the bulk of the attention here, examples of graphs and charts are also included.

Report Introduction

Perhaps the most useful and practical form of organization for a survey report is one that might be called the "newspaper" format. With this approach, the results are presented two or three times, rather than just once, but the level of detail increases substantially each time and the sections are divided and identified.

Executive Summary

The first section might contain an "executive summary" of the information. Often no more than a page or so, this first section includes only the major *highlights* of the results. It addresses only the most important information needs and presents a very brief sketch of the most valuable findings. An executive summary often uses *bulleted* paragraphs ranging in length from a single line to only a few lines.

Executive summaries may also be in brief form—paragraphs of no more than two or three sentences each, headed or titled with a key phrase to identify the type of information. The entire executive summary should take no more than a few minutes to read. It should only "hit the high points" of the information acquired in the survey and excite the interest and curiosity of readers, enticing them to look further to the next section.

Response Summary Questionnaire

Often the people seeking the information have participated in creating the questionnaire. If so, they're probably very familiar with the instrument. The questionnaire can be used effectively *in addition* to the executive summary. It's fairly easy and often useful to produce a facsimile of the questionnaire containing brief listings of the distributions of response. It's sometimes called a "Response Summary Questionnaire." It may be appended to the executive summary or included between that and the body of the report. It's *never* advisable merely to jot in the results on a blank questionnaire form. If it's to be used, it should be very neat and presentable.

The cosmetic aspects of the report may not seem to be very important compared to the contents and results. Wrong! The appearance of the report is *always* important. Every experienced researcher should be able to attest to that. The reason is simple: Sponsors are seldom experts at judging the technical performance of the survey designer or researcher. They ordinarily have some doubts concerning how accurate, reliable, and valid the results of the survey will be. They have very few ways to judge these things. Thus, they'll invariably place more confidence and

| **For Writing the Report Introduction** | **Guidelist 12–1** |

1. Begin with an executive summary of one or two pages.
2. Use bullets or brief paragraphs of two or three sentences each.
3. Cover only the major highlights and information needs.
4. Use headings or key phrases to identify sections.
5. The summary must stimulate interest and excite curiosity.
6. Use a *response summary questionnaire,* if appropriate.
7. Delete superfluous content from the response summary.
8. Type all entries and compose the summary very neatly.

value on any report that's neatly and carefully composed and presented than on one that's quickly or ineptly composed. Despite what those receiving reports may claim, and regardless of their impatience to receive the information, the researcher can be sure a haphazard appearance or the discovery of even minor errors or omissions will *seriously* jeopardize the confidence of those who read the report.

When a response summary questionnaire is included, the superfluous record format indications and precoding values should be deleted. Any instructions or notations that aren't relevant to understanding either the results or the way in which questions were asked should also be removed. The distributions of response to categorical items and the appropriate averages for continuous items should be *typed* in the proper places, next to the questions or items. The advantage of including a response summary questionnaire is that sponsors can turn to it later to see how the actual questions were phrased, the order in which they were presented, and the nature of the surrounding material. This can be quite helpful because the items are usually abbreviated or presented in a different sequence and context in the narrative and tabular report. The disadvantage of a response summary is that it's organized in a way that's convenient for respondents, rather than according to the categories of information needs or by the importance of the issues. Nevertheless, if there's any doubt about whether or not to include a response summary questionnaire, it's advisable to do so because it's so quick and easy to prepare. Basic guidelines for composing report introductions are outlined in Guidelist 12–1.

Narrative Reporting

The executive summary and response summary questionnaire should serve only as a prelude to the body of the survey report. This part, containing well-formed and composed tables and graphs, also includes a complete narrative discussion of the survey results. The text should be divided into major sections, according to the various types of information requirements, topics, or issues that were the focus of the survey. The narrative should refer to the tables or figures by number where appropriate. The tables or figures should appear only *after* they're referenced in the text. It's also important to avoid technical terms or phrases because sponsors aren't likely to be familiar with the jargon associated with survey research, data processing, or statistical analysis. With care and effort, even the most complex results can be expressed in lay terms. The objective of the report is to convey information, not to impress the reader with the writer's technical vocabulary. It's far better to violate every rule of grammar in order to say something clearly than to express it "correctly" but obscurely.

Use simple, direct sentences. They're more powerful and concise than long, flowing sentences. They make reading the report easier and more enjoyable for those seeking the information. Be *very* careful about identification of antecedents and object references. Don't use pronouns, such as *they, them, its, those,* and so on, unless it's perfectly clear what these pronouns refer to. Always use the noun to identify the person or thing being referenced if there might be doubt, even if it must be repeated in the same sentence. Refer to tables, graphs, variables, or items by name or number, even though it might seem obvious. Simply saying "The table indicates . . . " all too often leads the reader to ask, "*Which* table?" That's especially true if the table being referenced gets moved to another page when the document is reformatted for printing or publishing on a network.

The narrative text of the survey report should consist of a verbal description of the major results for each section or category of information needs. Even though those seeking the information may be well able to read and understand the tables or figures, the narrative is virtually always necessary and valuable. There are several reasons: First, the narrative text is *interpretive* rather than merely descriptive. The text indicates the meaning of the values and relationships revealed by the survey. Second, virtually everyone can communicate more effectively in words than in numbers or symbols. Those who seek the information constantly deal with concepts and images that are largely verbal and far less often numeric or symbolic in nature. Consequently, they can often perceive the meaning of facts and relationships expressed verbally much more readily than those expressed numerically or with symbols.

Third, the researcher can often provide additional insight, ideas, and information quite aside from the purely tabular or graphic portrayal of results. By virtue of having worked so closely and intimately with the project, the researcher report writer will probably acquire intuitive understanding or a "gut feeling" for certain facts or relationships. These insights can't be expressed in numeric form, but they can and should be stated verbally in the narrative text. Whenever the researcher offers opinions, suggestions, or recommendations based on judgment or intuition, rather than concrete survey results, that must be clearly noted in the text.

Lastly, researchers who are knowledgeable about survey research because of their past experience with such work can often provide very helpful and useful perspectives on the results. Researchers can draw freely from previous survey experience, provided they respect the proprietary nature of the actual results of other surveys conducted for other sponsors.

For each section of the survey report, the narrative text should provide a brief introduction to the information. This is usually done by citing the information need category or, more simply, by stating the questions in the mind of those seeking the information during the initiation of the survey. It's often advisable to say why the information was sought as well, if that can be expressed easily. For example, the narrative for a new section might begin:

Survey respondents were asked six questions to learn their attitudes toward the issue of new work rules. Their reactions were sought to gauge their potential acceptance of the proposed new policy.

Following this type of introduction to a section, the text would cite the tables or figures where the information was presented, then continue to identify and highlight the most important results. This is usually done by directing the reader's attention to the specific facts or relationships, thus:

Notice that the attitudes of new employees were markedly more positive than the attitudes of those who have been with the company for several years. This is very consistent with employee ratings of several other topics as well.

The researcher must often provide explanation and interpretation of the values shown in tabular or graphic form, but this is usually only part of the report writer's responsibility. At the very least, the researcher should be willing and able to identify the most relevant facts and relationships in the narrative text. For those with a grasp of the material being measured by the survey, much more extensive comment may be appropriate.

There may be a question concerning whether concrete recommendations should be included, whether merely suggestions would be appropriate, or whether only the bare facts should be noted. It's always advisable to ask those seeking the information for their preference and be guided by their wishes. When researchers provide concrete recommendations, there are two possibilities for problems: Those reading the report may feel the researcher has infringed on their prerogatives as executives or decision makers, or they place too much reliance on such recommendations, in the face of other, *contradictory* information. To avoid either extreme, the researcher can simply provide *suggestions* and identify the data that serve as a basis for them. That allows those reading the report to contradict when appropriate and to weigh the suggestions against their own background, experience, and body of accumulated information.

Each narrative report section should conclude with a very brief summary of the results for that section. These conclusions are usually only a few sentences. They're quite similar to the individual entries in the executive summary that heads the report. Thus, the narrative report process can be outlined in three steps for each section: (1) say what results will be presented, (2) present the results, and (3) summarize what was presented.

It's important to note that the narrative text shouldn't be too "dependent" on the tables and figures. Just as the reader should be able to gather the gist of the results from the tables and figures alone, so, too, should they be able to comprehend the major results by reading only the narrative text. Guidelist 12–2 summarizes the main guidelines for composing narrative text.

Tabular Reporting

The tables in the report should be edited versions of those generated by the analysis programs. Only the relevant values and entries should be included. The tables can usually be condensed so the results for many similar survey items can be contained in a single table or shown graphically on just one figure. The composition of meaningful, easily understood tables and figures is an art that can be cultivated and

For Composing Narrative Text   Guidelist 12–2

1. Divide the text into major sections according to the types of information needs, topics, or issues.
2. Include the tables after they have been referenced in the text, not before.
3. Avoid technical jargon used in statistics or processing in favor of the simpler, lay person's vocabulary.
4. Use short, simple, direct sentences rather than long, complex ones.
5. Use nouns repetitively to avoid any confusion about the antecedent of pronouns such as it, them, they, and so on.
6. In references to tables, figures, and other inclusions, identify them by their number or letter rather than by indefinite terms such as "*the* table."
7. Make the text interpretive rather than just descriptive of the results.
8. Introduce each major section by identifying its purpose or the reason for including it.
9. Discuss the major facts or relationships contained in each table or figure, but make the text fairly independent so it's meaningful without reference to tables.
10. Include additional ideas, conclusions, or suggestions, based on previous experience or intuition, but clearly note when they go beyond the actual results.

refined with practice. All it really requires is careful attention and concentration. Guidelist 12–3 summarizes the guidelines for creating report tables and figures.

There are two basic things the researcher must decide when composing tables or figures: The first is the *format* and the second is the *labeling* to use. When choosing a format, use space as effectively as possible. Arrange rows, columns, and sections so they contain *similar* material or apply to the same concept or topic. Allow enough "white space" so the tables or figures don't appear to be glutted with numbers or words. Separating different types of content helps the reader to recognize what's being presented.

It's usually best to use vertical rather than horizontal pages for the entire written report. Horizontal formats allow much more information on a single line, but it's often cumbersome for the reader who must turn the document to the side to read the contents. Another practical policy for writing tables is to use a *very consistent* format. This helps the report reader because, once familiar with the format, no further study is required to comprehend those that follow in a similar format. Lastly, it's good to remember a table can contain too much information. The general rule is that no one table or figure should require more than a very few minutes of study to comprehend.

The second major factor to consider when composing tables or figures is the *labeling*. Each table or figure in the report should be *named* and *titled*. Consecutive numbers make better indicators than letters or other symbols. Roman numerals are to be avoided unless the sponsor requires using them. The title should *say what's in the <u>body</u> of the table or figure*. If the body of a table contains frequencies, the table might be labeled, "Number of Respondents Indicating Each Alternative." If percentages are listed, they should be identified in the title. If averages are contained in the body of the table, the title must indicate not only that they're averages, but also *what* averages—the means, medians, or modes. For example, the title

For Composing Tables and Figures   Guidelist 12–3

1. Name each table and figure with a consecutive number, and preferably not with letters or Roman numerals.

2. Title each one with a brief description of exactly what's contained in the *body* of the table.

3. Label rows, columns, and sections with meaningful words, rather than codes labeled at the bottom of the table or graph.

4. Use a standard format whenever possible, so many tables are quickly recognized once the first is understood.

5. Use space and distance effectively to show relationships or provide identification.

6. Keep similar content in the same columns, rows, or sections, using space to separate distinct content.

7. Allow sufficient "white space" and don't contain too much information in one table or make it too dense.

8. Note statistical significance with an asterisk or letter superscript and note the probability level in a table footnote.

9. Use vertical rather than horizontal pages whenever possible, even if more tables or figures are needed.

10. Remember, each table or figure should virtually "stand alone," so it's meaningful without reference to text.

11. Always try to keep it *clean* and *simple.*

---

might be "Average (Mean) Estimates for Four Series." It's essential the title of the table or figure tells the reader exactly *what the table contains.* The reader should be able to understand clearly what's in the table *without* reference to the text or knowledge of any other part of the report.

The columns and rows of tables and the sections or parts of figures should also be labeled clearly. In order to conserve space, some report writers attach codes—1, 2, 3, or A, B, C, etc.—to the rows or columns. Then they list a key at the bottom of the table to show the items or categories to which these codes refer. This method is *never* advisable if it can be avoided. It's always better to include less information on each table and use as many different tables as needed. The only exception is when it's necessary for the reader to *compare* items. That can be accomplished more easily within a single table than among multiple tables. When there's no room or the actual probabilities can't be listed, statistical significance can best be shown in tables with the use of asterisks beside the appropriate values, such as 25*, or with letter superscripts, such as 25[a]. The significance is then noted in a footnote to the table (e.g., *Prob. < .05). This assumes all the report readers will know what statistical significance means. If not, the footnote might say something to this effect: "*The probability of this much difference resulting from sampling error is less than 5 percent."

Graphic Reporting

All types of graphic figures—graphs, charts, plots, and diagrams—have one thing in common, and it's their main advantage over tabular reports: They "map" quantities and relationships more directly than words or numbers. Graphics use size and shape to represent quantities. They use location and juxtaposition to display relationships visually. Cosmetic features are important for survey research reports, but graphics offer far more than just that. They can convey *configuration*—the *total* picture—in an instant. They can make meaningful to viewers what words and numbers couldn't possibly convey and do it very simply and elegantly. But of course, they do it at a price. They not only take considerable time and effort to produce, they may also take large amounts of space in a written report.

There are a wide variety of special-purpose charting and graphing programs for desktop computers of all kinds. They range from very basic, simple "utility" routines to highly complex and sophisticated programs. But regardless of their simplicity or complexity, learning to use them initially takes some time, effort, and patience. Once familiar with the program, however, most users find them fairly quick and easy to operate. Most spreadsheets and statistical analysis programs also include the ability to produce charts and graphs in basic formats such as those shown in Figure 12–1. These rather rudimentary models are very satisfactory for most survey research reports.

More sophisticated graphics programs have the ability to show depth, plot in three dimensions, overlay one set of data on another, display bars and areas in pictures, and display the information more colorfully, in both the figurative and literal sense of the word. The report writer must judge whether such enhancements are worth the time, effort, and expense involved in making them. There is also another consideration regarding color: Many computer systems include color printers and that encourages report writers to include colorful graphics. Unfortunately, color copy machines are far less common. It's not unusual for sponsors to find it necessary to make additional copies of research reports, ordinarily not in color. If they do, distinctions in color may fade into almost identical shades of gray, making the graphs and charts difficult to decipher. If color is to be used and there's a chance the report will be copies in black and white, it's advisable to use *both* color and *crosshatching* to be sure different elements are distinguishable.

The same recommendations that apply to naming, titling, and labeling tables apply as well to graphic figures, except that they are referred to as "Figure #" or "Exhibit #" rather than "Table #." Graphic figures should have their own, independent sequence of consecutive numbers. Rarely will there be a corresponding graph for every table, so there's no need for the numbers of tables and figures to correspond.

Graphics can play one of two roles in a report, relative to the tables: They may *replace* tables or they may *supplement* them. Using them as supplements is more common for written reports. For oral presentations using projected images, it's more common for graphic figures to replace tables. In the examples that follow, both tables and graphs or charts are provided. But this isn't to imply that they must always both be present.

The choice of the best type of graph to use in a given situation or to portray a specific set of information is a difficult one. There are no fixed rules or even firm guidelines about what kind of graph to use for data from a particular type of scale or item. At times it may be obvious that only one type is suitable and nothing else would do. At other times there may be a choice between two or more kinds of graphs. There are rare situations where *no* type of graph is really able to show the information effectively.

FIGURE 12–1   Graph and Chart Types

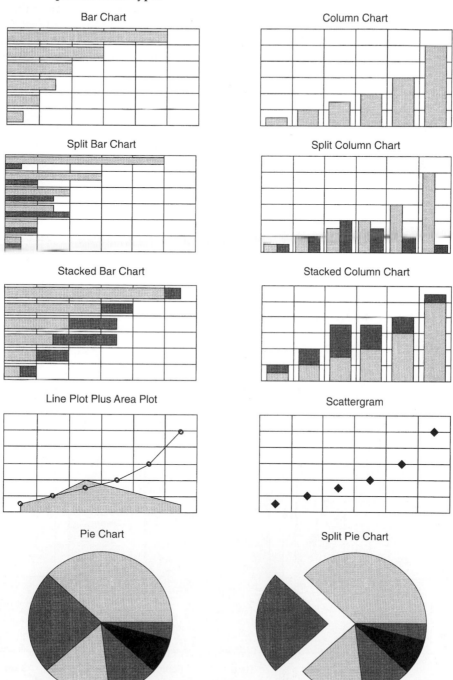

The following examples suggest the kinds of graphs or charts best suited to displaying the types of information contained in the corresponding tables. Once the type of graph has been chosen, the report writer must also decide what individual elements should be included on the graph. The basic anatomy of a graph is shown in Figure 12–2. Some of the individual elements shown there are optional. Others are almost always advisable to use. The guidelines for creating effective graphic figures are provided in Guidelist 12–4.

FIGURE 12–2 **The Anatomy of a Graph**

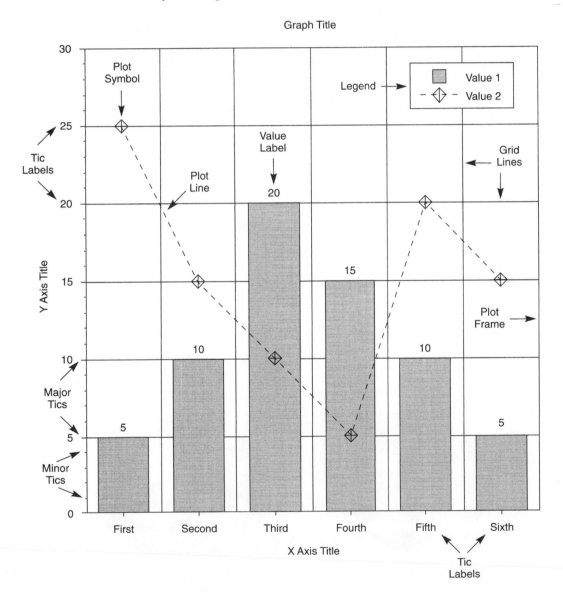

For Creating Graphic Figures	**Guidelist 12–4**

1. Name each graph or chart with a consecutive number, rather than with letters or Roman numerals.
2. Title each one with a brief description of exactly what *quantities* the *lines, bars,* or *areas* represent.
3. Use X axis and Y axis titles to indicate what spectrum or dimension each axis represents.
4. If multiple variables are plotted, label the plot elements or show a legend on or beneath the graph to indicate what each represents.
5. Include tic labels to show the levels, quantities, or proportions on the X axis and Y axis scale.
6. Use enough grid lines to allow the reader to estimate quantities but not so many as to make the graph dense or cluttered.
7. Including value labels on bars, plot points, or pie segments may allow the graph to *substitute* for a table rather than just supplement it.
8. Use the same graphic format consistently whenever possible so the elements are quickly recognizable once the reader is familiar with the first.
9. Use the same *proportions* and *scales* when results are to be compared from one graph to the next.
10. Allow sufficient "white space," and don't contain so much information on one graph as to make it overly complex.
11. Note statistical significance with an asterisk or letter superscript and note the probability level in a footnote below the figure.
12. Always try to keep it *clean* and *simple!* When there's a choice between a simple and a complex format, always select the more elementary one.

Reporting Data Description

The next section of this chapter contains a series of examples to serve as models for reporting the results of survey research. Sample results from each of the scale types shown in Chapter 5 are presented in a series of data description tables. An *alternative* or *supplementary* graph or chart is also provided. In addition, examples of narrative text that might accompany the tables and graphs are included. There's no one correct way to report results, but these examples are designed to provide report writers with suggestions for table, graph, and narrative format and content.

Reporting Multiple-Choice Items

Multiple-choice items such as those shown in Example 5–1 on page 119 are categorical data. They're usually described by listing the percentage of respondents choosing each category. Example 12–1 shows a variant of the frequency table discussed earlier. Only percentages are shown because ordinarily these proportions are generalized to the population by statistical inference. The number of respondents for the item is shown, so readers could calculate the number for each response if they wished to do so.

In Example 12–1, there were 7 percent who indicated some other, miscellaneous newspaper. Because there were so few and the frequency of any one

Single Response Item Table   Example 12–1

The kind of newspaper they *most often* read for business news	
Newspaper	**Percent**
National, daily paper	43%
Local, morning paper	22%
Local, evening paper	14%
Local, weekly paper	9%
National, weekly paper	5%
Other, miscellaneous papers	7%
Total	100%
Number = 160	

publication was usually only one person, the *others* are grouped into this miscellaneous category. Usually the others identified are recorded on a codelist and entered into the data file for processing, but they're not ordinarily listed in a report *unless* a substantial number of respondents select one particular "other" alternative or the sponsors express an interest in having these so-called *write-ins* reported. If they're needed, they could either be included in the table or listed in a separate table with the percentages based only on those who selected and entered some additional, miscellaneous alternative.

Notice the alternatives were listed in Example 12–1 with the modal category first, followed in descending order of percentages, with the "other" category always presented last. Alternatively, the sequence used in the questionnaire could have been maintained in the table if there were a logical order to the alternatives.

Figure 12–3 presents the tabular information of Example 12–1 in two graphic forms—a bar chart and a pie chart. Both provide good indications of the relative proportions of respondents in each category. The pie chart emphasizes the nature of a *single response* question—the percentages total to 100 with no overlap among categories. The choice between the two graphs depends on what the report writer wants to emphasize.

The narrative discussion of this information is likely to be brief. The table and/or graphs are largely self-explanatory. It's usually important only to identify the most popular categories, and perhaps to comment on the results if they're not intuitive, thus:

The national daily newspaper proved to be the single, most often used source of business news for the respondents in this population. The survey questions about

FIGURE 12–3
Single
Response
Item Graphics

Simple Bar Graph

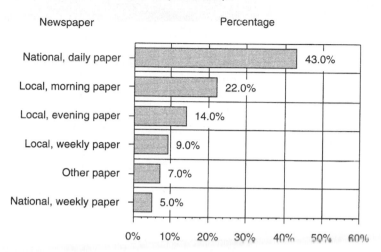

Simple Pie Chart

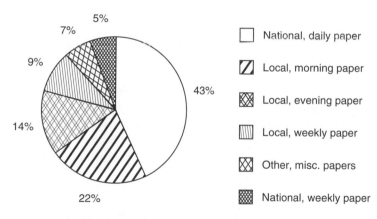

subscription, to be shown later, suggest *The Wall Street Journal* is by far the most popular, and probably four out of five who indicated a national daily paper here were referring to that newspaper. Nearly all the others are likely to be referring to *Barrons,* because there were few other national dailies to which respondents subscribed at home or at work. It's also interesting to note the local *evening* paper was less popular than was the morning paper, since the morning paper is generally more often read by business people than the evening paper.

Example 12–1 is a single response item, so it constitutes a single survey variable. The statistical analysis generates only one frequency table from which the percentages were drawn. In Example 12–2, the respondents could select more than one alternative. Consequently, this single survey question generates *six* variables, to which the respondents actually indicate "yes" or "no." Consequently, the analysis

Multiple Response Item Table   Example 12–2

Any and all types of newspapers they regularly read for business news		
Newspaper	Yes	No
National, daily paper	41%	59%
Local, morning paper	38%	68%
Local, evening paper	22%	78%
Local, weekly paper	7%	93%
Other, miscellaneous papers	3%	97%
National, weekly paper	2%	98%
Number = 160		

generates six frequency tables, one for each alternative that's a variable. Example 12–2 lists all six sets of percentages in a single table to save space and facilitate comparison. It wouldn't even be necessary to list the percentages in the "No" column, because this is easily recognized, given the percentage that did check the category. It would be presented as it is here and in Figure 12–4 only if there was as much interest in the proportion who did *not* read each paper as there was in who did. The narrative text to accompany this table or graph would be very similar to that for the previous ones, citing major categories and knitting the survey results together.

FIGURE 12–4
Multiple Response Item Bar Chart

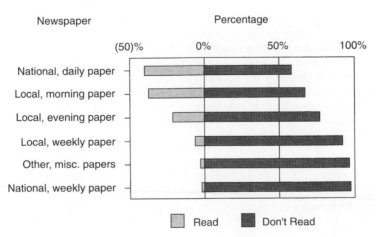

Percentage Who Read Each Kind of Paper for Business News

Tabular Likert Scale Report   Example 12–3

How much do you agree or disagree with each statement?	Strongly Agree	Agree	Neutral	Disagree	Strongly Disagree
A man should never cry in public	8.4%	11.5%	27.7%	36.5%	15.9%
A woman's place is in the home	12.9%	16.2%	19.1%	31.5%	20.3%
A man should help a woman in public	6.5%	19.4%	24.9%	29.6%	19.6%
Women should always pay their share	10.4%	18.0%	16.5%	26.2%	28.9%
Men must take the lead in sex matters	16.6%	18.3%	19.0%	22.1%	24.0%
Women should put family before career . .	21.5%	26.4%	18.2%	13.5%	20.4%
325 Respondents					

Likert Scale Item Reports

Multiple Likert scale items such as those shown in Example 5–2 on page 121 can also be shown in a single table. In Example 12–3, the scale categories are listed vertically to save space. It may be tempting to list the code values above the columns and print the scale below the table. That's never advisable in a final report if it can be avoided. It puts too much burden on the reader, and that's contrary to the basic objectives of survey reporting.

In Example 12–3, six items are shown in a single table, but many more could easily have been listed. This saves space and saves time for those reading the reports, but there's a more important reason for condensed tables like this: They allow the reader to make direct comparisons quickly and easily among comparable items. Such formats provide more information and enhance the value of the results. They require more work by the report writer, but they're well worth the extra time and effort.

Showing the entire distributions of response to Likert scale items in the fashion used here has both advantages and disadvantages. Ordinarily, the entire distributions are of interest. They should be listed if it would be useful to compare each *category* with the others. It takes more space and makes the comparisons among *items* more difficult because there are so many values to study. An alternative would be to list only the *median* values for each item. Using the median as a single indicator of the level of agreement is recommended to facilitate comparisons among *items* and to save space when there's no need to compare *individual categories*.

The distributions from Example 12–3 are shown in a stacked column chart in Figure 12–5. The scale is shown on the legend, while the items are slanted and listed above each column. The shading is graduated to correspond with the

FIGURE 12–5
Likert Scale
Stacked
Column Chart

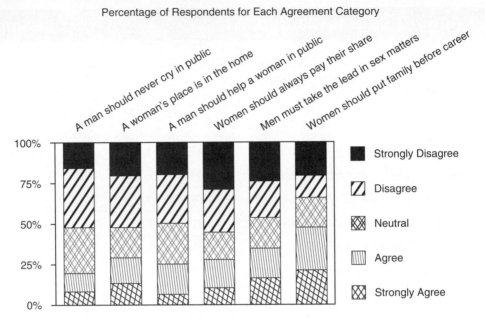

Percentage of Respondents for Each Agreement Category

amount of agreement. This kind of chart sacrifices precise, numeric detail to facilitate comparisons among variables and make the distinctions more vivid.

Verbal Frequency Scale Reports

Example 12–4 shows a tabular report of some of the data from the *verbal frequency scales* shown in Example 5–3 on page 122. As with the Likert scale, this scale generates *ordinal* data. The format in Example 12–4 is very similar to the previous one, except the names of the categories are short enough to be listed horizontally.

Only five verbal frequency items are shown in the table contained in Example 12–4, but of course many more might have been listed in the table. Analysis routines often generate one page for each such item, containing the frequency and percentage table and perhaps the median value. With such reports, comparisons among items are difficult. A table such as that in Example 12–4 is an excellent way to condense the information and make items very comparable with one another.

Figure 12–6 presents the data distributions from Example 12–4 graphically. The items in the table and graph haven't been rearranged, so their sequence represents the order of magnitude of the responses. Rather, the original order was retained here because it represented a rough "continuum" from minimal involvement in political issues to involvement. This is quite common with well-composed survey items and well-constructed questionnaires. The format and sequence permit the report reader to examine the *change* in the distributions from one item to the next, moving downward in the table or upward in the graph to detect patterns as the level of some underlying dimension increases or decreases. Thus, showing the items together enhances the meaning of the information to those seeking it.

Tabular Verbal Frequency Report   Example 12–4

How often do you do each of the following things?	Always	Often	Some-times	Rarely	Never
Seek information about candidates	5.3%	13.9%	22.4%	28.5%	29.9%
Vote in local elections	3.1%	6.4%	39.5%	17.8%	33.2%
Vote along strict party lines	8.4%	17.7%	19.5%	13.2%	41.2%
Contribute money to candidates	1.3%	3.9%	9.4%	6.3%	79.1%
Volunteer to work on campaigns	0.8%	1.6%	3.3%	16.6%	77.7%

?20 Respondents

Ordinal Scale Reports

Both the Likert scale and the verbal frequency scale generate ordinal data. The categories are listed in a sequence representing the increase or decrease in the order of magnitude, although intervals or "steps" between scale points aren't necessarily equal to one another. Other things besides the amount of agreement or the frequency of something can be arranged in a fairly large number of such sequential steps as well. When this is the case, the scale is called an *ordinal* scale because it shows *only* the order of things and generates ordinal data. Example 5–4 on page 125

FIGURE 12–6
Verbal Frequency Stacked Bar Chart

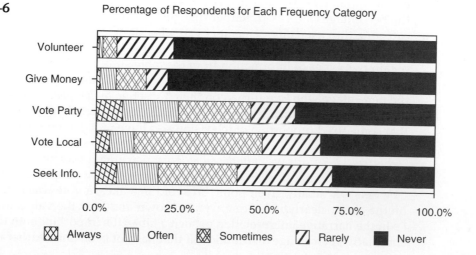

Percentage of Respondents for Each Frequency Category

Ordinal Scale Cumulative Table   Example 12–5

When TV is turned on, weekdays	Percent	Cumulative
The first thing in the morning	6.3%	6.3%
A little while after awakening	4.5%	10.8%
Mid-morning	5.2%	16.0%
Just before lunch	2.1%	18.1%
Right after lunch	11.8%	29.9%
Mid-afternoon	7.6%	37.5%
Early evening, before dinner	18.1%	55.6%
Right after dinner	21.0%	76.6%
Late evening	17.7%	94.3%
Usually don't turn it on	5.7%	100.0%
165 Respondents	100.0%	100.0%

shows a situation where the scale steps are times of day defined not by the hour and minute, but rather by daily activity patterns of respondents. It's not so important to sponsors to know the exact time of the occurrence according to the clock, because different families perform activities at different times of day. Rather the times, *relative to the families' daily activities,* are of greater importance.

Example 12–5 shows the tabular report of the data from the ordinal scale shown in the upper section of Example 5–4 on page 125. Notice that, as always, the number of respondents is listed clearly on the table so readers know the total on which the percentages are based. Rather than just listing the percentage distribution by category, the *cumulative* percentages are also shown. The cumulative percentages are often very revealing for ordinal scale items. The reader of the report can then obtain two types of information from the table simultaneously: the percentage of people who, in this case, turn on their TV set at a certain time of the day, and also the percentage who *have* turned on their TV set *up to that point* in the day. This latter piece of information is obviously very useful, especially given the assumption that some fixed proportion of television sets have remained on once they're originally turned on.

Figure 12–7 portrays *only the cumulative* percentages for the same variable reported in Example 12–5. Such a graph could easily be misperceived as showing "TV Sets On" at any given point. To avoid mistakes, a note was inserted directly on the chart, clearly indicating what's shown and how the values were derived.

In the narrative interpretation of such a table, it's important both to explain the cumulative percentage distribution, if that has not been done earlier in the report,

FIGURE 12–7
Ordinal Scale
Cumulative
Bar Chart

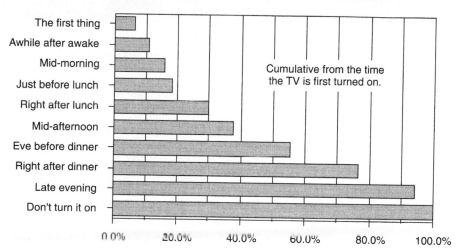

Percentage of TV's That Have Been Turned on at Each Point

Cumulative from the time the TV is first turned on.

and also to note the relevant results in terms of both category percentages and cumulative percentages. Notice how a typical narrative also makes suggestions and refers to cross-tabulation to check them:

> Respondents indicated the time during a typical weekday when they or someone in the family turned on the television set. They indicated they did so according to certain daily activities, rather than by the clock, because daily activity patterns differ widely from family to family. The results are shown in Table 5. The percentages are all based on 165 respondents who answered the question, and the largest percentage turned on their television sets *right after dinner,* but very nearly as many did so in the *early evening after dinner,* and in the *late evening.* The cumulative percentages indicate that less than one family in five had turned on the TV by *lunch time,* while over a third had done so by *mid-afternoon,* well over half by early *evening, before dinner,* and three quarters *right after dinner.* These results suggest very light morning viewership for this audience, and only moderate afternoon viewing for "soaps," the "game shows," and the "sit-com" reruns.
>
> On the other hand, the marked increase in the cumulative percentages just before dinner suggest a youthful audience coming in during late afternoon, perhaps after school, for the "cartoon" and "kid show" programming, as well as the early evening news for some stations and networks. These suggestions will be tested further when this item is broken down by family life cycle to measure differences in viewing patterns for those in different stages of the life cycle.

Forced Ranking Scale Reports

Ranking alternatives creates an ordinal variable for each item ranked. In Example 5–5 on page 126, four brands of cola were ranked according to the respondents' degree of preference. An analysis routine to generate frequency and percentage distributions might produce one table for each item ranked. These data can be condensed into a single table, such as in Example 12–6. The percentage distributions for each

Forced Ranking Scale Distributions · Example 12–6

Percentage Ranking Each Brand at Each Rank					
	1st	2nd	3rd	4th	Total
Coca-Cola	46.5%	44.0%	6.7%	2.8%	100.0%
Pepsi-Cola	31.2%	51.6%	11.3%	5.9%	100.0%
RC Cola	19.1%	3.1%	67.5%	10.3%	100.0%
Jolt Cola	3.2%	1.3%	14.5%	81.0%	100.0%
Total (119 Respondents)	100.0%	100.0%	100.0%	100.0%	

brand (variable) are shown by row, totaling to 100 percent at the far right. Each row of the table was derived from a frequency and percentage table for that particular brand or variable.

Aside from saving report space and reader time, there's another advantage to condensing tabular reports of rankings such as those shown in Example 12–6. Each respondent must rank each item, and no two items can be ranked the same. This is why the scale is called a *forced* ranking. If the data are edited properly, the rows should also total to 100 percent. Thus, those studying the relationships among the items can compare either the columns or the rows with one another.

The table provides those seeking the information with an entire "picture" of the *pattern* of preferences, rather than merely information about individual items. Thus, patterns are revealed merely by the choice and composition of the table format. This table *doesn't* show how those who ranked a particular item a certain way ranked the other items, but that can be determined by a set of cross-tabulations for each pair.

Figure 12–8 contains a stacked bar chart of the distributions shown in Example 12–6. The four brands are listed from the most to the least popular, and the legend identifies the rankings. The graph makes the distinctions more striking, but at the expense of the numeric precision found in the table. In such cases, where it's impractical to include value labels on the graph, *both* the table and graph might be used in the report.

Paired Comparison Scale Reports

Paired comparison scales are used only rarely in surveys because the data from them are difficult to analyze, as noted in Chapter 5. The items used in Example 5–6 on page 128 are the same cola brands used in Example 5–5. The object was to demonstrate the superiority of other scales to the paired comparison scale. However, there are some situations where it's appropriate to use paired comparisons because the scales actually mirror "real-world" choices the respondents must

FIGURE 12–8
Forced
Ranking
Stacked
Column
Chart

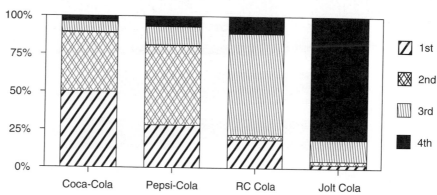

Percentage Ranking Each Brand at Each Rank

sometimes make. In Example 12–7, only three items and thus three pairs are listed. The items to be compared are three kinds of meat. There was an explicit reason for using the paired comparison scale. Both personal preference and dietary laws of some religions dictate certain choices. So, respondents are sometimes in a position of making a choice between such pairs.

In Example 12–7, there's a footnote indicating transitivity was forced by the elimination of intransitive cases. Since only three items and three pairs were used, there were very few such cases. *Intransitivity* results when a respondent indicates they prefer: A over B, B over C, and C over A. That's a logical impossibility, but it often happens with paired comparisons when many pairs are being rated. It's one of the main reasons paired comparisons are inferior to *rating* the items on an interval scale. When paired comparisons are used in surveys and reported in tables such as Example 12–7 or graphs such as Figure 12–9, either the *coefficient of transitivity* should be reported, or if the cases were eliminated, that should be noted.

Table of Multiple Paired Comparisons   Example 12–7

Percentage of Choice Between Pairs*				
Beef	82%	versus	18%	Pork
Beef	96%	versus	4%	Lamb
Pork	88%	versus	12%	Lamb
120 Respondents				
*Transitivity forced by deleting intransitive cases.				

FIGURE 12–9
Paired
Comparison
Stacked
Bar Chart

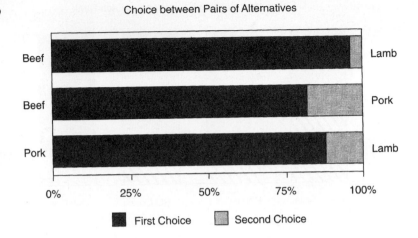

Choice between Pairs of Alternatives

The narrative should also briefly explain transitivity, at least the first time the term is referenced in the report, as well as explaining the meaning of the results, thus:

> Respondents rated their preference for beef, pork, and lamb when each was paired with one other variety of meat. There were two respondents who indicated they preferred beef to pork, lamb to beef, and pork to lamb, so their choices were intransitive and the data from these two cases were disregarded here. The results indicate: (1) A strong general preference for beef, as might be expected. (2) A fairly pronounced dislike for lamb. (3) A preference for lamb over pork by more than one in 10 people. The results suggest that if only two varieties are offered, beef and pork or beef and lamb would be much more acceptable than would pork and lamb. The choices seem to be governed by both preferences and prohibitions; by both "likes" and "dislikes" of respondents. Comparisons of these results with religious preference and affiliation may provide more evidence for this conclusion.

Comparative Scale Reports

When an absolute reference is lacking or inadequate and comparisons or *relative* measures are required, there's no necessity to use *paired* comparisons. Example 5–7 on page 129 shows a method for obtaining interval scale data based on a relative frame of reference rather than on an absolute standard. This scale can also be used for *multiple* comparisons. Example 12–8 reports the results of comparisons between the sponsor's retail store and six other shops. As in Example 5–7, a five-point scale was used, but instead of scale values ranging from one to five, they were oriented around zero and ranged from a negative two to a positive two. The table in Example 12–8 lists both the entire percentage distributions of response and also, since the scale is interval level, the average (mean) values.

When the percentage distributions are listed as they are in Example 12–8, those who read the table can easily make comparisons of *categories* of response across the rows. For a quick comparison of the *items* among one another, the averages can be compared more readily than the entire distributions. Finally, the averages also provide a quick and fairly indicative measure of the relationship between each competing shop and the "standard," the sponsor's own shop. The plus or minus sign

Multiple Comparative Scale Table   Example 12–8

Rating of Each Competitor Compared to This Shop						
Competitor	Very Inferior	Inferior	Very Similar	Superior	Very Superior	Mean
Abbot's	11.5	16.4	35.3	20.1	16.7	+0.14
Baker's	44.0	16.7	14.5	14.2	10.6	−0.69
Clark's	20.0	22.9	35.4	14.5	7.2	−0.34
Drake's	58.8	31.3	7.5	1.7	0.7	−1.46
Evert's	9.5	16.8	19.9	37.4	16.4	+0.34
Frost's	6.6	14.4	40.9	23.1	15.0	+0.26
175 Respondents						

provides a very visible indication of whether the other shop is regarded more or less favorably than the standard for comparison when the scale pivots on zero. The magnitude of the average value shows how much more or less favorably the other shops were perceived by respondents. Thus, this form of table provides a wealth of information to those seeking it.

The mean scores from Example 12–8 are graphed in Figure 12–10. Rather than listing the competitors in alphabetical order, as on the questionnaire, they're shown here in order of inferiority or superiority. Orienting the bar chart around the zero point representing the sponsor's store—the standard of comparison—highlights the direction and magnitude of the differences.

FIGURE 12–10
Mean
Comparative
Score Bar Chart

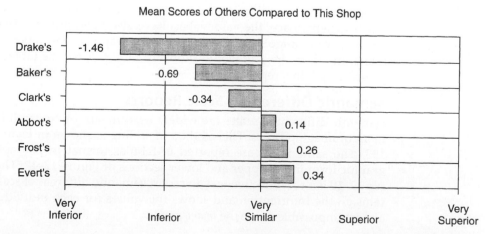

Mean Scores of Others Compared to This Shop

Linear, Numeric Scale Table   Example 12–9

Mean Importance Ratings When Choosing Sports Equipment*			
Factor Rated	**Mean**	**Factor Rated**	**Mean**
Quality of merchandise	4.8	Help and advice offered	3.5
Selection of brands	4.6	Speed of service	3.5
Variety of products	4.6	Store hours	3.4
Service after purchase	4.4	Location of store	3.2
Store guarantees	4.4	Size of the store	2.7
Price of the goods	4.2	Attractiveness of store	2.5
Courtesy of service	3.7	Availability of credit	2.2
*Five-point scale.		325 Respondents	

Linear, Numeric Scale Reports

Perhaps the most common scale used in survey research for continuous interval data is the linear, numeric scale, such as that shown in Example 5–8 on page 131. A tabular report of the results from such a scale, used to rate 14 attributes of sports equipment, is shown in Example 12–9. Because this scale has equal intervals, the mean values were computed and listed rather than the entire distribution for each item. The table also notes the range of the scale and the number of respondents for the item.

The linear, numeric scale data from Example 12–9 is plotted graphically in Figure 12–11. As in the tabular report, the items have been ordered from the most to the least important attributes. This provides a visual profile of the things that are important to those shopping for sports equipment. Since the plot in Figure 12–11 has sufficient space, the value labels have also been printed. There's no need to note the scale range since it's shown on the graph. The number of respondents is noted. In effect, the plot would probably *substitute* for the table rather than supplementing it in a report.

Semantic Differential Scale Reports

Semantic differential scales are widely used in survey research for the measurement of image profiles. This method of scaling is shown in Example 5–9 on page 133. The same items are reported in tabular format in Example 12–10 and in graphic form in the upper and lower sections of Figure 12–12. The table in Example 12–10 isn't an effective way to report semantic differential scale results. It contains all the information and shows the values for each individual item, but it's almost impossible to see the *image profile*.

FIGURE 12–11
Linear,
Numeric
Scale Plot

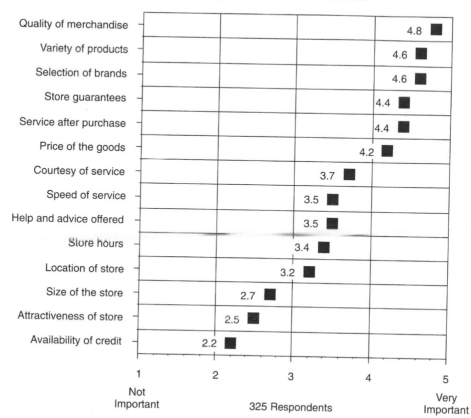

Mean Ratings of Importance on a Five-Point Scale

Quality of merchandise	4.8
Variety of products	4.6
Selection of brands	4.6
Store guarantees	4.4
Service after purchase	4.4
Price of the goods	4.2
Courtesy of service	3.7
Speed of service	3.5
Help and advice offered	3.5
Store hours	3.4
Location of store	3.2
Size of the store	2.7
Attractiveness of store	2.5
Availability of credit	2.2

1 — Not Important   2   3 — 325 Respondents   4   5 — Very Important

---

Semantic Differential Table   Example 12–10

Modal Ratings of the Pizza Served Here*

Adjective Pair Rated	Mode	Adjective Pair Rated	Mode
Hot . . . . Cold	2	Good . . . . Bad	2
Bland . . . . Spicy	6	Unattractive . . . . Attractive	6
Expensive . . . . Inexpensive	3	Fresh . . . . Stale	1
Moist . . . . Dry	1	Small . . . . Large	5
Soggy . . . . Crisp	4	Natural . . . . Artificial	3

*Seven-Point Semantic Differential
 Scale Labeled on Each Extreme.   168 Respondents

FIGURE 12–12
Modal
Semantic
Differential
Plots

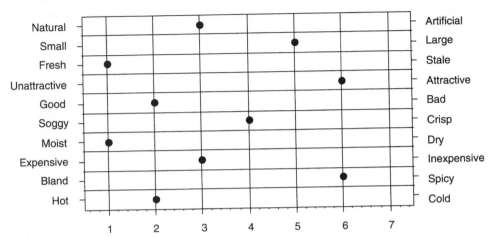

Plotted in Questionnaire Sequence and Direction

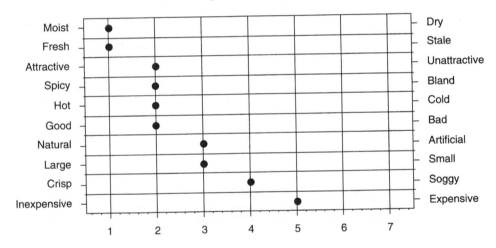

Plotted in Report Sequence and Direction

In the upper section of Figure 12–12, the items are listed *exactly* as they appeared in the questionnaire. The comparison of that plot with the one in the lower section of Figure 12–12 demonstrates an important objective of survey reporting. When the questionnaire was constructed, the survey items were ordered in a sequence dictated by the *response* task. Thus, the items were randomly ordered and some were listed with the positive adjective first while others were reversed. Consequently, when the modal values are listed in a table or plotted as they are, they don't actually form a *profile* for interpretation and reporting. It's difficult and time-consuming to understand the profile or form a mental picture of the results from either the table in Example 12–10 or the plot in the upper section of Figure 12–12.

In the lower section of Figure 12–12, the modal values are again shown, but there are two modifications in the plot: First, several of the items were "reflected" or reversed so all positive adjectives are shown on the left, with their negative counterparts listed on the right. Second, item pairs were reordered so those receiving the most positive responses were listed first and the less positive items followed in sequence down the page. In the data analysis for this example, the means were also computed. So, when two or more items had the same value for the mode, the one with the highest mean value was listed first to break the "tie."

A major goal when composing tables and graphs for reports is to enhance the information by facilitating the recognition of patterns and the comparisons among items. This often requires reordering and reflecting items. The plot in the lower section of Figure 12–12 much more readily portrays the image profile, by comparison with the table in Example 12–10 or the upper section of the figure. When the table or graph is composed properly, the reader easily gets a clear picture of the relationships shown.

Adjective Checklist Reports

The most simple and direct way to measure image attributes in a survey was shown in Example 5–10 on page 135, although it certainly isn't the best way in most cases. The price of the simplicity is that only categorical, dichotomous data are obtained for each item. Thus, the reports of such items consist only of the proportion of respondents who checked each item. Such a report is shown in tabular format in Example 12–11. If the data for the entire sample, combined, were to be shown in such a table, they would be obtained by generating an individual frequency table for each item, then listing only the percentage checking the item in the condensed, tabular report. In Example 12–11, the percentages are shown for each of two departments, using the same items as those shown in Example 5–10. Thus, the data shown are for two individual subsamples, and the proportions checking each item for the entire sample as a whole aren't shown because this would be "mixing apples and oranges" from the view of those seeking the information.

First selecting only one subsample or department and obtaining frequency tables, then repeating the computations for the second subsample or department could have obtained these percentages. This wasn't the procedure used here, however, because to do so requires doing the same analysis twice and doesn't provide a measure of the statistical significance of differences between the two departments. Rather than using frequency distributions, these data were cross-tabulated, so each table contained the percentages checking and not checking the item for each department. Consequently, Example 12–11 shows a data description report that was actually based on a measure of association—cross-tabulation. Notice the number in each department is listed at the bottom of the table and the statistical significance is shown in a footnote.

The original order of the items, used in the questionnaire and shown in Example 5–10, was retained in the tabular report in Example 12–11. For the graph in Figure 12–13, the items were sorted from those *most* often to *least* often checked by respondents in Dept. B, the larger of the two departments. Examination of the split bar graph shows even more dramatically how much the two departments differ in

Adjective Checklist Percentages   Example 12–11

Percentage of Each Dept. Checking Each Characteristic*					
Dept. A	Dept. B	Factor Rated	Dept. A	Dept. B	Factor Rated
9%	31%	Easy	91%	65%	Safe
88%	7%	Technical	55%	39%	Exhausting
3%	77%	Boring	74%	40%	Difficult
71%	12%	Interesting	62%	8%	Rewarding
12%	55%	Low-paying	41%	70%	Secure
8%	41%	Strenuous	3%	29%	Slow-paced
2%	88%	Routine	62%	17%	Enjoyable
16%	48%	Dead-end	5%	44%	Rigid
91%	12%	Changing	38%	21%	Pleasant
55%	9%	Important	59%	25%	Satisfying
79%	16%	Demanding	1%	14%	Degrading
1%	18%	Temporary	2%	17%	Risky

72   315 Respondents
*Differences between departments are all statistically significant, $P < 0.01$.

their image of their job. The narrative description of these results would point out the differential patterns between the two departments, based on comparisons between items and between departments.

Semantic Distance Scale Reports

Yet another method for measuring image profiles is the semantic distance scale, described in Chapter 5 and shown in Example 5–11 on page 136. Each distribution for each item could be described by generating a frequency and percentage table for each. But these items are actually continuous, interval level variables, so the averages for each can be used appropriately. The table in Example 12–12 shows the results of a series of semantic distance scale items listing attributes of a retail outlet. The median value was chosen as the appropriate average to list, based on the skewness and kurtosis of the distributions. The median is more representative of the most typical rating when the distributions are highly skewed, as they obviously were for these data, given the "floor" and "ceiling" effects. The mean is overly sensitive to the small number of extreme cases in the "tail" of the distribution furthest from the mode.

FIGURE 12–13
Adjective
Checklist
Split Bar Chart

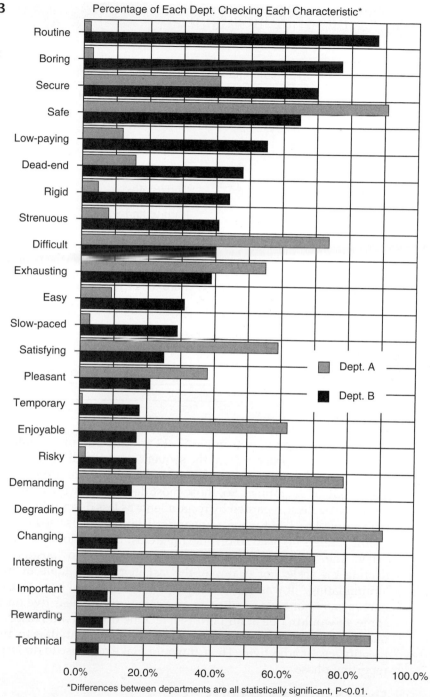

Percentage of Each Dept. Checking Each Characteristic*

*Differences between departments are all statistically significant, P<0.01.

Semantic Distance Tabular Report   Example 12–12

Median Ratings of This Shop*				
Characteristic Rated	**Median**	**Characteristic Rated**		**Median**
High quality products	4.9	Fast counter service		3.9
Neat and clean	4.8	Expensive goods		3.4
Wide selection	4.8	Bad location		2.6
Helpful staff	4.6	Understaffed		2.1
Friendly	4.5	Hard to find		2.0
Large	4.4	Deliveries often late		1.9
Ample parking	4.3	Short on experience		1.7
Fun to shop	4.2	Hard to reach, phone		1.7
Convenient hours	4.2	Unattractive		1.6
Easy to visit	4.0	Intimidating		1.1
*Five-point semantic distance scale from not descriptive to very descriptive.			325 Respondents	

In the table shown in Example 12–12 and the plot of the data in Figure 12–14, the items were reordered from the sequence used in the questionnaire. As in previous examples, the items in this example and figure are arranged by order of magnitude of the ratings. So, those most descriptive were listed first, followed in sequence by those regarded by respondents as less descriptive. This was also done in Example 12–11, but when a semantic distance scale is used to measure an image profile, there's no need to reverse the items. In fact, doing so would be inappropriate. The "negative" items shouldn't be converted to "positive" meaning by reflecting the scale. For example, the last item in the table in Example 12–12 is "Intimidating." It was least descriptive. If the item had been "Unintimidating, " it may or may not have resulted in an average rating near five on the scale. To assume so wouldn't be at all permissible. One of the main reasons for using a semantic distance scale, rather than a semantic differential, is to avoid the need to identify *bipolar* adjectives. Thus, it would make no sense to do just that during the reporting phase.

Fixed Sum Scale Reports

The fixed sum scale was described in Chapter 5 and shown in Example 5–12 on page 137. Such scales yield as many variables as there are items, but the objective is to show the *proportions* of each item, based on a specific total of incidents. To

FIGURE 12–14
Semantic Distance Profile Plot

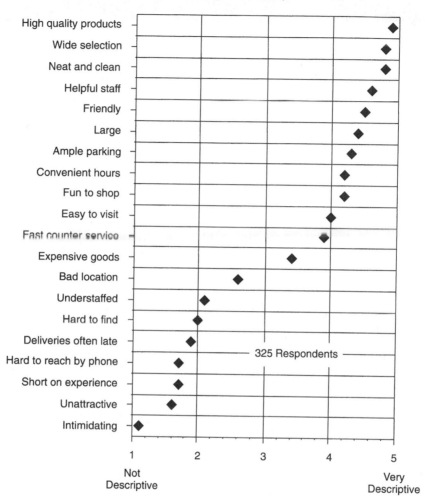

Median Ratings of This Shop

High quality products
Wide selection
Neat and clean
Helpful staff
Friendly
Large
Ample parking
Convenient hours
Fun to shop
Easy to visit
Fast counter service
Expensive goods
Bad location
Understaffed
Hard to find
Deliveries often late
Hard to reach by phone
Short on experience
Unattractive
Intimidating

325 Respondents

1   2   3   4   5
Not
Descriptive

Very
Descriptive

convey the complete meaning of the data, all the variables from the scale must be reported in a single table or chart, as in Example 12–13 and Figure 12–15.

The items in the table were sorted according to the magnitude of the proportions because they are merely types of food and don't stand in any logical sequence or relationship to one another. If they had some inherent orderly sequence, they should be presented in that sequence in the report.

Despite the fact that the items are individual variables, the data can be converted from whatever fixed sum or given total was used to a base of 100. So, the item *mean* values are actually percentages. The mean percentage is the appropriate average because the median or modal percentage values wouldn't necessarily total to 100 or any other fixed sum.

Pie charts such as that in Figure 12–15 lend themselves especially well to portraying results from fixed sum scales. In this split pie chart, the slice representing

Fixed Sum Scale Table   Example 12–13

Mean Percentage of Each Food Type Based on Last Ten Fast Food Meals	
Food Type (200 Respondents)	Mean Pct.
Hamburgers	41.8%
Pizza	28.4%
Sandwiches	15.0%
Chicken	8.3%
Some other	6.5%
Total	100.0%

pizza has been "split" or separated from the rest of the pie to emphasize the sponsor's product relative to the others.

The narrative description of the table or graph reporting a summary of the fixed sum scale should indicate the *actual value* of the given total used in the questionnaire if the proportions have been converted to percentages. It may also have to

FIGURE 12–15
Fixed Sum
Split Pie Chart

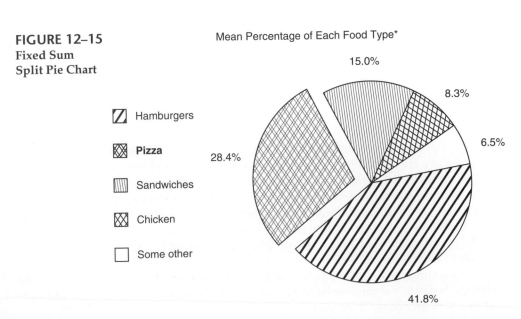

Mean Percentage of Each Food Type*

- ▨ Hamburgers
- ▧ **Pizza**
- ▥ Sandwiches
- ▨ Chicken
- ☐ Some other

15.0%

8.3%

6.5%

28.4%

41.8%

*Based on Last Ten Fast Food Meals by 200 Respondents.

explain the nature of the scale if it's the first time such data are presented in the report. By inserting such clarifications in the narrative text, the researcher can avoid confusion and the possibility that report readers might perceive the inconsistency in the table as an error, reducing the credibility of the survey. Thus, the narrative might begin:

> Survey respondents indicated the number of times they ate each type of food, out of the *last 10 times* they ate fast food. The average values were then converted to percentages, as shown.

Measures of Association

The previous discussion of survey reporting focused on *data description*, mainly for *individual variables.* Although the condensed tables and graphs typically show the results for a "family" of items with the same type of scale, the emphasis is mainly on the set of individual values rather than on the *relationship* between the variables.

When the relationship between variables is to be shown, the data reported within one table, graph, or section are often derived from different types of scales. The focus isn't so much on the description of each variable as on the *relationship* between the variables. The remainder of this chapter concentrates on reports of the *measures of association* between variables described in Chapters 10 and 11, including crosstabulation, analysis of variance, paired t-tests, correlation, and regression analysis.

Statistical analysis routines to measure the associations between variables almost always provide many more coefficients and values than needed in the final report. Some of that detail may be very important to the *research analyst,* but much of it wouldn't be understandable to report readers. So, the following discussion about reporting measures of association will emphasize not only what should be *included,* but also what can and should be *ignored* when writing the final survey report. It's important to note those conducting and reporting *academic* rather than *pragmatic* survey research may wish to provide their readers with more comprehensive and detailed reports of results than those for business, government, and organizational practitioners.

Cross-Tabulation Reports

When the relationship between two *categorical* variables is to be measured, crosstabulation is the appropriate method. Typical analysis routine printouts from this type of procedure are shown in Examples 11–3, page 312, and 11–4, page 313. The information from four such cross-tabs is reported in Example 12–14. This format is called a vertical banner because the same categories are listed on the columns for all four sections. The data are condensed in the table, both to save space and to facilitate comparison of the measures among the four different demographic variables.

Notice the table in Example 12–14 clearly identifies what row item in each section is being cross-tabulated with the item defining the columns of the table. These lines containing only section headings and no numbers are called "slugs." They effectively divide the table into sections to avoid confusion among several variables contained in a table.

Vertical Cross-Tabulation Table   Example 12–14

Time-of-Day Types by Demographic Characteristics					
400 Respondents	**Larks**	**Wrens**	**Owls**	**Total**	**Comb.**
Age Group*					
Under 35	44.5%	27.1%	28.4%	100.0%	38.7%
35 to 49	20.0%	30.6%	49.4%	100.0%	21.2%
50 and over	21.2%	30.6%	48.1%	100.0%	40.0%
Combined	30.0%	29.2%	40.7%	100.0%	100.0%
Education*					
No college	24.7%	32.5%	42.8%	100.0%	41.5%
Some college	40.0%	28.8%	31.2%	100.0%	31.3%
College graduate	26.6%	24.8%	48.6%	100.0%	27.2%
Combined	30.0%	29.2%	40.7%	100.0%	100.0%
Sex					
Males	31.4%	26.6%	42.0%	100.0%	51.7%
Females	28.5%	32.1%	39.4%	100.0%	48.3%
Combined	30.0%	29.2%	40.7%	100.0%	100.0%
Occupation					
White collar	43.9%	26.7%	29.4%	100.0%	63.8%
Blue collar	31.0%	33.8%	35.2%	100.0%	36.2%
Combined	30.0%	29.2%	40.7%	100.0%	100.0%
*Differences by *age* and *education* are statistically significant.					

The number of respondents is listed so readers know the total on which the percentages are based. In each section of the table, the *combined* percentages in the last column at the right show the percentage of respondents in each category, totaling to 100 percent for the entire sample. The combined percentages in the bottom row are the percentages of the entire sample within each column. They're the same for each section because the columns represent the same categories, but they're listed in each section so the row percentages for each category of the variable can be compared with the combined total, as well as with one another. All rows total to 100 percent, and the "Total" column is listed so readers will quickly recognize the percentages total *across* the rows and *not down* the columns. The first two demographic variables are listed with an asterisk and a footnote indicates the differences in the distributions are statistically significant. The other two cross-tabulations aren't significant.

The narrative text to accompany a table such as in Example 12–14 should *briefly* explain the format if it's the first table of its kind or the first time this format appears in the report. It would then note the statistical significance and identify the major results:

> There's less than a 5 percent chance that the distributions of Larks, Wrens, and Owls would differ as much as they do among age groups and among educational levels, for a sample such as this, if they actually did not differ in the whole population. Consequently, these differences are statistically significant and we can assume those in the population really do differ by age and education level in their time of day preferences. The differences between the sexes and occupational groups in this sample are not large enough to assume they exist in the population as well.
>
> The proportion of Larks, Wrens, and Owls differs very little between those who are in the middle and those in the upper age groups. By contrast, a much higher proportion of the youngest group tends to be Larks, a somewhat smaller proportion than the other groups are Wrens, and a markedly lower percentage are Owls.
>
> Educational level also seems to affect time of day preferences. It's interesting to note that those with no college and those who are college graduates have similar proportions of Larks, Wrens, and Owls, while those with some college are much more often Larks and less often Owls. But if education actually affects time of day preferences, and education certainly affects membership in occupational groups, then time of day preferences should also differ between blue- and white-collar occupations. They don't. To check further on this puzzling relationship, age groups were cross-tabulated with educational level. The results indicate that a large proportion of those with some college are young students, so the conclusion is that age is the most important determinant and education plays only a small role.

Another format for reporting several cross-tabs in the same table is shown in Example 12–15. In this format, the same four ratings define all *rows*. Each *pair* of columns shows the percentages for women and for men, for each variable or *brand*. Column percentages are listed in the body of the table, so they total downward to 100 percent. Since there were exactly as many women as men, there's no need to show the combined percentages for both sexes. The focus is directed exclusively to the comparison between the ratings of men and those of women for each brand. By presenting the distributions for all four brands in one banner, the comparison between brands is also facilitated, but it's important to note that measuring *significance* of differences *between brands* would require cross-tabulations between pairs of brands, for each sex, individually.

Analysis of Variance Reports

The statistical method for measuring the significance of differences among *mean* values of a continuous dependent variable for the categories of an independent variable is analysis of variance. A typical ANOVA table from an analysis program is shown in Example 11–5 on page 320. Reports of academic research ordinarily

Horizontal Cross-Tabulation Table   Example 12–15

Ratings of Four Brands by 100 Men and 100 Women*								
	Brand A		Brand B		Brand C		Brand D	
	Women	Men	Women	Men	Women	Men	Women	Men
Excellent ...	31%	19%	8%	12%	17%	26%	36%	44%
Good	42%	36%	21%	33%	40%	38%	51%	38%
Fair	19%	26%	39%	41%	32%	21%	10%	22%
Poor	8%	19%	32%	14%	11%	15%	3%	4%
Total	100%	100%	100%	100%	100%	100%	100%	100%

*Differences between sexes for all four brands are statistically significant.

show the results very much as they're listed in Example 11–5. Pragmatic survey research reports usually contain only the tables of mean values. Typically, they omit the analysis of variance table itself as in Example 12–16.

In the example, the actual probability is listed, rather than merely noting statistical significance. This is quite acceptable, providing the narrative explains the meaning of the probability, or the report readers are *all* very likely to know the meaning from an earlier explanation or previous training and experience. The footnote to the table in Example 12–16 indicates the other demographic variables in the survey did not prove to have significantly different test scores when they were analyzed. Thus, there was no purpose in showing the means for each category of those variables, because they're automatically assumed to be the same for all categories of each in the population.

The narrative text to accompany a tabular report such as that in Example 12–16 would typically identify the highest and lowest mean value for each category, for one variable at a time. Any trends or identifiable relationships among categories, in terms of the mean values, should be noted in the narrative, and the major differences by category should be discussed as well.

Paired t-Test Reports

When the significance of the difference between means is to be measured for a *pair* of continuous variables *both obtained from the same respondents*, a *paired* t-test can be used. The report of such an analysis from a statistical program is shown in the upper section of Figure 11–10 on page 331.

In Example 12–17, the analyses of the differences between the mean time respondents *actually* did four daily activities and the time they would *ideally* like to do them are reported in the same, condensed table. For academic survey research

Analysis of Variance Table of Means   Example 12–16

Breakdowns of: Lark-Owl Test Scores by Demographic Variables			
Group	**Probability**	**Mean**	**Number**
Age Group	.0000		
Under 20		2.09	11
20 to 29		5.14	97
30 to 39		6.18	73
40 to 49		7.00	59
50 to 59		6.72	78
60 to 69		6.90	51
70 and over		6.71	31
Combined		6.18	400
Marital Status	.002		
Married		6.67	215
Not married		5.60	185
Combined		6.18	400
Family Life Cycle	.0014		
Young single		5.19	113
Young couple		6.18	39
Child under 6		6.77	30
Child 6 to 15		6.18	44
Child over 15		6.72	54
Elder couple		6.97	74
Elder single		6.26	46
Combined		6.18	400
Scores not significantly different for other demographic items.			

Paired t-Test Table of Means   Example 12–17

Comparisons of Mean Actual versus Ideal Times for Activities				
Activity	**Actual**	**Ideal**	**Difference**	**Probability**
Get up	6:47 AM	7:12 AM	−25 Min.	.000
Start work	8:16 AM	8:35 AM	−19 Min.	.000
Finish work	4:02 PM	4:21 PM	−19 Min.	.000
Have dinner	6:31 PM	6:30 PM	+1 Min.	.598
Go to bed	11:00 PM	11:03 PM	−3 Min.	.126
400 Respondents				

reports, the table would probably contain much more detail. For more pragmatic survey research, the reports usually show only the mean values, just as with analysis of variance. It's also advisable to show the direction and magnitude *of differences* in means in paired t-test reports. Of course, there must be some notation of the statistical significance as well. Example 12–17 lists the actual probability for gauging significance.

In many cases, there's no need to list relationships that don't prove to be statistically significant. For example, the table in Example 12–16 merely notes that the means for the other demographic variables weren't significantly different. The actual means weren't listed. The table shown in Example 12–17 does show the actual and ideal *dinner times* and *bed times*, even though the differences are clearly not statistically significant. This is a case where it's just as important to recognize the *similarities* as it is to identify *differences* in mean values. Whenever such similarity in values is as notable or even more remarkable than are differences in values, the similar pairs of means should be listed, even though the differences aren't statistically significant.

The inclusion of five, comparable paired t-test analyses in one table, as in Example 12–17, allows the report to compare similarities and differences between pairs in the narrative text, thus:

> Survey respondents clearly indicated in their listings of actual and ideal times that they would prefer to arise in the morning about a half hour later than they do. The results shown in Table 17 also indicate they would like to start and finish their workday about 20 minutes later. By contrast, the results show they eat dinner in the evening at almost exactly the time they would like to do so, and also retire for the night at very nearly the ideal time.
>
> These relationships suggest two things: (1) The average individual in the population would like to start and finish work a little later than they're required to

Correlation Matrix Table   Example 12–18

Correlations Among Ratings of Self-Image for Five Attributes					
	Creative	Assertive	Patient	Outspoken	Cooperative
Creative		r = +.30 p = .001	r = +.01 p = .402	r = +.16 p = .001	r = +.09 p = .018
Assertive	r = +.30 p = .001		r = −.01 p = .014	r = +.48 p = .001	r = −.08 p = .032
Patient	r = +.01 p = .402	r = −.10 p = .014		r = −.19 p = .001	r = +.43 p = .001
Outspoken	r = +.16 p = .001	r = +.48 p = .001	r = −.19 p = .001		r = +.01 p = .408
Cooperative	r = +.09 p = .018	r = −.08 p = .032	r = +.43 p = .001	r = +.01 p = .408	
500 Respondents r = Correlation Coefficient p = Significance Probability					

do so. (2) The fact they must start work earlier than they would ideally like causes them to arise earlier than they want to, but they dine and retire in the evening when they would like. Thus, they sacrifice sleep time to meet work requirements.

Correlation Analysis Reports

When the *means* of two continuous variables that are both responses from the same respondents are to be compared, the paired t-test is used. When the relationship between such variables is to be measured in terms of their change or variance from one respondent to the next, *correlation* is the appropriate measure. Correlation analysis doesn't assume one is causing or determining the other. When the data are from interval or ratio level scales, product-moment correlation is used. When the data are from ordinal level scales, rank correlation is appropriate. The results are shown in reports and interpreted in exactly the same way, but when rank correlations are shown, it should be noted in the report table. If the table simply lists correlation coefficients, the assumption would be that the coefficients are product-moment correlations.

In Example 11–6, page 328, each pairing of five variables was reported in tabular form by the analysis routine. The variables were only identified by number and weren't labeled to indicate their meaning. The same results are shown in Example 12–18, but the table is labeled with the variables' names and the redundant "halves" of the matrix are both shown. Thus, readers can locate a pair by approaching from the top or the side of the matrix. In Example 12–18, the probabilities for assessing

Regression Analysis Report   Example 12–19

Regression of Actual on Estimated Expenditures in Dollars				
Variable	**Mean**	**Minimum**	**Maximum**	**Number**
Estimated expenditure	22.45	5.00	31.00	300
Actual expenditure	22.66	8.00	28.00	300
Item	**Symbol**	**Value**	**Std. Err.**	**Probability**
Mean difference	D	0.213	0.173	0.2180
Correlation	R	0.795		0.0000
Determination	R^2	0.633	2.829	0.0000
Slope	B	0.789	0.035	0.0000
Intercept	A	4.958	0.798	0.0000

Prediction equation: *Predicted Expenditure* = 0.789 times *Estimate,* plus $4.96.

statistical significance are listed. This assumes the readers are *all* completely capable of understanding and interpreting them. If that weren't the case, only the correlation coefficients would be listed. An asterisk would be attached to the significant coefficients and a footnote would indicate their significance. The narrative interpretations would merely identify the direction and intensity of each significant correlation.

Regression Analysis Reports

When the effect of one continuous variable on another is to be measured, regression analysis is the statistical method to do so. In Example 11–7, page 334, the relationship between *expected* and *actual* dollar expenditures is assessed and reported by the analysis routine. A less detailed tabular report of the same data is shown in Example 12–19.

It's always advisable to list the mean, minimum, and maximum values for the variable in regression analysis reports. The prediction equation is usually valid and accurate only within or very close to that range. The table in Example 12–19 also lists the difference in means and the probability for assessing the significance of the difference. This measure is the same as a paired t-test, and it's interpreted in the same way. It merely indicates that in this case, actual expenditures weren't significantly different from the expected expenditures. The correlation coefficient is also listed in Example 12–19, along with the probability for assessing its significance. The meaning is precisely the same as for product-moment correlation described earlier.

FIGURE 12–16
Regression
Scatterplot

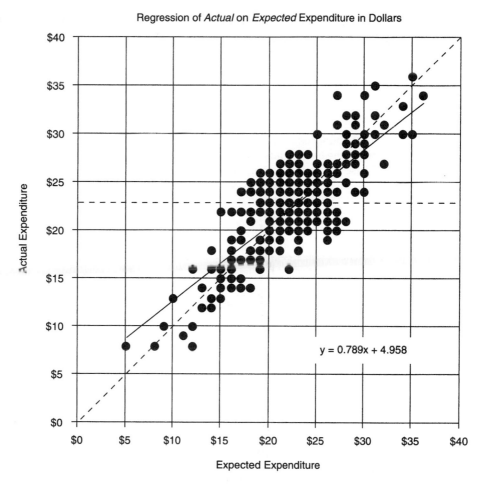

Regression of *Actual* on *Expected* Expenditure in Dollars

$$y = 0.789x + 4.958$$

The value of r-square is shown in the regression analysis report to indicate the degree to which the independent variable affects the dependent variable. It indicates the percentage of variance in the actual expenditures that's "explained" by knowing the expected value. It suggests how accurate a prediction based on the regression equation might be. The standard error of the estimate and the standard errors of the constant and the regression coefficient might also be included in the report, if the readers are sufficiently informed or familiar with regression analysis. In Example 12 19, the prediction equation is listed at the bottom of the table in verbal rather than symbolic form for those who aren't familiar with prediction equation symbols.

Regression analysis is a powerful tool, but it's also rather complex. Showing the data in a scatterplot such as that in Figure 12–16 sometimes makes it easier for information seekers to comprehend the more abstract numeric values. That way, they can actually see the relationship between the independent and dependent variables.

Regression analysis often requires a fairly complete and elaborate narrative explanation for report readers and sponsors who aren't completely familiar with statistical methods. If the focus of the information needs were on *measurement of the existing relationship,* the narrative would deal with that aspect. If *predictions of the dependent variable* were required, the narrative would place more emphasis on that. It would focus on accuracy and especially on meeting the requirements for valid application—such as staying within the range of values used to compute the equation. This narrative example focuses on both the relationship between the variables and on prediction:

> Three hundred of the newest homeowners within the complex who anticipated using the new facility were asked how much they *expected* to spend there per month. These values were recorded for each lot number. The lot numbers for those making subsequent, *actual* expenditures were also recorded with the amount spent. The results are shown in Table 19 and plotted in Figure 16. The average values for anticipated and actual expenditures were both very close to $22.50 per month. They didn't significantly under- or overestimate how much they would spend as a group.
>
> This might seem to suggest that we could estimate each new homeowner who moves in will spend about $22.66 per month at the facility, represented by the horizontal, dashed line in Figure 16. That would only be true on the average, over all newcomers. In fact, however, individual spending does vary substantially from one family to the next, as the plot shows. The regression equation indicates over 60 percent of that variation is "explained" by the differences in what they *expect* to spend. In other words, these people have a fairly good idea of what they'll *actually* spend at the facility.
>
> To predict how much each new homeowner will spend, we could simply ask them their expectations and take that as the estimate. If they *expected* to spend $15, we would predict $15, and if they *expected* to spend $30, we would predict $30. That way to predict is represented by the diagonal, dashed line in Figure 16. It's a much better predictor than the average for the group, but it's not the best way.
>
> The solid regression line plotted in Figure 16 shows that people who *expect* to spend less than the average actually underestimate their spending. They tend to spend a little more than they expected. By contrast, those who *expect* to spend more than the group average tend to overestimate. Their *actual* spending turns out to be less than they expected. So, the best predictor of how much a new family will spend is based on what they expect, but we would compute it with the regression equation.
>
> If they expect to spend $10 per month, we would multiply that by the slope of the line, .789, to get $7.89, then add the adjustment of $4.96. So we would expect them to spend $12.85 a month, not $10. Similarly, if they estimated $30, the prediction based on the regression equation would be $30 times .789 + $4.96 = $28.63. It's important to note this applies only to *homeowners* and only for predictions under $40. *Renters'* spending can't be predicted in this way. Nor do we have the data to predict how someone who *expected* to spend over $40 would *actually* spend.

This portion of a narrative text discussing the regression relationships in Example 12–19 and Figure 12–16 first cited the insignificant differences in mean values. Then it indicated the strength of the relationship, based on the r-square value. It compared a prediction based on the mean versus one based directly on the individual's expectation, the independent variable, making reference to the scatterplot to clarify the methods visually. Finally, it cited the regression equation as the best predictor and gave two examples of prediction calculations. The narrative did *not* discuss the confidence intervals around the regression prediction because that was beyond the scope of detail for the report. If the report's audience were knowledgeable about statistics, the narrative might have explained the prediction would be within $5.66 over 95 percent of the time and $8.49 over 99 percent of the time, based on the standard error of the estimate. The narrative report was also careful to note the restrictions on application of the regression equation, such as similar subjects (homeowners) and within the proper range (under $40.).

Concluding the Project

The final report of the results should be carefully edited and a clean copy typed using a dark print that can be copied clearly. Multiple copies are often required for sponsors and those seeking the information. The pragmatic survey research report should be headed with a title page that identifies the sponsor, project, and researcher or organization that conducted the survey. It's important to note on the title page the address and telephone number of the person or office responsible for the project, so they can be contacted at a later time for clarification, if that should be needed.

All of the pages within a survey report should be consecutively numbered, and the page numbers should appear in the same place on every page. When the report is of substantial size, an index should be included directly following the title page. The major sections of the report should be listed with the page number, and a list of tables or figures should follow the list of contents or index, if there are several.

Hard Copy Reports

Traditionally, the printed, hard copy survey research report was the most common report format. While online reporting via either the Internet or an intranet has become routine, hard copy reporting of survey results remains a popular option. There are several reasons: Some information seekers may not have access to an online report because they lack communications facilities or because of their location. In addition, some sponsors may have concerns about the security of online reports, either because they fear unauthorized access to the information or they worry that electronic files may be damaged or destroyed. Regardless of the reasons, hard copy reports remain common and researchers must know how to create them effectively.

If the final survey report consists only of a few pages, they should be stapled together in the upper left corner or attached in a small binder or folio to keep the document together and intact. When the report consists of many pages, it can be punched and contained in a ring binder or bound in some other form by a copy service. Larger reports stay neater and more readable when they're bound within durable covers. Ring binders are available with clear plastic "envelopes" on the covers so title pages can be inserted. The title is then visible from the outside. When the report is bound, it's advisable to label the front cover with the name of the report or use a clear plastic cover to make the report easily identifiable without opening it.

Online Report Generation

Perhaps the most expedient, though not the most elegant, means of publishing the written survey report online would be to write the document using a word processor such as Microsoft Word, then save it as a Web page. The program has a file option called "Web Page Preview." When selected, it launches the Internet Explorer Web browser (assuming it's the default browser on the system) and shows how the entire document will look as a Web page. This allows the report writer to adjust font, color, line spacing, and the like before saving the document. When saved as a Web page, the file is converted to a *HyperText Markup Language* (HTML) document, the language of the World Wide Web. The file can then be published on a website on the Internet or an intranet and viewed using any Web browser by anyone who has the appropriate access. Similarly, spreadsheet documents from programs such as Microsoft Excel® can be saved as HTML documents to be included on websites.

Survey research reports can also be contained and presented on websites using computer applications designed to create websites, such as Microsoft FrontPage® or Adobe PageMill®. In addition, if the researcher is to make one or more report presentations, described in Appendix C, the presentation manager program files, such as PowerPoint® presentations, can also be saved as HTML documents for viewing on the Web.

Another, somewhat more elegant approach to publishing survey research reports online is to compose or import them into a program called Adobe Acrobat®. This program creates *Portable Document Format* (PDF) files that can be saved on CD-ROM or made available to download from the Internet or an intranet. These files can be opened and read (though not modified) with Acrobat Reader®, a program that can be downloaded free from many locations on the Internet and that runs on all the popular operating systems and platforms. When PDF files are created in Acrobat®, there is more control of both text and graphics. These documents tend to have a clean, attractive appearance both on screen and when printed.

Wrapping Up the Project

The researcher should retain data files and documentation for a *substantial* period after completing a project. Very often sponsors or those seeking the information will have additional questions after studying the report. These additional information needs can usually be met quickly and inexpensively if the data files, programs, and documents are retained in good order. All of the survey materials, including the source documents, data files, special programs, and other materials obtained specifically for the survey, are the property of the sponsor unless otherwise specified in the contract. Thus, when these materials are clearly no longer of use to the researcher for the project at hand, the sponsor should indicate which are to be delivered to the sponsor's office and which are to be destroyed. In most cases of commercial survey research, all of the materials are regarded by the sponsor as proprietary information. Consequently, extra copies of the reports or other documents must usually be delivered to the sponsor or destroyed so they don't fall into the hands of those who aren't entitled to the information.

Whether the survey research project was conducted to meet academic requirements or professionally, as the result of employment or a contract, most experienced researchers find one source of "payment" to be very valuable. That's merely the sense of satisfaction and accomplishment that's inevitably achieved at the completion of a job *well done*. No matter how simple or mundane the content of a well-conceived and conducted survey might be, those who do the project can be assured of its value. This society both generates and consumes vast amounts of information. Our social, political, economic, and technical systems are heavily dependent on it. Consequently, those who use survey research to generate *information* that's both reliable and valid have contributed significantly to the progress and satisfaction of the society.

Summary

Generating the Final Report

A. Spend the time and effort. Avoid the temptation to rush through the report and do it carefully, even though sponsors may be overly anxious.

B. Keep it very neat. The appearance and cosmetic aspects of the report often indicate to readers, rightly or wrongly, the credibility of the survey results.

C. Use an executive summary. Pragmatic survey research reports should begin with a quick summary of the main highlights and major results.

D. Include a response summary. Prepare a blank questionnaire listing the simplest form of data description and removing any superfluous codes or instructions.

E. Compose tables first. Condense the information with clean, simple formats in a single page, so patterns and relationships can readily be perceived.

F. Display the information. Create charts, graphs, and diagrams when values and relationships can be represented more clearly by size and shape than by words and numbers.

G. Write a simple narrative. Avoid jargon and use plain vocabulary to describe the major findings revealed in each table, with introductions and summaries of each section.

H. Keep components independent. Tables and graphs should be clearly labeled and the narrative written so report readers can obtain the major gist of the results from either mode.

I. Conclude the project. Edit, copy, and bind the reports, including a title page for identification, and maintain data and documents until directed to deliver or destroy them.

Appendix A

Conducting Focus Groups

Focus Group Characteristics

Focus group discussions or conferences are usually called merely *focus groups.* A typical focus group consists of eight to twelve people seated around a conference table with a group moderator who *focuses* their discussion on a series of topics or issues of interest to the research sponsor, while the proceedings are being observed and recorded for analysis and interpretation later. Focus groups have a relatively short history, compared to survey research, but they have become an increasingly popular method of inquiry. Focus groups provide *qualitative* information rather than quantitative data. The results don't usually generalize reliably to the population as a whole. Consequently, focus group research is typically regarded as more *exploratory* and *preliminary* than conclusive.

Surveys are expensive and time-consuming. So, it's vitally important to ask the right questions and to ask them in the right way. By conducting one or more focus groups before initiating a survey, both sponsors and researchers may be able to get a better grasp of the problem and formulate the research questions more accurately. Well-conducted focus groups may also help the researcher to understand the potential survey respondents' general perspective on the issues, frame of reference, way of thinking, and typical vocabulary when dealing with the topics in question.

There are four key aspects of focus group inquiry that deserve attention: The agenda, the participants, the moderator, and the interpretations. The advantages and disadvantages of focus groups should be considered before turning to those issues.

Advantages and Disadvantages

There are both advantages and disadvantages to conducting focus groups before initiating a survey project. It's important for both sponsors and researchers to recognize the strong and weak points of this technique. Focus group research isn't

FIGURE A–1
Advantages of
Focus Groups

Spontaneity	Focus group participants typically respond very spontaneously, volunteering their opinions and reactions, sharing their experiences, and providing comments far beyond just responding to questions.
Subjectivity	Participants are encouraged to express their personal opinions and reactions freely in their own vocabulary, addressing what's most important to them rather than responding in someone else's terms.
Stimulation	Group participants usually fell free to reveal themselves, sharing personal experiences and disclosing personal reactions that stimulate others to describe their own views and reactions.
Speed	Moderators, facilities, and participants can be secured and focus groups can be conducted very quickly, so focus group inquiries may not seriously delay the start of a survey project.
Simplicity	Focus group results are expressed verbally and qualitatively, rather than in numeric, tabular reports, so both the process and the findings are readily understood by sponsors.
Structure	The inquiry is indeed focused and the conversation is centered on the specific topics and issues of greatest interest to the sponsor, covering each area in a meaningful, comprehensive way.
Specialization	Focus group inquiries can address very specific topics and issues in depth, dealing in great detail with the finer nuances and subtle ramifications of certain positions and special conditions.
Selectivity	The participation of people who represent special segments of the populations can often be obtained readily, allowing inquiries to be addressed to either opinion leaders or the common man or woman.
Secrecy	Since only a small number of people are involved, focus group inquiries can be conducted without revealing the existence, nature, and purpose of the anticipated survey to rivals or competitive firms.

always necessary or appropriate. When it is, the objective is to get the most from it while avoiding both the most common and the more obscure pitfalls.

Major Capabilities

The main advantages of focus groups are briefly outlined in Figure A–1. Focus groups tend to be very dynamic and spontaneous, compared to a one-on-one interview. Rather than just responding to the moderator, group members interact, engaging one another in conversation about the topics and issues in focus at the moment. These groups are large enough so no one person feels he or she holds the exclusive attention of the moderator. Yet they're small enough to be "conversational," so even those who are rather shy about speaking before a group aren't threatened by the situation. Since there's an agenda, the discussion is loosely, but not rigidly, organized. The moderator can direct the discussion toward the topics of major interest to the research sponsor. However, this doesn't preclude pursuing fortuitous, unanticipated avenues that often arise in the course of the group discussion.

The focus group moderator can probe and delve into the assumptions and feelings that underlie the attitudes and opinions expressed, so the results are richly textured with detail. The sponsor's representatives can observe the focus group, either directly or on video recordings. Nuances of voice, expression, and manner reveal more than just the verbal records of what group members said. The results often have a strong impact on interested survey sponsors and information seekers.

Focus group participants reveal far more than just their overt opinions and preferences—they also reveal *themselves*. In the course of conversation, they show something of their own, individual personality. So researchers and sponsors learn *who it is* that thinks, feels, and acts that way. Rather than seeing only a demographic profile of the respondents, focus group participants have names and faces. Their opinions and reactions are revealed in the context of their daily lives. So when survey research analysts, sponsors, and information seekers are making choices and decisions that depend on respondent reactions, they have a vivid picture in their mind's eye of the "real people" whose reactions are represented in the more abstract survey findings.

Major Limitations

Perhaps the primary disadvantage of focus group research is the limitation on the number of participants who can be included. Even if several focus group discussions are held, findings based on such a small sample can't be generalized to the population as a whole with any degree of confidence. Some sponsors and researchers do use focus groups as a substitute for survey research, rather than as a preliminary, exploratory method, but the qualitative results form such a limited number of people that they can't be regarded as conclusive. Consequently, generalization of focus group information to a broad universe of people is rarely if ever advisable.

Focus groups require a great deal of skill and expertise on the moderator's part. By comparison with field interviewers, focus group moderators should be much more thoroughly trained in the art of asking questions and guiding the discussion. It may *look* easy, but the task of moderating a focus group is vastly more difficult than it appears. There are often one or two people in a focus group who tend to dominate the conversation and overly influence the opinions of others, if they're allowed to do so. They have to be restrained without offending them. There are also likely to be a few who are rather shy and withdrawn—reluctant to give their own opinions and reactions. They must be drawn out and engaged, but without threatening them. Most important of all, the moderator must protect the *diversity* of opinion and reaction within the group, despite the strong tendency toward group *consensus* that inevitably emerges in any prolonged group interaction. These demands, among many others, make it difficult to find a competent focus group moderator. Yet, the validity and practicality of the information depend very heavily on the moderator's skill and expertise.

While focus groups are a relatively fast research method, they're also rather expensive. Each focus group among ordinary adults from the general public might cost the sponsor anywhere from a few thousand to several thousand dollars. Focus groups that include commercial, organizational, governmental, or professional executives or decision makers are much more expensive, ranging as high as many thousands of dollars each for special groups. Yet, one survey research project might call for several focus groups to be conducted, in order to cover the entire range of topics and the complete spectrum of potential participants from the population to be surveyed. In addition to the cost of this qualitative, exploratory information, the sponsor has to fund the survey itself to obtain more reliable and generalizable primary, quantitative data.

Focus Group Requirements

Informal or ad hoc focus group discussions are sometimes conducted at the sponsor's facilities or in public meeting rooms such as those provided by hotels and conference centers. So, focus groups don't really require special facilities and personnel, but they do benefit from using them. The vast majority of focus groups for businesses, organizations, and political sponsors are conducted by specialized personnel in facilities specifically designed for such research. Many, if not most, data collection agencies have special facilities for focus groups, and the majority of commercial focus groups are held in and conducted by data collection agencies.

Facilities and Equipment

Special-purpose focus group facilities usually include several components: A reception area and small waiting room, the conference room or rooms, adjoining observation rooms, administrative offices, bathrooms, and equipment storage rooms. The conference rooms themselves are more comfortably furnished than most meeting rooms. Usually there's conference table seating for a dozen or more people. To encourage a more intimate, relaxed atmosphere, some focus group rooms are furnished with couches, lounge chairs, and coffee tables rather than the conventional conference table and chairs. Microphones for recording the conversation are usually hidden from sight or at least rather obscure. That's not really to conceal the fact that the discussion will be recorded but to avoid making participants blatantly aware of the fact during the discussion. These rooms typically have one or more large mirrors that are, in fact, one-way windows between the conference room and the observation and/or camera rooms.

The observation rooms adjacent to the conference rooms often house and conceal audio and video recording equipment and technicians as well as observers. Researchers and sponsor representatives usually sit comfortably in semidarkness, watching and noting the focus group discussion while it's being conducted and speaking quietly among themselves without the notice of the participants in the next room. Some researchers and sponsors prefer to attend and observe the group discussion rather than merely to view the recording. It affords them a more direct and comprehensive impression.

Focus group discussions are sometimes only an hour or less in duration. Others extend over a little longer period. If so, the group may take a break at midpoint. If the researchers or sponsors are present, the moderator can speak briefly with them to gain their impressions and get suggestions concerning the avenues to be explored during the remainder of the focus group discussion. But whether they're present or not, focus group discussions are routinely video recorded for later study.

Special focus group facilities are desirable and widely available, but they aren't absolutely necessary. Focus groups can be conducted in a hotel, office, school, church, or public meeting room. If that's the case, the researchers, sponsors, and information seekers may still attend and observe, but they should *not* participate! Both their presence and that of the recording equipment and technicians should be as unobtrusive and inconspicuous as possible. The *more* the participants become or remain aware of their presence, the *less* validity and accuracy the results will have.

Personnel and Participants

The moderator plays a key role in focus group inquiries, although others are certainly involved in the process. The sponsors and information seekers help to identify the main topics to be discussed. The lead research analyst has overall responsibility for the focus group inquiry. The data collection agency or focus group center staff usually takes care of the preparation, recruitment, reception, and compensation of participants. Of course, the focus group participants who actually provide the information during the group discussions are central to the success of the focus group inquiry.

Research surveys of broad scope may include hundreds or even thousands of participants: No one of them has a noticeable effect on the outcome or the information obtained. But since focus groups by necessity include a few participants, the responses of each individual may represent a very large number of others who have similar views and reactions. Consequently, the recruitment, selection, and participation of each focus group participant should and usually do receive a great deal of consideration and attention.

Focus Group Agenda

The focus group agenda is a list of topics on which the discussion is to center. But the agenda for a focus group differs dramatically from a survey questionnaire. First, the questions on the agenda are framed much more loosely and broadly. Second, the agenda is much more flexible, since the discussion may suggest additional topics of inquiry to be pursued. Third, the topics and issues on the focus group agenda need not be approached in the order in which they're listed. The dynamics of relatively free-wheeling discussions dictate in large measure which topics and issues will precede or follow which others.

Translating Information Needs

The information needs to be satisfied by focus groups aren't necessarily the same as the ultimate information needs of the survey that might follow. Focus group inquiries may provide some directly applicable information to the research sponsor. However, their main objective is often to provide information to guide the survey research analyst and staff.

Identifying Key Issues

It was noted earlier that focus groups are typically an exploratory research method. Sponsor information needs are specified in the terms of the information seekers who will apply it to decisions and actions. But the questions addressed to survey respondents have to be expressed in the terms and couched in the conditions that are familiar to the public from which the survey sample will be selected. Thus, focus group inquiries are often designed to bridge that gap, to facilitate that translation.

The typical focus group agenda is expressed in very broad terms. Those composing the agenda first identify the key issues, the principal concerns and uncertainties of the research sponsor. The initial draft might be in the form of statements or phrases identifying discussion topics rather than as actual questions to be asked of the focus group participants. At this point, the effort is directed toward including all the key factors of concern.

Once the analyst is confident that all the main issues have been listed as topics, some weight or priority should be assigned to each, according to their degree of importance. Usually a simple, three-level breakdown is sufficient: (I) *Essential* information that's absolutely necessary, (2) *important* information that has substantial value to the sponsor and/or researcher, and (3) *supportive* information that amplifies and extends the value of the findings.

After identifying all of the key topics for discussion and assigning a priority to each to indicate the amount of time and degree of emphasis each one deserves, this skeleton framework can be fleshed out by listing the subsidiary issues and topics associated with each main category. So a two-level, or perhaps a three-level, outline constitutes the agenda.

Framing the Questions

The questions to be addressed to focus group discussants aren't designed to be answered with a single word or phrase, as they so often are on a survey questionnaire. Instead, the focus group agenda that the moderator brings to the discussion contains what might be called "trigger" questions, designed to draw out various opinions and stimulate a conversation about some issue. There are a couple of rather different approaches to writing such questions: One is to ask a question that will reveal participants' conclusions about the issue, then follow with a series of "probing" questions to learn what lies behind their opinions. The other approach takes just the opposite tack: first soliciting information about the background situation, then proceeding to inquire about the conclusive opinion that results under such conditions.

Some moderators are given strongly to one tactic or the other, but the best of them can approach a given issue either way, depending on what best fits the character of the group and the dynamics of the conversation during the discussion. Either way, the focus group questions should be rather loosely framed rather than tightly phrased and worded. The object is to tease out the *varying* perspectives and opinions on the topic. To do that, focus group questions often begin with a preamble that defines an entire spectrum of thought on the issue at hand, strongly implying that any and every position is as acceptable and respectable as any other. This helps to prevent the more dominant members of the group from leading or pulling others toward their own position, as though it were the only valid one.

Organizing the Schedule

The schedule of questions for a focus group discussion should be organized according to some principle so that the conversation doesn't jump abruptly from one topic or issue to a completely different one without a smooth transition. Without a well-defined train of thought, the discussion will be rather chaotic and disjointed. That makes the results far more difficult to interpret and it also inhibits the response of the participants. The mind abhors chaos and disorder. It doesn't readily move from consideration of one topic to a completely different and unrelated one without a meaningful connection or some advance warning. So, the analyst and moderator should plan smooth transitions and create "bridges" from one set of ideas to the next.

Schedule Flexibility

While some organization is necessary, it's a mistake to follow a rigid structure within a focus group discussion. Ordinarily, there are many incidents during the discussion where the participants themselves will take the conversation in an unexpected direction, following some train of thought the researcher or moderator didn't anticipate. By allowing that to happen, the inquiry benefits from the serendipitous information that comes forth. Were the moderator to adhere tightly to the schedule of questions, that opportunity would be lost.

When scheduling the questions, the objective is to provide organization when it's needed, yet not to impose a structure when it's not required. The moderator should willingly, even eagerly, let the conversation go where it will, providing it doesn't go too far afield of the main topics or issues. It also implies that the moderator must be able to find the way back to another topic on the agenda when the current conversation has exhausted the issue it spontaneously pursued. Thus, the adroit, well-practiced moderator has to be able to build such connections or bridges extemporaneously.

Generality to Specificity

The most effective focus group schedule moves from the general to the specific. For instance, the discussion of a topic might begin by focusing first on a very broad set of issues or principles, then move smoothly to consideration of various aspects or details of each. The participants might be questioned first about their general attitudes and policies concerning some issue, practice, or experience, then asked about specific instances and tactics. When the focus group discussion moves from one main topic category to another, the new set of questions should begin with the general issues, then explore the more specific, detailed opinions and actions. If the pattern were reversed, moving from the specific to the general, isolated examples or atypical details might dictate response to more general questions. By approaching the broader issues first, then ferreting out the specific incidents, the moderator helps prevent the participants from verbally "painting themselves into a corner."

Focus Group Participants

Recruitment and selection of the focus group members are certainly key elements, if not the most crucial elements of this exploratory method of inquiry. After all, it's they who will ultimately provide the information. Since there are so few participants, the information provided by each is a major part of the whole.

Selection Criteria

The focus group participants should be homogeneous in one respect and heterogeneous in another—similar in some respects but different in others. If the participants differ greatly in every way, they'll have a hard time relating to one another. By contrast, if most or all members of the group are of an almost identical ilk—if they're practically clones of one another—then they're likely to react as one. There would be too little diversity and too much redundancy.

Socioeconomic Composition

When all members of one focus group share a similar set of socioeconomic characteristics, that facilitates group interaction. For instance, a group consisting only of married women not working outside the home, who are mothers of two or more children, are likely to share many experiences and perspectives—they have the same problems and troubles, they face similar needs, and they enjoy about the same set of opportunities and satisfactions. This is especially true if their educations and family incomes are similar and they share other such demographic characteristics. Such group participants are more easily able to identify with one another and they're likely to interact freely with one another. They'll quickly and easily find a common ground. If, on the other hand, the group contained some such women, while others were younger, single, better-educated, and career-oriented women, the differences would be so large and so obvious they would inhibit a free, easy discussion of the topics at hand.

Obviously, there can be some diversity in the participants' backgrounds, but beyond some point, communication will be inhibited. If the population to be represented by the focus group participants consists only of one, fairly homogeneous socioeconomic segment, then a single focus group might represent the population quite well. If the population to be surveyed is quite heterogeneous, consisting of many diverse socioeconomic segments, it may be necessary to conduct several focus groups. When time or budget requirements preclude conducting several such focus group conferences, it's usually better to single out only the most important socioeconomic segments for study than to include widely diverse participants within only one or two focus groups.

Position Representation

While the similarity of the participants for any one focus group is desirable, the members should certainly not be identical to one another in their *reactions to the topics and issues* to be discussed. In other words, the group should provide varying views on the issues on which the discussion focuses. The objective, after all, isn't to obtain close consensus; just the opposite. The researcher should strive for a group composition that will represent various positions and views on the topics and issues to be discussed and to preserve that *diversity* in the information obtained.

With focus group inquiries, the goal isn't to measure and project the size or proportion of the population that takes each position or holds each view. That can be accomplished with the survey, but not by focus groups. Instead, the goal of each focus group is to discover and reveal the nature, range, and diversity of positions. Consequently, the criteria for selecting focus group participants might stipulate that a certain proportion of the people chosen must hold a certain view or have a certain kind of experience. It may even be necessary to prescreen candidates with a brief questionnaire to be sure various views or positions are represented.

Screening Candidates

Focus group participants are typically recruited by the data collection agency or focus group center where the inquiry will be conducted. The recruiters should be given the criteria for seeking and selecting the candidates. Whether or not the participants are to be screened before acceptance, it's incumbent on the sponsor or researcher conducting the inquiry to provide firm guidelines regarding who is and who isn't eligible. Lacking such guidance, those selecting participants are *very* likely to choose those who are the *quickest* and *easiest* to obtain. They probably won't represent the population to be sampled in the survey very well.

Conformity to Criteria

The criteria for selection of focus group participants might include either specification of the *groups* from whom participants are to be obtained or of the *individual* characteristics of those who are chosen. For instance, the directions for a focus group dealing with children's home study materials might state that the participants are to be obtained only from the P.T.A. roster of mothers of third and fourth grade elementary school pupils from a certain school. Alternatively, the directions might require that only mothers with children between nine and eleven years of age living within a certain area are eligible to participate.

In some cases it may be necessary to question potential participants with a brief screening instrument to ascertain whether they qualify for participation. Such questionnaires are neither as elaborate nor as formal as a typical survey instrument. Prospective participants might only be asked to indicate a few basic demographic characteristics, but they may also be questioned very briefly about their views or experiences. For instance, only those familiar with the issues or topics of interest to the sponsor might be eligible while all others may be disqualified and politely dismissed from further participation.

Participation and Payment

Survey respondents are only rarely paid for their participation, and then only under special circumstances. But responding to a survey questionnaire ordinarily takes very little time and effort. By contrast, taking part in a focus group discussion typically requires the person to visit a special facility at a specific time, to spend an hour or so there, and to participate much more actively with the others in the group. Consequently, focus group members often either receive monetary compensation for participating or they're given a substantial gift or premium for doing so.

Compensation is something of a two-edged sword: On the one hand, selection bias and error are *reduced* by compensation because desirable participants who would otherwise refuse can be induced to attend and participate. On the other hand, compensation might also *increase* bias and error. If they're given too much, it might encourage too favorable an attitude toward the issues, topics, or sponsor than would normally exist among those in the population to be surveyed. It might also result in greater representation of those who most need or want the money or gift, despite their actual lack of qualification or essential interest in the inquiry. To increase the positive effects and decrease the negative effects of compensating focus group participants, the sponsor or researcher should choose a level and type of compensation that's *proportionate* to the task and *commensurate* with the earning power of participants. The degree of effort participants have to put forth or inconvenience they must tolerate is only one factor. The other has to do with how much that time and effort is worth to *them!* Obviously, retirees with relatively low socioeconomic status should not be compensated at the same level as affluent, well-educated young professionals, nor vice versa.

There's one group of potential focus group participants who definitely *shouldn't* be selected—those who have ample time on their hands and greatly enjoy taking part in many such discussions. They may have participated many times in the past and make themselves readily available to the facility recruiting focus group participants. So, they become "professional" participants, and the more experience they gain, the greater their opinions, views, and reactions will vary from those of ordinary people in the population. If their participation isn't strictly prohibited, recruiters are likely to simplify their task by accepting one or several such easily identifiable and readily available "regulars."

The ideal number of focus group participants ranges from six or eight to as many as ten or twelve. Fewer people provide fewer opinions and less diversity, so the cost per item of information is increased. If only a few participants are present, there may be too few to encourage frank, open discussion. Each may see him- or herself as too obviously the center of attention, while a somewhat larger group affords some degree of inconspicuousness to the individual. On the other hand, groups that exceed about a dozen people become difficult for the moderator to manage: They often become fractionated and the more timid members become reluctant to express themselves before so many others. In addition, focus groups of eight or ten people are so common that most facilities are arranged to accommodate only about that number: Smaller groups would appear to be underpopulated or underattended while larger groups may crowd the space or cramp the facilities.

Usually about 10 or 15 percent of candidates who are recruited and selected probably won't show up (on time) to participate. It depends partly on the amount of compensation offered. Consequently, more participants are ordinarily solicited than will actually be required to compensate for the "no-shows." If, by some happenstance, all or nearly all those invited do show up for the focus group, it's best to exclude the excess, compensate them, and dismiss them, rather than including too large a number in the focus group session.

Focus Group Moderators

The single most important individual involved in a focus group is the moderator. The accuracy, utility, and value of the information obtained is directly dependent on the moderator's skill and ability. At first glance, the focus group moderator's job looks fairly simple and easy. In fact, it's deceptively difficult and exceedingly demanding. Even among very experienced moderators, only the best of them really do it well. To make matters even more difficult, a well-trained and very capable moderator might conduct one focus group very successfully, yet the same person might be completely inappropriate for a different group of participants and an agenda focusing on a different set of topics and issues.

Personal Attributes

A focus group moderator's potential depends in part on the nature of the personality. There are some personality traits that most or all effective moderators share and others that are virtually always absent in a good moderator. Yet the biographic characteristics of the best moderators tend to differ very markedly from one to the next—some are men, others women; some young, some elderly, and some middle-aged; some obviously glib and sophisticated, but others of the "salt-of-the-earth" type. There's a good reason for this diversity among focus group moderators.

Biographic Characteristics

Moderators tend to be more effective at obtaining information from the focus group members when they share many of the same biographic characteristics as most of the participants. The reasons are about the same as those for selecting participants with common socioeconomic or demographic characteristics: People are vastly more comfortable and at ease, and thus more candid and open, with people who are similar to themselves than with those who are quite different.

Even though some potential moderators might be exceptionally skilled and capable, their ability and experience would hardly compensate for perceived differences between them and the groups that were their demographic opposites. If necessary, it's best to sacrifice some degree of skill and experience in order to get a fairly close match between the demographic characteristics of the group members and those of the *moderator—providing the moderator possesses the basic qualifications.*

Personality and Temperament

The best and most effective focus group moderators tend to be fairly open, outgoing people. They're usually fairly bright, though they certainly shouldn't appear to be intellectual types. The more friendly and charismatic they are, the better, yet they shouldn't have a celebrity's demeanor. The more they're seen as "just one of the guys or gals," the more effective they're likely to be, unless, of course, the focus group participants are themselves an exceptional group. Good moderators appear to be more curious and inquisitive than knowledgeable or authoritative.

The most effective television talk show hosts maintain a certain naivetè—something of a "little boy" or "little girl" mentality. They show an ability to be intrigued or even dismayed. It allows the audience to identify with them, despite their celebrity status and years of association with famous and talented guests. The best focus group moderators have a similar image and demeanor. They have just enough authority to direct and control the flow of conversation but without directly affecting its content. They can engender enough trust so they don't threaten or embarrass the participants, but not so much familiarity that they lose respect or control.

Experience and Skill

The best and most effective moderators aren't necessarily the most experienced. Yet experience does count, and it takes a substantial amount of it for moderators to try different approaches and perfect their style and technique. The prospective moderator's track record is often the single most important indicator of skill and ability. Prospective focus group moderators should be able to provide the researcher with a client list identifying the types of research sponsors they have served, the nature of the focus group topics, and the recency of the experience. Confidentiality and the proprietary nature of research information may prohibit them from identifying each individual client firm. Yet they should be able to provide the identity of former client firms not competitive with the potential client together with the name and location of individuals within those firms who might be contacted for a recommendation. Sponsors or researchers who were former clients are vastly more reliable sources of information about prospective moderators than are the recommendations of data collection agencies, with whom they may be affiliated. Potential moderators may also be interviewed in person or by telephone, especially if they're to moderate several focus groups.

Figure A–2 contains a list of 24 key skills and attributes of an effective focus group moderator. These are the things to look for when interviewing prospective moderators. It's also advisable to evaluate moderators on these same factors after they've been hired and conduct a focus group. That way, moderators who perform well can be coached and advised so that they can improve their performance even further. Those who fail to meet acceptable standards can be avoided in the future. The moderator's level of performance can be taken into consideration when evaluating the accuracy and validity of the information obtained from the focus group.

FIGURE A–2
Focus Group Moderator Skills

Appear relaxed and comfortable	Politely control dominant members
Avoid alienating dislikable members	Prevent undue consensus formation
Avoid favoritism among participants	Probe to learn underlying factors
Avoid revealing own opinions	Pursue unanticipated avenues well
Build rapport with others quickly	Recognize socially desirable answers
Cover every agenda topic and issue	Recognize when a topic is exhausted
Encourage spontaneous reactions	Sense members' moods effectively
Enjoy the company of the group	Show genuine interest in responses
Follow a logical agenda sequence	Successfully obtain minority opinions
Listen attentively to speakers	Treat sensitive issues gently
Never threaten or intimidate members	Use self-disclosure effectively
Obtain comments from quiet members	Use simple, conversational speech

Focus Group Interpretations

The final aspect of focus groups to be considered is the interpretation of the information they generate. Survey *data collection* generates only "raw data" that must undergo substantial manipulation, analysis, and interpretation before it's usable—before it's transformed into *information* that's applicable. Focus group inquiries are quite different in that respect. Much of the "data" obtained is *directly* applicable, with little or no intervening manipulation or interpretation, to the task of survey planning as well as for some decision making and policy formation.

Monitoring and Recording

Focus groups are often monitored directly by researchers and perhaps by survey sponsors as well. That's especially true when only one or two groups are conducted within a short period of time in the same or in nearby locations. Direct observation provides more vivid and memorable impressions of the participants' reactions and comments. The "live" show conveys more immediate, detailed information and gives those attending a greater appreciation of the nuances and subtle cues inherent in the group discussion. In addition, the research analyst and information seekers can make suggestions and give direction to the moderator during a break in a session or between consecutive focus group sessions.

Video Recording

Focus groups are routinely videotaped so sponsors and information seekers who observed the session can refer to the record later and those who did not observe directly can view the tape at another time and place. Focus group centers at data collection agencies and other research facilities are equipped to make video recordings of focus groups inconspicuously, so the recording doesn't intrude on the discussions or inhibit participants.

When focus groups are held at hotels, conference centers, schools, or meeting rooms, it's more difficult to videotape the discussions unobtrusively. Yet it's important to make every effort to be as inconspicuous as possible. Camera operators and others taping the session may be experienced at recording weddings and other ceremonies, or even business meetings and conventions where the goal is to make the images and events as *attractive* as possible. If so, they need to be reminded that the technical quality of the recording is *completely* irrelevant. What does matter is that the sponsors obtain an accurate record that reveals opinions, attitudes, and re-actions *without* affecting them or their open expression by the participants.

Video-streaming

A relatively new form of focus group recording and reporting has become increas-ingly popular with the rapid growth of very fast, wide bandwidth connections to the Internet. When *video-streaming* is used, the focus group is video recorded digi-tally, rather than on tape. The video and audio are simultaneously transmitted to a host server on the Internet. All the sponsor's personnel who are authorized to ob-serve the group are given the time schedule, sign-on instructions, and passwords. They can watch the focus group on the computer from their own office or confer-ence room, either in "real time," or at any later date whenever they want to view the digital recording stored on the host computer.

There are several advantages to video-streaming focus group transmissions. There's no travel involved, which saves not only the travel expenses, but also the executive's valuable time. With this kind of reporting, several information seekers are likely to observe the group who wouldn't be able to do so or wouldn't find it worthwhile to do so if they had to attend physically. If several executives are watching the focus group while it's under way, they can "talk" to one another from their own offices in a private chat room running on their computer side-by-side with the video stream. They can also meet in a private chat room and confer while they watch the recording for the first time or review. Everything can be done from their own individual offices at any time that's individually or mutually convenient.

Online Focus Groups

There are many Internet research companies and sites that offer what they call *"Online Focus Groups."* Rather than recruiting participants to come to a central lo-cation and sit down to meet with one another and the moderator, participants are recruited to sign in at a private chat room on the Internet, where a moderator con-ducts a focused discussion among the participants. (Alternatively, some groups use a bulletin board where participants sign in two or three times a day, read the messages, and post their own observations, opinions, and comments over a period of several days or a few weeks.)

This procedure is much less costly than the conventional focus group because there's no travel involved. In addition, sponsor representatives can sign into the room as observers without the participants knowing they're present. It's the online equivalent to the observation room. As with video-streaming, sponsor representa-tives can also hold their own discussion among themselves, simultaneous with the online group discussion. The instant transcript that's saved during the discussion is another benefit of this method.

So-called online focus groups undoubtedly have value and will continue to grow in popularity as a method of acquiring *qualitative* data (as opposed to *quantitative* data). Nonetheless, many professional researchers feel the method departs so dramatically from conventional focus groups they would not recommend them to their clients as an *alternative* or *substitute* method of focus group inquiry. Some actually object to these procedures as being called "focus groups." Their objections are several:

- The speech and voice inflections of participants can't be heard.
- Body language and facial expressions can't be seen.
- It's impossible to know if the right people are participating.
- It's almost impossible to create any group dynamics.
- Attention to the topic can't be ascertained or controlled.
- Exposure to external stimuli is strictly limited.
- The moderator's role is highly restricted by the remote contact.

Even though these online cousins of conventional focus groups are not an adequate substitute for the original, this doesn't preclude their appropriate and effective use under certain circumstances: If qualified participants are so rare in the general population or so widely dispersed geographically, the online procedure may be better than no information at all. As with online surveys, the researcher has to be sure the potential participants to an online inquiry—those with the requisite computer skills and chat room or bulletin board savvy—are typical of the population they are assumed to represent.

Analysis and Application

Survey sponsors and information seekers can gain much by attending and observing focus groups or viewing the recordings. However, the research analyst normally has much more experience with focus group inquiries. The analyst can enhance the meaning and value of the information by providing a written or oral commentary that explains and interprets the focus group results.

The simple picture of "where people stand" on the topics and issues on which the group focused is often fairly obvious in the recording of the sessions. However, it's much more difficult for information seekers with little or no training and experience regarding focus groups to identify the relevant relationships between various aspects of the participants' responses. Consequently, the research analysts who analyze and interpret the information often concentrate on comparing and contrasting various opinions and reactions among individuals with different characteristics. The interpretive commentary should highlight the most relevant and indicative similarities and distinctions the focus group discussion reveals.

An effective focus group agenda will include both the "what" and the "why"—both what the participants think, feel, and do, and also why they respond that way. The search for the feelings, emotions, beliefs, and assumptions that underlie verbal opinions is a key aspect of the analysis and interpretation of focus group responses. The analyst should identify prototypical response patterns, then relate them to the factors or conditions that underlie each identifiable pattern.

Focus groups are often used to provide valuable preliminary, qualitative information to help researchers, sponsors and information seekers get a better grasp of

FIGURE A–3
Applying
Focus Group
Information

Area Affected	Questions to be Answered
Information Needs	What are the key issues or considerations in the minds of respondents? How do they think about these matters? What *feelings* do they have? How *important* are these things to them? What *belief* patterns, *experiences,* or *assumptions* will they bring to the response task?
Sampling Design	How much *diversity* is there in their thinking on these issues? How will that *variance* affect *sample size* and reliability? Must certain groups be represented? Does this suggest a *stratified* sample? Can they be reached and will they respond readily?
Instrumentation	What *vocabulary*—what *words or phrases*—did participants use when they spoke about each topic? How does this affect the *wording* of questions? What *range* or *spectrum* of opinions was revealed? What kind of scales does that imply? How much *instruction* will be needed?
Data Collection	*Can* and *will* these people respond to a self-administered, mail questionnaire? Will they require *personal* contact? *Telephone* contact? How much *probing* will they need? Will it be easy or difficult to build *rapport?* What kinds of *interviewers* would be best for this group?
Data Processing	Can the *range, diversity,* and *depth* of response be reflected *numerically?* How much *verbal* response will be needed, if any? What methods should be used to reveal *patterns* of response? How should the *associations* between variables be measured?
Report Generation	What report mechanisms are likely to portray survey responses from this group most effectively? Will a written report suffice? Would these *information seekers* respond better to an *oral presentation?* How much *graphic* material should be anticipated in the report?

the problems and formulate research questions more precisely for a subsequent survey. If that's the case, the researcher's goal is to learn more about the survey respondents' general perspective on the issues—about their frame of reference, way of thinking, and typical vocabulary when dealing with the topics to be covered in the survey. An effective focus group inquiry can provide the research analyst and staff with insights regarding *all six* steps in the survey research process. The areas affected and the relevant questions the researcher should ask when applying focus group information to the survey process are listed in Figure A–3. It certainly doesn't constitute an exhaustive list, but it does suggest many of the most important ways and means of applying the information gained in focus groups to the planning and execution of a reliable, valid survey.

Summary

Focus Group Inquiries

A. Focus groups are a popular form of *qualitative* research information because they're fast, flexible, and easily understood.

B. Focus groups are often conducted as a preliminary, exploratory inquiry to help researchers and information seekers plan a survey.

C. With so few respondents, focus groups may *not* be an adequate substitute for field surveys of a substantial sample of respondents.

D. Focus groups require *special expertise* and perhaps special facilities, so they can be costly, especially if several are required.

E. Most focus groups are conducted at *special facilities* or *centers* designed for that purpose, but they can also be held at hotels and meeting room facilities.

F. Focus groups are guided by an *agenda* of the *key issues and topics,* and it must be fairly *flexible,* rather than rigid.

G. Participants should be screened so the group will be demographically similar but still represent diverse views and opinions.

H. The role of the *moderator is critical* and the task requires a great deal of *skill* and *experience* to perform effectively.

I. Focus group sessions can be *observed directly* by sponsor representatives, and are routinely video recorded for later viewing.

J. Focus group discussions can be digitally recorded and video-streamed to information seekers at other locations for real-time or later viewing.

B

Conducting Experiments

Experimentation and Causality

Surveys, and to a lesser degree, focus groups allow the researcher and sponsor to make inferences about behavior and causality, based on what respondents or participants *say* about their actions and *why* they behave as they do. Experiments help to establish causality by measuring what people *do*, not what they say. By manipulating experimental conditions and measuring the effects, the experimenter can measure both the presence and the degree of the effect of one factor on another, without recourse to the self-reports of respondents.

Types of Experiments

There are two broad categories of experiments, based on where they are conducted: *laboratory* and *field* experiments. While many of the same principles and methods apply to both types, they differ not only in location, but especially in the degree of *control* the experimenter has on the procedures and extraneous influences.

Laboratory Experiments

Behavioral science laboratories and other labs used for measuring *human behavior* differ very widely, depending on the purpose for which they're designed. The prototypical behavioral science lab is similar in many respects to a focus group conference room—tables and chairs, perhaps some recording equipment, maybe a projector and screen, and of course the mirrored one-way window with an observation room behind it. But laboratory experiments are sometimes conducted in very plain conference room facilities, while other experiments may require very special facilities, such as test kitchens and dining areas, workshops to test home shop equipment, or optical equipment to measure pupil dilation and eye movement.

In a typical laboratory experiment the *"subjects"* are recruited to come to the facility where the experiment is to be held, in much the same manner as they would for a focus group. (Those who respond to surveys are called "respondents" and those who participate in focus groups are referred to as "participants," but those who take part in experiments—whether human or animal—are usually known as the "experimental *subjects*," or just plain "subjects.") In fact, the entire procedure, including recruitment, screening, scheduling, and compensation, are often very similar to those used for focus groups. Not infrequently, data collection agencies that conduct focus groups also have facilities for conducting experiments.

Terms such as "laboratory experimentation" and "human subjects" may sound strange and perhaps even a bit threatening to the average person. In fact, there's nothing very unusual or mysterious about experimentation. An example may clarify the procedure.

> A *survey* was conducted among patients who had been prescribed a particular medication for a common condition. The survey revealed many patients didn't take the tablets *regularly,* as directed. Comparison of the degree of regularity among those of various age groups revealed it was mainly the *elderly* who failed to adhere to the dosage schedule, but there was no obvious reason why.
>
> To discover why older patients took this medication only irregularly, the pharmaceutical company held a series of *focus groups* among elderly patients who were prescribed the drug. To the sponsor's surprise, most participants agreed they often didn't take their medication because *they had trouble opening the childproof, tamper-resistant container* it came in.
>
> Working with the container manufacturer, they arranged to have a sample of containers with six different types of lids or caps. All of them met the safety requirements, but differed widely in the way they had to be opened. A sample of elderly patients who had been prescribed the medication was recruited to visit a data collection agency at a time convenient to them. These experimental subjects didn't know this was an experiment, nor did they know it was connected in any way with the medication they were taking. They were told only that they would be asked to give their opinion on various shapes and colors of tablets for a new cold remedy.
>
> When each subject arrived, they were *randomly* assigned to one of the six "treatment conditions," corresponding to the six types of container lids. They were seated at a table in a small conference room and given eight containers, all with the same type of lid, but each containing a different shape and color of caplet inside. They were asked to open each of the numbered containers in sequence, examine the contents, and rate their opinion of the appearance of the caplets.
>
> In fact, the experimenter and sponsor had no interest in the ratings, whatsoever. This was merely a subterfuge, known as the experimental *ruse*. Instead, the subjects were videotaped as they opened each container to see how much difficulty they had, both initially and after opening several of them. Later, each was timed and their facial expressions, body language, and any utterances were rated on how much stress or confusion they indicated.
>
> Based on the experimental findings, the company selected a container that adult patients of all ages found to be easy to open and close. As a result, adherence to the dosage schedule subsequently increased markedly among the elderly.

Laboratory experiments have several important advantages over field experiments, but as with any measurement procedure, they also have limitations. The pros and cons of laboratory experimentation are outlined briefly in Figure B–1.

FIGURE B–1
Laboratory
Experiment
Pros and Cons

Advantages	Disadvantages
Relatively small number of subjects can be recruited more readily and sampled more precisely than large numbers.	Relatively small number of subjects demands greater sampling precision and limits the reliability of generalizations to the population.
Laboratory setting provides greater control of the environment and potential confounds.	Artificiality of the laboratory setting creates a threat to external validity of results.
Subjects can be *randomly assigned* to treatment and control conditions.	Special facilities and perhaps special equipment are required.
Subjects can be given instructions and questioned to be sure they understand.	Subjects are required to come to the facility and must be compensated for time and travel.
"Take" measures can be made to be sure the experimental treatment(s) has been properly administered and experienced by subjects.	Disruption of the subjects' daily routine may cause changes in moods, emotions, or psychological states.
Controlled conditions allow the experimenter to use more elaborate, complex experimental designs.	Knowledge their behavior is being measured or tested may sensitize subjects to experimental conditions and treatments.

Some of the terms used there may be unfamiliar, but they will be clarified later in the discussion of lab and field experiments.

Field Experiments

Laboratory experiment facilities differ from one venue to another, but the settings for *field* experiments are vastly more diverse. Those who participate in laboratory experiments may not know they are subjects in an experiment, as in the medicine container example, but they do know they are taking part in some sort of inquiry—that their actions or opinions are being measured. This may sometimes be so for field experiments, but more often than not, the experimental subjects don't even know they are part of an experiment. Instead, they're just going about their business as usual, without a clue that some aspect of their behavior is being measured and compared with that of others.

This aspect of field experiments may seem rather sinister, but it's not at all so. A few brief examples of field experiments may provide some reassurance: The traffic department of a large city randomly selected many street intersections with similar traffic volumes, randomly divided them into three groups, and set the traffic lights to stay red or green for 30 seconds, 45 seconds, and 60 seconds, respectively. Sensors then recorded the frequency with which drivers "jumped" the light

FIGURE B–2
Field
Experiment
Pros and Cons

Advantages	Disadvantages
A larger number of subjects provides greater reliability of the generalized results.	Random selection or assignment to treatment and control groups may be impossible.
The "real world" circumstances mean subjects may not even know they are participating in an experiment to measure their behavior.	The "real world" circumstances make it difficult to control potential confounds and threats to validity.
It's usually unnecessary for subjects to travel to a special location to participate.	Subjects can't be given instructions and questioned to be sure they understand.
Subjects need not disrupt their daily lives or activities in order to participate, so their actions may better reflect everyday behavior.	*"Take"* measures can't be used to be sure the experimental treatment(s) has been properly experienced by subjects.
The experiment often need not be completed in a matter of hours and may extend over days, weeks, or months.	Unexpected external events may jeopardize the experimental results or even the completion of the experiment.

before it turned green or "ran" the light after it had turned red. In addition, so-called "audit" vehicles joined the traffic to measure the rate of flow and duration of delay over several blocks. None of the signal violators were ticketed and probably none of the drivers even knew they were subjects taking part in a field experiment. (Incidentally, the 60-second duration led to the least delay and fastest overall flow, but also the highest rates of jumping and running the lights.)

Experiments such as these are constantly underway, ordinarily without anyone becoming aware of them: A fast food chain provides different versions of its menu to various stores; a school district tries a new textbook in some schools but not others and compares results with year-end testing; a judicial district compares two different types of parolee restrictions and compares recidivism rates; a supermarket chain modifies some store layouts and compares traffic patterns. These are all field experiments unbeknownst to those who are the subjects.

These and other such field experiments may appear to be fairly simple and straightforward. Some are, but most aren't. Like laboratory experiments, their counterparts conducted in the field have both advantages and disadvantages. The pros and cons of field experiments are briefly outlined in Figure B–2.

Experimental Designs

The goal of experimental design is to arrange the procedure so that any effect that's observed can be attributed *only* to the experimental treatment and *nothing else*. Suppose, for example, that an advertiser wanted to measure the effect of a

60-second television commercial, a 30-second television commercial, or no television commercial on the subjects' images of a brand of premium ice cream. An experiment is arranged to show the 60-second commercial to a group of men at a hotel conference room on a Saturday afternoon and get their image ratings. A group of women agree to view the 30-second spot and rate their images in a school classroom before a Wednesday evening PTA meeting. Lastly, a few weeks later, a group of elderly, retired men and women at a senior center who did not see either commercial serve as a "control group" by rating the ice cream brand on a Monday morning.

If there are differences in image ratings among the three groups of subjects, to what might those differences be attributed? Perhaps the 30-second and 60-second commercials did, in fact, *cause* the image ratings to differ. Perhaps. But is there anything else that might have influenced the ratings? Obviously there are several things:

- Differences in the average age of the groups may have had an effect on the subjects' image of ice cream in general or this brand in particular.
- Mothers of school children may all be more favorably disposed to ice cream than were those in the other two groups.
- People who rate their images of ice cream (or any other food) at one time of the day may rate it very differently at a different time.
- Those who participate at a hotel meeting room may at a senior center or at a school classroom provide different ratings if at a different location.
- The employment and income status of subjects may influence the way they view a premium (versus inexpensive) brand of ice cream.
- Those who take part in such an experiment at one time of the week or month may have different reactions on another day of the week or time of the month.

Anything other than the experimental treatment(s) that might cause or influence the post-measure or experimental results is called a *"confound"* because it's "mixed up" with the treatment. Thus, the alternative explanations for the results of the experiment listed above are potential *confounds.* Seven such threats to the internal validity of experiments are listed in Figure B–3. They threaten *internal* validity in the sense that they jeopardize the results *within* the experiment, itself, quite aside from generalization of the results to the population at large. Some experimental designs are able to control all or nearly all of these threats, while other seriously flawed designs are vulnerable to most or all of these threats.

Seriously Flawed Designs

Two pseudoexperimental designs are shown in Figure B–4. They're referred to as *pseudo*experimental because they only appear to be experiments. They're so seriously flawed they don't qualify as genuine experiments. They provide little or no control of the threats to internal validity.

With one-group designs, there is a treatment group only and no control or comparison groups. In the top section of Figure B–4 there is only a treatment and a postmeasurement. The treatment is *assumed* to have caused or affected the

FIGURE B–3
Threats
to Internal
Validity

Source of Bias	Means of Control
External Events over Time	
During the experiment, an external event other than the treatment may cause a difference between the premeasurement and postmeasurement.	Avoid the seriously flawed, "Experimental Group Only" design in favor of a genuine experimental and control group design.
Internal Processes over Time	
Changes within subjects during the experiment, aside from external events, may cause a difference between pre- and postmeasurement.	Task and measure both experimental and control groups in the same way, at the same time, and over the same time period.
Premeasurement Sensitization	
The premeasurement may cause subjects to be more or less sensitive to the treatment than they would be if there were no premeasure.	Randomly assign subjects to treatments and use a postmeasure only design or the four-group, six-measure design.
Measurement Instability	
The measurement instrument or person doing the measurement may change in the interval between premeasurement and postmeasurement.	Use the same, standardized measurement instruments and procedures and the same human observers over treatment and control groups.
Systematic Selection	
Subjects aren't randomly assigned to the treatment or control group, so prior to the treatment, there are systematic differences between groups.	Randomly assign subjects to treatment groups and when that's impossible, match or assign subjects to treatments as closely to random as possible.
Experimental Attrition	
Subjects assigned to some treatment groups withdraw at a higher rate than those in others or in the control group.	Strive to make the treatment and control groups' tasks and conditions equally difficult or demanding.
Regression to the Mean	
Some subjects have extreme premeasure scores merely by chance, so when they're tested again, the second measure will, on average, be less extreme.	Include the whole groups on pre- and postmeasures, rather than postmeasuring only those with extreme premeasure scores.

results—the postmeasurement. Suppose, for example, a trainer prepared a set of instructions for employees who are in training, on how to operate a particular piece of equipment. To ascertain if they understand the instructions, the trainer has them read the instructions, then watches to see if they use the equipment correctly. If they do, the instructor *assumes* the instructions have been clear and helpful. But

FIGURE B–4 Pseudoexperimental Designs

Postmeasure Only, Experimental Group Only

Group A ———————————————— Treatment ———————————————— Postmeasure A2

The treatment is assumed to have created the change.

Pre- and Postmeasure, Experimental Group Only

Group A ——————— Premeasure A1 ——————— Treatment ——————— Postmeasure A2

Difference between A1 and A2 is assumed to be caused by the treatment.

that's a shaky assumption at best. There's no way to tell if they would have used the device correctly whether or not they read the instructions.

In the bottom section of Figure B–4 there is, once again, only one group, but this time there are both pre- and postmeasures. While superior to the other one-group design, this one still has serious flaws. Suppose a group of new enrollees in an adult education class are given a proficiency test (the premeasure) at the beginning of the course. On completion, the test is administered once again to determine if the scores have improved. At first glance, this might appear to be an acceptable design, but look more carefully!

Five of the seven threats to internal validity listed in Figure B–3 are uncontrolled: An external event, such as a newspaper or television series on the subject of the course may have affected what the students learned. Internal process over time, such as the experience they gained outside the classroom, may have affected their performance on the postmeasure. They may have been sensitized by the initial test, so they responded differently to the course than if they hadn't been tested in the beginning. The testing might have been different the second time, so there was measurement instability. And some of the "poor" students or those least motivated may have dropped the course, leading to experimental attrition. Thus, this design leaves a very great deal to be desired.

Genuine Experimental Designs

Designs that *randomly* assign subjects to *treatment* and *control groups* are the most pure forms of experimentation. They provide the most complete information and greatest control over threats to internal validity.

Randomized Assignment Designs

The genuine experimental designs shown in Figure B–5 provide the highest degree of control over the threats to internal validity listed in Figure B–3. In the diagrams of experimental designs, the time line runs from left to right. Thus, measurements that are directly above or below one another take place at the same point in time. As a consequence, threats to validity such as *external events* and *internal processes* over time, as well as *measurement instability* and *experimental attrition* are controlled

FIGURE B–5 Genuine Experimental Designs

Pre- and Postmeasure, Experimental and Control Group

Group A ———— Random ———— Premeasure A1 ———— Treatment ———— Postmeasure A2

Group B ———— Random ———— Premeasure B1 ———— Control ———— Postmeasure B2

Difference between (A1 − A2) and (B1 − B2) is attributable to the treatment.

Postmeasure Only, Experimental and Control Group

Group A ———— Random ———— No Measure ———— Treatment ———— Postmeasure A2

Group B ———— Random ———— No Measure ———— Control ———— Postmeasure B2

Difference between A2 and B2 is attributable to the treatment.

because they have identical effects on both experimental and control groups with these designs.

The pre- and postmeasure design shown in the upper section of Figure B–5 provides control of all the threats to internal validity except *premeasure sensitization*. The *postmeasure only* design shown in the lower section of Figure B–5 controls for sensitization (as well as the other threats) because there are no premeasures. An example of the two designs may clarify the distinction between the two:

> In this example, the producer of a popular brand of frozen pizza sold in supermarkets is considering magazine advertising. Because it would be costly, the company wants to be sure the advertisement will have a positive effect on people's opinions of the quality of the brand. The researcher hired to test the ad's effectiveness suggests an experiment using a *postmeasure only, experimental and control group* design.
>
> A sample of subjects will be selected from among only those who are aware of the brand name. This will be relatively easy, since the brand is very well known in the area. The subjects will be randomly assigned to either the treatment or the control group and directed to separate rooms. The treatment group will be shown several magazine ads, including those of the pizza brand in question. At the same time, the control group will be shown the same group of ads, except that an ad for frozen desserts will be substituted for the pizza ad.
>
> After a set period of time, allowing them to finish reading all the ads, subjects in this *postmeasure only* design will be given a brief questionnaire to measure their opinion of the quality and flavor of the pizza brand. Any difference between the ratings of the treatment group (who read the pizza ad) and the control group (who read another ad, instead) can be attributed to the ad for the pizza brand.

Even though experienced researchers would agree this is the most appropriate experimental design for this kind of measurement, a problem may quickly emerge with the sponsor of the research. The question is simply this: *"How do we know the groups didn't have different opinions in the first place?"* That would be a legitimate question if the subjects hadn't been randomly assigned to treatment or control groups. But since they were randomly assigned, the probability of the groups differing purely by chance, because of sampling error, if the treatment didn't have an effect can be statistically determined. In this case, the researcher would use a *paired t-test,* discussed in Chapter 11, to determine the significance of differences between groups.

Despite the technical and statistical correctness of this design, the sponsor's concerns must remain a major concern for the researcher. In this case, the results could be seen as lacking *"face" validity:* In other words, they must *appear* valid "on the face of it." If those seeking the information are to base decisions on the findings with any degree of assurance, they must have confidence the results were obtained properly. If the process doesn't "look right," probably no amount of explanation (aside from a short course in probability statistics) would provide the necessary confidence on the sponsor's part.

One course of action open to an experimenter in this predicament would be to recommend the *pre- and postmeasure* design diagrammed in the top section of Figure B–5. The premeasures for the treatment and control groups could then be compared to be sure the groups were not significantly different from one another. Even if they were, the *difference* between the pre- and postmeasures for the treatment group can be compared to the corresponding difference for the control group, as indicated below the diagram in the upper section of Figure B–5.

While this might appear to be a sound solution to those training in experimentation, it would almost certainly *not* be the recommendation of experienced researchers. The reason is simple but compelling: This design doesn't control for the *premeasure sensitization* bias described in Figure B–3. In this example, those who were questioned closely about their opinion of the pizza brand *before* seeing the ad for it are very likely to view the ad quite differently from those who merely encountered it without being questioned in advance. In other words, the ad may have a positive effect on opinions, in part *because of the premeasure.* Thus, the sponsor might assume the ad would be effective in the "real world," when, in fact, it may fail because those in the population were not *sensitized* by being questioned before they saw the ad.

Ultimate Experimental Design

This is a classic case for the use of a *classic* experimental design: the *four-group, six measurement* design diagrammed in Figure B–6. It will be evident at first glance that this is a combination of the two designs shown in Figure B–5. But because both designs are used simultaneously in the same experiment, it becomes much more than just the sum of the two sets of results. The various comparisons this design yields are described below the diagram in Figure B–6. The first two sets are merely those of the individual designs shown in Figure B–5, but the three remaining comparisons focus on the effects of premeasures and their potential for sensitizing subjects to the treatment.

FIGURE B–6   **Ultimate Experimental Designs**

Four-Group, Six-Measurement Design

Group A ——— Random ——— Premeasure A1 ——— Treatment ——— Postmeasure A2
Group B ——— Random ——— Premeasure B1 ——— Control ——— Postmeasure B2
Group C ——— Random ——— No measure ——— Treatment ——— Postmeasure C2
Group D ——— Random ——— No measure ——— Control ——— Postmeasure D2

Difference between (A1 – A2) and (B1 – B2) is attributable to the treatment when subjects may have been sensitized by the premeasures.

Difference between A2 and B2 is attributable to the treatment when subjects have not been sensitized by the premeasures.

Difference between A2 and C2 is attributable to the effect of premeasurement on the treatment groups (A & C).

Difference between B2 and D2 is attributable to the effect of premeasurement on the control groups (B & D).

Difference between (A2 – C2) and (B2 – D2) is attributable to the effect of premeasurement on the effects of the treatment (i.e., the interaction between premeasurement and the experimental treatment).

Extended Experimental Designs

The genuine experimental designs shown thus far are in their simplest form: one treatment and a control group. Without violating their legitimacy, these designs can be extended by including multiple treatments. Figure B–7 contains two diagrams of such extended designs with four treatment groups, but many more could be included if a sufficient number of subjects are included in each group. Obviously the greater the number of treatment groups, the more taxing the process will be on both the staff conducting the experiment and the facilities where it is conducted. It's important to note that the treatments and measurements must be done simultaneously if *all* of the threats to internal validity, including *external events over time*, are to be controlled.

Imperfect Experimental Designs

The genuine experimental designs described above are the epitome of experimental precision and control; however, they come at a price. Such experiments typically require a laboratory, as opposed to a field environment. Even if a lab is available and suited to the kind of experiment the researcher wants to conduct, it might be difficult or impossible to meet all of the conditions necessary to a genuine experiment, such as random assignment, simultaneous measurements, or treatment and control conditions of equal duration. If it isn't feasible to conduct a genuine

FIGURE B–7 **Extended Genuine Experiments**

Pre- and Postmeasure, Extended Experimental Design

Group A ——— Random ——— Premeasure A1 ——— Treatment A ——— Postmeasure A2

Group B ——— Random ——— Premeasure B1 ——— Treatment B ——— Postmeasure B2

Group C ——— Random ——— Premeasure C1 ——— Treatment C ——— Postmeasure C2

Group D ——— Random ——— Premeasure D1 ——— Treatment D ——— Postmeasure D2

Difference between the premeasure and postmeasure for each treatment group is attributable to the respective treatments. Differences among postmeasure values are attributable to the differential effects of the treatments.

Postmeasure Only, Extended Experimental Design

Group A ——— Random ——— Premeasure A1 ——— Treatment A ——— Postmeasure A2

Group B ——— Random ——— Premeasure B1 ——— Treatment B ——— Postmeasure B2

Group C ——— Random ——— Premeasure C1 ——— Treatment C ——— Postmeasure C2

Group D ——— Random ——— Premeasure D1 ——— Treatment D ——— Postmeasure D2

Difference between the postmeasure values is attributable to the differential effects of the treatments.

experiment, it's often better to conduct an imperfect one than to abandon the method entirely.

Nonequivalent Groups

Earlier, in the discussion of pseudoexperiments, an example was cited where a trainer had employees read a new set of instructions on how to operate a particular device, then watched to see if they used the equipment correctly. Because there was no control group and this wasn't a genuine experiment, there was only the *assumption* the instructions caused or influenced subsequent performance. In such a case, it might be difficult or impossible to conduct a genuine experiment, but the researcher could do much better than the inadequate pseudoexperiment described.

   If the work environment prohibited the researcher from *randomly* assigning employees to either the treatment group (with the new instructions) or the control group (with the existing instructions), an *imperfect, nonequivalent groups design* such as that diagrammed in the upper section of Figure B–8 could be used. To do so, the experimenter might identify two manufacturing plants within the company that were "matched," or as similar as possible. The one designated as the treatment group would be given the new instructions. Meanwhile, during the same time period or as close as possible, those from the other plant, the control group, would be given instructions on some other device or task. Then, the performance of both

FIGURE B–8 Nonequivalent Groups Designs

Postmeasure Only, Nonequivalent Groups

Group A —— Matched ———————————— Treatment —— Postmeasure A2
Group B —— Matched ———————————— Control —— Postmeasure B2

Difference between between A2 and B2 is assumed to be attributable to the treatment.

Pre- and Postmeasure Only, Nonequivalent Groups

Group A —— Matched —— Premeasure A1 —— Treatment —— Postmeasure A2
Group B —— Matched —— Premeasure B1 —— Control —— Postmeasure B2

Difference between between (A1 – A2) and (B1 – B2) is assumed to be attributable to the treatment.

groups could be measured or systematically observed and the performance ratings for the two groups compared.

A refinement to this *postmeasure only, nonequivalent groups* design for this experiment is shown in the lower section of Figure B–8. By using the *pre- and postmeasure, nonequivalent groups* design, the experimenter could "match" the two units to take part in the test based on the premeasure. Premeasure performance ratings might be obtained from several plants or sites; then the two with the most similar ratings could be selected for the treatment and control groups. Similarly, if the experimenter wanted to test more than one set of instructions against one another and against the existing one, the extended version of the experiment diagrammed in Figure B–7 could be used but with matched rather than randomized assignment.

Time Series Designs

The experimental designs discussed earlier use only a single pre- and/or postmeasure. Time series designs, such as those diagrammed in Figure B–9, use multiple pre- and postmeasurements. Such designs are especially practical when the measurements already exist, such as in the form of internal accounting data or other routine, periodic measurements. Even if the measurements must be made as part of the experiment, time series designs are usually the best choice when both the *degree* and the *duration* of effects has to be measured. An example may clarify this kind of situation:

> A large, national department store chain is considering implementation of a series of "invitational sales." The proposed promotional program is both elaborate and costly. It entails sending e-mail and postal mail invitations to the store's largest and most frequent customers. The invitation-only, champagne cocktail party, fashion show and "appreciation sale," to take place "after hours," from 9:00 P.M. to 3:00 A.M., requires staff overtime, catering, entertainment, and, of course, substantial discounting of the latest, top-of-the-line fashions and accessories.

FIGURE B–9   Time Series Designs

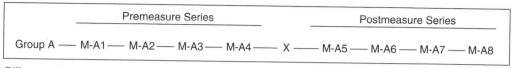

Single Group, Pre- and Postmeasurement Series

Premeasure Series	Postmeasure Series
Group A —— M-A1 —— M-A2 —— M-A3 —— M-A4 —— X ——	M-A5 —— M-A6 —— M-A7 —— M-A8

Difference between mean premeasures and mean postmeasures may be attributed to the treatment.

Two Nonequivalent Groups, Pre- and Postmeasurement Series

Premeasure Series	Postmeasure Series
Group A —— M-A1 —— M-A2 —— M-A3 —— M-A4 —— X ——	M-A5 —— M-A6 —— M-A7 —— M-A8
Group B —— M-B1 —— M-B2 —— M-B3 —— M-B4 —— X ——	M-B5 —— M-B6 —— M-B7 —— M-B8

Difference between (average premeasures minus average postmeasures) for Group A and Group B may be attributed to the treatment.

As with any such venture, there are many within the organization who are vigorously opposed to it and a nearly equal proportion who are enthusiastic advocates. All agree the cost of the event will almost certainly exceed the "one-time" sales revenue from it. Thus, the sale must result in increased revenue over the next several weeks to make it worthwhile.

This is a particularly difficult forecasting problem and business decision because, to some degree, discounted sales during the event will come, in part, from what would have been future sales. In the terms of the trade, it will "cannibalize" their own future sales, although it's impossible to predict the degree with any certainty. This factor makes a one-time measurement of effects even less helpful.

The research agency retained to provide data on the viability of such a promotional program proposes a *six nonequivalent groups, pre- and postmeasurement time series* design similar to that shown in the lower section of Figure B–9, with one exception: There will be three "treatment" stores which hold an event and three control stores with normal hours and advertising. Sales revenue by department and even by product line will be measured for several weeks prior to the event, at the event, and following the event.

By tracking the sales volume and comparing it with costs, the merchandiser obtained an accurate estimate of what profits (or losses) to expect if the program were extended to all the stores in the chain.

While highly beneficial, such field experiments are, by necessity, less precise and controllable than their laboratory counterparts. For example, the design controls for threats such as "global," external events that take place during the time series—those that are relevant or applicable to both the treatment and the control stores in the example. But of course, it *doesn't* control for an event that's unique to only one group, whether treatment or control. Thus, inclement weather at the site of one or more stores but not the others would confound the results.

Field experiments are also unable to reveal external factors over time that take place as the *result of implementation of the treatment*. In the store sale example, the events held as part of the experiment are likely to come as a surprise to rivals who would lack time to implement a response. On the other hand, if the program was implemented nationwide, there would almost certainly be competitive retaliation, and probably in multiple forms.

External Validity of Experiments

While field experiments are typically less able than laboratory experiments to control the main threats to *internal* validity, they're often less vulnerable to the most serious threats to *external* validity, namely *artificiality* and *reactivity*.

Artificiality and Generalizability

The term, "external validity" refers to the degree to which the results of an experiment can be *generalized to the population* from which the sample of experimental subjects was chosen. Thus, if all the threats to *internal* validity have been adequately controlled, the same or very similar results would be obtained if the experiment were replicated (i.e., repeated under identical circumstances). But that is *not* so that those in the population would necessarily behave in the same way outside the laboratory. An example of the danger of *artificiality* and *reactivity* may clarify this issue:

A food processing company created a frozen product called "breakfast cakes" that were neither pancakes nor waffles nor coffee cake. This "freezer-to-microwave-to-table" breakfast item was packaged in special materials to heat properly in a microwave oven. There were simple instructions on the package about how it should be opened, what should be removed, and how it should be placed in the microwave oven.

While the instructions were clear and simple, it was also very important to follow them closely. If not, the breakfast cakes were likely either to be doughy or burned. To test the consumers' ability to prepare breakfast cakes, as well as their preference for three flavors, the company conducted some experiments in their test kitchens. Women with various levels of cooking skill and experience were brought into the multistation test kitchen and asked to prepare breakfast cakes. When everyone had done so, the groups tasted the product and completed a questionnaire about their opinions of ease of preparation and palatability of the product.

The findings revealed three facts: (1) breakfast cakes were quick and easy to prepare, (2) all three flavors were rated from good to excellent, and (3) breakfast cakes were favored slightly over toaster waffles. The company was delighted and immediately implemented a limited, regional rollout of breakfast cakes. Initial sales were brisk. Subsequent sales were abysmal. The product was quickly withdrawn.

The company's test facilities had been geared to conducting taste tests, but not food preparation—an entirely different and more demanding form of behavior. The experimenters in this case didn't take into regard effects of artificiality and reactivity. When these women prepared the product, they knew they were being observed. They read the instructions carefully, arranged the package correctly, and set the microwave time precisely. The product tasted great!

When the typical consumer bought the product and prepared it at home, they often ignored some of the instructions, discarded some of the packaging they should have retained, sometimes put the cakes in a different dish, and used their own judgment about the time it should defrost and cook. The result was, of course, a distasteful or inedible product.

Too late, the experimenters and sponsor in this example realized subjects react very differently to the artificial setting of a laboratory than to their own, everyday "real world." Obviously, field experiments are much more likely to parallel the subjects' actual environment and circumstances. In fact, as it was noted earlier, field experimental subjects are likely to be unaware they are participating.

Blind Testing

The term "blind testing" refers to keeping the experimental subjects "in the dark" about what's being tested or rated. For instance, in a laboratory taste test of cola brands, the beverages in a blind taste test might be labeled only by random numbers or letters, rather than the brand names. And in a *double-blind* test, neither the subjects *nor those running the test* would know. Research indicates that when the persons actually conducting a human behavior experiment know which treatment is which, they may inadvertently influence the subjects' response by either their verbal or nonverbal actions. This, despite their best efforts not to influence the results. This influence is so pervasive it even extends to animal experiments where handlers unknowingly treat the animals in one group differently from another if they know to which treatment they have been assigned.

Because of its contaminating influence, blind and double-blind procedures are often used for laboratory experiments, but the *ultimate* blind procedure is a field experiment where the subjects don't even know they're participating. When subjects must be made aware of a field experiment to obtain their participation or cooperation, they should remain ignorant of exactly what's being measured or tested if at all possible. Whenever it's feasible to do so, keeping the subjects isolated from one another or inhibiting communications with other subjects is recommended. If experimental subjects communicate with one another during the experiment, the interaction may threaten validity in several ways. These are three of the most serious potential consequences:

1. The groups might have a tendency to *compete* with one another, which may reduce or eliminate the differential effects of the different treatments.

2. Subjects in one group may view those in another as being treated more favorably, making them *envious* or *resentful* and coloring their response to the treatment.

3. Groups may learn about the treatments to which other groups are assigned, so they *"share"* common treatments, blurring the distinctions between them.

Experimentation and Survey Methods

Some experiments, especially those conducted in a laboratory setting, are very different from research surveys. Others, and particularly field experiments that obtain self-reports of reactions to treatments, are almost identical to surveys. Regardless of their apparent similarity or dissimilarity with surveys, most experiments use some or all of the principles and methods that apply to survey research.

Project Initiation

Defining the information needs, planning the project, and designing the sample for an experiment are similar in many respects to the corresponding survey tasks. For an experiment, the breadth of information needs is likely to be more narrow. On the other hand, sponsors' understanding of experimental methods is typically more limited than for surveys. With survey research, response task, sample size, and design are usually more critical issues. But because experiments usually use much smaller samples, recruitment of subjects and assurance of their representation is often extremely important.

Measurement Instrumentation

When the measurements for an experiment consist partly or entirely of self-reports, the same questionnaire creation principles regarding wording, instructions, scaling, and composition apply to the experimental measurement instruments. It might appear, at first glance, that those same principles and techniques *wouldn't* apply to experiments that use observational measurement. But they do! After all, who does the observing and how are the observations to be recorded? So, with self-reports, the instruments are similar to the self-administered instruments for survey research. For observational measurements, the instruments are more similar to those created for interviewing, but instead of asking questions, the observers only record what they see or hear.

Analysis and Reporting

Surveys usually generate a much larger amount of data than experiments, but not always. So, data editing and processing is often quicker and easier for experimental projects. The statistical analysis tools used for experimental data are virtually identical to those used for survey projects, although the smaller sample and cell sizes may impose some rather more strict limitations.

As with definition of information needs, the breadth of experimental results is ordinarily much more narrow than for survey research. Thus, both written reports and oral or projected presentations are likely to include far fewer topics and issues. As a result, reporting is often more brief for experiments than for surveys. This factor is usually offset by the need for more extensive and detailed information about the selection and implementation of *procedures*. As noted earlier, sponsors of experimental research are less likely to be familiar with the experimental process, benefits, and requirements than are survey sponsors with the corresponding survey procedures.

Experimentation is an extremely flexible method of gaining a wide array of information, some of which is almost impossible to obtain in any other way. At first, the experimental process and especially the many different experimental designs might be somewhat daunting. Fortunately, it will quickly become apparent that they are almost all variations on the same or a very few basic themes: *selection* of subjects, *assignment* to treatment groups, maybe a *premeasure*, some form of *treatment*, and the final *measurement*. With a little study, the possibilities for additional variations are almost unlimited. Within the basic safeguards, the researchers' opportunities are limited only by the degree of creativity and enthusiasm they bring to the project.

Summary

Conducting Experiments

A. Know the method's capabilities and limitations. Experimentation is especially well suited to some types of information needs but ill-suited or incapable of satisfying others.

B. Evaluate a laboratory experiment's potential. Lab experiments provide much greater control over the threats to internal validity.

C. Examine a field experiment's promise. Experiments in the field provide a better parallel with the real world conditions of the population.

D. Avoid seriously flawed designs. Some designs are so faulty they're likely to yield information that is worse than none at all.

E. Consider genuine experiments first. Genuine experimental designs provide the greatest control over all the threats to internal validity.

F. Review the need for premeasures. If assignment to treatments is random and sponsors are comfortable with them, postmeasure-only designs are preferable.

G. Compromise when necessary. If genuine experimental designs aren't feasible, search for a viable design even if it's less than perfect.

H. Examine external validity. Lab experiments and field experiments that don't parallel the real world may suffer from artificiality and lack generalizability.

I. Apply appropriate survey research principles. Many of the same principles and techniques used in survey research apply equally well to experiments.

C

Presenting Survey Results

Why Do a Presentation?

Business and organizational presentations of all kinds have become increasingly popular. Despite the cost, time, and effort an effective presentation requires, there are many sound reasons for doing oral and projected presentations in addition to conventional written reports. By far the most compelling and important reason is simply that people recall a *vastly* higher percentage of what they see *and* hear than what they only see *or* hear.

The entire objective of survey research is to create and convey *information*. That means literally *informing* sponsors and information seekers about the findings of the project. Oral presentations lend themselves exceedingly well to reporting survey research results. But that's *not* to say they're always required or even always appropriate. Many times, a written report and perhaps a brief, informal meeting or conference is completely adequate. Each situation has to be evaluated, keeping the advantages and disadvantages of a formal presentation firmly in mind.

Presentation Advantages

The pros and cons of doing an oral presentation of survey research results are outlined in Figure C–1. The principal advantage—the tendency for sponsors and information seekers to retain more information for a longer time—was noted earlier. The fact that they bring everyone together in the same room at the same time is nearly as important. It would be almost impossible to establish the information needs for a survey at the beginning of the process without meeting or conferring by telephone as a group. A report presentation at the end of the project is a neat parallel that brings closure to the effort. Thus, the process "comes full circle," in a manner of speaking.

Presentation Disadvantages

The cost of report presentations is their main disadvantage. Their complexity and the demands they place on the research analyst and staff are close behind, and

FIGURE C–1
Pros and Cons of Report Presentations

Pros	Cons
Presentations *dramatize* the results of a survey, so they're recalled more vividly and in greater detail than written reports.	Report presentations are *costly* in terms of money, researcher time and effort, and the information seekers' time.
They're *interactive,* so the presenter can listen to questions, ask for clarification, and respond immediately.	They're *perishable* (when they're over, they're gone) so they're always *extra* or *supplementary* to a written report.
They provide audience *feedback,* so the presenter can be sure sponsors and information seekers understand results.	They're *demanding* on the researcher's expertise, not only on technical matters, but also at speaking before a group.
They address a *group* of information seekers simultaneously, allowing audience members to converse with one another.	They're *time and location specific,* so they may require rigid scheduling and travel by the researcher or information seekers.
They're *compelling* because the information can't be readily ignored, while written reports are often set aside.	They're *complex* and *difficult to control,* so there are many opportunities for something to go wrong or badly.

sometimes even more serious. Careful planning and preliminary work can control almost all the main threats to an effective presentation. They *can* be controlled, but they won't *all* be. There are almost always unanticipated problems that arise, but hopefully they won't be serious ones.

Planning and Preparation

The rather complex, demanding nature of a report presentation shouldn't discourage the researcher. Rather, it should prompt greater attention and advance effort. There are some aspects of a report presentation that are clearly beyond the researcher's control. Occasionally, serendipity will prevail. Both the information seekers and research staff may benefit from some fortuitous break. More often, however, a truly successful report presentation is the result of careful planning and preliminary work, rather than just good luck. That includes consideration of the many contingencies that might arise and how they will be handled.

One of the best ways to cope with unexpected circumstances or events during a presentation is to play "What if . . . ?" with colleagues. The game is akin to a negative brainstorming session. It's a simple but highly effective device. The lead analyst merely assembles a few others and asks them to envision every possible, *plausible* thing that might happen to diminish or disturb the report presentation. It isn't necessary to answer the "What if . . . ?" questions at the time, but they should be written down so solutions can be found for them at a later time. The person responsible for the presentation should examine the list, eliminate things regarded as implausible, and plan a strategy for handling the remaining threats or contingencies. This process will reduce the risks of problems during the presentation.

Oral presentations require more careful planning than written reports because they're "live." Written reports can be edited and reworked as many times as necessary to be sure they're accurate, complete, and effective. By contrast, once an oral report begins, what's said, done, and shown can't be recaptured and corrected. In effect, one can't "unring" the bell. There is one thing that can be done to be sure the presentation goes well. Every experienced speaker knows about it. Every effective speaker does it. Unfortunately, most inexperienced presenters are reluctant to do it. *It* is simply *rehearsal!* That means going through the entire presentation from start to finish *exactly as it will be done for the audience.* There's no substitute for thorough rehearsal.

Selecting Content

Written reports are in three phases: An *introductory* overview, followed by the *body* of the report, concluded by a brief *summary* of the findings. Oral presentations are rarely that repetitive or thorough because of the time limitations. The information needs dictate what should be in both the written report and the oral presentation. Originally, during the planning phase described in Chapter 2, the information needs were classified into three levels of importance: (1) *absolutely essential,* constituting the main reason for the project, (2) *highly valuable* for making important decisions, and (3) *supportive data* to enhance the understanding of decision makers and clarify the picture portrayed by the survey results.

The written report should be composed before the oral presentation is prepared. It includes all three levels of information. An oral presentation typically follows the same sequence as the written document, but only the first two levels of information priority are ordinarily included—*absolutely essential* and *highly valuable* information. Supportive data usually appear only in the written report.

Written reports almost always include both narrative text and numeric tables. They often include graphs and charts as well. During report *presentations,* the information is usually projected onto a screen for everyone to view simultaneously. So, the presentation often consists almost entirely of two kinds of content: *graphs* and *bullet charts.* Reading text that's projected onto a screen is *very tedious!* Reading tables that way is almost as difficult unless they're exceedingly simple. Consequently, the most effective presentations use very few numbers and words and a lot of pictures. Figure C–2 contains three typical slides for a survey report presentation. The guidelines for preparing bullet charts and graphic slides or transparencies are provided in Guidelist C–1 and C–2, respectively.

Choosing Presenters

Occasionally only one researcher conducts an entire survey research project. If only one person is responsible for the project, except for so-called outside services by external agencies, there won't be any question about *who* or *how many* people should present the information. However, most research projects are conducted by

FIGURE C–2
Typical
Report Slides
for
Presentations

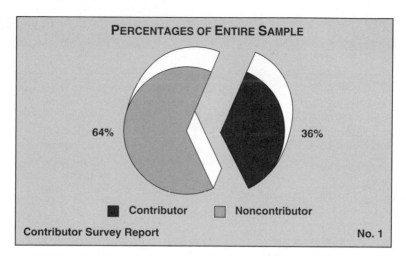

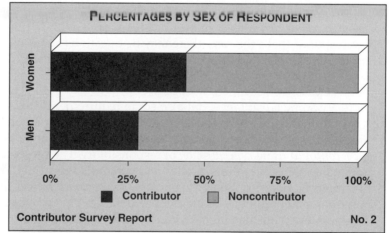

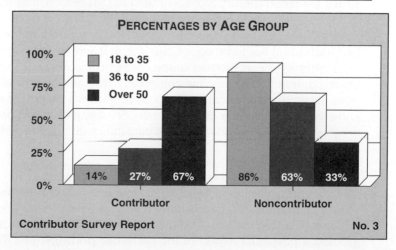

For Preparing Bullet Charts   **Guidelist C–1**

1. Limit the Content
   - Limit the number of . . .
     - words in each bullet
     - bullets in each section
     - sections on each slide
2. Organize the Material
   - Always move from the . . .
     - Most to the least important
     - General to the specific

- Chart Format
  - Keep it clean and simple
  - Use large, bold type
  - Indent to show levels
  - Use bullets to show levels
  - Use little or no punctuation
  - Title each chart slide
  - Number each chart slide

---

a project *team* or by a lead analyst or investigator with the help of a resident research staff. If that's the case, there may be questions about who should make the report presentation and how others might participate, if at all.

One Presenter

There are some advantages, but also some requirements that must be met, if one person from the project team is to make the report presentation to the sponsor and information seekers. The main advantages of using a single presenter are *consistency, continuity,* and *concentration* of responsibility. The presentation is likely to be more consistent throughout if only one person is reporting. There won't be any transitions from one presenter to another, so the *continuity* is almost automatic. If more than one person are doing the presentation, that requires more supervision to be sure everyone has prepared and rehearsed thoroughly. With only one presenter, the responsibility is concentrated in that person, and the individual is likely to be keenly aware of his or her responsibility.

When one person has the sole responsibility for making the actual presentation, that individual has to be completely familiar with every aspect of the report, and preferably with every aspect of the entire project. Even if the presenter knew the report content thoroughly and completely, it would be impossible to answer questions about sampling, data collection, or analysis unless he or she had firsthand knowledge of what was done and why. So, using only one presenter to do the entire job alone may put too much responsibility on one individual.

Multiple Presenters

Some survey research presentations call upon as many as five or six people to present various aspects of the project or different parts of the results. More than that would be inadvisable, and usually fewer take part in the presentation. The main advantage is that each may offer special expertise, background, or experience regarding a particular aspect of the project or findings. The disadvantages are the

For Preparing Graphics for Presentations   Guidelist C–2

1. Choose a clean, simple, *standard* format for every slide, including a background, presentation title, and slide title format.

2. Limit the number of graph *elements*—bars, segments, lines, or slices—that are included in each slide.

3. Add *value labels* to graph elements when it's feasible, to show the actual numbers without projecting tables.

4. Use distinctive colors or cross-hatching to make individual elements easily distinguishable from one another.

5. Use a sufficiently large *type size* and **bold print** for words and numbers so they can be read easily at a distance during projection.

6. Use shape, size, space, and location to portray quantities and relationships as clearly and accurately as possible.

7. Include enough "white space" to make the figures and labels stand out from the background of each slide.

8. It's better to use many, simple slides shown in sequence than to use fewer, more complex slides with too many elements on each.

9. Add color, depth, and pictures for a more dramatic effect *only* when they can be used *consistently, expertly,* and *attractively.*

10. Prepare a *title slide* identifying the presentation, sponsor, survey project, and presenter, to be projected prior to or at the beginning of the presentation.

11. Prepare "handouts" for the audience showing each slide in miniature so they don't have to write down the information that's projected.

12. When the final slides are complete, write notes for explanation of each one and *project the slides during REHEARSAL* to be sure everything is correct.

difficulties in controlling consistency, continuity, and concentration or responsibility, noted earlier.

One Plus Others

Often the best of both alternatives identified here can be obtained by having one person do the presentation while one or more others from the project team attend and participate during discussion or question and answer (Q & A) session. That puts fewer demands on the main presenter, since he or she can defer to a colleague to respond to technical questions beyond the presenter's familiarity or expertise.

If one person is *principally* responsible for making the presentation, who should it be? If the project director or lead analyst is also the most articulate and comfortable with speaking to a group, the problem is solved. Often that's not the case. It may be advisable to select the person who has the most poise and presence when making a presentation of this kind. If that's the choice, there are two conditions that apply: First, the person should be *reasonably knowledgeable* and technically capable regarding the project in particular and survey research in general. One wouldn't want to hire a professional master of ceremonies for the job, or pick someone from the project team who is only marginally qualified save for his or her skill at public speaking. Second, those who accompany the presenter and assist in answering questions must be thoroughly knowledgeable about their area and completely prepared to respond when needed.

Organization and Timing

There are usually three or perhaps four parts to a survey report presentation: The *introduction*, the *body* of the presentation, the *conclusions* by the analyst, and often a *Q & A session*. The sponsor should set the total duration of the presentation in advance. It's the analyst or presenter's responsibility to stay within the time allotted and to be available to respond during a Q & A session if that's desirable. Since almost everything takes longer than expected, the presentation should be planned and created to take only about *two-thirds* of the actual time allocated.

Report Introduction

It's always advisable to create a title slide to project on the screen prior to and during the beginning of the presentation. Usually a sponsor representative will introduce the presenter (or the *lead* presenter if more than one person will present the information). After greeting the group, the presenter should take a minute or so to outline the project *very briefly*. That will refresh the memory of those who worked with the project earlier. There may also be others in the audience who aren't at all familiar with the survey project.

This introductory sketch should indicate:

1. The main *reason* for the survey or the principal research *question* or *issue* the survey information obtained will help to resolve.
2. Who in the sponsoring organization arranged for or contracted for the project.
3. Approximately *when* the project began and *when* the data were collected.
4. *What population* was surveyed, together with how they were *sampled*, how the data were *collected*, how many were *sampled*, and how many *responded*.

Reference to the actual questionnaire and the items within it should be reserved for later discussion. At the discretion of the presenter, one or two slides may or may not be projected to outline the information provided in the introduction. Their appropriateness is directly related to the formality of the meeting, complexity of the project, and size of the audience.

Audience Handouts

What written material should be given to the audience, and *when* should it be provided? Although they may seem inconsequential, those are questions that deserve some consideration. Some speakers prefer to give the audience *nothing* in advance. They want the audience's undivided attention on what they're saying and they're projecting. They want to control the pace of the presentation and they don't want people to be looking ahead. A less rigorous approach is to give the audience "handout" copies of what's being presented. All the most popular presentation manager programs, such as Microsoft PowerPoint®, are capable of formatting the presentation with two, three, six, and even nine slides per page and printing them in gray scale or pure black and white so if they're copied, a color copier isn't necessary. The audience may also be given copies of blank questionnaires or the *response summary questionnaire* (discussed in Chapter 12) at the beginning of the presentation.

Ultimately, those who attend the presentation should receive copies of a *response summary questionnaire,* the handouts of the slides, and perhaps copies of the entire written report (if the sponsor requests its distribution). Most experienced presenters who have good command of audience attention prefer to distribute any handouts in their entirety at the beginning of the presentation. Alternatively, the presenter or a colleague can hand them out *in sections* during the course of the presentation. It's usually not advisable to distribute such material well in advance of the presentation. That tends to diminish enthusiasm for the presentation, and such things are almost never ready until the last minute anyhow.

The Body of Content

Presenting the main substance of the report should occupy about two-thirds to three-quarters of the time allotted to the entire presentation. The presenter projects each slide in sequence, identifying the main features of each graph or plot and "fleshing out" the brief phrases on bullet charts. Very simple, straightforward graphs such as those in Figure C–2 usually require only 20 or 30 seconds of explanation by the presenter and examination by the audience. More complex graphs or plots and lengthier bullet charts may take two or three minutes of study and discussion.

Some experienced speakers and presenters believe in what's known as "The Four-Minute Rule." It stipulates that audience attention and interest in any one topic or visual image drops *precipitously* after four minutes—more or less regardless of what the topic or image is! In other words, the limitations on audience attention span are *in the audience,* not in the content that's presented. This rule does appear to have some substance. If so, the presenter wouldn't want to approach that duration, let alone exceed it. None of the slides presented should be so complex as to require more than two or three minutes to explain and comprehend. Information requiring more extensive study should be broken into segments or conveyed in detail in the written report.

Audience Reactions

Whether questions, reactions, and discussion by the audience should be expressed *during* the body of the presentation or at the conclusion depends on sponsor preference and the nature of the material presented. It's important to note that *questions of clarification* should always be welcomed and answered *during* the presentation— at any point at all. These are questions about what's being said or shown. For instance, if someone in the audience is unsure whether a set of values shows frequencies or percentages, they should be encouraged to ask immediately. Similarly, if they want to know if the entire sample or only part of it is included on a chart, they should be encouraged to ask. If they're not sure where the question was asked in the questionnaire, they should feel free to inquire right away. They need that information to understand what's being presented at the moment.

Questions about *why* this group responded as they did or about *what the sponsor should do* given this information are quite another matter. Those are *questions of substance,* not clarification. Most presenters would prefer to approach such questions only after the entire body of information has been presented. Their reasons are several: Discussing such issues during the presentation may take so much time it will require rushing through the remainder of the information. The answers to such questions may become clearer after subsequent information has been presented. Some, and perhaps most of the audience, may want to move on rather than pause to discuss this particular issue. Dealing with the issue may result in discussion *among the audience* that would best be reserved for a later conference in the absence of the presenter or research staff.

If *substantial* questions are to be reserved for the conclusion or Q & A session to follow the presentation, the presenter should remind the audience that they can return to any particular slide or section, later. They should be encouraged to make a note of their question or comment, referring to the section or slide number, so the issue won't be neglected later. *They* should make note of it, since it's usually awkward for the presenter to pause and do so during the presentation; however, if other research staff are present, they may be assigned that job.

Summary and Q & A

It's customary for the presenter to provide a *very brief* summary of the main results and implications after the last of the body of information content has been presented. It's often effective to express such concluding material on one or two bullet charts that highlight all the main facts. After thanking the audience for their attention, the presenter would open the discussion to questions from the audience, if a Q & A session was planned and if time allows it. Guidelist C–3 offers several tips for enhancing one's credibility during both the presentation and the Q & A session.

If the slides or transparencies have been organized, labeled, and numbered carefully, it won't be difficult to refer back to the slide containing the information in question during the Q & A. Most presentation manager programs allow the presenter to merely enter the number of the slide and press *enter* while in the "slide show" mode. It's best to take the few seconds required to identify and project the appropriate slide unless the question is either very *quick* or extremely *general,* and so related to no one particular slide. When responding to questions of substance, and especially if they deal with *why* a certain response resulted, there are some basic rules presenters may find it beneficial to observe: First, there are times when the presenter or researcher can't be expected to *know* why. So, it may call for an admission that there's nothing within the data or the researcher's background or expertise that would provide an explanation.

The second rule is that sponsors and information seekers may *speculate* all they want. The researcher may *not.* There are few things more embarrassing in such situations than to move further and further out on a limb, only to eventually either have it sawed off or to break of one's own weight. In addition, to offer an opinion that proves to be patently unsound will jeopardize the credibility of the *entire presentation.*

For a More Credible Demeanor   Guidelist C–3

1. *Show confidence, but not arrogance.* Relax, smile, and converse with the audience as you would with a group of friends.

2. *Dress in business attire.* Even if the audience is dressed more casually, those in business suits or dresses gain respect and credibility.

3. *Don't wander about.* The presenter is almost always standing, but shouldn't be *walking* unless there's a reason to do so.

4. *Don't fidget!* Whether speaking or listening, your hands should either rest lightly on the lectern (not gripping it) or *hang at your sides.* (*This takes practice!*)

5. *Don't play with things.* If using a pointer, *put it down* when not in use. Keep pencils, pens, keys, and so on in pocket or purse where they belong.

6. *Keep your hands off your face.* Never, ever speak with your hand over your mouth. Don't play with your hair, rub your head, or stroke your chin, either.

7. *Stop and listen intently!* When someone speaks or interrupts, *stop.* Face them. Look *directly* at their face. Listen carefully and *wait* until they've finished.

8. *Pause before responding.* Don't be too quick to answer questions or respond to comments. Take *several seconds to think* before speaking in response.

9. *Restate what they say.* By repeating what you hear, you and they can be sure you understand. Only then should you reply to a question or comment.

10. *Don't use big words.* Talk as you would to a friend in a *social* situation, not as you would to a colleague on your project team.

11. *Don't be defensive.* Even if challenged rudely, it's better to respond with an understanding smile and quiet assurance than with a strident rebuttal.

12. *If you don't know, say so.* Don't ever try to "fake it" if you're puzzled or confused. Admit openly you don't know but will find out, then go on.

Rule three for responding to Q & A issues is to ask if additional data analysis might answer the question. For example, someone may want to know, "Why do you think one in five people responded in such-and-such a way?" An experienced researcher might frame that question very differently—in research terms: "Who are these people? How does this variable *relate* to other variables in the survey?" Thus, the researcher might suggest conducting some additional *measures of association* between this and other items to shed more light on the question.

Lastly, the researcher is forbidden to reveal *specific* information learned from other surveys. It was funded and it belongs to other sponsors—it's proprietary—and can't be released without written permission. But this certainly doesn't preclude researchers from bringing their professional background and expertise to bear on the question. It simply means the explanation should be couched in general terms. For example, mail surveys typically result in relatively low response rates—astoundingly so to many sponsors. Information seekers may want to know, and *should* want to know, what kind of nonresponse bias can be expected. They may ask how the response rate for this study compares with others.

Questions such as that are legitimate, appropriate, and intelligent inquiries. They can't be answered definitively, but they can and should be answered tentatively. The researcher must explain how this response rate compares with others, based on professional experience or familiarity with other studies of this kind. Based on his or her background and expertise, the researcher may explain that *typically* those who are most *positive* or most *negative*—those with *extreme* views or reactions—respond at higher rates than those "in the middle." Similarly, those with more involvement in the issues and with more time respond at higher rates, and so forth. Thus, researchers should be encouraged to share their knowledge and expertise with those less familiar with the survey research process and the results that it typically obtains.

Presentation Technology

The basic characteristics of an effective report presentation have remained the same over many years. However, the *technology* for creating and projecting audio-visual information has developed at an astounding pace. Constant exposure to highly sophisticated communication and information systems in their business and organizational lives also elevates audience expectations for a report presentation. The most important innovations in presentation technology are in presentation software and projection equipment.

Presentation Software

Several types of desktop computer programs are capable of generating graphs, plots, diagrams, and bullet charts for presentations. Many statistical analysis programs, spreadsheets, and graphic design programs can be used to compose or create presentation content; however, *presentation manager* programs are the most common and capable method for accomplishing what their name implies. Either the content of the presentation can be created within the presentation manager and its adjunct programs, or it can be imported from a word processor, analysis program, charting and graphing programs, or some other application program. Once the content is in place, the entire program can be organized and refined to create an informative and attractive presentation.

All the popular *presentation manager* programs have what are usually called "slide show" routines. When running the "slide show," the screen displays only the actual slide. It doesn't show other normal screen content such as scroll bars, menus, or toolboxes. These routines let the user project the slides of the presentation in sequence, moving from one to the next on a signal from the keyboard or after a preset time for each. They also allow the presenter to go to any slide in the presentation by number. This is especially useful during a discussion or Q & A session, when it may be necessary to refer back to slides that were shown earlier in the presentation.

Presentation manager programs provide special *transition* formats for moving from one slide to another, as well as animation of the slide content so that bullets charts or graphic figures can "build" in a present sequence and fashion. Presentations that use such special effects are time-consuming to produce and require considerable skill, but they're extremely dynamic and colorful. Despite their attractiveness, they probably don't add substantially to the audience's *understanding* of the information reported. They're probably more necessary for *persuasive* programs, such as sales presentations, than for more *informative* presentations. Nonetheless, it's important to recognize that constant exposure to media such as television and the Web has raised everyone's expectations regarding how information is conveyed. Consequently, the researcher or presenter should consider these so-called "cosmetic" presentation options carefully to judge how much time and effort are warranted.

Projection Equipment

The equipment for projecting the presentation may be at the facility where the presentation will take place, such as a conference room at the sponsor's offices, or it may be brought by the researcher. Research organizations that regularly make presentations usually have their own projection equipment, but those who rarely make presentations aren't likely to have a projector, even though they may have a laptop computer.

Liquid Crystal Display (LCD) projectors are the ideal device for making report presentation. The presentation manager program projects images directly from the computer using the "slide show" mode. Early models of the LCD projector were large, heavy, and fragile—they didn't travel well. What's more, they weren't very bright, so if the room wasn't darkened substantially, it was difficult to see the images from very far away.

Newer models of LCD projectors weigh only a few pounds, they fit into a case the size of an attaché case, and they're much less fragile and dramatically brighter. Those who do presentations often can travel easily with a laptop computer and portable LCD projector—everything needed to make a presentation. But many classrooms, meeting rooms, and conference centers have ceiling-mounted LCD projectors that are larger and commensurately brighter than the portable variety. As Guidelist C–4 suggests, the researcher should check with the sponsor or other venue where the presentation will be made to see what equipment is installed and what will be needed.

When an LCD projector isn't required, affordable, or available, the "old standby" is a conventional overhead projector for transparencies. They're still common in some school classrooms and they're often used at academic conferences where it's considered undignified to be too colorful or attractive. There are a few models that are portable but cumbersome. The ordinary kind is very bulky and not very portable. It also has a fan to cool the bulb, so it may be rather noisy in a small room. Overhead projectors are satisfactory for small- to medium-size rooms and audiences. Most such projectors don't provide enough illumination for a large room where those in the back of the audience are some distance from the screen.

The overhead transparencies themselves are quite easy and relatively inexpensive to produce. Ordinarily the slides are printed on special transparencies on a color copier. Alternatively, they can be printed in color on plain paper and copied onto special heat resistant transparencies at a copy center. Audience handouts are typically in black and white because multiple color copies may be too costly to be

BEFORE THE PRESENTATION

1. Ask the principal sponsor contact how many will attend and who they are. Learn as much as possible about the audience, and especially the "key" people.

2. Check the venue for the presentation in advance. Know how to get there, where to park, how to enter, move any equipment, and make it operational.

3. Check out the room where the presentation will be made in advance. Go to the lectern or place the presenter will stand and view the room from there.

4. If using a projector on a stand, try to arrange the seating or have it arranged so the projector isn't between the screen and anyone in the audience.

5. Several minutes before it's time to begin, check out the equipment one last time to be sure everything is adjusted, set, and working as it should.

6. *Don't* review notes or "go over" the material mentally while waiting to start. Instead, sit back, relax, and chat with others, preferably about other topics.

AT THE BEGINNING

7. Greet the audience, introduce yourself if you weren't introduced, and thank them for attending. Then, *begin immediately* in a pleasant, matter-of-fact way.

8. If anxious or nervous, *don't apologize or comment on it.* If it shows, they'll know it. If it doesn't, don't tell them. They *all* know *they* would feel that way, anyhow.

9. Keep your mind on the *material*—on the *information* you want to convey, without thinking about *how* you're doing it or how you've done so far.

DURING THE PRESENTATION

10. Follow the suggestions in Guidelist C–3 to maintain credibility. Be especially careful *never* to argue or be defensive.

11. If using a projector on a stand or table, avoid standing in front of the projected image or blocking anyone's view. If it's unavoidable, move to the side promptly.

12. Face the audience when speaking. If it's necessary to look at the projection screen, pause, do so, then turn and again speak to the audience.

13. If using an overhead projector, view the images from the transparency, not the screen. Point to items on the *transparency,* itself, using a pencil, not a finger.

14. If using transparencies, *keep them in order* after showing them by stacking them neatly, face down, so they can be easily located by number later, if needed.

15. If using an LCD projector, point to items on the screen with a light pen or with the computer's mouse and cursor arrow, but not by pointing with your hand.

16. Check a clock or wristwatch often. Strive to stay on schedule, and if the audience delays, remind them politely that there's more to cover.

DURING THE DISCUSSION OR Q & A SESSION

17. Gauge the time and keep your responses as brief as possible. Rarely should they require more than about 30 seconds. Don't say more than what's required.

18. Observe the suggestions in Guidelist C–3. Remember, you aren't expected to have all the answers. If you don't know, say so!

19. When questions arise that require more study or analysis, make notes of *what's* to be investigated and *who* in the audience wants to know.

20. If audience members converse among themselves, suggest *they* meet later, reserving *this* time for questions *you* can address (unless there's plenty of time).

AT THE CONCLUSION

21. Note any additional study or analysis that will be done and tell the audience *what* you will do, about *when* it will be done, *how* you'll report, and to *whom.*

22. Thank the sponsor and audience for the opportunity to do the study and make the presentation, and especially for their interest, attention, and participation.

practical. But usually it's sufficiently economical and well worthwhile to produce the transparencies in color.

There are also other modes of projecting survey results to an audience, but such devices as 35mm slide projectors, multiple computer monitors, or video monitoring equipment are only rarely used. The vast majority of projected presentations of every kind are made with either LCD or overhead projectors.

Making the Presentation

Much of what the presenter needs to know and do is implied in the recommendations for preparation and rehearsal. Guidelist C–4 contains an extensive set of suggestions and recommendations about what to do just before the presentation, at the beginning, during the presentation, during the discussion or Q & A session, and at the conclusion. There are three additional aspects of the presentation that deserve brief consideration: How to cope with *presentation anxiety*, use *notes* effectively, and control the *pace* and *timing* of the presentation.

Presentation Anxiety

There are a few—very, very few—who are quite comfortable speaking to a group of people they don't know. Almost all presenters, including even the most experienced, feel a little anxiety as the time to begin approaches. That's to be expected, but if the presentation has been well planned and *rehearsed* and the presenter is well prepared, any nervousness will almost certainly wane and disappear within a few minutes into the presentation.

So, the most important thing for the presenter to do to avoid anxiety and stress is to prepare thoroughly and *rehearse*—again and again. Sheer repetition is a potent enemy of anxiety. It's much easier to stay calm if one knows *exactly* what he or she will say and do at every point. The confidence gained from the experience of rehearsal will also lend a great deal of credibility to the presenter and the presentation. Guidelist C–4 lists several tips that will both reduce presentation anxiety and help ensure a fluid, effective presentation.

Using Notes Effectively

A presenter who needs no notes whatsoever is a rare exception. Those who make exactly the same speech or presentation again and again may not need any notes at all. Most presenters or research results depend on notes of varying detail to guide them while speaking. Yet probably the main guideposts for a report presentation are the visual slides that are projected. The best way to write and organize notes for a presentation is to take each slide in order and jot down a *few* words or phrases that are *cues* or *reminders* of what should be said about each.

Virtually all presentation manager programs have a "lecture notes" mode, so printed copies show both the slide and the notes the presenter has added to guide him- or herself. The notes should be *very brief*. More elaborate notes or actual *scripting* too often encourages the presenter to *read* from them. That's anathema to an interesting and informative presentation. The audience will hate it. If the presenter is sufficiently familiar with the material and has rehearsed thoroughly, he or she won't need more than an occasional glance or quick reference to the notes to bring the next topic to mind as a new slide is shown.

Pacing and Timing

One might mistakenly assume a presentation's pace should be determined almost exclusively by the time allotted and the material to be presented. In fact, that equation should have been achieved before the presentation was prepared. If the sponsor specified how much time was available, the presentation should have been geared to that duration. If the sponsor left it up to the researcher, the analyst should have estimated the time required and notified the sponsor. Typically, those arrangements are worked out in conversation between sponsor and researcher *well in advance*. Even so, it's impossible to anticipate precisely how long a presentation will take.

When a written survey report is read from the printed page, the pace is controlled entirely by the reader. Readers can move quickly or slowly, reviewing or scanning ahead at will. By contrast, presentations are *externally* paced from the audience's point of view. The presenter sets and maintains the pace. If the presentation moves too quickly, much of the material will escape the comprehension of the audience, or at least its slower members. If it moves too slowly, some are likely to lose interest and become distracted. So, the goal is to find a pace where *most* of the audience has sufficient time to comprehend the material but few become bored with it.

By watching the audience carefully for cues at the beginning of the presentation and any time the nature of the content changes significantly, the presenter can usually tell when it's time to move on, when to pick up the pace a little, and when to go more slowly. *Flexibility* is important! Sometimes inexperienced presenters adopt a *rigid* time schedule—in the worst case, a certain number of seconds or minutes for *each slide* of the presentation. That's absurd because some slides will obviously require more study than others. There's nothing wrong with calculating time to give to each slide on the *average,* but the emphasis here is on the *average* time. That should be only a *rough* guide to keeping pace and staying on schedule.

The two main threats to a well-timed presentation are *rambling presenters* and *digressing audience members*. If there's more than one presenter, *every one* must be assigned a *very specific* time, beyond which they *must not go!* If they do, the lead research analyst or presenter should politely but firmly ask them to summarize and finish their portion. If not, those who come later won't have sufficient time to present their material. All too often, one or more members of the audience will digress from the information at hand or want to discuss some issue of special interest to them. Unless it's the sponsor's chief representative, the presenter is well advised to remind the person or people that there's much yet to be covered and that there will be ample opportunity, *later,* to discuss such matters.

Concluding the Presentation

It's incumbent on the lead researcher or presenter to respect the sponsor's and audience members' time—to stay within the time limits set by the sponsor. It's also important to recognize that *everything always* takes longer than expected. *Everything* and *always* are strong generalizations. They make room for *no* exceptions. That's because there *are* no exceptions. Every experienced presenter knows that. So, it's vitally important to plan the presentation exactly as though there were only about two-thirds of the actual time allocated. That "extra" time must *not* be consumed during the early part of the presentation. The pace must be maintained. Inevitably, there will be sufficient questions, comments, and discussion by the audience at the end of the presentation. In the exceedingly unlikely event the presentation ends early and there's nothing more to say, certainly nobody would object in the slightest. There may be serious objections, however, if time runs out or the end comes late.

The sponsor's chief representative will usually signal when it's time to end the discussion of the project and terminate the meeting. They ordinarily don't just conclude it themselves. Rather, they give the presenter or participants a verbal cue that's usually easy to recognize. It's the presenter's job to recognize the cue and *promptly* conclude by thanking the sponsor for the opportunity to do the project and make the report. Then the presenter should turn to the audience and thank them cordially for their participation, interest, and comments.

As the report conference breaks up and people begin leaving, there may be some audience members who approach the researchers individually. They may even ask for a special meeting or report. That's not unusual, but it's a sensitive issue. In such circumstances, the researcher is well advised to seek the sponsor's chief representative or liaison and include him or her in the conversation and arrangements. Additional contact of this sort may or *may not* be welcome or acceptable to the sponsor.

Summary

Making Report Presentations

    A. Consider the pros and cons. Some projects *require* a report presentation and they're often of great value, but sometimes they're inappropriate or impractical.

    B. Plan and prepare *carefully.* Typically, 99 percent of the work and as much of the value is in the planning and preparation; 1 percent in doing it.

    C. Select only *major* content. The most salient aspects of the survey results should be presented, but the detailed information should be in written form.

    D. Choose an *effective* presenter. If there's a project team, it's often best to have one person make the presentation while others attend and respond to questions.

    E. *Logically* organize the material. Introduce the presentation, provide handouts, present the body of the report, and be prepared for discussion or Q & A.

    F. Check projection equipment needs. LCD projectors are prevalent and readily available to buy or rent, but sometimes only overhead projectors for transparencies are obtainable.

    G. Remember the cardinal rule: The probability of problems increases exponentially with the increase in complexity!

H. Expect presentation anxiety. Almost all speakers and presenters initially feel some anxiety, but it *can* be reduced and it will usually dissipate quickly.

I. Use notes effectively. They should be brief, providing only cues about what to say, and they should *never* be read verbatim.

J. Watch the pace and timing. The pace should be geared to time needed for audience comprehension; timing to the period allocated by the sponsor.

K. Conclude promptly and courteously. The sponsor usually signals the end of the conference, when the presenter should thank everyone and terminate.

Glossary

absolute frequency   The number of cases or respondents appearing in each category of a frequency distribution or an each cell of a cross-tabulation table.

absolute value   The value of a number, ignoring the plus or minus sign.

accessibility bias   One type of selection bias during sampling, where some respondents in the population are over- or underrepresented because they are more accessible or are less accessible than others.

acquiescence bias   Agreement or consent by respondents to what they believe an interviewer or sponsor would like them to think or say rather than giving their real opinion or reaction.

action component   One of the three basic components of an attitude, indicating the person's consistent tendency to take action regarding the topic or to remain passive about it.

adjective checklist   A scaling device that lists a series of adjectives that might be used to describe some person, place, or thing and asks the respondent to check any adjective that applies.

affiliations   The network of durable, formal, and informal associations an individual has with family, relatives, friends, and acquaintances.

affinity bias   A form of interviewer bias resulting from interviewers showing preference for certain types of people for whom they have an affinity, such as respondents who are similar to them or that they find attractive, and including them in the sample at higher rates than others.

aided recall   A form of questioning respondents about what they remember, where their memory is aided by presenting or describing the things they might recall.

all-inclusive categories   Response categories defined to ensure that every feasible answer will fit into a category; that there will be a category for every possible answer.

alpha level   The critical value, or probability level above which a relationship between variables will not be regarded as statistically significant because it is too likely that it could result only by chance from sampling error if the variables were actually not related in the population as a whole; also refers to the probability of a Type I error in academic research.

alphanumeric variable   A variable whose "values" are characters (words or letters) rather than numeric values.

alternative hypothesis   The proposition that some condition or relationship exists, accepted in scientific or academic research, if the results fail to support the "null hypothesis" that it does not exist.

analysis of variance (ANOVA)   A statistical measure of the association between a categorical independent variable and a continuous, numerical, dependent variable from an interval or ratio scale, used to assess the significance of differences among means for different groups.

area sampling   A form of cluster sampling where the region of the population is first divided into areas, some are randomly selected, and then respondents within those areas are randomly selected.

attitude   Relatively durable, psychological predispositions of people to respond toward or against an object, person, place, idea, or symbol, consisting of three components: their knowledge or beliefs, their feelings or evaluations, and their tendency toward action or passivity.

attitude scale   A scale used to measure attitudes, usually focusing on the respondents' feelings or evaluations toward one or more objects or copies.

auspices bias   The tendency for respondents to react toward the survey sponsor, if they know who the sponsor is, rather than providing their own, honest reactions to the survey questions themselves.

average   A measure of central tendency that represents the most typical case, usually referring to the arithmetic mean, but also applying to the median and the mode.

banner   A method for showing several cross-tabulations in one, condensed table in order to save space or facilitate comparison, ordinarily used only when one variable is cross-tabulated against several others.

bar chart A graphic portrayal of several quantities, such as frequencies or percentages, where the length of the horizontal or vertical bars represents the relative magnitudes of the values.

behavior The actions of people or objects in the past or at the present.

bias The tendency for some extraneous factor to affect the answers to survey questions or the survey results in general, in a systematic way, so that results are "pushed" or "pulled" in some specific direction.

bimodality The existence of two modes or peaks in a distribution of response, rather than a single modal value, often caused when the sample contains two, distinct populations or groups with differing reactions.

bipolar adjectives A pair of adjectives, such as those used in a semantic differential scale, that represent the polar extremes on one dimension or continuum.

bivariate relationship A relationship between only two variables.

bivariate statistics The statistics used to measure the relationship between only two variables and assess its statistical significance.

bottle scale A pictorial scale showing a series of bottles filled to varying levels, sometimes used when surveying those who may not always understand verbal or numeric scales, such as young children or those with reading impairments.

breakdowns A data analysis procedure that computes and reports the mean, standard deviation, and number of cases for a continuous numeric variable for each level of a categorical variable, ordinarily using analysis of variants to measure the statistical significance of differences in mean values.

callbacks The second and subsequent attempts to contact respondents by telephone or in person when they were not present to respond to the first attempt to contact them.

case A set of data obtained from one completed questionnaire or one respondent that serves as a single unit for analysis.

categorical data Nominal data where the values of the variables are merely the names of discrete,

independent categories and the numeric magnitudes have no meaning or stand in no fixed relationship, as opposed to continuous data.

categorical item A survey question coded with values that are merely the names of categories, so that the values do not represent magnitudes or stand in any ordered relationship with one another.

causality The potential influence or effect that one item or variable has on another.

ceiling effects The truncation or "chopping off" of the high side of a distribution because respondents' answers could go no further up the scale.

census Counting or taking measurements from all members of a given population, rather than sampling only a portion to represent the whole.

central systems Computer systems that do the actual processing at some central location accessible by communication to several operators or users.

central tendency measures Statistical averages that describe the most typical value or case, such as the mean, median, and mode.

chi-square A value, usually obtained from cross-tabulation of two items in survey research, that can be compared with the values of the chi-square distribution to obtain a probability for assessing statistical significance.

chi-square distribution The particular form of a distribution derived from a set of computations and defined by the number of "degrees of freedom," often listed in statistical reference tables.

classification variables Survey items, such as demographic variables, that are used to classify respondents into groups or categories for comparison.

closed-ended questions A structured survey question where the alternative answers are listed so that respondents must ordinarily pick only from among them.

cluster One group of individuals or sampling units that have proximity with one another within the sample frame in some respect, such as those within a given area.

cluster bias A form of selection bias resulting when a cluster sampling design selects respondents who are too closely related to one another within a cluster, so that they tend to give similar responses.

cluster sampling A technique often used in surveys to save travel or long-distance toll charges where the population is divided into clusters and a few clusters, each containing many respondents, are randomly selected.

codebook   The entire set of codelists for several variables from one survey.

codelist   The list of code values and category labels for a single survey variable that is generated by postcoding and used during analysis and reporting.

coding   The process of assigning code values to the various alternative answers to survey questions, either when constructing the questionnaire (precoding) or after the data collection (postcoding).

coefficient of determination   The square of the correlation coefficient, indicating the proportion of "shared" variance for correlation or the proportion of variance in the dependent variable that was "explained" by the independent variable in regression.

comparative scale   A scale using one entity as the standard by which one or more others are judged or evaluated.

computer hardware   The physical devices and components of computers, including both the central processing unit and the peripheral devices for inputting, storing, and outputting data.

computer software   The programs and coded instructions to the computer, including both the operating system that provides general control and the applications programs that perform specific computations.

conditional branching   Instructions or "go-to" statements in a questionnaire indicating the interviewer or respondent should skip items that don't apply, based on answers to previous questions.

confidence interval   The range around a numeric statistical value obtained from a sample, within which the actual, corresponding value for the population is likely to fall, at a given level of probability.

confidence level   The specific probability of obtaining some result from a sample if it did not exist in the population as a whole, at or below which the relationship will be regarded as statistically significant.

continuous variable   A variable that represents a continuum without any breaks or interruptions, so the numeric values could potentially take on an infinite number of values expressed in whole numbers and fractions.

convenience sample   A sample selected more on the bias of the researcher or data collection team's convenience than on the requirements for random selection with a known probability of inclusion and representation.

correlation analysis   A measure of the relationship or association between two continuous numeric variables that indicates both the direction and degree to which they co-vary with one another from case to case, without implying that one is causing the other.

correlation coefficient   The value computed with correlation analysis, ranging from zero to indicate no systematic relationship to plus or minus one, indicating a perfect linear relationship, where the positive or negative value shows if the relationship is direct or inverse, respectively.

correlation matrix   The correlation coefficients between each pair, for several variables, arranged so that each variable is identified on each row and on each column, with the coefficient listed in the cells defined by the rows and columns.

critical value   The probability level above which a relationship between variables will not be regarded as statistically significant because it is too likely that it could result only by chance from sampling error if the variables were actually not related in the population as a whole.

cross-tabulation   Plotting two categorical variables in the form of a matrix so that the values of one variable define the rows and the values of the other define the columns, with the cells containing the frequency of cases with a given value for each of the two items and from which a chi-square value can be computed to assess the statistical significance of the relationship.

curvilinear   A line or distribution of values that is continuous, but forms an arch, rather than a straight line.

data   Most often numbers, but also letters or words that symbolize or represent quantities, entities, or categories of things.

data analysis   The manipulation of numbers, letters, or symbols in order to suppress the detail and reveal the relevant facts or relationships.

data collection   The process of communicating questions and obtaining a record of responses from a sample, either by mail, telephone, or personal interviewing.

data field   The location and number of columns in a data file record required to contain the largest number of digits for any code value for a particular variable.

data point   A datum, or one single entry of a number, letter, or symbol, usually for one variable and one case or respondent.

data processing   Submitting the survey data to computer programs and routines in order to perform the statistical analysis and to generate reports, as opposed to hand tabulation of the data.

decisions   The process and/or results of individual evaluations, judgments, and choices among alternatives.

degrees of freedom (d.f.)   A parameter most often based on the number of cases or respondents, but slightly reduced to adjust for some earlier computations and used when checking reference tables or computing probability to assess statistical significance.

demographics   A set of conditions or attributes of people, often including age, sex, marital status, education, employment, occupation, and income, among others, usually measured in surveys to determine the types of people represented by the sample and to make comparisons of other results among demographic groups.

dependent variable   The variable that is viewed as being potentially influenced, affected, or determined by some other variable in a cause-and-effect relationship, based on the logic and meaning of the things represented by the variables.

depicted scale   Any scale that cannot be included within the survey question, so that it must be shown in the form of numbers, words, or pictures representing response alternatives.

descriptive research   Research that is designed primarily to describe rather than to explain a set of conditions, characteristics, or attributes of people in a population, based on measurement of a sample.

descriptive statistics   Statistics such as averages and measures of spread, used to suppress the detail in data files and to condense and summarize the data to make facts more visible, as well as to

indicate the degree to which the sample data are likely to represent the entire population.

desires   Express wishes or conscious urges of respondents that may be a topic for survey research measurement within the broader topic category of "needs."

desktop systems   Computer systems that do some or all of the processing right at the operator's desk or work station.

diagram scale   Any form of scale that uses a diagram to depict the response options or to obtain or collect answers to survey questions.

dichotomous question   A question with only two response alternatives, such as a yes/no question or an item that can either be checked or ignored.

discrete variable   A categorical variable yielding nominal data, where all of the answers must fall within a category and the code values stand in no ordered relationship to one another.

discriminant analysis   A statistical measure of the relationship between a continuous, numeric independent variable from an interval or ratio scale and a categorical dependent variable defining two or more groups, used both to assess statistical significance and also to compute the discriminant function, used to predict or classify new cases into groups.

discriminant function   The prediction or classification equation obtained from discriminant analysis, used to predict or classify new cases into groups when only the value of the independent variable is known.

dispersion   The range and degree of spread or variance in the distribution of data for a survey variable.

editing   The process of examining questionnaires or data against some set of criteria, to be sure the content is correct or appropriate.

executive summary   The first section of the final report, including only an outline of the major highlights of the results.

expected cell frequency   A value computed during or after cross-tabulation, based on the proportion of the data represented by the entire row and column on which the cell resides.

explicit scale   Any scale that is directly expressed or stated, either verbally or visually, as opposed to those that are only implied by the question.

extreme case   A response that is an outlier, with a value so extreme it is far distant from any other response, which may sometimes suggest there has been an error while recording or transferring the data.

extremity   The extreme or terminal point, limit, or part of something, such as the upper or lower limit of a scale or distribution of scores.

F-distribution   The particular form of a distribution derived from a set of computations and defined by two numbers of "degrees of freedom," often listed in statistical reference tables.

F-ratio   The ratio of a numerator and denominator value consisting of variance expressed as "mean squares," or the "sum of squares" divided by the degrees of freedom for each, usually computed with analysis of variance and compared to the F-distribution in a statistical reference table to assess statistical significance.

feeling component   One of the three main components of attitudes, consisting of the evaluations and judgments of the topic by the individual holding the attitude.

fixed sum scale   A particular type of scale where the respondent is asked to list the number of times each of a set of alternatives occurred or apply, out of a given total, so that the sum of the values must equal the total.

floor effects   The truncation or "chopping off" of the low side of a distribution because respondents' answers could go no lower on the scale.

forced ranking scale   A type of scale, yielding ordinal level data, where the respondents are instructed to rank a series of items in sequential order, with no "ties" or equal rankings allowed.

formatting   The design or a particular arrangement of words, numbers, or symbols, specifying their order or sequence, physical location, relative distance or proximity, and general form, often used in reference to the location of data fields within a file record.

frequency distribution   The number of cases that contain each of the scale values for a particular survey item or variable.

frequency table   A tabular presentation of the frequency distribution, often including percentage distributions based on the frequencies and the sample size, the number of valid cases, and the cumulative number of valid cases.

FTP   Abbreviation of *File Transfer Protocol*, the protocol used on the Internet for sending files.

goals   Specific objectives or ends sought by respondents that may be a topic for survey research measurement within the broader topic category of "needs."

go errors   An error that results when a decision maker goes ahead with a course of action and it proves to be costly or unsatisfactory.

grand mean   The arithmetic mean of the dependent variable for *all* of the cases in an analysis of variance, as opposed to the "group means," including only the cases in each category of the independent variable.

graphic data description   Portrayal of data distributions for individual survey variables with charts, graphs, or data plots rather than numeric tables.

graphic scale   Any scale with scale points portrayed as pictures or diagrams, rather than numbers, letters, or words.

hand tabulation   The statistical computations and analysis of survey data without the use of computer analysis routines, usually confined to frequency tables, cross-tabulation tables, and the statistics that can be obtained from them without the processing of continuous numeric variables with many scale values.

happy-sad face scale   One form of pictorial scale showing a series of simple sketches of faces with the mouth of each turned up in a smile to show pleasure or down to show displeasure in varying degrees, often used for surveying young children who may not be able to understand numeric or verbal scales.

histogram   A horizontal bar chart showing the frequency or percentage distribution of response for a survey item in graphic form, often generated by computer analysis routines if requested.

homoskedasticity   The required condition of a scatterplot of data for regression analysis, where the data points are spread around the regression line in approximately equal amounts at any given point on the line, forming an even corridor of data, as opposed to heteroskedasticity, such as a "funnel shaped" pattern of data round the regression line.

hostility bias Opposition, resentment, or resistance to an interviewer, survey sponsor, response task, or situational factor that negatively affects answers to one or more specific survey questions.

HTML Short for *HyperText Markup Language*, the authoring language used to create documents on the World Wide Web. HTML defines the structure and layout of a Web document by using a variety of tags and attributes.

hypothesis A conjectural statement about the value of some variable or the relationship between variables that will be tested and ultimately accepted or rejected on the basis of statistical analysis of survey results, most often used in formal scientific or academic research.

images The generalized or synthesized picture representation of some object, person, or idea held in the minds of people, based on partial information from previous experiences, perceptions, or evaluations, and often one of the major topics of survey research.

implicit scale Any scale that need not be explicitly stated in the question or presented verbally or visually to respondents because they automatically understand how they are to respond, such as asking one's age with the implicit understanding that it will be expressed in years since birth.

independence The condition between two variables or measurements where information about one gives no indication of the likely value of the other because they are unrelated.

independent variable The variable that is viewed as influencing, affecting, or determining the values of another variable when they are regarded as being in a potential cause-and-effect relationship.

inferential statistics Any statistical measure that can be used to make inferences or generalizations about a population, with a known level of probability, based on the values or conditions of a sample.

information needs The specific categories of information required by those sponsoring pragmatic survey research, in order to make decisions or choices or to set policy, or required by those conducting academic research to test a theoretical or conceptual hypothesis and enhance some body of knowledge or literature.

instrumentation The survey questionnaire and other devices, such as cover letters, rating cards, and the like, used to obtain data from respondents.

instrumentation bias The tendency for some aspect of the survey instruments to cause respondents to answer in a particular way or systematically "push" or "pull" the survey results in some given direction, thus reducing the survey validity.

instrumentation error The tendency for some aspect of the survey instruments to randomly affect the data in such a way that they are not true representations of the respondent opinions or conditions, but there is no specific direction or systematic influence, so that survey reliability is reduced.

integer A whole number, as opposed to a fractional or decimal value.

interpretation error Error that results when interviewers are asked to interpret responses during the interview or make judgments about the responses.

interrogation error Errors that occur when questions are expressed differently from one respondent to the next.

interval scale Any scale where the intervals between scale points are equal, even though there may be no zero value or zero does not represent a complete absence of the thing measured, such as the Fahrenheit scale.

interviewing bias The tendency for some aspect of the interviewing to cause respondents to answer in a *particular way* or systematically "push" or "pull" the survey results in some given direction, thus reducing the survey *validity*.

interviewing error The tendency for some aspect of the interviewing to randomly affect the data so they don't truly represent the respondents' opinions or conditions, thus reducing survey *reliability*.

judgment sample A sample selected on the basis of the researcher's judgment about what units or respondents should and should not be included, as opposed to random selection.

knowledge component One of the three main components of attitudes, consisting of the facts or beliefs the individual holds about the topic of the attitude.

kurtosis A statistical measure of the shape of a distribution that indicates whether the curve is more peaked or more flat than a normal, bell-shaped curve and how much so.

level of confidence The specific probability of obtaining some result from a sample if it did not exist in the population as a whole, at or below which the relationship will be regarded as statistically significant.

lifestyle   The general pattern of daily behavior, activities, choices, and preferences for an individual or family that might be used to characterize them and distinguish them in meaningful ways from those following a different pattern.

Likert scale   A type of scaling where the respondents are presented with a series of statements, rather than questions, and asked to indicate the degree to which they agree or disagree, usually on a five-point scale.

linear, numeric scale   A scale used when items are to be judged on a single dimension and arrayed on a scale with equal intervals, providing both absolute measures of importance and relative measures, or rankings, if responses among the various items are compared.

mail data collection   The mailing of questionnaires and their return by mail by the designated respondents.

maximum   The highest value for a variable that was actually obtained from a sample, often reported by analysis routines and used by analysts to assess range and likelihood of outliers or ceiling effects.

mean   The most common average or measure of central tendency, providing an indication of the most typical or representative value for the sample and the population as a whole, within a given confidence level.

mean squares   A value usually computed for analysis of variance to form an F-ratio to assess statistical significance, consisting of the total of the squared deviations from the mean for each data point, or sums of squares, divided by the number of cases or degrees of freedom.

measures of spread   Statistical indications of the dispersion of the data around the central point, such as the standard deviation.

median   An average or measure of central tendency, consisting of the value the middle case would take on if the cases were arrayed from lowest to highest value for the variable and the scale represented a continuum or could include an infinite number of points, used in preference to the mean for ordinal level data and often preferred to the mean for distributions that are highly skewed to one side or have outlying values.

mental set   The existing frame of mind, point of view, or train of thought adopted by a respondent at a given moment, used to judge a series of survey questions or items.

midpoint   The middle point on a scale with an odd number of scale points, sometimes reflecting neutrality on the spectrum of response.

minimum   The lowest value for a variable that was actually obtained from a sample, often reported by analysis routines and used by analysts to assess range and likelihood of outliers or floor effects.

minimum expected cell frequency   The lowest expected cell frequency in a cross-tabulation table, that must be at least five for valid use of the chi-square statistic to assess the significance of the relationship, computed by identifying the smallest row frequency and column frequency, multiplying the two, and dividing by the total frequency for the table.

mode   The only average appropriate to indicate the most typical case for a distribution of nominal data, consisting of the category with the highest frequency, and also representing the location of the peak or high point in a distribution of continuous numeric data with many scale values.

motives   The impetus or urge causing a person to take some action, that may be a topic for survey research measurement within the broader topic category of "needs."

multiple rating list   A survey item format used to save space and response time, designed so many items can be rated on the same scale.

multiple rating matrix   A survey item format used to save space and response time, designed so the same scale is used to rate multiple items on several dimensions.

multiple regression   Linear regression that uses a single dependent variable and two or more independent variables in the same analysis, in contrast to simple, linear regression using only one independent variable, so that both the effect of each independent variable and the effects of interactions among independent variables can be gauged.

multiple response item   A structured, multiple-choice survey question that allows the respondent to choose as many response categories as apply.

multivariate analysis   Statistical analysis techniques to assess the relationships or patterns among more than two variables simultaneously, including such methods as multiple regression, factorial analysis of variance, analysis of covariance, factor analysis, cluster analysis, multidimensional scaling, and the like.

mutually exclusive categories   Response categories defined to ensure a unique association between any given answer and only one category or alternative, so no response can fit into two or more categories.

namelist   A listing of names and addresses, often used for mail surveys, that may be accumulated or acquired from one of many namelist brokerage firms who accumulate and manage such lists for people with particular characteristics or in certain locations.

nay-sayer   An individual or respondent who persistently tends to respond in the negative more often than others, regardless of the question.

nay-sayer bias   The tendency for a set of survey results to be generally and artificially negative on a series of items because all items are inclined in the same direction, toward the positive or toward the negative, and negative responses to the earlier items were generalized to the remaining ones, thus reducing the validity.

need   A persistent or fundamental requirement of the individual in order to maintain physical, psychological, or social well-being, usually fluctuating over time in its degree of satisfaction, and often a topic for survey research measurement.

no-go errors   Errors that result when a decision maker either fails to take some action that would have positive results, or ignores an alternative that would be more positive, choosing some less positive course.

nominal scale   A scale that uses numbers, letters, or symbols only as the names of independent categories, so that the scale values do not stand in any ordered relationship to one another.

nonprobability sampling   A nonrandom sampling design such as convenience sampling, where the probability of selecting a given sampling unit from the population is neither known nor equal to the probability of selecting any other unit.

nonrespondents   Those in the population who were included in the sample but failed to respond because they refused or could not be reached, or for some other reason.

nonresponse bias   A systematic effect on the data reducing validity that results when those with one type of opinion or condition fail to respond to a survey more often than do others with different opinions or conditions.

normal curve   Any distribution that conforms exactly or very closely to a normal distribution.

normal distribution   A continuous, symmetrical distribution that forms a curve with a particular shape defined by a mathematical equation, often referred to as a "bell-shaped" curve, valuable as a statistical reference because the precise areas under the curve can be computed or obtained from statistical tables.

N-size   A commonly used term for the sample size or the number of cases included in an analysis or tabular report.

nth name sampling   A sampling design where the number of units in the sample frame is first divided by the desired sample size to obtain the value of n, a value between one and n is randomly selected as a starting point or first case to be selected, and then every nth name or unit is selected, yielding a random sample.

null hypothesis   The hypothesis stipulating there will be no significant relationship between two variables, which can be tested with survey or other data and rejected in favor of the alternative hypothesis if the relationship proves significant, and most often used in scientific or academic research.

numeric item   Any survey item with scale numbers that are meaningful and stand in an ordered relationship to one another, such as those from ordinal, interval, or ratio scales.

online focus groups   Participants sign in at a private chatroom on the Internet where they either join in a focused discussion with a moderator or read messages on a bulletin board and post their observations and opinions over a period of several days or weeks.

open-ended question   An unstructured survey question that does not include a list of alternative answers, so that respondents must answer in their own words.

order bias   The tendency for the order in which survey items are listed to affect respondents' answers in some systematic way, reducing validity.

ordinal scale   A particular type of scale where the response alternatives define an ordered sequence, so the first is less than the second, the second less than the third, and so on, yielding ordinal level data where the intervals between scale points are not known or necessarily equal.

outlier   An extreme case or data point that stands well above or well below its nearest neighbor and is highly atypical of the distribution as a whole.

paired comparison scale   A type of scale that presents respondents with one pair of alternatives at a time, instructing them to pick just one from each pair, yielding dichotomous, nominal data.

paired t-test   A technique for assessing the statistical significance of differences in mean values when both are obtained from the same respondents, and are therefore paired with one another.

panel data collection   A survey of a group of pres-elected respondents who agreed to be panel members on a continuous basis for a given period of time and provided initial demographic data, allowing selection of special groups and permitting the use of surveys to monitor responses over time.

parameter   A coefficient or value for the population that corresponds to a particular statistic from a sample and is often inferred from the sample.

PDF   Short for *Portable Document Format*, a file format developed by Adobe Systems. PDF captures formatting information from a variety of desktop publishing applications, making it possible to send formatted documents and have them appear on the recipient's monitor or printer as they were intended. To view a file in PDF format, you need Adobe Acrobat Reader, a free application distributed by Adobe Systems.

percentage distribution table   A table listing the percentage of respondents selecting each response category or scale point.

percentile   An indication of the position of a case or value within a distribution, based on the number of cases with a lesser value out of a total of 100 cases.

peripheral devices   Units of computer hardware, other than the central processing unit, used to input, store, and output data or information.

personal interview   Data collection accomplished with the interviewer in the presence of the respondent, so that they have visual contact, as opposed to telephone interviewing.

pictorial scale   Any scale with scale points portrayed as pictures or diagrams rather than numbers, letters, or words.

pie chart   A method for portraying results graphically, consisting of a circle divided by lines from the center to the perimeter, so that the angles between the lines and therefore the size of the "pieces" represent proportions.

pilot survey   A brief preliminary survey, often using a small, convenience sample, conducted to test the survey instruments and data collection method before the project details are finalized and the larger, formal survey conducted.

population   The definition of all those people or elements of interest to the information seekers and from among whom the sample will be selected.

population parameters   Values or coefficients such as the mean or variance that describe the distribution of a variable in the population, often estimated or inferred based on the corresponding values of *sample statistics*.

postcoding   The process of examining completed survey questionnaires, choosing response categories for items not precoded, assigning code values to them on the documents, and recording codes and category labels in a codelist.

precision   The range of the confidence interval at a given level of probability, expressed in absolute terms or as a percentage of the mean value.

precode   Assigning code values to the categories of structured questions and listing them for printing on the questionnaire prior to data collection.

preferences   Predetermined choices by respondents from among alternative goods, that may be a topic for survey research measurement within the broader topic category of "needs."

prestige   A condition of superior status, rank, or distinction relative to one's peers or society in general, constituting a basic human need, sometimes causing respondents to react to questions in ways they perceive to be more prestigious.

pretest   Preliminary trial of some or all aspects of the sampling design, survey instrumentation, and data collection method, to be sure there are no unanticipated difficulties or problems.

primary data   Data collected for a particular project to meet specific information needs, as opposed to data that already exist for general use or as the result of inquiries for other purposes.

probability sampling   Any sampling design where every element in the population has either an equal probability of selection, as with random sampling, or a given probability of being selected that is known in advance and used in analysis to assess significance.

process editing   Examining survey data with computer processing routines to be sure the data conform to the data file format and that all values are expressed in the proper form and are within the range of the scale for each item.

product-moment correlation   The statistical method of correlation that requires interval or ratio level data and is not appropriate for ordinal scale data, which require rank correlation.

qualification   The process of inspecting or interrogating potential respondents to be sure they are qualified to respond or that they fit the quota specifications for a particular interviewer.

qualitative research   Research obtaining data in the form of words or other indications that do not lend themselves to quantitative analysis and whose analysis and interpretation depend on subjective judgments by experts.

quantitative research   Research obtaining data in a form that can be represented by numbers, so that quantities and magnitudes can be measured, assessed, and interpreted with the use of mathematical or statistical manipulation.

questionnaire   The basic survey instrument containing instructions, questions, or items, response alternatives where appropriate, and specific means for recording responses.

quota   A set number or proportion of respondents with given characteristics or attributes sought in a sample or assigned to specific interviewers or field-workers.

quota sample   Any sampling design that requires a set number or proportion of respondents with given characteristics or attributes.

quota specification   The listing of quota requirements for the entire sample or for specific interviewers, including identification of the characteristics that define the quota, the manner in which they are to be ascertained, the method of qualification of respondents, and the number or proportion of respondents who are to have each attribute or combination of attributes.

random digit dialing   A sampling system for telephone surveys where all telephone numbers in households or all that have one of a given set of three-digit telephone number prefixes are regarded as the sample frame, and seven-digit or four-digit numbers are generated and dialed manually or automatically to obtain the sample.

random error   The result of extraneous factors, such as sampling error, affecting the survey results in no systematic pattern, so the answers are not consistently pushed or pulled in one specific direction.

random sampling   A sampling design that seeks to select respondents from the population or sample frame in a completely random fashion, so every respondent has an equal probability of being selected.

range   A measure of the spread in the distribution of data for a variable, defined as the maximum minus the minimum, plus one.

rank correlation   The statistical method of correlation appropriate when one or both of the variables are from only ordinal level scales, sometimes called Spearman rank correlation.

rank order scale   A scale essentially the same as the forced ranking scale.

rating card   A card or sheet containing a rating scale that is handed to or shown to respondents during personal interviews and from which they pick their response alternatives by number or letter.

rating scale   Any scale from which respondents choose values that represent their responses, ordinarily yielding interval or ratio level data.

ratio scale   Any scale that has the same characteristics as an equal interval scale, plus the fact that zero represents the complete absence of the thing being measured, so that a ratio of one scale value to another has meaningful and legitimate interpretation.

raw data   Data that has not been transformed or processed, although it may have been edited and transferred from one medium to another.

recode   The process of systematically assigning new code values to variables, based on the original values, usually done in order to group data into larger categories to obtain fewer code values.

record format   The specification of where the data field for each variable is to be keyed or recorded in a data file, including both the column(s) and the record numbers within a single case.

recording error   Error that may occur when interviewers are required to write down verbal answers by respondents, typically caused by unsatisfactory abbreviation when there is insufficient time to record entire verbatim answers.

regression analysis (simple linear regression)
A statistical measure of the effect of one interval or ratio level variable on another, used both to indicate the statistical significance of the relationship and to generate an equation to predict or estimate the value of the dependent variable for a new case, based only on the known value of the independent variable.

regression equation   The equation generated by linear regression analysis, expressed as a coefficient that can be multiplied by the value of the independent variable for a new case and a constant to be added to predict the unknown value of the dependent variable.

relative frequency   A term that is sometimes used to refer to the percentages listed in a frequency table, indicating the proportion of the sample in each category.

reliability   The degree to which the survey results are free from random error, as opposed to systematic bias, often expressed in terms of confidence intervals or confidence levels.

report generation   The process of arranging and condensing tabular survey results and expressing the written interpretations of the findings to provide information to those seeking it.

responding sample   The number of cases with valid responses to the survey or to an individual survey item, as opposed to the total sample size.

response bias   The tendency for some aspect of the response task, such as annoyance or a desire to please the interviewer, to cause respondents to answer in a particular way or systematically "push" or "pull" the survey results in some given direction, thus reducing the survey validity.

response error   The tendency for some aspect of the response task, such as boredom, inattention, or fatigue, to randomly affect the data in such a way that they are not true representations of the respondent opinions or conditions, but there is no specific direction or systematic influence, so that survey reliability is reduced.

response option error   Error resulting because interviewers read the alternative answers to respondents when they shouldn't do so or fail to read them when they should.

response rate   The percentage of those included in the sample who responded to the survey and provided usable, completed questionnaires.

r-square (r^2, Rsq)   The coefficient of determination obtained during regression analysis, indicating the proportion of variance in the dependent variable that is "explained" by the values of the independent variable.

runs test   A statistical process used in connection with regression analysis to determine the probability that the data are actually linear or arrayed evenly around a straight line if the data were plotted, by counting the "runs" of successive data points that are all on one side of the regression line.

sample   The number and/or identification of respondents in the population who will be or have been included in the survey.

sample frame   A listing that should include all those in the population to be sampled and exclude all those who are not in the population.

sample selection bias   Any form of bias resulting from the selection of respondents in a manner that deviates from random selection, so that some types of respondents are over- or underrepresented in the sample.

sample unit   The smallest unit of the sample to be surveyed or the unit that will constitute one case for analysis, ordinarily one respondent or questionnaire.

sampling design   The specification of the sample frame, sample size, and the system for selecting and contacting individual respondents from the population.

sampling error   The degree to which the results from the sample deviate from those that would be obtained from the entire population, because of random error in the selection of respondent and the corresponding reduction in reliability.

scale interpretation error   Error associated with the use of rating cards where respondents answer with the name of a category, rather than its number or code, and the interviewer records the wrong code value because the category names are not listed on the questionnaire.

scatterplot A graphic plot of the data points for two variables, usually generated on request by analysis routines during regression analysis, so that each data point is plotted horizontally according to the value of the independent variable and vertically according to the value of the dependent variable.

secondary data Data initially acquired for general use or for some purpose other than the information requirements of the project at hand.

selection bias A systematic effect on the data resulting from the selection of respondents in a manner that deviates from random selection, so that some types of respondents are over- or under-represented in the sample.

self-selection bias A systematic affect on survey results because some respondents voluntarily participate while others decline or refuse, so that those with certain opinions or conditions are under- or overrepresented in the sample.

semantic differential scale A scaling device that lists several pairs of bipolar adjectives, usually separated by a seven-point scale, and instructs respondents to rate the topic or object on each, ordinarily used to measure image and provide a profile.

semantic distance scale A scale listing several adjectives or phrases, where respondents are instructed to indicate how well each describes some object or topic based on a linear, numeric scale, often used to measure image and obtain a profile in much the same manner as the semantic differential scale is used.

sequential sample A sampling design that requires the collection of data in increments with a relatively small sample at each stage, so that analysis can be performed after each stage to determine when the sample is large enough to provide the required level of confidence or reliability.

shape The form or outline of a data distribution arrayed from lowest to highest value, portrayed in a data plot or described by statistical values such as the coefficients of skewness and kurtosis.

sight-edit The visual examination of the completed questionnaires immediately after data collection to determine if they are sufficiently complete and usable.

significance level The probability that the magnitude of the relationship might result in a sample of that size purely from sampling error if, in fact, it did not exist in the population.

simple random sample A sampling design that seeks to select respondents from the population or sample frame in a completely random fashion, so every respondent has an equal probability of being selected, and no clustering or stratification methods are used.

single response item A structured, multiple-choice survey question that requires the respondent to choose only *one* response category, such as one that represents the "best" or "favorite."

skewness A designation of the shape of a distribution, indicating the degree of symmetry or the degree and direction that the mode or peak "leans" toward one side, with only a few values extending well out toward the tail on the other.

slope In regression analysis, the "rise over the run" when the dependent variable is plotted on the vertical axis of a scatterplot, or the amount of increase or decrease in the units of the dependent variable for each unit of the independent variable, indicated by the regression coefficient.

social desirability The tendency for respondents to give answers to survey questions that are consistent with what the society believes is right, proper, correct, or acceptable, creating bias in the results whenever the true answers are suppressed to meet social norms.

spread The range and degree of dispersion or variance in the distribution of data for a survey variable, often described by the *standard deviation* of the distribution.

stair-step scale One type of pictorial scale graphically showing the scale points as a series of steps, appropriate for use with young children or other respondents who might have difficulty understanding a numeric or verbal scale.

standard deviation (S.D.) A computed measure of spread or dispersion in a distribution of data, based on the squared deviations of each point from the mean, that can be used to indicate the proportion of data within certain ranges of scale values when the distribution conforms closely to the normal curve.

standard error (S.E.) of the estimate   A computed value in regression analysis based on sample size and variance around the regression line, determining the confidence interval around a predicted value of the dependent variable at a given probability.

standard error (S.E.) of the mean   A computed value based on the size of the sample and the standard deviation of the distribution, indicating the range within which the mean of the population is likely to be from the mean of the sample at a given level probability.

statistic   Some value computed from sample data that may also be used to make inferences about the corresponding value or "parameter" for the whole population.

statistical analysis   The process of computation and manipulation of sample data in order to suppress the detail and make relevant facts and relationships more visible and meaningful, and to generate statistics in order to make inferences about the population as a whole.

statistical inference   The process of generalizing information from a sample to the population as a whole by estimating population parameters, based on their corresponding statistical values from the sample.

statistical significance   An explicit assumption by the analyst that a relationship revealed in the sample data also exists in the population as a whole, based on the relatively small probability that it would result only from sampling error if it did not exist in the population.

stratified sampling   A sampling design that divides the population into specific strata containing certain types of respondents, then selects subsamples of the required size for each strata.

stratum   The singular form of "strata," indicating one level of a stratified sampling design.

structured question   Any question that lists or prescribes the response alternatives from which respondents must choose, such as multiple-choice or true/false questions and items accompanied by rating scales.

subsample   One part of an entire sample that is singled out for special attention or analysis, often defined in terms of a demographic characteristic.

sum   The total of a series of values or the process of adding them.

sum of squares (S.S.)   A value computed for several forms of statistical analysis, such as computing the standard deviation, analysis of variance, regression analysis, and the like, where some mean is subtracted from each data point, this deviation is squared, and the squared values are added for all the cases.

survey   A research technique where information requirements are specified, a population is identified, a sample selected and systematically questioned, and the results analyzed, generalized to the population, and reported to meet the information needs.

systematic   A relationship or effect that is not random, but rather one that is consistent or in a given "direction."

systematic bias   A redundant term, since bias is defined as systematic effect, but commonly used to emphasize the nonrandom nature of a bias or to distinguish bias from random error.

systematic sampling   Another term for nth name sampling, where the number of units in the sample frame is first divided by the desired sample size to obtain the value of n, a value between one and n is randomly selected as a starting point or first case to be selected, and then every nth name or unit is selected, yielding a random sample.

system hardware   Any mechanical or electronic device linked in a computer system, including the central processing unit and "peripheral" devices such as printers and external disk drives.

t-distribution   A symmetrical statistical probability distribution, slightly flatter and wider than the standard, normal distribution, often listed in statistical reference tables and used to determine the significance of paired t-tests.

telephone interview   Interview data collection using the telephone to contact respondents, as opposed to personal interviewing where respondents are in the presence of the interviewer and have visual contact.

termination bias   Bias resulting when respondents of a certain type or with a certain orientation terminate their participation in a continuing study, such as a panel study, at greater rates than others.

threat   A source of bias or resistance resulting when respondents find survey items or topics intimidating or threatening, such as questions about financial matters, or instructions, questions, or scales that are confusing, suggesting the respondent is ignorant or incompetent.

t-test   A statistical method of assessing the significance of differences between two mean values for the same variable, as opposed to a paired t-test of values for two different variables for the same cases, yielding the same basic information as an analysis of variance with only two categories for the independent variable.

Type I error   In academic or scientific research (as opposed to pragmatic research), the probability of rejecting the "null hypothesis" that no relationship exists, and, therefore, accepting the "alternative hypothesis" that there is a relationship, when, in fact, no relationship exists in the population as a whole.

Type II error   In academic or scientific research (as opposed to pragmatic research), the probability of not rejecting the "null hypothesis" that no relationship exists, and, therefore, rejecting the "alternative hypothesis" that there is a relationship, when, in fact, a relationship does exist in the population as a whole.

unaided recall   A form of questioning respondents about what they remember, where the facts, objects, or events are not listed or presented to them to aid their recollection, as with aided recall.

unbiased   Free of bias or unaffected by any extraneous factor that would systematically affect the values or results.

unbiased estimate   A statistical term that indicates the value of a particular statistic, such as the mean, obtained from the sample, will be exactly equal to the corresponding value of the population parameter, on the average over an infinite number of such samples.

unconditional branching   Instructions that control the "path" of interrogation by directing all respondents who reach a specific place in the questionnaire, such as the end of a special section, to go to another location in the questionnaire, rather than merely continuing from that point.

unimodal   Having only one modal value for a distribution of categorical data or only one peak or mode for a continuous distribution.

univariate analysis   The statistical description or the analysis of just one variable at a time.

unstructured question   An "open-ended" survey question where the alternative answers are not listed and respondents must provide the answers in their own words.

URL   Abbreviation of *Uniform Resource Locator,* the global address of documents and other resources on the World Wide Web.

validation   A term commonly but incorrectly used by survey researchers and data collection agencies to indicate "verification" of responses.

validity   The degree to which the survey data or results are free from both systematic bias and random error.

variable   A measurement unit that can be taken on several different values, usually used to refer to the distribution of data for one survey item.

variance   A statistical term referring to the sum of the squared deviations of each data point from the mean (the sum of squares), divided by the number of cases or degrees of freedom (the mean squares), and also the value from which the standard deviation is computed by extracting the square root.

verbal frequency scale   A particular type of verbal scale where the frequency of an event to be indicated by the respondent is expressed verbally, ordinarily with the words "Always, Often, Sometimes, Rarely, and Never," rather than in numeric quantities.

verbal scale   Any scale whose points are expressed in words or whose numeric code values are labeled throughout the scale with words.

verification   The process of checking with respondents after they have been interviewed to be sure the person was actually interviewed and that the interview was done correctly and completely when and where it was supposed to be, and commonly but incorrectly called "validation."

video-streaming   A new form of digital communication sometimes used for focus group recording and reporting, in which the video and audio are simultaneously transmitted to a host server on the

Internet. The sponsor's personnel authorized to view the group are given the time schedule, sign on instructions, and password, so they can observe it from their own computer or conference room whenever they wish.

visibility bias   One form of selection bias, where a particular type of respondent is over- or underrepresented in the sample because they are more visible than others with different characteristics.

yea-sayer   An individual or respondent who persistently tends to respond in the affirmative more often than others, regardless of the questions.

yea-sayer bias   The tendency for a set of survey results to be generally and artificially positive on a series of items because all items are inclined in the same direction, toward the positive or toward the negative, and positive responses to the earlier items were generalized to the remaining ones, thus reducing the validity.

Index